"We Specialize in the Wholly Impossible"

"We Specialize in the Wholly Impossible"

A Reader in Black Women's History

Edited by
Darlene Clark Hine,
Wilma King,
Linda Reed

CARLSON PUBLISHING, INC. BROOKLYN, NEW YORK, 1995

Front Cover Photograph [Library of Congress]:

Nannie Helen Burroughs was only twenty-one years old when her speech, "How the Sisters Are Hindered from Helping," at the 1900 annual conference of the National Baptist Convention catapulted her to fame. The speech served as a catalyst for the formation of the largest Black women's organization in America—the Woman's Convention Auxiliary to the NBC.

In 1909 she founded the National Training School for Women and Girls in Washington, D.C. One of her mottos for the school, "We Specialize in the Wholly Impossible," serves as the title for this book.

Library of Congress Cataloging-in-Publication Data

We specialize in the wholly impossible : a reader in Black women's history / edited by Darlene Clark Hine, Wilma King, Linda Reed.
      p. cm. — (Black women in United States history ; v. 17)
      Includes bibliographical references and index.
      ISBN 0-926019-80-5 (hbk.) — ISBN 0-926019-81-3 (pbk.)
      1. Afro-American women—History. I. Hine, Darlene Clark.
II. King, Wilma, 1942– . III. Reed, Linda, 1955– . IV. Series.
E185.86.W435 1994
305.48'896073'09—dc20   94-41968

Typographic design: C.J. Bartelt

Text typeface: Adobe Janson Text

Composition: Joseph E.L. Fortt

Cloth and paperback case designs: Ann Harakawa

Index prepared by Scholars Editorial Services, Inc., Madison, Wisconsin.

Printed on acid-free, 250-year-life paper.

Manufactured in the United States of America.

First printing, January 1995.

*To our mothers
and
grandmothers*

Contents

Part IV: United States—Eighteenth Century

Part V: United States—Nineteenth Century

Part VI: United States—Twentieth Century

Introduction

This book was put together to reclaim, and to create heightened awareness about, individuals, contributions, and struggles that have made African-American survival and progress possible. We cannot accurately comprehend either our hidden potential or the full range of problems that besiege us until we know about the successful struggles that generations of foremothers waged against seemingly insurmountable obstacles. We can, and will, chart a coherent future and win essential opportunities with a clear understanding of the past in all its pain and glory.

Black women more than ever before need to challenge hateful assumptions, negative stereotypes, myths, lies, and distortions about our own role in history. Black women need to know the contradictions and ironies that our unique status presents to a country founded on the proposition that all men are created equal and endowed with the inalienable rights of life, liberty, and opportunity to pursue happiness. Yet it is not enough to know only about the injustices and exploitation Black women endured. We also owe it to ourselves to experience the thrill of knowing about Black women's accomplishments. As we are inspired by past and present Black women's lives, we acquire the power to construct a better future. The realities of history as unearthed and presented in these essays promise to liberate us all from ignorance, intolerance, and apathy, our most formidable enemies in the postmodern world.

This reader is designed to be used in African-American, American, and women's history courses. Although noteworthy exceptions exist, most women's history pays too little attention to the multifaceted dimensions of Black women's historical experiences beyond their enslavement and participation in the women's club movement. The essays included in *"We Specialize in the Wholly Impossible"* cover a range of topics across time and space, providing more than an introduction to the history of African-American women. This anthology showcases some of the most exciting and thought-provoking work in Black women's history through the diaspora. The vast majority of the essays were published in the 1990s, and this latest generation of historians challenges many long-held assumptions and beliefs. This is especially demonstrated in Jessie M. Rodrique's study of the Black community and its perception of and participation in the birth control movement.

A common thread connects all of the essays in this volume—the resistance of Black women to racial and sexual oppression and exploitation. Black women faced inhospitable forces. They deflected them through a willingness to struggle, a constant belief in their abilities to fashion a better world, and a refusal to submit to racism. The title *"We Specialize in the Wholly Impossible,"* a motto of Nannie Helen Burroughs, makes it abundantly clear that Black women did not view themselves as passive, powerless victims. Rather, they were active agents in fighting for changes that benefited themselves, their families, their communities, and their entire race. Yet it is equally important to underscore that hundreds of thousands of Black women also waged unsuccessful struggles against the powers of racism and patriarchy.

The selections included here will serve as the basis for discussions about the African background, the Atlantic slave trade, the nature of slavery in the Caribbean and in North America, the quality of freedom, resistance to oppression, and the transition to freedom for women of African descent. Post-emancipation subjects such as earning a living and gaining an education in the North and in the South receive attention, along with the women's self-expressions through clothes and club formation.

The essays in the first section call attention to the need for including race in the theoretical discussion of African-American women's history and to the need to rethink the cultural aesthetics underlying women's history and women's politics. Evelyn Brooks Higginbotham strongly urges feminist scholars to accept the challenge to give race a more prominent place in their analyses of power, while Elsa Barkley Brown notes that merely recognizing differences among women is insufficient for a full understanding of the relational nature of those differences.

The second section focuses on the African background and the transatlantic slave trade. Herbert S. Klein examines the place of women in the slave trade, and John Thornton examines the impact of the slave trade on family structures in exporting areas. Paul E. Lovejoy's study of concubinage in colonial Nigeria shows that the status of women under British rule remained essentially unchanged. Sylvia M. Jacobs's work on nine African-American women missionaries to Africa reveals the issues related to race, class, and gender they confronted as they sought to "civilize" and "Christianize" Africans in the late nineteenth and early twentieth centuries.

Too many studies of Africans in the diaspora give insufficient attention to women in the British Caribbean and Canada. Rhoda E. Reddock provides a feminist perspective on slavery in the Caribbean and Barbara Bush negates the notion that enslaved women passively accepted their conditions. Aside from tracing the women's daily responses to bondage, Bush shows linkages between their traditional culture and resistance. Andrea Starr Alonzo analyzes two slave narratives, allowing readers to hear the voices of Harriet Jacobs and of the Bermudian Mary Prince, whose *The History of Mary Prince* was the first slave narrative by a woman. Afua Cooper searches for information about Mary Bibb, an early Black schoolteacher in Canada. The essays in this section invite comparisons with those about women in the United States.

The paucity of articles about African-American women in eighteenth-century America challenges historians and others to mine the available resources to eradicate this void. Joan Rezner Gundersen's essay about Black and white women in a selected parish of colonial Virginia reveals much about the interactions of race and gender in their lives. Although the women shared commonalities, race and class kept them apart. Debra L. Newman's and Mamie E. Locke's essays focus on the role and treatment of African-American women as the colonies gained independence and adopted the Constitution of the United States.

The section covering the nineteenth century calls attention to differences among African-American women. Whittington B. Johnson and Loren Schweninger examine the lives of free Black women in the South, a surprising number of whom managed to accumulate property and own real estate. Susan A. Mann shows that sharecropping, although an improvement over slavery, was a mixed blessing. And John B. Reid describes Detroit women's insistence that education was a key factor in Black progress. Washerwomen and other household workers in Atlanta weren't passive either. Tera W. Hunter salutes their efforts to control their lives. At the same time, however, many Black women who moved west in hopes of freedom found themselves arrested and imprisoned for small crimes—or no crimes at all. Anne M. Butler vividly portrays the brutal conditions they faced. Finally, Nell Irvin Painter and Mary Beth Doriani examine Black women's biography/autobiography, delving into the stories of Sojourner Truth, Harriet Jacobs, and Harriet Wilson. And Patricia K. Hunt offers a rare look at the dress of Black Georgia women.

The final section of *"We Specialize in the Wholly Impossible"* focuses on the continuing battle of African-American women for civil, economic, and political rights. Gail Bederman demonstrates how Ida B. Wells successfully manipulated northern middle-class whites into supporting her campaign against lynching. Stephanie J. Shaw offers a fresh interpretation of the creation of the National Association of Colored Women. Linda Gordon compares Black and white women's activism, showing that both groups had different definitions of "help." Lillian S. Williams focuses on one group of women reformers in Buffalo, New York. In the 1920s Black women were intensely interested in the right to vote. Rosalyn Terborg-Penn highlights the difficulties they encountered—and ultimately overcame. Jessie M. Rodrique offers a new and important look at African-Americans' reaction to the early birth control movement. Contrary to previous studies, she shows that Black women embraced family planning and in fact took it out of the bedroom and into the community. Nupur Chaudhuri's interviews of Black senior citizens in Manhattan, Kansas, reveal that even in the West racism was strong. That it was subtle made it no less painful or destructive. More recently Ruby Doris Smith Robinson came of age as an activist in the Student Nonviolent Coordinating

Committee. Cynthia Griggs Fleming describes her efforts to combine that role with those of a wife and mother.

African-American women have always had a double burden. They were—and still are—discriminated against because of race *and* gender. Yet as all these essays show, even under the most brutal and "wholly impossible" conditions, they never lost the belief that working together they could improve their lives, the lives of their children, and the lives of all Black people. For them and for us, change is wholly possible.

Darlene Clark Hine
Wilma King
Linda Reed

November 1994

"We Specialize in the Wholly Impossible"

Part I
General Theoretical Essays

African-American Women's History and the Metalanguage of Race

Evelyn Brooks Higginbotham

Theoretical discussion in African-American women's history begs for greater voice. I say this as a black woman who is cognizant of the strengths and limitations of current feminist theory. Feminist scholars have moved rapidly forward in addressing theories of subjectivity, questions of difference, the construction of social relations as relations of power, the conceptual implications of binary oppositions such as male versus female or equality versus difference—all issues defined with relevance to gender and with potential for intellectual and social transformations.[1] Notwithstanding a few notable exceptions, this new wave of feminist theorists finds little to say about race. The general trend has been to mention black and Third World feminists who first called attention to the glaring fallacies in essentialist analysis and to claims of a homogeneous "womanhood," "woman's culture," and "patriarchal oppression of women."[2] Beyond this recognition, however, white feminist scholars pay hardly more than lip service to race as they continue to analyze their own experience in ever more sophisticated forms.

This narrowness of vision is particularly ironic in that these very issues of equality and difference, the constructive strategies of power, and subjectivity and consciousness have stood at the core of black scholarship for some half-century or more. Historian W.E.B. Du Bois, sociologist Oliver Cox, and scientist Charles R. Drew are only some of the more significant pre-1950s contributors to the discussion of race as a social category and to the refutation of essentialist biological and genetic explanations.[3] These issues continue to be salient in our own time, when racism in America grows with both verve and subtlety and when "enlightened" women's historians witness, as has been the case in recent years, recurrent racial tensions at our own professional and scholarly gatherings.

Feminist scholars, especially those of African-American women's history, must accept the challenge to bring race more prominently into their analyses of power. The explication of race entails three interrelated strategies, separated here merely for the sake of analysis. First of all, we must define the construction and "technologies" of race as well as those of gender and sexuality.[4] Second, we must expose the role of race as a metalanguage by calling attention to its powerful, all-encompassing effect of the construction and representation of other social and power relations, namely, gender, class, and sexuality. Third, we must recognize race as providing sites of dialogic exchange and contestation, since race has constituted a discursive tool for both oppression and liberation. As Michael Omi and Howard Winant argue, "the effort must be made to understand race as an unstable and 'decentered' complex of social meanings constantly being transformed by political struggle."[5] Such a three-pronged approach to the history of African-American women will require borrowing and blending work by black intellectuals, white feminist scholars, and other theorists such as white male philosophers and linguists. Indeed, the very process of borrowing and blending speaks to the tradition of syncretism that has characterized the Afro-American experience.

Defining Race

When the U.S. Supreme Court had before it the task of defining obscenity, Justice Potter Stewart claimed that, while he could not intelligibly define it, "I know it when I see it."[6] When we talk about the concept of race, most people believe that they know it when they see it but arrive at nothing short of confusion when pressed to define it. Chromosome research reveals the fallacy of race as an accurate measure of genotypic or phenotypic difference between human beings. Cross-cultural and historical studies of miscegenation law reveal shifting, arbitrary, and contradictory definitions of race. Literary critics, as in the collection of essays "Race," Writing, and Difference, edited by Henry Louis Gates, compellingly present race as the "ultimate trope of difference"—as artificially and arbitrarily contrived to produce and maintain relations of power and subordination. Likewise, historian Barbara Fields argues that race is neither natural nor transhistorical, but must rather be analyzed with an eye to its functioning and maintenance within specific contexts.[7]

Like gender and class, then, race must be seen as a social construction predicated upon the recognition of difference and signifying the simultaneous distinguishing and positioning of groups vis-à-vis one another. More than this, race is a highly contested representation of relations of power between social categories by which individuals are identified and identify themselves. The recognition of racial distinctions emanates from and adapts to multiple uses of power in society. Perceived as "natural" and "appropriate," such racial categories are strategically necessary for the functioning of power in countless institutional and ideological forms, both explicit and subtle. As Michel Foucault has written, societies engage in "a perpetual process of strategic elaboration" or a constant shifting and reforming of the apparatus of power in response to their particular cultural or economic needs.[8]

Furthermore, in societies where racial demarcation is endemic to their sociocultural fabric and heritage—to their laws and economy, to their institutionalized structures and discourses, and to their epistemologies and everyday customs—gender identity is inextricably linked to and even determined by racial identity. In the Jim Crow South prior to the 1960s and in South Africa until very recently, for instance, little black girls learned at an early age to place themselves in the bathroom for "black women," not in that for "white ladies." As such a distinction suggests, in these societies the representation of both gender and class is colored by race. Their social construction becomes racialized as their concrete implications and normative meanings are continuously shaped by what Louis Althusser terms "ideological state apparatuses"—the school, family, welfare agency, hospital, television and cinema, the press.[9]

For example, the metaphoric and metonymic identification of welfare with the black population by the American public has resulted in tremendous generalization about the supposed unwillingness of many blacks to work. Welfare immediately conjures up images of black female-headed families, despite the fact that the aggregate number of poor persons who receive benefits in the form of aid to dependent children or medicare is predominantly white. Likewise, the drug problem too often is depicted in the mass media as a pathology of black lower-class life set in motion by drug dealers, youthful drug runners, and addicted victims of the ghetto. The drug problem is less often portrayed as an underground economy that mirrors and reproduces the exploitative relations of the dominant economy. The "supply-side" executives who make the "big" money are neither black nor residents of urban ghettos.

Race might also be viewed as myth, "not at all an abstract, purified essence" (to cite Roland Barthes on myth) but, rather, "a formless, unstable, nebulous condensation, whose unity and coherence are above all due to its function."[10] As a fluid set of overlapping discourses, race is perceived as arbitrary and illusionary, on the one hand, while natural and fixed on the other. To argue that race is myth and that it is an ideological rather than a biological fact does not deny that ideology has real effects on people's lives. Race serves as a "global sign," a "metalanguage," since it speaks about and lends meaning to a host of terms and expressions, to myriad aspects of life that would otherwise fall outside the referential domain of race.[11] By continually expressing overt and covert analogic relationships, race impregnates the simplest meanings we take for granted. It makes hair "good" or "bad," speech patterns "correct" or "incorrect." It is, in fact, the apparent overdeterminancy of race in Western culture, and particularly in the United States, that has permitted it to function as a metalanguage in its discursive representation and construction of social relations. Race not only tends to subsume other sets of social relations, namely, gender and class, but it blurs and disguises, suppresses and negates its own complex interplay with the very social relations it envelops. It precludes unity within the same gender group but often appears to solidify people of opposing economic classes. Whether race is textually omitted or textually privileged, its totalizing effect in obscuring class and gender remains.

This may well explain why women's studies for so long rested upon the unstated premise of racial (i.e., white) homogeneity and with this presumption proceeded to universalize "woman's" culture and oppression, while failing to see white women's own investment and complicity in the oppression of other groups of men and women. Elizabeth Spelman takes to task this idea of "homogeneous womanhood" in her exploration of race and gender in *Inessential*

Woman. Examining thinkers such as Aristotle, Simone de Beauvoir, and Nancy Chodorow, among others, Spelman observes a double standard on the part of many feminists who fail to separate their whiteness from their womanness. White feminists, she argues, typically discern two separate identities for black women, the racial and the gender, and conclude that the gender identity of black women is the same as their own: "In other words, the womanness underneath the black woman's skin is a white woman's and deep down inside the Latina woman is an Anglo woman waiting to burst through."[12]

Afro-American history, on the other hand, has accentuated race by calling explicit attention to the cultural as well as socioeconomic implications of American racism but has failed to examine the differential class and gender positions men and women occupy in black communities—thus uncritically rendering a monolithic "black community," "black experience," and "voice of the Negro." Notwithstanding that this discursive monolith most often resonates with a male voice and as the experience of men, such a rendering precludes gender subordination by black men by virtue of their own blackness and social subordination. Even black women's history, which has consciously sought to identify the importance of gender relations and the interworkings of race, class, and gender, nonetheless reflects the totalizing impulse of race in such concepts as "black womanhood" or the "black woman cross-culturally"—concepts that mask real differences of class, status and color, regional culture, and a host of other configurations of difference.

Racial Constructions of Gender

To understand race as a metalanguage, we must recognize its historical and material grounding—what Russian linguist and critic M. M. Bakhtin referred to as "the power of the word to mean."[13] This power evolves from concrete situational and ideological contexts, that is, from a position of enunciation that reflects not only time and place but values as well. The concept of race, in its verbal and extraverbal dimension, and even more specifically, in its role in the representation as well as self-representation of individuals in American society (what psychoanalytic theorists call "subjectification"), is constituted in language in which (as Bakhtin points out) there have never been " 'neutral' words and forms—words and forms that can belong to 'no one'; language has been completely taken over, shot through with intentions and accents."[14]

The social context for the construction of race as a tool for black oppression is historically rooted in the context of slavery. Barbara Fields reminds us: "The idea one people has of another, even when the difference between them is embodied in the most striking physical characteristics, is always mediated by the social context within which the two come in contact."[15] Race came to life primarily as the signifier of the master/slave relation and thus emerged superimposed upon class and property relations. Defined by law as "animate chattel," slaves constituted property as well as a social class and were exploited under a system that sanctioned white ownership of black bodies and black labor.[16]

Studies of black women in slavery, however, make poignantly clear the role of race not only in shaping the class relations of the South's "peculiar institution," but also in constructing gender's "power to mean." Sojourner Truth's famous and haunting question, "Ar'n't I a Woman?" laid bare the racialized configuration of gender under a system of class rule that compelled and expropriated women's physical labor and denied them legal right to their own bodies and sexuality, much less to the bodies to which they gave birth. While law and public opinion idealized motherhood and enforced the protection of white women's bodies, the opposite held true for black women's. Sojourner Truth's personal testimony demonstrated gender's racial meaning. She had "ploughed, and planted, and gathered into barns," and no male slave had outdone her. She had given birth to thirteen children, all of whom were sold away from her. When she cried out in grief from the depths of her motherhood, "none but Jesus heard."[17]

Wasn't Sojourner Truth a woman? The courts answered this question for slavewomen by ruling them outside the statutory rubric "woman."[18] In discussing the case of *State of Missouri v. Celia*, A. Leon Higginbotham, Jr., elucidates the racial signification of gender. Celia was fourteen years old when purchased by a successful farmer, Robert Newsome. During the five years of his ownership, Newsome habitually forced her into sexual intercourse. At age nineteen she had borne a child by him and was expecting another. In June 1855, while pregnant and ill, Celia defended herself against attempted rape by her master. Her testimony reveals that she warned him she would hurt him if he continued to abuse her while sick. When her threats would not deter his advances, she hit him over the head with a stick, immediately killing him. In an act presaging Richard Wright's *Native Son*, she then burned his body in the fireplace and the next morning spread his ashes on the pathway. Celia was apprehended and tried for first-degree murder. Her counsel sought to lower the charge of first degree to murder in self-defense, arguing that Celia had a right to resist her master's sexual advances, especially because of the imminent danger to her health. A slave master's economic and property rights, the defense contended, did not include rape. The defense rested its case on Missouri statutes that protected women from attempts to ravish, rape, or defile. The language of these particular statutes explicitly used the term "any woman," while other unrelated Missouri statutes explicitly used terms such as "white female" and "slave" or "negro" in their criminal codes. The question centered on her womanhood. The court found Celia guilty: "If Newsome was in the habit of having intercourse with the defendant who was his slave, . . . it is murder in the first degree." Celia was sentenced to death, having been denied an appeal, and was hanged in December 1855 after the birth of her child.[19]

Since racially based justifications of slavery stood at the core of Southern law, race relations, and social etiquette in general, then proof of "womanhood" did not rest on a common female essence, shared culture, or mere physical appearance. (Sojourner Truth, on one occasion, was forced to bare her breasts to a doubting audience in order to vindicate her womanhood.) This is not to deny gender's role within the social and power relations of race. Black women experienced the vicissitudes of slavery through gendered lives and thus differently from slave men. They bore and nursed children and performed domestic duties—all on top of doing fieldwork. Unlike slave men, slave women fell victim to rape precisely because of their gender. Yet gender itself was both constructed and fragmented by race. Gender, so colored by race, remained from birth until death inextricably linked to one's personal identity and social status. For black and white women, gendered identity was reconstructed and represented in very different, indeed antagonistic, racialized contexts.

Racial Constructions of Class

Henry Louis Gates argues that "race has become a trope of ultimate, irreducible difference between cultures, linguistic groups, or adherents of specific belief systems which—more often than not—also have fundamentally opposed economic interest."[20] It is interesting that the power of race as a metalanguage that transcends and masks real differences lies in the remarkable and longstanding success with which it unites whites of disparate economic positions against blacks. Until the Civil Rights era of the 1960s, race effectively served as a metaphor for class, albeit a metaphor rife with complications. For example, not all Southern whites were slave owners. Nor did they share the same economic and political interests. Upcountry yeomen protested the predominance of planters' interests over their own in state legislatures, and white artisans decried competition from the use of slave labor.[21] Yet, while Southern whites hardly constituted a homogeneous class, they united for radically different reasons around the banner of white supremacy, waged civil war, and for generations bemoaned the Lost Cause.

The metalanguage of race also transcended the voices of class and ethnic conflict among Northern whites in the great upheavals of labor during the late nineteenth and early twentieth centuries. Amid their opposition, capital and labor agreed sufficiently to exclude blacks from union membership and from more than a marginal place within the emerging industrial work force.[22] Job ceilings and hiring practices limited the overwhelming majority of black men and women to dead-end, low-paying employment—employment whites disdained or were in the process of abandoning.[23] The actual class positions of blacks did not matter, nor did the acknowledgment of differential statuses (such as by income, type of employment, morals and manners, education, or color) by blacks themselves. An entire system of cultural preconceptions disregarded these complexities and tensions by grouping all blacks into a normative well of inferiority and subserviency.[24]

The interplay of the race-class conflation with gender evoked very different social perceptions of black and white women's work roles. This is exhibited by the concern about "female loaferism," which arose in the years immediately following Emancipation. Jacqueline Jones vividly exposes the ridicule and hostility meted out to black families who attempted to remove their wives and mothers from the work force to attend their own households. In contrast to the domestic ideal for white women of all classes, the larger society deemed it "unnatural," in fact an "evil," for black married women "to play the lady" while their husbands supported them. In the immediate postwar South, the role of menial worker outside their homes was demanded of black women, even at the cost of physical coercion.[25]

Dolores Janiewski calls attention to the racialized meaning of class in her study of women's employment in a North Carolina tobacco factory during the twentieth century. She shows that race fractured the division of labor by gender. Southern etiquette demanded protection of white women's "racial honor" and required that they work under conditions described as "suitable for ladies" in contradistinction to the drudgery and dirty working conditions considered acceptable for black women. Janiewski notes that at least one employer felt no inhibition against publicly admitting his "brute treatment" of black female employees.[26]

The most effective tool in the discursive welding of race and class proved to be segregation in its myriad institutional and customary forms. Jim Crow railroad cars, for instance, became strategic sites of contestation over the conflated meaning of class and race: blacks who could afford "first-class" accommodations vehemently protested the racial basis for being denied access to them. This is dramatically evident in the case of Arthur Mitchell, Democratic congressman to the U.S. House of Representatives from Illinois during the 1930s. Mitchell was evicted from first-class railroad accommodations while traveling through Hot Springs, Arkansas. Despite his protests, he was forced to join his social "inferiors" in a Jim Crow coach with no flush toilet, washbasin, running water, or soap. The transcript of the trial reveals the following testimony:

> When I offered my ticket, the train conductor took my ticket and tore off a piece of it, but told me at that time that I couldn't ride in that car. We had quite a little controversy about it, and when he said I couldn't ride there I thought I might do some good for me to tell him who I was. I said . . . : "I am Mr. Mitchell, serving in the Congress of the United States." He said it didn't make a damn bit of difference who I was, that as long as I was a nigger I couldn't ride in that car.[27]

Neither the imprimatur of the U.S. House of Representatives nor the ability to purchase a first-class ticket afforded Mitchell the more privileged accommodations. The collective image of race represented Mitchell, the individual, just as he singularly represented the entire black race. Despite the complicating factor of his representing the federal government itself, Mitchell, like his socially constructed race, was unambiguously assigned to the second-class car, ergo lower-class space.

A long tradition of black protest focused on such treatment of women. During the late nineteenth century, segregated railroad trains were emblematic of racial configurations of both class and gender; the first-class railroad car also was called the "ladies car." Indeed, segregation's meaning for gender was exemplified in the trope of "lady." Ladies were not merely women; they represented a class, a differentiated status within the generic category of "women." Nor did society confer such status on all white women. White prostitutes, along with many working-class white women, fell outside its rubric. But no black woman, regardless of income, education, refinement, or character, enjoyed the status of lady. John R. Lynch, black congressman from Mississippi during Reconstruction, denounced the practice of forcing black women of means and refinement out of first-class accommodations and into smoking cars. He characterized the latter accommodations as "filthy . . . with drunkards, gamblers, and criminals." Arguing in support of the Civil Rights Bill of 1875, Lynch used the trope of "lady" in calling attention to race's inscription upon class distinctions:

> Under our present system of race distinctions a *white woman* of a questionable standing, yea, I may say, of an admitted immoral character, can go to any public place or upon any public conveyance and be the recipient of the same treatment, the same courtesy, and the same respect that is usually accorded to the most refined and virtuous; but let an intelligent, modest, refined *colored lady* present herself and ask that the same privileges be accorded to her that have just been accorded to her social inferior of the white race, and in nine cases out of ten, except in certain portions of the country, she will not only be refused, but insulted for making the request. [Emphasis added][28]

Early court cases involving discrimination in public transportation reveal that railroad companies seldom if ever looked upon black women as "ladies." The case of Catherine Brown, a black woman, was the first racial public transportation case to come before the U.S. Supreme Court. In February 1868, Brown was denied passage in the "ladies car" on a train traveling from Alexandria, Virginia, to Washington, D.C. Brown disregarded the demand that she sit in the "colored car" instead. Her persistence in entering the ladies car was met with violence and verbal insults.[29] The resultant court case, decided in her favor in 1873, indicated not an end to such practices but merely the federal government's short-lived support of black civil rights during the era of radical Reconstruction. The outcome of Brown's case proved to be an exception to those that would follow.

Within a decade, Ida B. Wells sued the Chesapeake, Ohio, and Southwestern Railroad for physically ejecting her out of the "ladies" car. When the conductor grabbed her arm, she bit him and held firmly to her seat. It took two men finally to dislodge her. They dragged her into the smoking car and (as she recalled in her autobiography) "the white ladies and gentlemen in the car even stood on the seats so that they could get a good view and continued applauding the conductor for his brave stand." Although her lawsuit was successful at the lower court level, the state Supreme Court of Tennessee reversed the earlier decision, sustaining both the discrimination and the bodily harm against her.[30] The racist decision, like others of the courts, led to *Plessy v. Ferguson* in 1896 and the euphemistic doctrine of "separate but equal."

Racial Constructions of Sexuality

The exclusion of black women from the dominant society's definition of "lady" said as much about sexuality as it did about class. The metalanguage of race signifies, too, the imbrication of race within the representation of sexuality. Historians of women and of science, largely influenced by Michel Foucault, now attest to the variable quality of changing conceptions of sexuality over time—conceptions informed as much by race and class as by gender.[31] Sexuality has come to be defined not only in terms of biological essentials or as a universal truth detached and transcendent from other aspects of human life and society. Rather, it is an evolving conception applied to the body but given meaning and identity by economic, cultural, and historical context.[32]

In the centuries between the Renaissance and the Victorian era, Western culture constructed and represented changing and conflicting images of woman's sexuality, which shifted diametrically from images of lasciviousness to moral purity. Yet Western conceptions of black women's sexuality resisted change during this same time.[33] Winthrop Jordan's now classic study of racial attitudes toward blacks between the sixteenth and nineteenth centuries argues that black women's bodies epitomized centuries-long European perceptions of Africans as primitive, animal-like, and savage. In America, no less distinguished and learned a figure than Thomas Jefferson conjectured that black women mated with orangutans.[34] While such thinking rationalized slavery and the sexual exploitation of slave women by white masters, it also perpetuated an enormous division between black people and white people on the "scale of humanity": carnality as opposed to intellect and/or spirit; savagery as opposed to civilization; deviance as opposed to normality; promiscuity as opposed to purity; passion as opposed to passionlessness. The black woman came to symbolize, according to Sander Gilman, an "icon for black sexuality in general."[35] This discursive gap between the races was if anything greater between white and black women than between white and black men.

Violence figured preeminently in racialized constructions of sexuality. From the days of slavery, the social construction and representation of black sexuality reinforced violence, rhetorical and real, against black women and men.[36] That the rape of black women could continue to go on with impunity long after slavery's demise underscores the pervasive belief in black female promiscuity. This belief found expression in the statement of one Southern white woman in 1904: "I cannot imagine such a creation as a virtuous black woman."[37]

The lynching of black men, with its often attendant castration, reeked of sexualized representations of race.[38] The work of black feminists of the late nineteenth century makes clear that lynching, while often rationalized by whites as a punishment for the rape of white women, more often was perpetrated to maintain racial etiquette and the socioeconomic and political hegemony of whites. Ida Wells-Barnett, Anna J. Cooper, Mary Church Terrell, and Pauline Hopkins exposed and contrasted the specter of the white woman's rape in the case of lynching and the sanctioned rape of black women by white men. Hazel Carby, in discussing these black feminist writers, established their understanding of the intersection of strategies of power with lynching and rape:

> Their legacy to us is theories that expose the colonization of the black female body by white male power and the destruction of black males who attempted to exercise any oppositional patriarchal control. When accused of threatening the white female body, the repository of heirs to property and power, the black male, and his economic, political, and social advancement, is lynched out of existence. Cooper, Wells, and Hopkins assert the necessity of seeing the relations between histories: the rape of black women in the nineties is directly linked to the rape of the female slave. Their analyses are dynamic and not limited to a parochial understanding of "women's issues"; they have firmly established the dialectical relation between economic/political power and economic/sexual power in the battle for control of women's bodies.[39]

Through a variety of mediums—theater, art, the press, and literature—discourses of racism developed and reified stereotypes of sexuality. Such representations grew out of and facilitated the larger subjugation and control of the black population. The categorization of class and racial groups according to culturally constituted sexual identities facilitated blacks' subordination within a stratified society and rendered them powerless against the intrusion of the state into their innermost private lives. This intrusion went hand in hand with the role of the state in legislating and enforcing racial segregation, disfranchisement, and economic discrimination.

James Jones's *Bad Blood: The Tuskegee Syphilis Experiment* provides us with a profoundly disturbing example of such intrusion into blacks' private lives. Jones recounts how a federal agency, the Public Health Service, embarked in 1932 upon decades of tests on black men with syphilis, denying them access to its cure in order to assess the disease's debilitating effects on the body.[40] The federal agency felt at liberty to make the study because of its unquestioning acceptance of stereotypes that conflated race, gender, and class. By defining this health problem in racial terms, "objective scientific researchers" could be absolved of all responsibility. Some even posited that blacks had "earned their illness as just recompense for wicked life-styles."[41]

The Public Health Service's willingness to prolong syphilis despite the discovery of penicillin discloses not only the federal government's lack of concern for the health of the men in its study, but its even lesser concern for black women in relationships with these men. Black women failed to receive so much as a pretense of protection, so widely accepted was the belief that the spread of the disease was inevitable because black women were promiscuous by nature. This emphasis on black immorality precluded any sensitivity to congenital syphilis; thus innocent black babies born with the disease went unnoticed and equally unprotected. Certainly the officials of the Public Health Service realized that blacks lived amid staggering poverty, amid a socioeconomic environment conducive to disease. Yet these public servants encoded hegemonic articulations of race into the language of medicine and scientific theory. Their perceptions of sexually transmitted disease, like those of the larger society, were affected by race.[42] Jones concludes:

> The effect of these views was to isolate blacks even further within American society—to remove them from the world of health and to lock them within a prison of sickness. Whether by accident or design, physicians had come dangerously close to depicting the syphilitic black as the representative black. As sickness replaced health as the normal condition of the race, something was lost from the sense of horror and urgency with which physicians had defined disease. The result was a powerful rationale for inactivity in the face of disease, which by their own estimates, physicians believed to be epidemic.[43]

In response to assaults upon black sexuality, according to Darlene Clark Hine, there arose among black women a politics of silence, a "culture of dissemblance." In order to "protect the sanctity of inner aspects of their lives," black women, especially those of the middle class, reconstructed and represented their sexuality through its absence—through silence, secrecy, and invisibility. In so doing, they sought to combat the pervasive negative images and stereotypes. Black clubwomen's adherence to Victorian ideology, as well as their self-representation as "super moral," according to Hine, was perceived as crucial not only to the protection and upward mobility of black women but also to the attainment of respect, justice, and opportunity for all black Americans.[44]

Race as a Double-Voiced Discourse

As this culture of dissemblance illustrates, black people endeavored not only to silence and conceal but also to dismantle and deconstruct the dominant society's deployment of race. Racial meanings were never internalized by blacks and whites in an identical way. The language of race has historically been what Bakhtin calls a double-voiced discourse—serving the voice of black oppression and the voice of black liberation. Bakhtin observes: "The word in language is half someone else's. It becomes 'one's own' only when the speaker populates it with his [or her] own intentions, his [or her] own semantic and expressive intention."[45] Blacks took "race" and empowered its language with their own meaning and intent, just as the slaves and freedpeople had appropriated white surnames, even those of their masters, and made them their own.[46]

For African-Americans, race signified a cultural identity that defined and connected them as a people, even as a nation. To be called a "race leader," "race man," or "race woman" by the black community was not a sign of insult or disapproval, nor did such titles refer to any and every black person. Quite to the contrary, they were conferred on Carter G. Woodson, W.E.B. Du Bois,

Ida Wells-Barnett, Mary McLeod Bethune, and the other men and women who devoted their lives to the advancement of their people. When the National Association of Colored Women referred to its activities as "race work," it expressed both allegiance and commitment to the concerns of black people. Through a range of shifting, even contradictory meanings and accentuations expressed at the level of individual and group consciousness, blacks fashioned race into a cultural identity that resisted white hegemonic discourses.

The "two-ness" of being both American and Negro, which Du Bois so eloquently captured in 1903, resonates across time. If blacks as individuals referred to a divided subjectivity—"two warring ideals in one dark body"—they also spoke of a collective identity in the colonial terms of a "nation within a nation."[47] The many and varied voices of black nationalism have resounded again and again from the earliest days of the American republic. Black nationalism found advocates in Paul Cuffee, John Russwurm, and Martin Delany in the nineteenth century, and Marcus Garvey, Malcolm X, and Stokely Carmichael in the twentieth.[48] We know far too little about women's perceptions of nationalism, but Pauline Hopkins's serialized novel *Of One Blood* (1903) counterposes black and Anglo-Saxon races: "The dawn of the Twentieth century finds the Black race fighting for existence in every quarter of the globe. From over the sea Africa stretches her hands to the American Negro and cries aloud for sympathy in her hour of trial. . . . In America, caste prejudice has received fresh impetus as the 'Southern brother' of the Anglo-Saxon family has arisen from the ashes of secession, and like the prodigal of old, has been gorged with fatted calf and 'fixin's.' "[49]

Likewise Hannah Nelson, an elementary school graduate employed most of her life in domestic service, told anthropologist John Langston Gwaltney in the 1970s: "We are a nation. The best of us have said it and everybody feels it. I know that will probably bother your white readers, but it is nonetheless true that black people think of themselves as an entity."[50] Thus, when historian Barbara Fields observes the "Afro-Americans invented themselves, not as a race, but as a nation," she alludes to race as a double-voiced discourse.[51] For blacks, race signified cultural identity and heritage, not biological inferiority. However, Fields's discussion understates the power of race to mean nation—specifically, race as the sign of perceived kinship ties between blacks in Africa and throughout the diaspora. In the crucible of the Middle Passage and American slavery, the multiple linguistic, tribal, and ethnic division among Africans came to be forged into a single, common ancestry. While not adhering to "scientific" explanations of superior and inferior races, African-Americans inscribed the black nation with racially laden meanings of blood ties that bespoke a lineage and culture more imagined than real.

Such imaginings were not unique to African-Americans.[52] As nation states emerged in Europe during the fifteenth and sixteenth centuries, the concept of "race" came increasingly to articulate a nationalist ideology. Racial representations of nation included, on the one hand, "cosmopolitan" views that characterized each national grouping as contributing its own "special gift" to the complementarity of humankind, and, on the other hand, views of hierarchical difference that justified the existence of nation states and the historical dominance of certain groupings over others. Hence, Thomas Arnold could speak of the Anglo-Saxon's lineage in an 1841 lecture at Oxford: "Our English race is the German race; for though our Norman forefathers had learnt to speak a stranger's language, yet in blood, as we know, they were the Saxons' brethren: both alike belonged to the Teutonic or German stock."[53] Such cultural conceptions surely informed nineteenth-century African-American perceptions of the black nation as a site of group uniqueness.

Throughout the nineteenth century, blacks and whites alike subscribed to what George Fredrickson terms "romantic racialism."[54] Blacks constructed and valorized a self-representation essentially antithetical to that of whites. In his article "The Conservation of Races," published in 1897, Harvard-trained W.E.B. Du Bois disclosed his admiration for what he believed to be the "spiritual, psychical" uniqueness of his people—their "special gift" to humanity.[55] Twentieth-century essentialist concepts such as "negritude," "soul," and most recently "Afrocentricity" express in new and altered form the continued desire to capture transcendent threads of racial "oneness." Frantz Fanon described the quest for cultural identity and self-recovery as "the whole body of efforts made by a people in the sphere of thought to describe, justify and praise action through which that people has created itself and keeps itself in existence."[56] These efforts seek to negate white stereotypes of blacks and in their place insert a black worldview or standpoint. Of critical importance here are the dialogic racial representations effected by blacks themselves against negative representations—or more precisely, blacks' appropriation of the productive power of language for the purpose of resistance.[57]

Such a discursive rendering of race counters images of physical and psychical rupture with images of wholeness. Yet once again, race serves as myth and as a global sign, for it superimposes a "natural" unity over a plethora of historical, socioeconomic, and ideological differences among blacks themselves. This is not to understate the critical liberating intention implicit in blacks' own usage of the term "the race" when referring to themselves as a group. But the characterization obscures rather than mirrors the reality of black heterogeneity. In fact, essentialist or other racialized conceptions of national culture hardly reflect paradigmatic consistency. Black nationalism itself has been a heteroglot conception, categorized variously as revolutionary, bourgeois reformist, cultural, religious, economic, or emigrationist.[58] Race as the sign of cultural identity has been neither a coherent nor static concept among African-Americans. Its perpetuation and resilience have reflected shifting, often monolithic and essentialist assumptions on the part of thinkers attempting to identify and define a black peoplehood or nation.

Acceptance of a nation-based, racialized perspective even appears in the work of black women scholars, who seek to ground a black feminist standpoint in the concrete experience of race and gender oppression. Notwithstanding the critical importance of this work in contesting racism and sexism in the academy and larger society, its focus does not permit sufficient exploration of ideological spaces of difference among black women themselves. For example, sociologist Patricia Hill Collins identifies an ethic of caring and an ethic of personal accountability at the root of Afrocentric values and particularly of Afrocentric feminist epistemology, yet she does not investigate how such values and epistemology are affected by differing class positions.[59] In short, she posits but does not account for the *singularity* of an Afro-American women's standpoint amid diverse and conflicting positions of enunciation.

The rallying notion of "racial uplift" among black Americans during the late nineteenth and early twentieth centuries illustrates the problematic aspects of identifying a standpoint that encompasses all black women. Racial uplift was celebrated in the motto of the National Association of Colored Women—"lifting as we climb." The motto itself expressed a paradox: belief in black womanhood's common cause and recognition of differential values and socioeconomic positions. Racial uplift, while invoking a discursive ground on which to explode negative stereotypes of black women, remained locked within hegemonic articulations of gender, class, and sexuality. Black women teachers, missionaries, and club members zealously promoted values of temperance, sexual repression, and polite manners among the poor.

"Race work" or "racial uplift" equated normality with conformity to white middle-class models of gender roles and sexuality. Given the extremely limited educational and income opportunities during the late nineteenth–early twentieth centuries, many black women linked mainstream domestic duties, codes of dress, sexual conduct, and public etiquette with both individual success and group progress.[60] Black leaders argued that "proper" and "respectable" behavior proved blacks worthy of equal civil and political rights. Conversely, nonconformity was equated with deviance and pathology and was often cited as a cause of racial inequality and injustice. S.W. Layten, founder of the National League for the Protection of Colored Women and leader of one million black Baptist women, typified this attitude in her statement of 1904: "Unfortunately the minority or bad Negroes have given the race a questionable reputation; these degenerates are responsible for every discrimination we suffer."[61]

On a host of levels, racial uplift stood at odds with the daily practices and aesthetic tastes of many poor, uneducated, and "unassimilated" black men and women dispersed throughout the rural South or newly huddled in urban centers.[62] The politics of "respectability" disavowed, in often repressive ways, much of the expressive culture of the "folk," for example, sexual behavior, dress style, leisure activity, music, speech patterns, and religious worship patterns. Similar class and sexual tensions between the discourse of the intelligentsia (the "New Negro") and that of the "people" (the "folk" turned proletariat in the northern urban context) appear in Hazel Carby's discussion of black women novelists of the Harlem Renaissance during the 1920s.[63]

Today, the metalanguage of race continues to bequeath its problematic legacy. While its discursive construction of reality into two opposing camps—blacks versus whites or Afrocentric versus Eurocentric standpoints—provides the basis for resistance against external forces of black subordination, it tends to forestall resolution of problems of gender, class, and sexual orientation internal to black communities. The resolution of such differences is also requisite to the liberation and well-being of "the race." Worse yet, problems deemed too far astray of respectability are subsumed within a culture of dissemblance. The AIDS crisis serves as a case in point, with AIDS usually contextualized within a Manichean opposition of good versus evil that translates into heterosexuality versus homosexuality or wholesome living versus intravenous drug use. At a time when AIDS is a leading killer of black women and their children in impoverished inner-city neighborhoods, educational and support strategies lag far behind those of white gay communities.[64] Black women's groups and community organizations fail to tackle the problem with the priority it merits. They shy away from public discussion in large measure because of the historic association of disease and racial/sexual stereotyping.

Conclusion

By analyzing white America's deployment of race in the construction of power relations, perhaps we can better understand why black women historians have largely refrained from an analysis of gender along the lines of the male/female dichotomy so prevalent among white feminists. Indeed, some black women scholars adopt the term *womanist* instead of *feminist* in rejection of gender-based dichotomies that lead to a false homogenizing of women. By so doing they follow in the spirit of black scholar and educator Anna J. Cooper, who in *A Voice from the South* (1892) inextricably linked her identity to the "quiet, undisputed dignity" of her womanhood.[65] At the threshold of the twenty-first century, black women scholars continue to emphasize the inseparable unity of race and gender in their thought. They dismiss efforts to bifurcate the identity of black women (and indeed of all women) into discrete categories—as if culture, consciousness, and lived experience could at times constitute "woman" isolated from the contexts of race, class, and sexuality that give form and content to the particular women we are.[66]

On the other hand, we should challenge both the overdeterminacy of race *vis-à-vis* social relations among blacks themselves and conceptions of the black community as harmonious and monolithic. The historic reality of racial conflict in America has tended to devalue and discourage attention to gender conflict within black communities and to tensions of class or sexuality among black women. The totalizing tendency of race precludes recognition and acknowledgment of intragroup social relations as relations of power. With its implicit understandings, shared cultural codes, and inchoate sense of a common heritage and destiny, the metalanguage of race resounds over and above a plethora of conflicting voices. But it cannot silence them.

Black women of different economic and regional backgrounds, of different skin tones and sexual orientations, have found themselves in conflict over interpretation of symbols and norms, public behavior, coping strategies, and a variety of micropolitical acts of resistance to structures of domination.[67] Although racialized cultural identity has clearly served blacks in the struggle against discrimination, it has not sufficiently addressed the empirical reality of gender conflict within the black community or class differences among black women themselves. Historian E. Frances White makes this point brilliantly when she asserts that "the site of counter-discourse is itself contested terrain."[68] By fully recognizing race as an unstable, shifting, and strategic reconstruction, feminist scholars must take up new challenges to inform and confound many of the assumptions currently underlying Afro-American history and women's history. We must problematize much more of what we take for granted. We must bring to light and to coherence the one and the many that we always were in history and still actually are today.

NOTES

A number of people read earlier versions of this article. I am especially grateful to the insights, suggestions, and probing questions of Sharon Harley, Paul Hanson, Darlene Clark Hine, and Carroll Smith-Rosenberg.

1. See, e.g., Teresa de Lauretis, *Alice Doesn't: Feminism, Semiotics, Cinema* (Bloomington: Indiana University Press, 1984), and Teresa de Lauretis, ed., *Feminist Studies, Feminist Criticism* (Bloomington: Indiana University Press, 1986); Toril Moi, *Sexual/Textual Politics* (New York: Routledge, 1985); Joan W. Scott, *Gender and the Politics of History* (New York: Columbia University Press, 1988); Judith Butler, *Gender Trouble: Feminism and the Subversion of Identity* (New York: Routledge, 1990).

2. By the early 1980s women of color from various disciplines had challenged the notion of a homogeneous womanhood. A few include: Sharon Harley and Rosalyn Terborg-Penn, eds., *The Afro-American Woman: Struggles and Images* (Port Washington, N.Y.: Kennikat, 1978); Gloria T. Hull, Patricia Bell Scott, and Barbara Smith, eds., *But Some of Us Are Brave* (Old Westbury, N.Y.: Feminist Press, 1982); Barbara Smith, ed., *Home Girls: A Black Feminist Anthology* (New York: Kitchen Table: Women of Color Press, 1983); Cherrie Moraga and Gloria Anzaldua, eds., *This Bridge Called My Back: Writings by Radical Women of Color* (New York: Kitchen Table: Women of Color Press, 1983); Bonnie Thornton Dill, "Race, Class, and Gender: Prospects for an All-Inclusive Sisterhood," *Feminist Studies* 9 (Spring 1983): 131-50.

3. Charles Drew, in developing a method of blood preservation and organizing blood banks, contributed to the explosion of the myth that blacks were physiologically different from whites. See Charles E. Wynes, *Charles Richard Drew: The Man and the Myth* (Urbana: University of Illinois Press, 1988), 65-71; and C.R. Drew and J. Scudder, "Studies in Blood Preservation: Fate of Cellular Elements and Prothrombin in Citrated Blood," *Journal of Laboratory and Clinical Medicine* 26 (June 1941): 1473-78. Also see W.E.B. Du Bois, "Races," *Crisis* (August 1911), 157-58,

and *Dusk of Dawn: An Essay toward an Autobiography of a Race Concept* (New York: Harcourt Brace, 1940), 116-17, 137; Oliver C. Cox, *Caste, Class and Race* (1948; reprint, New York: Monthly Review Press, 1970), 317-20.

4. Michel Foucault, *History of Sexuality*, vol. 1, *An Introduction*, trans. Robert Hurley (New York: Vintage, 1980), 127, 146. Teresa De Lauretis criticizes Foucault for presenting a male-centered class analysis that disregards gender (see *Technologies of Gender* [Bloomington: Indiana University Press, 1987], 3-30). In both cases "technology" is used to signify the elaboration and implementation of discourses (classificatory and evaluative) in order to maintain the survival and hegemony of one group over another. These discourses are implemented through pedagogy, medicine, mass media, etc.

5. For discussion of race and signification, see Robert Miles, *Racism* (New York: Routledge, 1989), 69-98; also Michael Omi and Howard Winant, *Racial Formation in the United States from 1960s to the 1980s* (New York: Routledge, 1986), 68.

6. *Jacobellis v. State of Ohio*, 378 U.S. 184, 197 (1964).

7. Although Fields does not use the term "trope," her discussion of race parallels that of Gates. Henry Louis Gates, Jr., ed., *"Race," Writing, and Difference* (Chicago: University of Chicago Press, 1986), esp. articles by Gates, "Introduction: Writing, 'Race' and the Difference It Makes," 1-20; Anthony Appiah, "The Uncompleted Argument: Du Bois and the Illusion of Race," 21-37; and Tzvetan Todorov, " 'Race,' Writing, and Culture," 370-80. See also Barbara J. Fields, "Ideology and Race in American History," in *Region, Race, and Reconstruction: Essays in Honor of C. Vann Woodward*, ed. J. Morgan Kousser and James M. McPherson (New York: Oxford University Press, 1982), 143-47.

8. Michel Foucault describes the strategic function of the apparatus of power as a system of relations between diverse elements (e.g., discourses, laws, architecture, moral values, institutions) that are supported by types of knowledge: "I understand by the 'term' apparatus a sort of . . . formation which has its major function at a given historical moment that of responding to an *urgent need*. . . . This may have been, for example, the assimilation of a floating population found to be burdensome for an essentially mercantilist economy" (*Power/Knowledge: Selected Interviews and Other Writings, 1972-1977*, ed. Colin Gordon [New York: Pantheon, 1980], 194-95).

9. Louis Althusser, "Ideology and Ideological State Apparatuses (Notes toward an Investigation)," in his *Lenin and Philosophy, and Other Essays*, trans. Ben Brewster (New York: Monthly Review Press, 1972), 165.

10. Roland Barthes, *Mythologies*, trans. Annette Lavers (New York: Hill & Wang, 1972), 118, 120.

11. *Ibid.*, 114-15.

12. Elizabeth V. Spelman, *Inessential Woman: Problems of Exclusion in Feminist Thought* (Boston: Beacon, 1988), 13, 80-113.

13. M.M. Bakhtin, *The Dialogic Imagination: Four Essays*, ed. Michael Holquist, trans. Caryl Emerson and Michael Holquist (Austin: University of Texas Press, 1981), 352.

14. Bakhtin argues: "Language is not an abstract system of normative forms but rather a concrete heteroglot conception of the world." For my purposes of discussion, "race," therefore, would convey multiple, even conflicting meanings (heteroglossia) when expressed by different groups—the multiplicity of meanings and intentions not simply rendered between blacks and whites, but within each of these two groups. See Bakhtin on "heteroglossia" (293, 352),

15. Fields, "Race and Ideology in American History," 148-49.

16. Eugene D. Genovese, *Roll, Jordan, Roll: The World the Slaves Made* (New York: Pantheon, 1974), 3-7, 28.

17. Sojourner Truth's speech appears in Bert James Loewenberg and Ruth Bogin, *Black Women in Nineteenth Century American Life* (University Park: Pennsylvania State University Press, 1976), 235. For works on slave women, see Deborah Gray White, *Ar'n't I a Woman: Female Slaves in the Plantation South* (New York: Norton, 1985); Elizabeth Fox-Genovese, *Within the Plantation Household: Black and White Women of the Old South* (Chapel Hill: University of North Carolina Press, 1988), esp. chaps. 3 and 6.

18. Fox-Genovese, 326.

19. A. Leon Higginbotham, Jr., notes: "One of the ironies is that the master's estate was denied a profit from Celia's rape. Despite the court's 'mercy' in delaying execution until the birth of the child, the record reflects that a Doctor Carter delivered Celia's child, who was born dead" ("Race, Sex, Education and Missouri Jurisprudence: *Shelley v. Kraemer* in a Historical Perspective," *Washington University Law Quarterly* 67 [1989]: 684-85).

20. Gates, "Introduction: Writing 'Race' and the Difference It Makes," 5.

21. Fields, "Ideology and Race in American History," 156.

22. Abram Harris and Sterling Spero, *The Black Worker: A Study of the Negro in the Labor Movement* (1931; reprint, New York: Antheneum, 1968), 158-62, 167-81; Joe William Trotter, *Black Milwaukee: The Making of an Industrial Proletariat, 1915-45* (Urbana: University of Illinois Press, 1985), 13-14, 18, 39-79; Dolores Janiewski, *Sisterhood Denied: Race, Gender and Class in a New South Community* (Philadelphia: Temple University Press, 1985), 152-78; Jacqueline Jones, *Labor of Love: Labor of Sorrow* (New York: Basic, 1985), 148, 168, 177-79.

23. See Sharon Harley, "For the Good of Family and Race," *Signs: Journal of Women in Culture and Society* 15, no. 2 (Winter 1990): 340-41.

24. Patricia Hill Collins argues persuasively for the continued role of race in explaining social class position in her analysis of studies of contemporary black low-income, female-headed families. In her critique of the Moynihan report and the televised Bill Moyers documentary on the "vanishing black family," Collins argues that social class is conceptualized in both these studies as "an outcome variable" of race and gender rather than the product of such structural factors as industrial flight, mechanization, inadequate schools, etc. ("A Comparison of Two Works on Black Family Life," *Signs* 14, no. 4 [Summer 1989]: 876-77, 882-84).

25. For discussion of "female loaferism," see Jacqueline Jones, *Labor of Love*, 45, 58-60.

26. Dolores Janiewski, "Seeking 'a New Day and a New Way': Black Women and Unions in the Southern Tobacco Industry," in *"To Toil the Livelong Day": America's Women at Work, 1780-1980*, ed. Carol Groneman and Mary Beth Norton (Ithaca, N.Y.: Cornell University Press, 1987), 163.

27. *Mitchell v. United States*, 313 U.S. 80 (1941), app.; also see Catherine A. Barnes, *Journey from Jim Crow: The Desegregation of Southern Transit* (New York: Columbia University Press, 1983), 1-2.

28. See John R. Lynch's speech of the Civil Rights Bill of 1875 in U.S. Congress, *Congressional Record* (February 3, 1875), 944-45.

29. *Railroad Co. v. Brown*, 84 U.S. 445 (Wall) 445 (1873).

30. See Ida B. Wells-Barnett, *Crusade for Justice: The Autobiography of Ida B. Wells*, ed. Alfreda M. Duster (Chicago: University of Chicago Press, 1970), 18-20; for full discussion of this case and those of other black women on buses and streetcars, see

Willie Mae Coleman, "Black Women and Segregated Public Transportation: Ninety Years of Resistance," *Truth: Newsletter of the Association of Black Women Historians* (1986), reprinted in Darlene Clark Hine, ed., *Black Women in United States History* (Brooklyn: Carlson, 1990), 5:296-98.

31. For work by historians on sexuality's relation to class and race, see the essays in Kathy Peiss and Christina Simmons, with Robert Padgug, eds., *Passion and Power: Sexuality in History* (Philadelphia: Temple University Press, 1989).

32. Foucault, *History of Sexuality*, 1:14, 140, 143, 145-46, and *Power/Knowledge*, 210-11.

33. Nancy Cott calls attention to the role of evangelical Protestantism and, later, science in contributing to the image of "passionlessness" for American northern women ("Passionlessness: An Interpretation of Victorian Sexual Ideology, 1790-1850," *Signs* 4, no. 2 [Winter 1978]: 219-36); for changing Western representations, see Thomas Laqueur, *Making Sex: Body and Gender from the Greeks to Freud* (Cambridge, Mass.: Harvard University Press, 1990).

34. See discussion of Jefferson and larger discussion of Western views toward blacks in Winthrop D. Jordan, *White over Black: American Attitudes toward the Negro, 1550-1812* (New York: Norton, 1977), 24-40, 151, 154-59, 458-59.

35. See Sander L. Gilman, "Black Bodies, White Bodies: Toward an Iconography of Female Sexuality in late Nineteenth-Century Art, Medicine, and Literature," in Gates, ed., *"Race,"* 223-40.

36. Jacquelyn Dowd Hall, *Revolt against Chivalry: Jessie Daniel Ames and the Women's Campaign against Lynching* (New York: Columbia University Press, 1979), 129-57, 220; Ida Wells-Barnett, *On Lynching*, reprint ed. (New York: Arno Press, 1969); Joel Williamson, *A Rage for Order* (New York: Oxford University Press, 1986), 117-51; Howard Smead, *Blood Justice: The Lynching of Mack Charles Parker* (New York: Oxford University Press, 1986).

37. "Experiences of the Race Problem: By a Southern White Woman," *Independent*, vol. 56 (March 17, 1904), as quoted in Anne Firor Scott, "Most Invisible of All: Black Women's Voluntary Associations," *Journal of Southern History* 56 (February 1990): 10. Neil R. McMillen observes for the early twentieth century that courts did not usually convict white men for the rape of black women, "because whites generally agreed that no black female above the age of puberty was chaste" (*Dark Journey: Black Mississippians in the Age of Jim Crow* [Urbana: University of Illinois Press, 1989], 205-6).

38. A number of writers have dealt with the issue of castration. For historical studies of the early slave era, see Jordan, *White over Black*, 154-58, 463, 473; also discussing castration statutes as part of the slave codes in colonial Virginia, South Carolina, and Pennsylvania is A. Leon Higginbotham, Jr., *In the Matter of Color: Race and the American Legal Process* (New York: Oxford University Press, 1978), 58, 168, 177, 282, 413, n. 107. For discussion of castration during the twentieth century, see Richard Wright, "The Ethics of Living Jim Crow: An Autobiographical Sketch," in his *Uncle Toms's Children* (1938; reprint, New York: Harper & Row, 1965); and Trudier Harris, *Exorcising Blackness: Historical and Literary Lynching and Burning Rituals* (Bloomington: Indiana University Press, 1984), 29-68.

39. Bettina Aptheker, *Woman's Legacy: Essays on Race, Sex and Class in American History* (Amherst: University of Massachusetts Press, 1982), 53-77; Hazel V. Carby, " 'On the Threshold of Woman's Era': Lynching, Empire, and Sexuality in Black Feminist Theory," in Gates, ed., *"Race,"* 314-15.

40. James H. Jones, *Bad Blood: The Tuskegee Syphilis Experiment* (New York: Free Press, 1981), 11-29.

41. *Ibid.*, 22. Elizabeth Fee argues that in the 1920s and 1930s, before a cure was found for syphilis, physicians did not speak in the dispassionate tone of germ theory but, rather, reinforced the image of syphilis as a "black problem" (see her study of Baltimore, "Venereal Disease: The Wages of Sin?" in Peiss and Simmons, eds., *Passion and Power*, 182-84).

42. For a study of the social construction of venereal disease, from the late nineteenth century through the AIDS crisis of our own time, see Allan M. Brandt, *No Magic Bullet: A Social History of Venereal Disease in the United States since 1880* (New York: Oxford University Press, 1987); also see Doris Y. Wilkinson and Gary King, "Conceptual and Methodological Issues in the Use of Race as a Variable: Policy Implications," *Milbank Quarterly* 65 (1987): 68.

43. Jones, *Bad Blood*, 25, 28.

44. Darlene Clark Hine, "Rape and the Inner Lives of Black Women in the Middle West: Preliminary Thoughts on the Culture of Dissemblance," *Signs* 14, no. 4 (Summer 1989): 915.

45. Bakhtin, *Dialogic Imagination*, 293, 324.

46. On slave surnames, see Herbert G. Gutman, *The Black Family in Slavery and Freedom, 1750-1925* (New York: Pantheon, 1976), 230-56; also George P. Cunningham, " 'Called into Existence': Desire, Gender, and Voice in Frederick Douglass's Narrative of 1845," *Differences* 1, no. 3 (1989): 112-13, 117, 129-31.

47. Martin Robison Delany wrote in the 1850s of blacks in the United States: "We are a nation within a nation;—as the Poles in Russia, the Hungarians in Austria, the Welsh, Irish, and Scotch in the British Dominions" (see his *The Condition, Elevation, Emigration and Destiny of the Colored People of the United States*, reprint ed. [New York: Arno, 1969], 209; also W.E. Burghardt Du Bois, *The Souls of Black Folks* [New York: Washington Square Press, 1970], 3).

48. See, devoted to the subject of nationalism, John H. Bracey, Jr., August Meier, and Elliott Rudwick, eds, *Black Nationalism in America* (New York: Bobbs-Merrill, 1970); Sterling Stuckey, *Slave Culture: Nationalist Theory and the Foundations of Black America* (New York: Oxford University Press, 1987), and *The Ideological Origins of Black Nationalism* (Boston: Beacon, 1972); Wilson Jeremiah Moses, *The Golden Age of Black Nationalism, 1850-1925* (Hamden, Conn.: Archon, 1978).

49. Pauline Hopkins, "Heroes and Heroines in Black," *Colored American Magazine* 6 (January 1903): 211. The original publication of *Of One Blood* was serialized in issues of the *Colored American Magazine* between November 1902 and November 1903. See the novel in its entirety, along with Hazel Carby's introduction to the Oxford edition, in Pauline Hopkins, *Magazine Novels of Pauline Hopkins* (New York: Oxford University Press, 1988); see Hazel V. Carby, *Reconstructing Womanhood: The Emergence of the Afro-American Woman Novelist* (New York: Oxford University Press, 1987), 155-62.

50. See John Langston Gwaltney, "A Nation within a Nation," in *Drylongso: A Self-Portrait of Black America*, ed. John Langston Gwaltney (New York: Random House, 1980), 3-23; and Patricia Hill Collins, "The Social Construction of Black Feminist Thought," *Signs* 14, no. 4 (Summer 1989): 765-70. For a critique of race and essentialism, see Diana Fuss, *Essentially Speaking: Feminism, Nature, and Difference* (New York: Routledge, 1989), 73-96.

51. Robert Miles argues that both race and nation are "supra-class and supra-gender forms of categorization with considerable potential for articulation" (*Racism*, 89-90). Also, see Barbara Jeanne Fields, "Slavery, Race, and Ideology in the United States of America," *New Left Review*, no. 181 (May/June 1990), 115.

52. See Benedict R. Anderson's discussion of nation as "imagined" in the sense of its being limited (not inclusive of all mankind), sovereign, and a community, in his *Imagined Communities: Reflections on the Origin and Spread of Nationalism* (New York and London: Verso, 1983), 14-16.

53. Arthur Penrhyn Stanley, *The Life and Correspondence of Thomas Arnold, D.D.*, 12th ed. (London 1881), 2:324, quoted and cited in Reginald Horsman, *Race and Manifest Destiny: The Origins of American Racial Anglo-Saxonism* (Cambridge, Mass.: Harvard University Press, 1981), 66.

54. George Fredrickson discusses "romantic racialism" within the context of "benign" views of black distinctiveness. This view was upheld by romanticism, abolitionism, and evangelical religion and should be distinguished from "scientific" explanations or cultural interpretations that vilified blacks as beasts and unworthy of human dignity (*The Black Image in the White Mind* [New York: Harper & Row, 1972], 97-99, 101-15, 125-26).

55. W.E.B. Du Bois stated: "But while race differences have followed mainly physical race lines, yet no mere physical distinctions would really define or explain the deeper differences—the cohesiveness and continuity of these groups. The deeper differences are spiritual, physical, differences—undoubtedly based on the physical but infinitely transcending them" ("The Conservation of Races," in *W.E.B. Du Bois Speaks: Speeches and Addresses, 1890-1919*, ed. Philip S. Foner [New York: Pathfinder, 1970], 77-79, 84; see also Appiah's critique of Du Bois in *Uncompleted Argument*, 23-29.

56. Frantz Fanon offers this definition of national culture in contradistinction to one based on "an abstract populism that believes it can discover the people's true nature" (*The Wretched of the Earth* [New York: Grove, 1968], 233).

57. Raymond Williams asserts: "Language has then to be seen as a persistent kind of creation and re-creation: a dynamic presence and a constant regenerative process" (*Marxism and Literature* [New York: Oxford University Press, 1977], 31).

58. See Bracey, Meier, and Rudwick, eds., *Black Nationalism*, xxvi-xxx; Omni and Winant, *Racial Formation in the United States*, 38-51.

59. E. Frances White's perceptive analysis of African-Americans' contestation of the discursive representation of Africa calls attention to the conservative implications of Afrocentric feminism. See E. Frances White, "Africa on My Mind: Gender, Counter Discourse and African-American Nationalism," *Journal of Women's History* 2 (Spring 1990): 90-94; Patricia Hill Collins, "The Social Construction of Black Feminist Thought," 765-70, and *Black Feminist Thought: Knowledge, Consciousness, and the Politics of Empowerment* (Boston: Unwin Hyman, 1990), 10-11, 15. Also for a good critique, see bell hooks, *Yearning: Race, Gender, and Cultural Politics* (Boston: South End Press, 1990).

60. Evelyn Brooks Higginbotham, "Beyond the Sound of Silence: Afro-American Women in History," *Gender and History* 1 (Spring 1989): 58-59.

61. National Baptist Convention, *Journal of the Twenty-fourth Annual Session of the National Baptist Convention and the Fifth Annual Session of the Woman's Convention, Held in Austin, Texas, September 14-19, 1904* (Nashville: National Baptist Publishing Board, 1904), 324; also, I discuss the politics of respectability as both subversive and

conservative in Evelyn Brooks Higginbotham, *Righteous Discontent: The Women's Movement in the Black Baptist Church, 1880-1920* (Cambridge, Mass.: Harvard University Press, 1992), chap. 7.

62. Houston A. Baker, Jr., in his discussion of the black vernacular, characterizes the "quotidian sounds of black every day life" as both a defiant and entrancing voice (*Afro-American Poetics: Revisions of Harlem and the Black Aesthetic* [Madison: University of Wisconsin Press, 1988], 95-107); see also Houston A. Baker, Jr., *Blues, Ideology and Afro-American Literature: A Vernacular Theory* (Chicago: University of Chicago Press, 1984), 11-13. Similarly, John Langston Gwaltney calls the "folk" culture of today's cities a "core black culture," which is "more than ad hoc synchronic adaptive survival." Gwaltney links its values and epistemology to a long peasant tradition. See Gwaltney, ed., *Drylongso*, xv-xvii.

63. Carby, *Reconstructing Womanhood*, 163-75; also Henry Louis Gates, Jr., "The Trope of a New Negro and the Reconstruction of the Image of the Black," *Representations* 24 (Fall 1988): 129-55.

64. See Bruce Lambert, "AIDS in the Black Women Seen as Leading Killer," *New York Times* (July 11, 1990); Ernest Quimby and Samuel R. Friedman, "Dynamics of Black Mobilization against AIDS in New York City," *Social Problems* 36 (October 1989): 407-13; Evelynn Hammonds, "Race, Sex, Aids: The Construction of 'Other,'" *Radical America* 29 (November-December 1987): 28-36; also Brandt, *No Magic Bullet*, 186-92.

65. Anna Julia Cooper stated: "When and where I enter in the quiet, undisputed dignity of my womanhood without violence and without suing or special patronage, then and there the whole Negro race enters with me" (*A Voice from the South*, reprint of the 1892 ed. [New York: Negro Universities Press, 1969], 31).

66. Alice Walker, *In Search of Our Mothers' Gardens: Womanist Prose* (New York: Harcourt Brace Jovanovich, 1983), xi-xii; also see, e.g., Elsa Barkley Brown's introductory pages and historical treatment of Maggie Lena Walker, black Richmond banker in the early twentieth century, which reflect this perspective ("Womanist Consciousness: Maggie Lena Walker and the Independent Order of Saint Luke," *Signs* 14, no. 3 [Spring 1989]: 610-15, 630-33).

67. I am using "micropolitics" synonymously with James C. Scott's term "infrapolitics." According to Scott, the infrapolitics of subordinate groups not only constitute the everyday, prosaic, "unobtrusive" level of political struggle in contradistinction to overt protests but also constitute the "cultural and structural underpinning" of more visible discontent (*Domination and the Arts of Resistance: Hidden Transcripts* [New Haven, Conn.: Yale University Press, 1990], 183-92).

68. White, "Africa on My Mind," 82.

2

When Your Work Is Not Who You Are:

The Development of a Working-Class Consciousness Among Afro-American Women

Sharon Harley

May Anna Madison, a middle-aged former domestic quoted in John Langston Gwaltney's *Drylongso: A Self-Portrait of Black America*, declared: "One very important difference between white people and black people is that white people think that you *are* your work. . . . Now, a black person has more sense than that because he knows that what I am doing doesn't have anything to do with what I want to do or what I do when I am doing for myself. Now, black people think that my work is just what I have to do to get what I want."[1]

To the extent that attitudes toward wage work and occupational status are a reflection of racial and gender differences, Madison, a contemporary black female domestic, offers an accurate description of the traditional difference between how blacks and whites, women and men perceive the meaning of paid work in their lives—a perceptual difference that was present during the Progressive Era. As a consequence of both low status in the occupational structure and a desire to abide by conventional notions of women's proper role, the majority of black wage-earning women, especially mothers and wives, usually did not believe that their presence or their position in the labor force was an accurate reflection of who they were or of how they should be viewed by members of the black community. For most black women, opportunities for social status existed outside the labor market—in their family, neighborhood, and organizational and church lives.[2] Likewise, the development of a working-class consciousness among black women during the Progressive Era was affected by their domestic roles and occupational status, which differed somewhat from those of their white counterparts.

The operational definition of working-class consciousness as it is applied to black working women during the Progressive Era or in this paper is the expression of shared interests and the articulation of work-related concerns. Because of the racially exclusive practices of labor unions in the opening decades of the twentieth century, a working-class consciousness in the trade-unionist vein should not be expected of most black women and men of the period. Indeed, as sociologist Cynthia Costello indicates in a recent study of contemporary female clerical workers in a Wisconsin insurance company, the women who took collective action against their employer rarely identified with the concerns of the male-dominated trade union. They identified with the concerns of other working women. The seemingly contradictory nature of the working-class consciousness that characterized the women in Costello's study was even more apparent among black women, who were almost universally excluded from the major Progressive Era trade unions.[3]

Few would deny that the overwhelming majority of Progressive Era blacks were working-class in terms of their objective position in the class structure and their lack of control over the means of production. Undoubtedly, the social isolation and the work schedule of the majority of black working women, whether farmhands on southern plantations or domestics in private homes in the city, and their exclusion from trade unions impeded the development of a working-class identity and consciousness and the ability to act consistently on this consciousness during the early decades of the Progressive Era. Yet, individually and in organized groups, black women acted to improve their working conditions.

To what extent did black women identify themselves as wage-earners and express shared interests with other workers? How did black female wage-earners express their working-class concerns and consciousness? What impact did black women's self-perceptions and the black community's attitudes toward wage-earning women have on their labor activism?

The large representation of the black female population in the paid labor force reveals the importance of women's paid work to the economic survival of black families and households in the United States. During the period from 1880 to 1930, loosely defined as the Progressive Era, the black female wage-earning population rose steadily. The percentage of black women (ten years and older) in the paid labor market averaged 57 percent in the District of Columbia over the five decades of the Progressive Era. During the same period, the average proportion of employed black women in most large urban communities of similar size was approximately one-half that of the District.

Despite the large presence of black women in the labor market, a higher percentage of the black male population worked for wages in the United States. In 1910, 87 percent of the black male population in the United States was listed as gainfully employed, compared to only 55 percent of the female population. In the District of Columbia more black men (81 percent) worked than black women (60 percent) in 1910. Similarly, in Mississippi 90 percent of the black male population worked for wages, compared to only 68 percent of the black female population.[4]

Even in the poorest black families, husbands and fathers, not wives and mothers, were considered the primary breadwinners, regardless of the duration of their employment. Although seasonally unemployed, black men usually earned higher wages than black women. Since a married woman's proper place, even in the black community, was considered to be in the home caring for her children and her husband, black men were more likely to engage in work than women. When black fathers and husbands could not earn enough to make ends meet (which was often), black women, regardless of marital status, age, or the presence of children, joined the labor force. Of course, many never left.[5]

According to some blacks and whites, the presence of black mothers in the labor market was one of the most blatant examples of the lack of family stability and racial progress among the largely undereducated, rural black migrant class, regardless of the economic pressures on black households. Indicative of black male attitudes toward wage-earning wives and mothers were the views expressed by Giles B. Jackson and D. Webster Davis, authors of *The Industrial History of the Negro Race*, published in 1911. They argued: "The race needs wives who stay at home, being supported by their husbands, and then they can spend time in the training of their children."[6] In light of the precarious financial condition of most black households, this call for black mothers and wives to remain at home and be cared for by their husbands was an unrealistic expectation at best.

The racial barriers that black male wage-earners faced in the employment market forced a larger percentage of the married black female population to seek gainful employment. In 1890, approximately 23 percent of married black women in the United States participated in the labor force, compared to only 3 percent of the married white female population. The District of Columbia, with 43 percent of the married black female population in the labor force in 1890, had one of the largest work forces of this group, as well as a significantly higher percentage of married white women. By 1920, slightly more than 50 percent of the married black female population in the nation's capital was gainfully employed, compared to less than one-fourth of the married white female population. Similar ratios existed between black and white women in cities and towns throughout the United States during this period.[7]

Poverty, not a black cultural ethos favoring married women's wage labor, was the most significant explanatory factor for married black women's larger presence in the labor force. The difference in the level of employment of married black and white women reveals the degree to which racial identity affected an individual's economic condition. Greater economic pressures on black households, largely resulting from the low wages and seasonal employment of many black men, forced a larger number of married black women to work for wages. The financial survival of most black families and households (and not a small number of white households) prevented them from fully abiding by middle-class norms against married women in the paid labor market, especially in jobs outside the home.

Consequently, it would be incorrect to assume that a strong positive correlation existed between the large presence of married black women in the labor market and black male support for it. Black male response to working wives and mothers reveals a range of often contradictory emotions. Some black husbands forbade their wives to work for wages while others offered verbal support for such employment. Black male responses, though varied, can be characterized generally as reluctant acceptance rather than outright support. Despite a history of black female labor, total acceptance from black men was not forthcoming. Black women had often worked alongside their men in the antebellum and postbellum South. In addition, a religious and cultural tradition favorable to work existed in the black community, and black women's financial contributions to their households were important to their family's economic survival.

Although members of the black community knew the history of black women's work and, indeed, knew why married black women had to work for wages, they did not wholeheartedly support this activity. A married woman, especially if she had young children, who did not work for wages was a positive reflection of her husband's ability to provide for his family. Wives who worked, especially outside the home, only served to reinforce publicly the inability of black men to care for their families. Tensions increased within some black households as blacks became more aware of and affected by middle-class notions of women's and men's proper roles in society, as articulated by Jackson, Davis, and middle-class blacks.[8]

Black men were generally more "supportive" of their wives' employment than were men in other ethnic and racial groups, as fewer black men could make ends meet without their wives' financial assistance. A more important influence on married black women's labor, however, was the cultural ethos in the black community, which emphasized cooperation, sacrificing for kin, and "principal survival."[9] Members of the black community believed strongly that parents and adult relatives should sacrifice their own needs and wants for the advancement of their children and kin. The limited opportunities available to blacks for economic and social advancement without the benefit of a formal education and the importance that blacks generally attached to educating their youth contributed to the decision of black mothers to join the labor force in lieu of sending their children to work.[10]

Regardless of the noble purposes for married women's wage work, notions of acceptable behavior, especially among middle-class blacks and those aspiring to middle-class respectability and status, resulted in both public and private criticism of married women's employment. Negative responses came from diverse quarters: from middle-class, prominent black men like Jackson and Davis and from far less formally and professionally trained black men like Zora Neale Hurston's father. In her autobiography, *Dust Tracks on a Road* (1942), Hurston recounted that her father loved to boast to his male friends that "he had never let his wife hit a lick of work for anybody in her life."[11] The caveat was that Zora's mother had so many children (a fact about which her father also boasted) that it was virtually impossible for her to work for wages outside her home.

Male attitudes toward wage-earning married women reveal the dichotomy between the ideal and the real in the black community. The reality was that black women, irrespective of marital status, frequently had to work for wages, but this did not preclude members of the black community from articulating what they believed was the ideal role for married black women or from opposing married women's paid employment.[12]

28

Clearly, blacks were no more immune to middle-class white expectations about the roles of women than were many non-middle-class whites and members of various immigrant groups. Regardless of how many black mothers and wives worked and how much they needed to work for their family's economic survival, their presence in the labor force was not the ideal. Even among the poorest blacks, whose own standards of respectability were largely determined by the church and by the community in which they lived, their domestic ideology was not always diametrically opposed to middle-class norms of behavior.

Opposition to married women's wage work in the black community was generally strongest toward families who needed the income of a wage-earning wife or mother the most. Fewer professional black married women encountered such sentiments in their home, especially when married to professional men, although they likely encountered them in the workplace, especially when they competed with black men for jobs. The dissimilar response to professional married women, as opposed to other groups of wage-earning women, was based in part on their higher place in the occupational hierarchy. In addition, the presence in the paid labor force of an educated, professional black woman who was married to a professional man was less often viewed as a reflection of her husband's inability to care for his wife and family.[13]

How was it possible for a working-class consciousness to develop among black wage-earning women? The majority were domestic servants and farmhands, and many were married. They occupied low-status, unskilled jobs in the marketplace and, if married, were considered to be in violation of an acceptable code of behavior. They tended to view their work as temporary (regardless of their length of employment), and they were grossly discriminated against by most labor organizers as well as by other workers. Although the issue of low status obviously did not affect the consciousness of professional black women toward their employment, these women tended to de-emphasize, at least publicly, the wage-earning aspect of their gainful employment and instead emphasize their reform activities. Irrespective of a particular occupation or its place in the occupational hierarchy, the working-class consciousness of black women throughout the Progressive Era was seldom in the trade-unionist vein (which most labor and radical historians traditionally perceived as the only indication of the existence of a working-class consciousness).[14]

That wage-earning women of either race, and black men, for that matter, did not share with trade unionists a certain outlook about their status as workers and about the working class in general should not be surprising. It was difficult for women, regardless of race, and for black men to develop a working-class consciousness along the lines of a white male trade unionist while at the same time being denied membership in a white male-dominated union or, if granted membership, while being discriminated against. Besides, union organizing and strikes were relatively unknown phenomena for many rural southern-born blacks and for women in general. On this point Irene Goins, a black female organizer in the Chicago stockyards in 1918, remarked: "My people . . . know so little about organized labor that they have had a great fear of it, and for that reason the work of organizing has proceeded more slowly than I anticipated."[15]

The gender-based exclusionary practices and policies of Progressive Era trade union and labor organizations were compounded frequently by women's own ambivalence about their roles and status as wage earners. This ambivalence frequently encouraged them to deny, at least publicly, that they were wage-earning women or that their wage work was in any way a reflection of who they were. It was no accident that wage-earning women frequently referred to themselves as everything from "temporary helpmates" to "race uplifters" but less frequently as breadwinners or wage earners.[16]

While the economic motivation for their wage work was often similar to that of male wage earners, wage-earning women tended to view themselves as self-sacrificing mothers, wives, aunts, and sisters or as race uplifters rather than as workers. Their attitude toward their employment was, in part, an effort (not always conscious) to reconcile the domestic ideology about women's expected roles with the reality of their paid work lives and, in the case of domestic service workers, to de-emphasize the importance of their paid work lives to their everyday life and self-perception. Professional black women and their families were often as financially burdened as unskilled working-class families (although not always for the same reasons), but by couching their work roles in primarily racial uplift terms, they frequently sought a safe haven from criticism of their presence in the labor force.

Working women's often public disclaimers about their wage-earning roles should not be interpreted, however, as a lack of working-class consciousness or as a lack of concern about issues involving their lives as wage earners, their work conditions, and their wages. Expressions of working-class attitudes were revealed more often in private correspondence and conversations than in the public arena. Personal recollections of work-related concerns and activism have been divulged in recent personal interviews with black working women and in recent publications by women and labor historians.[17]

The private correspondence of female teachers revealed that, despite their public emphasis on the uplift nature of their wage work, issues concerning wages and occupational mobility were equally as important to them as they were to wage earners in general. In black women's public and private protests against the ban on married women teachers in the District of Columbia's public schools prior to 1918 and other forms of gender-based discrimination, the working-class attitudes and activism of professional black women were quite apparent.

The issues that female teachers emphasized in protest letters and public denunciations of sex discrimination were of an economic nature rather than an uplift nature—specifically, their inability to fulfill certain financial obligations. A female teacher in the District of Columbia public school system, who wished to remain anonymous for "obvious reasons," wrote Mrs. Raymond B. Morgan, a member of the Board of Education for the District of Columbia, to express her support for Morgan's opposition to the motion to reenact the ban against married female teachers. Questioning why women who had made enormous sacrifices for a professional career should be penalized for marrying, the anonymous correspondent declared that professional women's "personal obligations—to relatives, for example—do not cease with their marriage and, therefore, [they] have legitimate reasons for continuing to work." Besides, she warned, "in view of the high cost of living, the proposed motion would lead to secret marriages, fewer females, and fewer vacancies."[18]

The sentiments expressed in this letter reveal common concerns that professional black women shared with all black wage-earning women. Professional women needed to work for wages as much as the masses of uneducated black women and for many of the same reasons: to fulfill personal and familial obligations. The fulfillment of obligations to kin was considered a legitimate, even noble, purpose for women's employment. Attempts to restrict black women's employment and to pay them lower wages were issues that all black wage-earning women encountered, regardless of occupational and marital status.

Throughout the Progressive Era, despite their exclusion from or subordination within the major trade unions of the period, including those comprised of working women such as the International Ladies Garment Workers Union and the National Women's Trade Union League, black women took action to redress work-related grievances either on an individual basis or as members of various associations rather than as members of a trade-unionist group. Impressed by what the union did for women nurses, a black Chicago hospital worker decided to become a nurse. Knowing that she would be excluded from the existing nurses' union because she was black, this woman enrolled in a nurse's training program in anticipation of organizing black nurses at the hospital. Southern black women, not unlike their northern counterparts, also recognized the benefit of labor activism. Black women tobacco workers affiliated with the National Tobacco Workers Union participated in successful strikes in the late nineteenth and early twentieth centuries. In Florence, South Carolina, and Danville, Virginia, black female tobacco stemmers engaged in labor actions in 1898.[19]

Most middle-class black women showed their concern for working women and girls by establishing clubs and homes to assist them rather than by organizing black women workers into labor unions. In 1897, Victoria Earle Matthews, along with other prominent black women in New York City, formed the White Rose Industrial Association and established the White Rose Working Girls' Home. Yet, despite its reformist character, this home and association shared similar ground with trade unions of the period in seeking to prevent working women, largely domestic servants, from being exploited by employment agencies and potential employers.[20]

In addition, these Progressive Era working girls' associations and middle-class black women's clubs that dotted the urban landscape, primarily in the North, provided vocational training for working women and girls and offered day-care and kindergarten programs for the preschool children of working mothers. By offering child care and educational programs, the White Rose Association, the Colored Women's League of Washington, and similar groups were even more progressive than most traditional labor unions in meeting the needs of female membership then and now. The training and educational classes offered by black women's associations and clubs, while grossly underfunded, paralleled the apprentice programs that most unions offered their mostly white male members.[21]

Both black and white women were active in the Associations for the Protection of Negro Women, the 1905 brainchild of white philanthropist Frances Kellor. Located in New York City, Philadelphia, Norfolk, Memphis, Baltimore, and Washington, D.C., the association, which offered housing assistance, educational classes, and employment help, combined in 1901 to form the National League for the Protection of Colored Women. Willie Layten, a black woman who had been active in the Philadelphia association, became the new general secretary of the league, succeeding Kellor.[22]

In the spring of 1919, a conference was called in New York City by the National Association of Colored Women's Clubs, the major black women's reform organization, to deal with the plight of working black women. Black club women—particularly Nannie Helen Burroughs, founding president of the National Training School for Women and Girls—were concerned with the problems of working women, which led to the formation of the National Association of Wage-Earners in the 1920s. While reform-oriented, the association was no less radical than most of the trade unions of the period that sought relief for workers within the capitalist system, but this association was quite progressive in its publicly stated goals on behalf of women. It sought, among other purposes, "to secure a wage that will enable women to live decently" and "to influence just legislation affecting women wage earners."[23]

In the 1920s and 1930s, the closing decades of the Progressive Era, a growing number of black women who had had a long tradition of labor market activity and of individual and community-based protest action began expressing their working-class concerns more and more through traditional trade-unionist organizations. In 1920, at least ten union locals of black domestics in the South affiliated with the Hotel and Restaurant Employees' Union of the American Federation of Labor. Black women joined other labor organizations and formed auxiliaries to male labor unions. When given an opportunity to join with other working men and women to express their shared labor concerns and to engage in labor struggles, black women willingly did so.[24]

In the summer of 1933, black and white women workers at the Sopkin Dress Manufacturing Company in Chicago went on strike for higher wages and for an end to the racially segregated and unsanitary restrooms. Led by the Needle Trades Workers' Industrial Union, the strikers' demands were met: "25 cents of an hour for a forty-four-hour week, equal pay for equal work, and no discriminating between white and colored workers." While still victimized by racism within the unions, black women workers, who played a key role in the Chicago strike and in other strikes throughout the 1930s, were increasingly welcomed as members of the largely white and male-dominated labor unions.[25]

A history of working in exploitative situations and of dealing with racial oppression made it easier for black women to identify with the demands of labor organizations and with the plight of other oppressed workers. Their desire to promote their interests in workers led some black women and men to join the so-called radical wings of the labor movement and the Communist Party in the 1930s and 1940s rather than remain outside the labor movement or seek membership in organizations that did not fully promote their interests.[26]

Black women recognized the poor conditions under which they and black men operated in the labor market. Their many and varied expressions of dissatisfaction with their plight as wage earners reflected their working-class consciousness. The degree to which they did not publicly protest is more an indictment of racism and sexism in the American labor movement and of the social expectations for working women than it is an indicator of a lack of working-class consciousness among black women.

The black female domestic quoted in the opening paragraph was politically astute enough to recognize that there was an economic imbalance in the world, in the same sense that Marxists and socialists spoke of "haves" and "have-nots." Rather than encouraging revolutionary activity, however, she relied instead on her religious beliefs for a solution. She remarked: "If I were the Lord, I just wouldn't let nobody get but so rich and I wouldn't let nobody get but so poor. Life just seemed so unfair to me. It still does look that way to me. I have worked hard and tried to carry myself right, but I don't have very much to show for it. If I was the Lord, I wouldn't let things be like they are now. There wouldn't be any of this some-people-with money and some-people-with-nothing."[27]

With such a clear understanding of the inequities of the world, based on a lifetime of oppression and hard work, most black women and men, and oppressed people in general, needed less consciousness-raising to become part of the vanguard of a labor movement that sought to eradicate injustices against oppressed workers, regardless of color, gender, religion, and ethnic background. For a group of wage earners who had worked so hard all their lives, who daily experienced the sufferings of oppressed workers, and whose cultural and religious ethos embodied a deep respect for work, whether for pay or not, a working-class spirit and consciousness was always present. In order for it to surface more fully, it only needed to be encouraged and harnessed by the trade-unionist movement of the Progressive Era. Maybe if the trade unionist had responded, workers would have been the real victors in the struggle against industrial capitalism in Progressive Era America.

NOTES

1. John Langston Gwaltney, *Drylongso: A Self-Portrait of Black America* (New York: Vintage, 1981), 173-74. These narratives offer an excellent insight into the thinking of everyday, ordinary ("drylongso") black women and men on a variety of subjects.

2. According to Gwaltney, "the primary status of a black person is that accorded by the people he or she lives among. It is based upon assessments of that person's fidelity to core black standards." *Ibid.*, xxiii, xxx. On the subject of status, sociologist Bonnie Thornton Dill writes that "values in the Black community... attribute status to success along personal and family dimensions in addition to the basic ones of occupation, education, and income." See Dill, "The Means to Put My Children Through: Child-Rearing Goals and Strategies among Black Female Domestic Servants," in La Frances Rodgers-Rose, ed., *The Black Woman* (Beverly Hills, Calif.: Sage, 1980), 114.

3. While not having black women as their focus, several recent studies of women's labor market work have added to a general understanding of attitudes and life experiences of working-class women. These works represent an important shift in the scholarship in the field, which has traditionally been preoccupied with male wage-earners and white middle-class, professional women. In addition to Cynthia Costello, "Working Women's Consciousness: Traditional or Oppositional?" in Carol Groneman and Mary Beth Norton, eds., *"To Toil the Livelong Day": America's Women at Work, 1780-1980* (Ithaca, N.Y.: Cornell Univ. Press, 1987), consult Ruth Milkman, ed., *Women, Work and Protest: A Century of U.S. Women's Labor History* (Boston: Routledge & Kegan Paul, 1985).

4. For statistical data about the labor force participation of black men and women in the United States during this period, consult, for example, U.S. Department of Interior, Census Office, *Compendium of the Eleventh Census, 1890* (Washington, D.C.), pt. 3; U.S. Department of Commerce and Labor, Bureau of the Census, *Special Reports—Occupations at the Twelfth Census: 1900* (Washington, D.C.); U.S. Department of Commerce, Bureau of the Census, *United States Census of Population: 1910* (Washington, D.C.), vol. 4, *Occupations*; and U.S. Department of Commerce, Bureau of the Census, *Fourteenth Census of the United States, 1920: Population* (Washington, D.C.), vol. 4, *Occupations*. See also Joseph A. Hill, *Women in Gainful Occupations, 1870 to 1920*, Census Monograph IX (Washington, D.C.: GPO, 1929).

5. For wage figures, consult Elizabeth Ross-Haynes, "Negroes in Domestic Service in the United States," *Journal of Negro History* 8 (October 1928): 389-421.

6. Giles B. Jackson and D. Webster Davis, *The Industrial History of the Negro Race of the United States* (1911; reprint, New York: Books for Libraries Press, 1971), 133.

7. By contrast, the level of unmarried black and unmarried white female employment was comparable (75 percent and 70 percent, respectively). For statistical information about the married black female population in the labor force, consult U.S. Department of Commerce, Bureau of the Census, *Negroes in the United States, 1920-1932* (Washington, D.C.), 151-52.

8. For a discussion of the cultural basis for differences in black and nonblack (in this case, Italian) perception of married women's employment, see Elizabeth H. Pleck, "A Mother's Wages: Income Earning among Married Italian and Black Women, 1896-1911," in Nancy F. Cott and Elizabeth H. Pleck, eds., *A Heritage of Her Own: Toward a New Social History of American Women* (New York: Simon & Schuster, 1979).

9. See Gwaltney, *Drylongso*, for a discussion of core black cultural values, those shared by "the prudent black American masses." For a discussion of antebellum and postbellum black cultural ethos, consult Lawrence Levine, *Black Culture and Consciousness: Afro-American Folk Thought from Slavery to Freedom* (New York: Oxford University Press, 1977).

10. See Pleck, "Mother's Wages." Black children, especially teenagers, engaged in paid work but not nearly as much as children in immigrant families. The importance of sacrificing for one's children is addressed in Dill, "Means to Put My Children Through." Recognizing the obstacles that blacks were likely to face in the job market did not deter black mothers from sacrificing for their children's education. To black women interviewed for the study, Dill writes: "Education was seen as a means of equipping oneself for whatever breaks might occur in the nation's pattern of racial exclusion" (112).

11. Zora Neale Hurston, *Dust Tracks on a Road* (Philadelphia: Lippincott, 1942), 5.

12. Ambivalent feelings about a number of issues, including wage-earning wives, are prevalent among groups who live in oppressed ethnic and racial communities in which survival dictates one set of behavioral patterns and the "national marketplace of issues and ideas" (where white middle-class values predominate) dictates another. Gwaltney, *Drylongso*, xxvi.

13. Professional women maintained that educating the children of poor blacks was part of their moral and social obligation as educated women. The latter view is revealed in numerous published writings by professional women of the period. See, for example, Josephine Bruce, "What Has Education Done for Colored Women?" *Voice of the Negro* 1 (July 1904): 277-79, and Rosa D. Bowser, "What Role Is the Educated Negro Woman to Play in the Uplifting of Her Race?" in D.W. Culp, ed., *Twentieth-Century Negro Literature: Or, A Cyclopedia of Thought on the Vital Topics Relating to the American Negro* (Toronto: J.L. Nichols, 1920), 167-85. For an analysis of educated women's perceptions of their work in one urban community, see Sharon Harley, "Beyond the Classroom: The Organizational Lives of Black Female Educators in the District of Columbia, 1890-1930," *Journal of Negro Education* 51 (Summer 1982): 254-65.

14. The work attitudes and behavior of married black women often resembled that of the young white American wage-earners depicted in Leslie Woodcock Tentler, *Wage-Earning Women: Industrial Work and Family Life in the United States, 1900-1930* (New York: Oxford Univ. Press, 1979). Tentler's definition of working-class consciousness conforms to that of scholars who limit it exclusively to trade-unionist actions and collective bargaining. This issue is examined in Alice Kessler-Harris, "Where Are the Organized Women Workers?" *Feminist Studies* 3 (Fall 1975): 92-110. Motivated by a different set of historical and economic circumstances, black women have had a much longer and deeper history of developing survival strategies and protest than most white women. The class-consciousness and activities of wage-earning black women represent an extension of their "private troubles to the arena of public issues," as described in Cheryl Townsend Gilkes, " 'Holding Back the Ocean with a Broom': Black Women and Community Work," in Rodgers-Rose, *Black Woman*.

15. William M. Tuttle, Jr., "Labor Conflict and Racial Violence: The Black Worker in Chicago, 1894-1919," in Milton Cantor, ed., *Black Labor in America* (Westport, Conn.: Negro Universities Press, 1969), 98. The slow pace at which blacks joined labor unions can be attributed to a number of factors, including the racial antagonism

of union officials and white workers, manipulation by employers, and the availability of nonunion rather than union jobs for black workers. Focusing on black workers in Chicago, William M. Tuttle, Jr., discusses the obstacles to organizing black workers. Despite the barriers to organizing wage-earning women, Alice Kessler-Harris writes that, given the opportunity, women became active and committed union members. Trade unionists' failure, especially that of the American Federation of Labor, to seriously organize women is largely responsible for women's absence from the organized labor movement. See Kessler-Harris, "Where Are the Organized Women Workers?"

16. The idea of "helping out" was often an effort on the part of wage-earning women to lessen the importance of the market work and, if married, to overcome their husband's objections. See Pleck, "Mother's Wages," 386.

17. A rare look at the history of black women's collective actions is revealed in historian Rosalyn Terborg-Penn, "Survival Strategies among Afro-American Women Workers: A Continuing Process," in Milkman, ed., *Women, Work & Protest*. The frequently militant attitudes that black domestics express toward their work and work conditions are revealed in two recent studies, based largely on life histories obtained through oral interviews: Dill, "Means to Put My Children Through," and Elizabeth Clark-Lewis, "'This Work Had A End': African-American Domestic Workers in Washington, D.C., 1910-1940," in Groneman and Norton, *To Toil the Livelong Day*, 196-212. See also Verta Mae (Grosvenor), *Thursdays and Every Other Sunday Off* (New York: Doubleday, 1972). For information about black women's involvement in the American trade-unionist movement during the Progressive Era, consult Philip S. Foner, *Women and the American Labor Movement: From Colonial Times to the Eve of World War I* (New York: Free Press, 1979), and *Women and the American Labor Movement: From World War I to the Present* (New York: Free Press, 1980); Barbara Mayer Wertheimer, *We Were There: The Story of Working Women in America* (New York: Pantheon, 1977); and Jacqueline Jones, *Labor of Love, Labor of Sorrow: Black Women, Work, and the Family from Slavery to the Present* (New York: Basic Books, 1985).

18. "An earnest teacher," letter to Mrs. Raymond B. Morgan, Oct. 23, 1923, Terrell Papers, Box 4, Moorland Spingarn Research Center, Founders Library, Howard University, Washington, D.C. Letters to Mary Church Terrell and other board members reveal the depth of black professional women's concerns about wage and mobility issues in one urban community. See, for example, Frederick Douglass Sprague to Mary Church Terrell, Nov. 5, 1907, Terrell Papers, Ctr. 4, Library of Congress (LC); and Eva F. Ross to Mary C. Terrell, Jan. 5, 1907, Terrell Papers, Ctr. 4, LC.

19. For a discussion of labor efforts to "include" black women during the war years, see Foner, *Women and the American Labor Movement: From World War I to the Present*, ch. 1. Labor organizing was not a new phenomenon for black women during the Progressive Era. In the 1880s, black working women in such occupations as housekeepers, farmers, chambermaids, and washerwomen comprised fifteen women assemblies affiliated with the Knights of Labor. Assemblies of black domestics could be found in Washington, D.C., Norfolk, Virginia, Wilmington, North Carolina, and Philadelphia. See Foner, *Women and the American Labor Movement: From Colonial Times to the Eve of World War I*, and Jones, *Labor of Love*.

20. For a discussion of the White Rose Industrial Associations and other Associations for the Protection of Negro Women, consult Terborg-Penn, "Survival Strategies," 142-43.

21. See Harley, "Beyond the Classroom."

22. Terborg-Penn, "Survival Strategies," 143.

23. *Opportunity* 2 (Dec. 1924): 383, cited in Evelyn Brooks Barnett (Higginbotham), "Nannie Burroughs and the Education of Black Women," in Sharon Harley and Rosalyn Terborg-Penn, eds., *The Afro-American Woman: Struggles and Images* (Port Washington, N.Y.: Kennikat, 1978), 98-101.

24. Terborg-Penn, "Survival Strategies," 144.

25. Foner, *Women in the American Labor Movement: From World War I to the Present*, 274-75.

26. *Ibid.*

27. Gwaltney, *Drylongso*, 175-76.

3

"What Has Happened Here":
The Politics of Difference in Women's History and Feminist Politics

Elsa Barkley Brown

> My work is not traditional. I like it that way. If people tell me to turn my ends under, I'll leave them raggedy. If they tell me to make my stitches small and tight, I'll leave them loose. Sometimes you can trip over my stitches they're so big. You can always recognize the traditional quilters who come by and see my quilts. They sort of cringe. They fold their hands in front of them as if to protect themselves from the cold. When they come up to my work they think to themselves, "God, what has happened here—all these big crooked stitches." I appreciate these quilters. I admire their craft. But that's not my kind of work. I would like them to appreciate what I'm doing. They are quilters. But I am an artist. And I tell stories.
>
> —Yvonne Wells, quoted in *Stitching Memories: African American Story Quilts*

Questions of difference loom large in contemporary intellectual and political discussions. Although many women's historians and political activists understand the intellectual and political necessity, dare I say moral, intellectual, and political correctness of recognizing the diversity of women's experiences, this recognition is often accompanied with the sad (or angry) lament that too much attention to difference disrupts the relatively successful struggle to produce and defend women's history and women's politics, necessary corollaries of a women's movement. Like the traditionalists who view Yvonne Wells's quilts,[1] many women's historians and feminist activists cringe at the big and loose rather than small and tight stitches that now seem to bind women's experiences. They seek a way to protect themselves and what they have created as women's history and women's politics, and they wonder despairingly, " 'God, what has happened here.' " I do not say this facetiously; the fear that all this attention to the differences among women will leave us with only a void, a vacuum, or chaos is a serious concern. Such despair, I believe, is unnecessary, the product of having accepted the challenge to the specifics of our historical knowledge and political organizing while continuing to privilege a linear, symmetrical (some would say Western) way of thinking about history and politics themselves.

I am an optimist. It is an optimism born of reflecting on particular historical and cultural experiences. If I offer some elements of the cultural understandings underpinning those experiences as instructive at this juncture of our intellectual and political journey, it is because "culture, in the largest sense is, after all, a resource that provides the context in which [we] perceive [our] social world. Perceptions of alternatives in the social structure [can] take place only within a framework defined by the patterns and rhythms" of our particular cultural understandings. A rethinking of the cultural aesthetics that underlie women's history and women's politics is essential to what I perceive as the necessary rethinking of the intellectual and political aesthetics.[2]

And it is here that I think African American culture is instructive as a way of rethinking, of reshaping our thinking processes, our understandings of history and politics themselves. Like Yvonne Wells, Zora Neale Hurston—anthropologist, folklorist, playwright, and novelist—also addressed questions of cultural difference and, in the process, suggested ways of thinking about difference itself:

> Asymmetry is a definite feature of Negro art. . . . The sculpture and the carvings are full of this beauty and lack of symmetry. It is present in the literature, both prose and verse. . . . It is the lack of symmetry which makes Negro dancing so difficult for white dancers to learn. The abrupt and unexpected changes. The frequent change of key and time are evidences of this quality in music. . . . The presence of rhythm and lack of symmetry are paradoxical, but there they are. Both are present to a marked degree. There is always rhythm, but it is the rhythm of segments. Each unit has a rhythm of its own, but when the whole is assembled it is lacking in symmetry. But easily workable to a Negro who is accustomed to the break in going from one part to another, so that he adjusts himself to the new tempo.[3]

Wells and Hurston point to nonlinear ways of thinking about the world, of hearing multiple rhythms and thinking music not chaos, ways that challenge the notion that sufficient attention to difference leads to intellectual chaos, to political vacuum, or to intellectual and political void. Considering Wells's and Hurston's reflections on cultural difference might show us that it is precisely differences which are the path to a community of intellectual and political struggle.[4]

Also instructive is the work of Luisah Teish. In *Jambalaya: The Natural Woman's Book of Personal Charms and Practical Rituals*, she writes about going home to New Orleans for a visit and being met by her family at the airport: "Before I can get a good look in my mother's face, people begin arranging themselves in the car. They begin to talk gumbo ya ya, and it goes on for 12 days. . . . Gumbo ya ya is a creole term that means 'Everybody talks at once.'" It is through gumbo ya ya that Teish learns everything that has happened in her family and community and she conveys the essential information about herself in the group.[5] That is, it is through gumbo ya ya that Teish tells the history of her sojourn to her family and they tell theirs to her. They do this simultaneously because, in fact, their histories are joined—occurring simultaneously, in connection, in dialogue with each other. To relate their tales separately would be to obliterate that connection.

To some people listening to such a conversation, gumbo ya ya may sound like chaos. We may better be able to understand it as something other than confusion if we overlay it with jazz, for gumbo ya ya is the essence of a musical tradition where "the various voices in a piece of music may go their own ways but still be held together by their relationship to each other."[6] In jazz, for example, each member has to listen to what the other is doing and know how to respond while each is, at the same time, intent upon her own improvisation. It is in this context that jazz pianist Ojeda Penn has called jazz an expression of true democracy, for each person is allowed, in fact required, to be an individual, to go her or his own way, and yet to do so in concert with the group.[7]

History also is everybody talking at once, multiple rhythms being played simultaneously. The events and people we write about did not occur in isolation but in dialogue with a myriad of other people and events. In fact, at any given moment millions of people are all talking at once. As historians we try to isolate one conversation and to explore it, but the trick is then how to put that conversation in a context which makes evident its dialogue with so many others—how to make this one lyric stand alone and at the same time be in connection with all the other lyrics being sung.

Unfortunately, it seems to me, few historians are good jazz musicians; most of us write as if our training were in classical music. We require surrounding silence—of the audience, of all the instruments not singled out as the performers in this section, even often of any alternative visions than the composer's. That then makes it particularly problematic for historians when faced with trying to understand difference while holding on to an old score that has in many ways assumed that despite race, class, ethnicity, sexuality, and other differences, at core all women do have the same gender; that is, the rhythm is the same and the conductor can point out when it is time for each of us to play it. Those who would alter the score or insist on being able to keep their own beat simultaneously with the orchestrated one are not merely presenting a problem of the difficulty of constructing a framework that will allow for understanding the experiences of a variety of women but as importantly the problem of confronting the political implications of such a framework, not only for the women under study but also for the historians writing those studies.

I think we still operate at some basic levels here. This is an opinion which may not be widely shared among women's historians. For I am aware that there is a school of thought within women's history that believes that it, more than any other field of history, has incorporated that notable triumvirate—race, class, and gender—and has addressed difference. But my point is that recognizing and even including difference is, in and of itself, not enough. If fact, such recognition and inclusion may be precisely the way to avoid the challenges, to reaffirm the very traditional stances women's history sees itself as challenging, and to write a good classical score—silencing everyone else until the spotlight is on them but allowing them no interplay throughout the composition. We need to recognize not only differences but also the relational nature of those differences. Middle-class white women's lives are not just different from working-class white, Black, and Latina women's lives. It is important to recognize that middle-class women live the lives they do precisely because working-class women live the lives they do. White women and women of color not only live different lives but white women live the lives they do in large part because women of color live the ones they do.

Let me here grossly simplify two hundred years of Black and white women's history in the United States. Among the major changes we have seen has been the greater labor force participation of white middle-class women; the increasing movement of white middle-class women from the home to voluntary associations within the larger society to formal public political roles; the shift among Black women from agricultural labor to industrial, service, and clerical work; the emergence of Black working-class women from the kitchens of white women to jobs in the private sector; and the shift of middle-class Black women to jobs in the public sector. We could, and often do, set these experiences side by side, thus acknowledging the differences in the experiences of different women. And most often, whether stated or not, our acknowledgment of these differences leads us to recognize how Black women's life choices have been constrained by race—how race has shaped their lives. What we are less apt to acknowledge (that is, to make explicit and to analyze) is how white women's lives are also shaped by race.[8] Even less do I see any real recognition of the relational nature of these differences.

But white middle-class women moved from a primary concern with home and children to involvement in voluntary associations when they were able to have their homes and children cared for by the services—be they direct or indirect—of other women. White middle-class women have been able to move into the labor force in increasing numbers not just differently from other women but precisely because of the different experience of other women and men. The growth in white women's participation in the labor force over the last two decades and the increased opportunities for managerial and professional positions for white women have accompanied the U.S. transition from an industrial to a technological economy. This transition is grounded in the very deindustrialization and decentralization which has meant the export of capital to other parts of the world, where primarily people of color—many of them female—face overwhelming exploitation from multinational corporations' industrial activities and the flight of business from urban (particularly inner-city) areas within the United States and thus the tremendous rise in unemployment and underemployment among African American women and men.[9] It is precisely the connection between global industrial exploitation, rising unemployment and underemployment in inner-city, largely minority communities, and the growth in opportunities for the middle-class (and especially white middle-class women) which are likely to go unexplored. The change in the economy has meant not only the growth of the highly publicized "high-technology" jobs but also the tremendous growth in distinctly "low-tech" service jobs. The increased labor force participation of white middle-class women has been accompanied, indeed made possible, by the increased availability outside the home of services formerly provided inside the home—cleaning, food, health, and personal services. These jobs are disproportionately filled by women of color—African American, Latina, Asian American.[10] Middle-class Black women were hired to perform social service functions in the public sector at the same time that white middle-class women were moving from performing these functions, often as volunteer work, to better paid and higher status positions in the private sector.[11]

We are likely to acknowledge that white middle-class women have had a different experience from African American, Latina, Asian American, and Native American women; but the relation, the fact that these histories exist simultaneously, in dialogue with each other, is seldom apparent in the studies we do, not even in those studies that perceive themselves as dealing with the diverse experiences of women. The overwhelming tendency now, it appears to me, is to acknowledge and then ignore differences among women. Or, if we acknowledge a relationship between Black and white women's lives, it is likely to be only that African American women's lives are shaped by white women's but not the reverse. The effect of this is that acknowledging difference becomes a way of reinforcing the notion that the experiences of white middle-class women are the norm; all others become deviant—different from.

This reflects the fact that we have still to recognize that being a woman is, in fact, not extractable from the context in which one is a woman—that is, race, class, time, and place. We have still to recognize that all women do not have the same gender. In other words, we have yet to accept the fact that one cannot write adequately about the lives of white women in the United States *in any context* without acknowledging the way in which race shaped their lives. One important dimension of this would involve understanding the relationship between white women and white men as shaped by race. This speaks not just to the history we write but to the way we understand our own lives. And I believe it challenges women's history at its core, for it suggests that until women's historians adequately address difference and the causes for it, they have not and cannot adequately tell the history of even white middle-class women.

The objections to all of this take many forms but I would like to address two of them. First, the oft-repeated lament of the problems of too many identities; some raise this as a conceptual difficulty, others as a stylistic one. In either case, such a discussion reinforces the notion that women of color, ethnic women, and lesbians are deviant, not the norm. And it reinforces not just the way in which some histories are privileged but also the way in which some historians are privileged. In fact, in women's history difference means "not white middle-class heterosexual," thus renormalizing white middle-class heterosexual women's experiences. One result of this is that white middle-class heterosexual women do not often have to think about difference or to see themselves as "other."[12] Not only do people of color not have the luxury in this society of deciding whether to identify racially but historians writing about people of color also do not have the privilege of deciding whether to acknowledge, at least at some basic level, their multiple identities. No editor or publisher allows a piece on Black or Latina women to represent itself as being about "women." On the other hand, people who want to acknowledge that their pieces are about "white" women often have to struggle with editors to get that in their titles and consistently used throughout their pieces—the objection being it is unnecessary, superfluous, too wordy, awkward. Historians writing about heterosexual women seldom feel compelled to consistently establish that as part of their subjects' identity whereas historians writing about lesbian women must address sexuality. Does this imply that sexuality is a factor only in the lives of lesbian women, that is, that they are not only different from but deviant? These seem to me to be issues that historians cannot address separately from questions of the privilege some people have in this society and the way in which some historians have a vested interest in duplicating that privilege within historical constructions.

Another objection to the attention to difference is the fear, expressed in many ways, that we will in the process lose the "voice of gender."[13] This reifies the notion that all women have the same gender and requires that most women's voices be silenced and some privileged voice be given center stage. But that is not the only problem with this assumption for it also ignores the fact that gender does not have a voice; women and men do. They raise those voices constantly and simultaneously in concert, in dialogue with each other. Sometimes the effect may seem chaotic because they respond to each other in such ways; sometimes it may seem harmonic. But always it is polyrhythmic; never is it a solo or single composition.

Yet there is in the academy and society at large a continuing effort to uphold some old and presumably well-established literary and historical canon. Those bent on protecting such seem well trained in classical music; they stand on the stage and proudly proclaim: "We have written the score; we are conducting it; we will choose those who will play it without changing a chord; and everyone else should be silent." Unfortunately, much of the current lament among women's historians about the dangers, disruptiveness, and chaos of difference sounds much like this—reifying a classical score, composed and conducted this time by women.

This is not merely a question of whether one prefers jazz to classical music. Like most intellectual issues, this one, too, has real political consequences. We have merely to think about the events surrounding Anita Hill's fall 1991 testimony before the Senate Judiciary Committee. When Professor Hill testified, a number of women, individually and collectively, rallied to her support and to advance awareness of the issue of sexual harassment. Many of Hill's most visible supporters, however, ignored the fact that she is a Black woman, thirteenth child of Oklahoma farmers, or treated these as merely descriptive or incidental matters.[14] The National Organization for Women, feminist legal scholar Catharine MacKinnon, and others spoke forcefully and eloquently about the reality of sexual harassment in women's lives but in doing so often persisted in perpetuating a deracialized notion of women's experiences.[15] One wonders if many white feminists, especially, were not elated to have found an issue and a Black woman who could become a universal symbol, evidence of the common bonds of womanhood. Elevating Hill to such a status, however, required ignoring the racialized and class-specific histories of women's sexuality and stereotypes and our different histories of sexual harassment and sexual violence.[16]

In the end, I would argue, the ignoring of these racialized and class-specific histories became a political liability. Having constructed Anita Hill as a generic or universal woman with no race or class, and having developed an analysis of sexual harassment in which race and class were not central issues, many of Hill's supporters were unable to deal with the racialized and class-specific discussion when it emerged. This suggests how little our scholarship and politics have taught us about the construction of race in the United States, and I think this is connected to the failure to construct race as a significant factor in white women's experiences.[17] Once Clarence Thomas played the race card and a string of his female supporters raised the class issue, they had much of the public discussion to themselves.[18] Thomas and his supporters did not create a race and class context. They exploited it.

Thomas's analysis of Hill's charges and the committee hearings as "a modern day lynching based in white men's sexual stereotypes of black men hinge[d] on assuming that race should be considered only when thinking about his situation."[19] He, therefore, constructed himself as a Black man confronting a generic (read, for many people, "white" or "whitened") woman assisted by white men. "Thomas outrageously manipulated the legacy of lynching in order to shelter himself from Anita Hill's allegations"; by "trivializ[ing] and misrepresent[ing] this painful part of African American people's history," Thomas was able "to deflect attention away from the reality of sexual abuse in African American women's lives."[20] Such a strategy could only have been countered effectively by putting the experience of sexual harassment for Anita Hill in the context of her being a Black woman in the United States.[21]

Eleven years prior, Anita Hill embarked on her legal career. This was a woman who began her formal education before the Morris, Oklahoma, schools were integrated and who had gone on to graduate from one of the country's most elite law schools. When she confronted the sexual harassment, so painfully described in her testimony, the weight of how to handle these advances lay on Anita Hill not merely as "a woman or a Yale Law School graduate," but as "a young black woman, the daughter of Oklahoma farmers, whose family and community expected her to do well. It is essential to understand how this may have shaped both her experiences and her responses."[22] Hill's friend, Ellen Wells, herself the victim of sexual harassment on the job, explained much in her succinct statement before the committee: "You don't walk around carrying your burdens so that everyone can see them. You're supposed to carry that burden and try to make the best of it."[23]

Few Black women of Anita Hill's age and older grew up unaware of the frequency of sexual abuse as part of Black women's employment history. Many of us were painfully aware that one reason our families worked so hard to shield us from domestic and factory work was to shield us from sexual abuse. And we were aware that the choices many of our mothers made (or our fathers insisted upon) to forego employment were in fact efforts to avoid abusive employment situations. Sexual harassment as a legal theory and a public discussion in white middle-class communities may be a late 1970s' phenomenon, but sexual harassment has been not only a widespread phenomenon of Black women's labor history but also the subject of widespread public and private discussion within Black communities.[24] From the late nineteenth century on, Black women and men spoke out about the frequency of sexual abuse of Black women laborers, the majority of whom were employed in domestic service.

In fact, it is hard to read the politics of Black communities, especially Black women's organizations, in the late nineteenth and early twentieth centuries without recognizing this awareness of the reality of sexual harassment.[25] By the mid-twentieth century this was no longer as public a discussion in our communities as it had been in the late nineteenth and early twentieth centuries, but it was still a significant part of the private discussion and necessary socialization to being a Black female living in a racial and racist society.[26] A collective memory of sexual harassment runs deep in African American communities and many Black women, especially those born before the 1960s' civil rights movement, would likely recognize sexual harassment not as a singular experience but as part of a collective and common history.

Given the economic and racial circumstances, Black women understand from an early age that figuring out how to endure, survive, and move forward is an essential responsibility. As a newly minted, young, Black professional, the pride of one's family and community, the responsibility to do so would be even greater. You think, "they endured and so should I." You think you are expected to represent success. How can you dash your family's and community's joy at your achievements and their hopes that education, mobility, and a good job would protect you?[27]

Analyses which offered as explanation of Hill's long silence only that it was representative of the common tendency of women to individualize the experience, to feel isolated, and therefore not to report such incidents assume in fact a lack of socialization around these issues or a socialization which leads women to see themselves as alone, unique in these experiences; and they miss the complexity of such experiences for differing women.[28] By complicating the discussion past singular explanations or in ways that truly explored the differential dimensions and expressions of power, one might have expanded the base of support—support not based on a commonality of experience but on a mobilization that precisely spoke to particularities and differences.

Anita Hill experienced sexual harassment not as a woman who had been harassed by a man but as a Black woman harassed by a Black man. Race is a factor in all cases of sexual abuse—inter- or intraracial—although it is usually only explored in the former. When white middle-class and upper-class men harass and abuse white women they are generally protected by white male privilege; when Black men harass and abuse white women they may be protected by male privilege, but they are as likely to be subject to racial hysteria; when Black men harass and abuse Black women they are often supported by racist stereotypes which assume different sexual norms and different female value among Black people.[29] I think we understand this only if we recognize that race is operative even when all the parties involved are white.

But, recognizing race as a factor in sexual harassment and sexual abuse requires us particularly to consider the consequences of the sexual history and sexual stereotypes of African Americans, especially African American women. "Throughout U.S. history Black women have been sexually stereotyped as immoral, insatiable, perverse; the initiators in all sexual contacts—abusive or otherwise." A result of such stereotyping as well as of the political, economic, and social privileges that resulted to white people (especially white men but also white women) from such stereotyping is that "the common assumption in legal proceedings as well as in the larger society has been that black women cannot be raped or otherwise sexually abused."[30] This has several effects. One is that Black women are most likely not to be believed if they speak of unwarranted sexual advances or are believed to have been willing or to have been the initiator. Both white and Black women have struggled throughout the nineteenth and twentieth centuries to gain control of their sexual selves. But while white elite women's sexual history has included the long effort to break down Victorian assumptions of sexuality and respectability in order to gain control of their sexual selves, Black women's sexual history has required the struggle to be accepted as respectable in an effort to gain control of their sexual selves.[31] Importantly, this has resulted in what Darlene Clark Hine has described as a culture of dissemblance—Black women's sexuality is often concealed, that is, Black women have had to learn to cover up all public suggestions of sexuality, even of sexual abuse. Black women, especially middle-class women, have learned to present a public image that never reveals their sexuality.[32]

Further, given the sexual stereotyping of Black men, a young Anita Hill may also have recognized that speaking of the particularities of Thomas's harassment of her had the potential to restigmatize the whole Black community—male and female. This is not merely, as some have suggested, about protecting Black men or being "dutiful daughters." Black women sought their own as well as the larger community's protection through the development of a politics of respectability.[33] Respectable behavior would not guarantee one's protection from sexual assault, but the absence of such was certain to reinforce racist notions of Black women's greater sexuality, availability, or immorality, as well as the racist notions of Black men's bestiality which were linked to that.

Thomas exploited these issues. Only a discussion which explored the differences and linkages in Black and white women's and working-class and middle-class women's struggles for control of their sexual selves could have effectively addressed his manipulation of race and class and addressed the fears that many Black people, especially women, had at the public discussion of what they perceived as an intraracial sexual issue. Dismissing or ignoring these concerns or imposing a universal feminist standard which ignores the differential consequences of public discourse will not help us build a political community around these issues.

Attending to the questions of race and class surrounding the Thomas hearings would have meant that we would not have had a linear story to tell. The story we did have would not have made good quick sound bites or simple slogans for it would have been far more complicated. But, in the end, I think, it would have spoken to more people's experiences and created a much broader base of understanding and support for issues of sexual harassment. Complicating it certainly would have allowed a fuller confrontation of the manipulation and exploitation of race and class on the part of Thomas and his supporters. The political liability here and the threat to creating a community of struggle came from *not* focusing on differences among women and *not* seriously addressing the race and class dimensions of power and sexual harassment. It would, of course, have been harder to argue that things would have been different if there were a woman on the committee.[34] But then many Black working-class women, having spent their days toiling in the homes of white elite women, understood that femaleness was no guarantee of support and mutuality. Uncomplicated discussions of universal women's experiences cannot address these realities. Race (and yes gender, too) is at once too simple an answer and at the same time a more complex answer than we have yet begun to make it.

The difficulty we have constructing this more complicated story is not merely a failure to deal with the specifics of race and class; the difficulty is also, I believe, in how we see history and politics—in an underlying focus on linear order and symmetry which makes us wary, fearing that layering multiple and asymmetrical stories will only result in chaos with no women's history or women's story to tell, that political community is a product of homogeneity, and that exploring too fully our differences will leave us void of any common ground on which to build a collective struggle. These are the ideas/assumptions which I want to encourage us to think past.

I suggest African American culture as a means to learning to think differently about history and politics. I do this not merely because these are cultural forms with which I am familiar and comfortable. Rather, I do this because there is a lot that those who are just confronting the necessity to be aware of differences can learn from those who have had always to be aware of such. Learning to think nonlinearly, asymmetrically, is I believe essential to our intellectual and political developments. A linear history will lead us to a linear politics and neither will serve us well in an asymmetrical world.

NOTES

This is a revised and expanded version of a paper that was presented at the American Historical Association in New York in December 1990 and published as "Polyrhythms and Improvisation: Lessons for Women's History," *History Workshop Journal* 31 (Spring 1991): 85-90. For thinking through the original paper and/or this expanded version with me, I thank Deborah Britzman, Carol Boyce Davies, Marilynn Desmond, Evelyn Nakano Glenn, Tera Hunter, Robin D.G. Kelley, Deborah K. King, Jerma Jackson, Leslie S. Rowland, Susan Sterrett, and the editors of *Feminist Studies*.

1. See *Stitching Memories: African American Story Quilts*, Gallery Guide, Eva Grudin, curator (Williamstown, Mass.: Williams College Museum of Art, 1989), 1.

2. Elsa Barkley Brown, "African American Women's Quilting: A Framework for Conceptualizing and Teaching African American Women's History," *Signs* 14 (Summer 1989): 925-26.

3. Zora Neale Hurston, "Characteristics of Negro Expression," in *Negro: An Anthology*, ed. Nancy Cunard (London: Wishart, 1934); reprinted in Zora Neale Hurston, *The Sanctified Church* (Berkeley, Calif.: Turtle Island Press, 1983), 54-55.

4. My thinking that communities of struggle are created out of and sustained by difference as much as similarity is, in part, the product of my research on southern urban African American communities in the late nineteenth and early twentieth centuries. See Elsa Barkley Brown, "Weaving Threads of Community: The Richmond Example" (Paper presented at the Southern Historical Association, Fifty-fourth Annual Meeting, Norfolk, Virginia, 12 Nov. 1988); and " 'Not Alone to Build This Pile of Brick': Institution Building and Community in Richmond, Virginia" (Paper presented at The Age of Booker T. Washington: Conference in Honor of Louis Harlan, University of Maryland, College Park, May 1990).

5. Luisah Teish, *Jambalaya: The Natural Woman's Book of Personal Charms and Practical Rituals* (San Francisco: Harper & Row, 1985), 139-40.

6. Lawrence Levine, *Black Culture and Black Consciousness: Afro-American Folk Thought from Slavery to Freedom* (New York: Oxford University Press, 1977), 133.

7. Ojeda Penn, "Jazz: American Classical Music as a Philosophic and Symbolic Entity" (Faculty lecture series, Fifteenth Anniversary of African and African-American Studies Program, Emory University, Atlanta, Georgia, March 1986).

8. We need historical studies of white women in the United States comparable to the work begun by Alexander Saxton, David Roediger, Vron Ware, and Ann Laura Stoler—work which takes seriously the study of the racial identity of white U.S. men and white European women and men. See, Alexander Saxton, *The Rise and Fall of the White Republic: Class Politics and Mass Culture in Nineteenth-Century America* (New York: Verso, 1990); David R. Roediger, *The Wages of Whiteness: Race and the Making of the American Working Class* (New York: Verso, 1991); Vron Ware, *Beyond the Pale: White Women, Racism, and History* (London: Verso, 1992); Ann Laura Stoler, "Carnal Knowledge and Imperial Power: Gender, Race, and Morality in Colonial Asia," in *Gender at the Crossroads of Knowledge: Feminist Anthropology in the Postmodern Era*, ed. Micaela di Leonardo (Berkeley: University of California Press, 1991), 51-101.

9. Linda Burnham, "Struggling to Make the Turn: Black Women and the Transition to a Post-Industrial Society" (Paper presented at "Survival and Resistance: Black Women in the Americas Symposium," Schomburg Center for Research in Black Culture, New York City, 9 June 1989).

10. Evelyn Nakano Glenn, "From Servitude to Service Work: Historical Continuities in the Racial Division of Reproductive Labor," *Signs* (Autumn 1992).

11. Social service work in the late nineteenth and early twentieth centuries was often performed as volunteer work by Black and white women. With the development of the welfare state, white middle-class women increasingly were able to perform these functions as paid employees of the state and social service agencies. After World War II, as white middle-class women increasingly moved into private sector jobs, Black women were able, for the first time in large numbers, to move out of domestic and industrial work into clerical and professional positions. But they did so principally through their employment in the public sector providing social service functions for Black clients under the pay and scrutiny of local, state, and federal governments. See Teresa L. Amott and Julie A. Matthaei, *Race, Gender, and Work: A Multicultural Economic History of Women in the United States* (Boston: South End Press, 1991); Linda Gordon, "Black and White Visions of Welfare: Women's Welfare Activism, 1890-1945," *Journal of American History* 78 (September 1991): 559-90; Elizabeth Higginbotham, "Employment for Professional Black Women in the Twentieth Century," Research Paper No. 3, Memphis State University Center for Research on Women, 1985.

12. One result of this is that women of color often come to stand for the "messiness" and "chaos" of history and politics much as an "aesthetic of uniformity" led the Radio City Music Hall Rockettes to perceive the addition of Black dancers to their chorus line as making "it ugly ('unaesthetic'), imbalanced ('nonuniform'), and sloppy ('imprecise')." See Patricia J. Williams's wonderful discussion in *The Alchemy of Race and Rights* (Cambridge: Harvard University Press, 1991), 116-18.

13. See, for example, "Editor's Notes," *Journal of Women's History* 1 (Winter 1990): 7.

14. The discussion which follows should not be read as a critique of Hill's testimony but rather of those who set themselves out as political and intellectual experts able to speak with authority on "women's issues." It is concerned with public discussion in mainstream media by those identifying themselves as feminist activists, primarily white. My focus on such is a reflection of the scope of this essay and is not intended to hold white women solely or even primarily responsible for the state of public discussion. For my analysis that addresses and critiques developments within the Black community and among Black organizations, see "Imaging Lynching: African American Communities, Collective Memory, and the Politics of Respectability," in *Reflections on Anita Hill: Race, Gender, and Power in the United States*, ed. Geneva Smitherman (Detroit: Wayne State University Press, forthcoming). Finally, I am not naive enough to think the conclusion of the Thomas confirmation process would have been different if these issues had been effectively addressed. I do believe public discussion and political mobilization then and in the future could have been shaped differently by these discussions. Given that for two decades Black women have, according to almost all polls, supported feminist objectives in larger numbers than white women, I think we have to look to something other than Black women's reported antifeminism or privileging of race over gender for the answer to why an effective cross-race, cross-class political mobilization and discussion did not develop.

15. This is not to say that they did not acknowledge that Hill was Black or even, in Catharine MacKinnon's case, that "most of the women who have brought forward claims that have advanced the laws of sexual harassment have been black. Because racism is often sexualized, black women have been particularly clear in identifying

this behavior as a violation of their civil rights." See *People*, 28 Oct. 1991, 49. It is to say that having acknowledged this, race is not a significant factor in the analysis of women's experience of sexual harassment. For a more extensive analysis of this and other issues raised in this essay, see "Imaging Lynching," and Elsa Barkley Brown, "Can We Get There from Here? The Contemporary Political Challenge to a Decade of Feminist Research and Politics" (Paper prepared for "What Difference Does Difference Make? The Politics of Race, Class, and Gender Conference," Duke University-University of North Carolina Center for Research on Women, Chapel Hill, 31 May 1992).

16. For an analysis fully attuned to questions of race and class, see Kimberlé Crenshaw's participation in "Roundtable: Sexuality after Thomas/Hill," *Tikkun*, January/February 1992, 25-30. See also Crenshaw's analysis of Thomas's nomination pre-Anita Hill in "Roundtable: Doubting Thomas," *Tikkun*, September/October 1991, 23-30. It is useful to compare Crenshaw's analysis in the first with Ellen Willis's and in the latter with Catharine MacKinnon's.

17. In fact, race has been methodologically and theoretically written out of many analyses of sexual harassment. See, for example, the pioneering historical work of Mary Bularzik and the pioneering legal theory of Catharine MacKinnon. Bularzik is, quite appropriately, writing on white women and developing a discussion of the class dimension of sexual harassment; in the process, however, she offhandedly dismisses many Black women's understandings as false consciousness since they "often interpreted sexual harassment as racism, not sexism." See "Sexual Harassment at the Workplace: Historical Notes," *Radical America* 12 (July-August 1978), reprinted in *Workers' Struggles, Past and Present: A "Radical America" Reader*, ed. James Green (Philadelphia: Temple University Press, 1983), 117-35. MacKinnon acknowledges race as a factor only in cases involving persons of different races. See, for example, *Sexual Harassment of Working Women: A Case of Sex Discrimination* (New Haven: Yale University Press, 1979), 30-31. More importantly, her legal theory is built upon a notion of universal women and generic men which assumes that "men" are white and heterosexual.

> Over time, women have been economically exploited, relegated to domestic slavery, used in denigrating entertainment, deprived of a voice and authentic culture, and disenfranchised and excluded from public life. Women, by contrast with comparable men, have systematically been subjected to physical insecurity; targeted for sexual denigration and violation; depersonalized and denigrated; deprived of respect, credibility, and resources; and silenced—and denied public presence, voice, and representation of their interests. *Men as men have generally not had these things done to them; that is, men have had to be Black or gay (for instance) to have these things done to them as men.*

See *Toward a Feminist Theory of the State* (Cambridge: Harvard University Press, 1989), 160 (emphasis mine).

18. Thomas did this most significantly in his dramatic calling up of the lynching issue and situating himself, for the first time in the hearings, as a Black man, and also in his efforts to portray Hill as a Black woman who felt inferior to and threatened by lighter skinned and white women. The following analysis, for reasons of space, addresses the manipulation of issues of race; for a more extensive analysis of the class issues, see my "Imaging Lynching," and "Can We Get There from Here?"

19. Letter to The Honorable Senators of the United States from African American Academic and Professional Women Who Oppose the Clarence Thomas Nomination, 15 Oct. 1991; "Official Statement to All Members of the United States Senate from African American Academic and Professional Women: A Petition to Reject the Clarence Thomas Nomination," 15 Oct. 1991; see also, "Official Statement to All Members of the United States Senate—A Petition of African-American Professors of Social Science and Law," 12 Oct. 1991; all in my possession.

20. "African American Women in Defense of Ourselves," Guest Editorial in *New York Amsterdam News*, 26 Oct. 1991 and Advertisement in *New York Times*, 17 Nov. 1991; San Francisco *Sun Reporter*, 20 Nov. 1991; *Capitol Spotlight* (Washington, D.C.), 21 Nov. 1991; *Los Angeles Sentinel*, 21 Nov. 1991; *Chicago Defender*, 23 Nov. 1991; *Atlanta Inquirer*, 23 Nov. 1991; *Carolinian* (Raleigh, N.C.), 28 Nov. 1991.

21. The following discussion is not meant to speak for or analyze specifically Anita Hill's personal experience but to suggest the ways in which complicating the issues was essential to a discussion which would engage women from differing racial and class backgrounds.

22. "Official Statement to All Members of the United States Senate from African American Academic and Professional Women."

23. Ellen Wells, testimony before Senate Judiciary Committee, 13 Oct. 1991.

24. Mary Bularzik documents the longstanding recognition and discussion of sexual harassment of white working-class women but argues that white middle-class women were initially more reluctant to make public the sexual harassment that accompanied their employment. See "Sexual Harassment in the Workplace."

25. For public discussions of the connections between Black women's employment conditions and sexual abuse, see, for example, Maggie Lena Walker, "Traps for Women," Bethel A.M.E. Church, Richmond, Virginia, 15 Mar. 1925:

> Poverty is a trap for *women*, and especially for our women. . . . When I walk along the avenue of our city and I see our own girls employed in the households of the whites, my heart aches with pain. Not that I cast a slur, or say one word against any kind of honest employment, yet when I see the good, pure, honest colored girl who is compelled to be a domestic in a white man's family—while I applaud the girl for her willingness to do honest work in order to be self supporting, and to help the mother and father who have toiled for her, yet, I tremble lest she should slip and fall a victim to some white man's lust.

See Maggie Lena Walker Papers, Maggie Lena Walker National Historical Site, Richmond, Virginia. See Black female domestic workers' own public accounts. For example:

> I lost my place because I refused to let the madam's husband kiss me. . . . I believe nearly all white men take, and expect to take, undue liberties with their colored female servants—not only the fathers, but in many cases the sons also. Those servants who rebel against such familiarity must either leave or expect a mighty hard time, if they stay.

See A Negro Nurse, "More Slavery at the South," *Independent* 72 (25 Jan. 1912): 197-98. Black club women such as Fannie Barrier Williams talked publicly of the letters they received from Black parents urging them to work to secure employment opportunities that would save their daughters from "going into the [white] homes of the South as servants." See "A Northern Negro's Autobiography," *Independent* 57 (14 July 1904): 96.

26. The primary persons continuing these discussions were, of course, domestic workers themselves. See, for example, "When maids would get together, they'd talk of it. . . .They always had to fight off the woman's husband," in Florence Rice's interview with Gerda Lerner, quoted in *Black Women in White America: A Documentary History*, ed. Gerda Lerner (New York: Vintage Books, 1972), 275; or "nobody was sent out before you was told to be careful of the white man or his sons" in Elizabeth Clark-Lewis, " 'This Work had a' End': The Transition from Live-In to Day Work," *Southern Women: The Intersection of Race, Class, and Gender*, Working Paper No. 2, Center for Research on Women, Memphis State University, 15. It was common practice for domestic workers to gather together to socialize and/or to provide support and advice regarding working conditions, survival strategies, and so on. Because many of these gatherings occurred in the workers' homes, they were often overheard if not participated in by the young people in the homes. See, for example, Bonnie Thornton Dill, " 'Making Your Job Good Yourself': Domestic Service and the Construction of Personal Dignity," in *Women and the Politics of Empowerment*, ed. Ann Bookman and Sandra Morgen (Philadelphia: Temple University Press, 1988), 33-52; Paule Marshall, "From the Poets in the Kitchen," *New Your Times Book Review*, 9 Jan. 1983. Because the majority of Black women in the labor force up to 1960 were employed as domestic workers, a substantial number of African American women grew up with one or more family members who did domestic work and therefore were in frequent earshot of such conversations. In my own family a majority of my aunts and great-aunts were employed in either domestic or factory work; my mother, even though she had a college degree, when she took on paid employment to supplement the family income worked as a domestic or in a factory. For discussions of sexual abuse among Black women factory workers, see, for example, Beverly W. Jones, "Race, Sex, and Class: Black Female Tobacco Workers in Durham, North Carolina, 1920-1940, and the Development of Female Consciousness," *Feminist Studies* 10 (Fall 1984): 443-50. Robin D.G. Kelley suggests that the strategies adopted by Black female factory operatives to resist sexual harassment may have been passed down and developed out of domestic workers' experiences. " 'We Are Not What We Seem': Towards a Black Working-Class Infrapolitics in the Twentieth Century South" (unpublished paper cited by permission of the author).

27. These are obviously not just questions exclusive to African American women but suggest what may happen to any group of people when so few are able to succeed and what may happen when you see yourself, and are seen, as representing your community and not just yourself. I think of Chinua Achebe's protagonist in *A Man of the People*, of Alice Dunbar-Nelson's diary entries which reveal her awareness of her responsibility to maintain a particular image even when she had not the money to do so, and of Black male professionals employed in Richmond in the early twentieth century who told me of the difficulty they had making ends meet financially when their professional positions paid very little but their obligation to represent the potential for African American people's success meant that the Black community did not want them taking on second jobs as hotel waiters or janitors. All expressed an awareness that many people depended—not just financially but psychological—on their success and a belief that they needed to portray success and

hide all traces that mobility had not allowed them to escape the traps of any of the others.

28. See, for example, Catharine MacKinnon in "Hill's Accusations Ring True to a Legal Trailblazer," *Detroit Free Press*, 13 Oct. 1991, 6F.

29. One of the most egregious examples of the latter as related to this particular case can be seen in Orlando Patterson's argument that if Thomas said the things Hill charged he was merely engaging in a "down-home style of courting" which would have been "immediately recognizable" to Hill "and most women of Southern working-class backgrounds, white or black, especially the latter" but which would have been "completely out of the cultural frame of [the] white upper-middle-class work world" of the senators who would vote on his confirmation. See, "Race, Gender, and Liberal Fallacies," *New York Times*, 20 Oct. 1991, and the even more obnoxious defense of his position in *Reconstruction* 1,4 (1992): 68-71, 75-77.

30. "African American Women in Defense of Ourselves." For a good discussion of the sexual stereotypes of African American women in the late nineteenth and early twentieth centuries, see Beverly Guy-Sheftall, *Daughters of Sorrow: Attitudes toward Black Women, 1880-1920* (Brooklyn: Carlson Publishing, 1990), esp. chaps. 3 and 4. See also Patricia Morton, *Disfigured Images: The Historical Assault on Afro-American Women* (New York: Praeger, 1991).

31. Crenshaw, "Roundtable: Sexuality after Thomas/Hill," 29.

32. Darlene Clark Hine, "Rape and the Culture of Dissemblance: Preliminary Thoughts on the Inner Lives of Black Midwestern Women," *Signs* 14 (Summer 1989): 912-20.

33. The implications of this are explored in my "Imaging Lynching."

34. This became a common argument during and in the days following the hearings; see, for example, Barbara Ehrenreich, "Women Would Have Known," *Time*, 21 Oct. 1991, 104.

Part II
Africa

4

Sexual Demography:

The Impact of the Slave Trade on Family Structure

John Thornton

In the past few years, the study of the Atlantic slave trade has shifted emphasis from measuring its volume to judging its effects in Africa. In the recent seminar in African Historical Demography held in Edinburgh, the four contributions dealing with the slave trade assessed its effects on African population size, structure, and density (Diop 1981; Inikori 1981; Manning 1981a, 1981b; Thornton 1981). Emerging from this new concentration on the African side of the slave trade has been the realization that the slave trade had a significant impact on the role and life of women, and researchers are increasingly pointing out that the study of women, both as slaves and as free people in areas where slaving occurred, is a necessary corollary to the study of the slave trade as a whole (Manning 1981a).

The fact that the slave trade carried more men than women to the Americas, about two to three men for every woman according to those statistical series that are available, has long been seen as the cause of the inability of the slave population to grow in America. Low birth rates were largely a product of an extremely unbalanced sex ratio on American plantations, which when coupled with bad nutrition, few incentives to reproduce, and high abortion rates meant that slave populations could not keep ahead of their own mortality except by renewed imports from Africa (Sheridan 1975; H. Klein, this volume).

My own work on the Angolan population of the late eighteenth century suggested what were the effects of the very differently altered sex composition in Africa (Thornton 1980). In Angola, women outnumbered men by nearly two to one in the population left behind after the slave trade. However, unlike in the Americas, the skewed sex ratio did not result in a marked decline in population. Because of the established institution of polygyny, the almost undiminished numbers of women were able to counterbalance some of the losses to the slave trade by continued reproduction. In a study presented at the Edinburgh conference, I charted the probable effects of the slave trade on age and sex distribution in a model population with characteristics similar to those of the population of Angola (Thornton 1981). Then, operating on the assumption that the rest of western Africa had similar population structures, I tried to suggest what would be the effect on such a model population of withdrawing a number of slaves equal to the number known from studies of the volume of the slave trade. Working independently, Patrick Manning created another model, which, while differing in approach and assumptions, nevertheless arrived at similar conclusions (1981a and 1981b). Both models supported the conclusion that the population, although showing no long-term growth, suffered little long-term net loss. However, in both models the population, while not shrinking, did undergo fairly substantial alteration in structure, such that the group of males of working age was substantially reduced as a result of the specific demands of the slave traders and American purchasers for slaves in that age and sex group (Thornton 1980; Manning 1981b). In my own model, in which I tried to establish the minimum population densities necessary to support the known volume of slave exports in the interior behind each of several slave-exporting centers and then compared these densities with probable densities based on modern population size, I found that at the peak period of the slave trade in the late eighteenth century the demand for slaves must have come close to matching the maximum ability of all these regions to supply them. Moreover, in every region, the sex ratio in the age bracket 15-60 would have been only 80 men per 100 women, and in the hardest-hit area, Angola, as low as 40-50 men per 100 women (Thornton 1980).

The older debate on the slave trade had concentrated in one way or another on quantitative assessments of the population changes in Africa caused by the slave trade. Thus in Fage's many papers on the subject he insisted that the total volume of the trade was insufficient to offset natural growth and Africa was not depopulated (Fage 1975). Criticisms of Fage's approach, such as those of J.E. Inikori and L.M. Diop presented at the Edinburgh conference, maintained simply that Fage had underestimated the total number of slaves exported and that depopulation *had* occurred, with its most important negative effect being a less favorable land-to-labor ratio in the remaining population. The approach to the problem suggested by Manning and myself, on the other hand, involves investigation of the quality of the population left behind, and not simply its quantity. This approach supports an argument that the major impact of the trade was not so much the reduction of the total number of people remaining in Africa as fundamental alterations in the ratio of working to dependent populations or of male to female labor. In this reexamination, the position of women is highlighted, since it is they who suffered the most from the trade in Africa.

The alteration in the age and sex ratios affected women in Africa in two ways, both results of the age- and sex-specific nature of the demand for African slaves by the traders. First of all, since they retained their normal fertility, the burden of child care imposed on them was not lessened by the loss in population—all the more so since children younger than age fifteen or so were rarely taken by the slave traders. At the same time their own numbers, and more important the numbers of males who played a vital role in child support if not in child care, were declining. This can be clearly seen if we examine the change in the dependency ratio of a hypothetical population in which the working group aged 15-60 has been depleted by 10 percent (the effect of having a sex ratio of 80 men per 100 women in this age group). Before the onset of the trade, according to the model life table from which my work was constructed, about 60 percent of the population fell into this age bracket, while the other 40 percent were either younger and required child care, or older and were unable to participate in productive labor. Thus there were approximately 67 dependents for each 100 working people. After the distortion introduced by the slave trade, however, 54 percent of the population fell into the category of able-bodied workers, while 46 percent were dependent, giving a dependency ratio of 85 dependents for each 100 working people. Thus the burden of work falling on the productive members of society was greatly increased, forcing more and more of their time to be spent in purely subsistence activities and reducing their ability to produce surplus for commerce or to maintain an efficient division of labor.

Women were hit in another way as well, however, and this was due to the alteration of the sex ratios among the producers just at a time when the work load of all producers was increasing. The model suggests that there must have been 20 percent fewer males to perform work allocated to men during the slave trade era, work which would then have had to go undone, or be done by females, or compensated for by purchased items. For example, in central Africa women did agricultural work, but men did heavy clearing of the fields, chopping down trees and digging up roots. Without this clearing labor, the women would have had to plant less or move their fields less often, both of which would tend to reduce production (Thornton 1983:28-31). Likewise, because hunting, fishing, and the rearing of livestock were activities which many traditional African societies left to men, the loss of males resulted in a less protein-rich diet for the remaining people.

This model is, of course, an average calculation based on rather crude assumptions. The actual adjustment of particular African societies is much more difficult to determine. The model is a global one applied to all regions of western Africa that supplied slaves, and is based on data obtained from a few rather large areas. How the slave raids affected the population in smaller regions within these larger areas is not considered. For example, a society subjected to raids might lose men and women in equal numbers and the raiding society incorporate the women while selling off the men. Alternatively, slave raiding which matched military forces against each other might result in all the slaves procured by the victor being males of saleable age, since armies select for the same age and sex criteria as plantation managers. My model suggested that the societies that procured slaves selected men ahead of women, and left the societies which gave up slaves with unbalanced sex ratios, while Manning's model assumed that the victims of slave raiding lost men and women in equal numbers, and the unbalanced sex ratios affected the societies that did the raiding. In fact, a variety of different methods were used to procure slaves, from large-scale wars to small-scale kidnapping, including judicial enslavement and raids of organized military forces against disorganized villagers. Each of these methods might have resulted in a different mix of ages and sexes for both the aggressors and the losers, and hence a whole distinct constellation of resulting demographic structures.

In Angola, for example, slaves were procured by major wars between military powers, a method which would probably favor the acquisition of males by the group that sold the slaves (da Silva Corrêa 1782; Birmingham 1966), and smaller-scale kidnapping and raiding against villagers which would have resulted in the acquisition of both men and women (A.P.F. 1705). Moreover, the census data from Angola show unbalanced sex ratios and distorted age structures for both slaves and free people, suggesting that the depletion of males among victims and the incorporation of females by the groups that acquired slaves were going on simultaneously (Thornton 1980). Equally diverse means of slave procurement were probably being used in other regions as well, which future research may do much to clarify.

Although a focus on the age and sex distribution of affected African populations does not tell us as much about the qualitative social effects of the slave trade as we would like, it suggests some lines of research that could reveal more about those effects. For example, one result of the unbalanced sex ratios would be an alteration in the institution of marriage. Since the institution of polygyny was present in Africa at the time that the slave trade began (Fage 1980), the general surplus of women in the marriageable age group would have tended to encourage it and allow it to become much more widespread, driving down the bride wealth that women's families could demand and weakening the stability of the marriages in existence. It might also have favored men building up large households of wives through the purchase of female slaves; these slaves and their children, unprotected by their kin, would have been subject to abuses. This in turn might have had a detrimental effect on the status of marriage even for free women. These effects might vary according to whether the surplus of women was caused by an influx of female slaves, as in a society that was capturing slaves of both sexes but selling only the males to the Atlantic trade; or by a shortage of men, as in a society in which men were being drained off by warfare to the trade, leaving the women behind.

We can examine such qualitative changes in more detail by looking at one region, that of modern Guinea-Bissau (the Upper Guinea coast), for which descriptive data are available. By the early seventeenth century the region had become one of the foci of slave exporting from the western end of West Africa. Witnesses of the time commented on this fact, as for example the memorial submitted by the Jesuit priest Baltasar Barreira in 1606 (Brásio 1958-79, 4:190-98), or the group of Spanish Capuchins who submitted an open letter to the Pope and several other European rulers in 1686 (Labat 1728, 5:215-20; Texeira da Mota 1974:121-33). Extensive slave trade activity is confirmed as well by surveys of the ethnic origins of slaves landing in the New World, such as those compiled from notarial records in Peru by Frederick Bowser (1974:40-43). A fairly large percentage of the slaves leaving Guinea-Bissau were from the numerous small political units in the area (Texeira da Mota 1974:124-28).

From the written observations of many visitors to Guinea-Bissau, we can form some idea of the social ramifications of the slave trade there. It was the wealth of written evidence, much of it from residents hostile to the slave trade, that enabled Walter Rodney to write so poignantly and effectively about the distortion of life and justice caused by the slave trade in the region (1970:112-51). These hostile witnesses were mostly missionaries to the coast, which possessed a substantial settlement of Portuguese and Afro-Portuguese residents and was in need of clerical ministrations, and, as a non-Moslem zone, was open to attempts to missionize the African population. The Jesuits worked in the country from the start of the seventeenth century, and were joined by the Capuchins in mid-century (Brásio 1958-79; Carrocera 1957). Unlike lay residents, whose writing is also quite extensive, the missionaries took pains to describe daily life and customs, and were not indisposed to denounce the slave trade since it interfered with their successful proselytization as well as offended their sense of justice.

This corpus of writing allows us to see some of the ways in which women were affected by the Atlantic slave trade. Writing in 1684 in an enlarged recension of a manuscript he originally composed in 1669, Francisco de Lemos Coelho, a Portuguese resident of the area, made some interesting notes on the Bissagos Islands. Although he does not mention unbalanced sex ratios as such, Lemos Coelho noted that polygyny was so widespread there that "there are blacks there who have twenty or thirty wives, and no one has only one," and moreover, "the children in their villages are [as numerous as] a beehive" (Lemos Coelho 1953:178). Given the heavy slave trade in the area, the disproportionate number of women and children remarked by Lemos Coelho is not surprising. This unbalanced age and sex structure may also account for the very large share of work done by women on the islands, which astonished Lemos Coelho. After describing their complicated work in making cloth for clothes, he goes on to say: "They [the women] are the ones who work the fields, and plant the crops, and the houses in which they live, even though small, are clean and bright, and despite all this work they still go down to the sea each day to catch shellfish . . ." (Lemos Coelho 1953:178). Lemos Coelho was not the only observer to comment on the burden of work falling on the women of the Bissagos Islands. Over half a century earlier, André Álvares d'Almada made almost identical observations, noting, "they [the women] do more work than men do in other places" (Brásio 1958-79, 3:317). The men, it seems, were absorbed largely in war, which in this case meant slave raiding, while the women had to engage in production and perform more than the normal share of work. In the case of the Bissagos Islanders it seems probable that the real burden fell upon the extra women, those who had arrived as slaves, although Lemos Coelho's report does not distinguish between slaves and free women.

Elsewhere in the area, other witnesses explicitly drew a connection between slavery, an influx of women, and the peculiar status of slave wives. The Spanish Capuchins, who complained of the state of affairs in the region around Bissau in 1686, believed that the plenitude of female slaves encouraged concubinage (Texeira da Mota 1974:125; 131-32). Manuel Alvares, a Jesuit who wrote of conditions in the same area in 1616, observed, "All have many wives," again suggesting the generality of concubinage. Alvares also noted the special vulnerability of slave women: "If a noble takes his own slave for a wife, and she gives him some displeasure, he will sell her along with her child, even if the child is small, without any regard for the child being his own" (Texeira do Mota 1974:59-60). Others who had lived in Guinea noticed the ease with which subordinate family members might be sold for petty violations of custom (Texeira da Mota 1974:125), although Alvares added that upper-class women were protected from such dire measures. Much of this testimony was used years ago by Rodney to support his thesis that the slave trade had led to substantial legal distortion, and certainly this particular social custom would allow members of the upper classes to hold or sell subordinates at will and according to other needs or the demands of the trade (1970:106-10). Thus slaves held in marriage arrangements such as those described by Alvares could be mobilized for sale without costly wars or risk of retribution. Of course, most witnesses agree that warfare was still the major source of slaves (Texeira da Mota 1974:124-26), and one cannot help but suspect that the marriage customs were reported more for their shock value (and perhaps from isolated cases) than for the importance of their incidence.

Nevertheless, the slave trade brought many surplus women into coastal society in Guinea, and the Spanish Capuchins even noted that housing was inadequate, forcing male and female slaves to share quarters during peak periods of the trade (Texeira da Mota 1974:131). Inquisition authorities were aware that large numbers of slave women were affecting the Portuguese residents as well; in 1589, one Nuno Francisco da Costa was denounced to the Inquisition for having many *mulheres* (an ambiguous word in this case, meaning either women or wives) and reputedly saying that he cared more "for the fingernail of [a particular] slave woman than all the masses and confessions" (Baião 1906:251; Texeira da Mota 1976:15-16). Slavery and surplus women might even have altered the marriage patterns of theoretically monogamous Christians.

These scattered observations on female roles and marriage customs might be taken for no more than passing remarks of writers who were somewhat unsympathetic to African culture, were it not for their close agreement with our expectations based on demographic trends in the area. Just as Rodney's generalizations about the effects of the slave trade on class structure and the institution of slavery have been criticized as being atypical of West Africa (Fage 1980:289-91), so too might these remarks on women's roles and the status of marriage. The data are not quantifiable, and were obtained from observers who were antagonistic toward the slave trade and hence anxious to highlight its ill effects. But they do fit some predictions based on a knowledge of the demography of the slave trade, and as such must be taken with new seriousness.

Scholars interested in understanding the slave trade must undertake an investigation, covering as many areas and time periods as possible, of the status of women (both slave and free) and the institution of marriage in the context of our understanding of the population structure of societies participating in the slave trade. Similarly, it is an urgent task of those interested in the social history of Africa to investigate the nature and dimensions of the internal slave trade, and the strategy of its agents. To what extent did this internal trade involve the transfer of women from interior districts to the regions of the slave-trading states? Can we guess at the volume of this trade in females, which was fairly extensive in some regions? To what extent did the displacements of women within Africa and the siphoning off of men to the trans-Atlantic slave trade affect the precolonial population distribution, and what is the legacy of those effects today? We also need further exploration of how male and female roles were affected by the change in sex ratios.

In addition, more study of slave trades not involving shipment to the Americas might yield interesting results. For example, Olifert Dapper noted in the mid-seventeenth century that in every village along the Gold Coast from Allada to the Ivory Coast there were "three or four whores," recruited from female slaves, whose earnings went to the ruler of the village. To what extent was this widespread prostitution (prevalent in spite of the polygyny which Dapper also noted) a product of the trade in female slaves between Benin and the Gold Coast? (Dapper 1670:471). Was it due to the region's role as an importer of slaves (from the interior and other points of the coast), its growing role as an exporter of slaves (just beginning as Dapper wrote) (Rodney 1969), or the general concentration of strangers in the area that brought about the area's position as a marketplace between the zone controlled by interior merchants and that controlled by European traders? (Vasconcellos 1639:85).

We must accept that the full story of the effect of the slave trade on women in western Africa is well beyond the range of the sources available to us. Travelers' accounts, local chronicles, and even reports of residents often neglect descriptions of women's work and women's status, or present these in categories that are either an "ideal average" or a series of horror stories like those of the missionaries in Guinea-Bissau. Statistical evidence for any period save the very end of the precolonial era is likely to elude us. But we can learn considerably more about this aspect of Africa than we know now by reading over the sources available to us with a critical eye, informed by a knowledge of probable and possible effects of the slave trade. We can also try to develop models with greater predictive power than is possessed by the ones now in existence, models which, though perhaps not testable statistically, can be effectively tested by the documentation we do have.

REFERENCES

Unpublished Sources

A.P.F.: Archivio de Propaganda Fide (Rome). Bernardo da Firenze to Propaganda Fide, June 22, 1705. Scritture originali riferitenella Congregazione Generale, vol. 552, fols. 64v-65v.

Published Sources

Baião, A. 1906. *A Inquisição em Portugal e no Brazil. Subsídios para a sua história*. Lisbon.

Birmingham, D. 1966. *Trade and Conflict in Angola*. London.

Bowser, F. 1974. *The African Slave in Colonial Peru*. Stanford.

Brásio, A. 1958-79. *Monumenta Missionaria Africana*. 2nd series. 5 vols. Lisbon.

Carrocera, B. de. 1957. *Missiones Capuchinas en Africa. II. Missiones al Reino de la Zinga, Benin, Ardra, Guinea y Sierra Leone*. Madrid.

Dapper, O. 1670/1967. *Umbeständliche und Eigentliche Beschreibung von Africa*. Amsterdam.

Da Silva Corrêa, Elias Alexandre. 1782 (1937). *História de Angola*. 2 vols. Lisbon.

Diop, L.M. 1981. Méthode et calculs approximatifs pour la constitution d'une courbe representatif de l'évolution de la population de l'Afrique noire." In *African Historical Demography*, ed. C. Fyfe and D. McMaster. Edinburgh.

Fage, J.D. 1975. "The Effect of the Export Slave Trade on African Populations." In *The Population Factor in African Studies*, ed. R.P. Moss and R.J.A. Rathbone, London.

Fage, J.D. 1980. "Slaves and Society in Western Africa, c. 1455-c. 1700." *Journal of African History* 21:289-310.

Fyfe, C., and D. McMaster, eds. 1981. *African Historical Demography*. vol. 2. Edinburgh.

Inikori, J.E. 1981. "Underpopulation in 19th Century West Africa: The Role of the Export Slave Trade." In *African Historical Demography*, vol. 2, ed. C. Fyfe and D. McMaster. Edinburgh.

Labat, J.B. 1728. *Nouvelle relation de l'afrique Occidentale*. 5 vols. Paris.

Lemos Coelho, F. de. 1953. *Duas descrições seiscentistas da Guiné*. Edited by Damião Peres. Lisbon.

Manning, P. 1981a. "A Demographic Model of Slavery." In *African Historical Demography*, ed. C. Fyfe and D. McMaster. Edinburgh.

Manning, P. 1981b. "The Enslavement of Africans: A Demographic Model." *Canadian Journal of African Studies* 15:499-526.

Rodney, W. 1969. "Gold and Slaves on the Gold Coast." *Transactions of the Historical Society of Ghana* 10:13-28.

Rodney, W. 1970. *A History of the Upper Guinea Coast, 1545-1800*. Oxford.

Sheridan, R. 1975. "Mortality and Medical Treatment of Slaves in the British West Indies." In *Race and Slavery in the Western Hemisphere: Quantitative Studies*, ed. S.L. Engerman and E.D. Genovese. Princeton.

Texeira da Mota, A. 1974. *As Viagens de Bispo d. Frei Vitoriano Portuense a Guiné e a cristianização dos reis de Bissau*. Lisbon.

Texeira da Mota, A. 1976. "Alguns aspectos da colonização e do commércio marítime dos Portugueses na África ocidental nos séculos XV e XVI. *Centro de Estudos de Cartográfia Antiga. Series Separata* 97:15-16.

Thornton, J. 1980. "The Slave Trade in Eighteenth-Century Angola: Effects on Demographic Structures." *Canadian Journal of African Studies* 14:417-27.

Thornton, J. 1981. "Demographic Effect of the Slave Trade on Western Africa, 1500-1850." In *African Historical Demography*, vol. 2, ed. C. Fyfe and D. McMaster. Edinburgh.

Thornton, J. 1983. *The Kingdom of Kongo: Civil War and Transition, 1641-1718*. Madison.

Vasconcellos, Agustin Manuel y. 1639. *Vida y acciones del Rey Don Juan el Segundo*. Madrid.

Vogt, J. 1973. "The Early São Thomé–Principe Slave Trade with Mina, 1500-1540." *International Journal of African Historical Studies* 6:453-67.

5

African Women in the Atlantic Slave Trade

Herbert S. Klein

African women did not enter the Atlantic slave trade in anything like the numbers of African men. At all ages, men outnumbered women on the slave ships bound for America from Africa. As both contemporaries and later commentators have pointed out, far fewer women entered the slave ships of the Europeans than would have been the case if the Atlantic slave trade had operated randomly. Ever since the slave trade began, this disparity has elicited comments from all observers, and in recent years scholars have begun to pay serious attention to determining both its cause and its consequences.

In this short essay, I would like to examine the actual rates of participation of African women in the slave trade as seen from the experience of several European controlled trades, and to speculate on both the causes and consequences of this sexual disparity. As the reader will quickly realize, many of the hypotheses that I set forth are highly speculative because of the tentativeness and incompleteness of available records. Nevertheless, enough progress recently has been made on this problem so that some broad general features can be established even if the causes and consequences of these factors are still subject to extensive debate.

What recent research has now established is that contemporaneous observations of the slave trade, based upon limited experience, in fact hold for the entire history of the Atlantic slave trade. Women did not participate in the trade as fully as men; this was true of every period and every trade for which records are available. Only beginning in the late seventeenth century were systematic records kept of the sexual and age divisions among some African slaves. Fortunately for the purposes of this study, these records coincide with the most important phase of the Atlantic slave trade, when over three-quarters of the African slaves were shipped to America (Curtin 1969:265).

One of the earliest of the trades keeping sexual breakdowns was that of the Dutch at the end of the seventeenth and beginning of the eighteenth centuries. Among the over 60,000 slaves shipped from Africa to the West Indies in this period by both the West India Company and free trader ships, females were only 38 percent of the forced migrants. Even when slaves are examined by age group, the same disproportionate representation of males is apparent. Thus the adult sex ratio was 187 men for every 100 women, and the child ratio was 193 boys for every 100 girls.

Table 1

African Slaves Transported by Dutch Slave Ships, 1675-1795

Period	Men	Women	Boys	Girls
1675-1740[a]	22,682	10,132	2,442	865
1730-1795[b]	11,488	8,135	3,314	2,114
Total	34,170	18,267	5,756	2,979

Source: Postma 1979:257.

[a]Seventy-three shipments by vessels belonging to the West India Company.

[b]Ninety shipments by vessels belonging to free traders.

This same pattern can be seen among the slaves carried by the Danish slave traders in the second half of the eighteenth century. In the two decades of recorded trading, the Danes shipped from their own Guinean forts and from areas on the Guinean coast to the west of them some 15,000 slaves, of whom only 36 percent were females. Just as in the case of the Dutch, this sexual imbalance appeared among both adults and children, with 186 men to 100 women and 145 boys to 100 girls.

Table 2

African Slaves Transported by Danish Slave Ships, 1777-1789 (49 Ships)

Origin	Men	Women	Boys	Girls
Danish African Possessions	5,289	2,660	1,077	653
Non-Danish African Possessions	2,333	1,438	984	769
Total	7,622	4,098	2,061	1,422

Source: Green-Pedersen 1971:192-95.

In the last decade of eighteenth century, the British took some 83,000 slaves from the entire western African costal region. But even in this more broadly based sample of African slaves, the same discrimination against women which was evident in the more geographically limited Dutch and Danish trades is apparent. Among the British slaves, females represented only 38 percent of the slaves, with both adults (165:100) and children (164:100) showing the same bias toward males.

Finally, in the last trade for which we have extensive data on age and sex among the slaves, the same pattern emerges. Of the approximately 182,000 slaves arriving in Havana, Cuba, at the end of the eighteenth and beginning of the nineteenth centuries, only 29 percent were females. Especially among adults, women were severely underrepresented, with 251 men for every 100 women. Among the teens and children the rates were considerably less lopsided, being 153:100 and 200:100.

Being of both intra-Caribbean and African origin, the slave trade to Cuba presents special distortions which should be taken into account before these figures can be compared to those of the other African originated trades. To distinguish the origins of the slaves, unfortunately not listed by Spanish royal officials, I have taken African originated slaves to be any slaves who arrived on ships carrying 200 or more slaves per voyage. This procedure is based on a series of hypotheses about the trade and is supported by some alternative sources (Klein 1978, ch. 9). If these vessels are isolated from the totals, we are left with an estimated 102,000 slaves who arrived directly from Africa on some 322 vessels. The ratio of males to females among the Africans, 221:100 (with a much higher ratio among adults than among the two child categories—see Table 5), was slightly lower than among slaves of mixed African and intra-Caribbean origins. But what the disaggregated figures show is that there was an even more pronounced lack of women in the local interisland trade. Evidently, West Indian planters were reluctant to part with women now that the trans-Atlantic slave trade was coming to an end.

Table 3

Age and Sex of Slaves Carried from the African Coast in English Ships, 1791-1798

African Region	Men	Women	Boys	Girls
Senegambia	4,319	2,143	817	519
Sierra Leone	517	243	55	29
Windward Coast	4,526	2,414	383	215
Gold Coast	2,539	1,321	188	117
Bight of Biafra	14,375	10,971	435	384
Bight of Benin	304	189	9	10
Congo-Angola	11,596	6,144	968	509
Unknown	10,113	5,822	992	556
Total	48,289	2,947	3,847	2,339

Source: G.B.L., July 28, 1800. Figures are from the 272 ships (out of 332 listed) for which age and sex breakdowns were available.

Table 4

Age and Sex of Slaves Arriving in the Port of Havana, Cuba, 1790-1820

Period	Males			Females		
	Adults[a]	Teens[b]	Children[c]	Adults[a]	Teens[b]	Children[c]
1790-1794	14,985	1,587	3,885	3,531	1,173	2,062
1795-1799	11,805	1,537	2,846	2,662	763	1,031
1800-1804	18,344	2,548	4,320	6,218	2,004	2,334
1805-1809	6,727	1,172	2,405	1,738	520	931
1810-1814	8,712	2,133	3,711	2,494	1,289	1,823
1815-1819	22,606	7,910	12,558	9,171	5,251	6,603
1820	69	127	73	57	105	105
Total	83,248	17,014	29,798	25,871	11,105	14,889

Source: S.A.I., legajo 2207.

[a]Adults were listed in the traditional *piezas de indias* slave trade terminology, which means an age of eighteen or older.

[b]Teenagers, or *mulecónes* (f. *mulécas*), were defined as imported slaves aged eleven to seventeen years.

[c]Children, or *muléques* (f. *mulecónas*), were defined as imported slaves aged about seven to ten years.

Table 5
Sex Ratio and Percentage Children and Teens, by Route of Origin, of Slaves Arriving in Havana, Cuba, 1790-1820

Age Category	Routes[a]			
	Caribbean	Mixed	African	All Routes
Adults	479	302	283	322
Teens	229	160	139	153
Children	255	197	187	200
All Ages	376	244	221	251
(N =)	(38,629)	(41,652)	(101,644)	(181,925)
Children and Teens (%)	32	41	43	40

Source: S.A.I., legajo 2207.

[a]The routes were defined as follows: Those ships carrying from 1 to 99 slaves were assumed to be engaged in an intra-Caribbean trading; those with 100-199 could be either smaller African shipments or vessels engaged in broken voyages and mixing slaves from several sources; while any ship arriving with 200 slaves or more was considered to be coming directly from Africa to Cuba.

Thus in all trades, between two-thirds and three-quarters of all slaves arriving in America were males. But this general trend obscures some interesting internal variations. In some periods and from some regions more women were sent than was the norm. In analyzing the sources of the slaves bound for the West Indies in English ships in the 1790s, for example, it is evident that the Bight of Biafra supplied a much higher percentage of women than was common to the rest of the African exporting regions.

Interestingly, Table 6 does not support the correlation that might have been expected between the movement of women and of children. Thus Biafra, while contributing a very high percentage of women, was nevertheless contributing only an average percentage of children to the trade. This may be an accident of time and place, or it could mean that the factors influencing the flow of women were quite independent from those affecting the flow of children.[1] While no definitive pattern may be seen over time and across trades, the data do suggest that the very earliest (seventeenth-century) and very latest (nineteenth-century) periods of the mature slave trade may have been times of unusually low participation for women, or conversely that the mid- to late eighteenth century was a period of unusually high participation. But given the relatively nonrepresentative nature of the currently available samples of the trade which provided information on sex, such hypotheses can only be offered on the most tentative basis.

If, as now seems proven, women were disproportionately underrepresented in the Atlantic slave trade, the question remains why. Was this due to demand or supply considerations? Was there a planter preference for males which was based on labor, productivity, or other factors and reflected in price differentials? Or could it have been that women were more costly to transport than men and thus were less desired by the slave captains who made their purchases on the African coast? Or, finally, were the Africans themselves keeping women off the market despite demands for them from American planters and European slave captains?

Table 6
Average Sex Ratio and Percentage of Children Carried per Shipment in the English Slave Trade to the West Indies, 1791-1798

African Region of Origin	Sex Ratio	(Number of Shipments)	Children (%)	(Number of Shipments)	Mortality (%)[a]	(Number of Shipments)
Senegambia	210	(2)	10	(5)	3	(5)
Sierra Leone	210	(29)	22	(24)	4	(37)
Windward Coast	208	(15)	14	(9)	4	(15)
Gold Coast	184	(26)	12	(21)	3	(26)
Bight of Benin	187	(2)	6	(1)	4	(3)
Bight of Biafra	138	(79)	14	(22)	11	(105)
Congo-Angola	217	(60)	14	(39)	4	(63)
Unknown	188	(56)	12	(43)	2	(47)
Average	183		14		6	
(Total Shipments)		(272)		(164)		(301)[b]

Source: G.B.L., July 28, 1800.

[a]These are average mortality figures. There was a high degree of variance among the voyages in terms of mortality; thus the coefficient of variation for the 301 shipments for which complete data existed was 1.27. Individual regions ranged from .70 to 1.38. Biafra, which will be of concern later on in this essay, was at the lower end with a coefficient of variation of .91, which implies that its spread of mortality experience was on average lower than for the entire sample, and for most regions as well. Thus its high average mortality is not due to an unusual concentration of ships with high mortality experience.

[b]Only 272 shipments had complete age and sex breakdowns (of which only 164 carried children); the others simply gave total slave figures. This accounts for the discrepancy between the mortality sample and the sample from which the age and sex breakdowns were taken.

As early as the eighteenth century, administrators and analysts of the trade were concerned with this question and offered all possible answers, from explanations based on supply or demand considerations to speculations about differential mortality and costs of transport. Thus qualitative support for every possible causal model can be found in the eighteenth- and nineteenth-century records.

To deal with this crucial issue systematically, it is essential to outline the relevant variables. One of the more general concepts in the qualitative literature is that planters preferred men over women and paid higher prices for them. In the Parliamentary reviews of the trade, several experienced captains stressed this theme, along with the belief that the planters preferred men because women were useless in field labor.[2]

After some two decades of systematic analyses of slave prices and studies of working conditions of slaves in many American slave societies, it is evident that the perception of the captains on this point does not agree with the reality of the American experience. Several recent studies have shown that the earnings of male and female slaves differed little during the years of productive labor (Fogel and Engerman 1974, 1:75-77; Carvalho de Mello 1976, ch. 2; Fraginals et al., forthcoming). This was reflected in quite similar prices paid for male and female slaves in almost all major slave societies in the Americas. Prices for male slaves were usually somewhat higher than for female slaves, on the order of 10-20 percent in the prime working years. In almost all such societies, however, women were denied access to skilled occupations, and all skilled slaves were more highly priced than unskilled ones (Fogel and Engerman 1974; Carvalho de Mello 1976, appendix). Controlling for this differential access to skills, and comparing just unskilled fieldhand labor, the price differential between males and females is reduced almost to insignificance (Higman 1976:192). Women's prices in the prime years reflected a positive price for unborn children, and therefore may have compensated for whatever differences in physical potential might have existed.

Even if price differentials were not significant, is it possible that women could not be used in the harsh physical labor of plantation agriculture and were therefore needed less than men? Again on the contrary, all recent studies reveal that planters showed little or no sexual preferences in labor use, with women performing all the basic unskilled manual labor tasks that men worked at. Women in most American plantations were, in fact, overrepresented in all the brute force fieldhand labor occupations, and in mature plantation areas they tended to be the majority of actual field gang plantation workers. Thus, in both the sugar and coffee estates of early nineteenth-century Jamaica, the majority of women were found in field labor, and made up at least half of the gangs on most plantations (Higman 1976). In Worthy Park, one of the best studied of the larger sugar plantations, for example, from the late 1780s until 1838, women were never less than 54 percent of the total of the field hands, with two-thirds being the average ratio; and unskilled field labor—clearing, planting, weeding, and harvesting—occupied on average close to two-thirds of the women on the plantation (Craton 1978). A similar division of labor was found in nineteenth-century United States cotton plantations, and in late nineteenth-century Cuban sugar plantations and Brazilian coffee fazendas (Gray 1932, 1:547-49; Fraginals 1978, 2:42-43; Stein 1957:71).

Thus in terms neither of prices nor labor needs can the sexual imbalance of the African slave trade be explained by the actions of the American planters. Alternatively to explanations based on demand, could it be that transportation problems caused ship captains to take fewer females than males? The few studies available on the relationship between mortality and sex in the Atlantic slave trade make it evident that mortality rates of females were the same as or even less than those of males of the same age group.[3] Nor do any of the studies of the costs of transportation show any bias against women. Both men and women were allotted the same space between decks—though women were usually segregated from men for policing purposes—and both were fed the same foods on the trip. Since few infants were transported, there were no special transport problems or costs related to nursing mothers. In short, neither demand nor transportation factors can explain the sexual disparities in the trade.

That fewer women entered the Atlantic slave trade market than would have been purchased by the Europeans if the supply had been totally elastic is the obvious conclusion. But why they were kept out of this market can only be speculated upon. Women were enslaved within Africa itself. Also, there is now general agreement that a major internal slave market existed within Africa to supply local demands for slave labor. Some fragmentary price data which Philip Curtin has gathered from the interior of Senegambia suggest that there was a much higher local price paid for female than for male slaves.[4] If this was the case, then Africans could have been outbidding Europeans for females on the African markets. Or it could be that the higher prices reflected a much more limited supply of slave women, who in turn were being kept off the slave market either by their own societies or by their captors.

In support of this hypothesis of African demand for women, scholars talk of the vital importance of female agricultural labor in West Africa, while some also stress that in those societies where polygyny was important, the role of slave wives was crucial. Children born to such women were usually incorporated into the local society, and women in general were highly prized for their social and economic importance. Thus it has been suggested that the role of women in the economy and society gave them a higher value, especially as slaves, than men. In contrast it has been suggested that male slaves were not easily absorbed into the local labor systems, and thus represented a potential threat in terms of access to women and arms. They were therefore more easily put up for sale in the Atlantic slave market. If these various hypotheses ultimately prove to have some validity, it might be suggested that an indication of the viability of a given African region or state in the epoch of the Atlantic slave trade was its ability to retain women and keep them from the trans-Atlantic trade. The shipping of more women than normal might indicate a fundamental breakdown in the economic or social viability of the state. Some support for this position can be found in the English slave trade data for the 1790s, which show that the region of Biafra was then exporting the highest number of women of any African region, and also that the ships leaving from these shores experienced by far the highest rates of slave mortality at sea (see Table 6). Moreover, this mortality was consistently the highest of any region for every single age and sex category of slaves being shipped.[5]

In terms of the impact on American slave populations of the sexual distortions apparent in the trans-Atlantic slave trade, the implications are clearer. Since fewer women than men were arriving, and since those fewer women were already well into their adult years and brought with them few children, African populations in America were incapable of reproducing themselves. Most women had already used up some of their potential fecundity by the time they had arrived in America, and the problems of changing nutrition and cultural adjustment further reduced potential births. Supposing that there were on average only some fifty women for every hundred men, and the number of their children was also reduced, then African slave populations in America could only have experienced a negative growth rate.

The historical record of American slave populations, in fact, supports this finding. Every slave state with heavy direct importation of African slaves had a difficult time maintaining its servile laboring population. Only as the trade lessened and the creole slave populations grew were positive growth rates finally achieved. Thus negative growth rates of American slave populations are highly correlated with heavy rates of direct African importations.[6]

From this brief survey, it is apparent that determining the incidence of female participation in the slave trade is only the beginning of a long-term process in explaining its cause and understanding its impact. If it is primarily African supply considerations which determine the movement of women and girls into the trans-Atlantic trade, then the incidence of such females is an important, if indirect, index of African social and economic conditions. How that index is to be interpreted will differ from region to region, as the extreme fluctuations from the western African regions demonstrate. But that fewer women than men entered the trade and that Africans exercised a direct control over this movement cannot be doubted.

REFERENCES

Unpublished Sources

Carvalho de Mello, P. 1976. "The Economics of Slavery in Brazilian Coffee Plantations, 1850-1888." Ph.D. dissertation, University of Chicago.

G.B.C.: Great Britain, House of Commons, Parliamentary Papers.

G.B.L.: Great Britain, House of Lords, Record Office, Papers.

S.A.I.: Spain, Archivo general de Indias, Audiencia de Santo Domingo.

Published Sources

Craton, M.M. 1978. *Searching for the Invisible Man: Slaves and Plantation Life in Jamaica.* Cambridge, Mass.

Curtin, P.D. 1969. *The Atlantic Slave Trade: A Census.* Madison.

Curtin, P.D. 1975. *Economic Change in Precolonial Africa: Senegambia in the Era of the Slave Trade.* 2 vols. Madison.

Fogel, R.W., and S.L. Engerman. 1974. *Time on the Cross: The Economics of American Negro Slavery.* 2 vols. Boston.

Fraginals, M.M. 1978. *El Ingenio, complexo económico social cubana del azucar.* 3 vols.

Fraginals, M.M., S. Engerman, and H.S. Klein. Forthcoming. *Nineteenth Century Cuban Slave Prices in Comparative Perspective.*

Gray, L.C. 1932. *History of Agriculture in the Southern United States to 1860.* 2 vols. Washington, D.C.

Green-Pedersen, S. 1971. "The Scope and Structure of the Danish Negro Slave Trade." *Scandinavian Economic History Review* 19:150-97.

Higman, B.W. 1976. *Slave Population and Economy in Jamaica, 1807-1834*. Cambridge, Mass.

Klein, H.S. 1978. *The Middle Passage: Comparative Studies in the Atlantic Slave Trade*. Princeton.

Northrup, D. 1978. *Trade without Rulers: Pre-Colonial Economic Development in South-Eastern Nigeria*. Oxford.

Postma, J. 1979. "Mortality in the Dutch Slave Trade, 1675-1795." In *The Uncommon Market: Essays in the Economic History of the Atlantic Slave Trade*, ed. H.A. Gemery and J.S. Hogendorn. New York.

Stein, J. 1957. *Vassouras: A Brazilian Coffee Country, 1850-1890*. Cambridge, Mass.

NOTES

1. That this particular case may not have been the norm is seen in figures gathered for slaves seized off the Biafran coast in the 1821-39 period. Of some 24,000 slaves whose age and sex were known, the ratio of females remained a relatively high 100:195, but the ratio of children had now increased to 39 percent. Northrup 1978, appendix D.
2. G.B.C., Report on the Slave Trade, 1789, part I. While many captains stressed differential American prices and other demand-related factors, some two-thirds of them also spoke of the difficulty of procuring slave women on the African coast.
3. See, for example, Postma 1979:258. According to the House of Lords listing for the English Atlantic slave trade in the late eighteenth century, mortality among adult Africans averaged 6 percent for women and 5 percent for men. Among the children the mortality rates were higher, but differed little sexually, with females averaging 11 percent mortality in the Atlantic crossing and males 13 percent.
4. Curtin 1975:175-76. Recent demographic studies of Africa during the slave trade period have stressed the predominance of women on the coast and in so-called raider societies in the interior. See Thornton, this volume.
5. Both men and women leaving Biafra suffered 10 percent mortality on average, with boys having 28 percent and girls 33 percent. For girls only Congo-Angola, at 44 percent (5 ships), had a higher rate. For all other categories, the Biafra region was unique.
6. Klein (1978:243-46) provides detailed information on this issue for most American societies.

Concubinage and the Status of Women Slaves in Early Colonial Northern Nigeria

Paul E. Lovejoy

The establishment of British rule in Northern Nigeria (1897-1903) did not ameliorate the condition of female slaves, particularly concubines.[1] The policy of Indirect Rule, as implemented under the High Commissioner Sir Frederick Lugard (1900-6), required an accommodation with the aristocracy of the Sokoto Caliphate, which constituted most of the area that became the Protectorate of Northern Nigeria. Individual officials who opposed the conquest were deposed, but the aristocracy itself was kept in place. Indeed under colonial rule many of the powers of the aristocracy were enhanced. In order to achieve the support of the aristocracy, Lugard's administration had to compromise on many issues, and one of the most sensitive of these was concubinage. The issue touched the nerve of patriarchal Muslim society. Women in general held an inferior position in society, both legally and in fact. Concubines and other slave women were even worse off than free women. For the British, the treatment of women was not an important issue and there was virtually no reluctance in accepting the *status quo* to the extent that other policies allowed. The problem was that concubines were slaves, and British policy was committed to the reform and ultimate demise of slavery.[2] This article explores the tension between patriarchal Muslim society and British colonialism over the status of women. Concubinage was allowed to continue. It is apparent that women had to accept their subjugation, but sometimes they resisted.

Before the British conquest, slavery had been an important instrument for the recruitment of women, through capture and purchase, from outside the Sokoto Caliphate. Frequently, females had been brought into caliphate society at relatively young ages, often under the age of fifteen. Many of these slaves had been incorporated into the households of the aristocracy and merchant class as concubines. Others had been settled on rural estates as agricultural workers, but young girls, whether born on these estates or recently imported, had also been brought into the homes of the wealthy as concubines.[3] At the time of the conquest, some were court messengers (*jakuda* and *kuyangi*),[4] and often these women, too, had been concubines and only later were assigned political duties. Many households had a slave or two, usually women or girls, who worked in the compound. It was not unusual for these women to have spent at least part of their sexually mature years as concubines as well.

Under the Caliphate, concubinage, as a means of controlling women, accomplished three social aims. First, it concentrated women in the hands of the wealthy and powerful. Second, it increased the size of aristocratic and mercantile households as children were born to these women. Third, it helped consolidate the dominant culture of caliphate society. Women were brought into the caliphate from outside, forced to conform to urban, Muslim social norms, and contributed their children to the next generation of the commercial and political elite. British policy accepted the patriarchal structure of this social formation; there were no reasons apparent to colonial officials why any other policy should be adopted. In so doing, concubinage and the subordination of women were incorporated into the colonial system.

According to Islamic law and the customs of the Sokoto Caliphate, concubinage was a special category of slavery. Concubines were chosen for their sexual attraction to their masters, and they had rights which were denied other slaves. They were recognized in Islamic law. Men could have as many as four wives, who had to be free women, and they could have as many concubines, who were supposed to be slaves, as they could afford. The children of concubines were legally free, and a concubine was to become free on the death of her master, as long as she had borne a child and in some instances had shown signs of pregnancy or had miscarried.[5]

Although women were legally minors under Islamic law, there was a clear distinction between concubines and wives.[6] Concubines were slaves, and wives were not. As a slave, a concubine could not marry, own property, or inherit without the consent of her master. A wife, by contrast, had the rights of the free born, even though as a woman she had fewer rights than a male. The legal opinions of Muslim experts varied with respect to the propriety of free women owing land, the details of marriage contracts, and rules on inheritance. But free women did inherit and therefore could own land, although such ownership was often discouraged. There were a variety of marriage contracts between free women and free men, but the ease of divorce protected women from excessive abuse, at least in some cases. Inheritance practices theoretically followed Malikite norms, in which free women received half the male share of estates. There is no doubt that being a wife was preferable to being a concubine.

In the context of caliphate society, and indeed in the early years of colonial rule as well, wives not only had to be free-born or at least freed from slavery, they also had to be Muslims.[7] They had to have families with acceptable origins (*asali*). Marriage could not take place unless there was a guardian (*wali*) for the bride, usually her father, but sometimes the father's brother or the bride's older brother. The bride's family provided a dowry (*gara*), and the groom's family gave a number of presents to the bride and her family, the most important of which was *sadaki*, a cash payment that legalized the contract. There also had to be reliable witnesses. If a husband had more than one wife, he had to maintain nocturnal access, usually three nights in succession but sometimes four, and provide equal support for each.[8] Men did not always follow these norms, which is one reason why divorce was so common, but women from respectable families certainly could expect husbands to do so.

Colonial Policy Towards Women and Slaves

As part of general colonial aims to reform slavery, women received some protection from sale and excessive punishment, and the number of new slave recruits, including females, was steadily reduced. Those women, however, who were already slaves experienced life much as they had before the conquest. For Lugard and his staff of colonial officers, slavery presented a hazardous terrain fraught with the potential for serious social and economic dislocation.[9] Women as such were not considered a dangerous problem, but assuaging the fears of men—particularly those of the aristocracy and merchant class—was perceived as a necessary component of successful colonial rule. Sacrificing the interests of slave women was an easy, almost non-consequential act for Lugard and his staff.

British decrees on slavery affected both male and female slaves, but as will be demonstrated, female slaves were treated differently from males. The various slavery proclamations prohibited enslavement and the slave trade, abolished the legal status of slavery, and declared all children born after 1 April 1901 free. Slavery itself was not abolished nor were slaves as such emancipated. Instead, the British initiated policies to reform slavery with the intention of minimizing social dislocation and unrest.[10] As a result, keeping slaves in their place was a major concern, and because many female slaves were concubines, reinforcing the subordination of women to men inevitably become an unintentional but crucial dimension of British policy.

Females faced four distinct disadvantages. First, a clandestine trade in children and teenagers continued to supply some slaves, most of whom were females and many of whom became concubines. Secondly, as will be examined in detail below, the courts were used to transfer slave women to those men who could afford to buy concubines. Thirdly, girls born into slavery before 1901 were still legally available for concubinage as they reached puberty, which meant that there was a supply of girls, particularly from rural areas, until the mid-teens. Fourthly, even girls born after 1 April 1901 who should have been considered free were perceived as a pool from which new concubines could be drawn. Public opinion had discouraged the use of girls born into slavery as concubines, but with the difficulty of acquiring new slaves after 1901, many masters ignored public opinion.[11]

Colonial policy, as initially devised by Lugard, attempted to blur the distinctions between concubines and wives, even though it was well known that concubines were slaves and wives were free. Sometimes the wishful thinking of officials equated the two forms of relationship, thereby deliberately ignoring legal opinion and local practice, but it was not really expected that people would behave as officials sometimes wished. At least one colonial official wanted to believe that 'concubines are not really slaves'.[12] Lugard thought that matters relating to concubines were similar to those for women in general. 'It is a question of marriage rather than slavery.'[13] Women had to respect marriage and the dictates of their 'husbands'; running away was unacceptable for concubines, just as it was for wives in England, where according to Lugard a woman 'can be forced to return'. The intention was to prevent the growth of what Sciortini described as that 'very undesirable class of unattached females'.[14] Sir Percy Girouard, who succeeded Lugard as High Commissioner, charged that such women would 'drift into prostitution'.[15] The 'grown-up women' who were considered so undesirable, even to the point that they were not wanted as inmates at Freed Slaves' Homes, were girls as young as twelve.[16] The contradictions apparent in these quotations demonstrate that British officers—all male—rationalized their attitudes towards slave women and thereby provided a screen behind which Muslim males ran their households in much the same way as before.

Women and the Fugitive Slave Crisis

One of the reasons colonial officials tried to keep slave women, including concubines, in their place was because there was a mass exodus of slaves shortly after the conquest and for several years thereafter.[17] A recognizable and large portion of these fugitives were the very women who were supposed to be content with their lot, according to popular views of concubinage. That they were not is clear from the early colonial records. Temple reported in September 1902 that 'a number of domestic slaves, almost always women, have been running away to the Fort from their houses in Bauchi'.[18] Webster wrote of similar difficulties at Nassarawa in 1904: 'These runaways are all women; mostly concubines.'[19] The truth was clear; many women simply did not accept their status as slaves. They seem to have accepted better their subordination as women because many ran away with or to other men. Others attempted to reach their natal homes and relatives, which also meant attachment to males in most cases. Some did indeed become prostitutes, which required another kind of dependency even if it also offered independence from individual men.[20] As these actions of women demonstrate, male-female relationships were based on subordination, but there were different levels of subordination and women could and did move from one level to another.

When women ran away to their home communities, the British sent patrols and messengers to induce them to return. At Nassarawa, Webster used the courts to justify such punitive action.

> There have lately occurred a number of cases in which slave owners have complained to the Native Court or Emir of the desertion of their slaves or concubines and the course that follows is for the Sariki to send ordering the chief of the town in which they have taken refuge to send them in for the case to be decided. When if as in most cases matters can be amicably arranged the

runaway fugitive returns[;] if not a ransom is agreed on which generally is very low. The Toni towns have however lately refused point blank to send any in and driven out the Emir's messengers with insults or even blows.[21]

The patrols sent to retrieve the women charged these towns with contempt of court rather than harboring fugitive slaves. The effect was the same, of course. The colonial state was able to reinforce the relationship between concubine and master.

Supposedly, women could not be forced to return to masters who were responsible for cruelty or ill-treatment, and no woman could be made to go back if she absolutely refused. And there were women who did refuse, such as Agunge, aged thirty, who languished in irons in the Ilorin jail because she would not marry a cripple.[22] Agunge was allowed to go free in December 1906, without compensation to her master. Similarly, Ei-issa, aged twenty, was permitted to return to the home of her mother at Gindi, near Gwandu, in September 1905. She had been severely beaten by her master, who 'could give no good reason for the scars of whip cuts recently inflicted. She states that she ran from him to avoid this cruelty.' The master, however, was not prosecuted for assault 'as there was no evidence of corroboration'.[23] The intention was not to disrupt domestic relations, and if it was necessary to provide a safety valve, as in this situation, so be it.

The Courts and the Redemption of Women

The cornerstone of British policy was a decree that fugitive women had to obtain their freedom through the courts, which involved the payment of redemption money to their masters and the receipt of certificates of freedom. Otherwise a fugitive was returned to her master or placed under a guardian. In Nupe, Larrymore interpreted this decree in a fashion that was representative of other provinces. It should be noted that Larrymore's equation of 'husband' and 'master' reveals that dimension of British attitudes which attempted to obfuscate the difference between concubinage and marriage.

> In cases where a woman runs away from her husband or master, and the man she goes to can be found, an arrangement of the difficulty is easy enough, by making the latter compensate the original husband or master; the amount varies from £5-£10 [120,000-240,000 cowries]. But when, as sometimes occurs, no man is forthcoming, and the women still declines to return, a solution is more difficult. To allow her to have her own way and go free would simply mean increasing prostitution. I have now arranged to hand her over to the Emir's old mother. Her and her husband's [i.e. her master's] name and date of handing over are entered on a list kept in the Resident's office, and she is liable to be sent for at any time. In due course, as a rule within a month, a husband is found who is willing to pay the required compensation. The three are then brought up to the Resident, the new man's name duly entered up, the compensation handed over to the original husband [i.e. master], and the case

satisfactorily concluded. In cases where the man is forthcoming, but cannot afford to pay the amount demanded as compensation, the woman is allowed to go with him, but the Chief of the man's village is made responsible for the money.[24]

The redemption money could be paid in installments, as in the case of Alisu and Hawa, who were freed for sixteen bags of cowries (320,000 cowries), six bags down and the remaining ten bags to be paid over the course of two years.[25]

If slave women tried to attach themselves to soldiers or other government employees, the soldiers or employees had to pay the redemption money. In Katagum, for example, Isa, Biba and Kolo, aged seventeen, seventeen and fourteen respectively,

> were married to three soldiers . . . with the consent of their owner and in each case . . . in the presence of the Native Alkali [judge]. I [the Resident] warned the soldiers that these women were now free, and that they were responsible for their persons and must produce them at any time, unless for good reason shewn.[26]

The warning was an admission on the part of the colonial regime that the fate of slave women after they had been 'freed' could not easily be guaranteed. It must have been difficult, indeed virtually impossible, to keep track of women and thereby know for certain whether or not they had been resold into slavery, which usually meant concubinage. If soldiers and government employees could not pay, the fugitive women were restored to their owners, and as Temple reported from Bauchi in 1902, 'the returning of these women to their masters time after time became a serious nuisance'. As a result, he posted a notice in the market that slaves fleeing to the fort would first be punished and then would be sent back to their masters.[27]

Lugard carefully distinguished between the purchase money paid to masters and the dowry that was required for marriage—they were not the same thing—'but the woman may use it [dowry] for self-redemption if she desires to do so'. Lugard rested this interpretation on a ruling of a judge [alkali] in Bida. He considered the effect of the ruling 'far-reaching'. 'It amounts in fact to an abolition of the slave-concubine class (except in the case of a slave-girl who is voluntarily her master's concubine), and of a decree of emancipation for all women on marriage, except in the case of a woman slave who marries a fellow-slave.'[28] The logic of the argument went as follows: those born of slave parents (cucunawa) could not be sold anyway; women could no longer be obtained as slaves and concubines from pagan tribes, and hence it follows that practically all women are already emancipated. The law as it exists also recognizes that a slave woman who bears a child to her master is not only free at his death, but practically so during his life, and that even if she bears no child but is well behaved she is free at her master's death.[29]

Lugard's legal interpretation was straightforward: 'whenever a woman whose status is that of a slave marries a man, and any "dowry" is demanded by the owner of the woman, it must be regarded as purchase money, and the transaction is consequently illegal. It may, however, be paid as redemption-money, provided that the women is first freed with all proper formalities by the Native Court.'[30] In fact, however, this fine legal distinction was not always upheld, and practice varied considerably from one emirate to another.

In Yola, for example, local judges substituted the proper freedom papers for ones that stated that ransoming was done for purposes of concubinage, 'thereby perpetuating the state of slavery of the woman, and assisting in the purchase of a slave.'[31] Similar practices were followed elsewhere:

> The Courts have [in Sokoto at any rate] permitted women to be ransomed and freed, and yet to become the concubine of the ransomer by what amounts to a legal fiction. If the ransomer intends to marry the woman he says before the *alkali* [judge] *na pansa bauya to zama diya* [I ransom the slave woman she becomes free]. If it is intended, with her consent, that she shall become a concubine he says *na pansa bauya na sa ta daka* [I ransom the woman I set her in my private house]. The effect of the emancipation is thus held in suspense as long as she remains a member of the household, but takes effect the moment she leaves him. He cannot restrain her for she has been freed. She can leave her ransomer at will and marry whom she likes. She is even more free than the wife for she need get no divorce, and has no *Sadaki* to repay. Cases have occurred of girls inducing rich men to ransom them as concubines, in order that they may immediately leave them and marry someone else.[32]

Of course the number of concubines who actually took advantage of this legal fiction is unknown, and it is unlikely that many women were allowed to behave in the manner reported.

The 1905-06 Court Registers

The data for a study of concubinage and the fate of women slaves in general during the early years of colonial rule are decidedly biased. With the exception of one source,[33] all information is derived from males, whether they were colonial officials or informants. Courts discriminated against women; indeed the testimony of women was accepted only through male intermediaries. Hence there is virtually no direct testimony from women, and none from slave women. And the bits and pieces that reveal the attitudes of women are filtered through male eyes.

Registers of 627 freed slaves, 403 of whom were females, for 1905 and 1906 offer a rare view of how the British put into practice their policies for the treatment of slave women.[34] The registers record the names of slaves, their age and sex, the place of liberation, ethnic background, reason for emancipation and probable destination. Often these categories are incomplete, but in general the registers carry a tremendous amount of data of interest to social historians.

The registers were kept in order to keep track of freed slaves; the courts were a major instrument of reform under the colonial regime. Slaves who wished to purchase their own freedom were legally entitled to do so, although in practice there were numerous constraints which prevented many slaves from exercising this right.[35] Some oral traditions even deny that there was such a right, which is more consistent with the caliphate legal heritage.[36] The provisions of the slavery proclamations also allowed third parties to pay the redemption money on behalf of a slave, whereupon the slave was released in the custody of the redeemer. In this case the custodian was either a relative or an intended 'husband'. Slaves seized from traders were also released, although in these cases no ransom was paid. The courts issued certificates of freedom to each of the emancipated slaves.

The courts in question were of two types—local Muslim courts that existed under the Caliphate and continued to operate under the colonial regime and provincial courts set up by the British government. Most slaves seized from traders passed through provincial courts, while most other cases were handled by the Muslim courts, which were referred to as Native Courts. Kano, for example, had twenty-four Muslim courts in 1905-06.[37]

Undoubtedly many more slaves by far achieved their freedom without resort to the courts than are recorded in the 1905-06 registers; in addition to those who ran away in the first several years of colonial rule, many reached tacit understandings with their masters and mistresses whereby they gradually bought their own freedom through the payment of monthly installments. And still other slaves received their freedom as acts of charity on Islamic holidays and as death-bed bequests. Hence the registers are only a partial indication of a much larger process of change involving the slow decline of slavery. That these registers date to 1905 to 1906, relatively early in the colonial era, is of particular value historically, since many of the cases include people who were recently enslaved.

Although 64.3 per cent of the court sample was female, it is not safe to conclude that this percentage accurately reflected the proportion of slave women in caliphate society. Studies from the western Sudan do suggest such a conclusion there,[38] and it may well be that female slaves outnumbered males in the Sokoto Caliphate too. But because the courts offered a legitimate method for transferring women for purposes of concubinage and 'marriage', more women are registered than men, and hence projections of the relative proportion of males and females cannot be made on the basis of these figures.

Much of the information contained in the registers can be treated as reasonably accurate, with the normal allowance for human error. It can be assumed, for example, that age and ethnic identification are relatively accurate. If slaves did not know their ages, judges, court attendants and others offered their reasoned opinions. Ethnic awareness was clearly well developed; again slaves must have testified most of the time but others were highly informed about such matters. Redemption prices, statements of ill-treatment, seizure from slave traders, and similar information are probably accurate, too. Undoubtedly reasons for seeking emancipation were simplified in most cases, and ill-treatment, flight and other factors are likely under-represented in the registers. That these factors are mentioned at all is revealing. Their inclusion indicates that resistance to slavery was common, so common that court attendants and British officials alike saw little reason to hide such cases. They became immune to the implications of the mistreatment which was implied. A similar observation can be made about oral data collected in the 1970s. Informants readily volunteered evidence of severe punishment and poor living conditions for slaves, despite stereotyped statements about how willingly slaves accepted their status.

Certain other information in the 1905-06 registers must be treated cautiously, however. 'Marriage' was a common reason for freeing women, but what this meant in practice is open to interpretation. There is considerable circumstantial evidence that most 'marriages' were in fact cases of concubinage. Similar statements about relatives, adoption, and other situations implying dependency also have to be examined carefully. Besides the qualifications which limit a literal interpretation of some data, many officials failed to complete the registers, thereby reducing their comparative value. Nonetheless, the sample is large enough to allow considerable analysis of the plight of female slaves.[39]

Table 1

Age Profile of Female Slaves Freed Through Courts, 1905-06

Age	Number	Percent
0-5	25	7.4
6-10	37	10.9
11-15	64	18.8
16-20	77	22.6
21-25	40	11.7
26-30	44	12.9
31-35	16	4.7
36+	37	10.9
Total	340	100
Unknown	63	—

Source: Registers of Freed Slaves, 1905-06, SNP 15/1 Acc 90, Acc 121.

Fortunately, the registers provide considerable data on how female slaves were actually treated, although many questions remained unanswered. Of the 340 females in the 1905-06 registers whose ages are known (Table 1), 18.3 per cent were aged 10 and under. Children were a prime commodity in the slave trade, especially after the trade became illegal. They were relatively easy to move, there being little risk of escape or resistance. They could be disguised as children of the traders, and there was a ready market for children in southern Nigeria as well as in the northern emirates. Females between ages 11 and 25, the prime marriageable years as defined locally,[40] constituted 53.2 per cent of the cases. In fact most of these girls and women were probably destined for concubinage. If the women aged twenty-six to thirty are included then 66.1 per cent of the sample was in the category for which 'marriage' was a real possibility. Forty-four per cent of the 'freed' females were clearly destined for 'marriage,' although many of those women listed as redeeming themselves or otherwise 'freed' on their 'own inclination' were assisted by males and probably became concubines or otherwise 'married' (Table 2).

Table 2
Destination of Freed Female Slaves, 1905-06

Destination	Number	Percent
Marriage to Redeemer	145	39.4
Marriage—other	17	4.6
Restored to relatives	57	15.5
Freed Slaves' Homes	23	6.2
Missions	15	4.1
Custody of local officials	14	3.8
Court wards (children under 10)	8	2.2
Self-redemption	30	8.2
Adoption	3	0.8
Living with former mistress	5	1.4
Freed on own inclination	47	12.8
Escape	3	0.8
Died	1	0.3
Total	368	100
Unknown	35	—

Source: Registers of Freed Slaves, 1905-06, SNP 15/1 Acc 90, Acc 121.

Table 3
Ages of Females Redeemed for 'Marriage' to Redeemer, 1905-06

Age	Number	Age	Number
7	1	23	0
11	1	24	1
12	6	25	10
13	2	26	0
14	3	27	2
15	26	28	0
16	4	29	0
17	20	30	11
18	8	35	3
19	4	40	7
20	7	Youth	1
21	1	Unknown	18
22	4	Total	140

Source: Registers of Freed Slaves, 1905-06, SNP 15/1 Acc 90, Acc 121.

The age profile of females who 'married' their redeemers cannot be accepted as strictly accurate (Table 3). The bunching of ages indicates that many were estimates. Nonetheless, certain patterns are clear. Of the 121 cases where ages are given, seventy-five were under twenty and forty-six were aged twenty and over. Approximately half (sixty-two) of the women were in their mid to late teens. The youngest female headed for 'marriage' was seven; six twelve-year-olds were so intended.

For most females, women and children, freedom through the courts still meant some kind of dependency.[41] In 76.6 per cent of the cases, women ended up in the custody of others. Women who escaped, managed to purchase their own freedom or were released on their own recognizance constituted only 21.8 per cent. And many of these women probably established or re-established dependent relationships. The general policy was to encourage women to marry, return to relatives or maintain an ongoing association with their former masters and mistresses.

The question of controlling female slaves was implicitly connected with attaching women to men or surrogate males in the form of such colonial institutions as Freed Slaves' Homes and missions. Both the Islamic courts and the colonial infrastructure were brought to bear to achieve this end. The ideal was for a woman to have a 'husband'; whether she was a concubine or a wife did not matter to the colonial regime. If an unattached female was too young or no male was available, she was assigned a guardian, placed in a Freed Slaves' Home or handed over to one of the few mission stations. Sometimes girls under ten were assigned to Europeans as servants. Females in these various categories constituted 17.1 per cent of the sample. They were usually married as soon as prospective husbands were located.

Whenever relatives could be identified, unattached females were restored to their care, and usually the relatives were males; 15.5 per cent were so released.[42] The ransoming of relatives had been big business before the conquest and continued to be afterwards. Before 1903, free-born Muslims were retrieved from areas outside caliphate territory, and some neighboring pagans were able to secure the release of their kin within the Caliphate. Special market towns which had been considered politically neutral for purposes of ransoming captives were located at a number of places (between Maradi and Katsina and between Zaria and Ningi, for example).[43] After the conquest, it was possible for relatives to move more freely in search of kin. Hence at least four Jaba females and one Gwari woman were freed by relatives in the 1905-06 cases, which probably would have been more difficult to do, if not impossible, before the conquest.

Only twenty-two women (15.2 per cent) over age twenty-five were freed in order to 'marry'. Women over twenty-five were usually allowed to follow their own inclinations: women over thirty tended to ransom themselves. Some of these older women, at least, were concubines who were allowed to marry someone other than their master.[44] A master could make a declaration of intended emancipation upon his death. This declaration was known as *mudabbar*.

The master could continue to enjoy sexual access once the promise was given, but the woman could not be sold. Under some conditions, the woman could come and go as she pleased. These concubines were known as *wahayiya*.[45]

At least eighty-six cases (21.3 per cent) appear to be females who were seized from traders, the result of recent kidnappings, or otherwise enslaved since the British conquest. In most cases, however, the documents do not include evidence as to whether or not slaves were recently acquired. It is likely, therefore, that the proportion of new slaves was higher, perhaps much higher, than the data established.

The Cost of Redemption

The cost of redemption closely approximated the price of female slaves in the last years of the legal trade. In the 1890s, slaves generally cost between 100,000 and 300,000 cowries in various parts of the Caliphate.[46] The cost of redemption for 129 females in 1905-06 averaged 265,000 cowries, with the price of most women falling between 200,000 and 300,000 cowries (Table 4).[47] If small children and the one leper are excluded, than the average price was 275,000. There are several other anomalies in the sample which cannot be explained, such as the price paid for three women, apparently in a single court case, of 60,000 cowries each, a figure which is decidedly low. If these cases are omitted, then the average may well have been closer to 280,000. Because the British attempted to suppress the slave trade and did indeed prevent organized slave raiding, it might be expected that the cost of transferring female slaves through the courts would have been considerably higher than it was. That it was not suggests that the courts conspired to fix prices, since the supply of new slaves was decreasing and the demand for concubines continued to be high.

It is possible to break the 1905-06 prices down into several categories, including prices for women redeemed for 'marriage', prices for women redeemed by relatives, prices of self-ransom, and prices for cases of unknown or special reasons. The average price of ninety-two women redeemed for 'marriage' (excluding non-cowrie prices)[48] was 270,000 cowries; the average for those redeemed by relatives was 260,000; and the average for self-ransom was 270,000. The average price for the other cases, 190,000 cowries, includes a leper at 45,000 cowries, and if this case is excluded, then the average price for these other cases is not much lower.

There does not appear to be any correlation between price and the age of female slaves who were older than ten. The average price of girls aged eleven and twelve who were 'married', for example, was 266,000 cowries (sample: 5), although it might be expected that girls in this prime age group might have cost considerably more than other women. It should be noted that prices tended to bunch at four levels: 200,000 (ten cases), 250,000 (fifteen cases), 280,000 (sixteen cases) and 300,000 (fifty-three cases). These cases represent 71.7 per cent of the sample. The frequency of the 300,000 price seems to indicate that there was a standard price for the purchase of women; 40.5 percent of all cases were at this price.

Table 4
Cost of Redemption of Female Slaves, 1905-06

Cost (cowries)	Marriage (no.)	Relatives (no.)	Self-ransom (no.)	Other (no.)
45,000	—	—	—	1 (leper)
60,000	3	—	—	—
70,000	—	1 (baby)	—	—
90,000	—	—	—	1
130,000	—	—	1	—
180,000	1	—	1	—
200,000	7	3	—	—
210,000	3	—	—	—
217,000	—	—	1	—
220,000	1	1	—	—
240,000	1	1	—	—
250,000	9	2	4	—
260,000	4	—	—	1
270,000	5	—	2	—
280,000	11	1	2	2
290,000	1	—	—	—
300,000	42	2	9	—
310,000	—	1	1	—
320,000	1	—	—	—
330,000	1	—	—	—
350,000	2	1	—	—
£2.10s.	1	—	—	—
£3.10s.	—	1	—	—
£4.00	—	1	3	—
£20.00	1	—	—	—
Two cows	—	1	—	—
Mare, 3 clothes	—	1	—	—
Mare, 3 gowns	—	—	—	1
Total	94	17	24	6

Source: Registers of Freed Slaves, 1905-06, SNP 15/1 Acc 90, Acc 121.

While the 1905-06 prices seem to correspond with prices in the decade before the British conquest, it is not clear how long this price structure lasted. By 1917, for example, concubines cost £28, £20 compensation and £8 marriage payment, a total more than double the 1905-06 price.[49] Admittedly, the British no longer recognized cowries as legal tender by 1917 and hence the exchange rate had inflated considerably. The real price may well have been in line with earlier prices.

Some of the 1905-06 cases should be discussed further. The ransom price of the youngest girl to be 'married' to a redeemer—an eleven-year-old girl—was 300,000 cowries. The prices of the twelve-year-old girls, also 'married' to their redeemers, were 200,000, 250,000, 280,000, and 300,000. The prices of two others are not known. The oldest redemption cases included a seventy-year-old woman, ransomed by her daughter at Zaria for 350,000 cowries (one of the highest prices), a sixty-year-old woman who was repatriated to Mandara,[50] and a fifty-five-year-old woman who was released because of 'illegal transfer'. The low prices for redemption of some women for 'marriage' cannot be explained: three women were transferred at 60,000 cowries each; one was aged twenty-two years, the second twenty-four, while the age of the third is unknown. The details of one person ransomed at 90,000 cowries are not known. A 70,000-cowrie ransom for a one-year-old girl does not seem out of line, except that those born after 1901 were supposed to be free. The most expensive ransoms usually involved women who 'married' their redeemers, including prices of 320,000 cowries (fifteen-year-old), 330,000 cowries (eighteen-year-old), 350,000 cowries (fifteen-year-old), and 350,000 cowries (twenty-five-year-old). The only exception in the sample was the seventy-year-old woman ransomed by her daughter. The cases of redemption involving commodities did not end in marriage: two were by relatives and one was a case of self-ransom.

Ethnic Origins of Slave Women

Slave women came from a plethora of ethnic backgrounds. In the 1905-06 sample at least one hundred ethnic groups were represented, and no single ethnic group predominated. Ethnic identity or place of origin is known for 311 females. These include 277 ethnic affiliations, representing eighty-eight different ethnic groups, and thirty-four place names. Only twelve ethnic groups had five or more people; the greatest number was Jaba (31), followed by Hausa (26), Alago (21), Nupe (16), Kedara (15), Kanuri (14), and Gwari, Tangale, and Fulbe (10 each). Other significant identifications included Piri and Bashema (7 each), and Mada (5). Admittedly the sample is skewed, but it is unlikely that the inclusion of a greater number of slaves from emirates that are unrepresented or under-represented in the sample would change the general conclusion. Other ethnic groups would surely be included, and the numbers of each would change but not the extent of the variety.

The place names which are mentioned in thirty-four cases further suggest that the range of ethnic backgrounds was indeed large. Twenty of the thirty-four place names are from Adamawa, which was a large area with numerous ethnic groups. The other place names reflect the same pattern; slaves came from frontier emirates where pagan groups were scattered.

The reported identifications probably disguise even more varied backgrounds, moreover. Maguzawa, for example, is not included as a category, and females reported as 'Hausa' may well have included Maguzawa or have been second-generation slaves of other origins. Slaves of Kanuri origin represent a special category, since they were associated with neighboring Borno, not one of the non-Muslim societies that predominate in the sample. Nevertheless, in a few cases, perhaps 5 per cent, certificates of freedom were issued to slaves who had been kidnapped or caught in a raid from one of the enemies of the Caliphate and were therefore regaining their legitimate freedom under Muslim law.

Hausa, Fulbe and Nupe were the main ethnic groups associated with the Caliphate, and they represented 16.7 per cent of the sample. Of these, 8.4 per cent were described as Hausa, by far the largest ethnic group in the Caliphate, while 5.1 per cent were Nupe and 3.2 per cent Fulbe.

There is a relative absence of Muslim backgrounds. Only sixty-six cases are identified with ethnic groups that were predominantly Muslim; some other groups, such as the Ningi (four cases) were in part Muslim. In none of the cases, including Hausa, Fulbe, Nupe and Kanuri, did ethnicity and religion necessarily correspond. People were freed on the basis that they had been free and were Muslim. At least twenty females (5 per cent) were so released, but some Hausa, Nupe, Fulbe and Kanuri females may have been acculturated, second-generation slaves who were not entitled to emancipation on the grounds of religion. Despite the uncertainty of the data, it is clear that relatively few cases, probably less than 20 per cent, involved Muslims.[51]

The registers thereby confirm what has been known about the system of enslavement under the Caliphate.[52] Over 80 per cent of the females were clearly non-Muslim in origin, and an overwhelming proportion of these slaves were from small ethnic groups. A steady influx of new slaves from raided areas on the frontiers of the Caliphate maintained and indeed increased the population of the Caliphate. Enslavement served as a mechanism of demographic expansion and contributed to the consolidation of a Muslim, and largely Hausa, society. Such a policy reduced the size of the small ethnic groups on the periphery of the various emirates.

The ethnic categories also establish that most new slaves were settled within 100 km of their places of origin. Since the data do not address the question of slave movement directly, it is necessary to explain the reasoning behind this conclusion. First, the homelands of the various identifiable ethnic groups tended to be within 100 kms of the court where the slaves of those ethnic groups were freed, not a great distance. At least 21.3 per cent of the cases were females seized from traders, and even if they are removed from the sample on the assumption that the intention was to take them further afield and thereby increase the distance from the point of capture to final destination, the probable distance travelled by new slaves is hardly altered. Whether or not slaves were actually traded at some time between capture and emancipation, and many slaves were never traded but were distributed through official channels after emirate-sanctioned raids, slaves were often settled not far from home. It should be noted that these conclusions apply to males as well as females. Such information corrects the usual assumption that slaves often travelled great distances from point of capture to place of settlement.[53] While clearly many slaves did, many others did not.

People who lived in the areas bordering Zaria and Bauchi are more heavily represented in the sample than other regions that were also sources of slaves for the Caliphate (Table 5). The court cases at Zaria accounted for 158 (39.2 per cent) of all women freed; while those at Bauchi accounted for 107 (26.6 per cent). The third largest contributor to the sample was Yola (46 cases, 11.4 per cent), so that these three emirates, which formed a wedge through the non-Muslim middle belt of Nigeria, included 77.2 per cent of the cases. This skewing has to be taken into consideration in a number of the conclusions reached here. The degree of non-Muslim enslavement might not have been as severe if Kano, Sokoto and Gwandu were represented more fully, and the people on the fringes of these emirates, particularly Maguzawa and the Hausa of the independent enclaves of Maradi, Argungu and Tassawa would be in evidence. It is likely that more trade slaves found their way to Kano than to other emirates, because Kano Emirate dominated the commerce of the caliphate and relied less on raiding than Zaria, Bauchi and Yola for its slave supplies. Most slaves at Sokoto and Gwandu arrived as tribute from the other emirates, so that slaves there usually had travelled considerable distances. Only 12.5 per cent of the women from the court sample were freed in the northern emirates of Kano, Katsina, Katagum, Sokoto and Gwandu. Hence it is clear that the sample distorts the picture somewhat, but it is likely that the general conclusion would be the same if allowance is made for these important exceptions.

Table 5
Location of Court Cases for Freed Slaves, 1905-06

Emirate	1905		1906		Total		Percentage	
	Both	Females	Both	Females	Both	Females	Both	Females
Zaria	98	64	145	94	243	158	38.8	39.2
Bauchi	8	6	160	101	168	107	26.8	26.6
Yola	30	16	34	30	64	46	10.2	11.4
Sokoto	38	27	—	—	38	27	6.0	6.7
Muri	51	23	7	2	58	25	9.3	6.2
Bassa	14	8	—	—	14	8	2.2	2.0
Gwandu	7	7	—	—	7	7	1.1	1.7
Katagum	4	4	3	3	7	7	1.1	1.7
Kano	4	3	4	2	8	5	1.3	1.2
Katsina	—	—	6	5	6	5	1.0	1.2
Nassarawa	1	1	6	4	7	5	1.1	1.2
Ilorin	—	—	5	2	5	2	0.8	0.5
Borgu	2	1	—	—	2	1	0.3	0.2
Total	257	160	370	243	627	403	100.0	99.8

Source: Registers of Freed Slaves, 1905-06, SNP 15/1 Acc 90, Acc 121.

Slavery and Female Subculture

The diversity of ethnic origins for the slave women in the 1905-06 sample demonstrates well the fact that slavery was a process whereby non-Hausa females became acculturated. As is most clearly the case with respect to concubines, this process of forced assimilation frequently occurred within the extended families in which women were placed. Concubines, like wives, were kept in seclusion, so that free women had the primary responsibility of transforming non-Hausa slaves into Hausa concubines.[54]

Apprenticeship in household tasks and crafts, training in ceremonies associated with rites of passage, and co-operation in household activities brought wives and concubines together. The tensions and support inherent in these relationships were a crucial dimension of acculturation. While institutions of subordination had the function of promoting changes in ethnic identities, women had to interact in ways that provided solidarity based on gender, even if concubines usually had to obey the dictates of wives.

There is little known about important aspects of female subculture in the early years of colonial rule, particularly in matters relating to marriage, naming ceremonies and funerals. These rites of passage brought women together as women, and to some extent ethnic and class differences which separated women were temporarily ignored. *Bori*, a spirit-possession cult, reinforced a female subculture.[55] *Bori* ceremonies took place outside the acceptable (to most men) realm of Islam, and while some men participated in *bori* sessions, most *bori* adherents were women. Its dance, ritual and hierarchy offered an alternative world view to the male-dominated tradition of Islam. As with rites of passage, *bori* ceremonies helped undermine class and ethnic differences among women, although certainly *bori* did not always do so. Nonetheless, women participated in *bori* as women rather than as members of a specific class or a particular ethnic group.

A recognition of these women-centered activities serves as an important corrective to this study. In concentrating on slave women, I may well have displayed a tendency to underestimate the links between women of different classes. The cases in which mistresses freed their slave women, and the slaves stayed with the mistresses, suggest that something other than class was important to many women. Further research, set in proper historical perspective, is required to clarify the relationship between women in early colonial society.

The children of concubines had an advantage that was not shared by their slave mothers nor, indeed, by many free children of poor households. Despite the slave status of their mothers, their paternity not only guaranteed that children of concubines were free but also resulted in their being brought up in commercial or aristocratic households. These children were fully acculturated, and while they probably suffered some deprivation relative to their half brothers and sisters born of free mothers, they still had many opportunities not available to other children. The importance of the background of the concubine mother to the acculturation of her children is not certain, but the paramountcy of the paternal identity is very clear.

The ethnic backgrounds of concubine mothers were remembered well, according to the court records and oral testimony, but the significance of that identity other than as a label seems to have been slight. Women were cut off from their natal societies, and there were too many ethnic groups from which concubines were drawn to permit any particular ethnic identity from assuming a wider meaning for the women themselves.

Caliphate society was 'Hausa' in the sense that the dominant language of most parts of the Caliphate was Hausa. The greater diversity of ethnic backgrounds for slaves, particularly women, indicates that caliphate culture was constantly exposed to new influences in ways that are beyond the scope of this study. In fact many languages were spoken in the Caliphate; the aristocracy tended to speak Fulfulde as well as Hausa, and some emirates were outside the Hausa heartland. Nupe, Yoruba, Gurma and other languages were more common in these emirates, but everywhere Hausa was the commercial tongue. The extension of the Hausa language, Islam, and caliphate political ideology were parts of an interconnected cultural transformation which required the incorporation of slave women. This process of cultural change and expansion continued after the European conquest of the Caliphate. And the incorporation of alien women still was an important feature of this transformation in the early years of colonial rule.

Recruitment of Concubines, 1912-21

Concubines were still available in the clandestine slave markets for a least two decades after the conquest, although probably in restricted numbers. In Kano, Resident Carrow is remembered as the official who ended this trade in the years after 1919. According to Alhaji Mahmudu K'ok'i, a judge and intellectual who witnessed the events of this period,

> Before then trading in slaves, in concubines, went on in secret. It was done under the pretence of free marriage. It was when Mr Carrow arrived here [in 1919], that he was engaged in suppressing this. He went to Karaye, as the slave traders were numerous there. They used to go to Adamawa and bring back slaves from there. Mr Carrow would go right into the huts in their compounds where they were concealing slaves and fetch them out. And then the slave dealers were collected and told that they were to stop it. After that, the girls were divided among different house-holds. We were given some. My father was allotted two and they became like members of our family.[56]

As this testimony demonstrates, the practice of guardianship for freed slave women which had been established in the first years of colonial rule was still in force.

The courts provided a mechanism for the transfer of women well into the 1920s.[57] Christelow's analysis of court records from the Kano judicial council for 1913-14 demonstrates that unrelated males frequently redeemed slave women. In eleven of seventeen cases involving female slaves, a third-party male paid the redemption money.[58] By 1917 the Kano courts were heavily involved in the distribution of slave women, in striking contrast to the situation in 1905-06. Whereas only a few slave women were registered in Kano's twenty-four courts in 1905 and 1906, 1,027 were 'freed' in 1917 alone and a third of these were ransomed by prospective 'husbands', a proportion which is not much different from that for 1905-06 in other places.[59] As Alhaji Mahmudu K'ok'i remembered the situation, 'Before Carrow put a stop to slave trading, if a man had the money, and saw a young slave girl, he would offer to buy her, maybe [for] £20. Then the two would marry [sic] before an *alkali*; at that time the bride-price was fixed at £8—hence the *alkali* would write £8. A lot of women became concubines in this way.'[60]

In Sokoto in 1921, Edwardes still reported ransoming for purposes of concubinage, which were now considered cases of 'malpractice'.[61] Even then, however, the patriarchal attitudes of the British were not so very different from those of the Sokoto aristocracy:

> The ransoming of girls for concubinage undoubtedly still goes on. Several cases have come to my notice and I pointed out that the girl is born free and can marry whom she pleases. It is of course quite illegal, and must stop, but at the same time one cannot feel that any great harm is done. The girls are of low class, children of slaves of course, and as the concubines of rich men they have many luxuries denied to the wives of poor men. Such girls are freed by the court at the time, and can leave him whenever they wish. I have not punished any of the offenders, but have impressed on the Alkalai that it is their duty to satisfy themselves that a female produced for ransome [sic] is of age to be a slave, and that in any case the fact that the girl is free on leaving the court is to be made clear. I do not think that any subtleties of Moslem law as to the holding of a free woman in concubinage disturb the peace of either party.[62]

As Edwardes observed, 'The critical period passed three or four years ago. Now it is safe to say that there is not a virgin slave in the country, and any case of ransoming for concubinage is open to grave suspicion.'[63]

Despite the continued use of the courts, by the second decade of colonial rule, males had to rely increasingly on the recruitment of children born of slave parents as a source for concubines because newly enslaved girls became more and more scarce. It was necessary to impress girls into concubinage who technically should have been considered free, since they were born after 1 April 1901.[64] By then, however, the reform of slavery, even though directed at males, had been effective enough so that the recruitment of concubines could be overlooked. A new policy evolved which tried to keep such cases out of court. Concubines had to be recruited by other means.[65] Colonial attitudes towards women were such that the contradiction inherent in this policy scarcely mattered.

Summary

Court records from 1905-06 offer a rare view of the status of women slaves in early colonial Northern Nigeria. It is shown that British officials found it easy to accommodate the aristocracy of the Sokoto Caliphate on the status of these women, despite British efforts to reform slavery. Those members of the aristocracy and merchant class who could afford to do so were able to acquire concubines through the courts, which allowed the transfer of women under the guise that they were being emancipated. British views of slave women attempted to blur the distinction between concubinage and marriage, thereby reaffirming patriarchal Islamic attitudes. The court records not only confirm this interpretation but also provide extensive information on the ethnic origins of slave women, the price of transfer, age at time of transfer, and other data. It is shown that the slave women of 1905-06 sample came from over 100 different ethnic groups and the price of transfer, which ranged between 200,000 and 300,000 cowries, was roughly comparable to the price of female slaves in the years immediately preceding the conquest. Most of the slaves were in their teens or early twenties. The use of the courts to transfer women for purposes of concubinage continued until at least the early 1920s.

NOTES

1. This article arises from a joint research project into the impact of early colonial rule on slavery in which I am involved with J.S. Hogendorn. An earlier version was presented at the annual meeting of the Canadian Association of African Studies, Edmonton, June 1987. I wish to thank Elspeth Cameron, Michael Crowder, Martin Klein, Thomas Lewin, Beverly Mack, Catherine Coles and Richard Roberts for their comments.

2. For a discussion of British policy toward slavery, see J.S. Hogendorn and Paul E. Lovejoy, 'The development and execution of Frederick Lugard's policies toward slavery in northern Nigeria', paper presented at the annual meeting of the African Studies Association, Denver, November 1987, and Hogendorn and Lovejoy, 'The reform of slavery in early colonial northern Nigeria', in S. Miers and R. Robert (eds), *The End of Slavery in Africa* (Madison, 1988).

3. Muhammadau Rabi'u, interviewed at Fanisau, Kano Emirate, 13 July 1975 by Yusufu Yunusa; Garba Sarkin Gida, interviewed at Gandun Nassarawa, Kano Emirate, 14 September 1975 by Ahmadu Maccido; Abdulwahbu Dawaki, interviewed at Rano, Kano Emirte, 12 September 1975 by Aliyu Musa; and Bakoshi, interviewed at Hunkuyi, Zaria Emirate, 10 December 1975 by Ahmadu Maccido and Paul E. Lovejoy. All interviews, which are on deposit at the Northern History Research Scheme, Ahmadu Bello University, are on tape and have been transcribed. The interviews were conducted under the supervision of the author and/or J.S. Hogendorn.

4. Mahmood Yakubu, 'A century of warfare and slavery in Bauchi, *c*. 1805-1900: an analysis of a pre-colonial economy' (B.A. dissertation, unpublished, University of Sokoto, 1985), 64; and Beverly B. Mack, 'Service and status: slaves and concubines in Kano, Nigeria', in Catherine Coles and Beverly Mack (eds), *Hausa Women* (Madison, 1991).

5. For a fuller discussion of concubines and their place in Caliphate society, see Paul E. Lovejoy, 'Concubinage in the Sokoto Caliphate', in Coles and Mack, *Hausa Women*. Also see Douglas Edwin Ferguson, 'Nineteenth-century Hausaland, being a description by Imam Imoru of the land, economy, and society of his people' (Ph.D.

thesis, unpublished, UCLA, 1973), 231-33; and M.G. Smith, 'Introduction', in Mary Smith (ed.), *Baba of Karo. A Woman of the Moslem Hausa* (New York, 1954). It should be noted that Alan Christelow is wrong in stating that a concubine became free 'once she had born her master children'; see 'Slavery in Kano, 1913-1914: evidence from the judicial records', *African Economic History*, XIV (1985), 69.

6. For a general discussion of the place of concubines in Islamic society, see Joseph Schacht, *An Introduction to Islamic Law* (Oxford, 1964); Schacht, 'Umm-al-Walad', *Encyclopedia of Islam* (London, 1934), 1012-15; and Reuben Levy, *The Social Structure of Islam* (London, 1957), 69, 71-81, 105. For a comparison with the status of concubines in other Muslim societies, see Margaret Strobel, *Muslim Women in Mombasa, 1890-1975* (New Haven, 1979); Allan G. B. Fisher and Humphrey J. Fisher, *Slavery and Muslim Society in Africa. The Institution in Saharan and Sudanic Africa and the Trans-Saharan Slave Trade* (London, 1970), 97-109; E.R. Toledano, 'Slave dealers, women, pregnancy and abortion', *Slavery and Abolition*, II, 1, (1981), 53-68. For a further comparison with the status of women under slavery, see Claire C. Robertson and Martin A. Klein (eds), *Women and Slavery in Africa* (Madison, 1983).

7. For the place of concubines in Hausa society, see M.G. Smith, 'Social and economic change among selected native communities in northern Nigeria' (Ph.D. thesis, unpublished, University of London, 1951), 127-66. For an autobiographical account, see Mary Smith (ed.), *Baba of Karo*. For a description from 1905, see A.J.N. Tremearne, *Hausa Superstitions and Customs. An Introduction to the Folk-lore and the Folk* (London, 1913), 85-88. For local legal tradition in the first decade of colonial rule, see the notes on Muslim law, Hausa and English versions, in R.C. Abraham, *An Introduction to Spoken Hausa and Hausa Reader for European Students* (London, 1940), 120, 154-155, 158-159, 204-213. For a discussion of concubinage in more recent times, see Mack, 'Slaves and concubines in Kano'; also see Isa Wali, 'Concubines and slaves: the facts', *Nigerian Citizen*, 25 July 1956. For a discussion of the legal status of women, see Alan Christelow, 'Women and the law in early twentieth-century Kano', in Coles and Mack (eds), *Hausa Women*; Christelow, 'Slavery in Kano', 57-73.

8. Abraham, *Spoken Hausa*, 120, 150-53; M. Hiskett, 'Enslavement, slavery and attitudes towards the legally enslavable in Hausa Islamic literature', in John Ralph Willis (ed.), *Slaves and Slavery in Muslim Africa* (London, 1985), 1, 122; Abdulrazak Giginyu Sa'idu, 'History of a slave village in Kano: Gandun Nassarawa' (B.A. dissertation, unpublished, Bayero University, 1981), 45; Wada, interviewed in Kano City, 18 July 1975, by Yusufu Yunusa.

9. Hogendorn and Lovejoy, 'Lugard's policies toward slavery'; and Hogendorn and Lovejoy, 'Reform of slavery'.

10. *Ibid.*

11. Sa'idu, 'Gandun Nassarawa', 46-47, 131-32, 157; and Frederick Lugard, *Political Memoranda. Revision of Instructions to Political Officers on Subjects Chiefly Political and Administrative, 1913-1918* (London, A.H.M. Kirk-Greene (ed), 3rd edn, 1970), 288fn.

12. G.W. Webster, Report on Nassarawa Province, December 1904, SNP 7/5 346/1904. Unless otherwise noted, all archival references are to the Nigerian National Archive, Kaduna.

13. Marginal note to Webster's report of December 1904.

14. J.C. Sciortini, 10 May 1907, SNP 7/7 1648/1907.

15. Percy Girouard to Lord Crewe, 16 November 1908, CSO 1/27/8, Nigerian National Archives, Ibadan.

16. Sciortini, 10 May 1907.

17. Paul E. Lovejoy, 'Fugitive slaves: resistance to slavery in the Sokoto Caliphate', in G. Okihiro (ed.), *In Resistance: Studies in African, Afro-American and Caribbean History* (Amherst, Mass., 1986), 82-91; Hogendorn and Lovejoy, 'Reform of slavery'.

18. C.L. Temple, Report on Bauchi Province, September 1902, SNP 15/1 Acc 42.

19. Webster, Nassarawa Report, December 1904.

20. See, for example, P.G. Harris, Kano City Assessment 1921-22, SNP 7, where it is reported that the wealthy businessman, Mai Kano Agogo, owned a large lodging house in Fagge quarter which consisted of three quadrangles, each containing fifteen rooms. Some of the occupants were 'women of the prostitute class'. For a study of Hausa 'courtesanship', see Jerome Barkow, 'The institution of courtesanship in the northern states of Nigeria', *Genève-Afrique*, 10, 1 (1971), 1-16. Also see Abner Cohen, *Custom and Politics in Urban Africa: A Study of Hausa Migrants in Yoruba Towns* (London, 1969).

21. Webster, Nassarawa Report, December 1904.

22. Register of Freed Slaves, Ilorin Province, 1906, SNP 15/1 Acc 121.

23. Register of Freed Slaves, Sokoto Province, 1905, SNP 15/1 Acc 90.

24. H.D. Larrymore, Nupe Province, Report for Quarter ending 31 March 1907, SNP 7/8 2017/1907. Also see Stanley, Report on Sokoto Province, half year ending 30 June 1908, Sokprof 2/9 985/1908.

25. Register of Freed Slaves, Bauchi Province, May 1906, SNP 15/1 Acc 121.

26. Register of Freed Slaves, Kano Province, September 1906, SNP 15/1 Acc 121.

27. Temple, Bauchi Report, September 1902; Temple, Report on Bauchi Province, October 1902, SNP 15/1 Acc 43. Also see the case of Pattoo in Register of Freed Slaves, Kano Province, January 1905, SNP 15/1 Acc 90. In 1904, when Larrymore was Resident in Kabba Province, he instituted similar policies (Kabba Province Monthly Reports, March 1904, SNP 15/1 Acc 64):

> Freed Slave Women . . . [are] given to guardians in this place. One or two of them are a source of much trouble to the Resident at present. One [guardian, Mrs Williams] refused to do any work, has now commenced to refuse food, speaks no known language, and I am at a loss what to do with her. A police constable has apparently offered her marriage, by some means, and I am told that she is willing to marry the man. Will Your Excellency please sanction? [margin: 'yes'] She will be on the Police books as laid down. I think the woman is most fortunate in having found a suitor. I have seen her. Another is a girl freed slave (guardian, Mrs Hesse) after having been treated apparently with every consideration, in fact, as Mr. Hesse assures me, 'as one of the family' this young woman now refuses to reside with the Hesse household—she wants to marry Sergt Brown of the Police. I was assured however that she was too young to marry. I therefore offered to send her back to the [Freed Slaves'] home in Zungeru. She said, in Hausa, that if she were sent back she would cut her throat. She wants to live with the present Mrs Brown until old enough to marry Sergt Brown. Will Your Excellency sanction change of guardianship? [margin: 'It is a very puzzling case. I see no way of dealing with it except as you suggest.']

28. Frederick Lugard, *Instructions to Political and Other Officers, on Subjects Chiefly Political and Administrative* (London, 1906), 144.
29. *Ibid.*, 144.
30. *Ibid.*, 146. Also see Lugard, *Political Memoranda*, 228.
31. Lugard, *Political Memoranda*, 233.
32. *Ibid.*, 229, based on a report by Arnett.
33. Smith (ed.), *Baba of Karo*.
34. These registers are contained in two files, SNP 15/1 Acc 90, and SNP Acc 121.
35. Paul E. Lovejoy, 'Slavery in the Sokoto Caliphate', in Lovejoy (ed.), *The Ideology of Slavery in Africa* (Beverly Hills, 1981), 233-35; Lovejoy, 'Problems of slave control in the Sokoto Caliphate', in Lovejoy (ed.), *Africans in Bondage, Studies in Slavery and the Slave Trade* (Madison, 1986), 251-52; Hogendorn and Lovejoy, 'Reform of slavery.'
36. Lovejoy, 'Problems of slave control', 251.
37. Frederick Lugard, *Annual Reports, Northern Nigeria, 1905-06*, 411.
38. See Martin A. Klein, 'Women in slavery in the Western Sudan', in Claire C. Robertson and Klein (eds), *Women and Slavery in Africa* (Madison, 1983), 67-92.
39. Examples of court cases, taken from Register of Freed Slaves, Zaria Province, August 1906, SNP 15/1 Acc 90, include the following: Mahabauta, 10, Nruma [ethnic group], recently purchased, restored to relatives; Aliba, 30, Hausa, 'Freed by Emir of his own free will, having fallen to him as his share of Gado [inheritance]'; Kamahu, 25, Kedara, 'ransomed by Audu from Magaji for 220,000 [cowries] and married to him'.
40. Smith (ed.), *Baba of Karo*, 166.
41. For one of the clearest statements of this policy of enforced dependency, see H.R.P. Hillary, Sokoto Province Monthly Reports, January 1905, Sokprof 2/2 401/1905. Christelow, 'Women and the Law', also notes how important it was for males to speak on behalf of slave women who were seeking their freedom.
42. See, for example, the case of Yaganah, aged sixteen, Kanuri: 'Enslaved by some unknown man at Kukawa in 1903; exchanged in Bauchi shortly afterwards. Claimed by her brother. Freed to return with her brother to Bornu' (Register of Freed Slaves, Bauchi Province, August 1906, SNP 15/1 Acc 121). Also see the case of Pattoo, aged twenty-six from Bebeji in Kano Emirate: 'Freeborn Hausa woman, enslaved at Ningi, fled on the occasion of the 1904 Expedition [against Ningi]. Left to follow her own inclinations. A grown up woman well able to look after herself. She has been informed as the Regulations *re* marriage with govt servants' (Register of Freed Slaves, Kano Province, January 1905, SNP 15/1 Acc 90).
43. Lovejoy, 'Slavery in the Sokoto Caliphate', 235-36.
44. Yusufu Yunusa, 'Slavery in the 19th century Kano' (B.A. dissertation, unpublished, Ahmadu Bello University, 1976), 32-33.
45. G.P. Bargery, *A Hausa-English Dictionary and English-Hausa Vocabulary* (London, 1934).
46. David Carl Tambo, 'The Sokoto Caliphate slave trade in the nineteenth century', *International Journal of African Historical Studies*, IX (1976), 194, 216-17.
47. For a comparison with prices elsewhere in West Africa in the late nineteenth century, see Roberta A. Dunbar, 'Slavery and the evolution of nineteenth-century Damagaram,' in S. Miers and I. Kopytoff (eds), *Slavery in Africa: Historical and Anthropological Perspectives* (Madison, 1977), 164; Emmanuel Terray, 'Reflexions sur la formation du

prix des esclaves a l'intérieur de l'Afrique de l'Ouest précoloniale', *Journal des Africanistes*, 52, 1-2 (1982), 119-144; and Klein, 'Women in slavery', 67-92.

48. Cowrie-sterling exchange rates varied, but in 1906 a shilling was worth 1,200 cowries (*Annual Report, Northern Nigeria, 1906-07*, 522). At this rate £4 was worth 96,000 cowries but probably was meant to be the equivalent of 100,000 cowries. If this rate is correct, then sterling values were extremely low. Because of the problem of converting these values, the analysis here ignores these cases.

49. Summary of interviews with Alhaji Mahmadu K'ok'i of Kano by A.N. Skinner. Besides his career as a judge and scholar, Alhaji Mahmudu was also Bargery's principal collaborator in the compilation of the 1934 Hausa-English dictionary. I wish to thank Professor Skinner for a copy of these summaries. For a biography of Mahmadu K'ok'i, see Skinner (ed.), *Alhaji Mahmudu K'ok'i* (Zaria, 1977).

50. Register of Freed Slaves, SNP 15/1 Acc 90.

51. On the basis of ethnic identification, the upper limit of the percentage of female slaves who could have been Muslim, however defined, was 20 per cent.

52. Jan S. Hogendorn, 'Slave acquisition and delivery in precolonial Hausaland', in R. Dumett and Ben K. Schwartz (eds), *West African Culture Dynamics: Archaeological and Historical Perspectives* (The Hague, 1980), 477-93; and Michael Mason, 'Population density and "Slave raiding"—The case of the Middle Belt of Nigeria,' *Journal of African History*, X, 4 (1969), 551-64. For the debate on the drain of population from the Middle Belt of Nigeria as a result of enslavement, see M.B. Gleave and R.M. Prothero, 'Population density and slave raiding: a comment', *Journal of African History*, XII, 2 (1971), 319-24; and Mason's reply, 'Population density and slave-raiding: a reply', *Journal of African History*, XII, 2 (1971), 324-27.

53. Claude Meillassoux, *Anthropologie de l'esclavage. Le ventre de fer et d'argent* (Paris, 1986), 68-69; and Paul E. Lovejoy, *Transformation in Slavery. A History of Slavery in Africa* (Cambridge, 1983), 88.

54. For additional information on Hausa women, see Jermone H. Barkow, 'Hausa Women and Islam', *Canadian Journal of African Studies*, VI, 2 (1972), 317-28; Mack, 'Slaves and concubines and Kano'; Christelow, 'Women and the law'; Cohen, *Custom and Politics*; Catherine Coles, 'Muslim women in town: social change among the Hausa of northern Nigeria' (Ph.D. thesis, unpublished, University of Wisconsin, 1983); and Smith, *Baba of Karo*; and Isa A. Abba, 'Kulle (Purdah) among the Muslims in the northern states of Nigeria; some classification', *Kano Studies*, II, 1 (1980), 42-50.

55. On *bori*, see Michael Onwue Jeogwu, 'The cult of the *Bori* spirits among the Hausa', in Mary Douglas and Phyllis M. Kaberry (eds), *Man in Africa* (London, 1969), 279-305; and Christelow, 'Women and the law'.

56. Mahmudu K'ok'i, Summary of Interviews.

57. In 1906-07, at least 53 slave women were redeemed for purposes of 'marriage' in Kano Province; see F. Cargill, Kano Province Annual Report, 1907, SNP 7/9 1538/1908.

58. Christelow, 'Women and the law'. Christelow suggests that the main reason males ransomed unrelated women was because they acquired rights of *wilaya* (guardianship over the women and thereby could give them away in marriage, receiving in return the economic and social benefits which accrue to one who offers a bride. He does not consider the possibility that men obtained such women for purposes of concubinage. Any subsequent benefit acquired through marriage arrangements with other men must have been a secondary consideration, if it was a factor at all.

59. Chinedu Nwafor Ubah, 'Administration of Kano Emirate under the British, 1900-1930' (Ph.D. thesis, unpublished, University of Ibadan, 1973), 371.

60. Mahmudu K'ok'i, Summary of Interviews.

61. Edwardes, Sokoto Province Half Year Report, 30 September 1921, Mss. Afr. s. 769, Rhodes House.

62. *Ibid.*

63. *Ibid.*

64. Mack, 'Slaves and concubines'; Sa'idu, 'Gandun Nassarawa', 46-47, 131-32, 157.

65. By 1921, colonial officials had begun to expect that concubinage would be dealt with informally outside the courts. The *alkali* of Kano, Mohammadu Aminu, was removed from office in February as the result of 'a slave ransom case, in which he permitted a girl born in and brought from Ngaundare in the Cameroons to be treated as a slave, for purposes of ransom, thus contravening the code'. He received a jail term of three years. The *alkali* of Gwarzo, Kano Emirate, was likewise removed 'for permitting children born free, to be ransomed before him'. He received a similar sentence, See A.C.G. Hastings, Kano Province Report for 15 Months ending 31 March 1921, SNP 10/9 120p/1921.

7

Give a Thought to Africa:
Black Women Missionaries in Southern Africa

Sylvia M. Jacobs

The late nineteenth and early twentieth centuries witnessed the European partitioning and subsequent colonization of the continent of Africa. A small segment of the African-American community, including journalists, religious and secular leaders, diplomats and politicians, missionaries, and travelers and visitors, addressed themselves to the issue of the impact of the establishment of European imperialism in Africa. Although they may have viewed the different elements of imperialism (cultural, social, economic, political) in various ways, most middle-class blacks, believing that Africa needed to be "civilized and Christianized," generally concluded that if the interest and welfare of the indigenous African populations were being considered, European activity on the continent would be beneficial. They therefore supported the European imperialists in Africa as long as exploitation was not their only goal. Black American views on the European partitioning of Africa varied only slightly from tacit approval to partial rejection. This essay will discuss the response of one African-American group—black American women missionaries—to the European colonization of Africa, and how imperialism, gender, and race limited their roles as missionaries in Africa.

In the nineteenth century, white American and European Protestant church boards began to establish missions in Africa. These churches gave serious consideration to using African-Americans as missionaries on the continent. Thus began many successive attempts to appoint blacks to missionary work in their ancestral homeland. The largest number of African-American missionaries sent to Africa went during the late nineteenth and early twentieth centuries. Black American missionaries were affected by the prevailing Western image of Africa as a "Dark Continent" in need of "civilizing." Their relationship with Africa and Africans was both ambivalent and contradictory. On the one hand, these black American missionaries, women and men, believed that Africa needed to be "civilized and Christianized" and that it was their "duty," as descendants of the continent, to assist in that redemption. Race, then, was a factor in their commitment to Africans. But they had to wrestle with their Western orientation and their biases about African culture and society, and thus they initially held Africa and Africans at arm's length.

Although more than half of the American Protestant missionaries who went to Africa during this period were males, they were assisted by their wives, who were designated "assistant missionaries." But even single women sent as missionaries had secondary roles. The mores of the late nineteenth and early twentieth centuries prescribed that women missionaries be engaged in "women's work": that meant teaching in day, Sunday, and industrial schools; maintaining orphanages and boarding schools; making house-to-house visitations; and dispensing medical care to women and children.[1]

Between 1880 and 1920 almost eighty African-American women were assigned to or accompanied their husbands as missionaries to Africa. Of that number, fourteen went to five southern African countries: Angola and Mozambique, which were under Portuguese colonial rule; and the British colonies of Nyasaland, Southern Rhodesia, and South Africa. They represented six mission-sending societies. But only nine African-American women missionaries are discussed in this essay because there is little information on three of these women, who accompanied their husbands to South Africa—Celia Ann Nelson Gregg (1904-1906, 1924-1928), Mattie E. Murff (1906-1910), and Lucinda Ernestine Thomas East (1909-1920)—and the two others served the major portion of their terms of service after 1920—Julia Cele Smith (1918?-1948) and Bessie Cherry Fonveille McDowell (1919-1937). Were the views of these black female missionaries about European imperialism in Africa any different from their black male or white counterparts? Were there major differences in the experiences of African-American women missionaries in African mission work? Did these women have to adjust in any way to the European presence on the continent? Because of the nature of available sources, it is not always easy to distinguish the views of black female missionaries. Of the nine women discussed here, only five sent home letters or reports, or wrote about their experiences in Africa. What this means is that often we are left with only the writings of black male missionaries. Thus to understand the views of some of these women, we need to look at other things, such as applications, letters to newspapers and magazines, college and university catalogues and histories, and unpublished manuscripts.

The American Board of Commissioners for Foreign Missions (ABCFM) was the first American board to send missionaries to Africa. The ABCFM, one of several Congregational missionary societies, was organized in 1810 and two years later sent out its first foreign missionaries to India. At its 1825 annual meeting, the board voted to open a mission in Africa. In 1834 missionaries set up the first ABCFM mission at Cape Palmas, Liberia. ABCFM missionaries reached Natal in 1835 and subsequently set up the Zulu Mission, the first American-sponsored mission in South Africa.[2]

In 1882, the Reverend William C. Wilcox asked for and received permission from the board to explore the region around Inhambane, located between the cities of Sofala and Lorenço Marques in the southeastern corner of Mozambique, five hundred miles east of the Umzila kingdom and about six hundred miles north of Natal on the seacoast. Inhambane was at first a part of the Zulu Mission, but eventually the name East Central African Mission was adopted to designate this area, with the idea that it was only a stopover point from which an advance later would be made into the interior. Though not having received formal permission from the Portuguese Government to open the mission, representatives of the ABCFM secured a location a few miles out from the city of Inhambane and employed Africans to begin building mission houses. Several locations around the bay were ultimately occupied, and three African-Americans—Benjamin Forsyth Ousley, Henrietta Bailey Ousley, and Nancy Jones—pioneered one such station of the East Central African Mission at Kambini.[3]

Benjamin Ousley, born a slave of the brother of the Confederate States president, in Davis Bend, Warren County, Mississippi, was the first ordained black missionary of the ABCFM. Ousley earned a B.A. degree and an M.A. degree from Fisk University and a B.D. degree from Oberlin Theological Seminary.[4]

Henrietta Bailey was born to slave parents, Henry and Harriet Bailey, on October 4, 1852, in Washington County, Mississippi, although during the Civil War her family escaped to Knoxville, Illinois. She united with the African Methodist Episcopal (AME) Church in 1875 but was not fully accepted until 1878. Bailey studied at Knoxville High School and Fisk University, and before going to Africa she was employed as a teacher in Cornith, Mississippi. On August 14, 1884, she married Reverend Benjamin Ousley, who was under appointment by the ABCFM to the East Central African Mission. On her application of September 24, 1884, for mission service, in reply to the question—"When did you decide to go to the heathen, and what led you to think of the subject?"—Henrietta Ousley answered: "It had been brought to notice first by the departure of some missionaries for the West Coast of Africa, then an appeal was made to me personally by a friend to fit myself for a teacher for the Mendi Mission [mission of the American Missionary Association in Sierra Leone], then finally this request of Mr. Ousley's that I would share with him the life of a foreign missionary."[5] Benjamin Ousley apparently had sought a wife when he was commissioned to go to Mozambique. Henrietta Ousley, the first black woman sent out by the ABCFM, served in Mozambique with her husband from 1884 to 1893.

The last of the African-American pioneer missionaries in Mozambique appointed by the ABCFM was Nancy Jones. Jones, the first unmarried black woman commissioned by the American Board, was born in Christian County, near Hopkinsville, Kentucky, in 1860 and during her childhood moved with her family to Memphis, Tennessee. She was baptized at the age of fourteen while a student at Lemoyne Institute (Now Lemoyne-Owen College), and united with the First Colored Baptist Church of Memphis soon afterwards. Jones also attended Fisk University, graduating from the Normal Department course in 1886. At the same time, she taught in Alpika, Mississippi, commuting to Fisk. Although a Baptist, she applied to the Congregational American Board for a missionary appointment. In her letter of application she stated: "I have wanted to be a Missionary ever since I was twelve years old. . . . I have earnestly prayed to the Lord to teach me my duty, show me just what he would have me do and I received in answer to these petitions an urgent longing for work in a Mission field in Africa." Jones served the board in Mozambique, and later in eastern Rhodesia, from 1888 to 1897. The Ousleys and Jones worked together at Kambini for over five years. Henrietta Ousley and Jones had known one another at Fisk and apparently both had given some thought to their "duty" to assist in the "religious uplift" of Africa prior to their appointment.[6]

On September 25, 1884, the Ousleys departed from New York to join the East Central Africa Mission. They arrived at Durban, Natal Colony, South Africa, three weeks later, on November 14, and sailed for Inhambane on November 28, reaching the bay on December 2. Benjamin Ousley and William Wilcox traveled into the interior and Ousley selected the station at Kambini that he and his wife, and later Nancy Jones, eventually occupied. In the 1885 annual report of the East Central African Mission from the Kambini station, Ousley noted that because the Portuguese government in Mozambique was so restrictive of foreigners, missionary activities were limited to religious instruction, and only in those areas surrounding the mission; ABCFM missionaries were forbidden to preach outside these boundaries.[7]

In the Reports of Committees on the Annual Report in 1885, the Committee on Missions in Africa, chaired by James Powell, made the following observation:

> The East Central Mission . . . has been marked the past year by the exploration, selections of new stations, and the reinforcement of the mission by Mr. and Mrs. Ousley, colored graduates of Fisk University, Nashville; Mr. Ousley being also a graduate of Oberlin. We note the possible significance that the lives of the missionaries, trained in the schools of our denomination at the South, are to play in the future in the evangelization of the Dark Continent.[8]

Obviously, the Committee was reflecting the positive feelings, at that time, of the Congregational Church toward assigning African-Americans as missionaries to Africa.

In 1886, the Ousleys completed their mission compound at Kambini, and having learned to speak the Sheetswa language, opened a school, which numbered about 50 students by the end of the year. Henrietta Ousley's duties, because of her training, included teaching in the mission school. She taught alone in the mornings, but because of a larger number of students, Benjamin Ousley joined her in the afternoon. He spent his mornings studying and translating an English Bible study and a book of catechisms into Sheetswa, the language of the people around the bay of Inhambane. In view of the nature of nineteenth-century mission responsibilities for women, Henrietta Ousley also worked with the children and women of the area. But she found great disappointment in the work, partly because of her own Western biases. In a report to the board, Benjamin Ousley pointed out: "It is sad, but nevertheless true, that woman seems more degraded here, and harder to reach, than man. . . .

We often commiserate the degraded condition of these poor women; yet they do not appreciate our pity, or even desire to live different lives. They are satisfied with their present lot."[9]

A few explanations may help to clarify black missionaries' negative views about African women. First was the issue of labor roles. African-American missionaries were distressed over the fact that African women did agricultural work, which these missionaries viewed as "man's work." During slavery, African-American women had been forced to work side-by-side with male slaves in farming on plantations, and consequently, among African-Americans, female farm labor became an indication of low status. However, in African agricultural societies women who farmed had a high economic and social status. Second, black American missionaries viewed African women as inferior in African society because of polygamy. Often in African societies polygamy was beneficial to women because they assumed a higher social status as wives and because it resulted in the sharing of "women's work" among more persons. Because of their own cultural limitations, these missionaries failed to see the benefits to African women of agricultural work and polygamy. Third, African-American missionaries were disturbed by nudity and sexuality among African women.

On January 28, 1888, Francis W. Bates and his wife, Laura H. Bates, along with Nancy Jones, departed from Boston, the location of the headquarters of the ABCFM, to join the East Central African Mission.[10] In several letters written before her departure, Jones pondered her life's work. In one to President E.M. Cravath of Fisk University, she discussed missionary work and asked for his advice about her decision to go to Africa.

> I have prayed to the Lord and asked Him what He would have me to do ever since I became a Christian and I believe He has given me the work of a missionary and He directs my mind and heart to Africa the land of my Forefathers. To those who are calling to their sons and daughters to come and help them. . . . I am willing to go to Africa as a Missionary and I offer myself to any Missionary Society who wants some one to go to any Foreign Mission Station.[11]

Cravath directed Jones to the Congregational American Board, and she began communicating with Dr. Judson Smith, corresponding secretary of the ABCFM. She explained that she hoped to be useful to the Ousleys and would like to be associated with them in their mission work.[12]

After a short stay in Natal, Jones arrived at the Kambini station on May 18, 1888, immediately began studying the Sheetswa language, and soon began teaching with the Ousleys. After two weeks, she took charge of the school's primary department. Besides her regular school work, she also visited nearby areas and read to the village women. Like the Ousleys, Jones expressed regret that she had been unsuccessful in reaching the African girls and women. Unbeknownst to some missionaries, African women often viewed education as a male's prerogative, which may explain some of the resistance the missionaries encountered. Jones proposed setting up, on a small scale, a boarding school for the girls and boys, the "Kambini Home," and affirmed: "I do not know whether I shall be successful, but as it has not been tried here I feel that the good Lord will bless the effort." Unfortunately, Jones never realized her dream. Although she and the Ousleys took many abandoned and orphaned children into their homes, they were never successful in persuading the American board of the necessity and benefit of a boarding school. The Ousleys, however, did adopt one of the children and took him back to the United States with them when they returned.[13]

In July and August of 1888, Jones and Henrietta Ousley were left alone at the Kambini mission when Benjamin Ousley visited Natal for health reasons. Because there were not enough children in the Kambini school to keep both Henrietta Ousley and Jones busy, Jones, in October 1888, opened another school across a nearby stream, two miles from the Kambini station. Since a schoolhouse had not been built, the class met outside under a large tree, with over sixty children sitting on the ground. Jones taught them the commandments, the Lord's Prayer, verses of Scripture, reading, and sewing.[14]

Benjamin Ousley continued to suffer from an illness that he had contracted in the United States. Finally, in 1890, the Ousleys withdrew from Kambini, seeking medical relief in America and arriving in Boston on May 27.[15] During their absence, Jones continued the work among the younger children and visited the women in nearby villages. She criticized the Portuguese government for not providing food for the people that it had brought south to work. She declared, "I think it would be better for the people if this country was in the hands of a more judicious government." John D. and Hattie F. Bennett (who were white) joined Jones during the Ousleys' absence so that she would not be left alone on the Kambini station. The Bennetts and Jones took a furlough in Natal during the spring of 1891.[16]

In the 1890 Reports of Committees on the Annual Report, the Committee on Missions in Africa complimented the Ousleys and Jones for the work they were doing in Africa. It insisted that:

> From the colored students of our country are coming forward some of the most useful workers for this field [Africa], three out of five missionaries in the East Central African Mission being graduates of Fisk University. These facts emphasize the importance of larger work in this land, and suggest that we may properly expect that the gospel will be carried thence by the descendants of the African race.[17]

After six years' experience with the African-American missionaries in Mozambique, the American board evidently was pleased with the results.

Upon their return to Kambini, the Ousleys resumed their work at the mission, but found the situation somewhat worsened since they had left the station two years earlier. Because of the failing health of Benjamin Ousley, the Ousleys were again compelled to return to the United States. On July 8, 1893, they arrived in New York and later withdrew their connection with the ABCFM. They returned to Mississippi.[18]

The Inhambane region proved too unhealthy for continued missionary activity. Since missionaries of the East Central African Mission had not lost sight of their original plan for settling on higher ground away from the coast, the year 1893 was spent in selecting a new mission site in the elevated region of Gazaland. The area selected was located in eastern Rhodesia, on the northern slope of Mt. Silinda, at an elevation of four thousand feet above sea level, and nearly two hundred miles inland, at the mouth of the Pungwe River. Gazaland occupied the region adjoining the eastern coast from Delagoa Bay northward to the mouth of the Zambezi River. The new mission was within the jurisdiction of the British South Africa Company and its president, Cecil Rhodes, rented more than thirty thousand acres to the ABCFM for their mission station. Missionaries of this station were under British administration, while the remaining part of the mission field was subject to Portuguese control.

Jones joined the other members of the new Gazaland mission, and the Inhambane stations were permanently closed. The missionaries set forth from Durban on June 21, 1893; a portion of the party, including Jones, arrived at Mt. Silinda on September 25, 1893, and the remainder twenty-four days later. Houses were built, land cleared, crops planted, roads marked, and all of the main activities of mission work were begun.[19]

At Mt. Silinda, a day school was opened with Jones as teacher, and she continued to be in charge of the school throughout 1895 and 1896, despite poor attendance. She also organized a literary club among the people of the region. Although Jones's house was called "Silinda Hall" because of her continuing interest in caring for abandoned children, she again was unable to interest this mission station in the idea of a children's home and commented: "It seems that my hopes for seeing a Boarding school started for . . . girls and others will never be realized. Yet I am not discouraged entirely. It may not be in my time. But I feel that it will be established."[20]

On September 10, 1896, the Bateses and H. Juliette Gibson arrived at Mt. Silinda. Eight months later, on May 27, 1897, Nancy Jones submitted her resignation from the East Central African Mission to the Prudential Committee, giving as her reason: "on account of my aged mother needing my help and realizing that I am unable to work in harmony with the mission." On October 25, 1897, she arrived in Boston.[21]

Back in the United States, Jones admitted to Judson Smith, corresponding secretary of the board, that her reason for resigning was prejudice against her by several of the white missionaries who did not want to live with her at Mt. Silinda. After the Bateses and Gibson arrived on the station, Jones was no longer allowed to teach in the school or work with the children. Gibson took over these duties. At the same time, Jones was given the tasks of cooking, buying food, planting a garden, and supplying the mission with vegetables. The Bateses insisted that she pay for the room and board of the children and

African friends who visited her at the mission station. Jones complained that although she knew the language, and the people liked her, these missionaries were claiming that she was an unfit missionary. She admitted that their racism had made it so uncomfortable for her that she had resigned. But she asked the Prudential Committee to allow her to withdraw her resignation and assign her to an area where white missionaries could not live well. There, she claimed, she could work alone or with other African-American missionaries.[22]

Apparently, the Prudential Committee did not reconsider her resignation because Jones was never reassigned to Africa; she returned to her home in Memphis. In a series of addresses given in Alabama in 1898, Jones discussed pioneer missionary work on the coast of southeastern Africa. She testified that wherever white men were in control, Africans, as a rule, were discriminated against and treated with prejudice. Jones claimed that Africans regarded missionaries of their own race with confidence and asserted that Africa was a wide field that called loudly for intelligent, Christian African-American women and men, not only as teachers, but as leaders in every line of industrial, educational, religious, and social life. This was a view not held by all Africans, since some saw African-American missionaries simply as "white men and women in black skin."[23]

During this period, 1880 to 1920, two African-American women missionaries served in Angola, a Portuguese colony. Susan Collins, of the Methodist Episcopal Church's Pacific Coast Conference, was a graduate of the Chicago Missionary Training School (Illinois). Collins first was mentioned in the Methodist missionary report of 1890 as a missionary worker who was not a member of the Methodist Episcopal African Conference. She initially stopped at Dondo in the Angola District but immediately was transferred to Malanje. The missionaries in Angola were to plant industrial missions and establish nurseries for children in order to accomplish the dual mission goals—self-support and evangelism—of the third Methodist missionary bishop of Africa, William Taylor.[24]

Malanje, the last settled of the five original Methodist stations opened in Angola, was organized in September 1885. When Collins arrived in 1890 the church at Malanje had over twenty members. In 1893 Collins began working at Canandua. Mission property consisted of a house, two trading buildings, and farm land valued at over $2,700. At Canandua, Collins was a teacher at the girls' home. She was able to raise few vegetables in the gardens of the home toward their support.

On April 19, 1898, Collins was formally recognized by the Methodist Board of Managers as a missionary in Angola. The girls' school at Canandua was transferred and formed a part of the school at Quessua. After her certification by the church, Collins was transferred to the Quessua station. The station was opened in 1890 as part of Bishop Taylor's scheme of African industrial nursery missions. Originally connected with the Malanje Mission, it was called Munhall and eventually came to be known as Quessua. It was located at the foot of a mountain, about six miles from Malanje. To the Quessua mission house and farm there was ultimately added a common school and a nursery mission for Angolan girls. In the fields, sugar cane, Indian corn, and fruit trees were grown. At Quessua, as matron and teacher, Collins was in charge of the boarding school and orphanage for girls where there were about twenty students. She also did industrial work.[25]

In 1901, after a furlough in the United States, Collins returned to Angola under the auspices of the California branch of the Women's Foreign Missionary Society (WFMS) of the Methodist Episcopal Church. Management of the girls' home and school at Quessua had been assumed by the WFMS in 1901. By 1904 Collins taught over twenty girls in the WFMS school at Quessua. The WFMS home at Quessua, with Collins as matron, constantly housed about sixty girls by 1917, almost all of whom attended the WFMS school. Collins eventually was joined at Quessua by another African-American woman missionary sent out by the WFMS, Martha Drummer.

At Quessua there was a farm of over six hundred acres with an industrial school for boys and young men, taught by an Angolan helper, in addition to the WFMS home and school for girls. In 1918 an eight thousand-acre parcel adjoining the original property was secured by Quessua. The following year, Collins left Angola.[26] It is not clear why Collins was retired home, but it is possible that it was her advanced age, since she had been in the field twenty-eight years.

Martha Drummer, of Barnesville, Georgia, was graduated from Clark University (now Clark Atlanta University, Atlanta, Georgia) in 1901. She continued her training at Northeastern Deaconess Training School (Boston, Massachusetts), where she specialized in nurse training.

In 1906 Drummer sailed for Angola as a missionary of the Women's Foreign Missionary Society of the ME Church. She spent sixteen years at the Quessua station working at the girls' boarding home and school. She retired in 1922 from missionary service. On December 11, 1937, Drummer died in Atlanta, Georgia, with the last words: "Say Africa when you pray."[27] Apparently, neither Collins nor Drummer, as unmarried, black female missionaries with no church-related administrative responsibilities, had any dealings with the Portuguese government in Angola; rarely discussed European imperialism in their letters home.

Two other American churches initiated mission work in southern Africa during this period. The National Baptist Convention and the Seventh-Day Adventist Church opened mission stations in Nyasaland. The former, a black board, and the latter, white, both sent African-American missionaries into this area. The agents of the National Baptist Convention were Landon Cheek and Emma Delaney and the Seventh-Day Adventists were represented by Thomas Branch and his wife, Henrietta Paterson Branch.[28]

Black American Baptists first became interested in African mission work in the nineteenth century. After the organization of the Baptist Foreign Mission Convention in 1880, its first missionaries were sent to Liberia in 1883. In the late nineteenth century, the National Baptist Convention made plans to open an African Baptist industrial mission in the Shire highlands of Nyasaland.[29]

Reverend Landon N. Cheek was the first African-American missionary to arrive in Nyasaland. Cheek applied to the National Baptist Convention for a missionary assignment, was accepted in 1899, and after a year of soliciting funds from African-American churches, left New York on January 23, 1901, arriving in Nyasaland in April. In the Chiradzulu district in the southern province of Nyasaland, Cheek found an able and willing assistant in the American-educated African, John Chilembwe.[30]

When Landon Cheek arrived in Nyasaland in 1901, his advanced formal education, in conjunction with general European misgivings about African-American missionaries, assured colonial mistrust. In a letter to John Mitchell, Jr., editor of the *Richmond Planet* (Virginia), Cheek wrote: "The Negroes are looked upon [by the European colonialists] with suspicion as they hoist even the banner of Jesus in heathen Africa."[31]

The other National Baptist Convention missionary, and the second African-American missionary in Nyasaland, arrived in 1902, a year after Cheek. Emma Bertha Delaney was born in Fernandina Beach, Florida, in 1871, the same year as Cheek. She was graduated from Spelman Seminary (now Spelman College) in 1894 and its missionary training course in 1896. She spent six years completing the Spelman nurse training course, from which she received preliminary instructions for the mission field. After graduation, she worked for several years as a matron at Florida Institute (Live Oak). Delaney was sent out and supported by the Baptist women of Florida, serving in both Nyasaland (1902-1906) and Liberia (1912-1920).[32]

In an address delivered before she left for Africa, entitled "Why I Go As a Foreign Missionary," Delaney discussed mission work. She commented that, "my interest in missions was awakened in early childhood by a returned missionary who spoke on behalf of his work in Africa." She continued:

> At the age of thirteen, . . . I united with the [Baptist] church, and the spirit of missions increased. After entering Spelman Seminary and spending twelve years there, where our duty to God and humanity, both at home and abroad, is daily set forth, the mere desire for this work was changed to duty and a longing for the work that nothing else would satisfy. After more than three successful years of work at home, I stand to-night as a full-fledged candidate for Africa in obedience to the great command.[33]

At the Chiradzulu mission station, Delaney taught school. Eventually, extra teachers were added. Moreover, Delaney was influential in establishing a women's society and weekly sewing classes for girls. Certainly she was responsible for arousing interest among African-American women for African redemption, through her letters from Africa and her lectures in the United States. Four years after her arrival in Nyasaland, Delaney could see considerable improvement in the area surrounding the mission, and there were students in regular attendance at the schools.[34]

After Cheek and Delaney had been at Chiradzulu for two years, the mission station was renamed the Providence Industrial Mission (PIM). The arrival of these missionaries had shown Africans and European colonialists that the National Baptist Convention was prepared to support the mission financially and by 1904 regular remittances arrived from the church. Thus, by the time the missionaries left in 1906, a promising mission station existed. Cheek had married Chilembwe's niece, Rachael, and fathered three children, one of whom died before they left Africa. When Cheek returned to the United States, he took two PIM boys with him and educated them. Delaney was followed to the United States by one of her students, Daniel Malekebu, who earned a medical degree in the United States and returned to Nyasaland in 1926 as head of the reopened Providence Industrial Mission. With the foundations of the mission secure, Cheek, his family, and Delaney left Nyasaland in June of 1906 for a well-deserved furlough.[35]

Considering her visit to the United States in 1906 was only temporary, Emma Delaney asked the Baptist board to reappoint her to mission work in Nyasaland, but permission was denied by the British government. By this date the European imperialists were beginning to question the African-American and African-Caribbean presence in Africa. These colonialists feared the Africans would identify with their better educated, politically conscious brothers and sisters. Delaney then applied for a mission position in Liberia, was accepted, and worked there for eight years. Cheek, after his return to the United States, apparently did not reapply for African mission work.[36]

The Seventh-Day Adventist Church first sent six missionaries to Africa in July of 1887. Arriving in Cape Town, South Africa, this corps later was reenforced. In 1892 the South African Union Conference was organized with headquarters at Cape Town. Buildings were erected, a training school opened, an orphanage founded, and two periodicals, the *South African Sentinel* and the *South African Missionary*, were established. The first Seventh-Day Adventist to enter Nyasaland was George James, a student of Battle Creek College (Michigan) who went to that country in 1892. Unluckily, he died in 1894 of malaria on the return journey to the coast.[37]

At the beginning of 1902 the Seventh Day Baptists sold their missions near Cholo (about thirty miles south of the Blantyre region in southern Nyasaland) to the Seventh-Day Adventists. The third African-American missionary appointed to Nyasaland, Thomas H. Branch, and his wife, Henrietta, and family sailed from New York on June 28, 1902, on the *RMS Saxon*, arriving at Cholo, Nyasaland, on August 29, 1902. Branch had been chosen by the American missionary organization of the Seventh-Day Adventists to open their initial mission in Nyasaland. The Colorado Conference had recommended Branch and his family and had offered to support them in the field. Branch was sent as superintendent of the newly acquired Plainfield Mission Station in Nyasaland, a name given to it by the Seventh Day Baptists in honor of Plainfield, New Jersey, headquarters of that denomination. Branch was probably the first African-American Seventh-Day Adventist to be sent overseas as a missionary.[38]

Branch initially noticed that Africans were indifferent to alien religions but were eager to secure an education. It was for this reason that older missionary societies had established schools, which attracted many young men. In these mission schools, African students were exposed to Christianity and some accepted the new religion. Many Africans recognized a direct relationship between obtaining an education for the purpose of advancement within the colonial system and conversion to Christianity, and some were willing to convert as a means of securing that education. Branch hired teachers who had been trained by the older societies, and a Plainfield Mission school, with twenty-five students, was opened. Initially, the classes were held under the trees but eventually a school building was constructed. Henrietta Branch, and the Branches' daughter, Mabel, worked in the school. By the time the Branches left Nyasaland in 1907 the mission school numbered seventy-five pupils, and there were two out-schools located several miles from the mission.[39]

For five years the Branches faithfully carried on the work of the Plainfield Mission, but because Thomas Branch protested mistreatment and abuse of Africans, local journalists accused him of also being militant in his religious teachings. Because the Seventh-Day Adventist Church wanted the mission to be viewed in a positive light by the colonial government and remove all doubts of loyalty, in 1907 the General Conference decided to send a white man, Joel C. Rogers, to Nyasaland to take charge of the mission. Within four months of Rogers's arrival in May 1907, Branch and his family left Nyasaland. They worked a short time at the Seventh-Day Adventist South African Mission in Cape Town before eventually returning to the United States.[40]

On January 23, 1915, racism, taxes, forced labor, famine, drought, and conscription for World War I resulted in the highly significant but abortive Nyasaland Uprising led by John Chilembwe, who instructed his patriots "This very night you are to go and strike the blow and then die." Chilembwe and a few of his followers were killed and the uprising was crushed eleven days later on February 3, 1915.[41]

After the Chilembwe uprising many white colonialists in Nyasaland believed that the teachings of black American men and women missionaries in that country had induced a spirit of independence and insubordination among Africans. They argued that the protectorate had been free of such subversive elements until African-American missionaries entered the country, and they accused them of teaching revolution rather than religion. The six-member Nyasaland Native Rising Commission, appointed by the governor of the colony to inquire into the causes of the Chilembwe uprising, recommended that "only properly accredited missions should be allowed in the Protectorate" and stated that black American missionaries were "politically objectionable." The commission believed that black male missionaries encouraged African men to protest their political status and that black female missionaries made African women unhappy with their educational status.[42]

Another area in southern Africa where African-American women missionaries were stationed from 1880 to 1920 was South Africa. Mamie Branton of North Carolina married John Tule, a South African missionary educated in America, and the couple traveled to South Africa in 1897 as missionaries of the

National Baptist Convention. They were first located at Cape Town. In 1899 Reverend Tule transferred his affiliation and initiated the work of the Lott Carey Baptist Home and Foreign Mission Convention in South Africa. Little information exists on Mamie Tule's activities in the country but obviously she assisted in her husband's work.[43]

Lillie B. Johns, born in Wilmington, North Carolina, in 1877, traveled to Africa on January 26, 1897, with her husband, G.F.A. Johns, a South African missionary also educated in America, as missionaries of the National Baptist Convention. It is possible that Lillie B. Johns was the sister of Mamie Branton Tule. Both women were from North Carolina and bore a striking resemblance. After seven months in South Africa, three months spent in a sick bed, Lillie B. Johns died on September 21, 1897, only twenty years old. She had stated before she left the United States: "Should I not return home, do not grieve for me; it is just as near heaven from Africa as from America."[44]

Fanny Ann Jackson was born a slave in Washington, D.C., in 1837. Her freedom was purchased by an aunt and she was sent to New England to live with relatives. Jackson attended school in Massachusetts and Rhode Island. She earned an A.B. degree and an A.M. degree from Oberlin College. From 1865 to 1902 she taught at and eventually became principal of the Institute for Colored Youth in Philadelphia, Pennsylvania.[45]

In 1881 Jackson married Levi Jenkins Coppin, who was licensed to preach in the AME Church in 1876 and edited the *A.M.E. Church Review* from 1888 to 1896. Levi Coppin was elected the first bishop of South Africa in 1900 and assigned to the recently created Fourteenth Episcopal District (Cape Colony and Transvaal). His main responsibility was to oversee the merger of the South African Ethiopian Church with the American AME Church. Since it was common practice in the AME Church to assign a certain portion of missionary duties to wives, Fanny Coppin accompanied her husband to South Africa. The couple arrived at Cape Town on November 30, 1902.[46]

Before journeying to the continent, Fanny Coppin admitted that she thought of Africa, like most missionaries, black and white, as a place devoid of any religious development. Later, she was surprised to find that Africans had engaged in theological thought before the arrival of missionaries. She dedicated herself to preserving African indigenous cultures and felt that missionaries should structure religious training for Africans around the patterns that already existed. Many African-American missionaries came to respect African culture and society after their stays on the continent.

Fanny Coppin was involved in issues and activities relating to all aspects of African life, including living conditions for Africans in Cape Town, the establishment of a school and mission in the city, the development of women's organizations, and the impact of white colonial rule upon the lives of black South Africans. But most of her attention was directed toward the organization of Women's Christian Temperance Union Societies and Women's Mite Missionary Societies. She also formed small missionary groups among the wives of AME South African ministers.[47]

115

Like many black American missionaries working in Africa during this period, the Coppins questioned the benefits of European rule. Fanny Coppin asserted that after the imposition of British colonial rule in South Africa, no portion of the country remained the same. The Coppins were under constant surveillance by British officials. Fanny Coppin claimed that the British feared that religious and educational training would result in resistance by black South Africans to white rule. And she believed that repercussions could indeed be expected when colonial subjects became educated and began to question their inferior status in their society. She cautioned:

> I think, however, the authorities finally came to understand that we were missionaries pure and simple, and not politicians, and if there was any cause for alarm it must grow out of the fact that enlightenment does indeed enable people to see their true condition, and that they do sometimes become dissatisfied when convinced that injustice and a general lack of the Christian spirit of brotherhood, is responsible for much of their misery.[48]

Fanny Coppin felt that education was a vehicle for the expression of discontent among oppressed people. After the Coppins left South Africa, a 1915 law, passed by the Union of South Africa government, provided that "colored people, including missionaries, shall not immigrate" into the country.

It is clear from the applications, speeches, and letters written by these African-American women missionaries before they traveled to southern Africa that they believed that they were assisting in the redemption of the continent. They hoped to transfer Western gender-linked roles and functions to African women and many times they could not understand why African women rejected them and wanted to maintain their traditional way of life. Black American women missionaries often viewed African women's responsibilities and duties in their societies as foreign, alien, and even unacceptable.

A significant influence in their decision to pursue a missionary career was the colleges that they attended. Of the six women who are known to have received a post-secondary education, four graduated from southern black institutions. These schools promoted the idea that it was the "special mission" of African-Americans to help in the redemption of Africa. Fisk University, a privately controlled liberal arts institution, was founded in 1865 by the American Missionary Association (AMA) and historically has been associated with the Congregational Church. E.M. Cravath, Fisk's first president, was also field secretary of the AMA. Nancy Jones recalled the words on a banner in the dining room at Fisk, "Her Sons and Daughters are ever on the altar," and confessed that she felt that she was included in that number.[49] At Spelman College, a private women's school, students sang a song:

> Give a thought to Africa,
> 'Neath the burning Sun—

which typified a spirit prevalent throughout the institution, that of the duty of African-Americans to help "Christianize and civilize" their ancestral homeland. The motives of individual missionaries may have been various, but it is clear that the overriding theme of duty helped to explain why so many African-Americans volunteered for mission work in Africa. These African-American women who served in southern Africa, like most women missionaries, were trained as teachers, nurses and deaconesses.

Additionally, African-American women missionaries most times did not fully understand the nature of European imperialism in Africa. Missionaries had the goals of economic, social, educational, and religious development for Africans, but these did not coincide with the main objective of European imperialists in Africa before 1920, which was simply to maintain control in the African colonies, with as little cost as possible to the home governments. European administrators were not concerned about African societal growth. The Ousleys and Johns were critical of the Portuguese government in Mozambique for being restrictive, for not providing for African workers, and for being unfair in its dealing with Africans. Delaney, Cheek, and the Branches in Nyasaland and Fanny Coppin in South Africa reprimanded the British government for its lack of educational opportunities for Africans.

By the end of World War I, the general consensus of European colonialists in Africa, who by that date had occupied all of the continent except for the Republic of Liberia and Ethiopia, was that African-Americans caused too many disruptions to warrant their effective use as missionaries in Africa. Generally, there were no legislative restrictions directed against black American missionaries after 1920, but most European governments began to exclude them based on the belief that the African-American presence caused unrest among Africans and was dangerous to the maintenance of law and order on the continent.

European imperialists accused black missionaries of encouraging political revolts, and colonial governments, believing that they preached revolt rather than religion, discouraged their entry. But in southern Africa, where revolts occurred before 1920—such as the Herero Rebellion in Southwest Africa from 1904 to 1907, the Bambata (Zulu) Rebellion in South Africa in 1906, or the John Chilembwe Uprising in Nyasaland in 1915—African-American missionaries either were not present or did not exert enough influence to stage such uprisings. It is probably true, though, that the presence of educated black American missionaries was a constant reminder to Africans of the opportunities denied to them in their own land. Furthermore, by 1910, over 150 southern Africans had been educated in American black colleges and universities and exposed to African-American protest.

But other changes occurring in southern Africa and in the United States made the post-World War I world quite different from the pre-war one. In southern Africa, Africans began to form political organizations at the end of the nineteenth and beginning of the twentieth centuries. The principal one was the African National Congress (ANC), founded in 1912. In the United States, Booker T. Washington, the conciliatory black leader, died in 1915. A year later, the Jamaican Marcus Garvey arrived in the United States with his more militant stance. In 1919 W.E.B. Du Bois called the first Pan-African

Congress in Paris, emphasizing the poor conditions under which worldwide blacks lived and calling for unity among this group. The post-World War I period also witnessed an increase in black American self-consciousness with the New Negro movement and the Harlem Renaissance. Additionally, Africans and African-Americans had fought in World War I and returned to their countries after the war with a much more militant outlook. European imperialists, hoping to maintain law and order and develop Africa's resources with little resistance, feared the consequences if these two groups, Africans and African-Americans, both with increasing political awareness, were to get together. Europeans feared the rise of Ethiopianism, or the independent African church movement, in southern Africa. In the late nineteenth century, the Ethiopian Church united with the American based African Methodist Episcopal Church. Colonialists were also frightened by the popularity and spread of the Garvey movement throughout Africa with its "Africa for the Africans" philosophy. Attempting to keep "troublemakers" out of Africa, European governments in Africa concluded that African-American missionaries upset the status quo and were dangerous to the maintenance of law and order in Africa. Therefore, these colonialists discouraged the entry of not only black missionaries, but all black visitors to Africa.[50]

Black American women missionaries faced triple jeopardy. In addition to having to deal with European colonial policy in Africa, African-American women missionaries in southern Africa from 1880 to 1920 also faced sexism and racism from other American and European missionaries. Women were discriminated against as missionary workers. They were viewed by their mission boards and by their male colleagues as second-class missionaries. In this age of imperialism, racism also became a dominant issue in European and American thought. Whether they worked with white missionaries or a segregated mission stations, African-American missionaries were constantly being scrutinized by whites.

Some conclusions can be made about these African-American women missionaries who were stationed in southern Africa from 1880 to 1920. All served in countries—Angola, Mozambique, Nyasaland, Southern Rhodesia, and South Africa—with little or no previous experience with African-American missionaries. In almost all instances these women were among the first black women missionaries in the country (Ousley and Jones were the first in Mozambique, Jones was the first in Southern Rhodesia, Delaney and Branch were the first in Nyasaland, Collins and Drummer were the first in Angola, and Tule and Johns were among the first in South Africa). Five of the nine women were married (three of them wed immediately before they sailed with their husbands to Africa) and four were unmarried. The age when they went to Africa is known for five of the nine women. The average age for four of those was twenty-eight years old. Because Drummer was graduated from college in 1901, she probably also fit into this average. Coppin was sixty-five years old when she went to South Africa. Only the Branches took children to Africa with them. All of the women appeared to have been ignorant of the situation in

Africa before their arrival and not only had to adapt their attitudes to a partial acceptance of the African way of life in order to be effective among them, but also had to take care not to offend the European imperialists. In this age of imperialism and racism, the perceptions and experiences of African-American female and male missionaries in Africa were not dissimilar. With the assumption by Europeans of the "white man's burden" and the rise of Jim Crow in the United States, Africans and African-Americans were treated with the same prejudice. There was really no difference between the exploitation of and discrimination against Africans on the continent and the degradation and oppression of diasporic Africans throughout the world. African-American women missionaries in Africa faced this discrimination, as well as the sexism inherent in this imperialistic age.

NOTES

1. For a discussion of African-American views on the establishment of European imperialism in Africa during the late 19th and early 20th centuries, see Sylvia M. Jacobs, *The African Nexus: Black American Perspectives on the European Partitioning of Africa, 1880-1920* (Westport, Conn.: Greenwood Press, 1981). See also Sylvia M. Jacobs, "Afro-American Women Missionaries Confront the African Way of Life," in *Women in Africa and the African Diaspora*, ed. Rosalyn Terborg-Penn, Sharon Harley, and Andrea Benton Rushing (Washington, D.C.: Howard University Press, 1987), p. 122.

2. In *Black Americans and the Missionary Movement in Africa*, ed. Sylvia M. Jacobs (Westport, Conn.: Greenwood Press, 1982) there is a discussion of the role of African-Americans in the American Protestant mission movement in Africa before 1960. See also Wade Crawford Barclay, *History of Methodist Missions*, vol. 1: *Missionary Motivation and Expansion, 1769-1844* (New York: Board of Missions and Church Extension of the Methodist Church, 1949), pp. 165-66; and William E. Strong, *The Story of the American Board: An Account of the First Hundred Years of the American Board of Commissioners for Foreign Missions* (Boston: Pilgrim Press, 1910), pp. 124-25, 132.

3. Strong, *American Board*, p. 342; *The Missionary Herald, Containing the Proceedings of the American Board of Commissioners for Foreign Missions*, no. 73 (1883), p. 27; and "East Central African Mission," *Annual Report*, no. 74 (1884), pp. 20-21.

4. American Board of Commissioners for Foreign Missions Papers, Biography File, Benjamin Forsyth Ousley, Houghton Library of Harvard University, Cambridge, Mass. Samuel Miller, who taught in Angola from 1880 to 1884, was the first ABCFM black missionary.

5. ABCFM Papers, Memoranda Concerning Missionaries, volume 9, Henrietta Bailey Ousley, Houghton Library of Harvard University, Cambridge, Mass. "Notes for the Month," *Missionary Herald* 80 (Oct. 1884): 406 mentions the marriage of the Ousleys.

6. Strong, *American Board*, pp. 343-44 and Nannie Jones to Mr. E. K. Alden, July 19, 1887 (no. 612), ABCFM Papers, 6, vol. 35, Candidate File, Nancy Jones, Houghton Library of Harvard University, Cambridge, Mass. Nancy Jones's nickname was Nannie.

7. See "Notes for the Month" *Missionary Herald* 80 (Nov. 1884): 465; "Notes for the Month," *ibid.*, vol. 81 (Feb. 1885): 79; and Editorial Paragraphs, *ibid.*, vol. 81 (Apr. 1885): 135. See also "East Central African Mission, Kambini," *Annual Report*, no. 75 (1885), pp. 20-21.

8. "Reports of Committees on the Annual Report: The Committee on Missions in Africa" *Missionary Herald* 81 (Dec. 1885): 508.

9. See *Missionary Herald* 83, "East Central African Mission: A Day At Kambini" (Apr. 1887): 142 and "East Central African Mission: Degradation of Women" (Aug. 1887): 309. See also "East Central African Mission," *Annual Report*, no. 77 (1887), p. 60.

10. "Notes for the Month," *Missionary Herald* 84 (Mar. 1888): 127.

11. Nannie Jones to Pres. E. M. Cravath, March 20, 1887 (no. 610), ABCFM Papers, 6, vol. 35, Candidate File, Nancy Jones.

12. Nancy Jones to Dr. Judson Smith, November 1, 1887 (no. 63), ABCFM Papers, 15.4, vol. 12, East Central Africa File.

13. "Notes for the Month," *Missionary Herald* 84 (July 1888): 318; and "East Central African Mission: A Hopeful Outlook," *ibid.* (Sept. 1888): 387-88. See also "East Central African Mission," *Annual Report*, no. 78 (1888), pp. 19-21. Jones gives an account of her first four months at Kambini in Nancy Jones to Dr. Judson Smith, May 2, 1888 (no. 70); Nancy Jones to Dr. Judson Smith, May 29, 1888 (no. 72), ABCFM Papers, 15.4, vol. 12, East Central Africa File.

14. "East Central African Mission: Kambini," *Missionary Herald* 85 (Mar. 1889): 110 and Nancy Jones to Charles E. Swett, October 19, 1888 (no. 73), ABCFM Papers, 15.4, vol. 12, East Central Africa File.

15. "East Central African Mission: From Kambini," *Missionary Herald* 86 (June 1890): 237-38; "Notes for the Month," *Missionary Herald* 8 (June 1890): 296; "East Central African Mission," *Annual Report*, no. 79 (1889), p. 31; and Nancy Jones to Rev. Judson Smith, January 9, 1890 (no. 63), ABCFM Papers, 15.4, vol. 20, East Central Africa File.

16. "East Central African Mission," *Missionary Herald* 86 (Dec. 1890): 515; *ibid.*, vol. 87 (Feb. 1891): 62-63 and (Oct. 1891): 421; "East Central African Mission," *Annual Report*, no. 80 (1890), p. 28, and no. 81 (1891), p. 22; and Nancy Jones to Rev. Judson Smith, Feb. 6, 1890 (no. 64), ABCFM Papers, 15.4, vol. 20, East Central Africa File.

17. "Reports of Committees on the Annual Report: The Committee on Missions in Africa," *Annual Report*, no. 80 (1890), p. xv.

18. "Notes for the Month," *Missionary Herald* 89 (Aug. 1893): 336; and Nancy Jones to Judson Smith, Jan. 4, 1893 (no. 80), ABCFM Papers, 15.4, vol. 20, East Central Africa File. See also "East Central African Mission," *Annual Report*, no. 82 (1892), pp. 25-26; no. 83 (1893), pp. 26-27; and no. 84 (1894), p. 23.

19. Strong, *American Board*, pp. 342-44; Editorial Paragraphs, *Missionary Herald* 89 (Aug. 1893): 304; and *ibid.*, vol. 90 (March 1894): 96; and "East Central African Mission," *Annual Report*, no. 82 (1892), pp. 225-227; "Mt. Silinda (Gazaland)," *ibid.*, no. 83 (1893), p. 26; and *ibid.*, no. 84 (1894), pp. 23, 27.

20. "Letters From Mission: East Central African Mission, Gazaland," *Missionary Herald* 90 (July 1894): 286, *ibid.* (Oct. 1894): 462, and *ibid.*, vol. 91 (May 1895): 189-91; "East Central African Mission," *Annual Report*, no. 85 (1895), p. 31; and no. 86 (1896), p. 28; and Nancy Jones to Rev. Judson Smith, March 8, 1894

(no. 81) and March 26, 1895 (no. 82), ABCFM Papers, 15.4, vol. 20, East Central Africa File.

21. "East Central African Mission," *Missionary Herald* 93 (Feb. 1897): 68 and "Notes for the Month," *ibid.* (Dec. 1897): 523; "East Central African Mission," *Annual Report,* no. 87 (1897), p. 28; and no. 88 (1898), p. 28; and Resignation—Nancy Jones, May 27, 1897 (no. 87) and Nancy Jones to Rev. Judson Smith, Dec. 2, 1897 (no. 92), ABCFM Papers, 15.4, vol. 20, East Central Africa File.

22. Nancy Jones to Rev. Judson Smith, Nov. 1, 1897 (no. 90), ABCFM Papers, 15.4, Vol. 20, East Central Africa File.

23. "On the Dark Continent," *Indianapolis Freeman,* Feb. 5, 1898.

24. Collins is listed almost every year from 1890 to 1906 in the *Annual Report of the Missionary Society of the Methodist Episcopal Church.*

25. *Annual Report on the Board of Foreign Missions of the Methodist Episcopal Church* (1907-19), passim.

26. Walter L. Williams, *Black Americans and the Evangelization of Africa, 1877-1900* (Madison: University of Wisconsin Press, 1982), p. 14.

27. James P. Brawley, *The Clark College Legacy: An Interpretive History of Relevant Education, 1869-1975* (Atlanta: Clark College, 1977), p. 61.

28. I would like to extend sincere thanks to George Shepperson of the University of Edinburgh for his invaluable assistance in helping me to research this topic and for the priceless photographs of the Branch family in Nyasaland that he so generously shared with me.

29. W.E.B. Du Bois, ed., *The Negro Church* (Atlanta: Atlanta University Press, 1903), p. 111; Miles Mark Fisher, *A Short History of the Baptist Denomination* (Nashville: Sunday School Publishing Board, 1933), p. 117; Joseph R. Washington, Jr., *Black Religion: The Negro and Christianity in the United States* (Boston: Beacon Press, 1964), pp. 52-53; Edmund F. Merriam, *A History of American Baptist Missions* (Philadelphia: American Baptist Publication Society, 1913), p. 189; Henry C. Vedder, *A Short History of Baptist Missions* (Philadelphia: Judson Press, 1927), p. 270; Lewellyn L. Berry, *A Century of Missions of the African Methodist Episcopal Church, 1840-1940* (New York: Gutenberg Printing Co., 1942), pp. 225-28; and George Shepperson and Thomas Price, *Independent African: John Chilembwe and the Origins, Setting and Significance of the Nyasaland Native Rising in 1915* (Edinburgh: University Press, 1958), pp. 134-36.

30. Shepperson and Price in *Independent African* erroneously state that Thomas Branch was the first black American in Nyasaland, "arriving at the beginning of April 1901" (p. 135). My research has indicated, however, that Cheek arrived in April 1901 and Branch reached Nyasaland in August 1902. Kings M. Phiri in "Afro-American Influence in Colonial Malawi, 1891-1945: A Case Study of the Interaction Between Africa and Africans of the Diaspora," in *Global Dimensions of the African Diaspora,* ed. Joseph E. Harris (Washington, D.C.: Howard University Press, 1982), p. 255 repeats Shepperson and Price's mistake. See also Lewis Garnett Jordan, *Up the Ladder in Foreign Missions* (Nashville: National Baptist Publications Board, 1901), p. 132.

31. "Rev. Cheek Writes," *Richmond Planet* (Virginia), June 3, 1905; and Shepperson and Price, *Independent African,* pp. 137-38.

32. Florence Matilda Read, *The Story of Spelman College* (Atlanta, Ga.: n.p., 1961), pp. 352-53, 357-58; and C. C. Adams and Marshall A. Talley, *Negro Baptists and*

Foreign Missions (Philadelphia: Foreign Mission Board of the National Baptist Convention, U.S.A., Inc., 1944), p. 23.

33. See "Sketches of Spelman Graduates—Emma B. Delany," *Spelman Messenger,* Oct. 1901, p. 2; "Why I Go as a Foreign Missionary," *ibid.,* Feb. 1902, p. 5; and "Spelman Women in Africa," *ibid.,* Feb. 1945, pp. 2, 7, 8.

34. Read, *Spelman College,* pp. 354-55; Shepperson and Price, *Independent African,* pp. 139-41; Du Bois, *The Negro Church,* p. 120; and Adams and Talley, *Negro Baptists in Foreign Missions,* p. 23.

35. Shepperson and Price, *Independent African,* pp. 139-42. Roderick J. Macdonald in "Rev. Dr. Daniel Sharpe Malekebu and the Re-Opening of the Providence Industrial Mission: 1926-29; An Appreciation," in *From Nyasaland to Malawi: Studies in Colonial History,* ed. Roderick J. Macdonald (Nairobi, Kenya: East African Publishing House, 1975), pp. 215-33 discusses the reopening of the Providence Industrial Mission in 1926. There has been some recent controversy concerning the PIM. The question centered on the issue of whether Daniel Malekebu reopened the PIM in 1926 on his own or as a representative of the National Baptist Convention, U.S.A., Inc. (NBC). After his death, Malekebu's followers took over the mission property, despite the protests of the NBC. In the court decision, Judge L. A. Chatsika sustained the claim of the NBC. See William J. Harvey III, *Sacrifice and Dedication in a Century of Mission: A History of One Hundred Years of the Foreign Mission Board, National Baptist Convention, U.S.A., Inc., 1880-1980* (Philadelphia: Foreign Mission Board, National Baptist Convention, U.S.A., Inc., 1979), pp. 92-93; and Civil Case No. 319 of 1977, High Court of Malawi at Blantyre. The final court decision was given on Sept. 6, 1978, pertinent pages, 18-20.

36. Read, *Spelman College,* pp. 357-58. Emma Delaney's name is spelled DeLany in some publications.

37. M. Ellsworth Olsen, *A History of the Origin and Progress of Seventh-Day Adventists* (Washington, D.C.: Review and Herald Publishing Association, 1925), pp. 485-93; and V. E. Robinson, "Historical Sketch of the Work of the Seventh-Day Adventists in Nyasaland, 1902-1915," typescript, General Conference of Seventh-Day Adventists, Washington, D.C., pp. 3-4. I would like to thank Alta Robinson for a copy of her husband's manuscript.

38. S. S. Murray, *Handbook of Nyasaland* (London: Waterlow and Sons, 1932), p. 399; Olsen, *Seventh-Day Adventists,* p. 493; and N. Olney Moore, "Seventh Day Baptists and Mission Work in Nyasaland, Africa," (Plainfield, N.J.: Seventh Day Baptist Historical Society, n.d.), pp. 2-3. I am grateful to Thomas H. Merchant of the Seventh Day Baptist Historical Society for a copy of the latter report. See also Shepperson and Price, *Independent African,* pp. 86-87, 137.

39. The Branches wrote many letters and reports from Nyasaland which were published in the *Advent Review and Sabbath Herald* (Seventh-Day Adventist Church, Washington, D.C.) from 1902 to 1907.

40. Don F. Neufeld, *Seventh-Day Adventist Encyclopedia* (Washington, D.C.: Review and Herald Publishing Association, 1966), p. 151; William J. W. Roome, *A Great Emancipation: A Missionary Survey of Nyasaland, Central Africa* (London: World Dominion Press, 1926), p. 46; Olsen, *Seventh-Day Adventists,* p. 494; Murray, *Handbook,* p. 399; and Robinson, "Historical Sketch," pp. 10, 12. I am indebted to Maurice T. Battle, Associate Secretary, General Conference of

Seventh-Day Adventists, Washington, D.C. for his assistance in my research on Thomas H. Branch.

41. Robert I. Rotberg, ed., in *Strike a Blow and Die: A Narrative of Race Relations in Colonial Africa by George Simeon Mwase* (Cambridge: Harvard University Press, 1967), pp. 23-24 mentions Cheek and Delaney's relationship with Chilembwe. Chilembwe's uprising is discussed on pp. 29-52. See also Shepperson and Price, *Independent African*, pp. 267-319, 399.

42. Johannes Du Plessis, *Thrice through the Dark Continent: A Record of Journeyings across Africa during the Years 1913-1916* (London: Longmans, Green and Co., 1917), p. 346; Shepperson and Price, *Independent African*, p. 135; and George Shepperson, "Notes on Negro American Influences on the Emergence of African Nationalism," *Journal of African History* 1 (1960): 305. See also Native Rising Commission, *Report of the Commission [on] . . . the Native Rising within the Nyasaland Protectorate* (Zomba: Government Printer, Nyasaland Protectorate, c. Jan. 7, 1916), pp. 4, 6, 8. William J. Harvey III, executive secretary of the Foreign Mission Board of the National Baptist Convention, U.S.A., Inc., contends that his reading of Emma Delaney's letters and descriptions of her by other people led him to believe that she was very militant for her time and could have encouraged Africans at Chiradzulu to protest their position in Nyasaland. Interview, William J. Harvey III, March 9, 1983, Philadelphia, Pa.

43. Williams, *Black Americans and the Evangelization of Africa*, pp. 71, 190.

44. L. G. Jordon, comp., *In Our Stead* (Philadelphia: n.p., 1913), pp. 21, 36.

45. Fanny Jackson Coppin, *Reminiscences of School Life and Hints on Teaching* (Philadelphia: A.M.E. Book Concern, 1913), pp. 122-23; Martin Kilson and Adelaide Hill, *Apropos of Africa: Afro-American Leaders and the Romance of Africa* (Garden City, N.Y.: Doubleday and Co., 1971), pp. 281-82.

46. Margaret E. Burton, *Comrades in Service* (New York: Missionary Education Movement of the United States and Canada, 1915), p. 160; and Josephus R. Coan, "The Expansion of Missions of the African Methodist Episcopal Church in South Africa, 1896-1908" (Ph.D. diss., Hartford Seminary Foundation, 1961), pp. 293-94, 327-28.

47. Fanny Coppin, *Reminiscences*, pp. 125, 129-30; Burton, *Comrades*, p. 160.

48. Fanny Coppin, *Reminiscences*, pp. 124-128.

49. Nannie Jones to Mr. E. K. Alden, July 19, 1887 (no. 612), ABCFM Papers, vol. 35, Candidate File, Nancy Jones.

50. Jacobs, ed., *Black Americans and the Missionary Movement in Africa*, pp. 20-22.

Part III
Caribbean and Canada

8

Women and Slavery in the Caribbean:
A Feminist Perspective

Rhoda E. Reddock

Much has been written on the subject of New World slavery, and indeed it may seem that the time has come for all such considerations to cease. For the people of the Caribbean, however, slavery is a crucial aspect of their historical experience, and its existence and legacy are not confined to the distant past. In Cuba, for example, slavery still existed less than a hundred years ago. The study of history is important not for its own sake, but in order to acquire an understanding of the workings of society that we can apply to our present experience. In the women's movement throughout the world, women have had to reexamine and reinterpret history and often rewrite it in order to make women visible. In this article I shall attempt to reinterpret the history of slavery in the Caribbean from a woman's perspective. I hope by so doing to expose some of the ideology that conceals material oppression.[1]

Caribbean slavery has been attributed varying positions in Marxist mode-of-production analysis. To some (Padgug, 1976-1977; Genovese, 1967) it was a particular form of production within the worldwide capitalist system. To others (e.g., Post, 1978), however, it was a distinct mode of production, though it was incorporated into the sphere of exchange of the capitalist one. This view is justified by the fact that most, if not all, surplus value was derived from slave labor. According to Post (1978: 22-23), "It was based upon a particular combination of capital, land and labour-power, and as Marx showed, the mere presence of capital, even in conjunction with 'free' labour, let alone chattel slaves, does not make a social formation capitalist."

I take the position that New World slavery in general, and Caribbean slavery in particular, can be seen as the capitalist harnessing of an archaic form of economy. Whatever one's position, the relationship between New World slavery and the emergence of capitalism is clear, and Williams (1944) has shown that slave production provided much of the basis for European industrialization.

African-Caribbean slavery might be said to have begun in 1518, when Charles V of Spain, on the advice of Bartolomé de Las Casas, "protector of the Indians," formally granted permission for the importation of 4,000 African slaves to relieve the labor shortage in the Antillean mines. Portugal, Spain, Britain, France, the Netherlands, Denmark, and Sweden all took part in the slave trade that ensued and, with the exception of Sweden, in the slavery that was established in their colonies (Knight, 1978: 214).

Conditions varied somewhat from one area to the next, and the debate over the relative cruelty of the systems continues. What is important, though, is that at a particular time in history, the slave mode (or form) of production proved a most efficient means of capital accumulation for Western Europe in the sugar-plantation colonies of the Caribbean. Whatever tears may be shed at the thought of past brutality, economically for Western Europe there can be no regrets.

It is against this background, therefore, that we can approach the study of women in Caribbean slave society, where there was no necessity to conceal oppression or the profit motive. The facts revealed in this analysis, though derived from a very particular situation, are relevant to the study of the oppression of women internationally today.

Women in Social Production

Among slaves the housewife did not exist. From the age of 4, slave girls as well as boys worked on the estate. According to Orlando Patterson (1967: 157), "In Rosehall Estate (Jamaica) girls started work at four and remained in the Hogmeat Gang (which consisted of young children employed in minor tasks such as collecting food for the hogs, weeding, and the like) until the age of nine. Between the ages of 12 and 19 occupations varied." In one particular group, one girl aged 12 and two others aged 19 were in the field, two were attending stock, one was "with Mrs. Palmer," and another was a domestic. The majority of women in Jamaica between the ages of 19 and 54 worked in the fields. By the late eighteenth and early nineteenth century, women outnumbered men in the fields because of their lower mortality rates (Patterson, 1967; Craton, 1978; Dunn, 1972). By 1838, when slavery in the British colonies was abolished, the proportion of men in the fields had fallen below 40 percent (Craton, 1978). This is interesting when one notes that job discrimination on the basis of sex is often justified on the ground that women have lower physical strength and endurance.

In fact, according to Craton, slave women participating in field work similar to men's lived up to five years longer than men. In slavery, therefore, women were often as important as productive field laborers as men. In the words of Gwendolyn Midlo Hall (1971: 17), "slave manpower has been compared to plant equipment. The purchase price of the slave was the investment, and the maintenance of the slave was a fixed cost that had to be paid whether or not the slave was working." Therefore, says Patterson (1967: 67), "Slavery abolished any real social distribution between males and females. The woman was expected to work just as hard, she was indecently exposed and was punished just as severely. In the eyes of the master she was equal to the man as long as her strength was the same as his."

What was work like on these estates? In mid-nineteenth-century Cuba the working day in the grinding season was as long as twenty hours. Four or five hours' sleep was considered adequate. Women cut cane even during the ninth month of pregnancy (Knight, 1970: 76). According to Hall, by the end of the grinding season in Cuba even the oxen were reduced to mere skeletons, many of them dying from overwork. In Brazil, also a booming plantation society in the nineteenth century, one coffee planter calculated on using a slave for only one year (few on his estate could survive longer than that), during which he could get enough work out of the slave not only to "repay the initial investment, but even to show a good profit" (Hall, 1971: 19).

Despite their use in hard field labor, says Craton, women were always excluded from the more prestigious and skilled jobs, including, for example, work with the boilers, carpentry, and masonry. Patterson also noted that male slaves had a much wider range of occupations than female slaves, who were confined to being field hands, domestics, and washerwomen. The most prestigious jobs for women appear to have been those related to health, in particular, nursing. Tables for 1823 in Jamaica list two midwives and one woman doctor as being among the staff of one estate. This situation can be seen as the introduction of the sexual division of labor that had been instituted in Europe into one sector of slave society while not extending it to areas in which it was not economically advantageous.

A minority of women (and men) became "house slaves," participating mainly in domestic activities such as cooking and cleaning. In the hierarchy of slave societies, house slaves were a breed apart, and the class division between women who did household labor and those who did not may have started here. It is possible (although this is pure conjecture) that field slaves envied the position of the house slave not so much because of a love of housework as from a desire for a less strenuous existence and the higher status that went with proximity to white people. Patterson (1967) points out, however, that not all field slaves envied the house slaves' position. To many, the field offered more stability and relative freedom, for there they were not constantly at the mercy of masters and mistresses. These views would, of course, have varied from one plantation to another and over time.

Women and Reproduction

The main factor differentiating men from women is the capacity of women to produce human life. Throughout history the subordination of women has been centered around the necessity to control this important capacity. This question of reproduction, hitherto ignored in the social sciences, is now receiving increased attention with the emergence of academic studies on the subject of women, inspired by the women's movements of the 1970s.

Because of the crudeness of the social relations of production in slave society, the study of slave women and reproduction reveals much about the ability of the ruling classes to control the reproductive capacity of women to suit the economic necessity of the moment. Craton, in his sociodemographic study of Worthy Park Estate in Jamaica, identifies a "Christmas-tree effect" in population pyramids constructed from plantation records: the number of children is very small, whereas the middle-aged population is much greater and gradually tapers off into old age. He rejects the view that this situation reflects the planters' preference for "buying rather than breeding." Instead, he suggests that it is because of the long period of lactation among African women, during which sexual intercourse was taboo; high infant mortality rates because of disease and diet deficiencies; the biological and psychological effects of dislocation, stress, and overcrowding, analogous to conditions in a Nazi concentration camp; and the abortions performed by slave women who did not want to bring children into slave labor (Craton, 1978: 97-98). These are the factors he believes are responsible for the high frequency of sterility among slave women and the fact that more than half of them never gave birth at all.

Other writers, however, have seen this also as the result of definite preferences on the part of the planters. Noel Deere (1950: 227) noted that "natural reproduction of the slave population was not encouraged in sugar colonies; it was held to be cheaper to buy than to breed, since a child was an expense for its first twelve years of life." Similarly, Hall (1971: 24) reports:

> Sources from St. Domingue indicate masters calculated the work of a negresse during an eighteen-month period (that is, the last three months of pregnancy and the months during which she breast-fed her infant) was worth 600 lives, and that during this time she was able to do only half of her normal work. The master therefore lost 300 lives. A fifteen-month-old slave was not worth this sum.

Patterson attempts a more systematic discussion of the question, discussing the attitudes of slave owners toward reproduction in different periods of slave history. Using examples from Jamaica, he notes that during the early period, from 1655 until the beginning of the eighteenth century, estates were small and had few slaves. As a result, the treatment of slaves was better than it would become later, and "natural" reproduction was encouraged. During the eighteenth century, however, the rising planter class shifted to the large-scale monocrop production of sugar, and "natural" reproduction was abandoned. Thus by mid-century, Dr. Harrison could state that no encouragement was given to slaves to raise families, the general opinion being that it was cheaper to buy new slaves than to rear children. As late as the 1830s Henry Coor, a Jamaican millwright, estimated in the *West Indian Reporter* (March 1831) that the cost of rearing a slave to age 14 was £112 in Jamaica, £165 in Trinidad, £109 in Barbados, and £112 in Antigua (Patterson, 1967: 105). At this time the comparative market price of a field slave was £45 in Cuba (Hall, 1962: 306). Patterson further states that it was considered "a misfortune to have pregnant women or even young slaves." He also observed that "the attitudes of the owners were reflected in those of the slaves" (1967: 106). All the available data indicate that slave women disliked having children. At first this was limited to "creole" slaves, that is, slaves born in the region, but as the population of creole slaves increased, this attitude became more widespread. As a result of this, abortion and, to a lesser extent, infanticide were widely practiced (1967: 106-107).

The conditions of life and work for slave women physically discouraged reproduction. Gynecological disorders were rife because of the absence of facilities for pregnancy and childbirth, the poor sanitary conditions, the mistreatment of pregnant women, and the heavy labor for long hours. One of the most common disorders was amenorrhea (absence of menstrual periods); this was usually due to severe malnutrition, injury to the ovaries, or problems in the endocrine system caused by severe beatings. Another was menorrhagia (excessive flow at the period). These menstrual problems often resulted in early menopause and therefore in a reduced fertile time span. Thus the practices of the ruling class during the sugar era, determined by its production needs and international market opportunities, led to the emergence of a dominant ideology in which both masters and slaves found the costs of bearing and rearing children greater than the benefits. This ideology led to a practice by slave women that served the interests of the ruling class even though it was derived from different considerations.

In the Spanish Caribbean colonies, the same position was held by the planters, but it was manifested in different ways. Prior to the early nineteenth century there were very few women on slaveholding estates; in 1771 in Cuba the ratio was 1:1.9. A female slave, because of her risk of childbearing, was seen as a poor investment. As Francisco d'Arango y Perreneo, the father of the slave plantation system in Cuba, put it (quoted in Hall, 1971: 24), "During and after pregnancy, the slave is useless for several months, and her nourishment should be more abundant and better chosen. This loss of work and added expense comes out of the master's pocket. It is he who pays for the often ineffective and always lengthy care of the newborn." As a result, female slaves cost one-third the price of male slaves (Hall, 1971: 26). Nineteenth-century Spanish moralists justified this situation in terms of the undesirability of the coexistence of the sexes on the estates without marriage. Thus male slaves were condemned to celibacy (or homosexuality).

The nuclear family was actively discouraged by planters in all the Caribbean colonies. Where such families did develop, they could be easily destroyed through sale of members to creditors and/or to other plantations. In Jamaica, children were taken from their mothers after weaning and placed with a driveress[2] first in the grass gang[3] and then in other gangs as they grew older. Similarly, in Cuba slave mothers returned to work about six weeks after childbirth, at which time the child was turned over to the plantation nursery (Knight, 1970: 76). Patterson (1967: 167) notes with some regret that "the male head could not assert his authority as husband and father as his 'wife' was the property of another." This illustration lays bare the realities of marriage and the nuclear family. In this period in Caribbean history, this form of social organization did not meet the needs of capital. Therefore, there was no need to construct the ideological support for the nuclear family that conceals its fundamental nature even today.

In response to the attitudes of the masters, contempt for marriage was great among slaves, especially young ones (both female and male) in towns. Women in particular disliked marriage because, according to Patterson, it meant extra work and being confined to one man. Regular sexual activity began very early in life, especially for girls, and both men and women maintained multiple associations. One writer observed in 1823 that "the husband has commonly two or three wives, and the wives as many husbands which they mutually change for each other" (Patterson, 1967: 164). As old age approached, however, couples usually settled down into stable monogamous unions. It has been suggested that in the later years of slavery, when women were allowed to keep their children, the woman may have assumed a "matriarchal" position in the household, all the children being hers and not the man's.

Amelioration and Reform: New Laws and Women

As the last two decades of the eighteenth century drew near, the slave trade that had up to this point efficiently supplied the Caribbean slave owners with labor began to face difficulties. One source of these was the rise of industrial capitalism in Europe. It was at this time, after years of campaigning, that more attention was beginning to be paid to the abolitionists. In a controversial interpretation, Williams (1944) identified a contradictory relationship between monopoly slave-grown sugar production and new industrial production. The former, in giving rise to the latter, had sown the seeds of its own destruction because it was the capital accumulated from slavery that fueled industrialization. In addition to this, the increasing competition from "free"-grown sugar from India and the East Indies and the demand of British sugar producers in that region for equal treatment provided another source of support for the campaign against slavery and the slave trade.

Williams's book has been subjected to numerous criticisms, and the specific details of his interpretation of abolitionism are no longer reliable. But his general point—that the antislavery movement gained political force once it served the needs of a rising industrial capitalism—has held up well (Davis, 1975: 347-350). As Williams (1944: 136) states, the humanitarians

> could never have succeeded a hundred years before when every important capitalist was on the side of the colonial system. "It was an arduous hill to climb," sang Wordsworth in praise of [the abolitionist Thomas] Clarkson. The top would never have been reached but for the defection of capitalists from the ranks of slave-owners and slave-traders.

The struggle against monopoly and in favor of free trade was the main reason for the "defection of capitalists" in England from the cause of the planters. The new industrialists needed cheaper raw materials and markets for manufactured goods. A second difficulty with the slave trade was the growing shortage of slaves along the west coast of Africa, which forced slavers to go deeper inland in search of them and made slaves fewer and more expensive.

For these and other reasons, the colonial governments of all slave holding territories, whether French, Spanish, or English, sought to address themselves to this problem around the same time. In contrast with the short-sighted planters, the metropolitan ruling classes saw the slave plantation economy within the framework of their wider colonial interests. For example, the increasing incorporation of Africa as a supplier of raw materials and a producer of cash crops necessitated some control over the depletion of its labor force (Wallerstein, 1979: 28-29). In addition, possible slave revolts presented a continuing threat to the plantation system. In the words of Hall (1971: 112):

> The get-rich quick mentality of the planters and their managers generated conditions which were highly destructive to the slave population and undermined the stability of the colony. Revenues from these colonies, both direct and indirect, were vast, and the metropolis had a great deal at stake as it sought to prevent interest groups within the colonies from killing the goose that laid the golden eggs. Generally the metropolis embraced a broader, more long-range point of view than did the planter class.

Each of the three governments responded with a body of laws and regulations aimed at appeasing the abolitionists by "humanizing" slavery and increasing local reproduction of labor through measures directed at women and family organization. The British Amelioration Acts of 1787, the French Ordonnances de Louis XVI, and the Spanish Código Negro Carolino of 1785 and Código Negro Español of 1789 in general all advocated the same reforms: the encouragement of marriage and the nuclear family and the discouragement of "illicit" relations, which tend to reduce fertility; restrictions on the work hours of female slaves, especially pregnant and nursing ones; improvement in the nutrition of pregnant slaves; provision of facilities such as infirmaries for newborn slave infants; the allocation of "provision grounds" on which slaves could produce their own food; and the allocation of minimum yearly clothing allowances.

In general, the response of the planters to this was negative. Although they recognized the necessity to increase the "natural" reproduction of the local slave population, they resented any attempt to reduce their control over the life and labor of the slaves and their immediate profit. Resistance was greatest in the Spanish colonies, in particular Cuba, where the Cuban slave plantation economy was just gaining momentum. Consequently, the 1789 code, written for the entire Spanish empire, was never promulgated in any of the Spanish slave plantation areas of the Caribbean (Hall, 1971: 103). The planters of Havana justified this in terms of fears that if slaves heard about these reforms, instability would result. A Real Cédula of 1804 exhorting that slaves be treated humanely and that "female slaves be introduced on estates where there were only males until all desiring marriage were married" (Hall, 1971:

133

107) also failed to be published. A further slave code passed in 1842 reinforced some of the more oppressive aspects of slavery.

The results were similar where reforms were developed or supported by the local planter class. The attempts to increase local slave reproduction at best yielded only modest increases. In Tobago, for example, in 1798 (Williams, 1964: 60-62), a committee of both houses of the legislature set up to look into "the causes which had retarded the natural increase of slaves" made the following proposals:

(1) That the commodities and quantities which should be provided for slaves be fixed at:
   (a) 3 lbs. salted pork or 4 lbs. salted beef or 4 lbs. salted fish, or 4 lbs. good herring per week for each working slave and pro rata for children of different ages;
   (b) 7 quarts weekly of wheat flour or oatmeal or ground provisions such as Indian corn, peas, plantains, yams, potatoes or eddoes for each working slave and pro rata for children of different ages;
   (c) *For men* a cloth jacket, hat, frock and a pair of trousers in June and another frock and pair of trousers in December. *For women* a cloth jacket, hat and coarse handkerchief, a petticoat and a wrapper in June, and another petticoat and wrapper in December.

(2) A duty on all imported slaves above 25 years and a premium on all female slaves between the age of 8 and 20.

(3) The erection of a comfortable house on each estate with a boarded platform for the accommodation of slaves.

(4) Slave women should be prevented by law from taking young children into the fields and every estate is obliged to establish a nursery for the care of young children.

(5) The distribution of good land to the slaves, and the allocation of time to work on it.

(6) The erection of a comfortable house at the expense of the slave owner for a young woman on her marriage, plus a gift of livestock valued at $16 to $20 and clothing of a superior quality.

(7) That a law should be passed entitling a midwife to a fee of $1.00 for every child which she delivers alive.

(8) That a law be prescribed preventing women from working up to five weeks after having a child and then work to begin only on production of a surgeon's certificate.

(9) That mothers of six or more children be granted a total exemption of all labour.

(10) That overseers of the six plantations with the highest natural increase be given bonuses ranging from $100 to $50.

These measures, however, met with little immediate success (Patterson, 1967: 112): "slave women of child-bearing age, now largely creoles, were hardened in their anti-breeding attitudes with the result that most of the schemes for increasing the population by greater reproduction failed." The rather modest changes in the material reality of slave women's existence were not enough to change their dominant ideological positions. Thus although the planters desired increased reproduction, the slave women did not see it as in their interest to comply.

In Cuba, in response to the failure of the new measures to increase local reproduction, some planters resorted to slave breeding similar to that in the slave states of the United States of America. One writer identified the estate of Esteban Cruz de Oviedo at Trinidad (in Cuba) as the most shameless of these establishments. This "farm"—"served by its female blacks"—yielded an estimated thirty blacks a year, whereas its loss per year was only ten (Moreno Fraginals, 1976: 143). Hall notes in relation to this that a child of good stock was worth 500 pesos. This method nevertheless also proved unsuccessful, and the slave trade, abolished in 1819-1820, continued illegally.

The slave trade was abolished in the British colonies in 1807 and in the French in 1818. After this, methods aimed at increasing local reproduction were intensified. In most islands, more female slaves were imported during this period of illegal trade than prior to abolition. In many islands, abortion and infanticide were outlawed. In Jamaica, Sabina Park, a slave woman charged with the murder of her 3-year-old child, spoke in her own defense at the Half Way Tree Slave Court, saying that "she had worked enough for bukra (master) already and that she would not be plagued to raise the child . . . to work for white people" (Patterson, 1967: 106).

To forestall the growing demand for abolition, in 1823 the British government attempted once more to impose reforms on the British slave colonies. These were enforced in the crown colonies of Trinidad and British Guiana in 1824 but were attacked by the self-governing legislatures of Jamaica, Tobago, and Barbados. They included new rules on punishment, including abolition of the flogging of slave women and girls; provision of the slaves with two days off work, one for the Negro market, and Sunday for religion; manumission reforms, including mandatory freedom of slave girls born after 1823; and judicial changes allowing slaves to admit evidence in court, and establishing a "Protector of Slaves" who would keep a legal record of slave punishments (Williams, 1944: 197-198).

The planters strongly objected to most of these proposals, especially to the abolition of the Sunday market and of flogging for female slaves. They argued that "it was necessary to punish women. Even in civilised societies, they argued, women were flogged" (Williams, 1944: 198). A member of the Barbados legislature stated: "Our black ladies have rather a tendency to the Amazonian cast of character, and I believe that their husbands would be very sorry to hear that they were placed beyond the reach of chastisement" (Williams, 1944: 198). The Tobago planters similarly "condemned the prohibition of the flogging of female slaves as 'tantamount' to unqualified emancipation at this hour" (Williams, 1964: 130).

Attempts at reform and increased slave reproduction ran up against the resistance of slave women themselves and the reluctance of many planters to depart from their traditional means of exploiting and physically disciplining female slave laborers. The planter class, even when it accepted the necessity of biological reproduction of the labor force, considered harsh, physically damaging violence an indispensable weapon in its relations with slave women.

In the flurry of activity of the early nineteenth century, the slaves in the British islands came to believe that emancipation had been granted in England but withheld by the local planters. This led to a series of slave revolts, rebellions, and suicides in the region and eventually, in 1833, to abolition. To appease the planters, however, in addition to £20,000 in compensation which was to be divided among them, a five-year transition period was established during which the new "free wage laborers" were still tied to the estates as apprentices.

The Transition to Postemancipation Production and Reproduction

As early as the beginning of the nineteenth century, signs of the decreasing productivity of the slave plantation system had begun to be evident in the British Caribbean. This was usually attributed to the decline in sugar prices because of overproduction and increasing costs of production. Craton (1978), writing on Jamaica, suggests that two alternatives may have presented themselves to the planters, both based on economies of scale: to produce more with the same workforce or to produce the same amount with a smaller workforce. In view of their fear of overproduction, the latter solution was preferable, but trimming the workforce implied the substitution of "free wage labor" for slavery, something they were very slow to advocate (Craton, 1978: 172). For some years between 1815 and 1838, attempts were made to increase productivity by driving the workforce harder. This period was one of increasing alienation, forced labor, and rebellion. In Spanish Cuba, the 1820s saw the beginning of mechanization in sugar production. For the majority of planters only partial mechanization was possible, and large numbers of slaves were needed to maintain the level of production in the nonmechanized processes. These days have been described as "slavery's darkest hours," a rationalization process aimed at squeezing the last drop of work from the slave (Moreno Fraginals, 1976). With mechanization in all the colonies came increased specialization in particular skills of production. Women were more and more relegated to the manual and agricultural tasks whereas some men moved into the more highly skilled operations.

Examination of the transitional period immediately following slavery yields some insights into the direction in which female participation in the labor force was likely to develop. In his study of Worthy Park Estate, Craton (1978: 286) notes that discrimination between the sexes was established at the outset, the daily wage being determined by sex and seniority. Female ex-slaves were paid only half as much as men for equivalent tasks (Craton, 1978: 287). In order to appreciate the significance of this fact, earlier-mentioned ones have to be recalled: that at the time of abolition females represented nearly two-thirds of the slaves working on estates in the British colonies and that slave women worked as hard as the men and were punished as severely. Women continued to be 70 percent of the cane-cutting gang, while men moved up to the more skilled and prestigious jobs, which were more highly paid as well. In Worthy Park, one head field woman is recorded as being paid 1 shilling 6 pence per day, whereas head fieldmen were paid 2 shillings. This differentiation in wages might be seen as a change equally as important as the introduction of the wage itself. It concretized differences within the newly emerging agricultural working class. Its effects as far as men and women were concerned must also have been important, for the status of the male as the official breadwinner must have been strengthened by the differential wages and access to skilled positions.

As time went on, the participation of women in estate labor decreased as women continued to be relegated to the most menial and lowest-paid jobs. Planters and managers developed a marked preference for male laborers and justified this ideologically on the basis of the "relative unreliability of female labor." Craton (1978: 286-287) reports that "the most notable change in the composition of the 1842 workforce was the decrease once more in the proportion of women . . . the overall proportion of males rose from just under 40% in 1838 to over 60%, a return to the ratio of the earliest days of slavery." He notes, however, that at least 75 percent of the women continued as irregular workers during the early 1840s. One factor that contributed to the decline in the participation of women in social production was the continued introduction of new "labor-saving" technology, particularly in agricultural production. Around 1841, for example, the plough was introduced in Jamaica. The stipendiary magistrate[4] Bell (quoted in Hall, 1959: 49-50) wrote during this period:

> The constant and improved use of ploughs in this neighbourhood has and will save almost a fourth of the money formerly disbursed for the digging part of operation for canes for instance, opening and preparing 15 acres with the plough £15; digging etc., 15 acres with the hoe £60. This of course keeps money out of labourers' pockets, and accounts, with the dry weather, for the anxiety to get work.

Of course, the laborers referred to were mainly women by this time.

Concurrent with this development, Craton notes, was an increase in the frequency of marriages and stable monogamous unions and in the rate of natural population growth, now up to 50 percent higher than it had been during slavery. This situation, considered in conjunction with the earlier observations on differential wages, gives us some indication of the trends developing in ex-slave society. As far as the planters and the colonial state were concerned, the African ex-slave woman was moving into capitalist wage-labor society. Theoretically her primary economic activity was now to be not the production of commodities for exchange on the world market but the production of the labor force and the reproduction of labor-power, formerly the responsibility of the slave owner. Her position in the labor market was now only secondary to her responsibility in the household as a dependent "house-wife." Her labor was now to be exploited on an irregular basis and at the lowest terms (Augier et al., 1961: 188).

Women were defined as dependent housewives whether they were married or not. The main economic activities of women that emerged, therefore, were those that could be centered around the household (often self-employment) and that were compatible with child rearing: market gardening, petty trading, laundry work, dressmaking, and domestic work. This new sexual division of labor, though evident before emancipation, became more so after. Sidney Mintz (1974: 216-217), for example, reports that there is no evidence that prior to emancipation women were predominant in internal marketing in Jamaica, but this was definitely the case thereafter.

Thus, by attributing lower status to women as workers, planters were able to gain additional profits by paying lower wages to what was still a large proportion of the workforce. At the same time, they ensured that their new labor force and reserve army were continuously available.

Concluding Remarks

My aim in writing this article has not been simply to elucidate an interesting case. Rather, I hope that the lessons and inferences drawn from this study of Caribbean slavery will throw light on the mechanisms of control and oppression used on women internationally today.

Historically, the generative capacity of women has been the material basis for their subordination and oppression. Men, ruling classes, and states have sought to manipulate this capacity to suit their economic and political needs at various periods. This study presents one example, that of a planter class attempting to control the reproductive capacity of slave women in order to further its economic interests. The evidence is that its ability to do so, although great, was limited. Given the material conditions of slave life, women resisted pronatalist policies. Love of motherhood was neither natural nor universal.

My study also shows that changes in the approach to control over reproduction, women's participation in wage labor, and the family can occur within a relatively short time. Today this question is an international one, with many economic, political, and racial connotations. Although population control measures are being introduced among non-European women throughout the world, European women in Europe and elsewhere (e.g., South Africa) are confronting pronatalist policies. In some instances motherhood and the fatherland are being invoked, but in the majority of instances the incentives offered are physical and material—payments at childbirth or on the birth of a third child, one to three years of maternity with pay, attempts to roll back proabortion laws. These measures, like those of the planter class during its pronatalist period, underscore the political and economic importance attached to the female reproductive capacity.

Another issue of importance here is the degree to which oppressed peoples' notions of "good," "bad," "natural," and "unnatural" are determined by the ruling classes' control of the reproduction of ideology. This is seen here in the selective use of various conflicting ideological constructs in relation to marriage, the family, and motherhood as needs and patterns of production changed. On a deeper level, we note that the decisions of slave women regarding childbearing were determined largely by physical and material factors and not merely by ideas. Similarly today, many of the factors that force women to accept a certain course in life are material as well as ideological, even though they may be expressed only in ideological terms. Attempts to change this situation, therefore, cannot be successful at the level of ideological struggle and consciousness-raising alone, but must involve material changes in the organization of the family, the economy, and the society.

In relation to the family, a number of other interesting questions arise from this study of Caribbean slave women. One of major importance today is the relationship of the family to participation of women in wage labor. In relation to this, one has to examine the reasons it was necessary at some point to introduce the nuclear family, which had earlier been discouraged. The family, one might suggest, provided the niche within which the ex-slave woman could become a housewife and mother and into which she could fit when deprived of wage labor. This problem still confronts us today. Women's participation in wage labor is predetermined by their presumed relationship to a family, making them a permanent reserve army and an easily dispensable work force. Despite the fact that women field laborers in the British colonies showed a higher survival rate than the men in estate work and had proved themselves to be as efficient as male workers, they were from the outset paid lower wages than men on the ground of their "relative unreliability." Women's relative weakness has always been used as a justification for their position in the labor market and for the prevailing sexual division of labor. The example of slavery suggests that we should reject this view.

In the Caribbean, the attempt to impose the Western nuclear family on the ex-slave population largely failed. The ideal still prevailed until at least the 1970s, but the material circumstances of the majority of the people prevented this ideal, complete with its male breadwinner, from becoming a reality. Studies of the Caribbean family (e.g., M.G. Smith 1962; R.T. Smith, 1956; Clarke, 1957) have variously viewed it as deviant or as an aspect of Afro-Caribbean culture. On the basis of the analysis presented above, I would suggest that slavery, or at least the system of slavery that developed in the Caribbean, indirectly—by destroying the African family system, removing power and control over individual women from individual men, making men and women relatively equal producers, and removing the work of daily and generational reproduction of labor-power from individual women—caused a 200-year break in the transfer of African patriarchal control to the Caribbean. Attempts in the postslavery period to reinstate it either in a supposedly traditional African form or in a Western nuclear form have never been completely successful.

REFERENCES

Augier, R., S. Gordon, D. Hall, and M. Reckord
  1961   *The Making of the West Indies*. London: Longmans.

Clarke, Edith
  1957   *My Mother Who Fathered Me*. London: Allen and Unwin.

Craton, Michael
  1978   *Searching for the Invisible Man: Slaves and Plantation Life in Jamaica*. Cambridge, MA: Harvard University Press.

Davis, David Brion
  1975   *The Problem of Slavery in the Age of Revolution, 1770-1823*. Ithaca, NY: Cornell University Press.

Deere, Noel
  1950   *A History of Sugar*. Vol. 2. London: Chapman and Hall.

Dunn, R.S.
  1972   *Sugar and Slaves: The Rise of the Planter Class in the English West Indies*. Chapel Hill: University of North Carolina Press.

Genovese, Eugene
  1967   *The Political Economy of Slavery*. New York: Pantheon Books.

Hall, Douglas
  1959   *Free Jamaica*. New Haven: Yale University Press.
  1962   "Slaves and slavery in the British West Indies." *Social and Economic Studies*, 305-318.

Hall, Gwendolyn Midlo
  1971   *Social Control in Slave Plantation Societies*. Baltimore: Johns Hopkins Press.

Knight, Franklin W.
  1970   *Slave Society in Cuba during the Nineteenth Century*. Madison: University of Wisconsin Press.
  1978   *The Caribbean: Genesis of a Fragmented Nationalism*. New York: Oxford University Press.

Mintz, Sidney W.
  1974   *Caribbean Transformations*. Chicago: Aldine.

Moreno Fraginals, Manuel
  1976   *The Sugarmill: The Socioeconomic Complex of Sugar in Cuba, 1769-1860*. New York: Monthly Review Press.

Padgug, Robert A.
  1976-77 "Problems in the theory of slavery and slave society." *Science and Society* 40(1): 3-27.

Patterson, Orlando
  1967   *The Sociology of Slavery*. Rutherford, NJ: Fairleigh Dickenson University Press.

Post, Ken
    1978   *Arise Ye Starvlings: The Jamaica Labour Rebellion of 1938 and Its Aftermath*. The
            Hague: Martinus Nijhoff.

Smith, M.G.
    1962   *West Indian Family Structure*. Seattle: University of Washington Press.

Smith, R.T.
    1956   *The Negro Family in British Guiana*. London: Routledge and Kegan Paul.

Wallerstein, Immanuel
    1979   *The Capitalist World Economy*. Cambridge: Cambridge University Press.

Williams, Eric
    1944   *Capitalism and Slavery*. Chapel Hill: University of North Carolina Press.
    1964   *A History of the People of Trinidad and Tobago*. New York: Praeger.

NOTES

1. I am grateful to Sonia Cuales, Andy Vickerman, and Steve Stern for comments on earlier drafts of this article. I am, however, responsible for any errors caused by my stubborn adherence to certain positions.
2. A female head of a gang (the highest position among field slaves), who directed the work process, using force if necessary.
3. The group of slaves responsible for cutting grass on the plantation.
4. A special magistrate appointed and paid by the British government to enforce the rights of ex-slaves during the apprenticeship period.

9

A Study of Two Women's Slave Narratives:

Incidents in the Life of a Slave Girl and The History of Mary Prince

Andrea Starr Alonzo

$300 REWARD: Ran away . . . an intelligent, bright, mulatto girl, named
Linda, 21 years of age. Five feet four inches . . . Dark eyes, and black hair
inclined to curl . . . She can read and write, and in all probability will try to get
to the free states . . . [from the back cover of *Incidents*]

And she did, although at the time of this notice she was probably still in her
hiding place of seven years, which was no more than a few hundred yards from
her master's plantation. When she finally did engineer her escape, Harriet
Jacobs, under the pseudonym of Linda Brent, went on to write what was to
become the most celebrated slave narrative by a woman.

The slave narrative only recently has begun to receive some recognition
as a literary genre. As Henry Louis Gates points out in the introduction to his
volume, *The Classic Slave Narratives*, no other enslaved class in history has
produced such a voluminous amount of literature attesting to its plight as
human chattel. The narratives, which are the prose rendition of slave songs
and spirituals, mark the birth of the Afro-American literary tradition. Unlike
the songs, whose multiple purposes included anticipation of the afterlife as the
only foreseeable release from burden, the narrative's main objective was to
make known to all who would listen the gripping horror of a slave's earthly
condition. Moreover, the narrator denied the myth of the "contented slave"
and made clear the fact that every slave wished to be free. While the songs
were the voices of those still enslaved, the narratives of former slaves spoke for
those still in bondage who would not otherwise be heard.

Although the vast majority of slave narratives were written by men, several were by women as well. Two examples are those of Mary Prince, a West
Indian slave who has the distinction of being the first woman to publish a slave
narrative (*The History of Mary Prince*, 1831), and the U.S. slave Harriet Jacobs,
who wrote *Incidents in the Life of a Slave Girl* (1861) under the name of Linda
Brent. A skillful writer, Jacobs draws from the slave narrative genre and the
popular sentimental novel to tell her story. The story, of her seven-year hide-
out in her grandmother's tiny attic not far from her master, of the letters she

wrote and had sent to her master from Boston and New York, of her secret passage on a ship carrying her to freedom, and the miraculous reunion with her loved ones, has been reputed to be fiction. Only recently did scholar Jean Fagan Yellin prove to doubters that Jacobs's story is in fact her own.

Black literary scholars generally agree that slave narratives share a basic "formula." Based on the telling and retelling of similar stories, the narrative consists of roughly six stages. The first stage, an account of the narrator's birth, often begins with "I was born . . ." and frequently emphasizes the doubly dehumanizing factors of unknown date and parentage. Harriet Jacobs begins, "I was born a slave; but I never knew it till six years of my happy childhood had passed away" (6). Mary Prince also sticks to the formula: "I was born in Brackish-Pond, in Bermuda, on a farm belonging to Mr. Charles Myners" (187).

The second stage details the writer's life as a slave. Social as well as geographical information is chronicled, such as work details, lengthy examples of the master's treatment of slaves, a description of the writer's dwelling place and where, if known, other family members lived. While the fathers of both Jacobs and Prince lived on neighboring plantations, there were differences in their situations. Until the age of 12, Harriet Jacobs had relatively "kind" masters who taught her to read and write and didn't work her excessively hard. Indeed, she developed quite an affection for them. Mary Prince, on the other hand, had it rough from the beginning. The mistress of her early years wasn't so harsh, but the master was. In their early teens, when their mistresses died, both young women subsequently fell into the hands of crueler masters.

The usual third stage in the narrative focuses on the increasing recognition of the narrator's lowly status as a slave. One's station in life should be obvious from the beginning, perhaps, but a number of factors suggest why this might not be so. As in Jacobs's case, black children were often unaware of their status as slaves since they were frequently permitted to play freely with the children of their masters. Furthermore, if a slave were first owned by master who was not stern and then sold to one who was, her plight became all the more obvious. Another major factor in determining the slave's dissatisfaction with her status is degree of literacy. As hundreds, maybe thousands, of slave narratives will show, there is a marked link between a slave's opportunity to learn to read and the desire to be free. Those who managed even a modicum of education became distinctly more disgusted with their lives as chattel. Not all free blacks were literate of course; Jacobs wrote her own narrative, but Mary Prince related hers to a white editor.

In the fourth stage, then, the narrator resolves to escape and plans accordingly. In many cases, this took patience, years of planning, endurance of conditions sometimes harsher than those of slavery itself, and great imagination to carry out intricate plans. Jacobs, when threatened with the sale of her children for refusing her master's advances, ran away and hid for seven years in her grandmother's garret, an enclosure three feet high, nine feet long, and seven feet wide, before escaping north.

Next, in the fifth stage of the narrative, comes an account of the slave's actual escape. Frequently this account lacks extensive detail due to the narrator's desire to protect her complicitors and not to divulge escape secrets. Jacobs, however, does reveal some facts about her own miraculous escape.

Often while in what she called her prison she could clearly hear her children and grandmother moving about by day, and patrols and slave catchers (who would have been only too happy to capture her) roaming about at night. Eventually, however, a fellow slave and friend secured passage for her on a northbound vessel, claiming this to be her only possible chance. After numerous delays, indecision, and other complications, Jacobs finally sailed north to Philadelphia.

The sixth and last stage features the narrator's life as a free person, the perspective from which she is now writing. However, Mary Prince was not legally free at the time of the writing of her narrative. She had been turned out by her thankless master and mistress and was living in England, which was no longer a slave-holding country; her master and mistress did not believe she could survive there. Had she returned to her loved ones in Bermuda, she would have been remanded to slavery, a situation she was fighting at the time her narrative was written.

Though most slave narratives were published by men, there is a major distinction between male and female accounts of the slave experience. As Jacobs explains it, "slavery is terrible for a man, but it is far more terrible for a woman." Men and women were subjected to back-breaking toil, inadequate accommodations, clothing, and food; verbal abuse, whippings, and all kinds of physical, mental, and emotional brutality. The female slave, however, was further subjected to the humiliation and pain of sexual exploitation. Rape, concubinage, and the wrath of jealous mistresses were only a few of the indignities female slaves suffered just because they were women. Mary Prince told of repeated beatings and floggings: "Both my mistress and my master caused me to know the exact difference between the smart of the rope, the cart-whip, and cow-skin . . . to strip me naked—to hang me up by the wrists and lay my flesh open with the cow skin, was an ordinary punishment for even a slight offense." Yet, of her master's habits of stripping himself naked and commanding her to wash him in the tub, she says, "This was worse than all the licks."

To shun her master's advances, Harriet Jacobs deliberately became pregnant by another white man, a decision for which she obviously suffered tremendous guilt, as this heartfelt apology demonstrates.

> It was something to triumph over my tyrant even in that small way . . . Of a man who was not my master I could ask to have my children well supported . . . I also felt quite sure that they would be made free . . . Pity me, and pardon me, O virtuous reader! I know I did wrong . . . still . . . I feel that the slave woman ought not to be judged by the same standards as others. (56)

Note the double motive of survival as well as revenge.

The women's slave narratives also illustrate the importance of female bonding. A most poignant example of this is Jacobs's relationship with her grandmother and her loving relationship with her mistress, who was also a victim of the master's cruelty. Significantly, sisterhood crosses the color line, even in slavery, when despicable men are involved. Jacobs directly exhorts her female readership (both black and white) to sisterhood with an epigraph from Isaiah 22:9: "Rise up! ye women that are at ease! Hear my voice, ye careless daughters!" This expression of female bonding is strikingly recreated in a modern novel by Sherley Ann Williams, *Dessa Rose*. Dessa, not surprisingly, hates Ruth, the woman with whom she is entrusted, not because Ruth has done her any harm, but because she is white. On one occasion, while the two are guests in the home of a fellow southerner, Dessa wakes in the middle of the night to find their host is attempting to rape Ruth. Dessa finds herself helping fend off the man. She is awe-stricken to discover that white women are subject to the same humiliation as are black, and she softens in her attitude towards Ruth.

Chattel slavery may be over, but the slave narrative tradition has not died. Numerous black authors have drawn from this genre to shape their literature. In addition, a recent surge of black women writers has brought a fresher life to the slave narrative form, as many are writing about women in slavery: Williams, as mentioned above; Toni Morrison, in *Beloved*; and Gloria Naylor, in *Mama Day*. As long as there is Afro-American literature, its seed, the slave narrative, will be alive.

The slave narrative provides invaluable material for a number of classroom environments. Any course on U.S. or African-American literature, or black American history, would benefit from the narratives. The women's slave narratives would also enrich women's studies courses in literature, history, psychology, sociology, and anthropology. I have used excerpts for my own women's literature class, and read several in Afro-American literature.

Through these materials, students not only have an enriching experience with a vital part of America's past, but they also benefit from studying the structure of slave narratives, especially if a student is writing her own autobiography.

WORKS CITED

Brent, Linda. *Incidents in the Life of a Slave Girl*. New York: Harcourt Brace Jovanovich, 1973.

Prince, Mary. "The History of Mary Prince." In *The Classic Slave Narratives*. Ed. Henry Louis Gates. New York: NAL Penguin, 1987, 183-283.

10

Defiance or Submission?

The Role of the Slave Woman in Slave Resistance in the British Caribbean

Barbara Bush

The mechanisms of slave resistance in the New World have recently become a focus of interest for historians.[1] Although no one would now deny the fundamental importance of the theme of resistance to the study of slavery, there are few existing works that explore the specific role played by slave women. The assumptions of earlier historians as to the passive, acquiescent or even treacherous part played by slave women in slave resistance, overlaced with a strong ethnocentric and masculine bias, have left a negative and distorted picture. To redress this imbalance it is necessary to challenge the notion that slave women had a subordinate and ineffective role in slave resistance and emphasize, in contrast, the positive contribution they made in this crucial area of slave life.

The woman slave in history, like women in most cultures, has been the victim of historical invisibility. History has been written for men, by men and thus records only what men wish to see. Academic literature on the British West Indies has made little reference *per se* to the woman slave or has singled her out for special attention as an individual whose experience and reactions to slavery were intrinsically different from those of the male slave. Women have been described as 'more readily and firmly attached to the alien society of the whites' through concubinage,[2] meriting special treatment as slaves and in turn accommodating far more readily to the slave system than men. Thus women's role in slave resistance has been largely ignored in the belief that such physical proximity to white men placed them in a position encompassing 'the contradictory human possibilities of betrayal and devotion'.[3] Existing analyses of the woman's role in slave resistance have thus been obscured by over-emphasis on her sexual functions and the highly biased interpretations of these functions.

Recently, new works on the slave society have challenged some of the more prominent adverse racial and sexual myths about the slave woman, particularly in terms of her role in the slave family.[4] More emphasis has been placed on the strong influence of African cultural traditions described aptly by Walter Rodney as 'the shield which frustrated the efforts of the Europeans to dehumanise Africans through servitude'.[5] In the view of some authors, this traditional culture constituted a vital factor in resistance to white cultural impositions and acted as a fundamental catalyst in organized rebellions.[6] If traditional culture and slave resistance were interlinked thus, women as the foremost bearers of this culture would have made a crucial contribution to the slaves' struggle against white hegemony. It may be argued, then, that this important cultural role of slave women, strengthened by the relative equality of the sexes on West Indian slave plantations, ensured that the woman 'shared every inch of the man's physical and spiritual odyssey' in slave resistance, as in other areas of slave life.[7]

A reassessment of the slave women's role in slave resistance is fundamental to any more comprehensive study of their lives as slaves. From ship board insurrections to maronage and the African-led rebellions of the middle years, through the later Creole-led revolts, women had their part to play. From the early days of slavery, planters lived in fear of slave revolt and complained of the general everyday insubordination of slaves. Men and women alike were 'troublesome property' and thus slave control relied heavily on the operation of a harsh legal code and physical punishment. This paper, therefore, traces the responses of women to slavery within this framework of resistance and repression. The first section discusses everyday acts of non-cooperation—'day-to-day' resistance; the second section looks at the woman's role in organized slave uprising; and the final section explores the relationship between slave religion and slave resistance. The unifying thread is the African cultural heritage of the slave woman, the defence of which brought women frequently into conflict with the laws and values of the dominant white minority.

'Day-to-Day' Resistance[8]

Early works on slavery perpetuated and consolidated adverse contemporary images of blacks and portrayed the slave as a passive sambo/quashee figure possessing ascribed, inferior racial traits.[9] Such inferior traits are now more commonly viewed as evidence of non-cooperation and a refusal to accept the white man's code of morality, as subtle forms of everyday resistance to the harsh conditions under which slaves lived and labored.[10]

Slaves, both male and female, exasperated their masters in countless ways—shirking work, damaging crops, dissembling, feigning illness. Unlike outright revolt, these unspectacular routine acts of non-cooperation did not generally involve violence or the threat of violence against whites and have thus been termed 'passive' as opposed to 'active' forms of resistance.[11] Occasionally, individual acts of violence on the part of slaves did occur in the form of spontaneous reactions to overwork or severe punishment, willful poisoning, arson and, occasionally, murder, but it was the commonplace 'natural insubordination' of the slaves which daily chipped away at the whole fabric of the slave system.

In their formal definitions as slaves and as economic units, women were more or less equal to men and, likewise, far from becoming docile and submissive, frequently registered strong contempt for their white masters. Resistance to enslavement began from the moment of capture but intensified with the horrors of the middle passage. On board the slave ships, suicide, the ultimate rejection of an insupportable existence, was common for men and women alike. Slaves died not only from disease but also 'fixed melancholy', refusal to eat and drink or non-accidental drowning.[12] Such suicides were not simply evidence of apathy and despair but, according to West African religious belief, a positive means of attaining freedom.[13]

Although women were regarded by slave traders as less dangerous than men and hence were given more spacious quarters and kept in irons only if rebellious,[14] evidence suggests that they nonetheless resented their confinement. Women on board ship were reputedly 'sulky' and often had to be forced by 'threats and blows' to eat. Women when made to 'dance' upon the deck were observed to maintain their dignity and 'kept themselves aloof' showing 'an indignation which long-continued habit could not suppress when forced to behave childishly'. Sometimes if they refused to dance they were flogged.[15] Thus women reacted to the extremity of the middle passage, the misery, the overcrowding and total disorientation either by struggling to maintain their morale and dignity, or as Alexander Falconbridge noted, becoming 'raving mad', many of them 'dying in such a state'.[16]

After the initial disorientation of the 'salt water' period when mortality rates from illness and suicide were high, women showed little signs of resignation to their situation. Once established in their monotonous work roles on the plantation they often proved difficult and awkward to manage. Matthew 'Monk' Lewis, who was frequently castigated by his fellow planters for over-indulging his slaves,[17] made a number of references in his journal to the intransigence of his female slaves. One domestic servant failed to open the *jalousies* (outside shutters) despite being instructed repeatedly to do so. Other women refused to carry out their set tasks. One morning the women 'one and all' refused 'without the slightest pretence' to carry the trash away from the mill, one of the 'easiest tasks' set. As a result the mill had to be stopped. When the driver insisted on the women doing their duty '. . . a fierce devil of a Miss Whaunica flew at his throat and endeavoured to strangle him . . .' Having tried every way to satisfy his negroes and 'render them happy and secure', Lewis was forced to acknowledge the insubordinate nature of women slaves when the only individuals he found it necessary to punish were 'two female demons' for their aggressive and uncooperative behavior.[18]

Lewis was not the only planter to complain about difficult females. Accounts from varied sources relate how women shirked work, verbally abused overseers, feigned illness, stole and lied. Women were even accused of infecting their children with yaws (a common disease among slaves), 'that they might be released for a time from labour' and were thus viewed as instrumental in perpetuating this disease.[19]

An invaluable source of information about ordinary women field workers and their reactions to servitude are plantation journals and punishment lists. Those consulted here date from the early 1820s up to Emancipation and relate to the West Indian estates of Thomas and William King, merchants of London.[20] The Kings owned plantations in Grenada, British Guiana and Dominica and as absentee landlords, left the routine management of their estates to attorney/managers, who were required to keep meticulous records for the benefit of their employers. In plantation journals, managers had to enter all punishments meted out to individual slaves, the reasons why they were carried out, the names of the individuals who administered and witnessed them and the place and date. One particularly relevant column in these record books specified 'the nature and extent of punishment if female'. It indicates that while male offenders received an average 15 to 20 'stripes', the common punishment for female offenders was a varying period of time in the stocks or, alternatively, solitary confinement. This may reflect compliance with the ameliorative legislation passed throughout the Caribbean in the 1820s which banned or restricted the whipping of female slaves.[21]

Data from the records kept on the Kings' various plantations confirm the deep level of everyday resistance to slavery sustained by women slaves and show that, overall, during the late period of slavery they were frequently accused of insolence, 'shamming sick,' 'excessive laziness', 'disorderly conduct', 'disobedience' and 'quarrelling'. But perhaps the outstanding value of such records is the wealth of detailed information they yield about the defiant behavior of individual women. For instance, the Punishment Record Book of Plantation Friendship (Guiana), 1827, reveals that Katherine was punished on 11 and 30 November for insolence to the overseer and quarrelling in the field respectively; Henrietta was punished on 27 December for 'continually omitting to comply with her task' and had to spend a day and a night in the stocks.[22]

On the Kings' Success Plantation in Guiana, where out of 211 slaves, 93 were female, there appear to have been a number of consistently troublesome women. From January to June 1830, for example, Quasheba was punished repeatedly for 'refusing to go to work when ordered by the doctor' and on 4 May Caroline was punished for 'abusing the manager and overseer and defying the former to do his worst'. During the same period, one woman, Clarissa, is mentioned three times in connection with poor work and malingering. On the first instance, she was punished together with another slave, Lavinia, for 'leaving work unfinished and assigning no cause for so doing'. In the second instance she refused to do any work 'for having a seration [*sic*] on her finger' even when ordered so by the doctor and also used 'abusive language' to the manager. Finally, she was again punished for 'leaving three fourths of her day's work unfinished'. In Clarissa's case particularly, although her punishments increased in severity from 12 hours in solitary confinement to 60 hours in the stocks, her resistance to work remained undiminished.[23]

In all the above-mentioned incidents, punishment excluded the whip but there is some evidence that despite legislation and abolitionist pressure to ban its use on females, it was still employed on certain plantations. Under 'general observations' for 1823, for instance, John Wells, the attorney/manager of Baillies Bacolet Plantation in Grenada, noted that 'Eliza received 20 stripes for violent behaviour in the field . . . and for excessive insolence to myself when reprimanding her in the presence of the gang'. As late as 1833, women were still liable to be whipped on the same plantation. The Record of Punishment for that year notes that on 19 February Germaine was given 15 'stripes' for 'wilfully destroying canes in the field and general neglect of duty'.[24]

Official records may have conveniently 'overlooked' harsher punishments inflicted on women although this cannot be substantiated. Certainly, the temptation to use the whip must have been there, for the complaints of planters about the unruly behavior of slave women is amply supported by evidence from the Kings' estates. Women, if anything, were more trouble than men. The Punishment Record Book of Sarah Essequibo, for instance, shows that in the six-month period from January to June 1827, 34 slaves (out of a total of 171 from the plantation as a whole) were punished, of whom 21 were women. The women, moreover, tended to be more persistent offenders than the men and several of them were punished three times and one woman four times during the said period.[25]

As the threat of punishment proved little or no deterrent to these defiant slave women, perhaps the planters were right in their defense of the whip as the only viable means of keeping females in order and forcing them to work. But there is no guarantee that the whip would have had any greater effect on breaking this spirited resistance than other more common and allegedly more humane forms of punishment. In lieu of the whip women still had to suffer the humiliation and discomfort of the 'hand and foot' stocks or solitary confinement, sometimes with the additional degradation of wearing a collar. If the whip was short and sharp, alternative punishments lasted anywhere from a few hours up to three days, and in very serious cases a longer period was recommended.

Whip or no whip, a significant proportion of women slaves continued to risk the wrath of their white masters, most commonly by refusing to work, or engaging in verbal abuse and insolence. Sometimes individual women were accused of the more serious crime of 'exciting discontent in the gang'; others were punished for leaving the estate without permission, some of them for long periods. This rebellious behavior testifies to a refusal on the part of the ordinary field hands to accept the harsh conditions of their servitude but domestic servants who, in theory at least, led an easier and more privileged life, seldom proved contented and obedient slaves either. They, too, refused to acquiesce gracefully to white authority, though the methods they used to frustrate their masters and mistresses may have been more subtle and devious.

Despite the threat of relegation to field work, domestic servants[26] in the West Indies, the majority of whom were women,[27] were frequently troublesome, especially to planters' wives who were in constant contact with them. Mrs. Carmichael, the wife of a Trinidadian planter, was, for instance, sorely tired by the grumblings, lies and deceitful behavior of female domestics. Of all her 'troublesome establishment' she felt the washerwomen to be 'the most discontented, unmanageable and idle'.[28] Her comments may reflect a certain intra-sexual antagonism but they are staunchly supported by other West Indian commentators who cited domestic slaves as 'particularly difficult'. Edward Long believed the 'propensity to laziness' among slaves was chiefly conspicuous among house servants, while 'Monk' Lewis complained of their inefficiency and noted that attempts to correct faults were 'quite fruitless'. According to John Stewart, domestics, although 'in general' well treated, were continually disobedient and would 'seldom do their duty' except under duress. He added that because these domestics were so 'refractory, vicious and indolent', the white woman, in managing her household, was 'a greater slave than any of them'.[29]

Of all slaves, domestic servants probably exhibited the greatest degree of duality of behavior. Because of their close proximity to whites, they outwardly conformed and adopted European values to a greater degree than the more autonomous field slaves, but, covertly, they rejected such values and the system they were allied to. Peter J. Wilson observed a similar duality in modern Caribbean society. He outlined a marked dichotomy between what he terms 'reputation' and 'respectability'. Reputation (Afro-Caribbean value-orientated) often undermined respectability (European value-orientated) and can thus be viewed as a form of resistance to European domination.[30] Wilson's analysis is valid for slave society, particularly in terms of 'day-to-day' non-cooperation and subtle forms of resistance to cultural brain-washing on the part of individual slaves. It is particularly applicable to female domestics, who were in a constantly ambiguous position *vis-à-vis* whites, a factor complicated by contemporary attitudes to inter-racial sexual behavior. The nature of the unenviable position of such women is reflected in contemporary references to the cruel punishments many of them were subjected to.[31]

On West Indian slave plantations, women, domestic or field workers, thus used many ploys to frustrate their masters and avoid work. Their ingenuity would appear to be boundless. For instance, one particular woman on a Trinidadian plantation miraculously exhibited a different colored tongue each time she visited the plantation doctor. The doctor became suspicious, the tongue was wiped clean with a damp cloth and revealed to be 'completely clean and healthy'. In consequence the woman was flogged, the standard punishment for 'shamming and idling'.[32] Occasionally women even went as far as to mutilate themselves in order to avoid work.[33]

Individual women sometimes committed acts which carried a high risk of severe punishment or even death by execution. One such example is provided by 'Monk' Lewis. On a visit to a Slave Court he witnessed the trial of a black servant girl accused of attempting to poison her master. Lewis was appalled by her 'hardened conduct' throughout the trial and observed that when found guilty she heard the sentence pronounced 'without the least emotion' and 'was seen to laugh' as she was escorted down the courthouse steps.[34] Such lack of repentance, like ingratitude, was anathema to the planters for it underscored the fact that no individual could ever be completely controlled by another human being. But penalties for such 'delinquency' and 'lack of respect' were harsh. To laugh in the face of white laws, a blatant expression of free-will, demanded much courage and resolution.

Other forms of more subtle resistance existed, however, which did not actually jeopardize the slave's life. Mrs. Carmichael described the consistently difficult behavior of one particular female slave on her husband's estate. She was a domestic servant, who 'although a clever and superior person' was 'next to impossible to manage'. Relegated to field work for insubordination, she one day made such a commotion that she was placed in the stocks. When this failed to subdue her rage, the driver was obliged to admit that she would never work for him 'or any other Massa'. But despite her intransigent attitude to her official role as a slave, in her private domestic life she was energetic and positive, owning extensive provision grounds kept 'in beautiful order' and running 'a complete huckster's shop' on the estate.[35]

Such behavior is a good example of the dual response of slaves to their situation, negative in their 'official' role but positive in terms of their 'unofficial' role within the slave community itself, where African-orientated norms and values dominated. In terms of this 'unofficial' role, slave women were of vital importance, for instance, to the internal marketing system of Caribbean slave islands, in both the cultivation of provision grounds and the marketing of goods. Through these activities, they were able to assert their individuality and independence within the slave context, but also to contribute positively to the development of Creole society as a whole. The internal marketing activities and other small 'business' enterprises of women slaves represented a valuable contribution to the creation, in the midst of hardship and oppression, of a positive 'underlife' for the slave family and community.[36]

Everyday resistance to slavery was thus an important facet of the slave woman's life. In her official work role, particularly, this resistance was counteracted by punishment. In the West Indies, field gangs, the 'backbone' of the slave labor force, were predominantly female.[37] Labor was extracted only through coercion, often in the form of physical punishment. Given the contemporary belief that 'the indolent only and the ill-disposed encounter punishments',[38] women must have been frequent victims of the overseer's whip, under which 'neither age nor sex found any favour'.[39] Women may even have resisted punishment itself. Although references to this are rare in Caribbean literature, accounts from the antebellum South, where conditions were arguably less harsh, make numerous references to slave women resisting floggings.[40]

As plantation records cited above indicate, in terms of everyday resistance, women were arguably more troublesome individually than men. Mrs. Carmichael believed this to be the case,[41] as did the Trinidadian planters who resented the law of 1823 which banned the whipping of female slaves. Women, the planters declared, were 'notoriously insolent' and only kept in 'tolerable order' through fear of punishment. According to one colonial official in Trinidad, female slaves 'more frequently merited punishment than males'.[42] Thus women slaves, despite the 'peculiar burdens' of their sex, proved far from acquiescent and submissive and showed their resentment towards their masters in many different ways during their day-to-day existence. 'Quasheba'[43] was as much a creation of white ethnocentricism as a 'Quashee'.

Traitor or Amazon? The Woman's Role in Slave Uprisings

The specific contribution made by women slaves to slave uprisings is a contentious area of study. From contemporary evidence, it cannot be disputed that the leaders of slave revolts were generally men. For instance, after a slave conspiracy was exposed in Antigua in 1736, out of 47 slaves only one woman was executed.[44] Absence of the names of female slaves from contemporary records of slave uprisings does not constitute proof that they played no active part, but such 'historical invisibility' presents grave difficulties in determining their actual role. A further complicating factor is that in the rare contemporary references to slave women in the context of slave plots, they are frequently indicted as traitors to the slave cause. The conspiracy in Antigua for instance, was allegedly disclosed to the authorities by a female slave, as was a slave plot in Montserrat in 1768. The Report of the 1816 Barbados uprising also refers to this informant role of slave women.[45]

It may be argued that the close proximity of slave women to whites, through concubinage, directed women towards betrayal rather than active support of the conspiracies of fellow slaves. But certain important points can be made which qualify such over-generalization of the 'traitor' role of women slaves. For instance, there is little strong evidence which suggests that women were any more likely to betray fellow slaves than were male slaves. Any assumptions to the contrary may merely reflect personal prejudices about women on the part of contemporary observers. Furthermore, if on occasion women did disclose information to whites, this information may have been extracted only under duress. The 1736 Antiguan conspiracy was allegedly discovered as a result of 'voluntary information' given by one Phillida who was 'taken up on suspicion of some virulent Expressions, used upon her Brother's Account', and subsequently revealed the existence of 'secret Saturday night meetings'. The anonymous author later revealed that torture was used to extract information from slaves, which may explain why a woman who was apparently committed to the conspiracy suddenly turned traitor.[46] Women may have been singled out for such torture because of their assumed vulnerability and lack of physical endurance. A more balanced and realistic appraisal of the woman's role in slave uprisings needs to move away from the previous evaluations, which often involve negative ethnocentric judgments, and introduce new dimensions to the analysis, in particular the influence of African cultural factors.

The spirit of revolt among slaves did not develop sporadically but was part of a continuum of resistance which linked Africa to the New World.[47] In the context of traditional West African society, it was not unknown for women to have engaged in armed confrontation. Equiano, reminiscing upon his West African childhood, mentioned that the women of his tribe (the Ibo) were also warriors and 'march boldly out to fight along with the men'. Similarly, women of the Ibibio tribe were noted for their fearlessness. John Adams recorded that, among the Ibibios of the early nineteenth century, women were 'equally mischievous and ferocious' as men.[48] Later Victorian works also mentioned the martial role of women from some West African societies, particularly Dahomey and Southern Nigeria;[49] in more recent times, the ability of West African women to engage in physical confrontation was manifested during the Aba riots or 'Women's War' of 1929 in Nigeria, when a number of Ibo women were killed protesting against a tax imposed upon them by the British Government.[50]

Women in certain areas of West Africa have a tradition of participation in communal resistance against outside aggression. Far from being passive in community affairs, moreover, they frequently take a significant part in decision-making processes. Traditional women's political organizations are as prominent as men's and consulted by men on important issues. In some tribes, such as the Ashanti of Ghana and Mende of Sierra Leone, individual women wield great influence and, in the latter tribe, are eligible to become village headmen and chiefs.[51] In this cultural context women shipped to the West Indies would have been equipped to take an active role in communal acts of slave resistance. Thus the woman's role in slave uprisings must be determined from three broad perspectives: her African cultural background, her experience as a slave and the actual dynamics of organized slave resistance.

Slave revolts in the British West Indies can be broadly categorized on a typological and chronological basis into maronage, the African-led revolts of the middle period and the creole-led revolts of the last years of slavery. The aims and nature of slave rebellions changed as slave society developed. Within the dialectic of conflict, the specific role of slave women also altered as slave society developed and matured.

During the early period of slavery, slave resistance often took the form of the establishment, in the mountains or other inaccessible areas, of maroon settlements, by slaves who had fled the plantations. From these runaway communities guerrilla warfare was waged against the whites.[52] Source material relating to the specific role of slave women in maroon activities is scarce but the story of the legendary Jamaican windward maroon, Nanny, offers some insight into one possible function certain women may have had. Nanny was an Obeah woman after whom two maroon settlements were named. One contemporary observer, Phillip Thicknesse (who accused her of sentencing a white emissary to death), described this formidable woman in the following way:

> The Old Hagg . . . had a girdle round her waist, with (I speak within compass) nine or ten different knives hanging in sheaths to it, many of which I doubt not had been plunged into human flesh and blood. . . .[53]

Allowing for Thicknesse's obvious bias,[54] the little contemporary evidence which exists suggests that she undoubtedly held considerable political influence, if she did not actually displace the headman. She was reputed to have slain English soldiers in battle and her supernatural feats are still discussed by windward maroons.[55]

The attitude of British Colonial authorities towards Nanny can perhaps shed some light onto why so little documentation exists which refers to the active participation of women in slave rebellions. The British refused to accept spiritual leaders such as Nanny and recognized only the authority of the head-man, expecting the latter to perform duties that in the past fell to her.[56] Hence, the influence and power certain black women held over slaves may have been ignored or overlooked by European men conditioned to believing in the total political and social subjugation of their own women.

On a more mundane and widespread level, maroon women in general may have played an important part in promoting and maintaining the spirit of resistance. Thicknesse observed how maroon mothers were 'responsible for transmitting to their "pecananes" an animosity towards whites'. The children he came in contact with poked fingers against his chest and shouted 'becara—becara' (white man) in derision. Their mothers, he alleged, openly flaunted such animosity, wearing the teeth of slain soldiers as ankle and wrist bracelets. Writing at a much later date, Robert Dallas also mentioned the contempt maroon women in the British Caribbean had towards whites.[57] Evidence for women actually taking up arms is scant. But women did actively fight alongside men in French and Dutch Guiana,[58] and it is unlikely that the situation was any different in the British West Indies. If caught as rebels, women were brutally punished. In Surinam in 1728, a large group of 'fugitive negroes' known as the 'Seramica rebels' took refuge in the woods and for two years pillaged estates 'with lances and firelocks'. According to John Stedman, of eleven 'unhappy negro captives' executed in 1730 for their participation in this unrest, eight were female. Six women were broken alive on the rack and two young girls were decapitated. Stedman averred that 'such was their resolution' under these tortures that they submitted to them 'without uttering a sign'.[59]

Women also stoically endured the hardships and insecurity which characterized maroon life. For instance, after a crushing attack by the whites in 1735, the windward maroons of Jamaica retreated from their main base, Nanny Town, and split into two parties. According to Robert Dallas, one of these groups—about three hundred strong, including many women and children—marched a hundred miles over densely wooded and precipitous mountains to join Cudjoe's Leeward band. The colonial authorities found out about the march and sent parties to 'disperse and destroy' the group but the marchers 'fought and forced their way on' and succeeded in their objective.[60] Moreover it was women who ensured the physical survival of maroon communities for it was they who were chiefly responsible for the cultivation of provision grounds, in keeping with the traditional economic role of African women.[61] Without women, and their vital contribution to stability and cultural cohesion, maroon communities would have been little more than impermanent groups of runaways.

As in maroon uprisings, the role of women in the African-led slave revolts of the eighteenth century[62] was markedly influenced by West African cultural traditions, with two important qualifications. Firstly, maroon women were free and therefore able more easily to readopt their traditional roles than were slave women. Secondly, whereas maroons were generally successful in their struggles against whites, the African-led slave rebellions had an aura of 'heroic impossibility' and little chance of success. Thus, in contrast to the role of women in the struggles of the maroons, women's participation in contemporaneous slave revolts was influenced by their slave status on the plantation.

The African-led revolts of the middle period of slavery undoubtedly drew inspiration from the maroon uprisings and if the maroons had legendary women leaders such as Nanny, a spiritual if not actual military head, slave rebellions likewise produced women whose personal contribution to specific uprisings was noted for posterity. Edward Long, for instance, in his account of the serious rebellion in Jamaica in 1760 relates a curious anecdote about a slave woman named Cubah which hints at her possible function in the unrest. During the rebellion, a wooden sword 'of a peculiar nature', purportedly used among 'Coromantins' as a signal for war, was found in Kingston. It was subsequently revealed that the Coromantins had raised Cubah to the rank of royalty and dubbed her 'Queen of Kingston'. At their meetings she 'sat in state under a canopy, with a sort of robe on her shoulders and a crown on her head'.[63]

Long viewed Cubah as a frivolous carnival character, not to be taken seriously. She may have been only a symbolic figurehead but her position did not lack traditional significance. In the account of the 1736 Antigua conspiracy, for instance, the leader is described as a "Coromantee' slave named Court. He was said to have worn 'a good sabre' by his side with a red 'scabbard' and a 'peculiar cap' made of green silk. According to the anonymous author, Court was dressed in keeping with 'Coromantee rites' performed when a king was resolved upon war and, like Cubah (who was dressed in a similar fashion), conducted his affairs 'under an umbrella or canopy of state'.[64] Rattray recorded the use of a similar ceremonial apparel at the courts of the Ashanti (Coromantee) kings in the 1920s.[65] Given the matrilineal structure of Ashanti society and the high degree of equality between men and women in affairs of state, exemplified by the high status of the Queen Mother,[66] it is arguable that Cubah was not merely a colorful, carnival-style figurehead, but effectively one of the true leaders of the 1760 rebellion.

Although it is difficult to determine the true nature of Cubah's role in the 1760 Jamaican Rebellion, given the paucity of the available evidence, her personal commitment to the uprising is hard to dispute if Long's testimony is accepted. 'When her majesty was seized and ordered for transportation, . . .' he recorded, 'she prevailed upon the Captain of the transport to put her ashore again on the Leeward part of the island' and continued her subversive activities for some time until she was eventually recaptured and executed.[67]

Allusions to similar participation of individual women in rebellions are unfortunately very rare. But this 'invisibility' of slave women does not necessarily imply inactivity. On the contrary, accounts of various rebellions indicate that women did join in uprisings and maintained a strong loyalty to the slave cause.

During the Antiguan slave revolt of 1736, for instance, it was reported that '. . . a number of slave women . . . were willing to fight in the revolt' and a certain councillor Vallentine Morris allegedly claimed that the slave women 'by their insolent Behaviour and Expressions had the utter Extirpation of the white as much at heart, as the Men, and would undoubtedly have done much Mischief by Butchering all the women and children'.[68]

In the later 1760 rebellion, it was recorded that slaves of all sexes and ages joined the rebels. From William Beckford's Esher Estate, one of the early flash-points of unrest, the rebellion quickly spread to other plantations until the 'whole party, including women' had increased to about 400.[69] According to Monica Schuler, the general records relating to armed revolt among the slaves in the eighteenth century indicate a similar broad spectrum of participants— male, female, young and old, plantation slave and urban slave. The common denominator was that they were all, in the main, Africa-born.[70]

By the end of the eighteenth century, the character of slave rebellions began to change subtly in response to the increasing creolization of slave society and the spread of Christianity and literacy. The influence of abolitionism and the example of the French Revolution became increasingly in evidence in slave unrest. As the nature of organized slave resistance changed, so too did the specific role of slave women.

Literature from the period refers frequently to the verbal and physical aggressiveness of women slaves in connection with conspiracies and uprisings. For instance, a negro plot was discovered in the vicinity of Monk Lewis's estate; before the imprisoned offenders were executed, the overseer of a property adjacent to Lewis's had occasion to find fault with a female fieldhand. In response to his criticism, 'she flew at him with the greatest flury', grasped him by the throat and suggested to her fellow slaves that they should murder him there and then. The suddenness of this attack 'nearly accomplished her purpose' before other slaves came to the overseer's assistance. The woman was executed.[71]

As the egalitarian political ideals of the French revolutionaries diffused throughout the Caribbean, the example of Saint Domingue (Haiti) became highly significant to the slaves. In Trinidad these dangerous influences were exceptionally pervasive and greatly perturbed the planters, many of whom had fled from the French islands with their slaves. Vidia Naipaul cites a reference to one such planter who was disturbed while bathing in a stream on his plantation by twelve black women walking along a nearby path. Shaking *chac-chac* pods they sang a patois song as they danced along. 'Vin, c'est sang beque', they chanted, 'Nous va boire sang beque'. The chorus was 'San Domingo'.[72]

Verbal incitation to revolt appears to have been a particular forte of women slaves during the latter decades of slavery. A striking example of this is the involvement of a certain woman slave named Nanny Grigg in the insurrection in Barbados in 1816. According to the confessions of Robert, a slave from one of the implicated plantations, this dangerous woman had informed the blacks that she had read in the newspapers that all the Negroes would be freed on New Year's Day; she was 'always talking about it' and told the slaves they were all 'damned fools' to work. When the blacks had not been freed by New Year, she declared that the only way they could achieve freedom was to fight for it by setting fires 'the way they did in Saint Domingo'.[73]

In many ways, late slave uprisings could be termed prototype peasant revolts and slave women accordingly adopted a role similar to women involved in such struggles. Hence they were verbally aggressive, acted as go-betweens, participated in a number of subversive activities and were prepared to join in physical confrontation with white authority. Described often as 'turbulent and rebellious' they were not infrequently put on trial for 'sedition and mutiny'.[74]

Contemporary accounts of the 1831 Rebellion in Jamaica illustrate this point. Bernard Senior, who wrote a biased but informative account of the rebellion, accused women he encountered on his sorties with the Militia of 'concealing information'. One such woman allegedly led Senior's party straight into a rebel ambush. Another woman they apprehended had been sent as a guide with a rebel foraging party as she was well acquainted with provision grounds in the area.[75]

Senior's observations suggest that during the late period of slavery women were particularly prominent as guides, spies and messengers, aided perhaps by the unusual physical mobility they were afforded to carry out marketing activities and the cultivation of provision grounds.[76] As was the case during earlier slave uprisings, women charged with 'discontent and mutiny' risked cruel physical punishments.[77] Though it is not within the scope of this article, research into the punishment lists pertaining to rebel slaves may yield valuable information as to the nature of the participation of women slaves in slave uprisings in general. Conversely, as such lists were drawn up by whites, they may reflect the double-standard of European men (applied to Nanny, the maroon leader, at the end of the First Maroon War) which would detract from their value as source material.

'Obeah', Slave Religion and Resistance to Slavery: The Slave Woman's Contribution

In the area of slave resistance it has been stressed that cultural traditions inherited from Africa were of major significance. Some of the strongest African survivals were embodied in slave religion, which played an important part in organized slave revolts and constituted 'a determined resistance to the pressures of despair and dehumanisation' on the part of the slaves.[78] In this area of predominantly cultural resistance, black women in the Caribbean were highly active, particularly in the traditional African-based religions such as obeah and myalism. This was in keeping with the prominent positions women, particularly older women, held as priests in some contemporary West African societies.[79]

The single term 'obeah' was used by contemporary observers to describe the 'pagan' rites of slaves and it is therefore important to distinguish between obeah (worked by individual priests using magic and fetish) and myalism (group worship, often used as an 'antidote' to the more harmful aspects of obeah). There was a strong association between slaves of Ashanti origin, myalism and slave revolts[80] and the 'Obeah man or woman' was regarded by whites as a 'very wicked and dangerous' person on the plantation who wielded a great influence over the slaves.[81] Bryan Edwards noted that in the 1760 revolt in Jamaica, 'the influence of the professors of the Obeah Art' induced 'a great many' of the slaves to rebellion. Edward Long made a similar observation.[82]

As Monica Schuler has pointed out, traditional African religious practice, myalism particularly, lent itself quite well to organized rebellion, acting as a unifying element and providing an acceptable excuse for the gathering of slaves.[83] John Stedman described in vivid detail one such gathering of women spiritual leaders. 'The slaves,' he wrote:

> . . . also have amongst them a kind of Sybils, who deal in oracles; these sage matrons dancing and whirling round in the middle of an assembly with amazing rapidity until they foam at the mouth and drop down convulsed. Whatever the prophetess orders to be done during this paroxysm is most sacredly performed by the surrounding multitude which renders these meetings extremely dangerous, as she frequently enjoins them to murder their masters or desert to the woods . . .[84]

Such subversive activities were probably most marked in the African-led revolts of the eighteenth century. During this period the 'Obeah' man or woman may have been less of a magician and more of a priest.[85] Their 'priestly' activities, blanket-termed 'obeah' and condemned as pagan 'fanaticism' by the whites, were forbidden by law and severely sanctioned. All legal codes in the Caribbean incorporated clauses aimed at suppressing 'the many mischiefs that may . . . arise from the wicked art of obeah men and women' and slaves who attempted to use supernatural powers 'to promote the purpose of rebellion' were to be punished by death, transportation, 'or other such punishment'.[86] The use of poison 'during the practice of Obeah or otherwise' was also legislated against,[87] a reflection of the planters' almost paranoid fear of such 'sinister' and 'irrational' practices which in their estimation were implicated in many cases of willful poisoning of black and white alike. For instance, planters blamed the sudden loss of large numbers of slaves on 'the abominable belief in obeah'. Women, particularly domestic servants and plantation 'nurses' (female slaves who tended the sick), were frequently implicated in such 'mass poisonings' which were usually seen as part of wider 'negro conspiracies'.[88]

Allowing for a degree of irrational suspicion on the part of a white minority in an overwhelmingly African-orientated society apparently dominated by witchcraft, actual poisoning incidents may not have been uncommon.

The blacks in the West Indies had an extensive knowledge of indigenous poisonous plants some which killed very quickly but 'may be so order'd as not to kill a person in many Days, Months or Years' and which produced symptoms in victims 'very similar' in their effect to 'the influence of . . . malign diseases such as plague, cholera and yellow fever. . . .'[89] Female domestics were often accused of administering such poisons to white victims, as they were easily able to conceal them in food and drink.[90]

The practice of 'obeah' was clearly associated with willful poisoning in the eyes of the local whites, 'ever since the colonist became acquainted with [negroes].'[91] Obeah was implicated wherever inexplicable deaths occurred, even if poison was not actually cited. One Jamaican planter reporting to the Select Committee on the Slave Trade of 1789 recalled that a dying negro on his plantation had confessed that her stepmother 'a woman of the Popo country (Dahomey), above eighty years old but still hale and hearty' had 'put Obi on her' as she had done to others who had recently died. The old woman had, reputedly, practiced 'obi' for 'as 'many years' as the dying woman could remember.[92]

Despite their laws and 'instruments of torture' planters were unable to control such acts. No threat of punishment could suppress the highly influential and subversive religious practices of the slaves. Contemporary observers were agreed that from the earliest days of slavery to Emancipation, slaves were 'addicted to witchcraft' and in great awe of their 'necromancers and conjurors of both sexes' who were 'artful' and had a 'great ascendency' over other negroes.[93] 'Obeah' constituted a major area of resistance to imposed cultural values and often acted as an essential catalyst in slave uprisings. In the early and middle period of slavery 'Obeah' practitioners openly defied slave laws and set an example of insubordination to fellow slaves. Thus, because of their position of power and authority within the slave community, individuals, such as Nanny, the maroon Obeah woman, made ideal rebel leaders.

But if it was the older women who tended to become prominent individuals in the vanguard of slave resistance, women slaves of all ages were also reported to have been 'well acquainted with all the customs and mythology of their native country' and generally more suspicious than male slaves of Christianity.[94] This was particularly noticeable in the later period of slavery when missionary activity was more widespread. Christian conversion was most popular among elite slaves, the vast majority of whom were men. Ordinary slave women had little to gain from Christian religion with its Pauline doctrines of female inferiority and subordination which contrasted sharply with the relative egalitarianism of West African religions.

During this period, women appear to have been particularly suspicious of Christian baptism and burial, on the part of both themselves and their children.[95] There is some evidence which indicates women were reluctant to enter into Christian marriage for fear that it would reduce their independence of action and render them inferior to their husbands, giving the latter licence 'to beat and ill-treat them'.[96] In this resistance to Christianity, creole slaves were no less stubborn than African-born women.[97] One such creole woman slave on Lewis's estate, for instance, adamantly refused to be christened 'having imbibed strong African prejudices from her mother'. In Lewis's opinion this was 'a common attitude' among women slaves.[98]

Until the last two decades of slavery, West Indian slaves adhered primarily to traditional African-derived religions and remained largely ignorant of Christianity, despite the creolization process. Even after exposure to Christian beliefs, many black men and women remained 'involuntary proselytes' and clung to their old beliefs.[99] Christian indoctrination of slaves was intimately linked with the control of the black community as it stressed submissiveness, obedience and the acceptance of the status quo.[100] Thus, the retention of a high degree of African content in slave religion represented an important aspect of general resistance to slavery.

As emancipation approached, slaves may have outwardly accepted Christianity but the content of their religion remained essentially African. In keeping with African-based tradition, many of the syncretic black religions which developed during this period have retained a certain degree of sexual egalitarianism and women remain prominent as leaders.[101] Thus from the early days of slavery through the Emancipation and beyond, black women played a significant role in slave religions and hence resistance to white domination. In so doing they not only contributed to organized slave resistance but ensured the cultural continuity of the slave community which helped to cohere the slave family and shield the individual slave from total dehumanization.

Conclusion

An old Ibo legend tells of how God decided not to allow women to fight wars since they were so fierce that they might have wiped out the world.[102] In the context of the Caribbean there is a grain of truth in this legend. The defiant stance of black women was marked throughout the period of slavery. They contributed positively to slave resistance at all levels and in so doing presented a strong challenge to the slave system and all that it represented.

In their formal sphere as plantation workers, sheer force of circumstance rendered women equal to men and evidence indicates that on a day-to-day basis they fiercely fought the system. There is little factual basis to support the contention that they were treated differently from men or that they proved more pliable and submissive. It is unlikely that their unenviable sexual position *vis-à-vis* white men caused them to turn traitor to the slave cause. On the contrary, in view of their strong commitment to their families and the wider black community, traitors among them were probably the exception rather than the rule.[103]

From this fresh perspective, the substantial role played by black women in organized slave revolt can no longer be ignored. From maronage to the creole-led revolts which preceded Emancipation, women were actively involved with the slave cause. Indeed, as Edward Brathwaite has observed, the black woman was from the beginning as deeply committed as her brother to 'the art and act of subversion and liberation'.[104]

In their response to slavery and the methods of resistance they adopted, women were heavily influenced by African cultural traditions. Black women in the New World have been designated by some authors as the 'principal exponents' and protectors of traditional African-derived culture.[105] It was largely through the preservation of these cultural traditions, aided by the pivotal role of women in the slave family, that the theme of resistance first developed and was subsequently transmitted to children by their mothers in song and oral tradition.

Without the consciously rebellious black woman the strong tradition of resistance could not have become so thoroughly interwoven into the fabric of the slave's daily existence. In their unwillingness to cooperate, in raising their voice in satirical song, in verbally abusing their masters and refusing to behave submissively, women showed much courage and strength. In slave revolts they may not have been 'Amazons' but neither were they traitors and because of their important status in traditional African-derived religions, were often instrumental in fomenting unrest. Overall, women slaves had, on the evidence available, as deep, if not a deeper commitment to 'puttin on (ol') Massa' and preserving their human dignity as any of their male counterparts. It is for a proper recognition of this commitment that I have been arguing in this paper.

NOTES

1. For a general survey of recent historiographical trends in the history of slavery see, for example, Michael Craton ed., *Roots and Branches: Current Directions In Slave Studies (Historical Reflections*, vol. 6, no. 1, Summer 1979); 'Comparative Perspectives in New World Plantation Societies', *Annals of the New York Academy of Sciences*, vol. 292 (June, 1977).

2. Peter J. Wilson, *Crab Antics: The Social Anthropology of English Speaking Negro Societies in the Caribbean* (London, 1973), p. 193.

3. For a critique of this portrayal of slave women see, for example, Mae C. King. 'The Politics of Sexual Stereotypes, *The Black Scholar*, vol. 4, nos. 6 & 7 (March-April, 1973), p. 12. According to this author, such divided loyalties could generate 'suspicion, guilt and degradation' around individual women.

4. See, for instance, relevant chapters in Eugene Genovese, *Roll, Jordan, Roll: The World the Slaves Made* (New York, 1974); Herbert G. Gutman, *The Black Family in Slavery and Freedom, 1750-1925* (New York, 1976); Barry Higman, *Slave Population and Economy in Jamaica 1807-1834* (London, 1976); Michael J. Craton, *Searching for the Invisible Man: Slaves and Plantation Life in Jamaica* (Cambridge, Mass., 1978).

5. Walter Rodney, 'Upper Guinea and the Origins of Africans Enslaved in the New World', *Journal of Negro History*, vol. LIV, no 4 (October, 1969), p. 345.

6. See, for instance, Edward Brathwaite, *The Development of Creole Society in Jamaica* (Oxford, 1971); John W. Blassingame, *The Slave Community: Plantation Life in the Antebellum South* (New York, 1972); Oruna de Lara, 'Resistance to Slavery from Africa to Black America,' *Annals of the New York Academy of Sciences*, vol. 292 (27 June

1977), p. 464; Monica Schuler, 'Ethnic Slave Rebellion in the Caribbean and the Guianas', *Journal of Social History*, 3 (1970), p. 379; Wilson, *Crab Antics*.

7. This point is forcibly argued by Lucille Mathurin in her article, 'The Arrivals of Black Women,' *Jamaica Journal*, vol. 9, nos. 2 & 3 (February, 1975), p. 2. Lucille Mathurin has produced one of the few works to date which explore the role of the slave woman as a rebel—*The Rebel Woman in the British West Indies During Slavery* (Kingston, 1975). This is a short book written in a lively style which provides a good general introduction to the subject.

8. This term was first used by A. Raymond Bauer and Alice Bauer in 'Day to Day Resistance to Slavery', *Journal of Negro History*, vol. XXVII (1942).

9. See, for instance, Lowell J. Ragatz, *The Fall of the Planter Class in the British Caribbean, 1763-1833* (New York, 1928); Frank W. Pitman, *The Development of the British West Indies, 1700-1763* (New Haven, 1917); Ulrich B. Phillips, 'A Jamaican Slave Plantation', *American Historical Review*, vol. XIX (April 1914).

10. See, for instance, Kenneth Stampp, *The Peculiar Institution: Slavery in the Ante-bellum South* (New York, 1956); Orlando Patterson, *The Sociology of Slavery: An Analysis of the Origins, Development and Structure of Negro Slave Society in Jamaica* (London, 1967). Other more recent relevant works include Brathwaite, *Development of Creole Society*; Blassingame, *Slave Community*; Genovese, *Roll, Jordan, Roll*.

11. See William Rivère, 'Active and Passive Resistance to Slavery' (Unpublished paper, University Library, University of the West Indies, St. Augustine, Trinidad, 1972).

12. See, for instance, Alexander Falconbridge, *An Account of the Slave Trade on the Coast of West Africa* (London, 1788), p. 7; William Snelgrave, *A New Account of Some Parts of Guinea* (London, 1734), pp. 167, 173, 190, 191; Anon, 'The Ballad of a Repentant Sailor' (Bristol, 1779), cited in John Riland, *Memoirs of a West Indian Planter* (London, 1837), pp. 68-69.

13. Sir Hans Sloane, for instance, observed that 'Negroes from some countries think they return to their own country when they die . . . and therefore regard death but little, imagining they shall change their condition by that means from servile to free and so for this reason often cut their throats'. (See Sir Hans Sloane, Bart, *A Voyage to the Islands Madera, Barbados, Nieves, S. Christophers and Jamaica, with the natural history . . . of the last of those islands; to which is prefixed an introduction wherein is an account of the inhabitants . . . trade, etc.*, 2 vols. [London, 1707-25], 1, xvii.) According to Daniel Mannix, contemporary reports indicate that slaves had to be watched at all times to prevent them from committing suicide. He cites a Captain Phillips who corroborates Sloane's earlier observation that slaves believed that when they died they returned home to their own country and points out that this particular belief was reported from various regions, at various periods of the slave trade, but seems to have been especially prevalent among the Ibo of Eastern Nigeria. See Daniel P. Mannix in collaboration with Malcolm Crowley, *Black Cargoes: A History of the Atlantic Slave Trade, 1518-1865* (London, 1962).

14. See Bryan Edwards, *The History, Civil and Commercial of the British Colonies in the West Indies . . .* , 3rd ed. (ed. by Sir William Young), 3 vols. (London, 1801), II, p. 51; Riland, *Memoirs of a West Indian Planter*, p. 65.

15. Riland, *Memoirs of a West Indian Planter*, pp. 68-69, 51, 59-61; Falconbridge, *Account of the Slave Trade*, p. 23.

16. Falconbridge, *Account of the Slave Trade*, p. 32.

17. This point is made by Richard R. Madden, *A Twelve Month Residence in the West Indies . . .* , 2 vols. (London, 1835), II, pp. 24-25.

18. Matthew Gregory Lewis, *Journal of a Residence Among the Negroes of the West Indies* (London, 1845), pp. 77, 175, 304-5, 103.

19. This allegation is made by John Stewart in *A View of Jamaica* (London, 1823), pp. 304-5. According to Bryan Edwards, however, this practice was, in effect, a form of inoculation. A 'female Koromantyn slave' had told him that the women inoculated their children with a mild dose of yaws by an incision in the thigh. The children became slightly ill, recovered and were henceforth immune to the disease. (Edwards, *History of the British Colonies*, II, p. 69).

20. These plantation records are part of the Atkin's slavery collection which is housed in Wilberforce House, Hull. The main sources consulted were Baillies' Bacolet Plantation Returns (Grenada), 1820-1833 and the Punishment Records Books from the Kings' Guiana plantations—Friendship, Sarah and Good Success, 1823-1833.

21. For examples of these laws and the reactions to them, see 'Abstract of the Jamaican Slave Law, 1826', No. 37, cited in Bernard M. Senior, *A Retired Military Officer* (London, 1831), p. 145. *C.O. 295/60 C.O. 295/66* Commandant of Chaguanas to Woodford, 20.8.1823, quoted in Bridget Brereton, 'Brute Beast or Man Angel: Attitudes to the Blacks in Trinidad 1820-1888' (Unpublished Paper, University of the West Indies, St. Augustine, Trinidad, 1974), p. 11.

22. Punishment Record Book of Plantation Friendship, 1827.

23. Punishment Record Book of Good Success, 1830.

24. Baillies Bacolet Plantation Returns, 1823.

25. Punishment Record Book of Plantation Sarah, 1827.

26. The term 'domestic servant' is here restricted to the lower grades of house slaves. I have omitted from my analysis the powerful 'housekeeper' who often wielded much power over white men. Frequently light-colored and sometimes free, her special status demands a separate analysis.

27. This conclusion is based on quantitive data derived from Jamaican plantation records kindly made available to me by Michael Craton (University of Waterloo). The same point is also made by a contemporary observer, William Beckford, in *Remarks Upon the Situation of Negroes in Jamaica* (London, 1788), p. 13.

28. Mrs. A.C. Carmichael, *Domestic Manners and Social Condition of the White, Coloured and Negro Population of the West Indies*, 2 vols. (London, 1833), I, pp. 256, 258, 118, 119; II, pp. 268, 334.

29. Edward Long, *A History of Jamaica . . .* , 3 vols. (London, 1774), II, p. 145; Lewis, *Residence Among the Negroes*, p. 175; Stewart, *View of Jamaica*, pp. 246, 172.

30. Wilson, *Crab Antics*, pp. 4, 9, 58, 99-105.

31. Several examples of such punishments are cited by Captain John Gabriel Stedman in his *Narrative of a five years expedition against the revolted Negroes of Surinam from the year 1772 to 1777*, 2 vols. (London, 1796), I, pp. 77, 179 ff., and Henry Coor in *British Sessional Papers*, XL, 1791-92, no. 745, p. 34.

32. Mrs. Carmichael, *Domestic Manners*, II, p. 102.

33. See, for instance, Lewis, *Residence Among the Negroes*, p. 92.

34. *Ibid.*, p. 104.

35. Mrs. Carmichael, *Domestic Manners*, I, pp. 184-186.

36. For useful descriptions of the cultivation of provision grounds by slaves, see William Beckford, *A Descriptive Account of the Island of Jamaica; with remarks upon the cultivation of the sugar-cane . . .* , 2 vols. (London, 1790), II, pp. 151-160, 187; and Robert C. Dallas, *The History of the Maroons—From Their Origin to the Establishment of their Chief Tribe in Sierra Leone*, 2 vols. (London, 1790), I, cviii, cix. A useful

discussion of the internal marketing activities of slaves, which stresses the significant part played by slave women, can be found in Sidney Mintz and Douglas Hall, 'The Origins of the Jamaican Internal Marketing System,' in Sidney Mintz, ed., *Papers in Caribbean Anthropology* (New Haven, 1970), pp. 3-26.

37. This predominance of women is revealed in plantation lists which give a breakdown of the occupational status of slaves. For this information I am indebted to Michael Craton.

38. Beckford, *A Descriptive Account*, II, pp. 383-84.

39. Thomas Cooper, *Facts Illustrative of the Condition of Negro Slaves in Jamaica* (London, 1824), p. 20.

40. See for instance, Genovese, *Roll, Jordan, Roll*, p. 619.

41. Mrs. Carmichael, *Domestic Manners*, II, p. 119.

42. Brereton, 'Brute Beast or Man Angel', p. 11.

43. The female equivalent of 'Quashee', used as a tag sometimes in the British West Indies to describe a characteristically adverse composite stereotype of the individual slave, in a similar way to the use of the name 'Sambo' in the Old South. Both 'Quashee' and 'Quasheba' are derived from common names found among the Akan-speaking tribes of what is now modern-day Ghana.

44. Anon., *A Genuine Narrative of the Intended Conspiracy of the Negroes of Antigua* (Dublin, 1737), pp. 21-22.

45. *Ibid.*, pp. 19-20; Thomas Southey, *Chronological History of the West Indies*, 2 vols. (London, 1827), II, p. 396; *The Report from a Select Committee of the House of Assembly, appointed to inquire into the origin, causes and progress of the late insurrection* (Barbados, 1817), p. 8.

46. *A Genuine Narrative* . . . , pp. 19-20.

47. Oruna de Lara, 'Resistance to Slavery,' p. 464.

48. Olaudah Equiano, *Equiano's Travels*, abridged and edited by Paul Edwards (London, 1967), pp. 9-10; John Adams, *Sketches Taken During Ten Voyages to Africa, Between the Years 1786 and 1800* (London, n.d.), pp. 140-41.

49. See, for instance, Sir Richard Burton, *A Mission to Gelele, King of Dahomey*, 2 vols. (London, 1893), II, pp. 42-57.

50. For reference to this incident see Sylvia Leith-Ross, *African Women: A Study of the Ibo of Nigeria* (London, 1939), p. 165; S.O. Esike, 'The Aba Riots of 1929', *African Historian*, vol. 1, no. 3 (1965), p. 308; Azikiwe Nnamdi, 'Murdering Women in Nigeria', *Crisis*, no. 37 (May 1930), p. 164.

51. Analyses of the political status of certain West African women can be found in Judith van Allen, 'Sitting on a Man: Colonialism and the Lost Political Institutions of Igbo Women', *Canadian Journal of African Studies*, vol. VI, no. 2 (April, 1972), pp. 165-81; and Carol P. Hoffer, 'Mende and Sherbro Women in High Office', *ibid.*, pp. 151-64. See also Daryl Forde, 'Kinship and Marriage Among the Matrilineal Ashanti,' in Alfred Radcilffe-Brown and Daryl Forde, eds., *African Systems of Kinship and Marriage* (London, 1956), p. 267 ff.; Kenneth Little, *The Mende of Sierra Leone* (London, 1965), pp. 64-68.

52. For a general discussion of maronage in slave colonies in the New World, see Richard Price, ed., *Maroon Societies* (London, 1973); Eugene Genovese, *From Rebellion to Revolution: Afro-American Slave Revolts in the Making of the Modern World* (Baton Rouge, 1979), pp. 51-82.

The term maroon is derived from the Spanish *cimarones* (mountaineers). Many of these maroons came originally from tribes from areas which today constitute the countries of Nigeria and Ghana. For example, in Jamaica the Ashanti were prominent whereas in Brazil it was the Yoruba. Maroons carried on a protracted struggle against whites which was, arguably, a form of slave revolt (see Orlando Patterson, 'Slavery and Slave Revolts,' in Price, *Maroon Societies*, pp. 246-75). Eventually the maroons entered into peace treaties with the whites.

In Jamaica, for instance, under a Treaty signed in 1738, the maroons were granted freedom and autonomy along with the possession of designated lands in return, among other things, for returning runaway slaves and helping whites to suppress slave revolts. According to Genovese this 'divide and rule' policy implemented by whites in Jamaica successfully warded off the possibility of any successful, large-scale black uprising—such as that which occurred in Saint-Domingue in 1795. (Genovese, *From Rebellion to Revolution*, pp. 67-68.)

53. Phillip Thicknesse, *Memoirs and Anecdotes of P. Thicknesse*, 2 vols. (printed for the author, London, 1788), I, p. 123.

54. When sent out to fight the maroons in Jamaica, Thicknesse was a junior officer in the Army. Much of his book is a vindication of his character in response to the 'libellous' accusations of a fellow officer who called Thicknesse a coward. In view of this it would naturally have been in his interest to stress the ferocity of the maroons and the fact that 'all the regular troops in Europe could not have conquered the wild negroes for force of arms' (Thicknesse, *ibid.*, I, p. 91).

55. See Barbara K. Kopytoff, 'Jamaican Maroon Political Organisations: The Effects of the Treaties', *Social and Economic Studies*, vol. 25, no. 2 (June, 1976), p. 90. For an additional comment on Nanny see Alan Tuelon, 'Nanny—Maroon Chiefteness', *Caribbean Quarterly*, vol. XIX (December, 1973), pp. 20-27.

56. Kopytoff, 'Jamaican Maroon Political Organisations,' p. 101.

57. Thicknesse, *Memoirs*, I, pp. 119, 120; Dallas, *History of the Maroons*, I, p. 73.

58. Evidence pertaining to women taking up arms in these areas can be found in 'A Rebel Village in French Guiana: A Captive's Description,' in Price, *Maroon Societies*, pp. 317, 319; Stedman, *Narrative*, I, pp. 46, 275.

59. Stedman, *Narrative*, I, pp. 33, 34.

60. Dallas, *History of the Maroons*, I, p. 73.

61. *Ibid.*, pp. 112-14; 'Observations on the Habits . . . of the Maroon Negroes of the Islands of Jamaica', in Edwards, *History of the British Colonies*, I, Appx. no. 2, pp. 540-41. An Outline of the traditional economic role of West African women can be found in Leith-Ross, *African Women*, 65 ff, and Melville J. Herskovits, *The Myth of the Negro Past* (1941, repr., New York, 1967), 58 ff.

62. These rebellions were often of a 'national' or 'ethnic' character, the rebels having a clear sense of identity and a set of goals which often excluded other groups of slaves. See Schuler, 'Ethnic Slave Rebellions', pp. 377-78, and another article by the same author, 'Akan Slave Rebellions in the British Caribbean', *Savacou*, I (1970), pp. 8-31.

63. Long, *History of Jamaica*, II, p. 445.

64. *A Genuine Narrative* . . . , pp. 6-8.

65. Robert S. Rattray, ed., *Religion and Art in Ashanti* (Oxford, 1927), pp. 257-79. According to Rattray, the Ashanti kings sat under 'a state umbrella' on a special chair and wore a 'chaplet of silk' around their heads.

66. *Ibid.*, pp. 134 ff., 198, 264 ff. See also Forde, 'Kinship and Marriage among the Matrilineal Ashanti', pp. 271-73.

67. Long *History of Jamaica*, II, p. 445.

68. Cited from *Calendar of State Papers*, vol. XLI, nos. 314, ii, 227, in David Barry Gaspar, 'The Antigua Slave Conspiracy of 1736: A Case Study of the Origins of Collective Resistance', *William and Mary Quarterly*, 3rd ser., vol. 35, no. 2 (April, 1978), p. 314.

69. Long, *History of Jamaica*, II, p. 449.

70. Schuler, 'Ethnic Slave Rebellions', p. 379.

71. Lewis, *Journal*, p. 93.

72. See Vidia S. Naipaul, *The Loss of Eldorado* (London, 1973), pp. 292-93. It translates as 'wine is white blood; we are going to drink white blood'.

73. Report on the 1816 Barbados insurrection, Appx. D. 'The Confession of Robert, a slave belonging to the Plantation called "Simmons"'.

74. See, for instance, evidence from Colonial Office documents cited in Richard Frucht, 'Emancipation in St. Kitts, 1834,' in *Science and Society*, vol. 1, no. 2 (Summer, 1975), pp. 208, 209.

75. Senior, *Retired Military Officer*, pp. 180, 204-7, 212-16.

76. The laws of Jamaica as applied to slave markets and marketing activities and the mobility these afforded are discussed in Mintz and Hall, 'The Origins of the Jamaican Internal Marketing System', pp. 15 ff.

77. A sample of this is cited in John Jeremie, *Four Essays on Colonial Slavery* (London, 1831), p. 6.

78. Genovese, *Roll, Jordan, Roll*, p. 183.

79. The significant part played by women in West African religions is mentioned in Adams, *Sketches*, 12, and stressed in Walter Rodney, *A History of the Upper Guinea Coast, 1545-1800* (Oxford, 1970), p. 103. For modern anthropological data on the powerful position of women—particularly older women—in West African religions, see Forde, 'Kinship and Marriage among the Matrilineal Ashanti', pp. 256, 269-70; Van Allen, 'Sitting on a Man', pp. 151, 165; Leith-Ross, *African Women*, pp. 26 ff.

80. An excellent analysis of this association can be found in Schuler's 'Ethnic Slave Rebellions.' Schuler has since further refined her analysis of myalism, ethnicity and slave resistance in 'Afro-American Slave Culture', in *Roots and Branches*, pp. 121-37, in particular, pp. 127-35.

81. Stewart, *View of Jamaica*, p. 278.

82. Edwards, *History of the British Colonies*, II, p. 99; Long, *History of Jamaica*, II, p. 475.

83. Schuler, 'Ethnic Slave Rebellions', p. 383.

84. Stedman, *Narrative*, II, pp. 304-5.

85. See Schuler, 'Ethnic Slave Rebellions.'

86. Examples of such laws are given in Edwards, *History of the British Colonies*, II, Appx. XI, pp. 177-78 (Law XLV 1792) and Stedman, *Narrative*, II, pp. 304-5.

87. *Ibid.*

88. Examples of such incidents are cited in Edwards, *History of the British Colonies*, II, p. 114, and Naipaul, *Loss of Eldorado*, pp. 296-98.

89. Sloane, *Voyage to the Islands*, II, p. xii; Madden, *Twelve Month Residence*, II, pp. 70-76.

90. Allusions to these sinister activities of female domestics can be found in Lewis, *Journal*, pp. 74-77, Long, *History of Jamaica*, II, p. 428; Edwards, *History of the British Colonies*, II, p. 114, Sloane, *Voyage to the Islands*, I, p. ix.

91. This is made quite apparent in the questions on Obeah put to witnesses from Jamaica by the Select Committee on the Slave Trade in 1789. Their answers are particularly detailed and give a colorful, if somewhat biased view of the Obeah arts

of Jamaican slaves. See for example, *British Sessional Papers*, Commons, Vol. XXVI (1789) 646a, Part III, Jamaica, Ans. No. 22.

92. *Ibid.*, Section A.

93. The actual phrases quoted here are from Thomas Atwood, *The History of Domenica* (London, 1791), p. 269, although they could well have come from several other commentaries on West Indian slavery from the same period; Sir Hans Sloane had made a very similar observation almost a century earlier (*Voyage to the Islands*, I, cxiv).

94. See, for instance, Riland, *Memoirs of a West Indian Planter*, p. 104.

95. For relevant examples of female resistance to Christianity, see Lewis, *Journal*, p. 53; Edwards, *History of the British Colonies*, II, p. 84.

96. This is remarked upon by Riland, *Memoirs of a West Indian Planter*, pp. 186-7; Cooper, *Condition of Negro Slaves*, pp. 42-47; Senior, *Retired Military Officer*, pp. 42-43.

97. Although variations among slaves undoubtedly existed on an individual and ethnic basis as well as between creole and African-born, these may have been less important than has hitherto been assumed, especially in the area of slave relations and slave resistance. Edward Long, for instance, believed that little difference existed between African and Creole in view of the latter's 'frequent intermixture with the native African' (*History of Jamaica*, II, p. 407). This binding African culture had among slaves has been commented on by Sidney Mintz and Richard Price. They suggest that there were 'deep-level cultural principles, assumptions and understandings' which were shared by Africans in the New World Colony and which acted as a vital catalyst in the development of creole institutions. See Gutman, *The Black Family*, p. 329.

98. Lewis, *Journal*, p. 121.

99. Long, *History of Jamaica*, II, p. 429; Riland, *Memoirs of a West Indian Planter*, p. 104.

100. For a fuller discussion of this link between social control and Christianity, see Gwendolyn M. Hall, *Social Control in Slave Plantation Societies: A Comparison of St. Domingue and Cuba* (Baltimore, 1971), pp. 32 ff., 50-51.

101. See, for instance, Frances Henry and Pamela Wilson, 'The status of Women in Caribbean Societies: An Overview of their Social, Economic and Sexual Roles', *Social and Economic Studies*, vol. 24, no. 2 (June, 1975), pp. 356-92; Martha Beckwith, *Black Roadways: A Study of Jamaican Folk-Life* (New York, 1969, First Published, 1929), pp. 160, 172.

102. *Equiano's Travels*, p. 179.

103. See, for instance, Brathwaite, 'Submerged Mothers', p. 48: 'I suspect that many less women than men—even though by 1815 they were demographically equal on plantations—were guilty of such weaknesses.'

104. *Ibid.*

105. See, for instance, Melville J. and Frances S. Herskovits, *Trinidad Village* (New York, 1947), pp. 8, 9; Wilson, *Crab Antics*, p. 135.

11

The Search for Mary Bibb, Black Woman Teacher in Nineteenth-Century Canada West

Afua Cooper

The decision to write an article on Mary Bibb was influenced by my study of the history of women and education in nineteenth-century North America. A study of Black female teachers who taught in Canada West during this period presented itself as a viable task. After finding names such as Matilda Nichols, Sarah and Mary Anne Titre, Mrs. J.E. Grant, Mary Ann Shadd, and Mary Bibb herself, I decided for several reasons to study only one of these women, Mary Bibb.[1] Mary Bibb and Mary Ann Shadd were probably Canada West's most prominent Black women leaders during the eighteen-fifties and sixties. Moreover, Mary Bibb was married to Henry Bibb, another leader in the Black community. Mary Shadd, however, has been the subject of several biographical works, and even though more could be written about her, at least she has not been subsumed under someone else's history. The same cannot be said of Mary Bibb, about whom no biographical work exists. My research, then, on Mary Bibb, is an attempt to correct this imbalance.

The search for Mary Bibb, as it came to be, was both frustrating and rewarding. Although she has been described in the relevant literature as "widely known," those that described her that way failed to give details of her life. Thus the dearth of evidence in itself became a kind of evidence in the attempt to put the pieces of her life together. Since there are large gaps in parts of the story and only scanty evidence for other parts, her life history is not a continuous narrative, but a story with some parts missing.

There is more evidence about the life of her husband, Henry Bibb. In fact, the comparison of their life histories is a telling reminder of the peripheral place that women occupy in history, especially if the women are non-white. Burt James Loewenberg and Ruth Bogin remark in *Black Women in Nineteenth-Century American Life*,

> Omission of woman's role and woman's story shrivels the evidence at hand for analysis and dilutes the full validity of the segments presently available. Neglect of the history of black women—Harriet Tubman and Sojourner Truth are notable exceptions—is a crucial instance of distortion. . . . Recovery of the

black past is itself a force shaping the black future, yet the full range of experience of black women still awaits discovery and assessment.[2]

The writers comment further on the fact that historians have been content to permit the men of the race to represent the women in almost every significant category. "Thus it is the male who is the representative abolitionist, fugitive slave or political activist. The black male is the leader, the entrepreneur, the politician, the man of thought."[3]

Hence, in the writing of history, it is the man that assumes center stage. Therefore we know of Mary Bibb, an articulate and educated woman, mainly through the activities of her husband. It is not known if Mary Bibb left any written speeches, diaries, or autobiographical account, though we know that she wrote articles for her husband's newspaper and may have written editorials too. She also wrote letters to leading abolitionists of the day. Despite this lack of a personal account, she still deserves historical treatment, if only because she was one of the chief participants in Black community life in Canada West during those crucial mid-century years. But, unlike thousands of other North American women, Mary Bibb did not completely disappear from the scenes of history, even though the odds were against her.

Mary Elizabeth Bibb was born Mary Elizabeth Miles, around 1820 in Rhode Island, to free Quaker parents. She was their only child. Not much is known about her early life or education, but probably she was taught by her parents and attended a Quaker school or a private institution for Black children. In 1827, when she was seven years old, a survey by the Black newspaper *Freedom's Journal* found that in Providence, Rhode Island, with a colored population of fifteen hundred, there was not one African free school.[4] Therefore if Mary grew up in Providence or its environs, she must have had her early schooling by other means. If she lived in Newport, she probably attended the private high school there for Black students.

However, Mary attained her early schooling and qualified for entry into the Massachusetts State Normal School at Lexington. Like many other Blacks who had access to higher education, she probably viewed teaching as a mission for the uplifting of her race.[5] Certainly many free young Black women like Mary Miles who had some education were encouraged by their parents and other supporters to take up teaching, which conferred a higher status than domestic work. Since Mary Miles was an only child, her parents were probably willing to provide a "suitable" education for her. Gerda Lerner, in her book *Black Women in White America*, comments,

> In the Negro's long struggle for survival, education was always a foremost goal, both as a tool for advancement and acceptance in the general society and as a means of uplifting and improving life in the black community. . . . By the 1830's, the number of black female graduates of schools run by whites had increased sufficiently to staff black schools in many communities.[6]

On the other hand, it was not easy for aspiring young Black women to receive advanced education in the United States, North or South. Emma Willard and Catharine Beecher, white educators who started female seminaries, did not admit Black girls to their schools. The same can be said of the managers of Mt. Holyoke seminary.[7] Even at Oberlin College, which was interracial and co-educational from its inception in 1833, very few Black women were able to take advantage of this opportunity before 1871.[8] The closing of Prudence Crandall's school in Connecticut by the state because she admitted Black girls points succinctly to the difficulty Black women had in pursuing higher education.[9]

Nevertheless, Mary Miles and other Black women from the North did manage to obtain a post-secondary education.[10] Mary Miles's experiences at normal school are not known but we do know that after graduating she taught at several Black schools in the North and Northeast. It was in New York City that she met Henry Bibb, whom she later married. The couple moved to Sandwich, Essex County, in Canada West after the passing of the fugitive slave law of 1850.

Upon her arrival in Canada West, Mary Bibb opened a school for Black children. But her interest in advancing the status of Blacks reached beyond education, for she was also involved in establishing and publishing, with her husband, Canada West's first sustained Black newspaper, the *Voice of the Fugitive*. She was one of the Canadian directors of the Refugee Home Society, a colonization scheme to settle landless refugees, and was also active in the temperance, Sabbath school, anti-slavery, and emigrationist movements.[11] During the latter part of her life in Canada, after the death of Henry Bibb, Mary Bibb married Isaac Cary and continued her teaching. By 1865, however, she was no longer teaching but was operating a fancy goods business. In the early 1870s she left Canada for Brooklyn, New York, where she spent the rest of her life.

Searching for Mary Bibb was like looking for the proverbial needle in a haystack. My first channels of inquiry were secondary sources, including the *Black Abolitionist Papers*, which provided useful clues. They contained brief biographical sketches of her, mentioned her in endnotes, and reprinted a letter from her to the white abolitionist Gerrit Smith. But this information was inadequate. Since she was born in Rhode Island and attended normal school in Massachusetts, I turned to books on those places, attempting to discover something of her early life; this attempt proved to be fruitless.

The *Black Abolitionist Papers* announced that after normal school Mary taught at several schools in the American North and Northeast. Although they mention only Albany, Cincinnati, and Boston, they imply that she also taught in other places.[12] Given this piece of information, I was able to find her in an endnote in Carleton Mabee's *Black Education in New York State: From Colonial to Modern Times*: "Mary Bibb then known as Mary Miles taught at the Albany

Black public school in the mid-1840s."[13] Nothing was discovered about her sojourns in Cincinnati and Boston.

While attending an anti-slavery meeting in New York City in 1847, Mary Miles met Henry Bibb, with whom she started corresponding; they were married the next year.[14] Two years later they moved to Sandwich in Canada West and into a leadership vacuum in the growing Black community there. Mary seemed to become more visible in the years she was married to Henry Bibb, even though he occupied center stage most of the time. The *Black Abolitionist Papers* record her participation in various community activities; in *Freedom Seekers*, Daniel Hill documents some aspects of her teaching career; in *Narratives of Fugitive Slaves*, Benjamin Drew writes fondly of her and her private-school venture; Jim Bearden's and Linda Jean Butler's book, *Shadd*, contains information about Mary Bibb's teaching but also makes unflattering comments about her character.

In *Black Utopia*, William and Jane H. Pease detail the history of the Refugee Home Society and Mary Bibb's involvement with it. Floyd Miller and Herbert Aptheker, in *The Search for a Black Nationality* and *A Documentary History of the Negro People in the United States* respectively, confirm that she was a delegate at the 1854 emigrationist convention in Ohio. Miller states, "Of the women delegates, only Henry Bibb's widow, Mary, was widely known."[15] Since Robin Winks's *The Blacks in Canada* is required reading for anyone studying the Black experience in Canada, I turned to it for information on Mary Bibb's life here and found a discussion of her along with her husband and their involvement with the Refugee Home Society. Winks also tells the reader where to find readings on Henry Bibb's life, but about Mary he is silent.[16]

As Mary Bibb was a government teacher for the year 1853 in Sandwich, I perused the superintendent's report for common schools in that township but found no record of her. The superintendent stated in his summary that the trustees for the separate colored school where Mary taught did not meet and that the parents of the school could not afford to maintain it.[17]

At this point I might have abandoned the search if some tantalizing clues had not fallen into my hands. The 1851 Sandwich census returns reveal the Bibbs living in a two-story frame house. Mary's occupation is not given, but Henry is listed as "editor of publications." The Bibbs are listed as Methodists with one servant named Charlotte Bibb. The returns do not say whether Charlotte was a relative.[18] Here finally was "primary source" proof of Mary Bibb's existence in Canada West.

She also appears in the 1861 census for Windsor as wife of Isaac N. Cary.[19] Again the census fails to show if she was practicing a profession, but when the Black abolitionist and writer William Wells Brown was touring Canada West in 1861, he found Mary Bibb still teaching.[20] Did she continue to teach throughout the sixties? Since her school was private, I consulted the Dun and Bradstreet business directories, where I found Mary Bibb, not as a teacher but as a business woman operating a "fancy goods" shop. Her business is listed in the directories from 1865 to 1871.[21] She also appears in the 1871 Windsor census, still married to Isaac N. Cary.

What made the search for Mary Bibb particularly frustrating was the fact that, although she was very well-known, I could find no sustained documentation of her life. Information is available only in bits and pieces, and several segments of her life, especially the earlier periods, are missing. The historians and writers, though acknowledging her popularity, concentrated on her husband, Henry Bibb. It became clear that in attempting to study the life of Mary Bibb, I would have to trace her through the life of her husband, who was more prominent, because whatever he did during the years they were married she did too. Although Mary Bibb was an independent and historically important person in her own right, because she was married to a man with a dynamic personality who was favored by the writers of history, a great deal of what Mary did was subsumed under her husband's history. The fact that the emphasis was on her husband is an indication of the male bias of the writers and historians (which is not to discount Henry Bibb's achievements).

In spite of the difficulties of writing about a person about whom very little evidence is available, it is nevertheless possible to do so, precisely because the very lack of evidence can be interpreted as evidence. Here, for example, the invisibility in the literature of someone who is supposed to have been conspicuous is a telling comment on the manner in which historians ignore persons who are seen to be handicapped by sex, race, or both.

After some consideration I decided to concentrate on Mary Bibb's teaching career, since this was a profession that she practiced throughout most of her life. Her experience as a teacher also assisted her greatly in other parts of her life.

The teaching career of Mary Miles Bibb Cary probably started before she entered normal school, for many young girls in the nineteenth century worked as "pupil-teachers" or were school mistresses before acquiring formal training.[22] Not much is known about Mary Bibb before normal school. It would be useful, for example, to know who paid her fees and how she supported herself while at the institution. What was the curriculum like? How many years did she spend there? How did she view her experience at the school? What grade of certificate did she obtain? It is certain that she had graduated by the mid-forties since Carleton Mabee had her teaching in Albany then. On leaving normal school, she taught, according to the *Black Abolitionist Papers*, "at several schools, including an Albany, New York, school for Blacks, and Hiram S. Gilmore's Cincinnati high school. She later taught in Boston."[23] What subjects did she teach at Albany? What were her wages? Why did she leave Albany? Was her move to Cincinnati prompted by better job opportunities? Perhaps it was, as the Cincinnati high school established for Black children by the white philanthropist, Hiram S. Gilmore, had a wide and excellent reputation. The school is described by Wendell P. Dabney:

175

No expense was spared to make this school a success. Good teachers were employed, and besides the common branches of an English course, Latin, Greek, music and drawing were taught.... Pupils were prepared for college, and quite a fair proportion of them went to Oberlin and such colleges as drew no color line on matriculation.[24]

It is therefore quite probable that Mary moved to the Cincinnati school, given its success, for a better teaching position. What were the reasons for her move to Boston? Boston was the seat of the anti-slavery movement in the Northeast and was also the home of Henry Bibb, whom she had married. Her move to that city, I believe, was engendered by her marriage and her involvement in abolitionism. It is therefore quite reasonable to believe that in Boston she combined teaching with abolitionist work.[25] Boston appeared to be the final place she taught in the United States, for soon after she married and moved to that city she and her husband immigrated to Canada West.

Mary's moving from one place to another, from school to school, was not uncommon; in fact, the itinerant teacher was the norm in many North American communities.[26] As schools became more widespread in North America in the last century, teachers followed the imperatives of the profession, going where work could be found and, perhaps more important, where wages were better. Mary did not marry until she was twenty-eight; thus for a good part of her adult life she supported herself and was an independent woman. This was not uncommon for the period. Many young female teachers, both Black and white, supported themselves and sometimes family members throughout much of their lives. Quite a few of these teachers did not marry, and a large proportion of those who did marry did so relatively late in life.[27]

The man Mary Miles married was a leading abolitionist and a fugitive slave. Henry Bibb was born in Kentucky in 1815 to a slave mother, Mildred Jackson, and a white master, James Bibb. Never content with slavery, Henry Bibb escaped more than five times but was recaptured. In one instance when he was trying to free his wife, Malinda, and his daughter, Mary Frances, all three were caught and sold separately. Bibb made his final and successful flight from slavery in 1842, when he escaped from his Texan master and journeyed to Detroit, where anti-slavery leaders helped him, unsuccessfully, to try to free his wife and child.

Once Bibb was settled in Detroit, he toured Michigan and the Northeastern United States, "lecturing against slavery and campaigning for the liberty party."[28] He became one of the abolition movement's most influential speakers and was ranked with the likes of Frederick Douglass. It was reported that after one of Bibb's speeches the audience "cheered, clapped, stamped, and wept in turns."[29] From Detroit Bibb moved to Boston, where, having given up hope of ever rejoining his family, he married Mary Miles. In 1849 he wrote his autobiography, *The Narrative of the Life and Adventures of Henry Bibb, an American Slave*.[30]

In 1850 the United States congress enacted a fugitive slave law that gave slave masters the right to pursue and capture their escaped slaves who had sought refuge in the North. Free Blacks were not safe either, as they too could be kidnapped and sold into slavery:

> This law was so heavily weighted against the fugitive that even free Negroes of the North were seriously endangered. The Negro claimed as a fugitive—by a master's affidavit presented before a United States judge or commissioner—was given no jury trial. And the Official's fee was ten dollars if he found the Negro to be a fugitive; five dollars if he did not! Moreover, all residents were required by this law to prevent the rescue or escape of the condemned fugitive.[31]

In this atmosphere of intimidation and fear, thousands of Blacks left their homes, families, possessions, and secure jobs, and a great number of those that left came to Canada.[32] As a known fugitive, Henry Bibb thought that Canada was the best place for him at that time;[33] he also felt that it was his mission to labor among the many fugitives who had fled to Canada. He wrote to one of the founders of the American Missionary Association, Lewis Tappan:

> Soon after the law was passed fugitives were fleeing to Canada in such vast numbers that I was induced by friends of humanity to come here & commence an organ through which their wants & conditions might be made known to our friends in the States, & which should be devoted to the elevation of the condition of our people generally. I here enclose the prospectus.[34]

The organ Henry Bibb mentioned is the newspaper he established, the *Voice of the Fugitive*.

Mary Bibb also felt it was her mission to help the fugitives, as she said in a letter to Gerrit Smith, dated November 8, 1850:

> My Dear Friend
>
> Will you aid us by sending as many subscribers as convenience will permit, There are hundreds of slaves coming here daily. My husband & self consider this the field for us at present. He is about to engage in this. I expect to take a school next week—any aid from the friend will be very acceptable. Please let me know what you think of the movement. In haste,
>
> M.E. Bibb[35]

One way to help the fugitives was through education, and shortly after she arrived in Canada West, Mary Bibb opened a school for Black children in her home. Did she start the school the week of November 13, as she stated in her letter to Smith, or did she open it at a later date? Daniel Hill records that she

> opened a classroom in her home in Sandwich in January 1851. Within a month the enrolment jumped from 25 to 46 pupils. In February, Bibb managed to find a larger room for her pupils, but it was . . . ill-ventilated, with uncomfortable seats and a shortage of desks and apparatus. Besides, Mrs. Bibb

had to carry firewood quite a distance to heat the classroom. . . . Her salary as teacher-caretaker was $10 for a whole eight-month term![36]

What did Mary Bibb teach? What were the ages of her pupils? Was her pay so low—just over one dollar a month—because the parents of these children could not afford to pay more for their schooling? This question brings into focus the financial circumstances of the Black community in Essex County, of which Sandwich was a part. If the majority of the parents were recent arrivals in Canada, having fled the tyranny of the fugitive slave law, it is more than likely they did not have great means.[37]

By providing the children with some education, Mary Bibb was performing a valuable service to the community, for the educational opportunities available to Black children in Canada West were meager. Just before the Bibbs arrived in Canada West, the legislature had made legal provision for separate schools for Black children. Previously, Black children in several parts of the province were barred from the common schools by white school supporters. Their parents then had no choice but to establish separate schools for these children. The Separate School Act of 1850 was a recognition by the government that segregated schooling already existed in the province.[38] However, Black schools were poorly funded, and even in some places with sizeable Black populations none existed. As a result many Black children were left without schooling.[39]

Neither Mary Bibb's good intentions nor the parents' desire for an education for their children were sufficient to keep the school alive. The school lacked necessary apparatus and books, as Henry Bibb mentioned in his letter to Lewis Tappan: "My wife just commenced teaching a school in Sandwich . . . she has a large school, but has not a suppy [sic] of books for the children."[40] Lacking most of what was necessary for survival, the school foundered by the beginning of 1852.[41]

The opening of a school by Mary Bibb in her house was certainly not unusual in Canada West. Susan Houston and Alison Prentice write in *Schooling and Scholars in Nineteenth-Century Ontario*, "One way or another teachers were at the centre of Upper Canadian quest for schooling. Theirs was an entrepreneurial spirit. Young or old, married or single, female or male, they were often the creative forces behind their schools."[42] These historians also comment on the closeness that usually developed between the teacher and the community she worked for.[43] Mary Bibb must have become very close to her charges as a result of their common origin. From her experiences at this particular school there also emerges a picture of what teaching entailed in that era in Canada West. She had to carry firewood and maintain the school as well as teach, not because hers was a Black school but because that was the nature of many schools in Canada West as the educational state started to grow and expand.[44] But the problems of the Black schools were compounded as they received little or no financial support from the government.

After Mary Bibb lost her school, she "worked as a dressmaker until the spring of 1853, when she took charge of a flourishing government-sponsored black school of sixty-nine students."[45] It is noteworthy that Mary was a practical and resourceful woman who, having lost her school, did not throw up her hands in despair. She no doubt acquired her skill as a dressmaker as part of her early training or normal school education. Beth Light and Alison Prentice note, "[In the eighteenth and nineteenth centuries], British North American schools with female students felt the need to provide training of a practical sort in needle skills."[46] The same was true in the United States for that period. Joan M. Jensen writes that many Quaker female teachers who instructed Afro-American girls taught them to read, spell, and sew.[47] Being a Quaker child herself, Mary Bibb was probably instructed in the needle arts at a Quaker school. The fact that she worked as a seamstress may also be an indication that Henry Bibb's earnings as editor and lecturer were not enough to support the family.

The "flourishing" government school of which Mary Bibb took charge was the colored separate school at Sandwich. After perusing the relevant superintendent's report for Sandwich schools for the year ending December 31, 1853, the local superintendent of schools, one Mr. Vervais, concluded tersely regarding the colored school, "No school, no meeting for the last two years." The trustees for the school did not meet, and hence nothing could be written about it. In short, the Black school was neglected. In a final remark Vervais noted, "They have not the means to keep the school and they do not agree."[48]

The various education acts promulgated in Canada West in the mid-nineteenth century provided for the taxation of parents and other persons for the maintenance of the common schools. Were the parents of the sixty-nine scholars unable to pay the common rate that was to be directed toward the upkeep of the school? If the parents were recent immigrants that may well have been the case. What is meant by Vervais's statement that school supporters did not agree? Could he be referring to the issue of segregation that was being debated in the Black and wider communities and had split the Black communities? Did some Black parents in Sandwich withdraw their children from Bibb's school because they were opposed to separate schooling?[49] Whatever is meant by Vervais's statement, by March 1854, when the report was sent to the Education Office in Toronto, the school was closed and Mary Bibb was out of a job. The school has been described as "flourishing," but in light of this evidence that description was an overstatement.

Mary Bibb's change from being her own employer to being an employee of the state was part of the nineteenth-century movement of women teachers from domestic teaching or private schools into public schools. Prentice writes that many teachers who became servants of the state thought the change would mean more stability and professionalism,[50] but for Mary Bibb this turned out not to be true. Mary must have felt disheartened at the loss of two schools where she had taught. No doubt she was also disillusioned at the state of education for Black children in Canada West.

August 1, 1854, was a turning point in Mary Bibb's life, for on that day her husband died at the age of thirty-nine.[51] With his death the Black community lost one of its most dynamic leaders and spokespersons. But Mary Bibb, who was thirty-four at the time, lost a husband, a companion, and a colleague. Having to support herself, she started another private school. By this time she had moved from Sandwich to Windsor. In 1855 the Boston abolitionist and journalist, Benjamin Drew, who was touring the Black communities of Canada West, found Mrs. Bibb teaching: "Mrs. Mary E. Bibb, widow of the late lamented Henry Bibb, Esq., has devoted herself to teaching a private school in Windsor, and with good success. During the last spring term, she had an attendance of forty-six pupils, seven of whom were white children."[52] Teaching in the nineteenth century can be said to have been training for life. Many women, whether married, single, or widowed, who were in financial straits turned to teaching for survival; Mary Bibb was one of them.

Sometime after 1855, Mary married Isaac N. Cary (sometimes spelled Carey), brother of Thomas Cary, husband to Mary Ann Shadd.[53] There had been a personal and ideological conflict between Miss Shadd and the Bibbs, but it is not known if under these circumstances the women patched up their differences.[54] In the 1861 census for Windsor, Mary Bibb appears as Mary E. Carey, forty, with her occupation listed as "wife." Her husband is listed as a barber. Also living with them was a Julia Carey, for whom no age is given; nor is there any indication of who Julia Carey was. The Carys occupied a two-story frame house and are listed as Methodists.[55]

In the last century, census takers did not usually give the occupation of a married woman who worked outside the home. She would simply be categorized as "wife," or the space would be left blank. Only if a woman was a widow or single (but not part of a family) would a job be listed for her. It is almost as if the census takers were saying that they did not recognize the work of women outside the home and that these women should stay home and follow the wifely role they were destined for. This male bias of the census takers has served to bury the lives of countless women and remove them from the scenes of history.

We do know, however, that Mary Bibb was working as a teacher in 1861, even though this information was not documented by the census. We know this because William Wells Brown, who toured the Black communities of Canada West in 1861, wrote a description of the Carys and their activities:

> Mr. Cary is one of the most enterprising and intellectual men in Canada, and is deeply interested in the moral, social, and political elevation of all classes. Mrs. Cary, is better known as the beautiful and accomplished Mary E. Miles, afterwards, Mrs. Henry Bibb. Her labors during the lifetime of Mr. Bibb, in connection with him, for the fugitives, and her exertions since, are too well known for me to make mention of them here, Mrs. Cary has a private school, with about 40 pupils, mostly children of the better class of Windsor.[56]

This was the third educational venture that Mary Bibb Cary had engaged in in Canada West, and it was the most sustained, having lasted six years or more. Was it because its patrons were of the "better class" of Windsor and could afford to pay well for the services of a teacher? As Mary Bibb Cary was also "accomplished," was the instruction she imparted superior to that of the common school? Was it a racially mixed school? If this is the same school where Drew found her teaching, then white children did attend. The poorer Black children must have attended the colored government school, since by 1861 rates had been abolished and therefore the cost of an education would no longer have been too burdensome for their parents. Brown's last statement can also be interpreted to mean that Mary Bibb Cary, knowing that a middle class existed in the Black community, was consciously catering to it.[57]

Brown's sketch of Mary Bibb indicates not only that she had a high profile when she was married to Henry Bibb but that she had also been well-known when she was Miss Miles. It would be helpful if he had mentioned her many "exertions." And his description of her as "beautiful" is also the first reference to her looks that I have found.

By 1865 Mary Bibb was no longer a teacher. Did she grow tired of teaching? Did her pupils move away? Since by all indications, that was the most successful of her schools, why did she give it up and open a "fancy goods" store?[58]

This article on Mary Bibb, though limited in many aspects, shows that with determined research it is possible to construct a profile of individuals who, for a variety of reasons, including their race and sex, have been "hidden in history." Since so many women, especially non-white women, have been ignored in the writing of Canadian history, it is important to continue doing historical research along these lines.

NOTES

To Mary Bibb, though long dead. If she had not existed, the material for this would be unavailable. To Alison Prentice, my professor and thesis supervisor, for encouraging me to submit this article on Mary Bibb to *Ontario History*.

1. Mention of Matilda Nichols can be found in Jim Bearden and Linda Jean Butler, *Shadd, The Life and Times of Mary Ann Shadd* (Toronto: N.C. Press, 1977), 122-23; of the Titre sisters in J.I. Cooper, "Mission to Fugitive Slaves at London," *Ontario History*, 46 (April 1954), 135-39; of Mrs. J.E. Grant in the *Voice of the Fugitive*, Apr. 9, 1851; and of Mary Ann Shadd in Bearden and Butler, *Shadd*, and Jason Silverman, "Mary Ann Shadd and the Struggle for Equality," in Leon Litwack and August Meier, eds., *Black Leaders of the Nineteenth Century* (Urbana: University of Illinois Press, 1988), 87-100.
2. Burt James Loewenberg and Ruth Bogin, eds., *Black Leaders in Nineteenth-Century American Life* (Philadelphia: University of Pennsylvania Press, 1976), 3-4.
3. *Ibid.*, 4.
4. Dorothy Sterling, *We Are Your Sisters: Black Women in the Nineteenth Century* (New York: W.W. Norton, 1984), 180.

5. For Black women teachers' views on "race uplift," see *ibid.*, 180-213 and 261-301; and Gerda Lerner, *Black Women in White America* (New York: Pantheon, 1972), 118-46.

6. Lerner, *Black Women in White America*, 73-76.

7. For Emma Willard and her school, see Anne Firor Scott, "The Ever Widening Circle: The Diffusion of Feminist Values from the Troy Female Seminary, 1822-1872," *History of Education Quarterly*, 19 (Spring 1979), 3-23; for Catharine Beecher, see Kathryn Kish Sklar, *Catharine Beecher: A Study in Domesticity* (New Haven: Yale University Press, 1984); for the Mt. Holyoke institution, see "Professional Scholars in Isolated Splendor," in P.M. Glazer and Miriam Slater, *Unequal Colleagues: The Entrance of Women into the Professions, 1880-1940* (New Brunswick: Rutgers University Press, 1987), 25-67.

8. Lerner, *Black Women in White America*, 76. In an article on Blacks and Oberlin, W.E. Bigglestone also writes, "In reality the college never enrolled many negroes. They made up four or five percent of the student body between 1840 and 1860, rose to seven or eight percent during the decade after the civil war, and then declined to five or six percent." "Oberlin College and the Negro," *Journal of Negro History* (1971), 198-219.

9. For information on Prudence Crandall's school, see Sterling, *We Are Your Sisters*, 181-82.

10. *The Journal of Negro Education*, 51 (1982) devoted the entire issue to the experiences of American Black women and higher education. Detailed descriptions of Black women and their struggle for advanced education can also be found in Lerner, *Black Women in White America*, 73-146, and Sterling, *We Are Your Sisters*, 181-213 and 261 305.

11. For information of the Bibbs and the Refugee Home Society, see William and Jane H. Pease, *Black Utopia* (Madison: Historical Society of Wisconsin, 1963); Peter Carlesimo, "The Refugee Home Society: Its Origins, Operations, and Results," M.A. thesis, University of Windsor, 1973; for Mary Bibb and the temperance movement, see Bearden and Butler, *Shadd*, 34; for the Sabbath school movement, see *Voice of the Fugitive*, Aug. 13, 1851; for anti-slavery, see C. Peter Ripley, ed., *The Black Abolitionist Papers*, vol. 2 [hereafter *BAP*] (Chapel Hill: University of North Carolina Press, 1986), 222-23; and for Mary's involvement in the emigrationist movement, see Floyd Miller, *The Search for a Black Nationality* (Urbana: University of Illinois Press, 1973), 145.

12. *BAP*, 110.

13. Carleton Mabee, *Black Education in New York State: From Colonial to Modern Times* (Syracuse: Syracuse University Press, 1979), 312.

14. Henry Bibb himself talks about their meeting, engagement, and marriage in his autobiography, though he does not say in what city they were married. Gilbert Osofsky, ed., *Puttin' On Ole Massa: The Slave Narratives of Henry Bibb, William Wells Brown, and Solomon Northrup* (New York: Harper and Row, 1969), 190-91.

15. Miller, *The Search for a Black Nationality*, 145.

16. Robin Winks, *The Blacks in Canada* (New Haven: Yale University Press, 1971), 205, 372.

17. Annual Report of the Local Superintendent of Common Schools, Township of Sandwich, 1853, RG 2, F 3 B, Archives of Ontario [hereafter AO].

18. Manuscript Census for the township of Sandwich, 1851, AO.

19. Manuscript Census for Windsor, 1861, AO.

20. William Wells Brown was an escaped slave from Kentucky who became an ardent abolitionist and anti-slavery orator. He is also credited with being the first African-American novelist; his two novels, *Clotel* and *St. Domingo*, were written during the 1850s. In 1861-62, he undertook a tour of the Black settlements of Canada West. *BAP*, 460.

21. Dun and Bradstreet Reference Books, AO.

22. For one discussion of the youth of female teacher trainees, see Alison Prentice, " 'Like Friendly Atoms in Chemistry,' Women and Men at Normal School in Mid-Nineteenth Century Toronto," in David Keane and Colin Read, eds., *Old Ontario: Essays in Honour of J.M.S. Careless* (Toronto: Dundurn, 1990), 295.

23. *BAP*, 110.

24. Wendell P. Dabney, *Cincinnati's Colored Citizens* (New York: Negro Universities Press, 1970), 103.

25. *BAP*, 110.

26. Susan E. Houston and Alison Prentice, *Schooling and Scholars in Nineteenth-Century Ontario* (Toronto: University of Toronto Press, 1988), 169-70, 184.

27. Scott, "The Ever Widening Circle," 15-19.

28. Robert C. Hayden, ed., *A Salute to Historic Black Abolitionists* (Chicago: Empak, 1985), 7.

29. *Ibid.*

30. Henry Bibb's experiences as a slave and his life as a freeman are described in his autobiography, *The Narrative of the Life and Adventures of Henry Bibb, an American Slave* (Boston, 1849), which is reprinted in Osofsky's *Puttin' On Ole Massa*.

31. Herbert Aptheker, *A Documentary History of the Negro People in the United States* (New York: Citadel, 1951), 299.

32. See Fred Landon, "The Negro Migration to Canada After the Passing of the Fugitive Slave Act," *Journal of Negro History* (1920), 22-36.

33. Henry Bibb was a well-known abolitionist, and one of his former masters knew his whereabouts because they had corresponded. See the *Voice*, Sept. 23, Oct. 7, and Nov. 4, 1852; *BAP*, 217-20.

34. *BAP*, 114.

35. *Ibid.*, 108.

36. Hill, *Freedom Seekers*, 156.

37. Not much is known about the financial position of the fugitive population. But William Wells Brown stated during his tour of the Black settlements of Canada West: "There is a fair proportion of wealth among the colored people, especially when we take into consideration the indigent circumstances under which so many came to Canada. I found one man in Toronto, said to be worth $120,000. . . . Others whose wealth was estimated at from $5,000 to $40,000 were also given to me." *BAP*, 463.

38. See Robin Winks, "Negro School Segregation in Ontario and Nova Scotia," *Canadian Historical Review*, 50 (1959), 164-91.

39. Jason Silverman and Donna Gillie, " 'The Pursuit of Knowledge Under Difficulties': Education and the Fugitive Slave in Canada," *Ontario History*, 74 (1982), 95-111.

40. *BAP*, 111.

41. *Ibid.*, 110.

42. Houston and Prentice, *Schooling and Scholars*, 61.

43. *Ibid.*

44. Elizabeth Graham gives an instance of one nineteenth-century female teacher, Lizzie Overend, who "was faced not only with an inadequate and rundown schoolhouse, but also with such day to day maintenance problems as sweeping the floor, disposing of garbage, hauling water and repairing broken utilities. Elizabeth Graham, "Schoolmarms and Early Teaching in Ontario," in Janice Acton, Penny Goldsmith, and Bonnie Shepard, eds., *Women at Work, Ontario, 1850-1930* (Toronto: Canadian Women's Educational Press, 1974), 182-83.

45. *BAP*, 111.

46. Beth Light and Alison Prentice, eds., *Pioneers and Gentlewomen of British North America, 1713-1867* (Toronto: New Hogtown Press, 1980), 69.

47. Joan M. Jensen,"Not Only Ours but Others: The Quaker Teaching Daughters of the Mid-Atlantic, 1790-1850," *History of Education Quarterly* (Spring 1974), 7.

48. See Supt. report for Sandwich schools, 1853, AO.

49. Many Black parents of the province who were opposed to segregated schools often withdrew their children from them. Sometimes the schools collapsed as a result. See "Petition of the Black Residents of Camden Against a Separate School," Jan. 13, 1856; "Petition of Colcheser Black Inhabitants Against a Separate School," Nov. 28, 1857, RG 2, C 6 C, AO. Alexander Murray in his splendid thesis also describes the split in the Black community regarding segregated schools. But he also makes it very clear that in most instances Blacks had no choice but to ask for and attend this type of school. Alexander Murray, "Canada and the Anglo-American Anti-Slavery Movement," Ph.D. dissertation, University of Pennsylvania, 1960, 328-35.

50. Alison Prentice, "From Household to School House: The Emergence of the Teacher as a Servant of the State," *Material History Bulletin* (1983-84), 19.

51. Coincidentally, Henry Bibb died on the anniversary of the emancipation of the slaves in the British Empire. *BAP*, 110.

52. Benjamin Drew, *The Narratives of Fugitive Slaves in Canada* (Cleveland, Ohio: John P. Jewett, 1856), 321-22.

53. *BAP*, 380.

54. In *Shadd*, Bearden and Butler give a rather lopsided view, in favor of Mary Shadd, of the rift between the Bibbs and her; however, Peter Carlesimo's perceptive thesis presents a more balanced discussion of the issue. Peter Carlesimo, "The Refugee Home Society: Its Origin, Operations, and Results."

55. Census returns for Windsor, 1861, AO.

56. *BAP*, 478.

57. Brown's comment that Bibb taught children of the better class has to be placed in context. A government separate school was opened in Windsor only two years before Brown visited Windsor, and Black parents had had to find schooling for their children before that time. Bibb's school was the only one before 1859 that provided an education for Black children. Perhaps the parents of Bibb's pupils had been long established in Windsor and had some means to pay tuition. For information on the Windsor Black separate school, see the superintendent's report for Windsor schools, 1859, RG 2, F 3 B, AO.

58. In 1863 as the United States federal army began to recruit Black men to fight on the side of the Union in the Civil War, hundreds of Black men in the province of Canada West took up the call. After the war many Black families also returned to the United States to find lost relatives and friends and help in the Reconstruction. As a result numerous children of school age also left the province. Jonathan W. Walton, "Blacks

in Buxton and Chatham, Ontario, 1830-1890: Did The 49th Parallel Make A Difference?", Ph.D dissertation, Princeton University, 1979, 164-69.

It is also possible that Mary Bibb was worn out from teaching. In 1865 she was forty-five years old and had been a teacher for at least twenty years. The adverse conditions under which many nineteenth-century teachers labored contributed to ill health and "burn-out" in many. Mrs. Bibb may have felt that a fancy goods store was easier to manage than a school. For teacher burn-out see Marta Danylewycz and Alison Prentice, "Teachers' Work: Changing Patterns and Perceptions in the Emerging School Systems of Nineteenth- and Early Twentieth-Century Canada," *Labour/Le travail*, 17 (Spring 1986), 71-73.

Part IV
United States—
Eighteenth Century

12

The Double Bonds of Race and Sex:

Black and White Women in a Colonial Virginia Parish

Joan Rezner Gundersen

Phillis, a black slave, and Elizabeth Chastain LeSueur, her mistress, worked and raised families together for over thirty-two years in King William Parish, Virginia. In their small world, about thirty miles west of Richmond, shared ties of gender created a community of women but not a community of equals. The bonds of race and slavery provided constraints that divided the experience of Phillis from that of Elizabeth. Like most women of their day, they left but a faint trail through the records. Elizabeth Chastain LeSueur was probably the older, born about 1707, while all that is certain about Phillis is that she was born before 1728. Both women died sometime after David LeSueur's estate went through probate in early 1773. Both bore and raised children, worked at the many domestic tasks assigned to women in the colonies, and experienced the growth of slavery in their region. The similarities and differences between their lives (and the lives of the other women of the parish) reveal much about the ways gender and race interacted in the lives of colonial women.[1]

The lives of black women such as Phillis have yet to be explored in depth by the new social historians. We have, however, learned something about the lives of women like her mistress, Elizabeth Chastain LeSueur.[2] In recent years historians have examined the life expectancy of seventeenth-century blacks, the effects of demographics and demand upon the introduction of slavery in the Chesapeake, the impact of a black majority upon South Carolina development, the patterns of slave resistance in eighteenth-century Virginia, and the structure of eighteenth-century slave families.[3] In all of this the black woman appears as a cipher, notable in the seventeenth century and first part of the eighteenth by her absence and by her lack of overt resistance to slavery; she seems essential only to the study of fertility. But just as the experience of white women such as Elizabeth Chastain LeSueur differed from that of white males in the colonies, the black female's experience in slavery differed from the male's, and to ignore that difference would be to misunderstand the nature of slavery. Gender not only separated female slaves from males, it also forged bonds with white women. After all, black women lived among whites, and in order fully to understand their lives, it is necessary to compare their experiences with those of white women. Only then can we begin to understand what it meant to be black and female in colonial Virginia.

This essay looks at slavery from a comparative female perspective in King William Parish during the eighteenth century. The findings suggest that the bonds of a female slave were twofold, linking her both to an interracial community of women and setting her apart as a slave in ways that make evident the special burden of being black and female in a white, patriarchal society.[4] The local parish records, including tithe records for nearly every year between 1710 and 1744, provide a unique opportunity to illuminate the role of the black woman in a small plantation setting and to document the development of slavery within a new community just as it became the major labor source for the colony.[5]

The slave women who arrived at King William Parish in the early eighteenth century did not make a simple transfer from an African past to an English colonial present (even with intermediary stops). Rather, they came to a community itself in transformation from a French Protestant refugee culture to an English colonial one. The Virginia House of Burgesses created King William Parish for Huguenot refugees who settled at Manakin Town in 1700. Changing county boundaries placed the settlement at various times in Henrico, Goochland, Cumberland, and Chesterfield counties before 1777. The tiny handful of slaves present before 1720 belonged to a community in which French was the dominant language.[6] The decade of the 1720s, during which the first expansion of the slave population occurred, is also the period in which the Huguenot community leadership and property passed into the hands of those who, like Elizabeth Chastain LeSueur, either had arrived in Virginia as infants or had been born there.[7] An epidemic in 1717-1718 greatly disrupted the community and its institutions, speeding the transfer of leadership to a new generation.[8]

The economy of King William Parish, based on wheat and other grains, was also in transition, and the adoption of slavery was a reflection of this change. The first black women thus had to adapt to both a culture and an economy in transition. In the 1720s some land passed into English hands, and tobacco became a secondary crop. Slavery and tobacco together grew in importance in the parish over time. English interlopers did not introduce either slavery or tobacco, but they did provide a bridge to the agricultural patterns of the rest of the colony. The first slaveholding families in the community, including Elizabeth LeSueur's family, were French, and the purchase of slaves signified their claim to be members of the gentry.[9]

When Abraham and Magdalene Salle purchased Agar, an adult black female, in 1714, she joined a handful of other blacks at Manakin. The only other black woman, Bety, had arrived in the parish the year before. Agar began and ended her three decades of service in Manakin as part of a black female population outnumbered by black men, but for a decade in the middle (1720-1730), she was among the majority or was part of an evenly divided black population. Since black and white women in the Chesapeake were also outnumbered by men, Agar was part of a double minority. In King William Parish the circumstances of immigration had created nearly even sex ratios for both races. By 1714, for example, the white community had only slightly more adult men than women.[10] Recent studies throughout the Chesapeake have documented the shortage of black women in slave communities, and while the sex ratio at King William Parish favored men, it was seldom as severe as that reported for other areas. Thus the sense of being part of a female minority was less obvious than elsewhere in the colony.[11]

Table 1
Number and Sex Ratio of Adult Blacks in Manakin, 1711-1744

Year	Males	Females	Unknown	Sex Ratio
1711	2	0	0	2:0
1712	5	0	0	5:0
1713	3	1	0	3:1
1714	4	2	0	2:1
1715	4	3	0	4:3
1717	6	3	0	2:1
1719	6	3	0	2:1
1720	3	4	0	3:4
1723	11	11	0	1:1
1724	11	11	0	1:1
1725	8	9	0	8:9
1726	8	7	0	8:7
1730	31	21	6	3:2
1731	28	19	10	7:5
1732	30	21	0	11:7
1733	33	24	3	4:3
1735	45	22	0	2:1
1744	66	51	0	11:8.5

Source: Tithe lists, King William Parish Vestry Book; 1744 Tithe List in Brock, ed., *Documents*, 112-16.

The King William Parish slave population grew slowly. The originally unbalanced black population achieved a better balance between the sexes, then became more one-sided, and finally returned to a nearly balanced state (see Table 1). By 1720 Agar was one of four black women out of a total of seven slaves in the community. Throughout the 1730s the adult sex ratio became more skewed, leaving women outnumbered 2:1, but well before the Revolution it had balanced.[12] Overall, from 1710 to 1776, the parish's adult sex ratio for blacks was 6:5, or nearly even.[13] This is very close to the ratio that the whites of the parish had achieved by 1714. Thus only early in the settlement's history did the majority-minority experience of black and white women diverge.[14]

Interplay between patterns of importation and natural increase explain the shifting sex ratios. The more balanced sex ratios of the early years were an unintentional outgrowth of purchase patterns for imported slaves. Upriver slave purchasers received the leftovers from importation. Since adult males were the most desirable, and also available in greater numbers, the Tidewater planters purchased nearly all males in the early part of the eighteenth century.[15] Conversely, the slaves who reached the Piedmont in these earlier years included proportionately more women and children. By mid-century the majority of imports went to the Piedmont, providing an expansion of male field labor and unbalancing the sex ratios.[16] As a native-born slave population came of age in the 1750s, the ratio was once more evenly balanced.[17]

Throughout Agar's life at Manakin (1714-c. 1748) she was constantly part of a racial minority, for whites outnumbered blacks until after 1750. By the late 1730s black men and women comprised half of the tithables of King William Parish. Since white women were excluded from the count of tithables, and since there were many more white children than black, Agar and other blacks were still part of a minority in the community, but among a majority of those who worked the fields. Agar probably died in the late 1740s, a few years after the LeSueurs purchased Phillis. Phillis lived in a community almost evenly divided between whites and blacks and between men and women, but belonging to a numerical majority did not loosen either the bonds of slavery or gender.

Ironically, black women had an opportunity for a more normal family life than did black men because they were less desirable purchases. Because black women were outnumbered by men in King William Parish, it was easier for women to form families. Even so, the evidence suggests that black women took their time.[18] Several factors complicated a black woman's search for a partner. The dispersed patterns of ownership meant few black women lived in a slave quarter or with other blacks. Initially blacks, and especially black women, were scattered singly or in small groups among those families who owned slaves. Over one-third of the families owned some slaves or rented them.[19] No family before 1744 paid taxes on more than six blacks over age sixteen. Before 1744 only two or three families owned enough slaves to have both adult males and females. Thus black women had to search for mates on nearby farms. Furthermore, many black women lived relatively short times in Manakin, disappearing from the tithe records after only a few years. Bety, the first female slave in the parish, for example, appears only on four tithe returns. Such transience delayed the process of forming a family. In the early years this experience did not necessarily set black women apart from whites; immigrants of whatever race tended to marry later. As the community aged, however, the black woman's delay in starting a family did set her apart, for native-born white women began families earlier than their immigrant sisters, black or white.

There is only fragmentary evidence to suggest whether the slaves of Manakin were imported directly from Africa, or the West Indies, or if they were purchased from other colonial owners. Almost all slaves bore Anglicized names. The names of the slaves do suggest that the same kinds of compromises between African and English cultures that Peter H. Wood found in South Carolina also existed in colonial Virginia.[20] The process of having the county courts decide the age of young immigrant slaves had identified a small percentage of the black population in King William Parish as imports. Importers usually registered newly arrived Africans at a county in the Tidewater and then brought them upriver for sale. Thus the records in the King William Parish area do not normally distinguish between slaves imported from abroad and those born elsewhere in Virginia.[21]

Whatever these names may reveal about the origins of Manakin's black residents, black and white women were subjected to the same gender-imposed cultural restraints in naming. Of course, only white males had the security of a stable surname, but putting that issue aside, naming patterns reveal a subtle power structure in which gender played as important a role as did race. It is fitting that the first black woman resident in King William Parish was called Bety, because Bett (Beti, Bety, Betty) would prove to be one of the most common names for slave women in the parish. Of the 737 blacks studied, the 336 women bore only 71 names. Nine of these names were used seventeen times or more and account for over half of all the women. Conversely, the 401 men bore 117 names, only 5 of which were used seventeen times or more, representing only one-quarter of all male names. Thus the men bore more individualistic names. The men's names included those with more recognizable African roots such as Ebo, Manoc, and Morrocco. The women's names were more Anglicized. The most common female names among slaves were western names that closely resembled African ones, such as Betty and Jude. Hence the names represent a compromise of cultures. It is possible that the lack of recognizable African roots reflected the insistence by owners that black women fit the cultural norms for women while accepting the idea that black men might be "outlandish."[22]

Slave naming patterns may have been affected by the French community. Manakin whites bear frustratingly few names, especially among women. Nine women's names account for over 90 percent of the more than 600 white women associated with the Manakin community before 1776. While both black and white women drew their names from a much smaller pool than did men, the pool of black names had a diversity to begin with only eventually matched by white families who added new names through intermarriage. That black women shared the same names more frequently than black men parallels the pattern of the white community. But there was a further commonality among women's names that cut across racial lines. Slave names were often the diminutives of white names, for example, Betty for Elizabeth and Will for William. White women also were known by diminutives such as Sally, Patsy, and Nancy. They appear this way even in formal documents such as wills. Nicknames and diminutives are not used for adult white males. Hence diminutives were shared by women, both black and white, but not by all groups of men. White women shared in unaltered form several common names with black women, including Sarah, Hannah, and Janne. Male slaves did not bear the same names as white males, although a white youth might be called by a nickname such as Tom, which was also a common slave name. On legal documents and at adulthood, however, white men claimed the distinction granted by the formal versions of their names. Slaveowners apparently found it more necessary to distinguish between white and black males than to distinguish between white and black females by changing the form of their names or choosing names for slaves not used by whites. Such distinctions in naming patterns helped to reinforce the status and power of white men.

The records unfortunately do not reveal who did the naming of black women, whether immigrant blacks influenced the choice of names assigned them or whether owners or mothers chose the names of black children. Control over the power of naming was an important indicator of the power relationship that existed between owner and slave, but general cultural constraints also shaped the choices made by whoever exercised that power. Tradition greatly limited the naming patterns of whites. The oldest children bore grandparents' names, the next oldest were their parents' namesakes, and younger children were named for siblings of their parents. Occasionally a family would use the mother's family name as a first name for a younger child.[23] However, the important point is that general cultural constraints determined naming patterns, not individuals, and the gender constraints of Virginia meant that women of both races shared a naming experience that offered them fewer choices, accorded them less individuality, and reinforced a dependent status.

Childbirth is an experience shared by women of all races, but in King William Parish the patterns of childbearing reveal another way in which black women lived within a community of women and yet encountered a separate experience. Next to the ordinary rhythms of work, childbirth may have been the most common experience for women. Pregnancy, childbirth, and nursing provided a steady background beat to the lives of women in the colonies. Recent research has shown that colonial white women made childbirth a community event, infused with rituals of support by other women, and that these rituals of lying-in were shared with black women.[24] The evidence from Manakin, however, suggests that the risks of childbirth were greater for black women than for white. Although they may have participated in the rituals surrounding childbirth, black women were the center of attention less frequently because they had fewer children; moreover, participation in this women's culture required them to abandon some of their African traditions. Truly, childbirth was a bittersweet experience for black women.

The fragmentary King William Parish Register includes the records of births of slaves among forty-eight owners for the years from 1724-1744.[25] The parish register reveals only the owner's name, not the mother's, but since most white families claimed only one or two black women it is possible to trace the childbearing history of individual women.[26] The average birth interval was about 28 months, but was often less than two years. The experience of Marie, a slave of Jean Levillain, illustrates this point. Marie's first two children were born 19 months apart, followed by intervals of 24, 25, 11, 14, and 30 months.[27] In general, for the black women of Manakin, the most frequent interval was 20 months. Fifty-six percent of the birth intervals were between 15 and 34 months. However, another quarter of the intervals fell into a block running 36 to 47 months. The interval between births, however, was much more ragged than these figures suggest. Many women had long gaps in their childbearing histories. Other women had few or no children. For example, Pegg, the slave of Barbara Dutoy, had only one child in twelve years.

Table 2
Birth Intervals for Women Associated with Manakin

Interval in Months	Black Births 1724-1744		White Births 1701-1783	
	Number	Percent	Number	Percent
0-8	0	0	2	1
9-14	6	9	5	3
15-19	10	14	23	11
20-24	12	17	58	29
25-29	15	21	44	22
30-34	3	4	25	12
35-39	8	12	22	10
40-44	7	10	4	2
45-49	3	4	5	3
50-54	1	2	6	3
55-59	0	0	2	1
60+	5	7	6	3
Total	70	100	202	100

Source: King William Parish Register in Brock, ed., Documents; William Macfarlane Jones, ed., The Douglas Register (Richmond, Va., 1928).

While the average and median for childbirth intervals were similar for black and white women in the parish, there were also major differences. The black woman was much more likely to have an intermittent history of childbirth with long gaps, ending much sooner that it did for the whites of Manakin. Birth intervals for whites were more tightly clustered around 24 months than black births. Seventy-four percent of the white births fell in the interval between 15 and 34 months (see Table 2). Elizabeth Chastain LeSueur, for example, bore children every two to three years with almost clockwork regularity from 1728 to 1753, while her slave Phillis had two children 30 months apart and then had no more children for at least seven years.[28]

The child-spacing patterns for black and white women of King William Parish provide important clues to the adaptation of black women to American slavery and their participation in a community culture surrounding childbirth. African customs of nursing were different from those of Europeans. In Africa women often nursed children for more than three years, abstaining from sexual relations during that period. Black women continued these patterns in the Caribbean slave communities, as did seventeenth-century blacks in the Chesapeake. The secondary cluster of birth intervals of three to four years suggests that a number of immigrant black women, including Phillis, continued that tradition in the Manakin area. European women, however, nursed for a shorter time and had resultingly closer birth intervals of about two years.[29] Marie and a number of other black women in the parish adopted the shorter European traditions of nursing. Whether this adoption of European custom came at the urging of owners or as part of a cultural accommodation by black women, the result was that Marie and others like her had one more bond with white women.

In another way, however, the birth intervals explain how childbirth set black and white women apart, for black women had many fewer children per mother than the white women did. Childbearing histories for twenty-eight black women and fifty-five white women appear in Table 2. Twice as many white women provided almost three times the number of birth intervals as did black women. The difference may be a result of fewer black births, owners more frequently forgetting to register black births, or a combination of the two. All of the possibilities suggest a different experience for black women. Other evidence, such as estate inventories, suggests that fewer births account for most of the difference. Because many black women lived in King William Parish for fewer than their total childbearing years, it was necessary to transform the raw figures into data for a stable community in order to make comparisons with the experience of whites. A stable population would have been represented by just under nineteen black women living in the parish continuously throughout the twenty-year period. They would have averaged 6.01 children to produce the births actually registered. While this compares favorably with figures for total children born to the French immigrant generation at King William Parish, it is considerably lower than the average number of children born by the later generation of white settlers at Manakin. Some white women also ended their childbearing after only a few children, or had long gaps due to the death of a spouse or physical problems, but most produced a steady stream of children spaced two years apart.[30] If black women had borne children spaced at the average interval without interruption, it would have taken only 14.2 years to reach the family size indicated by the stable population calculations.

That most black women were immigrants and most whites were native-born accounts for some of the difference in numbers of children, for immigrant women often delayed starting families while searching for mates or found their marriages disrupted. Others reached menopause before they had been in the Manakin area twenty years. The gaps in the middle of black women's childbearing years, however, are at least as significant as any shortening of the years at risk by late starts. Those mid-life gaps in childbearing were due in part to black life expectancy. Africans and other immigrants to the South had high death rates, even in the more healthful eighteenth century. Disruptions caused by the death of a partner could inhibit the total number of children a woman bore, especially while the black community was small, for finding a new partner might take years. Although white women also lost partners, by 1730 the population of King William Parish was colonial-born and more resistant to the endemic fevers. Thus their marriages were more stable. The slave population, however, continued to be heavily immigrant and thus continued to have a higher rate of marriage disruption. Transfers of ownership and removal to other areas increased the possibility of separation from partners and hence lowered the number of children born.

Childbearing was a part of the rhythm of a woman's life, but that rhythm had a different beat for black women. All twelve of Elizabeth LeSueur's children were born in October, November, or December. Phillis's known childbirths, however, were in April and October. Two-thirds of King William Parish's black births, however, occurred between February and July. The months of August through January saw relatively few black births. Black women, then, usually conceived during the months of May through October. The white women of Manakin show a much different pattern of births. Births were heavy in the fall and early spring and lowest in June, July, and August (see Figure 1). White conceptions were lowest in the fall; blacks were lowest in the deep

Figure 1
Birth Months for Manakin Children, 1724-1750

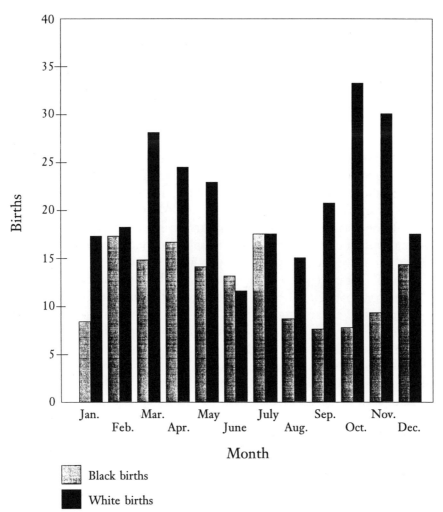

Black births

White births

winter.[31] Black women thus were in the later stages of pregnancy during the heavy labor season of spring planting. Surely this affected their health.

The puzzling question of why black women had their children on a different cycle from white women has no ready solution. Black women were certainly not planning their pregnancies in order to receive reduced work loads during the spring, because there is evidence that the loads were not reduced. It is possible that black men and women had more contact with each other during the summer and fall while they were tending and harvesting crops. In the cold months black women may have been kept close to the plantation house working on domestic projects such as spinning, and thus were not free to meet with their partners. White women had no such constraints. Opportunity for conception increased when the cold months brought white men closer to the hearth fires.

The white women of Manakin expected their children to survive to adulthood.[32] A black woman could not. King William Parish death records are fragmentary, so slave deaths appear only in a few cases where the record of birth includes a note of the infant's death.[33] Circumstantial evidence, however, suggests high infant and child mortality. Only 44 out of 151 of the slave children whose births were recorded in the parish register appear in any other legal and church record, and for some that second appearance was as a child. Death explains many of the disappearances.[34] For example, Beti, slave of Gideon Chambon, bore children Jean (John) in 1727 and Marye in 1733. When Chambon's estate inventory was filed in 1739 neither child appeared on the list. Given Chambon's age and economic conditions, the most likely explanation is that the children died, not that he sold or gave them away. Similarly, Magdalene, born in 1744, does not appear in any records after the filing of John Harris's will when she was seven. Owners registered two and three children by the same name over the years. John Chastain, for example, registered the births of black newborns named Fillis on March 24, 1745/6 and June 12, 1753. Only one slave of that name appears on his estate inventory. Likewise, Bartholomew Dupuy's slave Sara bore sons named Jack in both 1727 and 1730. Apparently they were doing what many families also did following the death of a white child, that is, replacing it by another of the same name.[35]

The work patterns of black women fostered the high death rate among their children by exhausting mothers and making infant care difficult. The experiences of Aggy, a slave of the Levillain family, provide some clues to the relationship between work, childbearing, and infant mortality. Aggy (Agar) had been born in Manakin on August 7, 1733, as the slave of Jean Levillain; she passed by will to Jean's son Anthony Lavillain in 1746.[36] Four years later, when Aggy was seventeen, Anthony died intestate, leaving Aggy the property of Anthony's newborn daughter Mary and the subject of an administered estate for the next fifteen years. Aggy's first child was born when she was eighteen. Two years later she had another. Throughout those years she worked in the fields, while the administratrix of the estate, Elizabeth Lavillain Young Starkey, recorded expenses for "nursing" both small children. The youngest, a girl, died by age three. In 1763 Aggy, by then thirty, again became pregnant. The pregnancy was not easy, however, for the records show payments to Mrs. Chastain for treating Aggy "when sick" and attending Aggy's lying-in.[37]

Aggy's life illustrates the black pattern of work and childbearing in King William Parish. Beginning in her teens Aggy had two children spaced two years apart, but then there was a ten-year gap before she had another child. From 1754 to 1756 Aggy was hired out. Then she returned to work with the other slaves growing tobacco, wheat, and corn for the estate. John Levillain, Anthony's brother and, after 1754, Mary's guardian, did see that Aggy got medical treatment during her difficult later pregnancy, but the records Levillain filed with the court for income to the estate credit her with the same share of work on the crops as other slaves, so he had not reduced her work. Such practices would increase the risk of infant mortality.[38]

The records for the Manakin area do not reveal much about the birth customs for black women, but Charlotte Chastain's appearance during Aggy's lying-in was not the only time a white midwife was paid for the delivery of a black woman's baby in the Manakin area.[39] Thus while the Manakin families might not have been rich enough to provide the elaborate lying-ins for black women that Mary Beth Norton has described, the birth experience was not left entirely to the black community.[40] Since we also know that black women helped at the births of white children, the physical act of giving birth may have been one of the most significant ways in which black and white women served each other in a single community.

As with the other aspects of their lives, work both separated and brought black women together with whites. Virginia's tithe laws made clear the distinctions. White women such as Elizabeth Chastain LeSueur were not counted in figuring the tithe. In fact, they only appeared on the tithe lists when widowed with slaves or male children sixteen years or over. On the other hand, black women like Phillis were counted. Ironically, it is easier to trace black women from year to year in the community since they are listed on the tithes than it is to trace white women. Eventually, in 1769, free black women received the same exemption as white women, but slave women remained a part of the tithe. In other words, black women were considered a basic part of the agricultural labor force in a way that white women were not.[41] Undoubtedly, Phillis had spent part of her time working in the LeSueur fields. When the LeSueurs purchased her they had no children old enough to help with farm work, and David and Elizabeth LeSueur were planting without any regular help. Phillis's arrival assured Elizabeth that she could withdraw from occasional help in the fields to her many household duties and garden.

While white women seldom worked away from home, black women sometimes did. Slave rentals kept the labor supply flexible, cut costs for care by owners, and provided an income for widows and orphans. Two major sources for rental slaves were estates managed to provide an income for widows and orphans, and wealthy farmers who hired out their surplus women and children slaves. Women slaves hired out more frequently than men.[42] Thus black women might be separated from family and friends in order to secure the income that allowed a white woman to remain on the family farm. Agar, who had arrived at Manakin in 1714, spent the 1730s hired out by the widow Magdalene Salle, while the family's other adult slave, Bob, stayed on the plantation. Only when Magdalene's son came of age and assumed management of the plantation did Agar return to the plantation. Widow Barbara Dutoy also rented her slaves to other residents of Manakin from 1726 to 1733. In both cases rental gave the widow an income without the worry of planting. It allowed minimum disruption to the widow's life, but at the expense of disrupting the slave woman's life.[43]

Surviving orphans court records and wills document other hiring out of slaves in the Manakin area. Jean Levillain hired out Aggy from 1754 to 1756 for a charge of about £4 each year. Some hiring was short-term. James Holman hired out a black woman for two weeks' time while managing Peter Martin's estate. In addition, nine children's births appear in the parish register without their owners paying tithes on an adult woman. The mothers were probably rented out and appeared under the renter's name on the tithe list.[44] A hired slave could move frequently; for example, Lucy seems to have been hired by Abraham Salle in 1724, Jack Griffin in 1732 and 1733, and Pierre Louis Soblet in 1734 and 1735.[45] The rental of female slaves thus seems to have been an integral part of the Manakin labor system, allowing aspiring farmers to add to their small labor forces while providing income for widows and orphans. Once again the community's perception of black women primarily as field hands set black and white women apart.

Phillis might have spent much of her time in the fields, but she also worked with Elizabeth LeSueur on the many tasks associated with women's work. Domestic work was not a single occupation but a variety of highly skilled tasks shared by women on the plantation.[46] For example, clothmaking occupied both white and black women in the Manakin area. When David LeSueur died in 1772, the family owned working farms in both Buckingham and Cumberland counties. Only the home plantation in Cumberland, however, had cotton, wool and cotton cards, a wool wheel, two spindles, four flax wheels, and parts for two looms. Elizabeth obviously oversaw and worked with Phillis and Phillis's two grown daughters in the making of a variety of cloth.[47] The LeSueurs were not unusual, for inventories throughout the Manakin region mention several crops including flax, the tools necessary to produce linen thread, and somewhat less frequently, looms for weaving.[48] The Lavillain estate, for example, purchased two spinning wheels. The wheels were for the use of Aggy and Nan, slaves of the estate who continued to be credited with a share of the crops of tobacco and grains. John Levillain simply added cloth production to the women's field duties.[49] The usefulness of women in the tasks of cloth production may have encouraged owners to purchase women slaves. From its beginning the colony at Manakin provided Virginia cloth, used to clothe slaves and the poor. Black women worked with white women in this production on the small farm, thus providing another way in which a community of women cut across racial lines.

The smallness of slaveholdings and the relatively short life expectancies of owners created major instabilities in the lives of black women that exceeded the uncertainties of life for their white mistresses. Although owners recognized that black families existed, and while there is convincing evidence that kinship ties were strong among blacks, the value of slaves as property meant that black family stability was tied to the life cycle of their owners.[50] Short life expectancies and parental willingness to establish adult children on farms of their own as soon as possible accelerated the cycle in the Manakin area. Life patterns in the late seventeenth and early eighteenth centuries were such that most Chesapeake parents expected to die before all their children came of age.[51] One result of this expectation was the willingness of parents to give adult children their shares of the estate when they came of age or married. For example, Elizabeth Chastain's brother John and sister Judith were already living on their shares of land when their father Peter wrote his will.[52] Thus even a long-lived owner was no guarantee of stability in a slave family.

Most blacks in the Manakin area changed hands upon the death of an owner or the coming of age of a child of the owner. Because slaves were valuable legacies to children, they were often divided among several heirs. Daughters, especially, received slaves as their share of the estate, either as dowries or legacies. With slaveholdings small, black families were divided at each period of change within the white family. Most bequests in the Manakin area (except for life interests to widows) were of one or two slaves. David LeSueur, for example, granted each of his eight surviving children one slave. Phillis, her two oldest children, and another male (probably husband to her daughter) stayed with their mistress, Elizabeth Chastain LeSueur, but all of Phillis's younger children and grandchildren were scattered.[53] Owners when possible left very small children with slave mothers or bequeathed the slave mother to a married son or daughter and the slave's children to the children of the son or daughter. Thus black women received some recognition of bonds with children not accorded to men. In fact, the estate appraisers often perceived infants and mothers as one, giving a single value to a mother and her small child. Frequently they did not even bother to list the infant's name.[54]

Black women might wait for years before the pain of such divisions became real. While the marriage of older children of the owners caused some separation among black families, the major estate divisions came when the owner died. Many estates remained intact for years awaiting the coming of age of minor children or the remarriage or death of a widow. Thus the fate of black women (and men) depended on the fate of their white mistresses.[55] For example, Kate was a slave of Anthony Rapine when he died in 1737. Rapine gave his wife, Margaret, a life interest in half the estate with all eventually to go to his daughter, Maryanne Martin. Since Maryanne and her husband lived with the Rapines, Kate's life went on unchanged. In 1740 she bore a daughter, Hannah. Three years later Maryanne Martin was widowed and soon after she remarried. She deeded Kate and Hannah to her year-old son, Peter Martin, shortly after remarrying. In 1747, ten years after Anthony Rapine died, the estate was finally divided between Margaret Rapine and Thomas Smith, who had married the now-deceased Maryanne. Kate and Hannah (by then age seven) were listed together on the inventory and passed into Smith's possession. He then turned Kate and Hannah over to Peter's new guardian in 1749. At last, after twelve years, Kate and Hannah were forced to move.[56] The black woman on a larger estate had a better chance of remaining with kin following the death of an owner. The few large estates included in the study divided slaves on the basis of where they lived, often giving a particular farm and its slaves to an heir.[57]

The slave woman lived and worked in a very small community at Manakin. Since each family owned only a few slaves, a black community could not exist on a single plantation. The farms at Manakin were small enough (the original allotments were 133 acres each) that visiting between farms would be possible, and thus a wider community might have existed. The birth patterns, however, suggest that such visiting was limited. Although the dispersed black population might have hindered the formation of a black community, the tasks of the black woman put her in constant contact with whites. Family members on a small farm labored in the fields alongside the slaves, and women's chores such as spinning might be done with the wife and daughters of the owner. Historians have speculated that slaves who lived on small plantations or in areas isolated from a black community probably adopted white values and customs more readily than those who could fashion a creole life-style with other blacks.[58] For the black woman this meant partial acceptance into the special world of women's society. Such acceptance made more poignant the contrast in birth rates, child mortality, and family stability between blacks and whites.

Life for black women in the Manakin area was filled with insecurity. Some risks, such as childbirth, were shared with white women, but others were not. As part of a double minority black women enjoyed a favorable marriage market, but dispersion of holdings threatened the families formed by black women with separation. Some slaves on large plantations could begin to develop distinct creole societies near Manakin, but that was possible only after 1750 and only for a small proportion of slaves. Slave rentals, which affected women more than men, added another dimension of instability to that ensured by the short life spans of spouses and owners. The decisions made by widows to remarry, farm, or hire out slaves for income not only determined whether white families would remain intact, but whether black ones would too. Most black women in the Manakin area lived on small farms or quarters where their field work was supplemented by sharing in the household tasks of the white women on the farm. The "bonds of womanhood" surrounded her life as much as the bonds of slavery, beginning with the very choice of a name. Childbearing was especially frustrating for the black woman, filled with the pain of frequent infant death, heavy workloads when pregnant, and separation from children. But childbirth also meant sharing in a woman's network that stretched across racial lines. The life of a black woman was thus constantly subjected to the cross-pressures of belonging to a woman's subculture without full membership.

NOTES

1. Elizabeth was the daughter of Pierre and Anne Soblet Chastain. I approximated her birth date from the known birth years of male siblings and the order of children as listed in Pierre's will. In other words, the only clues to her age come from records about males. Phillis had to be sixteen or older in 1744 when she appears on the King William Parish Tithe List. "June, 1744—A List of King William Parish," in R. A. Brock, ed., *Documents Chiefly Unpublished, Relating to the Huguenot Emigration to Virginia and to the Settlement at Manakin-To*wn . . . (Richmond, 1886), 113, hereinafter cited as 1744 Tithe List; will of Pierre Chastain, November 20, 1728, Deeds and Wills, Goochland County (Virginia State Library, Richmond), microfilm; the Virginia State Library has microfilm and photostatic copies of all extant colonial records from the state, hence all subsequent references to county records will refer to the holdings in the Virginia State Library; will of David LeSueur, February 24, 1772, Wills, Cumberland County; inventory of David LeSueur, April 26, 1773, Wills, Cumberland County.

2. For a general discussion of the experiences of antebellum black women see Jacqueline Jones, *Labor of Love, Labor of Sorrow: Black Women, Work, and the Family from Slavery to the Present* (New York, 1985), and Deborah Gray White, *Ar'n't I A Woman?: Female Slaves in the Plantation South* (New York, 1985). The work on the colonial plantation mistress begins with the classic study by Julia Cherry Spruill, *Women's Life and Work in the Southern Colonies* (Chapel Hill, 1938). Recent studies include Lois Green Carr and Lorena S. Walsh, "The Planter's Wife: The Experience of White Women in Seventeenth-Century Maryland," *William and Mary Quarterly*, 3d Ser., XXXIV (October 1977), 542-71; Joan R. Gundersen and Gwen Victor Gampel, "Married Women's Legal Status in Eighteenth-Century New York and Virginia," *William and Mary Quarterly*, 3d Ser., XXXIX (January 1982), 114-34; Daniel Blake Smith, *Inside the Great House: Planter Family Life in Eighteenth-Century Chesapeake Society* (Ithaca, N. Y., 1980); Darrett B. and Anita H. Rutman, " 'Now-Wives and Sons-in-Law': Parental Death in a Seventeenth-Century Virginia County," in Thad W. Tate and David L. Ammerman, eds., *The Chesapeake in the Seventeenth Century: Essays on Anglo-American Society* (Chapel Hill, 1979).

3. For a discussion of the origins of the black family in the Chesapeake that includes information on women, although not written from their perspective, see Allan Kulikoff, "The Beginnings of the Afro-American Family in Maryland," in Aubrey C. Land, Lois Green Carr, and Edward C. Papenfuse, eds., *Law, Society, and Politics in Early Maryland* (Baltimore, 1977). Russell R. Menard, "The Maryland Slave Population, 1658 to 1730: A Demographic Profile of Blacks in Four Counties," *William and Mary Quarterly*, 3d Ser., XXXII (January 1975), 29-54; Edmund S. Morgan, *American Slavery, American Freedom: The Ordeal of Colonial Virginia* (New York, 1975), 295-315; Peter H. Wood, *Black Majority: Negroes in Colonial South Carolina from 1670 through the Stono Rebellion* (New York, 1974); Gerald W. Mullin, *Flight and Rebellion: Slave Resistance in Eighteenth-Century Virginia* (New York,

1972), 103-105; Herbert G. Gutman, *The Black Family in Slavery and Freedom, 1750-1925* (New York, 1976), 1-230. Gutman uses material from 1750 to 1860 as though it were part of one general period.

4. See Gutman, *The Black Family*, 335-39, and T. H. Breen and Stephen Innes, *"Myne Owne Ground": Race and Freedom on Virginia's Eastern Shore, 1640-1676* (New York, 1980), 22-23, for other historians who note that blacks and whites might be part of a community together.

5. This essay is part of a larger community study that includes use of family reconstitution techniques. King William Parish was an Anglican parish created especially for the Huguenot settlers at Manakin. The parish always received special treatment, including exemption from paying the salary for clergy set by law, but its vestry and clergy were under Anglican discipline. The basic records available include the King William Parish Vestry Book (with tithe lists), 1707-1750, the King William Parish Register (births), 1724-1750, and profiles of black and white members of the community drawn from the county records of Henrico, Goochland, Cumberland, Chesterfield, and Powhatan counties. These records include estate inventories, wills, deeds, guardian accounts, estate administrations, and white family records. I have traced the blacks in the community after 1744 by identifying the white families in the area and then using their estate records to find blacks. Miscellaneous records from other counties and parishes have filled specific gaps. The study ends in 1776, but in order to complete profiles of the people I have used materials after that date. The King William Parish Vestry Book is a single volume, in French, housed at the Virginia Historical Society in Richmond. The King William Parish Register is printed in Brock, ed., *Documents*, 77-111.

6. Vestry records and church services were in French. The parish used a French translation of the Anglican prayerbook while continuing Huguenot traditions of limited admission to communion. Beginning in 1719, at the request of Robert Jones, one service in six was given in English. The wills of Manakin settlers filed before 1720 were all in French. King William Parish Vestry Book, December 26, 1718. The vestry book has been translated and published, but because of errors in the published version's tithe lists I have used the original manuscript.

7. David LeSueur was a second-generation Huguenot refugee, but he was born in London in 1703. He came to Virginia about 1724. William and Susan Minet, eds., *Livre des Tessmoignages de L'Eglise de Threadneedle Street, 1669-1789* (London, 1909), 175. There was a major changeover in the vestry at this time. Eight new vestrymen were elected August 25, 1718. King William Parish Vestry Book, August 25, 1718.

8. The church records are very thin for this period, and there is also a gap in the county records. Later evidence indicates that most of those who disappeared from the records in this period died. For example, a dispute over land revealed that the husband and all four sons of the Mattoon family died in quick succession, leaving sole ownership with the wife Susannah. Petition of Susannah Carner, June 17, 1730, and June 12, 1734, in H. R. McIlwaine, Wilmer L. Hall, and Benjamin J. Hillman, eds., *Executive Journals of the Council of Colonial Virginia* (6 vols., Richmond, 1925-66), IV, 222, 326.

9. For example, the Salle family was the first to own slaves in the community, and Abraham Salle served as a justice of the peace appointed specially for the French community. Elizabeth Chastain LeSueur's father, Pierre Chastain, was the other special magistrate. He bought his first slave in 1713.

10. A census of white inhabitants in 1714 included 71 men, 62 women, 85 boys, and 70 girls, for a total of 288. The lower number of girls may reflect early ages of marriage (some out of the community) for women. I have corrected the totals of boys and girls to include the orphans. The census listed them by name but counted them only in the grand total. "List Generalle de tous les François Protestants Refuges, Establys dans la Paroisse du Roy Guillaume, Comte d'Henrico en Virginia, y Compris les Femmes, Enfans, Veuses, et Orphelins," in Brock, ed., *Documents*, 74-76.

11. Menard, "The Maryland Slave Population," 32-34.

12. There are no tithe lists for 1716, 1721-22, 1727-28, and 1740-43. The lists for 1729, 1734, and 1736-40 record only the number of tithes charged to each head of a family rather than list individual names. Part of the 1744 list also was returned this way, but by using other records I could determine the slaves involved for most of those families.

13. Tithe Lists, King William Parish Vestry Book; 1744 Tithe List, in Brock ed., *Documents*, 112-15. In 1730 the tithe lists showed fifty-two slaves with a ratio of about three men for every two women. In the next several decades the ratio rose so that men outnumbered women 2:1. The parish tithe lists are not available after 1750, but evidence from estate inventories and wills suggests that the numbers of men and women had again become more equal by 1776.

14. The numbers are approximate because it was not possible to be sure that I had made all record linkages for a particular slave. Thus the figures inevitably include a bias enlarging the total. On the other hand, since the birth and tithe records are incomplete, the study also has missed a random number of slaves drawn from both sexes. The major sources for the profiles of slaves are the tithe lists 1710-44, wills and inventories of people associated with Manakin, and the King William Parish Register in Brock, ed., *Documents*, 77-111.

15. Allan Kulikoff, "The Origins of Afro-American Society in Tidewater Maryland and Virginia, 1700 to 1790," *William and Mary Quarterly*, 3d Ser., XXXV (April 1978), 233-34.

16. Allan Kulikoff, "A 'Prolifick' People: Black Population Growth in the Chesapeake Colonies, 1700-1790," *Southern Studies*, XVI (Winter 1977), 391-94. Kulikoff notes that the period 1710-40 was a transitional one, moving from importation of West Indian slaves to direct importation from Africa. This shift skewed sex ratios to produce a heavier male bias.

17. The evidence suggests that despite slower growth of the total slave population, Manakin went through the initial patterns of growth and importation at about the same time and with less trauma than the Tidewater counties studied by Allan Kulikoff. Kulikoff, "The Origins of Afro-American Society," 226-59.

18. Russell R. Menard has argued that a predominantly male population inhibited family formation among blacks in early Maryland. This is true only if one views the matter from the perspective of a male slave or defines a family as headed by a male. Menard, "The Maryland Slave Population," 34-35.

19. The tithe list for 1730 includes seventy-three white family units. Of these, twenty-six included blacks. 1730 Tithe List, King William Parish Vestry Book.

20. Wood, *Black Majority*, 181-86.

21. The problems encountered by Stephen Chastain over the payment of duties for a boy he purchased in 1714 support this hypothesis. Chastain thought that the duty had been paid by the ship captain and tried to collect compensation from the captain after

a court ruled Chastain liable. Order Book, July 6, 1714, August 1714, and October 1714, Henrico County.

22. The most common women's names were Betty, Hannah, Jenny, Sarah, Jude, Lucy, Moll, Nann, and Jane or Janne. The most common men's names were Will, Tom, Dick, Frank, and Jack. These are not the same names that Herbert G. Gutman found most common among nineteenth-century blacks, despite naming patterns that should have reproduced family names in the next generation. Gutman did find that women's naming patterns were different from men's. Gutman, *The Black Family*, 187. Darrett and Anita Rutman found very similar naming patterns among the slaves of Middlesex County, Virginia, from 1650 to 1750. Darrett B. and Anita H. Rutman, *A Place in Time: Explicatus* (New York, 1984), 98-99.

23. For example, the names of the children of David and Elizabeth Chastain LeSueur included David and Elizabeth (each used twice due to the death of a child), Chastain, Peter (her father's name), Catherine (his mother's), John (her brother's), James (her uncle's), Samuel, Tell, and Martell. The last three names may have been new to the family or were a part of David's background.

24. Mary Beth Norton, *Liberty's Daughters: The Revolutionary Experience of American Women, 1750-1800* (Boston, 1980), 78; Richard W. Wertz and Dorothy C. Wertz, *Lying-In: A History of Childbirth in America* (New York, 1977), 4-6; Catherine M. Scholten, " 'On the Importance of the Obstetrick Art': Changing Customs of Childbirth in America, 1760 to 1825," *William and Mary Quarterly*, 3d Ser., XXXIV (July 1977), 426-45. Norton's work specifically mentions southern birthing experiences; the others look at childbirth as a general social custom brought from England.

25. By comparing the tithe lists and parish register it was possible to determine that sixty-four black women over age sixteen lived in the parish during at least part of the years covered by the register. There were 151 births registered. 113 during the period 1724-44.

26. Nothing illustrates the patriarchal nature of society better than a birth registration system that has infants born to males. The church records record only births, not baptisms, making clear that the owners registered these births so that there would be proof of age, an important factor when the slave would become taxable at sixteen.

27. King William Parish Register, in Brock, ed., *Documents*, 80-100. Marie was Levillain's only adult female slave until 1735, when Nan was added to the tithes. Marie's last two childbirths overlap with the first of Nan's, but it is possible to sort out which births belong to each mother. The information on black births is taken from the parish register, with what support is available elsewhere. The information for white births includes wills, family records, and records of other parishes. The birth intervals for blacks are thus limited to the period covered by the King William Parish Register, but white births covered the whole eighteenth century.

28. The LeSueurs registered births in King William Parish in 1728, 1733, 1735, 1738, 1740, 1744, 1747, and 1750. David LeSueur's will included three children not in this listing, twins born in 1753 and a daughter who must have been born in 1742, given her own date of marriage and history of childbirth. The LeSueurs were out of the parish in 1730 and may have had a child then too. As for Phillis, the last seven years of the parish register include no slave births for the LeSueur family.

29. Menard, "The Maryland Slave Population," 38-41; Herbert S. Klein and Stanley L. Engerman, "Fertility Differentials between Slaves in the Unites States and the

British West Indies: A Note on Lactation Practices and Their Possible Implications," *William and Mary Quarterly*, 3d Ser., XXXV (April 1978), 368-72.

30. It is difficult to get complete information on the childbearing histories of women from King William Parish, but I have compiled secure evidence on 101. The 28 immigrant women on whom I have information bore 138 children, or an average of 4.9. The 45 native-born women bore 484 children, or an average of 10.75. I deliberately have not used completed family size since that figure is based on intact marriages. I have chosen instead to compile the complete childbearing histories of women, even if they were cut short by death or continued through several marriages, because this views the topic through the eyes of the woman.

31. A similar pattern was reported by the Rutmans and Charles Wetherell for Middlesex County, Virginia. Darrett B. Rutman, Charles Wetherell, and Anita H. Rutman, "Rhythms of Life: Black and White Seasonality in the Early Chesapeake," *Journal of Interdisciplinary History*, XI (Summer 1980), 29-53. I have chosen to chart the actual births rather than the cosine measure of variance from the expected average because the actual births provide a clearer picture for those who are not demographers. The cosine pattern for King William Parish, however, is a reasonable fit with the Rutman data.

32. The infant mortality rate for Manakin families is low. Many families saw all of their children reach adulthood. Infant mortality seems restricted to a few families and probably reflected conditions specific to those families.

33. Examples of infant deaths are the births of Moll, born December 31, 1740, and died January 11, 1740/1, slave of Martha Chastain; and Judith, born April 9, 1740, and died June 19, 1740, slave of John Villain, Jr., King William Parish Register, in Brock, ed., *Documents*, 99-100. In this area Elizabeth LeSueur and Phillis reversed the common patterns. The two children of Phillis whose births were recorded in the parish register both were still with the family thirty years later. Elizabeth LeSueur's first two children died before age twenty-one. A third died unmarried at age thirty-one. *Ibid.*, 81-104; will of David LeSueur III, June 26, 1769, Wills, Cumberland County, and will of David LeSueur I, February 24, 1772, *ibid*. Because of the repeated use of first names within a family I have adopted a system of identifying those with the same first and last names by Roman numerals assigned by order of birth.

34. Gutman found a similar mortality level among nineteenth-century blacks. Gutman, *The Black Family*, 124. The county records of the counties for the years Manakin was included in each of their bounds include only one deed of gift of a King William Parish slave and no outright sales of blacks living in Manakin. In fact, there are few transfers of blacks other than by will in these records for anyone. It is possible that such sales were not normally recorded, but the lack of evidence for slave sales in the region from the *Virginia Gazette*, the fact that slaves do not appear as property to be sold in estate sales reported to the courts, that so many slaves can be traced through transfers by will and estate records, the existence of a few recorded deeds, and the curious provision of Virginia law that slaves were real estate, not personal property, all add weight to the conclusion that few slave children disappeared from these records because of sales.

35. Chambon was illiterate. His name appears in the records with several different spellings. I am using the form that appears most often, King William Parish Register, in Brock, ed., *Documents*, 80, 88, 105-106, 110, 79, 84; inventory of Gideon Chambon II, August 21, 1739, Wills, Goochland County; inventory of John Harris, March 26, 1753, Wills, Cumberland County.

36. The father and son spelled their last names differently. I have used the spelling each man preferred. King William Parish Register, in Brock, ed., *Documents*, 89. Will of John Levillain, June 17, 1746, Deeds and Wills, Goochland County.

37. Anthony Lavillain's widow, Elizabeth Jones Lavillain, remarried twice while administering the estate. Her name changed on different sections of the records filed with the court. Anthony Lavillain estate management records, August 21, 1754, August 25, 1755, September 1757, and August 24, 1764, Will Book, Orphans Court, Cumberland County.

38. Anthony Lavillain estate management records, August 24, 1764, Will Book, Orphans Court, Cumberland County.

39. There were several adult Chastain women in the area, but Charlotte Judith Chastain, wife of the clerk of the vestry and local surgeon (and sister-in-law to Elizabeth Chastain LeSueur), was the most likely to have been a midwife. The records for management of the Frances Bernard estate include payments to Mrs. Robertson for "Delivering her [Mary Bernard's] Negro Woman" and to Mrs. Burnett for the same. Frances Bernard estate management records, August 1755 and August 1760, Will Book, Orphans Court, Cumberland County.

40. Norton, *Liberty's Daughters*, 66-67.

41. William Waller Hening, [ed.], *The Statutes at Large: Being A Collection Of All The Laws of Virginia, From The First Session Of The Legislature In The Year 1619* (13 vols., Richmond, 1819-23), VIII, 393.

42. The Manakin evidence is very similar to that reported by Sarah S. Hughes for the late eighteenth century. Hughes, "Slaves for Hire: The Allocation of Black Labor in Elizabeth City County, Virginia, 1782 to 1810," *William and Mary Quarterly*, 3d Ser., XXXV (April 1978), 268-72.

43. Several of the tithe lists from the 1730s do not list dependents by name, so it is hard to trace slaves. Magdalene Salle inherited Bob and Agar in 1730/1. In 1733 Agar appears as a tithe of John Martin, whereas Bob appears under Magdalene Salle's name. In 1744 Magdalene Salle is credited with two tithes, presumably Bob and Agar. Joseph and Pegg were slaves of Pierre Dutoy. His widow Barbara inherited them, but only once do they appear under her name. They are listed with several different families until 1733, when they appear under Barbara's new son-in-law, Thomas Porter. King William Parish Vestry Book, 1723-36; will of Abraham Salle II, March 1, 1730/1, Miscellaneous Papers, Henrico County; will of Pierre Dutoy, October 3, 1726, Deeds and Wills, Henrico County.

44. Anthony Lavillain estate management records, August 25, 1755, August 24, 1764, Wills, Orphans Court, Cumberland County; Peter Martin estate management records, March 19, 1754, Deeds and Wills, Orphans Court, Goochland County. The slave births were to Joseph Bingley, James Brian, David LeSueur, Daniel Perault, Thomas Porter, Nicholas Soulie, Jacob Trabue, and Giles Allegre. King William Parish Register, in Brock, ed., *Documents, passim*. The births were not to mothers under sixteen. Nicholas Soulie registered his first slave birth in 1728 but had no slave tithes until 1732. It is unlikely that one of his slaves gave birth at age twelve.

45. Tithe lists, 1724, 1732-35, King William Parish Vestry Book.

46. Menard, "The Maryland Slave Population," 53. Menard argues that while male slaves had a variety of skilled occupations to draw them away from the fields, women had only domestic work and cloth production. Domestic work, however, in the eighteenth century was made up of quite diverse, highly skilled activities. For a good

description of the many skills of colonial domestic work see Laurel Thatcher Ulrich, *Good Wives: Image and Reality in the Lives of Women in Northern New England, 1650-1750* (New York, 1982), 11-86.

47. Despite David LeSueur's status as a vestry member, his seventeen slaves, and landholdings of more than a thousand acres, his inventory is that of a simple farming family with only a few luxury items. There is little doubt that Elizabeth Chastain worked at household tasks and did not just supervise them. Inventories of David LeSueur, April 26, 1773, Wills, Cumberland County.

48. See for example the inventory of Peter Faure, April 16, 1745, Deeds and Wills, Goochland County.

49. The two black women were the only women for whom the estate might have purchased the wheels. The heiress, Mary, was away at school. Anthony Lavillain estate management records, August 24, 1764, Will Book, Orphans Court, Cumberland County.

50. Herbert G. Gutman develops this insight extensively in his book, *The Black Family*, 154-55, 138.

51. Rutman and Rutman, " 'Now-Wives and Sons-in-Law'," 153-82.

52. Will of Peter Chastain, November 20, 1728, Deeds and Wills, Goochland County. Joan R. Gundersen, "Parental Control and Coming of Age in Virginia," paper read at the Winona Conference on Changing Images of the American Family, Winona, Minn., November 1979.

53. LeSueur owned seventeen slaves, mostly members of two black families. Will of David LeSueur I, February 24, 1772, Wills, Cumberland County; and inventories of David LeSueur, April 26, 1773, *ibid.*

54. See the inventories of Isaac Salle, August 17, 1731, Deeds and Wills Goochland County; David LeSueur, April 26, 1773, Wills, Cumberland County; Peter Harris, February 26, 1776, *ibid,*; Peter Guerrant, September 1750, *ibid.*; and John Harris, April 26, 1753, *ibid.* See the wills of Peter Harris, August 28, 1775, *ibid.*; James Holman, September 24, 1753, *ibid.*; Stephen Watkins, *c.* 1759, Wills, Chesterfield County; John Martin, May 3, 1736, Deeds and Wills, Henrico County; Jacob Trabue, *c.* 1772, Wills, Chesterfield County; and Abraham Salle, March 1, 1730/1, Miscellaneous, Henrico County.

55. See the wills of Stephen Chastain, August 21, 1739, Deeds and Wills, Goochland County; Francis Flournoy, *c.* 1770, Wills, Chesterfield County; and Peter Anthony Lookado, July 25, 1768, Wills, Cumberland County.

56. Deed of Gift, Maryanne Martin to Peter Martin, September 20, 1743, Deeds, Goochland County; division of Rapine estate, September 17, 1747, Wills, *ibid.*; Order Book, September 16, 1747, *ibid.*; Order Book, November 27, 1749, Cumberland County. Anthony Rapine died in 1737. Will of Anthony Rapine, November 15, 1737, Deeds and Wills, Goochland County.

57. See for example the wills of Jacob Michaux, June 27, 1774, Wills, and John James Dupuy, February 27, 1775, Wills, both of Cumberland County.

58. Kulikoff, "The Origins of Afro-American Society," 229, 245.

13

Black Women in the Era of the American Revolution in Pennsylvania

Debra L. Newman

It is undeniable that the era of the American Revolution saw the passage of the Gradual Abolition law in Pennsylvania. It is also undeniable that this law made a significant difference in the lives of Afro-Americans even if the material aspects of freedom were worse for some. After all, who would argue that slavery was better than freedom? No other single law or action in this period would have a greater impact on the lives of Afro-Americans. One of the cogent reasons for the passage of this law was the effort of the Pennsylvania abolitionists to erase the contradiction that the institution of slavery caused in the American people's struggle for independence from England. Their pressure augured an era of experimentation, of change. In order to assess the changes that the American Revolution made for black women in Pennsylvania, it is necessary to study their lives during the decades before the war and in the period immediately after it.

Black women were a small but important segment of eighteenth-century Pennsylvania society. This is not a study about black women as victims of the social and legal system of the colony under the institution of slavery nor about the abolitionist movement but an attempt to provide some information about the fabric of these women's lives—information about what they could and did do in spite of slavery. Few records were generated by blacks themselves prior to the Gradual Abolition law, and only scattered records with information about individual blacks were kept: some baptism and marriage records, wills and deeds which mention blacks, newspaper advertisements for sale of blacks or for runaways, tax records, censuses, slave manifests and merchants' records, diaries of observers, court records and emancipation, indenture and other legal protection papers. None of these records alone provide a well-rounded view of the black woman; using some of them collectively only gives a sketch of their existence. There are enough records, however, for a statement to be made with an attempt to evoke the point of view of the women themselves.

The eighteenth-century Pennsylvania black women were fettered on all sides by behavioral constraints whether they were slaves, indentured servants, or free persons. Lacking real freedom these women exercised limited personal liberty by rebelling against their masters, by running away, feigning sickness or being generally uncooperative. Finding futility in recalcitrance in many cases, black women could decide to work creatively in their limited spheres, act as wife and mother as effectively as they could, take advantage of a few legal rights and maintain a circumscribed social life. This statement does not imply that the treatment of the black women, slave or free, was benevolent or just, rather that no matter what the intent of the builders of the peculiar institution, in order to survive the black women had to deal effectively with all phases of life. They could not be swept along by the social and legal proscriptions of slavery.

Most Afro-American women came to Pennsylvania in the eighteenth century when slavery was flourishing in the colony. Some were brought by ship from other colonies, especially South Carolina, and from Jamaica, Barbados, Antigua, St. Christopher, Nevis, Anguilla and Bermuda. From mid-century, blacks were forced immigrants to the colony directly from the African continent. Up to 1729 only a few blacks, about two or three, came on each ship. From the time of the Seven Years War, however, when the number of white servants was reduced because of participation of white male servants in the fray, the numbers of blacks brought into the colony aboard ships increased until 1766 when the trade had slowed significantly but not completely.[1] Records of the Bureau of Customs indicate that blacks were imported and exported through the port of Philadelphia until the 1860s—often illegally. The schooner, *Prudence*, brought seventeen African men, women and children in 1800 and the ship, *Phoebe*, 100 Africans in the same year in defiance of the section of the Gradual Abolition law which expressly forbade the trade.[2] The ships' records for the eighteenth century generally yield some physical information about the individual women. Sometimes the records just indicate that there were black women aboard the ship, other times they give the individual's first name, (surnames are rare), sex, age, height, color and owner. For example, the description of Nelly states that her age is 13, her height 4'9" and her complexion, yellow. Collectively the records describe most of the women as teenagers or in their early twenties with varied complexions represented as bright mulatto, mulatto, yellow, black or African. Their different hues point to the preference of Pennsylvanians for second generation Africans who they felt could better adapt to their society and to the climate.[3] Many of the women had smallpox marks. Of the thousands of blacks imported or smuggled into Pennsylvania, it is virtually impossible to determine the number of women or their proportion to the men because too many of the records give numbers of blacks aboard the ship without giving specific numerical breakdowns by sex.[4]

Black women came into Pennsylvania overland with their owners. Free blacks and runaways came to Pennsylvania of their own volition during the course of the century because the harsh work-gang plantation system of labor of the South was rare in this colony, because of the Gradual Abolition in 1780 and because of the limited opportunities for employment and for political and social life.[5] Most of the blacks in the colony were concentrated in six southeastern counties: Philadelphia, York, Bucks, Lancaster, Chester and Montgomery.[6] Any statement of the numbers of blacks in the colony made before the first federal census of 1790 represented an estimate since no comprehensive count was made before that time. Green and Harrington in *American Population Before the Federal Census of 1790* give estimates of 2,000 to 30,000 Afro-Americans for various years between 1715 and 1775 based on views of contemporary observers and county tax records.[7] Some county tax records give information about the number of blacks taxable as property between 1772 and 1783: Bedford, 28; Berks, 164; Cumberland, 649; Lancaster, 439; Washington, 448; and York, 448.[8] Gary Nash explains that taxable blacks were generally between the ages of twelve and fifty.[9] Nash, in his article, "Slaves and Slaveowners in Colonial Philadelphia," estimates the size of the black population by using burial records, Philadelphia tax records and comparisons with censuses for the black population in New York.[10] The following is a chart of burial statistics in Philadelphia for the first half of the eighteenth century:

Average Burials per Year[11]

Year	White	Black	%Black
1722	162	26	13.8
1729-32	396	94	19.2
1738-42	418	51	10.9
1743-48	500	64	11.3
1750-55	655	55	7.7

The next table is Nash's estimate of the population for the latter half of the century:

Burials in Philadelphia 1756-1775[12]

Year	Average Burials		
	White	Black	%Black
1756-60	917	91	9.2
1761-65	990	87	8.1
1766-70	856	87	9.2
1771-75	1,087	87	7.4

The latter table shows a decline in the black population of Philadelphia. Nash contends that the decline was caused by the inability of the slave population to reproduce itself because of limited familial contact, males outnumbered females, a high infant mortality rate and because many females were beyond childbearing age. The slave population is estimated at 1,392 in 1767 and 673 in 1775. When slave importation slowed after the 1760s, it became more obvious that natural reproduction among the black population was limited.

According to the 1790 census the total number of blacks in Pennsylvania was 10,301—6,540 free and 3,761 slave. So many blacks throughout the colonies flocked to Pennsylvania in order to enjoy a life of freedom after 1780 that between 1790 and 1800 the black population of Philadelphia increased more than 176 percent.[14] The underground railroad which was at its inception directed to Pennsylvania and freedom became active in the last fifteen years of the eighteenth century, and blacks themselves were active directors and helpers during these dramatic flights to freedom which brought many more Afro-Americans into the colony.[15] Afro-Americans were still brought into Pennsylvania as slaves after the passage of the Gradual Abolition law but were sometimes freed and made indentured servants until the age of twenty-eight.[16] In 1800 the total black population was 16,270 with 14,564 free and 1,706 slave.[17] The 1820 census was the first one to enumerate the black population by sex. The number of black females was 15,398 while the number of males was 14,804 with most concentrated in the Philadelphia area. There were 6,671 black females and 5,220 males in Philadelphia County and 4,426 females and 3,156 males in the city.[18]

From 1700 to 1780 most black women in the colony were held as slaves. Those who were free were constrained by a web of laws woven with the intent of limiting the activities of all black people. The intent of the laws is easy to isolate. Duty acts and trade regulations relating to black people were directed to slave traders and owners. Restraining laws were addressed to blacks, slave and free. As the century progressed, the laws regarding blacks became more and more restrictive. In 1700 special courts were established for blacks who were from this time until abolition denied trial by jury. Blacks could not carry arms without special license, and Afro-American men received severe penalties for assaults on white women. In 1721 laws were passed stipulating that no liquors were to be sold to Afro-Americans without the permission of their masters and another prohibiting Philadelphia blacks from shooting guns without a license.[19]

A group of laws passed in 1726 provided that vagrant free persons could be bound out to indentured service, provided fines for free blacks who harbored slaves and forbade trade between free blacks and slaves who did not have their master's consent to do so.[20] These provisions suggest that the free black was sufficiently concerned with the plight of his enslaved brothers and sisters to make laws necessary to restrict conspiracies for freedom. The harboring of slaves by free blacks was less effective than trading because trading could provide the slave with money necessary to purchase his own freedom whereas the harbored slave could only change his status by eluding the authorities for a period long enough to pass as free.

A free black person could be sold into slavery for life for marrying a white person. The laws of 1726 also discouraged manumission. Although the laws of 1700 and 1726 forbade blacks to assemble in companies, in 1732, 1738 and 1741 the Philadelphia City Council passed acts prohibiting slave "tumults" on Sundays and in the court house square at night.[21] These "tumults" were generally social gatherings, parties, funerals, or church services which were led by self-appointed black religious leaders who wandered about the vicinity of Philadelphia and through the colony preaching to the black population.[22] Because black people became skilled in many areas of endeavor, white workers petitioned the Pennsylvania assembly in 1708 and 1722 to forbid the employment of black mechanics or skilled workers. In 1726 a law was passed forbidding masters to hire out their slaves.[23]

The major legal action of the century for blacks was the Gradual Abolition Act. The preamble to the act cites the tyranny of Great Britain as a moving force in Pennsylvania's efforts to reduce tyranny against blacks. The preamble also mentions that slavery cast blacks "into the deepest affliction by an unnatural separation and sale of husband and wife from each other and from their children. . . ."[24] The act provided that no child born after the passage of the act would be a slave; that black and mulatto children were to be servants until 28 years of age; that all slaves were to be registered; that owners of slaves, though not registered, were to be liable for their support; that blacks were to be tried in court like other inhabitants; that the jury would value a slave in the case of a sentence of death in order to pay the owner; that the reward for blacks who captured runaways would be the same as that for white servants; that none would be deemed slaves but those registered except runaways from other states; that slaves taken from the state could be brought back and registered and that no blacks or mulattoes other than infants could be bound to indenture for longer that seven years.[25] The law was later amended to provide for the forfeiture of ships employed in the slave trade, for a prohibition against masters separating husbands, wives and their children and for penalties against taking blacks or mulattoes out of the state.[26]

Unfortunately, so many people sought to evade the act that the act itself ushered in a new set of legal protection certificates which were absolutely necessary for freed blacks. Since slave states surrounded Pennsylvania and master and slave dealers saw free blacks as potentially valuable for reenslavement, it was necessary to find ways of protecting the expanding free black population. Emancipated blacks were given certificates; and indentured servants were provided with papers stating the terms of their indenture. These papers had no value to blacks, however, if they could be stolen from them or destroyed. The Pennsylvania Society for Promoting the Abolition of Slavery and for the Relief of Free Negroes served as a registry for the legal protection papers of free blacks in Pennsylvania and blacks in neighboring states.[27] The Society kept marriage and birth certificates, certificates of freedom, of identity, statements of character, certificates allowing blacks to seek employment, passes and passports, certificates to prevent impressment and indenture papers.

Certificates of freedom showed that blacks gained their freedom in many different ways such as birth, will, manumission, purchase by themselves, their family or by benevolent persons or groups and then freed. Some were freed when their masters left with the British. Others gained freedom through work agreements, through indenture or by attaining a certain age.[28] Some masters brought their slaves into Pennsylvania after the Gradual Abolition Law was passed so that the slave would be freed:

> The bearer, Nancy, with her daughter, Hagar, were brought by me to Philadelphia from Dover in June 1785 where they remained with me until this day,

having by the laws of Pennsylvania become free in six months after they came into the state. When I brought them up it was my intention they should become free by their stay in Pennsylvania. Nancy received wages from me for the time she has been with me here.

May 14, 1788 Edward Telshman[29]

Some were cruelly freed when they were obviously too old to take care of themselves for any extended period. Mercy Candwell was freed when she was 87 years old after "a servitude of the greater part of her life."[30] The certificates of freedom and manumission papers sometimes listed the possessions of their owners especially if they consisted of goods, livestock or property which were inconsistent with the material level of blacks during the period. The Society used these records to act as legal counsel for blacks who were wronged or kidnapped if the unfortunate victim could establish contact with the Society.[31]

Within the confines of slavery black women worked hard and suffered many trials. For some the English language was difficult, and diseases aggravated by the harsh Pennsylvania winters took many lives.[32] Blacks who were free were sometimes not given the opportunity of employment; so they fed, clothed and housed themselves with difficulty. Some women went to the poorhouse; others ended up in jail. The Pennsylvania Abolition Society petitioned for the release of Dinah Nevil and her children from the Philadelphia workhouse on May 29, 1775.[33] There was also the everpresent threat of being kidnapped and taken to the South, a practice which became alarmingly common after abolition. The Pennsylvania Legislature urged by the Abolition Society took a strong stand in the matter of kidnapping. In May of 1791 the Society sent a memorial to the Congress protesting the kidnapping of free blacks and asking for the relief of a man named John who was being unlawfully held as a slave in Virginia. In June of the same year the governor of the state sent a letter to his counterpart in Virginia protesting the seizure of John by three men who were attempting to sell John as a slave and requesting that the governor of Virginia help restore the man's freedom. This letter is followed a month later by a demand from the governor of Pennsylvania to the governor of Virginia to deliver the three men who forcibly seized John.[34]

The occupations of most Afro-Americans did not vary much after abolition. Most blacks in the colony worked on farms or as domestic servants. Often farmers utilized a slave or a free family along with their own for field and house work, but more often blacks worked in urban centers. In the era of the American Revolution in Philadelphia about one in every five families owned a slave.[35] It was fashionable in the colony, especially in Philadelphia, to employ black women as housekeepers and cooks. This is the principal reason why black women were more numerous than black men in the Philadelphia area. The women's tasks as housekeepers included washing, ironing, tending children and waiting table. Some women were skillful with needlework or spinning. Black women worked as laundresses, nurses, dressmakers, seamstresses and cooks. A few were employed outside the city in ironworks.[36] The 1790 census lists occupations for a few Philadelphia free black women: Miss Arthur and Jane Mullen were milliners; Susanna Hammil worked in a tavern; Ann McNeil was a housekeeper; Phoebe (no surname given) was a huckster or peddler and Margaret Woodby was a cake baker.[37] Another source lists Ann Poulson as a laundress and Terra Hall as a hatter.[38]

Newspaper advertisements tell even more about the various occupations of black women. Owners often stressed (and probably sometimes exaggerated) the areas in which a black woman excelled in order to facilitate her sale. An advertisement from an owner in Carlisle, Pennsylvania, reads, "To be sold, a strong, healthy mulatto wench, 16 years old, she has had the small pox, measles, can cook, wash and do most sorts of housework."[39] A Lancaster woman is described as a good cook and dairy worker and another younger woman in the same advertisement "about 27 years old is an excellent house servant and besides washing and ironing can spin wool and flax, knit, etc., understands the management of a dairy and the making of butter and cheese."[40] A 17-year-old girl is described as having had the smallpox and measles, as healthy, strong and lively, "would suit the country or town, she can do all sorts of housework, and might soon be made a good cook."[41] One woman is advertised as a good cook "who can be recommended for her honesty and sobriety."[42]

Character references for blacks which are among the records of the Pennsylvania Abolition Society list the numerous household skills of black women.

> Rachael Roy is slave belonging to Dr. Gardener of Charleston, South Carolina. Sometime past her master went to England and left her with three children. . . . She has schooled them all and taught them all plain needlework.[43]

> This is to satisfy whom it may concern that Negro Tamer has leave to hire with whom she pleases and receive her own wages. She is a good weaver and spinner and knitter. She can wash and iron well, is acquainted with house business.[44]

Many women who were freed chose to become indentured servants, or were freed under the condition that they became indentured servants, or were indentured by their parents. The years of indenture varied greatly, but black women were usually indentured for "housewifery." January 27, 1786 Margaret, a mulatto free woman, indentured herself for three years, occupation, housewifery. Jane Pernall with the consent of her father was indentured for nine years of housewifery including sewing, knitting and spinning. Phoebe, about 25 years old, was indentured to Adam Lantzinger for 16 years of housewifery.[45]

The eighteenth century found most black women doing various types of domestic work. Neither the Revolution nor the Gradual Abolition Law caused a significant change in occupation. By mid-nineteenth century there was still no meaningful change; women were effectively lodged in the same types of occupations. Of 4,429 women over 21 in 1848, 1,970 were laundresses, 486 were seamstresses and 786 domestic workers. The rest were in trades, housewives, servants, cooks and rag pickers.[46]

Although it was not uncommon for black families to be sold apart in Pennsylvania, the family structure remained strong and marriages were frequent. Among the archives of the colony a number of marriages of black men and women are recorded. Various churches listed marriages among Afro-Americans. A large number were registered in Swedes' Church, St. Paul's Church and St. Michael's and Zion Church, all of Philadelphia. The registration sometimes indicated whether blacks were slave or free, mulatto, black or African, or whether they had the consent of their masters and sometimes listed the masters' names. Two recorded marriages took place in January of 1756. William Derrham and Mary Waldrek, both free mulattoes, had their marriage registered in St. Michael's and Zion Church as did John, who was freed by John Sin Clear (St. Clair), and Mary Ann. The next year John, the servant of Mr. Bankson, and Jane, a servant of Mr. Master, were wed in the same church.[47] Forty-eight black marriages were recorded in this church's records between 1756 and 1794.[48] The only occupation given is servant or slave except for one man who is listed as a cooper.[49] The distinction between the meaning of slave and servant is often unclear.

There are thirty-nine marriages listed for St. Paul's Church between 1768 and 1792.[50] The record keeper for St. Paul's sometimes added an additional comment to the marriage records. For instance, in recording the marriage of Edward Talbert and Alice David, both free blacks, he wrote, "That is good." For another couple who he had probably forgotten to register right away, he gave the date "about April 23, 1791." For the marriage of Rebecca Wood and Samuel Berry he indicates that he gave them no certificate.[51] In these records the racial designation "African" seems to be distinct from that of "Negro." Samuel Carson and Sophia Hand, Africans, were married on February 8, 1795 and Jan Ellis and Samuel Robeson, Africans, were wed in May of 1793 while Thomas Yervis and Philis Cox, Negroes, registered on May 5, 1783.[52]

The Moravian Church in Bethlehem, Pennsylvania married Magdalena Mingo and Samuel Johannes on April 20, 1757. Johannes was described as a "Malabar" presumably from eastern India.[53] Andreas, *ein Mohr*, and Maria, *eine Mohrinn*, were married in November of 1742 in Bethlehem.[54] Other churches registered a few blacks. Some of the records do not indicate either the church or the place of the marriage. Cuff and Judith, two blacks belonging to Messrs. Mifflin and Elves, were married on November 2, 1764.[55] It is probably also true that many of the records were not kept or simply do not indicate race. Black churches under Richard Allen and Absalom Jones performed wedding ceremonies also in the last years of the eighteenth century. On July 1, 1798 Luke Johnson and Sabarah Smith were married by Absalom Jones, rector of

St. Thomases Church.[56] Several resolutions passed in the last decade of the century by the Philadelphia Free African Society suggest that there was a number of people who did not bother with the marriage ceremony at all.[57] There are certainly enough records, however, to point out that the black women had a value for solidifying the family structure according to the laws of the colony especially since women held as slaves had to have the permission of their masters in order to wed.

Probably throughout the century women acted as family leaders alone. The 1790 census lists fifty black women family heads with a total of ninety-four dependents. Some of the women were widows; most had dependents; only eleven were listed as the only person in the family.[58] The 1800 census gives seventy-six black women as heads of families. It is rare that the same women who appear in the 1790 census as women alone show up again in the one for 1800.[59] This is an indication of either geographical or social mobility (or unfortunately, of the census takers' mistakes). They probably had either moved out of the state, were married, or lived with another person, even a male minor over sixteen, who was considered head of a household.

In most cases, the responsibilities accompanying marriage or heading a family had to be secondary for the black woman because she had other houses to maintain, other families to feed and other children to tend. Nevertheless, she persevered. A number of women, however, did strike out for freedom before and after the passage of the Gradual Abolition Law. Newspaper advertisements tell the stories of the numbers who ran away, which many probably did by melting into the crowds of Philadelphia.

> Runaway on the night of the eighth of March [1778] from the subscriber, of Thornbury Township, Chester County, Pennsylvania, a mulatto woman named Rachel, of a middle size, about 30 years of age....Took with her one black bonnet and four gowns.[60]

Some women married free men who purchased their freedom for them. Others married to slaves, like the wife of Absalom Jones, were brought out of slavery first since the children followed the condition of the mother.[61] Dinah Jones of Chester County was freed when her husband purchased his liberty.

Pennsylvania black women had their share of more daring escapes too. While some women waited for their husbands and sons to return from fighting the colonists' battle, others joined with the British during the occupation of Philadelphia in 1777 and in 1783 left with them to seek a better life in Nova Scotia, England or the West Indies. The British had promised freedom to all blacks who joined their ranks.[63] The Continental Congress demanded in 1783 that the British make a list of all of the Afro-Americans removed from the United States so that reparations could be made to the owners at a later date.[64] The British complied, creating an "Inspection Roll" of blacks with information about their ships' destinations, and personal information such as age, description, indication of slave or free status and, finally, whose possession they were in at the time of embarkation. A large proportion of blacks in Philadelphia left with the British. Some of the women who went were Tinah Leech, 25, who was formerly the property of George Leech of Philadelphia, and Catherine, 30, formerly the property of a doctor in Philadelphia from whom she had been separated for five years in 1783. Bellah Miles, 44, and Sally Miles, 10, were probably mother and daughter. Isaac Bush and Lucy Bush, both 35, and probably husband and wife, also left.[65]

It is obvious that during the time blacks lived within the British lines, and sometimes it was for as long as seven years or more, there was an active social existence. Couples were married and a number of children were born. The children are listed in the records as "born free within British lines." For example, Ralph and Nancy Henry had a daughter, Molly, who was 4 years old in 1784 and was described as a fine child. She had been born free behind British lines. Peter and Betsy Johnson had a son four and one two years old. Johnson had left Robert Morris of Philadelphia six years before; so both of the family's children were born out of captivity probably within British lines. John Jones left Virginia in 1776 with Lord Dunmore and Lucretia, Jones' wife, had left Philadelphia with the British troops. They had a daughter, Charlotte, who was three years old. Some mothers came with their children but no fathers. One father, Cato Cox of Frankford, Pennsylvania, came with his son to the British lines and married a New York woman there.[66]

Some women whose lives span part of both the eighteenth and nineteenth centuries opted to join with those who returned to Africa from 1820 to 1840. Mary Smith, Elizabeth Small, Ann Poulson, Elizabeth James, Jane Hawkins, Terra Hall, and Mary Butler, all of whom were literate, were among those who left. Other women were Matilda Spencer, Sara Smith, Elizabeth Carey, Charlotte Cain and Charlotte Brown. Terra Hall was 55 and Charlotte Brown was 60 years old. Mrs. Black, Nancy Bantam and Nancy Augustine also made the trip. They went alone or with their families to face the inhospitable African climate. Most were destined for Liberia, but some went to Sierra Leone and many died of fever shortly after they had arrived.[67] These women were not escaping slavery for there were few slaves left in Pennsylvania by 1820; they wanted an alternative to being a free black woman in a white-ruled land.

Not all women sought physical emancipation. Some tried to escape through education. By the last decade of the century the black church and black benevolent societies were sponsoring schools for blacks.[68] Earlier, in 1770, Anthony Benezet had provided for a school for free blacks and mulattoes. Other Quakers provided educational facilities for blacks and by 1797 had seven schools for them. A school for black women was established by the Society for the free instruction of blacks in 1792.[69] The school in Cherry Street was taught by Helena Harris, a black woman "of considerable parts, who had been for several years employed as a teacher of white children in England."[70]

A roll from the Society's Girls' School demonstrates some interesting facts about this early education.

List of the Girls in the Black School Under the Care of the Committee of Education of the Abolition Society, July 2, 1800[71]

Name	Age (yrs.)	Sent by	Time	Subject
Charlotte Johnson	16	John Richards	Half day	Reading, writing
Rebecca Harrison	16	John Richards	Half day	Reading, writing
Sarah Lewis	16	Parents	All day	Writing, arithmetic
Catherine Still	14	D. Dupuy	Half day	Writing, arithmetic
Abby Macclan	16	A. Howell	Half day	Spelling
Nancy Ellis	14	M. Wilcocks	Half day	Spelling
Jane Nash	8	J. Folwell	All day	Spelling
Mary Lewis	8	Committee	All day	Letters
Minte Liston	6	Committee	All day	Letters
Elizabeth Sewel	12	Committee	All day	Letters
Elizabeth Still	16	D. Dupuy	Half day	Spelling, reading, writing
Rebecca Lewis	17	Parents	All day	Spelling, reading
Patty Pennington	3	Parents	Half day	Letters

Most of the young women were taught academic subjects rather than household skills, although these skills were sometimes a part of the curriculum. The roll for the Girls' School was short in this year, but among the sponsors are three parents (or two; perhaps Sarah Lewis and Rebecca Lewis were sisters), black parents who had the means to send their children to school. The roll for the Boys' School is about twice as long. Six of the boys were sent by their parents.[72]

The Society noted the enthusiasm the black community had for increased schooling and sometimes pooled their efforts with the free black community in Philadelphia in matters of education. Many women were later able to attend the Clarkson School. The roll for this school for the years 1820-23 lists over fifty pages of women aged 16 to 50.

The Society also helped the free black community with their efforts for employment. The Society's minutes report that they were able to find jobs for black adults and children and that they sometimes had more applications from the Afro-American community than they could fulfill.[74]

The most significant change accompanying abolition for Afro-Americans in Pennsylvania was that blacks finally had the legal right to organize. In November 1787 Richard Allen and Absalom Jones organized the Free African Society, which was a mutual aid association, and began their independent church movement.[75] Men and women joined together to start working to help take care of their own people. The society made special provisions for the support of widows and orphans of members. In addition to establishing churches, schools and benevolent societies, by the end of the century blacks in Philadelphia owned nearly one hundred houses.

The greatest transition for the black woman during the era of the American Revolution was the move from slavery to freedom. Economic improvement was practically nonexistent for all but a few of these women who were frugal enough to save a little money and to buy property or those who ran small establishments. Although abolition was gradual, by 1820, forty years after emancipation, there were only 211 slaves in the state of Pennsylvania and 150 of those were over 45 years old. Freed blacks tended to stay with their masters after emancipation. This seems especially true of York County where there were 847 free blacks listed in 1790 but none as heads of families. The occupation of black women in the eighteenth century, servant, was not one that they could leave behind with the coming of emancipation or the passage of more than a century. It was during the eighteenth century that the patterns of oppression of the black women were designed, a pattern which would continue into the twentieth century. It was also during the last two decades of this century that black women were first given opportunities for organizational leadership. These opportunities were provided by the church, benevolent societies and social groups. A few black women were given opportunities for basic education. Slavery did not devastate the black woman. She performed her occupational duties, played her role as mother and wife and interacted with other Afro-Americans inside and outside of the legal and social confines of slavery.

NOTES

1. Darold Wax, "Negro Imports into Pennsylvania, 1720-1766," *Pennsylvania History*, 32 (July 1969), pp. 254-87.
2. Slave Manifests for Philadelphia, 1800 to 1860 in the Records of the Bureau of Customs, National Archives and Records Service, Washington, D.C. Hereafter, NARS.
3. Darold Wax, "Quaker Merchants and the Slave Trade in Colonial Pennsylvania," *The Pennsylvania Magazine of History and Biography*, 86 (April 1962), pp. 153-56.
4. Slave Manifests, NARS; and Wax, "Negro Imports," pp. 254-87.
5. Leon Litwack, *North of Slavery* (Chicago: University of Chicago Press, 1961), pp. 69, 80; W.E.B. Du Bois, *The Philadelphia Negro* (New York: Schocken Books, 1967), pp. 46-47; Edward R. Turner, *The Negro in Pennsylvania, 1639 to 1861* (New York: Arno Press, 1969), pp. 83, 253.
6. Bureau of the Census, *Heads of Families at the First Census of the United States Taken in the Year 1790, Pennsylvania* (D.C.: Government Printing Office, 1908), pp. 9-11; Turner, *Negro in Pennsylvania*, p. 12.
7. Evarts B. Greene and Virginia D. Harrington, *American Population Before the Federal Census of 1790* (New York: Columbia University Press, 1932), pp. 114-19.
8. *Ibid.*, p. 119.
9. Gary B. Nash, "Slaves and Slaveowners in Colonial Philadelphia," *William and Mary Quarterly*, 30 (April 1973), p. 232.
10. *Ibid.*, pp. 223-56.
11. *Ibid.*, p. 226.

12. *Ibid.*, p. 231.
13. *Ibid.*, p. 238.
14. 1790 Census of Pennsylvania; *Second Census of the United States, Pennsylvania,* Records of the Bureau of Census, microfilm, NARS.
15. Turner, *Negro in Pennsylvania,* p. 241; Wilbur H. Siebert, *The Underground Railroad from Slavery to Freedom* (New York: Macmillan Co., 1898), pp. 431-34.
16. Stanley I. Kutler, "Pennsylvania Courts, the Abolition Act and Negro Rights," *Pennsylvania History,* 30 (January 1963), p. 14.
17. 1800 Census of Pennsylvania.
18. *Census for 1820,* compendium (D.C.: Gales and Slaton, 1821), Table 11.
19. *Pennsylvania Statutes-at-Large,* Chapters 49, 56, and II, 250.
20. *Ibid.,* IV, 59.
21. Du Bois, *Philadelphia Negro,* p. 414. (Appendix B. Legislation, etc. of Pennsylvania in Regard to the Negro, pp. 411-18.)
22. Charles Wesley, *Richard Allen* (D.C.: Associated Publishers, 1969), p. 9; Turner, *Negro in Pennsylvania,* p. 45.
23. *Pennsylvania Statutes-at-Large,* IV, 59; and Du Bois, *Philadelphia Negro,* p. 412.
24. Pennsylvania Society for Promoting the Abolition of Slavery (Hereafter PAS), *The Constitution of the Pennsylvania Society for Promoting the Abolition of Slavery and the Relief of Free Negroes Unlawfully Held in Bondage and the Acts of the General Assembly of Pennsylvania for the Gradual Abolition of Slavery* (Philadelphia: J. Ormrod Printer, 1800), pp. 8-15.
25. *Ibid.*
26. *Ibid.*, p. 26.
27. PAS, Committee for Improving the Condition of Free Blacks (Hereafter, Committee), Minutes, 1790-93, p. 17, September 1790. Historical Society of Pennsylvania, Philadelphia, Pa. (HSP).
28. PAS Papers, HSP.
29. Manumission Books, May 1788, PAS Papers, HSP.
30. Character References for Blacks file, PAS, HSP.
31. Case Files, PAS Papers, HSP.
32. Wax, "Quaker Merchants," p. 156.
33. Minutes of the Society for the Relief of Negroes, p. 2. Cox-Parrish-Wharton Papers, HSP.
34. Papers of the Continental Congress, Vol. II, pp. 565, 575, 579, NARS, microfilm.
35. Nash, *Slaves and Slaveowners,* p. 242.
36. Some mention of women in ironworks is made in Darold Wax, "The Demand for Slave Labor in Colonial Pennsylvania," *Pennsylvania History,* 34 (1967), pp. 331-45.
37. 1790 Pennsylvania Census, pp. 208-45.
38. Tom W. Shick, *Emigrants to Liberia, 1820-43, An Alphabetical Listing* (Newark, Del.: Liberian Studies Assn., Inc., 1971), pp. 41, 77.
39. *The Pennsylvania Packet or General Advertiser,* Lancaster, Pa., February 18, 1778.
40. *Ibid.*, Mar. 18, 1778.
41. *Dunlap's Pennsylvania Packet or the General Advertiser,* Phila., Pa., January 24, 1774.
42. *Ibid.*, March 21, 1774.
43. Character References for Blacks file, PAS, HSP.
44. *Ibid.*
45. Indenture Papers, PAS, HSP.
46. Du Bois, *Philadelphia Negro,* p. 143.

47. *Records of Pennsylvania Marriages Prior to 1810, Pennsylvania Archives*, II, Vol. 8 and 9 (Harrisburg: Hart, 1878, 1880), Vol. 9, pp. 300, 324, 332.

48. *Ibid.*, Vol. 9, pp. 300-411.

49. *Ibid.*, Vol. 9, p. 370.

50. *Ibid.*, Vol. 9, pp. 453-92.

51. *Ibid.*, Vol. 9, pp. 463, 467, 483.

52. *Ibid.*, Vol. 8, pp. 325, 340, 361.

53. *Ibid.*, Vol. 9, p. 116.

54. *Ibid.*, Vol. 9, p. 120.

55. *Names of Persons for Whom Marriage Licenses Were Issued in the Province of Pennsylvania Previous to 1790, Pennsylvania Archives*, II, Vol. 2 (Harrisburg: Hart, 187-), p. 63.

56. Marriage Certificates, PAS, HSP.

57. Wesley, *Richard Allen*, pp. 93, 95.

58. 1790 Census of Pennsylvania.

59. 1800 Census of Pennsylvania.

60. *The Pennsylvania Packet*, March 18, 1778.

61. Sidney Kaplan, *The Black Presence in the Era of the American Revolution* (New York: New York Graphic Society, Ltd., 1973), p. 83; Wesley, *Richard Allen*, p. 59.

62. Certificates of Freedom, PAS, HSP.

63. Papers of the Continental and Confederation Congresses, Vol. 68, p. 445, NARS.

64. *Ibid.*, PCC 212, pp. 59-62.

65. "Inspection Roll of Negroes Taken on Board Sundry Vessels at Staten Island, 1783," Papers of the Continental and Confederation Congresses, NARS.

66. *Ibid.*

67. Shick, *Emigrants to Liberia.*

68. Committee Minutes, PAS, HSP; Wesley, *Richard Allen*, pp. 91-92; Turner, *Negro in Pennsylvania*, pp. 129-30, 191-92.

69. Turner, *Negro in Pennsylvania*, pp. 128-29.

70. *Phildelphia City Directory, 1794* (Philadelphia: Jacob Johnson and Co., 1794), p. 225.

71. Roll of the Girls' School, PAS Papers, HSP.

72. Roll of the Boys' School, PAS Papers, HSP.

73. Committee Minutes, PAS, HSP.

74. Wesley, *Richard Allen*.

75. *Ibid.*, p. 58; Turner, *Negro in Pennsylvania*, p. 125.

14

From Three-Fifths to Zero:

Implications of the Constitution for African-American Women, 1787-1870

Mamie E. Locke

During the summer months of 1787, in Philadelphia, Pennsylvania, 55 men argued, debated, suggested, compromised, and eventually hammered out a document that would form the basis of the government of the United States of America. In 1788, the requisite number of states had ratified this document—the Constitution. The Constitution has been called a living, flexible piece of work that is the cornerstone of American democracy. It has been argued that the Constitution established the privileges and rights of citizenship, raised to new heights the rights of individuals, and acknowledged the fundamental principles of life, liberty, and the pursuit of happiness. In the bicentennial year of the ratification of the United States Constitution, a simple question can be posed: Was the primacy of individual rights and equality truly reflected in the Constitution as it was written in 1787? The response to this question is equally simple: no, given the omission, for various reasons, of more than half the population. At the bottom of the heap of omissions was to be found the African-American woman.

In his controversial remarks on the bicentennial of the Constitution, U.S. Supreme Court Justice Thurgood Marshall argued that the meaning of the Constitution was not "fixed" in 1787; furthermore, the wisdom, sense of justice, and foresight of the framers who were being hailed in celebration were not all that profound, particularly since they created a defective government from the beginning. Marshall further stated that there were intentional omissions, namely blacks and women (Marshall 1987, 2). It is the purpose of this paper to discuss a group of people encompassing both characteristics of exclusion—African-American women. It is also the purpose of this paper to elaborate on Justice Marshall's interpretation of the meaning of the Constitution, specifically as it relates to the document's exclusion of African-American women in 1787 and again in 1870. Also to be discussed are African-American women's struggles against peripheral status and the consequences of exclusion.

The framers of the Constitution were careful to avoid using terms designating sex or color. The words "slave," "slavery," and "female" are not to be found in the original document. What one does find are phrases such as "persons held to service or labor" (Article IV, section 2) or "three fifths of all other persons" (Article I, section 2). Those persons held to service or labor and designated as three fifths were African-Americans, females and males. Thus the African-American woman started her life in this new government created by men of "wisdom, foresight and a sense of justice," as three-fifths of a person. The struggle for wholeness was begun almost immediately, yet the African-American woman usually found herself on the periphery of such struggles. She participated, but she watched as her status moved from three-fifths, in the 1787 document, to zero—total exclusion—with the passage of the Fifteenth Amendment in 1870.

Once, when a speaker at an antislavery meeting praised the Constitution, Sojourner Truth, that prolific sage of the nineteenth century, responded in this way:

> Children, I talks to God and God talks to me. I go out and talks to God in de fields and de woods. Dis morning I was walking out and I got over de fence. I saw de wheat a holding up its head, looking very big. I goes up and talks holt of it. You b'lieve it, dere was no wheat dere. I says, "God, what is de matter wid dis wheat?" and he says to me, "Sojourner, dere is a little weasel in it." Now I hears talkin' bout de Constitution and de rights of man. I come up and talks holt of dis Constitution. It looks mighty big, and I feels for my rights, but dere ain't any dere. Den I say, "God, what ails dis Constitution?" He says to me, "Sojourner, dere is a little weasel in it." (Bennett 1964, 146)

Thus, when the Constitution was written, it advocated equality, opportunity, and the rights of all, yet it condoned the institution of slavery, where men and women alike were reduced to property. Or were they persons? In the Federalist #54, James Madison argued that slaves were considered not only as property but also as persons under the federal Constitution. According to Madison, "the true state of the case is that they partake of both these qualities; being considered by our laws, in some respects, as persons, and in other respects, as property . . . the Federal Constitution . . . views them [slaves] in the mixt character" (Madison 1961, 337). In this essay, Madison sought to explain the use of such "weasel" phraseology as "three fifths of all other persons" and "the migration or importation of such persons" (Article I, section 9).

When antislavery advocates compromised their principles and allowed the institution of slavery to be sanctioned by the very foundation of the new government, the Constitution, they relegated the African-American to a status of insignificance. The three-fifths compromise, by counting African-Americans for the purpose of taxation and representation, created an interesting paradox. It gave to African-Americans the dual status of person and property—however, more property than person.

What did all this mean for the African-American woman? Involuntary servitude had a tremendous impact on African-Americans, as it was both an economic and a political institution designed to manipulate and exploit men and women. As active participants in the labor market during the slavery era, African-American women worked not only in the plantation fields and in the masters' homes but in their own homes as well. They took on many roles and virtually had to be everything to everybody. They were, inter alia, mothers, lovers (willing and unwilling), laborers, and producers of labor. After 1808, the supply of slaves abated somewhat due to congressional legislation prohibiting the importation of Africans into the country. Consequently, the source of additional slave labor was to be effected through natural increase. Once again the onus was on the shoulders of the African-American woman, who fell prey to further victimization and exploitation. Her fertility was viewed as an asset, yet she had no control over the children born to her; they, too, were the property of the slave owner, to be bought and sold at the owner's demand.

Interpretation of the Constitution and state laws and statutes merely reinforced the notion of the property rights of slaveholders. For example, the defeminization of African-American women made it easy for them to be exploited: They "were never too pregnant, too young, too frail, to be subject to the harsh demands of an insensitive owner" (Horton 1986, 53). African-American women were not allowed the protections that were accorded to white women. They were expected to work hard for the slave owner and to maintain their own homes as well. Their status can be summed up in the folk wisdom given to Janie Sparks by her grandmother in Zora Neale Hurston's novel, *Their Eyes Were Watching God*:

> De white man throw down the load and tell de nigger man to pick it up. He pick it up because he have to, but he don't tote it. He hand it to his women-folks. De nigger woman is de mule of the world so far as Ah can see. (Hurston 1969, 29)

The seeds of this reality for the African-American woman were planted in slavery. Hence, African-American women had few illusions that they held the favored position accorded white women.

African-American women did not complacently accept their lot in life. They engaged in resistance in many ways (see Davis 1971 and Hine and Wittenstein 1981). They also initiated their own groups such as literary societies and temperance, charitable, and education groups, and of course antislavery groups. Although some white feminists of the nineteenth century, such as Lucy Stone and Susan B. Anthony, invited African-American women to participate in the women's struggle, the reform groups actively discriminated against African-American women. Their dislike of slavery did not extend to an acceptance of African-Americans as equals. For example, attempts by African-American women to participate in a meeting of an antislavery society in Massachusetts nearly caused the collapse of that group. According to historical documents, African-American men were more readily accepted into the inner sanctums of abolitionist societies than were African-American women. It is no surprise, then, that the most well-known advocates of women's rights among African-Americans were males, e.g., Frederick Douglass, James Forte (Sr. and Jr.), and Robert Purvis. The most prominent female was Sojourner Truth (Terborg-Penn 1981, 303). African-American women did, however, participate through their own initiative in both the antislavery and women's movements.

Armed with beliefs such as "It is not the color of the skin that makes a man or woman, but the principle formed in the soul" (Stewart 1973, 565), women such as the Forten sisters, Maria Stewart, and Milla Granson, to name a few, spoke out against racial and sexual injustices. For example, Maria Stewart often attacked racial injustice in the United States. Her outspokenness was accepted and applauded by African-American men until her criticisms were aimed at them for not doing as much as they could for the race. Stewart realized then the limitations placed on her as an African-American woman. She could speak out on behalf of civil rights and abolition but could not address sexism among African-American men. This dilemma, or duality of oppression, is a burden that African-American women still bear.

In the period preceding the Civil War, African-American and white men and women worked together as abolitionists. All saw a future where slaves and women would be liberated and elevated to equal status under the Constitution of the United States. But would this Constitution incorporate women and slaves? Political abolitionists and Garrisonian abolitionists (followers of William Lloyd Garrison) debated the role and the significance of the Constitution. Many felt that the American political system was corrupt and that this corruption stemmed from the Constitution. As a Garrisonian, Frederick Douglass felt that supporting the Constitution was also supporting slavery. He argued that endorsement of the Constitution meant that one served two masters, liberty and slavery. This argument was articulated also by abolitionist Wendell Phillips. Phillips felt that one should not hold an office in which an oath of allegiance to the Constitution was required. He argued that, since the Constitution was a document upholding slavery, anyone who supported it was a participant in the moral guilt of the institution of slavery (Hofstadter 1948, 148; Lobel 1987, 20).

Douglass later moved away from the Garrisonian view and came to support political abolitionists' natural-law theory. This view of the Constitution justified participation in the political process (Garrisonians argued for nonparticipation in government), which would allow radical lawyers and judges to argue against and eventually end slavery. It is the natural-law interpretation of the Constitution that led Douglass to assert that the three-fifths compromise "leans to freedom" (Lobel 1987, 20). But did it in fact? According to Chief Justice Roger Taney in the case of *Dred Scott v. Sandford* (1857), persons of African descent were not citizens under the Constitution. Taney reemphasized the Declaration of Independence's and Constitution's denial of African-American citizenship, for the Constitution, he argued, clearly showed that Africans were not to be regarded as people or citizens under the government formed in 1787; they were, and would continue to be, property.

Even before the *Dred Scott* decision, a future president was voicing his opposition to suffrage and equality for African-Americans: In a letter to the *New Salem Journal* in 1836, Abraham Lincoln wrote that he supported suffrage for all whites, male and female, if they paid taxes or served in the military. In 1858, a year after the infamous *Dred Scott* decision, Lincoln confirmed this view by stating that he in no way advocated social and political equality between whites and blacks and that he was as much in favor as anyone of whites having a superior position over blacks (Catt and Shuler 1969, 70; Hofstadter 1948, 116).

Armed with political agitation, men and women, whites and African-Americans, toiled long and hard toward the quest for equality and liberation. This agitation culminated in a bloody Civil War that ended with the South in ruins and another struggle in store. Who would secure political rights in the postwar period—white women, African-Americans, or both? Where would the African-American woman be, once the smoke cleared?

The democratization of America, it has been said, has not been the result of the Constitution, or of the equalitarian ideals of voters, or even of the demands of nonvoters; however, these things have played a role, albeit a secondary one. What, then, has brought about democratic change in American society? To some observers, the motivating force behind the major democratic reforms has been partisan advantage. Those reforms thought to be advantageous to a political party have passed; others have been shelved (Elliott 1974, 34).

An all-important question during the period following the Civil War was "What is to be done with the freedman?" Senator Charles Sumner of Massachusetts felt that African-Americans should be given the ballot and should be treated like men. Thaddeus Stevens of Pennsylvania said they should be given 40 acres of land and should be regarded as human beings. Abraham Lincoln suggested deportation but was told that idea was virtually impossible (Bennett 1964, 186-187). So what was to be done?

Two groups saw advantages to using the freedmen for their own purposes. First, leaders of the women's rights movement saw an opportunity to channel constitutional discussions around universal suffrage. They supported passage of the Thirteenth Amendment (which ended slavery) and continually pointed out that universal suffrage was a direct outgrowth of the principle of unconditional emancipation. The doors that had formerly been closed to African-Americans were slowly opening. As both federal and state constitutions were amended to accommodate the African-American, women pushed forward, hoping that they could pass through the same doors as the freedmen (DuBois 1987, 845; Papachristou 1976, 48). Women were not to be as lucky as the freedmen, however. With the doors closing to them, conflict was brewing that would lead to an irreparable schism between women and African-Americans, a schism that would carry over to the twentieth-century struggles of blacks and women.

The second group looking for personal gain on the backs of the freedmen was the Republican Party. Republican leaders saw an opportunity to consolidate their power base by enfranchising the freedmen. It was felt that African-Americans, out of gratitude, would support the party with their votes. So the wheels were put into motion to enfranchise the freedmen. Were women to be included? Would suffrage be universal?

In 1863, Angelina Grimké stated that the civil and political rights of women and of African-Americans were closely connected. She declared that she wanted to be identified with African-Americans, because women would not get their rights until African-Americans received theirs (Weld 1970, 80). Did this include African-American women, or just men and white women?

President Andrew Johnson opposed granting suffrage to any African-American, male or female. In a meeting with George Downing and Frederick Douglass in 1866, Johnson made his position clear:

> While I say that I am a friend of the colored man, I do not want to adopt a policy that I believe will end in a contest between the races, which if persisted in will result in the extermination of one or the other.... Yes, I would be willing to pass with him through the Red sea to the Land of Promise, to the land of liberty; but I am not willing . . . to adopt a policy which I believe will only result in the sacrifice of his life and the shedding of his blood. (Fishel and Quarles 1970, 276)

Despite Johnson's position, the radical Republicans circumvented any of his actions, to the point of impeaching him and nearly convicting him and ousting him from office.

There were national and state fights brewing over the issue of universal suffrage. At the state level, several states, including Kansas and New York, proposed changes to their constitutions advocating suffrage for African-Americans and women. In Kansas both proposals were rejected, whereas in New York the proposal for women was rejected. At the national level, after the Thirteenth Amendment ended slavery, the Fourteenth Amendment was proposed. This amendment created a serious controversy between women suffragists and men. The major area of contention was the wording of the Fourteenth Amendment, which granted suffrage specifically to males. For the first time, the Constitution explicitly defined voters as men. Section 2 reads,

> Representatives shall be apportioned among the several states according to their respective numbers, counting the whole number of persons in each state.... But when the right to vote at any election . . . is denied to any of the male inhabitants of such state, being twenty-one years of age, and citizens of the United States . . . the basis of representation therein shall be reduced in the proportion which the number of such male citizens shall bear to the whole number of male citizens twenty-one years of age in such state.

Speaking before the annual meeting of the Equal Rights Association in 1866, Frederick Douglass argued that acquisition of the franchise was vital for African-American men, whereas it was merely desirable for women (Terborg-Penn 1981, 305). Although Douglass attempted to keep the support of white women behind the movement for African-American suffrage, the rift between the two groups was widening.

The greatest controversy arose over the proposal and passage of the Fifteenth Amendment. White women continued to press for universal suffrage but were being told to wait until the suffrage amendment for African-American males had been passed. This time period was deemed the "Negro's hour" (Stanton 1970). The controversy over the Fifteenth Amendment polarized the Equal Rights Association. The Fifteenth Amendment aided the freedmen and rejected women. Where did this leave African-American women? They remained on the periphery as discussion centered on African-American men and white women.

The Equal Rights Association drifted into two factions, the old abolitionists (headed by William Lloyd Garrison, Wendell Phillips, and Frederick Douglass) and the ardent suffragists (headed by Susan B. Anthony and Elizabeth Cady Stanton). The former group argued for support of the Fifteenth Amendment and urged women not to jeopardize the freedmen's opportunity to obtain suffrage. The latter group opposed the Fifteenth Amendment and started its own newspaper, *The Revolution*. This suffragist faction also joined forces with George Train, a racist Democrat (Papachristou 1976, 56); the association with Train exacerbated the already growing rift between the two groups.

The suffragists used *The Revolution* and other forums to voice their opposition to passage of the Fifteenth Amendment. This excerpt from *The Revolution* summarizes their point of view and also includes their views on the position of African-American women:

> Manhood suffrage? Oh! no, my friend, you mistake us, we have enough of that already. We say not another man, black or white, until woman is inside the citadel. What reason have we to suppose the African would be more just and generous than the Saxon has been? Wendell Phillips pleads for black men; we for black women, who have known a degradation and sorrow of slavery such as man has never experienced. (Papachristou 1976, 57)

The issue of African-American women was discussed further in an exchange between Douglass, Anthony, Stanton, and others at a meeting of the Equal Rights Association where the subject of debate was the Fifteenth Amendment. Douglass argued that there was not the same sense of urgency for women as for the freedmen. He indicated that women were not treated as animals, were not insulated or hanged from lampposts, and did not have their children taken from them simply because they were women. When asked if the same things did not happen to African-American women, Douglass replied that they did—but because they were black, not because they were women. Thus Douglass underscored the primacy of race over sex. Elizabeth Stanton argued that if African-American women in the South were not given their rights then their emancipation could be regarded simply as another form of slavery (Papachristou 1976, 64; Stanton 1970, 81). Even though African-American women were victims of both racism and sexism, they were being put in a position of having to choose which oppression was the more debilitating.

Responding to Douglass's remarks, Phoebe Couzins stated, "While feeling extremely willing that the black man shall have all the rights to which he is

justly entitled, I consider the claims of the black woman of paramount importance . . . the black women are, and always have been, in a far worse condition
than the men. As a class, they are better, and more intelligent than the men,
yet they have been subjected to greater brutalities, while compelled to perform
exactly the same labor as men toiling by their side in the fields, just as hard
burdens imposed upon them, just as severe punishments decreed to them, with
the added cares of maternity and household work, with their children taken
from them and sold into bondage; suffering a thousandfold more than any man
could suffer" (Papachristou 1976, 64). Couzins was one of the few white women
who identified with the plight of African-American women and spoke on their
behalf. Along with other suffragists, she advocated universal suffrage and felt .
that the Fifteenth Amendment should not be passed unless women were included. She felt that men were not any more intelligent nor any more deserving
than women:

> The Fifteenth Amendment virtually says that every intelligent, virtuous woman
> is the inferior of every ignorant man, no matter how low he may be sunk into
> the scale of morality, and every instinct of my being rises to refute such doc-
> trine. (Papachristou 1976, 64)

African-American women were themselves divided over the issue of suffrage. Sojourner Truth spoke for those doubly oppressed by race and sex:

> There is a great stir about colored men getting their rights, but not a word
> about the colored women; and if colored men get their rights, and not colored
> women theirs, you see the colored men will be masters over the women, and it
> will be just as bad as it was before. So I am for keeping the thing going while
> things are stirring; because if we wait till it is still, it will take a great while to
> get it going again. (Truth 1973, 569)

Truth supported the Fifteenth Amendment but voiced her concern about men
being granted suffrage over women.

The suffragist Frances Harper posed the question whether white women
were willing to encompass African-American women in their struggle, to which
Anthony and others replied that they were. Harper supported passage of the
Fifteenth Amendment; she declared that, if the country could only address one
issue at a time, she would rather see African-American men obtain the vote
(Papachristou 1976, 64). The debate raged, but when the smoke cleared African-American men had obtained the vote and all women were disenfranchised
and remained effectively outside the foundation of the American political
system.

It has been argued that the Reconstruction Era focused more attention
on the rights of African-Americans and women than ever before (see DuBois
1987, 846). However, it is apparent that the focus was more on the rights of
African-American men and white women. African-American women were
pushed to the periphery of any discussions, or were acknowledged only nomi-

nally, despite the fact that they existed as persons who were both female and black. According to bell hooks (1981), the support of African-American male suffrage revealed the depth of sexism, particularly among white males in American society. To counter this sexism, white women began to urge racial solidarity in opposition to black male suffrage. This placed African-American women in the predicament of choosing between discriminatory precepts—white female racism or African-American patriarchy (hooks 1981, 3). As Sojourner Truth knew, sexism was as real a threat as racism. This issue remains unsolved.

Because they were excluded from the constitutional furor of the Reconstruction period, especially the controversy surrounding the Fourteenth and Fifteenth Amendments, white female suffragists amplified racist themes in their struggles. They claimed that enfranchising black men created "an aristocracy of sex" because it elevated all men over all women. Women suffragists criticized the Fifteenth Amendment because "a man's government is worse than a white man's government" and because the amendment elevated the "lowest orders of manhood" over "the higher classes of women" (DuBois 1987, 850). They, of course, meant white women.

Passage of the Fifteenth Amendment did not grant universal suffrage, just as the framers were not the proclaimed visionaries who created "a more perfect union." Passage of the Fifteenth Amendment elevated African-American men to a political status that thrust them into the patriarchal world. White women remained on their pedestals, cherished positions to be revered and envied. African-American women had once again been omitted from the cornerstone of American democracy, the Constitution of the United States. There was a difference made in 1870, however: She was no longer to be counted as three-fifths of a person; she was zero.

REFERENCES

Bennett, Lerone. 1964. *Before the Mayflower: A History of the Negro in America, 1619-1964.* Baltimore: Penguin Books.

Catt, Carrie Chapman, and Nettie Rogers Shuler. 1969. *Woman Suffrage and Politics.* Seattle: University of Washington Press.

Davis, Angela. 1971. "The Black Woman's Role in the Community of Slaves." *The Black Scholar* 2:3-14.

Dred Scott v. Sandford. 1857. 60 U.S. 19 Howard 393 (1857).

DuBois, Ellen Carol. 1987. "Outgrowing the Compact of the Fathers: Equal Rights, Woman Suffrage, and the United States Constitution, 1820-1878." *The Journal of American History* 74:836-862.

Elliott, Ward E. Y. 1974. *The Rise of Guardian Democracy: The Supreme Court's Role in Voting Rights Disputes, 1845-1869.* Cambridge: Harvard University Press.

Fishel, Leslie Jr., and Benjamin Quarles. 1970. *The Black American: A Documentary History.* Glenview, IL: Scott, Foresman and Company.

Hine, Darlene, and Kate Wittenstein. 1981. "Female Slave Resistance: The Economics of Sex." In *The Black Woman Cross-Culturally*, ed. Filomina Chioma Steady. Cambridge, MA: Schenkman.

Hofstadter, Richard. 1948. *The American Political Tradition*. New York: Vintage Books.

hooks, bell. 1981. *Ain't I a Woman: Black Women and Feminism*. Boston: South End Press.

Horton, James Oliver. 1986. "Freedom's Yoke: Gender Conventions Among Antebellum Free Blacks." *Feminist Studies* 12:51-76.

Hurston, Zora Neale. 1969. *Their Eyes Were Watching God*. New York: Negro Universities Press.

Lobel, Jules. 1987. "The Constitution and American Radicalism." *Social Policy* 18:20-23.

Madison, James. 1961. "Federalist 54." In Alexander Hamilton, James Madison, and John Jay, *The Federalist Papers*, ed. Clinton Rossiter. New York: New American Library. (Original work published in 1788.)

Marshall, Thurgood. 1987. "Justice Thurgood Marshall's Remarks on the Bicentennial of the U. S. Constitution." *Signs* 13:2-6.

Papachristou, Judith. 1976. *Women Together: A History in Documents of the Women's Movement in the United States*. New York: Alfred A. Knopf.

Stanton, Elizabeth Cady. 1970. "This Is the Negro's Hour." In *Voices From Women's Liberation*, ed. Leslie B. Tanner. New York: Signet Books.

Stewart, Maria. 1973. "What If I Am a Woman?" In *Black Women in White America*, ed. Gerda Lerner. New York: Vintage Books.

Terborg-Penn, Rosalyn. 1981. "Discrimination Against Afro-American Women in the Women's Movement, 1830-1920." In *The Black Woman Cross-Culturally*, ed. Filomina Chioma Steady. Cambridge, MA: Schenkman.

Truth, Sojourner. 1973. "I Suppose I Am About the Only Colored Woman That Goes About to Speak for the Rights of Colored Women." In *Black Women in White America*, ed. Gerda Lerner. New York: Vintage Books.

Weld, Angelina Grimké. 1970. "The Rights of Women and Negroes." In *Voices From Women's Liberation*, ed. Leslie B. Tanner. New York: Signet Books.

Part V

United States—
Nineteenth Century

15

Free African-American Women in Savannah, 1800-1860:

Affluence and Autonomy Amid Diversity

Whittington B. Johnson

For most Savannahians, the dawning of the nineteenth century brought few changes of any substance. But for a very small minority of African-American women who had only recently gained their freedom, the new century marked the dawn of a new life. They knew only too well the customary roles that had been assigned to the city's black women since Africans accompanied Georgia's first settlers in the 1730s.

Very early in their lives, female slaves were trained to meet the needs of their masters, mistresses, and their families; little consideration, if any, was given to their own personal needs. They often suffered under oppressive task-masters, worked long arduous hours, were sexually abused, whipped for the slightest provocation, and witnessed the sale and subsequent separation of their children and husbands.

The experiences of slave women have in recent years been the focus of increased scholarly attention.[1] But still largely unexplored are chronicles of their non-enslaved sisters, those black women who, for a variety of reasons, obtained their freedom, yet continued to live and work in the midst of a slaveholding society that made aberrations of their newly won status.[2] Free black females generally pursued the same vocations and suffered much of the same exploitation they had known under bondage. But at the same time, they enjoyed considerable advantages and escaped much of the oppression suffered by their enslaved counterparts. Taking advantage of the legal rights and social and economic opportunities available to them in an urban environment, the free black women of Savannah made substantial contributions to their community, which maintained its position as Georgia's most progressive black community throughout the antebellum period.

Savannah also boasted the state's largest free black populace. The city's free African-American population increased by nearly 50 percent between 1800 and 1810 (from 224 to 329), and continued to grow, although less spectacularly, until 1860, when it reached 705, or 20 percent of the state's total number of free blacks.[3]

The lone black religious institution in Savannah at the turn of the century, the First African Baptist Church, founded in 1788,[4] quickly felt the impact of the population increase as the number of worshipers (including a huge slave following) outgrew the edifice, causing Andrew Bryan, its founder, to consider organizing another black Baptist church. This was accomplished in December 1802 under the leadership of Henry Cunningham, a former slave and McIntosh County native, who had moved to Savannah and joined the First African Baptist Church.[5] Joining Cunningham in organizing the new church were nine other free African-Americans, including five women: Elizabeth (Betsy) Cunningham (his wife), Susan Jackson, Silva Monnox, Leah Simpson, and Charlotte Walls.[6] These women were among the more affluent free blacks in the community and they contributed to the spiritual life of their new church, the Second African Baptist Church. Other free women were active in First African Baptist Church, [7] and later Third African Baptist Church, while still others attended biracial churches—Christ Episcopal Church, the Independent Presbyterian Church, and St. John the Baptist Catholic Church—where they had less important roles than in the African churches.[8] When the Andrew Methodist and St. Stephen's Episcopal churches established chapels for blacks, free African-American women became active in those congregations.[9]

It was in the Baptist church, Savannah's only autonomous black religious institution, however, where free women were most visible, valuable, and influential. They were church mothers, a position which may have carried as much influence and respect as its male counterpart, the deacons; they formed their own benevolent and temperance societies, sang in the choir, and taught Sunday School.[10] Although men dominated offices in the black Baptist churches, females enjoyed voice and vote in the monthly business conferences, the governing body of each Baptist congregation. Since majority rule prevailed, and there were no distinctions between males and females, or clergy and laity, females exercised influence commensurate with their considerable numbers, thus partially overcoming the male dominance of church office.[11]

Free black women did not enjoy the same good fortune in the job market. Women outnumbered their male counterparts in the work place, but faced far more limited opportunities. Unlike most white families, social and economic pressures in free black households often forced females to work. A serious shortage of free black males forced some women to either remain unmarried, marry slaves, or become mistresses of whites, all of which could contribute to economic hardships. Since African-American males were squeezed into the least financially rewarding segment of the economy, many women had to supplement the family income. In addition, jobs were not plentiful and were intended mainly for males; professions and some business positions were not available to African-Americans at all.

The 49 males listed in Savannah's Register of Free Colored Persons in 1823 included eighteen occupations in which they were gainfully employed, whereas the 107 females listed only two more, twenty.[12] Even if the females' list had included such occupations as teaching and prostitution, which were illegal and hence unlisted, or selling milk, common but also unlisted, this disparity would not have changed significantly.

The list of free black female occupations in 1823 indicates that washerwoman (30) and seamstress (26) were the most common vocations; these were followed by 17 cooks, 11 sellers of small wares, 5 housekeepers, and 4 nurses. No more than two persons were employed in the remaining occupations.[13] The 1860 census, however, reveals significant changes in vocational preferences (which probably resulted from the law of supply and demand): seamstress/dressmaker (121) far outnumbered washerwoman as the most common, with the latter a distant second (44); domestic servants (32) and pastry cooks (20) emerged as popular vocations; and the number of nurses (10) more than doubled. Teaching, prostitution, and selling milk still were not listed.[14]

More black women sold fruits, cakes, and other foods in the streets and in the market than the figures in 1823 and 1860 reveal. Hawking, the name for this practice, had been a popular enterprise since the previous century. In 1812, the city council became so annoyed with black females who spent time "hawking," that it passed a resolution indefinitely suspending the issuance of badges and ordered constables to incarcerate all African-American females caught, "selling cakes, apples," without a badge. The council was evidently concerned that by engaging in such activities, the women were unavailable to nurse whites during the approaching "sickly season of the year," a situation that would have caused great suffering among whites if allowed to continue.[15] The resolution exposed the tenuous position of free women and illustrated one of the multiple ways in which they were manipulated by whites.

In spite of the disadvantages encountered in the job market, women were well represented among real estate owners in the black community. As Loren Schweninger maintained in his study of southern black property owners, African-Americans placed great importance upon owning property, which they perceived as an indicator of prosperity and an important way to gain the respect of whites.[16] The high visibility of black females among the propertied class is thus positive evidence of their prosperity, which, in turn, was a key factor in the economic growth of their community.

Over the years, black women acquired a numerical advantage among real estate owners in all categories, but especially those in the most highly assessed property. In 1820, thirty-six free blacks in Savannah owned homes that were assessed at a minimum of $200 each, for a total of $31,250. Women home owners (21) comprised a majority of this group, their holdings totaling $17,700 or 56 percent of the total. In 1820, a majority of home owners (5 of the 9) in the $1,000 and higher category also were women.[17] After 1830 when the number of free (male and female) home owners decreased, females still retained their lead and actually increased their proportion of higher priced real estate ($1,000 and higher). In 1858, seventeen of the nineteen home owners in that category were women who, combined, owned property valued at $37,750, nearly 90 percent of the total ($41,950) owned by this group.[18] Schweninger offered a sound reason for the large presence of women among property owners: "free women sought to acquire property as a means of protection, economic independence, and self-sufficiency."[19]

Home ownership made free African-American taxpayers, rather than taxable personal property, another major and meaningful distinction between free and slave status. In the nineteenth century, real estate taxes were the primary source of revenue for state and local governments. Since women owned the majority of, and the most valuable, property in the black community, they paid more taxes than the free black males, propertyless whites (males and females), and slaves, who were ineligible to own land. The tax digests reveal that free African-American women acted responsibly in discharging this important civic responsibility.

Buying real estate became more difficult for African-Americans after 1830. Encumbrances to home ownership had existed, including an 1818 law that prohibited African-Americans from owning real estate in Savannah.[20] But the number of black home owners declined after the 1820s. This decline was due to the influx of European immigrants during the antebellum period who also sought housing, thereby causing prices to escalate. Just when houses were becoming more expensive, some African-Americans were falling on hard times. Some died intestate and the state sold their property; some were victims of one or more of the panics that hit the American economy in 1819, 1837, and 1857.[21] Finally, the local racial climate became more hostile toward African-Americans following the Missouri Compromise debate in 1820; David Walker's 1829 *Appeal to the Colored Citizens of the World*, which called for violent action to overthrow slavery, was circulated widely in Savannah; and Nat Turner's rebellion in 1831. Collectively, these circumstances created an environment much more hostile toward African-American economic progress.

The manner in which black women took advantage of opportunities afforded by free status—while coping with changing racial attitudes and economic environment—is best revealed by examining individual examples. Susan Jackson, Frances Carley, and Nancy Golding were among the early successful pastry cooks in Savannah. Frances Carley's real estate was assessed at $1,000 in 1854, but it slipped to $700 in 1860, at which time she was seventy-five years old and had managed over the years to live comfortably by selling pastries.[22] Nancy Golding, a Liberty County native, moved to Savannah in 1808 and joined the Independent Presbyterian Church in 1841. A huskster turned pastry cook, she was so successful that by 1854 her real estate in Yamacraw was assessed at $1,000 and four years later at $1,550, before taking a precipitous decrease in 1860, when the property was assessed at $500.[23] Since she owned the same property during those years, the assessment reflected a decrease in value rather than in the size of her holding. She, like Frances, was among a small minority of black property owners whose real estate value declined in 1860, but none as much as Nancy Golding's.

In his reminiscences, William Harden recalled the "delicious ice-cream of the most popular flavors" purchased from Aspasia Mirault's bakery and confectionery on the northeast corner of Bull and Broughton streets. This shop "was well patronized by the white people" which enabled Aspasia, who had left revolution-ravished Haiti in 1800, to live comfortably. She did, however, experience some financial problems at times: in 1847 for instance when she failed to pay her taxes.[24] Georgia Conrad, the granddaughter of a former Georgia governor, patronized a different pastry cook, but her compliments were just as laudatory as Harden's; she described the unnamed proprietress as "the best cake maker and baker . . . whose fruit cakes had such a reputation that they were sent for from many places, England included."[25]

In the 1850s two younger black women, Catherine Baty and Richard Ann (Houstoun) Butler, joined this group of older successful pastry cooks. Catherine Baty, who was born in 1801, owned real estate on Pierce Street in Oglethorpe Ward that was assessed at $1,000 in 1854, and at $1,150 in 1860.[26] Richard Ann, the younger daughter of Richard Houstoun, a free black tailor, was taught to bake by Susan Jackson and later married James Butler, a Liberty County carpenter, in 1842. A year later she gave birth to her only child, a baby girl, Margaret, who died at the age of three.[27] Richard Ann and James Butler must have made a good team because when he died in 1859, they owned the old Houstoun family home on Broughton and Houston streets, which Henry Cunningham had bought from her mother, and at least three other houses that were rented.[28] She remained a faithful member of Second African Church throughout her life and, judging from the inventory of her estate, she lived a simple life, nothing fancy, no gigs, buggies, horses, fine jewelry, or slaves even though she could have afforded them.[29]

Dressmaking proved more profitable than pastry making. African-Americans had gained a reputation for lavishly spending money on clothes, especially on so-called "Sunday clothes," which led a local newspaper publisher to comment that blacks were driven to "extravagant gratification" to satisfy their desire to dress up, adding that "this ambition to dress is absolutely a disease."[30] Thus, with a clothes loving group of black customers serving as a core and white customers amply supplementing it, a relatively large group of free black women were engaged as seamstresses, and by the 1820s and 1830s, several did quite well financially.

One was Leah Simpson, a founding member of Second African Baptist Church, who owned four slaves and real estate on Farm Street assessed at $2,000 in 1819; she purchased another slave in 1820 but the value of her real estate dropped to $800. Another, Catherine Deveaux, a native of Antigua, owned real estate in Greene Ward, the location of Second African Baptist Church, where her husband was a leader; she subsequently purchased property in Columbia Ward as well as in Warren Ward.[31] Her property in Columbia Ward included a "negro house," probably for her slaves.

Other successful seamstresses of her generation included Betsy Baptist, Manette Tardieu, Betsy Cunningham, Sarah Marshall, and Ann Morel. Betsy Baptist was brought as a slave to this country from Africa in 1795, but by 1837 she had gained freedom and owned one-half a lot on which she had built a house assessed at $500.[32] Manette Tardieu, who also came to Savannah in

1795, was a native of Santo Domingo. Having arrived free, unlike Betsy Baptist, she was able to acquire land more quickly and by 1830 her property was assessed at $300.[33] It is difficult to isolate the property holdings of the other seamstresses since they all had successful husbands: Elizabeth Cunningham was the wife of Andrew Marshall, the venerable pastor of First African Baptist Church; and Ann Morel was the wife of Andrew Morel, a tailor from Santo Domingo.

By the 1850s a new group of successful free African-American seamstresses in their forties, or younger, had emerged to augment their older counterparts. Georgia Conrad saved Margaret Blodsett from oblivion when she proclaimed Blodsett's dainty work "was not to be excelled.[34] Louisa Marshall learned to sew while she was single and this skill became useful after her husband, Joseph, Andrew Marshall's son, died just as his dray business had begun to flourish. Although she was left in a comfortable state, Louisa's resources were insufficient to maintain her former lifestyle. She was able, however, to supplement the income from her husband's estate with money earned from sewing. In 1858, her home was assessed at $1,500.[35]

Hannah Cohen was left in a comfortable financial state by her mother, Maria Cohen, who had raised and sold produce from her garden. Hannah, however, was a seamstress. In 1860, Hannah's property was valued at $1,000, and she owned a slave.[36] Unlike Hannah, Georgiana Guard followed the vocation of her mother, June Guard, a former seamstress. A member of the Independent Presbyterian Church, which she joined in 1843 at the age of twenty-three, Georgiana built upon the modest financial resources her mother had left, and in 1860 owned real estate assessed at $1,050 and one slave over twelve years of age.[37] Another of these new generation seamstresses, Estelle Savage, was the oldest of three children (two girls and a boy) born to Phyllis Savage, from Santo Domingo. Both sisters were seamstresses, but Estelle was more successful. In 1858, Estelle's real estate was assessed at $2,600, while propertyless Tharsville and her brother lived rent free in houses owned by their older sister.[38]

The youngest of this second generation of seamstresses was Sarah Ann Black, who, only in her mid-twenties in 1860, owned a large lot outside the city limits on Gaston Street between Jefferson and Montgomery streets on which she built two "good houses" and two "shanties," which were probably rented. Sarah maintained a common law arrangement with an out-of-town white cotton salesman. Living outside the city limits allowed Sarah to keep cows on her premises; by selling milk to the public, she supplemented the income she received from sewing, her primary occupation.[39]

Rose Jalineau, another of the many emigrés from Santo Domingo who came to Savannah and did quite well financially, had a benefactor, Francis Jalineau, a free mulatto merchant, who left her property in Cuba. In 1830s Rose, a seamstress, probably had financial problems because she sold valuable land in Greene Ward to High Cullen, a white man, for $1,000.[40] This was only a temporary solution to her financial woes; in 1844, failure to pay $15 in delinquent taxes resulted in the auction of her property located at the corner of Congress and Price streets, which was brought by Orlando A. Wood, Esquire, for $300.[41] Seventy-seven-year-old Rose Jalineau switched occupations in 1848, washing clothes and other articles, which she continued to pursue until 1864 when she died propertyless at the age of ninety-three. She was buried in the Cathedral Cemetery, rather than the city's black cemetery.[42]

Rose's age may have contributed to her inability to acquire real estate after 1848, but her new occupation, while common among women, did not produce as many success stories as others, especially in view of the relatively large number who practiced it. Washing required only marginal skill; as one former Georgia slave described the process, "We took clothes out'n the suds, soaped them good and put them on the blocks and beat them with the battlin' sticks, which were made like a paddle. On wash days you could hear those battlin' sticks pounding every which-way."[43] This may account for the droves of black women it attracted, which, along with their numbers, kept wages low. Washing kept females from starving but seldom allowed them to earn enough to live comfortably.

Mary Spiers probably earned as much as any washerwoman and had accumulated enough money in the 1820s to purchase five slaves and real estate assessed at $400. Another washerwoman, Hannah Pray, owned a house and lot in North Oglethorpe Ward. Even though the property was assessed at only $70 in 1847, she was unable to pay her taxes; in 1860, the property's value had increased to $300. She, nevertheless, paid the taxes.[44]

Perhaps the most successful free African-American female of her generation (pre-1850) was Susan Jackson, owner of valuable real estate in the city and a thriving business. She was evidently a very astute person, for in 1812 her husband Simon, a successful tailor and community leader, entrusted her with the responsibility of going to Charleston, South Carolina to close the deal on their house and lot in Reynolds Ward, which they were able to purchase for $1,500 with a loan secured from Richard Stites, a prominent Savannah lawyer who handled Simon Jackson's legal matters. After her husband's death, Susan Jackson paid both the balance on the mortgage (about $600), and a long-standing debt of $200 that Simon Jackson had secured by using their real estate as collateral. This allowed her to gain clear title to the property. She earned the money to meet those obligations by operating a pastry shop and renting property. Susan Jackson died of heart disease on January 12, 1862 at the age of eighty-two.[45]

Ann H. Gibbons was the most successful of the post-1850 women, but her life is something of a mystery. Although she had a daughter, Claudia, in 1820, and she owned the most valuable real estate among African-Americans in 1860, neither the father of her child nor the source of her income is known. After appearing on the tax digest in 1833 as propertyless, she started her climb up the economic ladder in the 1840s and, by 1850, she declared two lots containing dwellings and four slaves. In 1852, her slaves were assessed at $2,200, placing her second to Anthony Odingsell (whose nine slaves were assessed at

$2,700) among the small group of black slaveholders in the Chatham-Savannah area. In 1860, Gibbons owned two lots in North Oglethorpe Ward, one in Middle Oglethorpe (with a total value of $9,000) and three prime slaves.[46]

Although records reveal that Savannah's black community included a small group of slaveholders, the practice was not pervasive. In 1860, for instance, nine black slaveholders owned a total of 19 slaves, a small fraction of the 15,417 slaves in Chatham County; except for Anthony Odingsell, who lived on Little Wassaw Island and owned 8 slaves, no African-American owned more than 2 slaves.[47] Black slaveholders were interested in owning slaves primarily to assist in their enterprises, which accounts for the seeming anomaly of a slaveholding washerwoman. Records for Savannah do not indicate that black-owned slaves performed personal services for their masters as their primary duty, unlike the situation in Charleston.[48] The differences between the two groups may have resulted more from socioeconomic factors than from attitudes concerning the use of slaves. The black community of Charleston was much older, more affluent, and more sophisticated than Savannah's, and Charleston's free African-Americans had been more successful in narrowing the standard of living gap between themselves and whites than had black Savannahians.

By 1820 free black women in Savannah outnumbered males as slaveholders. This was less a result of greater female activity in the slave trade than it was a consequence of female longevity—husbands died and left their wives real estate and personal property, including slaves. For instance, Richard Cohen and John Gibbons, owners of seven and five slaves respectively, bequeathed them to their widows—Maria Cohen and Chloe Gibbons. Even when the number of black slaveholders decreased after 1830, females still constituted a majority.[49]

There is no evidence that black slaveholders in Savannah mistreated their slaves. Local newspapers and published journals of visitors to antebellum Savannah, which vented their displeasure with other alleged inappropriate behavior among African-Americans and could be expected to comment on any abuse of slaves, were silent on the subject.[50] Generally, slaves kept in the city received better treatment, food, and clothing than their country sisters and brothers.[51]

Black slaveholders outnumbered black teachers. In view of the hostile conditions under which the latter labored and the fact that legislation prohibited teaching African-Americans to read, it is hardly surprising that a more sanguine environment existed for black slaveholders than for schoolteachers. Savannah lacked a professional class of black teachers and up-to-date school buildings. The formal learning process was conducted in small classroom settings, usually comprised of marginally trained black teachers and a mixed group of free and slave children, with all grades taught in the same room. Although educating blacks was illegal, the laws were discreetly ignored.[52] As Charles C. Jones, noted Presbyterian minister and native Georgian, observed in the 1840s:

> Their [free African-Americans] advantages for education and consequently
> access to the written word of God, are more limited in the slave states . . . on

account of laws against the education of colored persons; but notwithstanding in the slave states the free Negroes do have schools for their children, or some private instruction. . . .[53]

Free persons of color in Savannah did, indeed, operate schools for black children. In addition to three free black males, Catherine Deveaux and her daughter, Jane, of Second African Baptist Church, Mary Woodhouse of St. Stephen's Episcopal Church and Mary Beasley also taught school. These teachers conducted their schools clandestinely and pupils took special care to avoid detection while going to and from school. They loitered around the playground, then individually walked off inconspicuously to a designated place; they carried buckets as though on an errand; they wrapped their books in newspaper; they picked chips on their way to school (the poor used chips as fuel); and they took circuitous routes to and from school.[54]

Catherine Deveaux was probably among the early black females to teach in Savannah. Her husband, John, was a deacon and later preacher in Savannah and she tried to help his ministry by teaching children to read the Bible. Catherine passed the torch to her daughter, who apparently successfully expanded the scope of the educational experiences to which pupils were exposed. Jane Deveaux conducted her school for almost thirty years and was never forced to close its doors. A surprised group of Union troops found the school operating when they captured Savannah in 1864; the Freedmen's Bureau subsequently hired her to teach in the school which it established for freedmen.[55] Mary Woodhouse taught school in the house on Bay Lane between Habersham and Price streets, which her mother-in-law, Susan Woodhouse, had purchased in the first decade of the nineteenth century. When the young Woodhouse operated the school in the 1850s, she had between twenty-five and thirty pupils (free and slave) and was assisted by her daughter, Mary Jane. The pupils usually spent one or two years there learning the basics before transferring to the school which Mary Beasley operated, where they were given what could be considered an upper level elementary education.[56] Obviously the census taker erred in 1860 when he said only seven African-Americans, all free, attended school that year.[57]

Female black teachers were in the vanguard of efforts to educate black children in Savannah. It was a challenging job, but the burning desire to learn, which many of their pupils brought to school despite public officials' efforts to keep them ignorant, and the high value that the black community placed on education made teaching a rewarding experience. Although their schools lacked up-to-date books, chalkboards, and maps, teachers created a wholesome learning environment and provided their pupils with educational experiences that left a lasting impression. This training was especially important because many of the pupils, the first generation in their families to receive schooling, subsequently became community leaders. Without question, female teachers performed a valuable service to the black community.

Thanks to the efforts of these women and other interested persons in the city—blacks and whites—black education made its inauspicious beginning in

Savannah. These pioneer educators were rewarded for their efforts as a considerable number of African-Americans (slave and free blacks), although the accurate number is unknown, learned to read, and a smaller number learned to read, write and cipher. One of the young ladies who benefited from the educational opportunities clandestinely offered African-Americans was Hettie Sabattie. A twenty-four-year-old seamstress when the Civil War began, she returned to Darien, Georgia after the war and taught in one of the first schools for blacks in the hometown of her mother, Mary Gary, a free African-American and member of Christ Episcopal Church.[58]

The window to freedom which free black females presented must have encouraged female slaves to seek manumission. If that were not achievable, they might alternatively seek permission to hire their own time. This privilege allowed them to live with their families and away from their masters, who, in return, were paid a stipulated amount, usually nine dollars each month, plus a smaller amount to hire the time of each teenage child. The exact number of slaves allowed to hire their time is unknown, but if the number of former slaves who filed claims with the Southern Claims Commission concerning alleged property losses sustained at the hands of the Union Army constitutes a representative sample, they could have outnumbered free African-Americans.[59]

The considerable amount of freedom enjoyed by the sizable group of nominal slaves in Savannah may also account for the colonization movement's small following in the black community. Since slaves enjoyed this privilege at the pleasure of their masters, they were careful to avoid indulging in behavior which might have alienated their benefactors and caused withdrawal of the privilege. It is not surprising, therefore, that during the peak years of the exodus to Africa, 1848-1856, the American Colonization Society transported only 297 free blacks (males and females) and 529 slaves to Liberia; only a fraction of this small number were Savannahians.[60]

Even though African-American females did not play a major role in the colonization movement, one of their number deserves mention. Cecilia D'Lyons was the mulatto daughter of Samuel Benedict, a former Savannah resident and eventual chief justice of the Liberia Supreme Court. Cecilia, then a thirty-five-year-old mother with five children ranging in age from seven to sixteen, joined a small group of black Savannahians who departed for Liberia from ports outside Georgia.[61] She did not have enough money to pay for passage on a ship that left in 1847; she subsequently moved to Maryland and departed on a ship the following year. Before leaving Savannah, however, she persuaded several other blacks to emigrate. One gathers from the tone of one of her letters to an official of the society that Cecilia D'Lyons, too, was a victim of the vulnerability which Suzanne Lebsock so aptly described in *The Free Women of Petersburg*.[62] In that letter the despondent black mother said: "We had not means yet . . . had I been justly dealt with however I should have had some means to go upon[,] but unfortunately the weak and powerless have to yield to all who are ungenerous enough to take advantage of them."[63]

The economic exploitation to which Cecilia D'Lyons alluded was just one of a number of problems faced by free black females in Savannah. They also were confronted with a shortage of free males, but this was less serious than some of the other problems because of the availability of eligible adult male slaves. Marriages between free black females and slaves were common. This arrangement was not as undesirable as it might seem because children of mixed marriages involving free black females and slaves were born free. Many of those slave husbands hired their own time, hence provided almost the same male presence in their homes which free black males did. Added to these factors was the high probability that the family would remain together since separating families by selling the male slave partner out of the city occurred infrequently. The number of mixed marriages is unknown, but some of the more ambitious slaves in the city were partners in such a union. For instance, William J. Campbell, slave pastor and successor to Marshall as leader of First African Baptist Church, the largest Baptist church (1,500 members in 1860) in Savannah, and Ulysses L. Houston, slave pastor of Third African Baptist Church (now known as First Bryan Baptist Church), were married to free mates.[64]

Because slave husbands could not legally head households, these men were not listed in the censuses in that capacity. Contrary to what the census takers reported, however, these men were the decision makers, breadwinners, and heads of their families. The number of households that fell into this category is hard to determine, but it was not restricted to just a few. This means that the number of female-headed households was lower, maybe even significantly, than that drawn from the census. It is accurate to conclude, moreover, that free wives to nominal slaves generally enjoyed a normal marital relationship.

An important health statistic favored free African-American females in Savannah: longevity of life. Between 1830 and 1860 at least thirty-six African-Americans (slaves and free persons) reached their ninetieth birthday, and nine of those, or 25 percent, were free African-American females, even though this group comprised less than 10 percent of the total black population. Next in order of longevity were female slaves who were also disproportionately represented among the ninety and over group, but to a smaller degree than the free black females; the males were in a minority.[65] Black females in Savannah who survived their childbearing years lived longer than adult males, and free black females outlived all other adult blacks. The reason(s) for this is unknown.

It is very clear that free African-American women in Savannah often prospered in spite of the hostile environment in which free status was not an inalienable right. Because women usually outlived their mates, the responsibility for preserving their gains, however meager, fell upon their shoulders. After 1830, when circumstances tightened and manumissions declined precipitously, the blood of free African-American women flowing through the veins of their newborn infants assured freedom, regardless of their fathers' status. This factor contributed significantly to the continued growth of the free black population in Savannah, despite legislation to effect just the opposite. Free women defied bans on teaching blacks how to read, thus breaking barriers and, in the process, instilling a desire among blacks to obtain an education after the Civil War. Furthermore, they met their civic responsibility by paying their share of real estate taxes.

Free women, therefore, enjoyed certain privileges that were denied slave females and one that even was denied other African-Americans, whether free or slave; these women, moreover, served as role models for their daughters, showed slave females, and others, a different role which black women could perform, helped build the black church, and generally contributed to the growth, progress, and prosperity of the black community. Thus, free status created opportunities for African-American women in Savannah, 1800-1860, to live distinctively different from slave females.

NOTES

1. The most significant literature on slave women includes Angela Davis, "Reflections on the Black Woman's Role in the Community of Slaves," *Black Scholar* 3 (December 1971); Dorothy Sterling, ed., *We Are Your Sisters: Black Women in the Nineteenth Century* (New York, 1984); Deborah Gray White, *Ar'n't I a Woman?: Female Slaves in the Plantation South* (New York, 1985); Minrose Gwin, *Black and White Women of the Old South: The Peculiar Sisterhood in American Literature* (Knoxville, 1985); Jacqueline Jones, *Labor of Love, Labor of Sorrow: Black Women, Work and the Family from Slavery to the Present* (New York, 1986); and Elizabeth Fox-Genovese, *Within the Plantation Household: Black and White Women of the Old South* (Chapel Hill, 1988). On slave women in the Savannah area, see Betty Wood, "Some Aspects of Female Resistance to Chattel Slavery in Low Country Georgia, 1763-1815," *Historical Journal* 30 (September 1987): 603-22. The author wishes to thank his colleague Janet Martin for her helpful suggestions.

2. The fullest treatment of free black women to date is Adele Logan Alexander, *Ambiguous Lives: Free Women of Color in Rural Georgia, 1789-1879* (Fayetteville, Ark., 1991). Works that deal at least in part with free black women in the urban South include Suzanne Lebsock, *The Free Women of Petersburg: Status and Culture in a Southern Town, 1784-1860* (New York, 1984); Michael P. Johnson and James L. Roark, eds., *No Chariot Let Down: Charleston's Free People of Color on the Eve of the Civil War* (Chapel Hill, 1984); and Loren Schweninger, "Property-Owning Free African-American Women in the South, 1800-1870," *Journal of Women's History* 1 (Winter 1990): 13-44.

3. *Second Census of the United States, 1800* (Washington, D.C., 1801); *Aggregate Amount of Persons within the United States in 1810* (Washington, D.C., 1811), 80-81; and *The Population of the United States in 1860: Eighth Census* (Washington, D.C., 1863), 79.

4. On the history of this church, see George White, *Historical Collection of Georgia . . .* (New York, 1854), 313; James Simms, *The First Colored Baptist Church in North America* (Philadelphia, 1888), 19; Walter Brooks, "The Priority of the Silver Bluff Church and its Promoter," *Journal of Negro History* 7 (April 1922): 187.

5. "Letters Showing the Rise and Progress of Early Negro Churches in Georgia," *Journal of Negro History* 1 (January 1916): 86-87. Henry Holcombe, *The First Fruits*

in a Series of Letters (Philadelphia, 1812), 83; Edgar G. Thomas, *The First African Baptist Church of North America* (Savannah, 1925), 29.

6. Reverend E.P. Quarterman, former pastor of Second Baptist Church, to Whittington B. Johnson, October 18, 1981. Mabel Freeman La Far, "The Baptist Church of Savannah, Georgia: Records and Register," 1:135 (typescript), Georgia Historical Society, Savannah (hereinafter cited as GHS). The minutes of the August 5, 1808 business conference state that dismissal letters had been sent for this group.

7. Simms, *First Colored Baptist Church*, 85-86.

8. Christ Episcopal Church of Savannah Parish Registers, 1822-1851; Independent Presbyterian Church Sessional Minutes, Books 1 and 2, 1828-1851; St. John the Baptist Catholic Church Parish Register, 1796-1816; all on microfilm at Georgia Department of Archives and History, Atlanta (hereinafter cited as GDAH).

9. Haygood S. Bowen, *History of Savannah Methodism: From John Wesley to Silas Johnson* (Macon, 1929), 59; *Journal of the Proceedings . . . of the Protestant Episcopal Church, 1856* (Savannah, 1856), 45.

10. Thomas, *First African Baptist Church*, 141; Milton C. Sernett, *Black Religion and American Evangelicalism* (Metuchen, N.J., 1975), 138; Fredericka Bremer, *The Homes of the New World: Impressions of America*, 2 vols. (New York, 1853), 1:354.

11. Brief of Evidence in *Richard Baker, et al. vs. Peter Houston, et al.*, March 1881, First African Baptist Church Minutes, Collections, Dues, and Funerals, 1871-1889, GHS; see also Larry M. James, "Biracial Fellowship in Antebellum Baptist Churches," in John B. Boles, ed., *Masters and Slaves in the House of the Lord* (Lexington, Ky., 1988). The essay focuses on biracial churches, but many of those practices were followed in black churches. Minutes of the Sunbury Baptist Association, 1818-1938 (microfilm), University of Georgia Libraries, Athens; also see minutes of the 1840 convention.

12. Chatham County Register of Free Persons of Color, 1817-1829, GDAH. The Georgia Historical Society, formerly an independent agency, is now part of the Georgia Department of Archives and History. Many of the original public documents and church records housed at the Society and the Savannah Courthouse are on microfilm at GDAH.

13. *Ibid.*

14. *Eighth Census of the United States, 1860.*

15. Savannah City Council Minutes, 1812-1822, GDAH.

16. Loren Schweninger, *Black Property Owners in the South, 1790-1915* (Champaign, Ill., 1990).

17. City of Savannah Tax Digest, 1820, GDAH. Some of the women home owners in the $200 category may have had slave partners who actually owned the property, but the number of such couples probably was not large enough to have given male owners a majority.

18. *Ibid.*, 1858. Simon and Josephine Mirault, whose real estate was valued at $3,500, are included among the owners in the high-value real estate category, but Josephine Mirault is not included among the seventeen women. The total number of black home owners in all categories (43) was down in 1858 from the number in 1823 (64). See *ibid.*, 1823.

19. Schweninger, "Property-Owning Free African-American Women," 30. The high visibility of African-American women among real estate owners in Savannah was consistent with the practice throughout the South. See Schweninger, *Black Property*

Owners in the South, 84-87. The percentage of women real estate owners, however, was much higher in Savannah than the regional average.

20. Thomas Cobb, *A Digest of the Statutes of the State of Georgia* (Athens, 1851), 995; Ralph B. Flinders, *Plantation Slavery in Georgia* (Chapel Hill, 1933), 236. An 1810 Georgia statute required free African-Americans to have guardians. Special bonds often developed between free blacks and their guardians who usually acted as the principal parties in the purchase of real estate, which they subsequently deeded to the African-Americans.

21. City of Savannah Tax Digest, 1820, 1823, 1848, and 1860. More free African-Americans owned homes in 1820 than in 1860. Although there were more black home owners in 1848 (65) than in 1823 (64), there was a considerable decrease proportionately, since the free black population had grown significantly over that twenty-five-year period.

22. Chatham County Tax Digest, 1854, GDAH; *Eighth Census of the United States, 1860.*

23. Chatham County Register of Free Persons of Color, 1817-1829, 1826-1837; Chatham County Tax Digest, 1858; City of Savannah Tax Digest, 1858, 1860.

24. William Harden, *Recollections of a Long and Satisfactory Life* (Savannah, 1934), 48-49; City of Savannah Tax Digest, 1847.

25. Georgia Bryan Conrad, *Reminiscences of a Southern Woman* (Hampton, Va., n.d.), 16.

26. City of Savannah Tax Digest, 1854, 1860.

27. Chatham County Register of Free Persons of Color, 1837-1849.

28. City of Savannah Tax Digest, 1858.

29. Bureau of Refugees, Freedmen, and Abandoned Lands, Account of Richard Ann Butler, #638, Record Group 101, Registers of Signatures of Depositors in Branches of the Freedmen's Bureau Savings and Trust Company, M816, Roll 9, National Archives, Washington, D.C. (hereinafter cited as BRF&AL). Estate of Richard Ann Butler, December 1869, Central Records Office, Chatham County Courthouse, Savannah (hereinafter cited as CRO). See also Inventories and Appraisements, 1862-1874, Chatham Court of Ordinary, GDAH. She sold a lot for $600 in 1868 which does not show in the appraisement. Deeds, Vol. 4A, 1868, Chatham County Superior Court, CRO.

30. *Savannah Republican*, June 6, 1849.

31. City of Savannah Tax Digest, 1810, 1820, 1824.

32. Chatham County Register of Free Persons of Color, 1826-1835; Chatham County Tax Digest, 1837.

33. Chatham County Tax Digest, 1810; Chatham County Register of Free Persons of Color, 1826-1835.

34. Conrad, *Reminiscences of a Southern Woman*, 16.

35. City of Savannah Tax Digest, 1858.

36. Chatham Register of Free Persons of Color, 1823-1829; *Eighth Census of the United States, 1860.*

37. Independent Presbyterian Church Sessional Minutes; Chatham County Register of Free persons of Color, 1826-1835; City of Savannah Tax Digest, 1860.

38. Chatham County Register of Free Persons of Color, 1826-1835; City of Savannah Tax Digest, 1858; Estate of Estelle Savage, 1891, CRO.

39. *Eighth Census of the United States, 1860*; Claim of Sarah Ann Black, Southern Claims Commission Case Files, Chatham County, Georgia, #18222, RG 217, National Archives, Washington, D.C.

40. Estate of Francis Jalineau, 1824, CRO; Deeds, Volume 2V, 1837-1838, 100, *ibid.*

41. Deeds, Vol. 3B, 1843-1844, 329-30.

42. Chatham County Register of Free Persons of Color, 1837-1849; see also City of Savannah Tax Digest for the years 1848-1864; Savannah Board of Health Minutes, 1830-1864, GDAH. Also see the volume for 1859-1864.

43. Interview with Sally Hunt of Commerce, Georgia, Ex-Slaves Interviews, W.P.A., Hargrett Rare Book and Manuscript Library, University of Georgia Libraries.

44. Chatham Register of Free Persons of Color, 1817-1829; City of Savannah Tax Digest, 1847, 1860; *Eighth Census of the United States, 1860*; Harden, *Recollections*, 49.

45. La Far, "The Baptist Church of Savannah, Georgia," 1:135; Simms, *First Colored Baptist Church*, 57; Simon Jackson Account, Wayne-Stites-Anderson Papers, GHS; Richard M. Stites to William Drayton, Savannah, December 3, 1811, Wayne-Stites-Anderson Papers; Deeds, Vol. K, 1823-1834, 508-509; Inventories and Appraisements, 1862-1874, Chatham County Court of Ordinary, 96; Savannah Board of Health Minutes, 1859-1864; City of Savannah Tax Digest, 1860. Susan Jackson is not listed in the 1860 census.

46. Chatham County Register of Free Persons of Color, 1837-1849; City of Savannah Tax Digest, 1833, 1860; Chatham County Tax Digest, 1852. Estate of Ann Gibbons, CRO. Claudia B. (Anderson) Gibbons, Ann Gibbons' daughter, was her sole heir. Ann Gibbons was not the daughter of John (Jack) and Chloe Gibbons, hence she did not inherit their property. See note 49.

47. Black slaveholding in Savannah peaked in 1823, when 20 slaveholders owned a total of 58 slaves. See Chatham Register of Free Persons of Color, 1817-1829; City of Savannah Tax Digest, 1860; Chatham County Tax Digest, 1860; *Eighth Census of the United States, 1860*.

48. Thomas S. Bonneau, a highly regarded black schoolteacher, owned house servants. See the will of Thomas S. Bonneau, Record of Wills, Vol. 43, 1826-1834, Charleston County Courthouse, Charleston, S.C. For a discussion of black slaveholders in Charleston, see Michael P. Johnson and James L. Roark, *Black Masters* (New York, 1984), 203-205 and *No Chariot Let Down*.

49. Chatham County Register of Free Persons of Color, 1817-1829; Richard Cohen is listed as the owner of seven slaves in 1823 and Maria Cohen is listed at the same address. In the City of Savannah Tax Digest, 1850, Maria is listed as the owner of six slaves. John Gibbons, a carpenter, is listed as the owner of five slaves and Chloe Gibbons resided at the same address. According to the 1810 Savannah Tax Digest, she was his wife. In 1834, Chloe Gibbons owned six slaves, Chatham County Tax Digest. In 1813, however, male slaveholders outnumbered females, City of Savannah Tax Digest.

50. *Savannah Republican*, May 17, 1849, contains a complaint about blacks gathering to celebrate the departure of friends for Liberia; *ibid.*, June 6, 1849, contains a complaint concerning the ostentatious dress and smoking habits of blacks, and their refusal to yield sidewalks to whites; *Savannah Daily Morning News*, June 4, 1861, contains a complaint about blacks' lack of support of the Confederate cause. The following are just a few of the contemporary accounts of life in antebellum Savannah: Bremer, *The Homes of the New World*; Emily Burke, *Pleasure and Pain: Reminiscences of Georgia in the 1840s* (Savannah, 1978); Conrad, *Reminiscences of a Southern Woman*; and Charles Lyell, *A Second Visit to the United States*, 2 vols. (New York, 1868).

51. This characterization of black slaveholders is different than the experience of William Ellison, a Sumter County, South Carolina planter and owner of over sixty slaves, who allegedly did not feed and clothe his slaves properly. See Johnson and Roark, *Black Masters*, 107-52.

52. Ronald Killion and Charles Waller, eds., *Slavery Times When I Was Chillun Down on Master's Plantation* (Savannah, 1973), 4; Savannah City Council Minutes, August 25, 1817.

53. Charles C. Jones, *The Religious Instruction of the Negroes in the United States* (Savannah, 1842), 121-22.

54. Sister M. Julian Griffin, *Tomorrow Comes the Song: The Story of Catholicism Among the Black Population of South Georgia, 1850-1978* (Savannah, 1978), 17-18.

55. Simms, *First Colored Baptist Church*, 256; Griffin, *Tomorrow Comes the Song*, 18; BRF&AL, Affidavits, Miscellaneous Records, Contracts, 1865-1872, Savannah, Record Group 105, Superintendents Monthly Report.

56. Susie King Taylor, *Reminiscences of My Life in Camp* (Boston, 1902), 5.

57. "Statistics in the United States in 1860," *Eighth Census of the United States, 1860*, 507.

58. See Whittington B. Johnson, "A Black Teacher and Her School in Reconstruction Darien: The Correspondence of Hettie Sabattie and J. Murray Hoag, 1868-1869," *Georgia Historical Quarterly* 75 (Spring 1991): 90-105.

59. See Southern Claims Case Files, Chatham County, Georgia, RG 217, National Archives. These files contain depositions of persons who alleged that the Union Army confiscated their property when it captured Savannah in 1864. See also Edward Ayers, *Vengeance and Justice: Crime and Punishment in the 19th Century American South* (New York, 1984), 103; this author estimates that nearly 60 percent of the slaves in Savannah lived away from their masters; Jones, *The Religious Instruction of Negroes*, 139; Jones does not state how many slaves were hired out but he suggests the number was considerable. See also Wade, *Slavery in the Cities*, 49.

60. James M. Gifford, "The American Colonization Movement in Georgia, 1817-1860" (Ph.D. dissertation, University of Georgia, 1977), 89.

61. Thomas C. Benning to William McLain, Savannah, November 19, 1847, American Colonization Society Records (microfilm), University of Georgia Libraries.

62. For a discussion of the vulnerability of black women in another southern community, see Lebsock, *The Free Women of Petersburg*, 87-111.

63. Cecilia D'Lyons to William McLain, Savannah, November 3, 1847, American Colonization Society Records.

64. Claim of Celia Boisfeillet, #3751, RG 217, Southern Claims Commission Case Files; Claim of Edward Hornsby, #13, *ibid.*; Minutes of the Sunbury Baptist Association, 1860. After the war, Houston was elected to the Georgia legislature.

65. Savannah Board of Health Minutes, 1830-1864. There are gaps in the minutes (five years are missing), and the minutes were only kept from May through October each year.

16

Property Owning Free African-American Women in the South, 1800-1870

Loren Schweninger

"A reasonable reward will be paid for the recovery of any part of the articles missing," a notice in the *Columbian Museum and Savannah Advertiser* announced on April 11, 1814. "Silver Smith's and other persons dealing in silver, gold or plated ware, answering the description of the above, are requested to stop the same, and to give to either of the subscribers information of the same." It took nearly a full column to list the missing articles: a dozen large spoons, half-dozen tea spoons and one soup ladle, all of silver, a dozen tea spoons and ladle stamped Carrol [of Philadelphia] and engraved with the letter L, two pair of decanter stands, three mahogany dining room tables, a tea table, round stand, three chests of drawers, a dozen chairs, six feather beds, four Marseilles quilts with fringe, one large blue and white counterpane, two lace shawls, one large laced quilt, a dozen wine glasses, four fluted decanters, a mahogany case with two rows of brass hoops, a spy glass marked London with mahogany case, clothing, jewelry, a tambour frame, and numerous other items. The notice explained that on the first night of spring a fire had swept through the residence of Selinah and Lydia Levingston. With the help of neighbors, the two women had carried their belongings into the street, but in the confusion that followed many of their possessions had been carried off by thieves.[1]

Such notices were common enough during the early years of the nineteenth century, as fires and thefts plagued nearly every town and city in the South. What set this incident apart was that the two subscribers were free women of color. Their plea was entered under the names of their white "guardians." But how could two black women in Savannah acquire such a large personal estate? And how common was it for African-American women to own property? It seems doubtful that the Levingstons could have amassed such holdings by selling embroidered goods, as the listing of a tambour frame might suggest. It also seems doubtful that they could have acquired such items working at the menial occupations common to most free black women in the city. It is probable that they were somehow connected with whites, perhaps as mistresses of their male guardians. In any event, the record is not clear concerning how they obtained their possessions, only that they owned a remarkable list of valuables.

Until recently, historians have paid little attention to the subject of property ownership among African-American women (or any women for that matter) during the nineteenth century. Early studies of slavery concentrated primarily on their role as "matriarchs" of slave families, while later investigations during the 1970s often focused on "black culture" and "black consciousness," emphasizing how, despite being sexually exploited by their white masters, African-American women played an important role in passing down a unique set of cultural values from one generation to the next.[2] Similarly, the literature on free African-Americans—from the early twentieth century university studies, to Carter G. Woodson and his followers, to the growing number of dissertations, articles, and books written during the 1950s, 1960s, and 1970s—contains information on a broad range of subjects but only fleeting references to the special economic role of women.[3]

During the 1980s, this has slowly begun to change as scholars have turned their attention to the "internal slave economy" and free blacks in an urban setting. In their articles on slave property holding and market networks, historians Philip Morgan and Lawrence T. McDonnell have showed how some female slaves became actively engaged in buying and selling various goods. In her important analysis of free women of color in Petersburg, Virginia, Suzanne Lebsock noted that among the free blacks who managed to accumulate property, "a high proportion—40 to 50 percent—were women." In their studies of urban free blacks, Leonard Curry and Whittington B. Johnson discovered that black women were "quite visible" as property owners in Charleston, Louisville, Baltimore, Savannah, and other cities. In addition, Morgan, McDonnell, and others have examined the motives that prompted women to acquire property: slaves could provide better shelter and clothing for their children, add fruits and vegetables or store-bought items (coffee, tea, sugar, liquor) to their diets, travel by horse or wagon to visit relatives; a few could achieve a measure of autonomy within the "peculiar institution" or save enough to purchase themselves or loved ones out of slavery; free women of color could better defend themselves against the oppressive laws and institutions, seek legal redress within the court system, and sometimes secure white guardians and "protectors." They, too, were sometimes able to purchase loved ones out of bondage.[4]

Despite these recent studies, our understanding of the special economic role of black women is still in its infancy.[5] It appears that slave women were just as active as slave men in the domestic slave economy and slave marketing systems in the South. They bought, sold, and traded garden crops, rice, cotton, corn, tobacco, sugar, hogs, cattle, horses, sheep, poultry, eggs, honey, fish, fruits, meats, pies, breads, cakes, and a long list of other items.[6] It also appears that these slave economic networks were more prevalent than historians had previously believed, and that slave women were probably more active than men in what might be called the retail side of this trade.[7] In towns and cities and some rural areas, black women established stands, stalls, and even small stores to sell various items; they also peddled fruits and vegetables from carts and wagons.[8] While most of their business came from white customers, there is some evidence that the networks stretched from the countryside into towns and cities and included sales from market women to female domestic servants who were charged with the responsibility of obtaining groceries and other goods for the households of the white slaveowning aristocracy. As yet, however, we have achieved only a glimpse of the unique economic activities of slave women.[9]

While further research on this subject, as well as female slave hiring, self-hire, and self-purchase, will enlarge our understanding of black women's history, the purpose of this essay is more modest. It seeks to explore the nature and extent of property ownership among the relatively small group (compared with the slave population) of *free black women* in the South during the pre-Civil War period, and to assess the impact of the war on this group. What significance did free black women attach to owning property, how did their acquisitions differ in rural and urban areas, in different sections of the South, among blacks and mulattoes? What occupations did property owning free women of color follow? How did these occupations change over time? How much property did they accumulate and how did their holdings compare to those of men—black and white? How was property ownership connected to their attitudes toward marriage and their families, toward the region of their birth, toward dominant whites? What particular circumstances did they face in attempting to acquire property; how did they respond to those circumstances; and what does their response reveal about the social, cultural, and economic milieu in which they lived? As will be shown in the pages that follow, the unique and changing profile of free black women who owned property reveals a great deal about the nature of southern society.

I

The ability of free women of color to enter the property holding class varied considerably in different sections of the South. Though this changed from one generation to the next, and especially so after emancipation, and though any geographical division tends to minimize the significant diversity within the South, even within different states and counties, the subject can best be understood by analyzing two sub-regions within the South. In the Lower South, stretching from South Carolina to Louisiana and Texas, the free black population had emerged from a highly selective emancipation process or had arrived as immigrants from the Caribbean. They were often of mixed racial origin, skilled, and had received some education. Moreover, in South Carolina, Georgia, and the Gulf states, only a tiny proportion of the total black population—3.5 percent in 1820 down to 1.5 percent in 1860—claimed free status. In the Upper South, most free blacks were part of a large-scale indiscriminate manumission process during the late eighteenth and early nineteenth centuries. They were often black as opposed to mulatto, unskilled, and illiterate.

They represented a substantially larger portion of the region's total black population, 10.6 percent in 1820, rising to nearly 13 percent four decades later.[10]

During the early decades of the nineteenth century, even in the lower states, only a small number of free women of color entered the property owning class. Working as laundresses, seamstresses, and servants, or in some instances managing small shops and stores, they struggled merely to provide a subsistence for themselves and their families, much less to acquire real estate and other property. They also confronted increasingly hostile legislative acts prohibiting them from selling certain types of food and beverages (beer, whiskey, wine, fruit, cakes, candy), managing certain types of businesses (coffee houses, retail liquor stores), or moving about from one location to another. In 1818, Georgia lawmakers denied free blacks the right to purchase or acquire real estate, or slaves, by conveyance, will, deed, or contract. Though this law was later repealed (except in Augusta, Darien, and Savannah) with regard to real property, it indicated the extraordinary lengths whites in some areas were willing to go to keep free blacks in a subordinate economic position.[11]

The few extant tax assessment lists for communities in the Lower South reveal the difficulties free women of color had in acquiring an economic foothold. In 1820, the census listed 237 free black women over age fourteen in Chatham County (Savannah), Georgia. While some of them lived in families with male household heads, tax listings during the 1820s showed only thirty property owning black women. Most of them owned between fifty dollars and two hundred dollars worth of property, usually listed in the names of white trustees. Only a few—Catherine Richards, Mary Habersham, Hannah Lewis, and Fanny Williams—possessed property worth at least five hundred dollars. In other towns and cities, as well as scattered rural areas, the profile of property owning black women was much the same. Only in Charleston, New Orleans, and a few rural Louisiana parishes did more than a small number of free black women enter the tax rolls.[12]

Gradually during the antebellum period, however, free women of color in the Lower South expanded their property holdings. This was especially true in towns and cities where some free women of color entered more profitable occupations. In some instances, they were given a start by white husbands or fathers; in other cases, they were aided by white benefactors. As a consequence, some free women of color established hairdressing shops, confectioneries, bakeries, coffee houses, and boarding houses. A few managed large-scale enterprises or owned highly profitable businesses. It is ironic that some white men deemed it inappropriate for white women to enter the business world (and occasionally passed laws to this effect) but did not forbid black women from establishing enterprises.[13]

In Charleston, several free women of color, including Margaret Noisette, Marie Weston, and Ann Seymour, owned business establishments and rental buildings. They also acquired small slave labor forces. In Savannah, Susan Jackson ran a pastry shop in Reynolds Ward, the leading business section of the city, and eventually purchased her place of business, a brick building appraised at ten thousand dollars. Her neighbor, free mulatto Ann Gibbons, the descendant of a West African Ibo chieftain, lived comfortably on the income from her various rental properties. In New Orleans, Eulalie d'Mandeville Macarty, for many years the mistress of white businessman Eugene Macarty, established a wholesale mercantile and dry goods store, purchasing various manufactured items from abroad, housing them at her depot in Plaquemines Parish, and distributing them through a network of slaves to various retail outlets in the state. A shrewd businesswoman, she purchased stock, real estate, and discounted bank notes, eventually accumulating a personal fortune of $155,000.[14]

One of the most remunerative occupations for free women of color was the hotel and boarding house business. Following the death of Charleston hotel owner Jehu Jones in 1833, the old Burrows-Hall Inn was taken over by Jones's stepdaughter, Ann Deas, and a few years later by Eliza Seymour Lee, who had previously operated a boarding house. The guests at this popular establishment included aristocratic slaveowners, Northern merchants, and virtually every distinguished foreign traveller who visited city. The famous English actress Fanny Kemble, who married Pierce Butler, the wealthy grandson of the Revolutionary War veteran and signer of the Declaration of Independence, was greatly impressed by her accommodations in Charleston in 1839 and complimented Eliza Lee as "a very obliging and civil colored woman who is extremely desirous of accommodating us to our minds." Lee's counterparts in the Crescent City included Lucy Ann Cheatham, Elizabeth Reid, Mary Harby, and Martha Johnson, all of whom kept comfortable and attractively decorated rooming and boarding houses. By 1860, including those who rented or leased their establishments, there were ninety-four free women of color who ran rooming houses in Louisiana alone. Their average total estate—real and personal property—reached nearly eighteen hundred dollars.[15]

In the rural Lower South, a few free women of color entered the planter class. Most of them were directly related to whites, of French or Spanish and African heritage (creoles of color), or had at one time cohabited (since marriages between the races were illegal in every state) with a white planter. Usually they had either inherited their land or been given a start by a white benefactor. Yet it took financial ability and business acumen to expand their holdings. During the decades before the Civil War, a few women in South Carolina, Mississippi, and Louisiana managed highly profitable plantations. South Carolina rice planter Margaret Mitchell Harris, who had inherited twenty-one slaves from her father, the mulatto son of a white planter, produced 240,000 pounds of rice in 1849. During the 1850s, Ann Johnson, the wife of a Natchez, Mississippi, free African-American barber who had been murdered by a free black, owned a small slave labor force and managed a plantation a few miles from town. In Louisiana, Plaquemines Parish sugar planter Louise Oliver, Iberville Parish slaveowner Madam Cyprien Ricard, Natchitoches Parish planter Marie Suzanne Metoyer, St. John the Baptist plantation owner Louisa Ponis, and

West Baton Rouge slaveowner Agnes Mahier were among the most prosperous free persons of color in their communities. They owned rice, sugar, and cotton estates, large herds of livestock, and valuable farm machinery.[16]

To manage their plantations, these women acquired increasing numbers of slaves. While occasionally manumitting a bondsman for long years of service or purchasing a family member to keep a slave family together, they generally bought and sold slaves as a matter of economic necessity. Like their white neighbors, they purchased, sold, mortgaged, willed, traded, and transferred fellow African-Americans, demanded long hours in the fields, and severely disciplined recalcitrant blacks. On sugar estates where the harvesting and pressing of the cane demanded, as it did in the Caribbean, sixteen and eighteen hour work days, they pushed their bondspeople incessantly; when slave women were unable to work such long hours, they stocked their plantations with young men. Among the twenty-eight field hands on Louise Oliver's estate, the men outnumbered the women three to one; in the age group fifteen to thirty-six, the ratio was four to one; only two slave women had any children. Nor were these African-American women averse to selling off a few slaves for a quick profit. Seeing such an opportunity, the heirs of St. Landry Parish slaveowner Felicite Oursol auctioned several field hands when prices rose during the 1850s. Similarly, the heirs of Francois Allain, of Pointe Coupée Parish, sold five slaves to pay some debts following Francois' death in 1839. One laconic sentence told of their eventual fate: "Desires, American negro girl aged about 15 years, was set up for sale and after crying her for some time and receiving frequent bids, therefor was finally Struck off to Joseph B. Bourgeat [Bourque]."[17]

Those who managed profitable businesses, owned farms or plantations, or had become large slaveholders represented only a tiny portion of the free black women in the Lower South. Among the 10,123 adult free black women in the region in 1850, only 561 were listed in the census as realty owning heads of households. Among them, three out of four (427 of 561) lived in one state—Louisiana—and a near majority (257) in one city—New Orleans. Others were scattered in fifty-four counties from Georgetown, South Carolina, to Jackson County, Texas. They owned $1,671,400 worth of real estate, an average of $2,979 per landholder, ranging from $736 in Georgia to $3,602 in Louisiana. A decade later, while the adult female free African-American population rose five percent, from 10,123 to 10,620 the number of real estate owners increased twenty-four percent, from 561 to 694, but now only half of them lived in Louisiana (359) and only twenty-eight percent (193) in the Crescent City. They owned $1,870,200 in realty, $2,695 per owner, ranging from $897 in Florida to $3,884 in Louisiana (see Appendixes 2 and 3). While other free women of color who owned property lived in families headed by free black men or property owning white men, only six percent of the adult female free African-American population in the region was separately listed in the census returns as real estate owners and household heads on the eve of the Civil War.[18]

The decline among female property owners in New Orleans and Louisiana reflected the increasing economic pressures free women of color confronted is some sections of the Lower South during the late antebellum period. In the midst of new restrictive laws, racial hostility, and increasing competition for skilled and semiskilled jobs, some women were forced to sell off some of their holdings, while others went into debt to continue their operations. A few became so fearful of the anti-free black enactments and pronouncements (there was sentiment in some quarters to remand free blacks to slavery) that they migrated to the North or the Caribbean. Some property owning free women of color were probably among the 291 emigres—described in a New Orleans newspaper as "literate and respectable free colored people"—who left the Crescent City in 1859 and early 1860 bound for the black republic of Haiti.[19]

Yet to describe the late antebellum era in the region as one of decline among property owning free women of color would be only partially correct. While some women lost their holdings or experienced financial reversals, others were able to maintain their real estate intact, and a few, especially in South Carolina, Georgia, and Alabama, actually expanded their estates or entered the property owning class for the first time. The number of women in South Carolina listed as real estate owners jumped from 56 to 198 during the 1850s, and their average holdings went from $1,132 to $1,581. This rise was in part a reflection of the probable undercount among property owners in the 1850 census; even so, such a substantial rise reflected economic advancement for some women. In Georgia, the number of real estate owners more than doubled, and in Alabama it increased nearly three-fold, and there was also a corresponding rise in mean value of their property, which, while not keeping pace with the inflation in land values, was significant considering the numerical increases. Thus, even in the midst of racial turbulence, free women of color who owned real estate outside of Louisiana were able to maintain their earlier gains and in some instances improve their economic position. Their ability to do so bore witness to their remarkable achievements even under the most adverse circumstances.

II

Free black women in the upper states possessed few of the economic advantages of their counterparts in the Lower South. They were rarely assisted by whites, possessed few skills, and sometimes had spent many years in slavery. Not only were they forced to deal with oppressive laws and legal restrictions, but in some areas they faced strong competition from other free blacks and slaves for even the most menial jobs. Among those who established small businesses, only a few were able to capture a profitable white clientele as were free women of color who ran boarding houses in the Gulf region and South Carolina. Among those who owned farms, only three—Frankey Miles in Amelia and Priscilla Ivey in Mecklenburg counties Virginia, and Lydia Mangum of Wake County, North Carolina—could be classified as "planters." In the upper states, the vast majority of free black women, even in the property owning group, worked as laundresses, seamstresses, cooks, waitresses, domestic servants, and farm laborers; even those who entered "higher" occupations labored as nurses, midwives, milliners, or hairdressers.[20]

During the early decades of the nineteenth century, despite a five-to-one population differential, fewer free black women in the Upper than in the Lower South were able to accumulate property. In rural areas of Virginia, in 1820, out of a total adult female free black population of more than seven thousand, probably not more than a few dozen free women of color in the entire state possessed real estate. In rural Maryland, North Carolina, Kentucky, and Tennessee, much the same was true, while in towns and cities, the number of free black women who purchased lots or houses remained negligible. In the District of Columbia, in 1825, a tax assessment list revealed that only six African-American women paid taxes on real estate. "The main explanation for this," historian Luther Porter Jackson observed, "lay in the fact that the [pre-]1830 generation of free Negroes had not been free long enough to establish themselves as property owners."[21]

Following 1830, increasing numbers of free women of color were able to enter the property holding class. Now a generation removed from bondage, taking advantage of increased market demands for semi- and unskilled workers (as some slave men were sold away in the lower states for higher prices), and, except in 1837-1843 and 1857-58, living in a period of general prosperity, free black women gradually began to acquire real estate and other property. In 1830 in Petersburg, Virginia, seven of the twenty-three black lot owners were women, including Mary Eppes, Kitty Smith, and Rebecca Brown, who owned between sixty and nine hundred dollars worth of realty. Thirty years later, in 1860, the number of black women who owned real estate in the city had risen to ninety-two, nearly 40 percent of the 231 total owners. Among the latter group, thirteen owned at least one thousand dollars worth. In Frankfort, Kentucky, among the small group of property owners in 1842 were several women, including Winny Lewis and Sally Chiles, who ran laundries and had saved enough to purchase their own homes valued at one thousand dollars each. Eighteen years later, ten of the thirty-five black realty owners in Franklin County (Frankfort) were women. In other towns and cities, including Baltimore, District of Columbia, Richmond, Nashville, Lexington, and St. Louis, there were similar rises in the number of women who entered the tax rolls during this generation.[22]

The expansion of property ownership among free women of color in the upper states was clearly revealed in the census returns of 1850 and 1860. At mid-century, there were 695 free black women in the Upper South who owned a total of $362,100 worth of real estate, or an average of $521. While census takers often failed to list the occupations of these landholders, most worked as washerwomen and seamstresses, and only twenty-seven owned at least two thousand dollars worth of land and other property. A decade later, while the adult female free black population had increased only twelve percent (from

53,183 to 59,459), the number of realty owners rose seventy-six percent, from 695 to 1,223. They owned a total of $912,500 worth of real estate, or $746 per owner. Though their occupational status had not improved significantly, increasing numbers of free women of color owned large farms, plantations, or businesses. The number of female household heads who boasted at least two thousand dollars worth of real estate rose 237 percent, from twenty-seven to ninety-one. Of course, considering the fact that the adult female free black population in the region stood at 59,459 in 1860, only a tiny number of free black women had entered the property holding group, but, as in the lower states, the number of individual property owners does not take into account the wives of property owning free African-American men (numbering more than 5,100 in the upper states), and the few free African-American women who cohabited with property owning white men.

As these figures suggest there was a sharp contrast between the Upper and Lower South with regard to property ownership among free women of color. In the upper states, three out of five were listed in the census as "black" rather than "mulatto," and about the same (sixty-three percent in 1850 and fifty-five percent in 1860) could neither read nor write, while in the lower states, only one out of four was listed as "black" and between forty-six and twenty-seven percent (1850 and 1860) as being illiterate. Not only were they more likely to be listed as black and illiterate, but property owning free women of color in the upper states controlled less than one-third of the average real estate of their counterparts in the deep South, and, compared with the total adult female black population, they were less likely to own any realty.[23]

Yet the censuses of 1850 and 1860 also revealed the beginnings of a shift as free black women in the upper states enlarged their holdings more rapidly than their counterparts in the Lower South. Expanding economic opportunities, the increased availability of land in some sections, and inflation of land values for those who had previously acquired real estate accounted for some of the Upper South's expansion, but the rise was primarily due to the relentless drive on the part of free black women to gain an economic stake. While the medial realty holdings in both sections remained the same, the average value for women in the upper states rose forty-three percent, while in the lower states it was slowly declining. There was also a significantly greater increase in the number of property owners in the upper states compared with the Lower South (see Appendixes 1 and 2). Even working at the most menial tasks (which, unlike the lower states, most of them continued to do), frugal and industrious women could earn as much as their male counterparts—day laborers and farm hands—and, increasingly, they put their extra earnings into the acquisition of land.

III

Not only did some free women of color exert great effort to enter the property owning class, they controlled a substantial portion of the South's antebellum free African-American wealth. According to the census, free black women owned real estate worth $2,033,500 in 1850, or twenty-seven percent of the total owned by blacks. A decade later they owned $2,782,700 of $12,807,100 in real property, or twenty-two percent. The small percentage decline was due mainly to the marked expansion of property holding among men in the Upper South rather than any significant drop in the number of female owners. Moreover, they owned, on average, more property than their male counterparts. In 1850, the difference was $1,619 compared with $1,169. During the 1850s, with the surge into the property owning group in the upper states, the gap narrowed, but black women still controlled slightly larger average estates in realty ($1,452 vs. $1,303) than free African-American men. Both of these measurements—the large proportion among the property owning class and the greater average real estate wealth—reflected the unique condition of free black women during the antebellum era.

It is difficult to make comparisons with whites since the most accurate analysis of middle-period wealth holding includes only men, and since the census returns, from which averages are derived, used a typical American household as a frame of reference—that is, male family head. But the fact that all except a small portion of white wealth was controlled by males is itself important. Free black women control a substantially larger share of the black wealth than white women controlled of the white wealth. Compared with whites, as would be expected, their holdings were minuscule. At mid-century, the average real estate owned by white males over twenty-one in the nation stood at about one thousand dollars and during the next decade it rose fifty percent, to about fifteen hundred dollars.[24] Among all adult free black women, a total of more than 63,306 in 1850, the mean holding was only thirty-two dollars (excluding women living with men); a decade later, among the 70,079 adult free black women, it had risen to only forty dollars, less than three percent of the figure for white men. But the average real estate holdings for the nearly two thousand free women of color who were listed in the returns as realty owners, which stood at $1,452 in 1860, bore witness to the remarkable achievement of a small group of black women, all the more remarkable since some of them started out as slaves.[25]

These averages do not include the several hundred free black women who lived with propertied white men, bore their children, and shared, at least to some extent, in their wealth and accumulations. Most interracial couples lived in the lower states, but a sizeable group lived in the Upper South. Free black women lived with men who were comparatively well off by the standards of the day. On the eve of the Civil War, the average real estate holdings of property owning whites who cohabited with black women (at least those who were listed in the census in such a manner, approximately 233 in 1860) stood at $3,296 in the upper states, and $3,580 in the lower tier. Several of these women lived with men who were extremely prosperous. Thirty-eight-year-old Antoinette Angelette of Plaquemines Parish, Louisiana, for example, bore the children of sixty-year-old sugar planter Sylvestre Dobard, while New Orleans free mulatto Lucy Cheatham (who later changed her name to Lucy Ann Hagan) lived part of the time with financier and cotton merchant John Hagan who controlled assets of $160,000. Mary Fenno, the wealthiest black woman in Arkansas, was the virtual wife of Joseph Fenno, a prosperous Little Rock businessman, while Lucy Bedford of Nashville was left an estate in excess of $85,000 by trader, businessman, and slaveowner William Bedford who lived with Lucy most of his adult life. While not legally married, most of these women of color shared their white mates' wealth or received some property at the time of their deaths.[26]

The unique status of free women of color in the South before the Civil War, their ability to carve out a niche in the local economies, and their relations with whites had a dramatic effect on the free black family. For a variety of reasons, property owning free black women remained circumspect about committing themselves to marriage. Those who had saved some money, acquired real estate, or operated a business could lose everything by the wrong choice of a mate since the courts invariably recognized the property rights of men. Those who were attempting to purchase a loved one out of bondage often did not wish to assume the additional family responsibilities of marriage. Some black women chose to live with a partner without formalizing marital vows. Others chose to live alone or with their children. Property owning women sometimes required African-American men to sign "a conveyance in trust" promising not to disturb the property they brought to a union. Some of the more than 400 free black women listed in 1850 and 1860 census returns as having separate property holdings, though living with a male head of family, had probably made some sort of prenuptial arrangements about their holdings. In addition, "marriage" to a slave could bring heartache and financial difficulties, even though the children of such a union would be free; and in most locations, especially in cities and in states like Georgia, Alabama, Mississippi, and parts of Louisiana, free black women greatly outnumbered free black men of marriageable age, further limiting opportunities for "normal" family relations.[27]

Even when property owning black women did commit themselves to marriage, they faced the destructive forces of disease and death that were so prevalent during the nineteenth century. The moving testimony of forty-two-year-old Hillery Deering following the death of his sister, Sophie Jackson, involving the distribution of Sophie's estate reveals the difficulties confronting other free black women. Their father had died in 1846 when they were still quite young, and their mother in 1858 or 1859. "Sophie Jackson, Matilda Bartlett and I are the only children my mother had," Deering explained. "Moses Jackson, the husband of Sophie, died in St. Louis about fourteen years ago [1854, and] their children all died when young, none of whom married. The husband of Matilda Bartlett & she & their children are all dead. None of the children married. I am the only relative of Sophie Jackson living."[28]

Thus, the social, economic, and demographic pressures working against monogamous free African-American life were substantial. While economic pressures made it advantageous for white families to live together—the more children the more workers on the farm or partners in a business—just the opposite was true for the free black family. Spouses and children became a liability and an economic drain. A profile of female black property owners at mid-century suggests some of these difficulties. As a group they were extremely old, over fifty in the Upper South, and over forty-eight in the lower states. Only one out of four was in her teens, twenties, or thirties, while nearly one out of three in the upper states and one out of four in the lower states was age sixty or older. This was at a time when the life expectancy for white men who reached age twenty-one was under fifty, and the average white wealth holder was six or eight years younger than the average black woman who owned property. While the census did not list the family relationships within each household, these women had fewer than two children living with them at the time of the listing. In part, this was due to their age, but even younger property owning women, those in their thirties and forties, had fewer children than either slave or white families.[29]

Their unique situation also had an effect on their attitudes toward their home communities. Most property owning free black women had spent many years building up their estates and acquiring reputations of honesty and frugality in their communities. Consequently, few were willing to leave familiar surroundings to migrate to a neighboring state or leave the South. At a time when white Southerners, often leading coffles of slaves, moved restlessly from one location to another, free women of color stayed in the towns and rural areas where they had been born and had lived all their lives. The vast majority of the black female property owners—seventy-five percent in 1850 and eighty-two percent in 1860—owned their land in the state of their birth.[30] Some of those born out-of-state, especially in Kentucky, Tennessee, and Missouri, had been originally carried to the west as slaves. Their attitudes toward their home communities were summarized by Elvira Jones, a free black in Richmond, Virginia, who had acquired a small house on the outskirts of town and purchased her two children out of bondage. When she learned that she might have to emigrate because of a law requiring her children, as recently emancipated slaves, to leave the commonwealth within a year, she petitioned the legislature. "Tis with anxious and trembling for[e]bodings then that your Petitioner presents herself before the Legislature to supplicate of their liberality and clemency, permission to herself and children to live and die in the Land of their nativity." She argued that she had acquired, through "great frugality," some "small pecuniary resources." It was her opinion that the "endearments of kindred and of home" were more important to the "humble and obscure" than "to persons more elevated in life."[31]

The plea of Elvira Jones to remain near "kindred" and "home" suggests the unique and ambiguous condition of property owning free women of color in the antebellum South. For some, the long road from slavery to freedom had consumed their most productive years; for others, it took a substantial effort to extricate their children or family members from bondage. They were forced to deal with oppressive laws, the violent hostility of whites, tenuous and some-times volatile relationships with black men, and the difficulties of maintaining "normal" family relations in the midst of slave society. Yet they struggled to overcome these difficulties through hard work and the acquisition of property. In the Upper South, where their economic opportunities were limited, they controlled relatively small estates, but in the lower states, where there were better opportunities, some black women became relatively prosperous. In all, free women of color made substantial economic gains in the decades leading up to the Civil War.

IV

The social and economic forces that had created a unique environment for property ownership among free black women were swept away by emancipa-tion. The changing profile of female black property owners during the 1860s not only indicates the new developments occurring during the postwar era but suggests how these developments differed in the Lower and Upper South among former slaves and former free persons of color. In both the lower and upper states, freedom brought an infusion of former slave women into the property owning ranks. While not a precise indicator of former status, the changes in color and literacy at least point to the ability of some freedwomen to acquire real estate. Prior to the war, more than three out of four property owners in the lower states were described as persons of mixed racial ancestry, and the same proportion as literate. A decade later, more than half of the women who owned property in the region were listed as black (836 of 1,562 or 53.5 percent), and two out of three were illiterate. In the Upper South, the changes were less dramatic, but there was a rise among those listed as black, from fifty-eight percent to sixty-five percent, and among those who could neither read nor write, from fifty-five percent to seventy-seven percent.

The movement of freedwomen into the property owning class can also be seen in an analysis of the changes in the total estate holdings among black women. Prior to the war, free black women in the lower states who owned at least one hundred dollars worth of real *and/or* personal property controlled more than three million dollars worth of wealth (Table 1), nearly three times as much as their counterparts in the upper states. But by 1870, not only did their total holdings decline slightly, but black women in the upper states surged ahead in total estate and mean holdings (Table 2).

Table 1
Total Estate Holdings Among Property Owning Free Black Women in the South, 1860

	Sum	Mean	Cases
Lower South	$3,082,800	$2,597	1,187
Upper South	$1,315,200	$713	1,844
Total	$4,398,000	$1,451	3,031

Table 2
Total Estate Holdings Among Property Owning Free Black Women in the South,
1870

	Sum	Mean	Cases
Lower South	$2,737,800	$560	4,892
Upper South	$2,921,200	$654	4,470
Total	$5,659,000	$604	9,362

Source: Computed from USMSPC, 1860, 1870.

These changes, as well as the substantial increases in both sections among those who owned only a few hundred dollars worth of property (see Appendixes 4-6), point to both a rise in the number of freedwomen among property owners and the postwar transformation among former property owning free women of color.[32]

In the Lower South, antebellum free women of color experienced a decline in their property holdings during the war and in its immediate aftermath. Some lost their plantations and slaves in the wake of Union advances between 1862 and 1865, while others suffered from crop failures, droughts, labor problems, and unsettled economic conditions during the Reconstruction period. They found it extremely difficult to obtain loans to rebuild or expand their plantations. In urban areas, the changing nature of race relations—the entry of blacks into politics, racial unrest and violence, racial separation in churches and schools—made it difficult for free African-American businesswomen to maintain their former clientele of white planters, businessmen, and professionals who were themselves experiencing economic problems. Moreover, the breakup of the prewar clans during the Reconstruction period and the changing nature of the paternalistic bonds between former free women of color and whites left property owning black women more vulnerable to creditors or whites who sought to lay claim to their property. In a number of instances, former free women of color found it more difficult to defend their holdings after the war than they had during the antebellum period.[33]

Within five years after the war, most free women of color in South Carolina and Louisiana who had once owned large farms and plantations or managed successful businesses had either lost their holdings or suffered significant financial reversals. Even in towns and cities, where most free black women had invested in real estate rather than slaves, they suffered losses. There are obvious difficulties in seeking to trace women from one census to the next, but only a few of those listed in 1860 as realty owners remained as property holders a decade later. Partially reflecting this decline was the drop in the mean real estate holdings among all property holding black women in the Lower South, from $2,695 in 1860 to $1,120 in 1870 (see Appendixes 2 and 3)—a decline greater than the general depreciation in the South's land values.[34]

In the Upper South, there was more continuity from the antebellum to the postbellum periods among property owning free black women. In some areas, especially the western states of Kentucky and Missouri, whites were less opposed to black proprietorship than in the more densely populated black belt regions of the lower states. In some border cities, economic activity had increased substantially during the war. While cities such as Columbia, Charleston, Mobile, and New Orleans had experienced the brunt of Union artillery or burning and destruction, Baltimore, the District of Columbia, Lexington, Louisville, Nashville, and St. Louis had witnessed an economic boom during the war years. As a result, a number of antebellum free black women in the region, including, among others, North Carolina seamstress Martha Armstrong, District of Columbia laundress Elizabeth Bean, and Kentucky housekeeper Milly Lewis, survived the war with their holdings intact or slightly improved. Reflecting this continuity was the rise in the average holdings of female black real estate owners in the upper states between 1860 and 1870, from $746 to $887.[35]

Even more revealing in measuring these changes are comparisons of median (fiftieth percentile) holdings and standard deviations (dispersion from the mean) among female real estate owners in the two sections. Prior to the war, the median real estate value for the group in the upper states was three hundred dollars, compared with one thousand dollars in the lower states, and the standard deviation of 18.53 compared with 93.71 in the Lower South. Following the war, the median in both sections stood at five hundred dollars, and the dispersion from the mean was almost exactly the same (see Appendixes 5 and 6). In short, while there were increasing numbers of former slave women entering the property owning rolls in both sections, the changes in the median holding and the standard deviation pointed to a much stronger prewar continuity in the upper states than in the Lower South.

The infusion of freedwomen into the property owning class and the changing profile of former free African-American property owners, however, paled with respect to the relative decline among all female black realty owners compared with their male counterparts. In the lower states, the proportion among black realty owners who were women dropped from 30 percent to 7.6 percent; in the upper states, from 17 percent to 11 percent. Even with increases in the Upper South, the total value of female-held black realty rose only 43 percent, from $2,782,700 in 1860 to $3,984,000 a decade later, this at a time when the real estate owned by black men rose nearly 200 percent. By 1870, black women controlled only twelve percent of the black-owned real estate in the South, compared with twenty-two percent a decade earlier.

This relative decline during the early postwar years, despite the huge numerical increase among free women in the wake of emancipation, tells us a good deal about black women during the nineteenth century. Former slaves could now legally marry black men. Former free women of color could now choose from a larger number of possible partners. Not only did the proportional drop among female property owners correspond with a substantial rise in male land owners in the region, but unlike the antebellum period, when more than half of the black real estate owners were free women of color or free black men living alone or without a spouse, now more than eighty percent of the land owners lived in family units of husband and wife (at least as suggested by the surnames listed in the population censuses) and children. Thus the destructive forces on the family during the slavery era, which affected not only the slave but the free African-American family, were largely eliminated during the postwar years. As a result, black women overwhelmingly chose to live in stable families with their husbands and children. Ironically, however, this decreased their personal autonomy as their separate property holdings diminished.[36]

Proportion of Female Black Realty Owners, Upper and Lower South

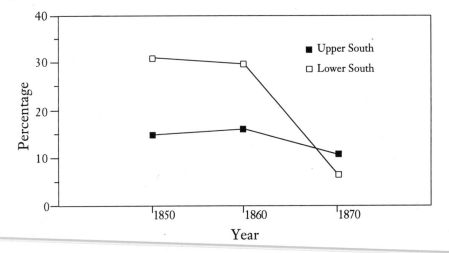

Thus, during the first seven decades of the nineteenth century, the profile of property owning black women changed dramatically. In the Lower South, a small group of free women of color, mostly mulattoes who had been assisted by whites, emerged as property owners early in the century, but by the 1840s and 1850s, they found it increasingly difficult to expand their holdings. In the Upper South, it took a generation of freedom before free black women, usually unskilled and rarely assisted by whites, were able to begin acquiring property. The Civil War accelerated the sectional leveling that had begun during the late antebellum period. Perhaps most importantly, there was a significant proportional decline among women compared with men during the early postwar era. The unique and special role of free black women, then, grew out of the peculiar conditions they confronted in a society based on slavery. Forced to acquire a subsistence for themselves, thrust into a position of family head and provider, or at least a co-equal with men in these regards, sometimes not able to find a suitable mate, free black women sought to acquire property as a means of protection, economic independence, and self-sufficiency.

In 1874, *The New York Times* ran a half-column article (extracted in large part from the Atlanta *Herald*) titled "Negro Property Holders: Some Interesting Statistics From Georgia." After discussing the rise of black property ownership among former slaves following the Civil War, the newspaper noted a curious phenomenon, the significant amount of property controlled by black women. Among the fifteen most prosperous blacks in Georgia, those with holdings of at least five thousand dollars, the paper listed eight women: Claudia Gibbons, Eliza Fowler, and Celia Middleton of Chatham County, Eliza Woodiff and Louisa Henderson of Macon, Nora Butterfield and Isabella Maxell of Richmond, and Mary Ann Todd of McIntosh. Indeed, one of the subheadings asserted: "The Women The More Thrifty."[37] Like most newspapers during the period, the *Times* had its facts jumbled, presented erroneous statistics, and poked fun at African-Americans, including one property owner who paid taxes on five dollars worth of property. But it had unwittingly pointed to an important historical phenomenon. Two generations after the notice of Selinah and Lydia Levingston had appeared in the Savannah *Advertiser*, the lingering legacy of property ownership remained, a legacy that revealed the peculiar position and remarkable industry and enterprise of black women living in the midst of a slave society.

Appendix 1
Female Black Realty Owners in the Upper South, 1850

State	Owners	arph*	trph**
Delaware	39	$921	$35,900
District of Columbia	30	$507	$15,200
Kentucky	119	$534	$63,500
Maryland	111	$363	$40,300
Missouri	19	$911	$17,300
North Carolina	112	$400	$44,800
Tennessee	31	$629	$19,500
Virginia	234	$537	$125,600
Total	695	$521	$362,100

Female Black Realty Owners in the Lower South, 1850

Alabama	16	$813	$13,000
Arkansas	7	$743	$5,200
Florida	17	$929	$15,800
Georgia	22	$736	$16,200
Louisiana	427	$3,602	$1,538,100
Mississippi	13	$1,338	$17,400
South Carolina	56	$1,132	$63,400
Texas	3	$767	$2,300
Total	561	$2,979	$1,671,400
Total in South	1,256	$1,619	$2,033,500

Source: Computed from USMPC, 1850.

*average real property holdings
**total real property holdings

Appendix 2
Female Black Realty Owners in the Upper South, 1860

State	Owners	arph	trph
Delaware	55	$465	$25,600
District of Columbia	116	$1,138	$132,000
Kentucky	139	$688	$95,600
Maryland	243	$465	$113,100
Missouri	36	$3,422	$123,200
North Carolina	185	$428	$79,200
Tennessee	58	$1,628	$94,400
Virginia	391	$638	$249,400
Total	1,223	$746	$912,500

Female Black Realty Owners in the Lower South, 1850

State	Owners	arph	trph
Alabama	40	$1,080	$43,200
Arkansas	—	—	—
Florida	30	$879	$26,900
Georgia	46	$1,065	$49,000
Louisiana	359	$3,884	$1,394,300
Mississippi	13	$2,015	$26,200
South Carolina	198	$1,581	$313,000
Texas	8	$2,200	$17,600
Total	694	$2,695	$1,870,200
Total in South	1,917	$1,452	$2,782,700

Source: Computed from USMPC, 1860.

Appendix 3
Female Black Realty Owners in the Upper South, 1870

State	Owners	arph	trph
Delaware	91	$989	$90,000
District of Columbia	189	$2,142	$404,800
Kentucky	402	$923	$371,200
Maryland	469	$756	$354,500
Missouri	243	$994	$241,500
North Carolina	307	$464	$142,400
Tennessee	297	$889	$263,900
Virginia	517	$709	$366,500
Total	2,515	$889	$2,234,300

Female Black Realty Owners in the Lower South, 1870

State	Owners	arph	trph
Alabama	116	$1,211	$140,500
Arkansas	69	$900	$62,100
Florida	68	$541	$36,800
Georgia	223	$724	$161,400
Louisiana	439	$1,967	$863,600
Mississippi	248	$723	$179,200
South Carolina	305	$836	$254,900
Texas	94	$545	$51,200
Total	1,562	$1,120	$1,749,700
Total in South	4,077	$977	$3,984,000

Source: Computed from USMPC, 1870.

To obtain property owners with estates valued at from $100 to $900, a sample of 7,855 propertied blacks was used.

Appendix 4

Distribution Analysis Among Female Black Real Estate Owners in the Lower South, 1850

Value	Frequency	Percentage	Cumulative Percentage
$100-200	58	10.3	10.3
$300-400	68	12.1	22.5
$500-600	56	10.0	32.4
$700-900	44	7.8	40.3
$1,000-1,900	124	22.1	62.4
$2,000-2,900	61	10.9	73.3
$3,000-4,900	64	11.4	84.7
$5,000 or more	86	15.3	100.0

Mean = $2,979   Median = $1,000   Std. Dev. = 68.99
Minimum = $100   Maximum = $92,000

Distribution Analysis Among Female Black Real Estate Owners in the Upper South, 1850

Value	Frequency	Percentage	Cumulative Percentage
$100-200	283	40.7	40.7
$300-400	195	28.1	68.8
$500-600	99	14.2	83.0
$700-900	33	4.7	87.8
$1,000-1,900	58	8.3	96.1
$2,000-2,900	12	1.7	97.8
$3,000-4,900	11	1.6	99.4
$5,000 or more	4	.6	100.0

Mean = $521   Median = $300   Std. Dev. = 10.28
Minimum = $100   Maximum = $20,000

Appendix 5

Distribution Analysis Among Female Black Real Estate Owners in the Lower South, 1860

Value	Frequency	Percentage	Cumulative Percentage
$100-200	56	8.1	8.1
$300-400	70	10.0	18.2
$500-600	94	13.5	31.7
$700-900	46	6.6	38.3
$1,000-1,900	204	29.4	67.7
$2,000-2,900	90	13.0	80.7
$3,000-4,900	54	7.8	88.5
$5,000 or more	80	11.5	100.0

Mean = $2,695   Median = $1,000   Std. Dev. = 93.71
Minimum = $100   Maximum = $200,000

Distribution Analysis Among Female Black Real Estate Owners in the Upper South, 1860

Value	Frequency	Percentage	Cumulative Percentage
$100-200	456	37.3	37.3
$300-400	245	20.0	57.3
$500-600	174	14.2	71.5
$700-900	95	7.8	79.3
$1,000-1,900	162	13.2	92.6
$2,000-2,900	37	3.0	95.6
$3,000-4,900	32	2.6	98.2
$5,000 or more	22	1.8	100.0

Mean = $746   Median = $300   Std. Dev. = 18.53
Minimum = $100   Maximum = $50,000

Appendix 6
Distribution Analysis Among Female Black Real Estate Owners in the Lower South, 1870

Value	Frequency	Percentage	Cumulative Percentage
$100-200	363	23.2	23.2
$300-400	283	18.1	41.4
$500-600	292	18.7	60.1
$700-900	141	9.0	69.1
$1,000-1,900	242	15.5	84.6
$2,000-2,900	92	5.9	90.5
$3,000-4,900	82	5.2	95.7
$5,000 or more	67	4.3	100.0

Mean = $1,120   Median = $500   Std. Dev. = 22.38
Minimum = $100   Maximum = $50,000

Distribution Analysis Among Female Black Real Estate Owners in the Upper South, 1870

Value	Frequency	Percentage	Cumulative Percentage
$100-200	540	21.5	21.5
$300-400	703	28.0	49.4
$500-600	472	18.8	68.2
$700-900	208	8.3	76.5
$1,000-1,900	357	14.2	90.7
$2,000-2,900	115	4.6	95.2
$3,000-4,900	59	2.3	97.6
$5,000 or more	61	2.4	100.0

Mean = $887   Median = $500   Std. Dev. = 20.02
Minimum = $100   Maximum = $50,000

(Source for Appendixes: Computed from USMSPC, 1850, 1860, 1870). Methodological Note: During the middle-period, census takers were instructed to record the estimated value of real (1850-70) and personal (1860-70) property held by every household head and individual property owner in the United States. An individual's real and personal property combined comprise the total estate as cited above. While the method of personal inquiry resulted in rough estimates rather than precise valuations, there is little doubt that the censuses are unique and extremely valuable documents for estimating wealth holdings. In his exhaustive study of Edgefield County, South Carolina, Orville Vernon Burton praised the 1870 census takers in that locale as extremely knowledgeable and conscientious. Their work, he said, provided the most detailed, accurate, and complete information available on the county's population—black and white. Economist Lee Soltow has described the middle-period census returns as "unique" and "precious" not only in helping us understand American inequality but also in permitting us to comprehend the basic nature of capitalism and individualism. Unlike tax assessment volumes and other types of local records concerning property ownership, the census returns are the only source that consistently connect gender, racial identity, and wealth for the South as a whole. Blacks with more than five thousand dollars worth of property were usually checked in at least one other source. For the purposes of citation, I have used the printed page numbers or the hand-written page numbers in the upper right-hand corner of the right-hand page. The page cited includes both the page on which the number appears and the unnumbered facing page. For wealth holders with between one hundred dollars and nine hundred dollars worth of property in 1870, a sample was taken from every twentieth printed page of the manuscript volumes. The sampling procedure is subject to a small margin of error. (See Raymond Jessen, *Statistical Survey Techniques* [New York: John Wiley and Sons, 1978], 407; and Frank Yates, *Sampling Methods for Censuses and Surveys*, 4th ed. [New York: Macmillan Publishing Co., 1981], 140.) All of these data were analyzed with SPSSX (the most recent version of Statistical Package for the Social Sciences). The program used to generate a profile of the lower group in 1870 utilized the "do if" and "loop" commands. After perusing the census returns, I occasionally ran across the name of a property owner missed by the census takers (or whom I missed). These names were added to my census data and are cited as "Computed from USMSPC" although they came from county court records, scattered assessment lists, and several reliable secondary sources. Thus, in 1860, among the 1,971 female real property owners, ninety-three, or five percent, were derived from sources other than the census. I have checked my data against the findings of Lee Soltow and other historians who have used the census for investigations of particular states and locales and find them to be generally compatible.

NOTES

1. *Columbian Museum and Savannah Adviser*, April 11, 1814, Museum of Early Southern Decorative Arts, Winston-Salem, North Carolina.

2. E. Franklin Frazier, *The Negro Family in the United States* (Chicago: University of Chicago Press, 1939), 40-41; and "The Negro Slave Family," *Journal of Negro History* 15 (April 1930), 198-259; Stanley M. Elkins, *Slavery: A Problem in American Institutional and Intellectual Life* (Chicago: University of Chicago Press, 1959), 53-54; Richard C. Wade, *Slavery in the Cities: The South, 1820-1860* (New York: Oxford University Press, 1964), 117-21; John Blassingame, *The Slave Community: Plantation Life in the Antebellum South* (New York: Oxford University Press, 1972); Eugene Genovese, *Roll, Jordan, Roll: The World the Slaves Made* (New York: Pantheon Books, 1974); Herbert Gutman, *The Black Family in Slavery and Freedom, 1750-1925* (New York: Pantheon Books, 1976); Lawrence W. Levine, *Black Culture and Black Consciousness: Afro-American Folk Thought from Slavery to Freedom* (New York: Oxford University Press, 1977); Jacqueline Jones, *Labor of Love, Labor of Sorrow: Black Women, Work, and the Family from Slavery to the Present* (New York: Basic Books, 1985), 8; Bettina Aptheker, *Woman's Legacy: Essays on Race, Sex, and Class in American History* (Amherst: University of Massachusetts Press, 1982), 89-110; Darlene Clark Hine and Kate Wittenstein, "Female Slave Resistance: The Economics of Sex," in *Black Women Cross-Culturally*, ed. Filomina Chioma Steady (Cambridge, Mass.: Schenkman, 1981); Deborah G. White, "Female Slaves: Sex Roles and Status in the Antebellum Plantation South," *Journal of Family History* 8 (Fall 1983): 248-61; Dorothy Sterling, ed., *We Are Your Sisters: Black Women in the Nineteenth Century* (New York: W.W. Norton, 1984).

3. See: John H. Russell, *The Free Negro in Virginia, 1619-1865* (Baltimore: The Johns Hopkins University Press, 1913); James M. Wright, *The Free Negro in Maryland, 1634-1860* (New York: Columbia University Press, 1921); Rosser Howard Taylor, *The Free Negro in North Carolina* (Chapel Hill: University of North Carolina Press, 1920); Carter G. Woodson, *Free Negro Owners of Slaves in the United States in 1830* (Washington: Association for the Study of Negro Life and History, 1924); Luther Porter Jackson, *Free Negro Labor and Property Holding in Virginia, 1830-1860* (Washington: American Historical Association, 1942); John Hope Franklin, *The Free Negro in North Carolina, 1790-1860* (Chapel Hill: University of North Carolina Press, 1943); Donald E. Everett, "The Free Persons of Color in New Orleans, 1830-1865," Ph.D. dissertation, Tulane University, 1952; Edward F. Sweat, "The Free Negro in Antebellum Georgia," Ph.D. dissertation, Indiana University, 1957; Letitia W. Brown, *Free Negroes in the District of Columbia, 1790-1846* (New York: Oxford University Press, 1972); Herbert E. Sterkx, *The Free Negro in Ante-Bellum Louisiana* (Rutherford, N.J.: Fairleigh Dickinson Press, 1972); Ira Berlin, *Slaves Without Masters: The Free Negro in the Antebellum South* (New York: Pantheon, 1974).

4. Philip D. Morgan, "The Ownership of Property by Slaves in the-Mid-Nineteenth-Century Low Country," *Journal of Southern History* 49 (August 1983), 399-420; Lawrence T. McDonnell, "Money Knows No Master: Market Relations and the American Slave Community," in Winfred B. Moore, Jr., et al., eds., *Developing Dixie: Modernization in a Traditional Society* (Westport, Conn.: Greenwood Press, 1988); Suzanne Lebsock, *The Free Women of Petersburg: Status and Culture in a Southern Town, 1784-1860* (New York: W.W. Norton and Co., 1984), 90; Leonard

P. Curry, *The Free Black in Urban America, 1800-1850* (Chicago: University of Chicago Press, 1981), 44; Whittington B. Johnson, "Free Blacks in Antebellum Savannah: An Economic Profile," *Georgia Historical Quarterly* 64 (Winter 1980): 426-27.

5. See: Caroline Matheny Dillman, "The Sparsity of Research and Publications on Southern Women: Definitional Complexities, Methodological Problems, and Other Impediments," in Dillman, ed., *Southern Women* (New York: Hemisphere Publishing Co., 1988), 1-18; and Carolyn E. Wedin, "The Civil War and Black Women on the Sea Islands," *ibid.*, 71-80.

6. Testimony of Linda Roberts, January 30, 1870, Claim R21,467, Southern Claims Commission, in William Paine Papers, Georgia Historical Society, Savannah, Georgia; Morgan, "The Ownership of Property," 405, 417; Virgil Hillyer to J.B. Howell, March 22, 1873, Records of [Southern] Claims Commission, Records of the Treasury Department, Record Group 56, reel 3, National Archives; Hillyer to Asa Aldis, February 21, 1874, reel 4, *ibid.*; William Paine to Charles Benjamin, June 24, 1876, reel 11, *ibid.*; William Allen to R.R. Gurley, December 29, 1836, in Records of the American Colonization Society, reel 26, Library of Congress.

7. McDonnell, "Money Knows No Master," 33; George Rawick, ed., *The American Slave: A Composite Autobiography*, supplement, ser. 2, 10 vols. (Westport, Conn.: Greenwood Publishing Co., 1979), Vol. 2, pt. 2, 26; Rawick, ed., *The American Slave: A Composite Autobiography*, 19 vols. (Westport, Conn.: Greenwood Publishing Co., 1972), Vol. 7, pt. 1, 111; John W. Blassingame, ed., *Slave Testimony: Two Centuries of Letters, Speeches, Interviews, and Autobiographies* (Baton Rouge: Louisiana State University Press, 1977), 363; John Liddell to Oran Mayo, September 4, 1849, Liddell Papers, Louisiana State University, Baton Rouge, Louisiana; Oran Mayo to John Liddell, March 4, 1852, *ibid.*; Charles Vinzent to Julian S. Devereux, April 6, 21, 1853, Julien Sidney Devereux Family Papers, Barker Texas History Center, Austin, Texas; Abigaile Curlee, "A Study of Texas Slave Plantations, 1822-1865," Ph.D. dissertation, University of Texas, 1932, 82, 141-43; Henry William Ravenel, "Recollections of Southern Plantation Life," *Yale Review* 25 (June 1936): 750-51; *A Digest of the Laws of the State of Georgia* (Philadelphia: Towar, J. and D.M. Hogan, 1831), 310; *Acts Passed at the First Session of the Twenty-Third General Assembly of the State of Tennessee* (Nashville: J. George Harris, Printer to the State, 1840), 82-83; Helen T. Catterall, ed., *Judicial Cases Concerning American Slavery and the Negro*, 5 vols. (Washington: W.F. Roberts Co., 1932), 2: 240.

8. "Presentment of the [Charles Town] Grand Jury, 1733-34," in *South Carolina Historical and Genealogical Magazine* 25 (1924): 193; Peter Wood, *Black Majority: Negroes in Colonial South Carolina from 1670 through the Stono Rebellion* (New York: W.W. Norton and Co., 1974), 207; Ulrich B. Phillips, "The Slave Labor Problem in the Charleston District," in Elinor Miller and Eugene Genovese, eds., *Plantation, Town and Country: Essays on the Local History of American Slave Society* (Urbana: University of Illinois Press, 1974), 13; Jonathan Beasley, "Blacks—Slave and Free—Vicksburg, 1850-60," *Journal of Mississippi History* 28 (February 1976): 1-32; William L. Richter, "Slavery in Baton Rouge, 1820-1860," *Louisiana History* 10 (Spring 1969): 125-45; Roger Fischer, "Racial Segregation in Ante-Bellum New Orleans," *American Historical Review* 74 (February 1969); 926-37; Lester Shippe, ed., *Bishop Whipple's Southern Diary, 1843-1844* (Minneapolis: University of Minnesota Press, 1937), 103; William Preston Johnson to ?, August 22, 1861, Johnson Family Papers, Filson Club, Louisville, Kentucky; Charles L. Perdue, Jr.,

Thomas E. Barden, and Robert K. Phillips, eds., *Weevils in the Wheat: Interviews with Virginia Ex-Slaves* (Charlottesville: University of Virginia Press, 1976), 316-17.

9. For comparisons with other parts of the Americas, see: Sidney W. Mintz, "The Caribbean as a Socio-cultural Area," in *Peoples and Cultures of the Caribbean: An Anthropological Reader* (Garden City, New York: The Natural History Press, 1971), 29; and *Caribbean Transformations* (Chicago: Aldine Publishing Company, 1974), 155; David Barry Gaspar, "Slavery, Amelioration, and Sunday Markets in Antigua, 1823-1831," *Slavery and Abolition: A Journal of Comparative Studies* 9 (May 1988): 1-28; Ciro Flamarion S. Cardoso, "The Peasant Breach in the Slave System: New Developments in Brazil," *Luso-Brazilian Review* 25 (Summer 1988): 49-57; Stuart B. Schwartz, "Resistance and Accommodation in Eighteenth Century Brazil: The Slaves' View of Slavery," *Hispanic American Historical Review* 57 (1977): 69-81. For how these attitudes toward property differed from those of their West African ancestors, see: Martin R. Delany, *Official Report of the Niger Valley Exploring Party* (New York: Thomas Hamilton, 1961), sect. 13; Robert Campbell, *A Few Facts Relating to Lagos: Abeokuta, and Other Sections of Central Africa* (Philadelphia: King and Baird, 1860), 6, 10; R.J.M. Blackett, *Beating Against the Barriers: Biographical Essays in Nineteenth-Century Afro-American History* (Baton Rouge: Louisiana State University Press, 1986), 164. Also see: Legislative Records, Petition of the Inhabitants of Orangeburg District to the South Carolina Legislature, December 4, 1816, #95, South Carolina Department of Archives and History; General Report of the Committee on Colored Population, *ca.* 1858, #2848, *ibid.*; George Rawick, ed., *The American Slave: A Composite Autobiography*, supplement, ser. 2, Vol. 7, pt. 1, 111.

10. Ira Berlin, "The Structure of the Free Negro Caste in the Antebellum United States," *Journal of Social History* (Spring 1976): 297-319; Benjamin Klebaner, "American Manumission Laws and the Responsibility for Supporting Slaves," *Virginia Magazine of History and Biography* 63 (October 1955): 443-53.

11. David Thomas, "The Free Negro in Florida Before 1865," *South Atlantic Quarterly* 10 (October 1911): 340; Berlin, *Slaves Without Masters*, chap. 10; *Digest of the Laws of the State of Georgia* (Milledgeville: Grantland and Orme, 1922), 467-69.

12. *Census for 1820* (Washington: Gales and Seaton, 1821), 28; Tax Digest, Chatham County, Georgia, 1821-1827, Georgia Department of Archives and History, Atlanta, Georgia; Ralph Flanders, "The Free Negro in Ante-Bellum Georgia," *North Carolina Historical Review* 9 (July 1932): 267.

13. "Pursits &c of the Free People of Color in the Town of Frankfort," July 16, 1842, Filson Club, Louisville, Kentucky; Laura Foner, "The Free People of Color in Louisiana and St. Domingue: A Comparative Portrait of Two Three-Caste Societies," *Journal of Social History* 3 (Summer 1970): 406-40; *General Index of All Successions, Opened in the Parish of Orleans, from the Year 1805, to the year 1846,* compiled by P.M. Bertin (New Orleans: Yeomans and Fitch, 1849), *passim;* James Robertson, ed., *Louisiana Under the Rule of Spain, France, and the United States, 1785-1807; Social, Economic, and Political Conditions of the Territory Represented in the Louisiana Purchase,* 2 vols. (Cleveland: Arthur H. Clark Co., 1910-11; reprint ed., Freeport, New York: Books for Libraries Press, 1969), 1: 218.

14. "Register of Free Persons of Color, Chatham Co., Ga.," 1823, 1824, 1825, 1826, Georgia Historical Society, Savannah, Georgia; USMSPC, Chatham Co. Ga., 1850, 297, 299; *ibid.*, Savannah, 1st Dist., 1860, 47; RCPC, Chatham Co., Ga.,

Estates, #J125, December 15, 1869; *List of Tax Payers of the City of Charleston for 1860* (Charleston: Evans and Cogswell, 1861), 333, Koger, *Black Slaveowners*, 36, 43; Catterall, ed., *Judicial Cases*, 3: 292, 589, 611-12; Juliet E.K. Walker, "Racism, Slavery, and Free Enterprise: Black Entrepreneurship in the United States before the Civil War," *Business History Review* 60 (Autumn 1986): 350.

15. Bernhard Karl, *Travels Through North America, During the Years 1825 and 1826*, 2 vols. (Philadelphia: Carey, Lea and Carey, 1828), 2: 4-5; Thomas Hamilton, *Men and Manners in America* (London: T. Cadell, 1833), 347-48; Frances Anne Kemble, *Journal of a Residence on a Georgia Plantation in 1838-1839* (New York: Harper Brothers, 1863; reprint ed., ed. by John A. Scott, Athens: University of Georgia Press, 1984), 41; Malcolm Bell, Jr., *Major Butler's Legacy: Five Generations of a Slaveholding Family* (Athens: University of Georgia Press, 1986), 255-69; USMSPC, Charleston, S.C., St. Phillip and St. Michael Parishes, 1850, 99; *ibid.*, 4th Ward, 1860, 312; Albert and Harriett P. Simons, "The William Burrows House of Charleston," *South Carolina Historical Magazine* 70 (July 1969): 172-74; USMSPC, New Orleans, La., 1st Mun., 2nd Ward, 1860, 209, 214, 265; Records of the Parish Probate Court (hereinafter RPPC), New Orleans, La., Successions, #22,076, March 2, 1851. Total estates in Louisiana were computed from USMSPC, 1860. An unusual example in the upper states was Nancy Lyons' boarding establishment for "aristocratic" free blacks. See Cyprian Clamorgan, *The Colored Aristocracy of St. Louis* (St. Louis: n.p., 1858), 12-13.

16. Koger, *Black Slaveholders*, 121-22; USMSPC, Adams Co., Miss., Natchez, 1850, 14; *ibid.*, 1860, 44, 120; William Ranson Hogan and Edwin Adams Davis, eds., *William Johnson's Natchez: The Ante-Bellum Diary of a Free Negro* (Baton Rouge: Louisiana State University Press, 1951), 62-63; RPPC, Plaquemines Parish, La., Inventories, Vol. 1846-1858 (May 6, 1857), 404-09; Sterkx, *The Free Negro*, 204-07; RPPC, Natchitoches Parish, La., Successions, #335, September 7, 1838; USMSPC, St. John the Baptist Parish, La., 1850, 279; RPPC, West Baton Rouge Parish, La., Successions, #176, July 18, 1829.

17. RPPC, Plaquemines Parish, La., Inventories, Vol. 1846-1858 (May 5, 1857), 404-09; *ibid.*, St. Landry Parish, La., Successions, #2256, September 9, 1859; *ibid.*, Pointe Coupée Parish, La., Successions, #176, April 5, 1839; *ibid.*, #355, January 31, 1844.

18. Computed from USMSPC, 1850, 1860; Calculated from *The Seventh Census of the United States: 1850* (Washington: Robert Armstrong, 1853), xliii; *Population of the United States in 1860: Compiled from the Original Returns of the Eighth Census* (Washington: Government Printing Office, 1864), 594-95.

19. Robert Reinders, "The Decline of the New Orleans Free Negro in the Decade Before the Civil War," *Journal of Mississippi History* 24 (April 1962): 95-96.

20. Jackson, *Free Negro Labor and Property Holding in Virginia*, 122, 127-28, 216-17, 224; Claim #18,049, Henry F. Harrison (administrator of Frankey Miles's estate), *ca.* 1877, Records of the Treasury Department, Records of the Southern Claims Commission, Record Group 56, reel 9, National Archives; USMSPC, Wake Co., N.C., Northwestern District, 1860, 115.

21. Jackson, *Free Negro Labor and Property Holding in Virginia*, 138.

22. *Ibid.*, 139, 239-46; "Pursuits &c of the Free People of Color in the Town of Frankfort," 1842; Computed from USMSPC, Franklin Co., Ken., 1860.

23. Computed from USMSPC, 1850, 1860.

24. Lee Soltow, *Men and Wealth in the United States, 1850-1870* (New Haven: Yale University Press, 1975), 64.

25. Computed from USMSPC, 1850, 1860.

26. USMSPC, Plaquemines Parish, La., 1850, 272, 276, 279; *ibid.*, New Orleans, La., 1st Mun., 5th Ward, 1860, 710; RPPC, New Orleans, La., Wills, Vol. 0 (June 19, 1856), 357-68; RCPC, Pulaski Co., Ark., Estates, #184, November 17, 1866, in Arkansas Historical Commission State Archives, Little Rock, Arkansas; USMSPC, Davidson Co., Tenn., Nashville, 10th Dist., 1860, 186; Loren Schweninger, ed., *From Tennessee Slave to St. Louis Entrepreneur: The Autobiography of James Thomas* (Columbia: University of Missouri Press, 1984), 65.

27. Lebsock, *The Free Women of Petersburg*, chap. 4; RCPC Charleston, S.C., *Miscellaneous Land Records*, bk. L8 (September 14, 1814), 31, in Museum of Early Southern Decorative Arts, Winston-Salem, North Carolina; RCPC, ST. Louis, Mo., Marriage Records, Vol. 13 (February 12, 1868), 222; Berlin, *Slaves Without Masters*, 136-37; RPPC, New Orleans, La., Successions, #361, April 19, 1879, at New Orleans Public Library. In the above succession (estate) it was noted that Louisa Boisdore was allowed to retain the eighteen hundred dollars she had brought to her marriage twenty-eight years before. In the South as a whole, adult free women of color (twenty years and older) in 1850 and 1860 represented fifty-five percent of the free Negro population. Calculated from *The Seventh Census of the United States: 1850* (Washington: Robert Armstrong, 1853), xliii; *Population of the United States in 1860: Compiled from the Original Returns of the Eighth Census* (Washington: Government Printing Office, 1864), 594.

28. RCPC, St. Louis, Mo., Estates, #8741, July 13, 1869.

29. Computed from USMSPC, 1850, 1860. The census did not note family relationships. The data include those living in the same household with the same surname whose relative age would indicate probable son or daughter relationship. While it is difficult to determine relationship in some instances, a fairly accurate estimate of the number of children in the same household can be made in most cases. For the comparative demographic literature on free black households and the role of women, see: Frank F. Furstenberg, Jr., Theodore Hershberg, and John Modell, "The Origins of the Female-Headed Black Family: The Impact of the Urban Experience," *Journal of Interdisciplinary History* 4 (Autumn 1975): 211-33; Crandall A. Shifflett, "The Household Composition of Rural Black Families: Louisa County, Virginia, 1880," *ibid.*, 236-60; Paul J. Lammermeier, "The Urban Black Family of the Nineteenth Century: A Study of Black Family Structure in the Ohio Valley, 1850-1880," *Journal of Marriage and the Family* 35 (August 1973): 440-56; George Blackburn and Sherman L. Ricards, "The Mother-Headed Family among Free Negroes in Charleston, South Carolina, 1850-1860," *Phylon* 42 (March 1981): 11-21; Lebsock, *The Free Women of Petersburg*, 89, 280.

30. Computed from USMSPC, 1850, 1860. These percentages include the District of Columbia. For 1860, there are sixty-five missing cases (3.4 percent) for individuals who were taken from local probate records. Thus the percent born in-state is the *valid percent* and excludes the missing cases.

31. Legislative Records, Petition of Elvira Jones to the Virginia General Assembly, Henrico County, December 5, 1823, Virginia State Library, Richmond, Va.; see also John Dungee to Virginia General Assembly, December 19, 1825, in James Hugo Johnston, *Race Relations in Virginia and Miscegenation in the South, 1776-1860* (Amherst: University of Massachusetts Press, 1970), 278.

32. Computed from USMSPC, 1860, 1870. The proportion of free Negroes and slaves of mixed racial ancestry in the general population in 1860 was as follows: free Negroes in the Lower South, 76 percent; slaves in the Lower South, 8.5 percent; free Negroes in the Upper South, 35 percent; slaves in the Upper South, 13.4 percent. See Berlin, *Slaves Without Masters*, 178.

33. Koger, *Black Slaveowners*, chap. 10; Records of the General Tax Return, Charleston, S.C., 1865-67, State Department of Archives and History, Columbia, S.C.; RCPC, Chatham Co., Ga., Estates, #R-278, May 12, 1886; Diary of Catherine Johnson, August 16, 1864, January 1, 1865, May 30, 1866; Nathan Willey, "Education of the Colored Population of Louisiana," *Harper's New Monthly Magazine* 33 (June to November 1866); 244-50; RPPC, Pointe Coupée Parish, La., Successions, #205, July 11, 1865; *ibid.*, Plaquemines Parish, La., Successions, #252, April 27, 1867; *ibid.*, New Orleans, La., Successions, #28,620, January 11, 1867; *ibid.*, Successions, #21,696, July 11, 1887; *ibid.*, Successions, #34,148, November 10, 1870; Mills, *Forgotten People*, 237-39; RCPC, Pulaski Co., Ark., Estates, #184, November 17, 1866, in Arkansas Historical Commission State Archives, Little Rock, Arkansas.

34. Soltow, *Men and Wealth in the United States*, 64.

35. USMSPC, New Hanover Co., N.C., Wilmington, 1860, 343; *ibid.*, 1870, 412; *ibid.*, District of Columbia, 7th Ward, 1860, 879; *ibid.*, 1870, 450; *ibid.*, Jefferson Co., Ken., Louisville, 2nd Ward, 1860, 586; *ibid.*, 4th Ward, 1870, 340.

36. Computed from USMSPC, 1860, 1870. To obtain property owners with estates in 1870 valued between one hundred dollars and nine hundred dollars, a sample of 7855 propertied blacks (from every twentieth printed page in the manuscript census) was used.

37. *The New York Times*, November 4, 1874.

17

Slavery, Sharecropping, and Sexual Inequality

Susan A. Mann

One of the main purposes of women's studies, as Joan Kelly succinctly put it, is to "restore women to history and to restore our history to women."[1] This study follows Kelly's suggestions for restoring women to history by examining how changes in major forms of production affected the respective roles of men and women in different classes and racial groups.[2] Specifically, this article examines how the transition from slavery to sharecropping affected the position of freedwomen in the American South.[3]

Since sexism is a distinct form of oppression that can cut across race and class lines, analyzing sexism within oppressed groups has presented feminists with a number of theoretical and political dilemmas. For example, given the central thesis of Marxist theory that private property is the root of women's oppression, socialist feminists have had great difficulty explaining the distinct nature of patriarchal oppression when it has been manifest in both propertied and propertyless classes.[4] Similarly, discussions of Black women's domination by Black men in writings by women of Color have generated a good deal of intraracial controversy and debate. This controversy received national publicity in response to the enormously popular film version of Alice Walker's *The Color Purple*, which candidly portrayed domestic violence and incest within Black households.[5]

Because oppression within a group marked by sex, race, class, or ethnicity is divisive of group solidarity, it must be acknowledged and understood in order to preserve the health of the community. Indeed, the roots of the modern feminist movement stem, in part, from sexism within the civil rights and "new left" movements, just as the women's movement of the nineteenth century arose, in part, from sexism within the abolitionist movement.[6] Recognition of this oppression is thus an integral part of reconstructing women's history. Yet, such recognition can reinforce racist and classist stereotypes or make the just demands of oppressed groups vulnerable to external racist, classist, and sexist manipulation. Moreover, conflict about giving priority to one social critique over another in strategies for political action can itself divide progressive groups and impede social change. Consequently, analyzing oppression within oppressed groups is like "dancing on a minefield."[7]

There are no easy solutions to these political dilemmas. Some feminist theorists, like those in the Combahee River Collective, have sought to resolve these dilemmas by formulating theories about the multiple dimensions of Black women's oppression, arguing against horizontal hostilities that split the solidarity of oppressed groups.[8] Other writers have tried to establish a contextual understanding of multiple oppressions as exemplified by Ann Petry's "Like a Winding Sheet," a moving short story that shows how racism and oppressive working conditions fostered wife abuse.[9] This article looks at historically specific relationships between oppressions experienced by Afro-American women during the transition from slavery to sharecropping in order to reconsider Joan Kelly's historical work on women. Kelly argues that historical periods traditionally characterized as eras of "progressive" social change, such as the Renaissance or the American Revolution, often have not been progressive for women and instead have entailed greater restrictions on the scope and power of their social roles. Although this thesis calls into question many key assumptions regarding the nature of historical development, it has received a good deal of substantiation from recent scholarship on women.[10]

While the abolition of slavery was clearly a major progressive transformation for both Black men and women, sharecropping was not the most progressive available alternative following the Emancipation. Rather, the sharecropping system was a compromise solution to serious conflicts between landowners and the emancipated slaves.[11] Indeed, the failure of radical land reform, the demise of any hopes for "forty acres and a mule," and a continuing concentration of land ownership resulted in a strictly controlled system of production and marketing. Sharecroppers had little control over which commodity was produced and sometimes had little control over their labor, depending on the amount of assets, such as land or machinery, furnished by the landowner. In turn, usurious credit arising from the crop-liens system often locked croppers into a system of virtual debt peonage. These factors, when combined with legal and informal controls over Black labor, such as the notorious Black Codes, created production and exchange relations reminiscent of semifeudal or semifree precapitalist forms of labor.[12]

Nevertheless, in relative terms, sharecropping was an important advance over slavery. The legal and institutional rights to human property were abolished so that human beings could no longer legally be bought, sold, tortured, or murdered under the sacred penumbra of private property. The diet, education, leisure time, and general standard of living of the emancipated improved. For example, the per capita reduction in working hours for the Black population after the Emancipation was between 28 and 37 percent.[13] In addition, freedmen and women were able to make their own consumption decisions—an important freedom often taken for granted by a nonslave population.

Kelly has also argued that whenever private and public domains have become more differentiated, sexual inequalities have increased.[14] According to Kelly, the separation of work into "production for subsistence" and "production for exchange" affects the sexual division of labor and women's "equal relations to work or property with men of their class."[15] Under both slavery and sharecropping, domestic labor or work inside of the home was labor geared toward production for subsistence, while agricultural labor or work outside of the home was directed primarily toward the production of commodities for exchange.[16]

Sharecropping presents a particularly interesting case for examining Kelly's thesis, since production for exchange under the sharecropping system was often predicated on the labor of the entire family. Relative to other types of production units, family labor enterprises blur the distinction between private and public spheres of social life. However, relative to slavery, Black women's commodity-producing field labor was reduced in sharecropping, even though this labor still made a significant contribution to household income. As in many other family labor enterprises, it also appears that male croppers controlled the labor of family members, and, hence, held more power than women held over income and property.[17]

For this comparative analysis of the effect the transition from slavery to sharecropping had on sexual equality, it seems appropriate to use some of the same criteria Kelly suggested for gauging the relative contraction or expansion of the powers of women.[18] Because it is not possible to examine all of the criteria suggested by Kelly in an article-length essay, this study will be limited to an evaluation of how changes in economic roles, domestic power relations, violence against women, reproductive freedom, and access to education affected Afro-American women.[19] Because few historical studies of the post-Civil War South include a sustained account of Black women sharecroppers, my own study is necessarily methodologically exploratory.[20] To overcome some of the methodological difficulties of studying slaves and sharecroppers, whose voices are not a part of the existing historical record, I have interwoven available quantitative data with more qualitative types of data, such as oral histories.[21] Through combining these methodologies, this study attempts to piece together the social fabric of these people's lives and to place their lives within the larger context of economic and social history.

Gender Differences in Economic Roles

An abolitionist sympathizer noted with bitter irony that slaveowners made a "noble admission of female equality" in their attempts to wrench as much labor as possible from *both* female and male slaves.[22] It is estimated that in the Cotton Belt slave women spent approximately thirteen hours a day in fieldwork, engaged in such diverse and traditionally masculine tasks as plowing fields, dropping seeds, hoeing, picking, ginning, sorting, and moting cotton.[23] Yet, as Deborah White points out, those who reported that women and men did the same work seldom reported the ages of the women. White suggests that, although women of childbearing age did plow and do heavy labor, the middle ages or post-childbearing ages were the most labor-intensive years of a woman's life.[24] In this way slaveowners tried to maximize bondswomen's capacity to labor and to be in labor by matching production demands to family and biological life cycles.

The fact the slaveowners tried to exploit as much profit as possible from both female and male labor did not mean that a division of labor by sex was absent in the slave community. In fieldwork, most women were ranked as three-fourths hands and pregnant or nursing women as one-half hands, regardless of their individual productivity.[25] While women performed many traditionally masculine tasks, those tasks that demanded sheer muscle power were often exclusive to men, such as clearing land or chopping and hauling wood. In addition, very few women served in high-status positions, such as those of skilled artisans and mechanics or supervisors and drivers of male (or even female) slave crews.[26]

Male slaves also regarded many traditionally male tasks as unsuitable for bondswomen, just as they regarded many domestic tasks as unsuitable or degrading for themselves.[27] Leslie Owens describes how one means of humiliating male slaves was to require them to do certain types of domestic labor, such as making them wash clothes. She writes, "So great was their (the male slaves') shame before their fellows that many ran off and suffered the lash on their backs rather than submit to the discipline."[28] Apparently, even slave husbands in cross-plantation marriages, who saw their wives only on weekends, did not do their own laundry. One observer described how on "Saturday night, the roads were . . . filled with men on their way to the 'wife house,' each pedestrian or horseman bearing his bag of soiled clothes."[29]

It has been argued that because the slave's own household was one of the few realms of social life where labor took place outside of the strict supervision and purview of whites, domestic activities, though arduous, offered Black women a degree of personal autonomy and fulfillment. This is exemplified by the remark of one slave about her mother and grandmother, "Dey done it 'cause dey wanted to. Dey wuz workin' for deyselves den."[30] Nevertheless, if this domestic labor is included in estimates of total labor time expended, slave women worked longer hours per day than slave men.[31]

Moreover, because slaveowners placed a higher priority on agricultural production than on the day-to-day reproduction of their slave labor force, slaves were allowed little time for their own domestic labor.

> On many plantations women did not have enough time to prepare breakfast in the morning and were generally too tired to make much of a meal or to give much attention to their children after a long day's labor. Booker T. Washington's experience was typical: "My mother . . . had little time to give to the training of her children during the day. She snatched a few moments for our care in the early morning before her work began, and at night after the day's work was done. . . ." Fed irregularly or improperly, young black children suffered from a variety of ills.[32]

To increase the efficiency of slave labor time, cooking and child rearing were sometimes carried out communally, particularly on larger plantations.[33] While slaveowners probably cherished their own private life-styles, they preferred these more efficient and less costly communal arrangements for their slaves. In contrast, slaves were quite insistent about their preference for eating in their own separate households. Consequently, even though communal tasks added to the solidarity of the slave community, slave women often felt deprived of their ability to cook for their kinfolk or to discipline their children.[34]

Some feminists may view the existence of collective child care and communal kitchens as fostering improvements in the social position of women, since privatized domestic labor reduces women's ability to participate in the larger community, increases their isolation, and makes them more vulnerable to patriarchal dependency and abuse.[35] However, the communal facilities established by slaveowners were created both to reduce slave subsistence costs and to increase slave labor time—not to benefit slave women. Consequently, the demise of these communal facilities with the rise of sharecropping would suggest a mixture of both gains and losses for freedwomen.

After the Civil War there were numerous abortive attempts to replace slavery with a system of production based on wage and/or share labor organized into gangs or squads. Gerald Jaynes provides an excellent account of the various social and economic factors that resulted in the demise of gang labor and the rise of family sharecropping as a "compromise solution" to ongoing conflicts between white landowners and newly freed Blacks.[36] Along with his discussion of ex-slaves' struggle for more autonomy and their rejection of the centrally controlled wage/gang system, Jaynes also explains how gender-related issues helped to foster the rise of family sharecropping.

One of these gender-related issues involved landowners' acute concerns about the labor shortage that resulted once many women and children left fieldwork after the Civil War. By the 1870s, the number of freedmen, women, and children working in the fields dropped to as low as one-quarter of the antebellum level. Freedwomen often refused to work in the fields because they were paid even lower wages than men and because gang or squad labor put them in close proximity to white landowners and overseers who continued to abuse them.[37]

Blacks preferred the more decentralized system of family sharecropping because it removed them from direct control and supervision by whites. Landowners tolerated sharecropping because it provided a means of dealing with the female and child labor shortage. As one landowner commented, "Where the Negro works for wages, he tries to keep his wife at home. If he rents land, or plants on shares, the wife and children help him in the field."[38] In short, landowners recognized the usefulness of the male sharecropper's patriarchal authority in putting women and children to work in the fields.

Indeed, as Jaynes points out, kinship relations and "an authoritarian paternal figure" proved more powerful for ensuring labor discipline than the impersonal relations between overseers and wage laborers.[39] While no doubt emotional commitments to family well-being may have enhanced labor productivity, the use of force should not be ignored. Unlike landowners and overseers who were now forbidden to use the lash, husbands and fathers could legally use corporal punishment to discipline their wives and children. As an observer noted, "One man, this year, felt obliged to give his own son a tremendous beating, for not performing his share of the labor."[40] Such obligations for disciplining family members were even contractually specified. For example, cropper Thomas Ferguson agreed in his share contract to "control [his] family and make them work and make them behave themselves."[41]

The rise of family sharecropping, then, increased Black women's involvement in field labor in the decades following the Civil War. In this way, sharecropping women were direct victims of this oppressive way of organizing agricultural labor. Sharecropping clearly combined classism, racism, and patriarchy—giving white, well-to-do males control as landowners and giving Black males control as family patriarchs. However, when compared to slavery, the sharecropping system still enabled freedwomen to divide their time between fieldwork and housework in a way that more often reflected their families' needs than the needs of landowners.[42]

If domestic labor is taken into account, sharecropping women probably worked longer hours than men every day. Elizabeth Rauh Bethel's analysis of both domestic and field labor under sharecropping suggests that women's total working hours were longer than those of men, particularly in poorer sharecropping households where women were likely to engage in more field labor than did other sharecropping women.[43] Consequently, while Black women gained some release from field labor and from control and supervision by white males, their gains relative to Black males, in terms of total labor time expended, appear to be directly related to the wealth of sharecropping households.

The decline in female field labor meant that in the Black sharecropping household the sexual division of labor was more marked than in the slave household. Moreover, as compared to slaveowners, sharecropping families placed greater priority on women's role in household labor, which further reinforced a traditional sexual division of labor.[44] Consider, for example, the view of sharecropper Ned Cobb (alias Nate Shaw): "I was a poor colored man but I didn't want my wife in the field like a dog. . . . I considered I was the mainline man to look at conditions and try to keep up everything in the way of crops and stock and outside labor."[45]

Despite the fact that freedwomen's fieldwork was generally more seasonal than that of freedmen, Black women in the post-Civil War era worked outside of the home more often than did white women. In 1870, in the Cotton Belt, 98.4 percent of white wives reported to the census that they were "keeping house," while 40 percent of Black wives reported "field laborer" as their occupation.[46] In the poorest sharecropping households, most Black women worked in the fields, with some estimates in later years approximating 90 percent.[47]

However, even though a significant number of Black women worked in the fields, husbands controlled the economic rewards from farm labor. As Ruth Allen observed from her analysis of women in Texan cotton production in the 1920s, "It is practically a universal situation that the money received from the sale of the crop is the man's income."[48] In addition, as in the antebellum era, landowners valued the commodity-producing labor of sharecropping women less than that of men regardless of any individual's productivity. This sexual discrimination is reflected in the fact that landowners allocated land to share-cropping households on the basis of the sex and age of household members, with more land being allocated for men than for women and children.[49] Hence, gender inequalities existed even in labor directed toward production for ex-change—inequalities that were buttressed both by the prejudices of landowners and by the power sharecropping husbands gained from controlling the income produced by family labor.

Sharecropping women were more likely than men to switch roles and do traditionally male tasks (particularly in poorer households)—their male coun-terparts seldom did household tasks.[50] Zora Neale Hurston's fictional account of an exchange between husband and wife captures the complexity of this situation where gender inequalities existed alongside the interdependence of husbands' and wives' work:

[Ned, the husband]: "Is dat air supper ready yit?"

[Amy, the wife]: "Naw hit ain't. How you speck me tuh work in de field right long side uh you and den have supper ready jiz az soon ez Ah git tuh de house? Ah helt uh big-eye hoe in my hand jez ez long ez you did, Ned."[51]

While field labor was generally more arduous than household labor, the conditions under which sharecropping women performed household chores were extremely primitive since they owned few pieces of household equipment and lacked running water, adequate insulation, or sanitary facilities. Surplus earnings were more likely to be invested in farm equipment than in domestic labor-saving devices. This could reflect a shared economic interest in investing in types of property that lead to capital accumulation; however, it could also reflect the fact that males controlled farm income.[52]

While the sexual division of labor was more marked in sharecropping than in slavery, oral histories suggest that Black women preferred both the sharecropping system and the ability to devote more time to the reproduction of their own and their families' labor. As one freedwoman remarked when contrasting her work under slavery with her work under sharecropping, "I've a heap better time now'n I had when I was in bondage."[53]

Bethel argues that there were certain advantages for households in which the adult women spent more time in housekeeping tasks. These advantages included the ability to spend more time preparing food, tending gardens, and caring for young children. These reproductive activities not only provided a more varied and balanced diet but also contributed to the material well-being of the family.[54] Yet, while entire families benefited from the time women devoted to domestic activities, it is still not clear whether or not women benefited relative to men. Indeed, there appears to have been a complex con-tradiction between women's desire to be relieved from the arduous commodity-producing labor of fieldwork and the fact that, by moving into a traditional household role, Black women enabled Black men to have more control over family income.

Domestic Power Relations and Violence Against Women

Under both slavery and sharecropping, landowners recognized the Black male as head of his family.[55] Herbert Gutman discusses how religious rules also imposed a submissive role upon married slave women. He describes an incident in which a Black woman had been dropped from a church for refusing "to obey her husband in a small matter." She was readmitted to the church but only after she made "a public apology before the whole congregation."[56] Since slaves were often required to attend the churches of their masters as a means of social control, it is unclear whether these church rules were a product of ruling class hegemony or whether they were in fact part of the slaves' own values and beliefs (as Gutman suggests).[57]

Lawrence Levine provides some insight into American slaves' values and beliefs in his discussion of how slave folk tales often denigrated aggressive women and celebrated the father as the family's chief protector. While he argues that these folk tales must be taken into consideration in any understanding of male-female relations under slavery, he is careful to point out that knowing "one's lot and identity" was a practical necessity for survival and was not confined to women.[58]

This is not to say that slave and sharecropping women were merely passive victims of domestic authority and violence. To the contrary, there is much evidence that individual Black women stood up to their husbands and defended themselves against personal abuse, just as they resisted and fought against the domination and violence wielded by whites.[59] Moreover, relations between Black males and females must be viewed within the context of the fact that under both sharecropping and slavery, the oppressions of Black patriarchy paled beside those of racism and classism. Hence, Black males and females depended on each other and their families to work together in solidarity and resistance. Nevertheless, a number of historians (including feminist and Afro-American historians) suggest that it was normative behavior for Black women slaves and sharecroppers to accept male domestic authority.[60]

Modern studies of family decision making generally find that the spouse who makes the major decision is also the spouse who contributes the most income to the household.[61] If this was also true for the sharecropping era, the facts that women engaged in agricultural commodity production less than men and that they (however voluntarily) did most of the domestic labor would suggest that men held greater decision-making power in sharecropping households, including decision making about family income and property. Since male croppers also were held legally responsible for crop production and for meeting share agreements, this male decision making was buttressed by the state.[62] However, it appears that at least some household property was recognized as belonging to the wife, given the story told by sharecropper Ned Cobb about keeping his wife from signing any share agreements to prevent creditors from "plundering" all of their property.[63] It is possible that ownership of household property was legally recognized if it constituted property the woman brought into the marriage. Nevertheless, personal property, like the household goods Cobb was referring to, must be distinguished from income-producing property, such as land or income from crop production, in terms of relative significance for family power relations.

Though there was a shift from matrilineal descent under slavery to patrilineal descent under sharecropping, this did not prove as significant for Black women as one might expect. Indeed, slaveowners introduced matrilineal descent neither to legitimate African traditions nor to benefit slave women. Rather, they used matrilineality as a formal mechanism for determining property rights over the progeny of cross-plantation unions.[64] Nevertheless, patrilineality and the legalization of marriage for Blacks after the Emancipation allowed Black men to gain control over their wives' property and earnings, to assume custody of children, and to discipline their wives forcefully. Moreover, rights to divorce were limited even in cases of abandonment or domestic violence.[65]

The issue of violence against women raises other serious questions regarding the dominant roles of both white and Black men under American slavery and sharecropping. Clearly, violence was an ever-present threat to slave families.[66] Moreover, slaveowners made no distinction in meting out physical punishment: neither pregnancy, motherhood, nor physical infirmity precluded this violence. For example, a particularly odious method of whipping pregnant women involved digging a depression in the ground to protect the fetus while ensuring the ability to discipline the mother violently.[67]

Even though the sharecropping system provided greater protection for Blacks than had slavery, violence against Black women by whites was also rampant in the racially motivated terror that accompanied the Reconstruction Era. For example, inadequate legal protection of Black rape victims is reflected in the fact that "from emancipation through more than two-thirds of the twentieth century, no Southern white male was convicted of raping or attempting to rape a Black woman" despite knowledge that this crime was widespread.[68] Given the complacency of the white legal system toward this violence and toward the flagrant lynching of Blacks—female and male—it is not surprising that the Black community placed a much greater emphasis on racism than sexism.

In the face of such violence perpetrated by whites, Black women tended to stay within the confines of their kin, neighbors, and fellow church members. As the daughter of a Black landowner commented, "Women didn't go into town much."[69] Yet some of these women, particularly those in poorer sharecropping households, did private household work to supplement their families' incomes, while others (often widows and single women) migrated to urban areas to do domestic work. Consequently, the risk of sexual abuse by white males was exacerbated by Black women's need to supplement their families' incomes through domestic service. As a Black servant remarked in 1912: "I believe that nearly all white men take, and expect to take, undue liberties with their colored female servants—not only the fathers, but in many cases the sons also. Those servants who rebel against such familiarity must either leave or expect a mightily hard time, if they stay."[70]

It is not possible to determine whether sexual and physical abuse by Black males was normative or whether it increased or decreased following the Emancipation since there are few data on the frequency of abuse during these two eras. However, historical evidence suggests that wife and child abuse by Black husbands was prevalent under both slavery and sharecropping.[71] As one Black woman commented in 1912, "On the one hand, we are assailed by white men, and, on the other hand, we are assailed by black men, who should be our natural protectors."[72] Similarly, Ned Cobb described his parents' relationship: "If I had a twenty-dollar bill this mornin for every time I seed my daddy beat up my mother and beat up my stepmother I wouldn't be settin here this mornin because I'd have up in the hundreds of dollars. Each one of them women—I didn't see no cause for it."[73]

Since social isolation is associated with spouse abuse, it is possible that the greater isolation of sharecropping households, as contrasted to slave quarters and the more centralized plantation system, might have provided less opportunity for community observation or intervention in case of spouse abuse.[74] Indeed, sharecroppers' voices make clear that domestic misery and violence were frequent components of everyday life in the rural South. Based on thousands of pieces of oral and written testimony documenting the interpersonal lives of southern farm people during the first half of the twentieth century, Kirby concludes: "There are assuredly scenes of satisfaction, security, sometimes bliss. . . . But the corpus of this large, if haphazard, collection of testimony contains far more instances of unhappiness, *especially among women*. Marriage was a cruel trap, motherhood often a mortal burden; husbands were too often obtuse, unfaithful, drunken, and violent. the collective portrait is less one of bliss than of pathos."[75]

Reproductive Freedom Under Slavery and Sharecropping

Reproductive freedom generally refers to the ability to choose when and if one wants to have a child. Today, there is a tendency to focus primarily on family planning issues as the major concerns constituting reproductive freedom.[76] However, information about Afro-American women slaves' and sharecroppers' use of birth control and abortion is scant.[77] Consequently, assessing the reproductive freedom of Black women in these earlier historical eras will have to focus more broadly on identifying when (or if) these women were in a position to make choices about their sexual activities and their sexual partners, as well as evaluating the general health care they received during pregnancy and childbirth.

Because of their interest in the physical reproduction of human capital, slaveowners intervened in even the most intimate of slave family ties. While there is some evidence of slave breeding, this does not appear to have been the norm, although a rudimentary form of eugenics was practiced through the slaveowners' intervention in the marriage ceremonies and broomstick rituals that slaves continued to conduct. The brutality of this class-based control is all too evident in the tragic stories from slave narrative where arranged marriages were forced on unwilling slaves.[78] Since slave marriages had no legal status and property rights over slave children were determined matrilineally (whereby the economic advantage fell to owners of slave women in cross-plantation marriages), in the interests of capital accumulation owners encouraged marriages between slaves on the same plantation.[79]

Another incentive for encouraging slave marriages on the same plantation came from the fact that slaveowners used family affection and solidarity to discipline family members and to reduce the likelihood of escape or rebellion.[80] The fact that more fugitive slaves were male than female may reflect slave women's greater responsibility for child rearing and, hence, a more traditional sexual division of labor.[81]

Most historians agree that relative to other health issues, health care was at its best for pregnant slave women because of slaveowners' direct interest in the physical reproduction of human capital. Prospective mothers' health, along with their work loads and diets, all became more acute investment concerns after Congress outlawed the overseas slave trade in 1807.[82] Despite these concerns, health care for slave women was extremely inadequate. For slaveowners, short-term productive interests generally took priority over long-term reproductive interests. For example, during cotton boom years, there was a significant decline in slave fertility rates and an increase in slave miscarriage rates. Indeed, in general, in the prewar South, the more agriculturally productive regions characteristically had lower than average Black fertility rates.[83]

Compared to slavery, sharecropping arrangements reduced white male control (direct and indirect) over Black women's reproductive activities. Black women were able to choose their mates freely, to spend time with their children, and to engage in family relations without the constant threat of family separation. These women bore an average of five or six children.[84] Such large families did not necessarily reflect ignorance of birth control or irrational family planning. Rather, children were an economic asset—they augmented the household's labor supply and provided security for parents in old age. As one observer noted, "Children thus may be said to cost the cotton farmer less and pay him more."[85] Nevertheless, since child rearing was predominantly a female task, young children meant additional demands on women's labor, especially when these children were too young to work.

Some sharecropping landowners arranged for doctors to serve their tenants, but this was not the norm. As under slavery, childbirth was normally attended by midwives who were cheap and nearby, while mothers generally took care of other medical needs. The fact that medical treatment patterns did not change significantly is actually an indication of a relative drop between slavery and sharecropping. That is, the absence of professional medical care for sharecropping families may have been more significant than its absence in the slavery era, since the medical exigencies of Civil War battlefields resulted in major advances in the skills of professional medical practice[86]—advances that did not find their way into sharecropping communities.

Gender Inequalities in Access to Education

According to John Hope Franklin, the Freedmen's Bureau's greatest success came through its efforts on behalf of Black education. By 1867, schools had been set up in even the most remote counties of each of the confederate states.[87] However, schooling for sharecropping children was often merely a brief interlude between infancy and adulthood. Most children never had the opportunity to attend school with any regularity, since they began working in the fields around the age of ten or twelve. Girls were more likely to get a formal education than were boys because of the greater demand for male field labor,[88] but landlords pressured sharecropping families to keep all of their children in the fields.[89]

Thus while girls had greater access to formal education than did boys, this education was extremely inadequate, not only in terms of the limited amount of time sharecropping children spent in school but also in terms of the overall quality of the education they received.[90] The introduction of home economics and its ideology of female domesticity into southern public schools in the 1880s and 1890s took place first in Black schools in order to prepare Black women to labor not only in their own households but also as household servants for white families.[91] Though working in white homes was a choice of last resort, there is some evidence that the ideal of female domesticity within Black households had some support among Blacks. Black newspapers urged the "development of a womanly nature" as a means of "elevating and refining" the race, and a number of Black leaders during this era advocated traditional, subservient roles for women.[92]

Despite the inadequate quantity and quality of Black education, the advances in access to education for freedwomen clearly exceeded the slave era when formal instruction in schools was illegal for slaves in most slave states. Franklin captured the class nature of the slaveowners' fear of educating slaves when he pointed out how the laws against teaching individual slaves were often disregarded and viewed as not very serious, "but the instruction of slaves in schools [established specifically] for that purpose was another thing."[93]

Variations in Patriarchy

With the rise of sharecropping the position of freedwomen improved, even though the sexual division of labor and women's roles in production inside the home became more marked.[94] These women gained more control over their working hours and reproductive freedom than they had in the slave era when white male slaveowners had controlled and/or intervened in these aspects of Black women's lives. It also appears that white males had fewer opportunities to abuse Black women physically and sexually, even though this abuse clearly continued. Relative to Black men, women increased their access to formal education. However, it does not appear that Black sharecropping women experienced an improved quality of life in terms of economic power, domestic authority relations, domestic violence, and their total number of working hours inside and outside the home.

The fact that the position of Black women appears from this study to be subordinate to that of Black men on certain dimensions under both slavery and sharecropping questions the conclusions of some major feminist historians who have documented women's roles during these eras. For example, Deborah Gray White concludes from her analysis of the lives of female slaves that slave households involved an "equal partnership" between males and females—an equality which was predicated on and buttressed by the absence of property in these households.[95] Yet her description of the lives of female slaves, which included wife battering, black-on-black rape, and husbands who "set 'round talkin' to other mens" while their wives worked even longer hours doing domestic chores, undermines her argument.[96]

White is not alone in offering such contradictory portrayals. Other feminist writers, such as Elmer Martin, Joanne Martin, and Angela Davis, also maintain that slave households were egalitarian units, despite their descriptions of unequal gender roles.[97] For example, Martin and Martin discuss how "slavery equalized the black man and woman" such that "the black man did not do any work that the black woman did not also do." However, on the very same page they quote Leslie Owens's observation that there "were certain duties considered women's work that men declined to do."[98] Thus it appears that, although slave women experienced a masculinization of their roles, slave men did not experience a corresponding feminization of their roles, despite all the attention academics have paid to the so-called emasculated Black male and the corresponding myth of Black matriarchy in discussing Black family structures. Indeed, rather than either the equality or matriarchy claimed by some writers, it seems that slave households were in fact characterized by patriarchy.[99] As hooks notes, failure to acknowledge this patriarchal reality fosters blindness to the fact that "the damaging effect of racism on black men neither prevents them from being sexist oppressors nor excuses or justifies their sexist oppression of black women."[100]

With few exceptions, patriarchy also has not been adequately acknowledged in writings on sharecropping women. For example, another feminist historian, Jacqueline Jones, is explicitly hesitant to characterize Black sharecropping households as patriarchal. While she admits that there was inequality in "domestic authority," she argues that the term "patriarchy" is inappropriate when Black males had little control over most significant economic resources;

when escaping from poverty was often precluded by racism regardless of the amount of an individual's hard work; and when many whites continually tried to deprive Black males of all meaningful types of authority and power.[101]

Both White and Jones tend to base their arguments primarily on the fact that the propertyless nature of slave sharecropping households, which was persistently maintained by racist restrictions on the accumulation of wealth and power by Blacks, precluded the existence of any meaningful notion of patriarchal domination. In turn, although both of these writers provide evidence of interpersonal inequalities in power, they seem unwilling to equate this with institutional patriarchal domination.

It is possible that due to racist restrictions on the accumulation of wealth or power by Blacks, slaves and Black sharecroppers may have experienced relatively more sexual equality than middle- or upper-class whites. That is, these restrictions precluded Black husbands and wives from being separated by the more extreme gender-based differentials in economic rights and privileges that well-to-do whites experienced. However, this greater relative equality should neither be exaggerated nor romanticized given the fact that it was premised on the poverty and deprivation of both sexes.

Moreover, both slavery and sharecropping existed within the context of a larger capitalist mode of production predicated on private property. Consequently, these propertyless classes were under the hegemony of a legal system and other institutions that were property oriented. Male control over women and children in slave and sharecropping households was backed not merely by individual force but also by mechanisms of social control enforced by ruling classes, churches, and the state. Unfortunately, some feminist thinkers have ignored this more complex relationship between property and patriarchy, presenting instead a rather mechanistic equation that argues that, if an individual lacks property, this precludes the existence of patriarchy. Yet major critics of private property, like Marx, Engels, and Lenin, recognized the existence of patriarchy within propertyless classes, even though these same critics have been accused of being blind to gender issues.[102] Indeed, Marx, Engels, and Lenin all recognized that patriarchy, like private property, was institutionalized and not simply a characteristic of individuals.

Institutionalization entails not only objective constraints on social behavior but also subjective constraints internalized through socialization. Consequently, it is not surprising that male domestic authority and the relegation of females to traditional sex roles were often fostered by Afro-American folk tales or newspapers and accepted by female slaves and sharecroppers. This is not meant to resurrect either a "blame the victim" approach or the view that the history of Black women is merely a history of passive victimization. Rather, the point of recognizing the subjective dimensions of institutionalization is to highlight the more subtle, yet still coercive, nature of sex-role socialization.

Because property-oriented legal and institutional mechanisms of social control also govern interpersonal life, interpersonal inequalities of power that disadvantage women implement institutional patriarchal domination. Domestic violence and authoritarianism are political forms of institutionalized domination, buttressed by gender inequalities in socialization practices, access to material resources, and existing marriage or family law. While such interpersonal and domestic issues were major concerns of both the nineteenth-century women's movement and the temperance movement,[103] modern feminists have even more emphatically rejected any dichotomy between public and private spheres of social life when recognizing political oppression. If one takes seriously a major tenet of modern feminist thought that "the personal is political,"[104] then in light of this research on Black women it must also be concluded that the political is personal.

Some writers have argued that because male and female roles are complementary in family labor enterprises, couples are more dependent on each other's labor, and hence, more equal.[105] Though male and female roles may have been complementary under sharecropping, this complementarity was not synonymous with equality.[106] The division of labor under sharecropping was such that female labor was directed more toward production for use, while male labor was directed primarily toward production for exchange. This differentiation is of particular political and economic significance in a market economy precisely because production for use is by definition unpaid labor, regardless of its intrinsic value. As numerous feminist debates over domestic labor have long recognized, this places women in a subordinate position.[107] Such a sexual division of labor was a major organizing principle of the American family sharecropping system.

Even when Black women sharecroppers engaged in a significant amount of production for exchange, control over income generated from agricultural production was in the hands of men—even if this income was produced by the labor of the entire family. Male control over this income, coupled with the domestic decision-making power this entailed, meant that Black women could only have been in an inherently unequal relation to Black men. This situation is not unique to sharecropping but, rather, is characteristic of many family enterprises—both rural and urban.[108]

Slave and sharecropping households alike were organized patriarchally, and this sexual inequality was buttressed by the larger patriarchal society in which these households existed. This is not to dismiss the cultural and historical specificity of racial or class oppression in the lives of Black women but, rather, to argue that patriarchy should be viewed as historically and culturally diverse. That is, the notion of patriarchy should be reconceptualized to include a number of patriarchies. The degrees of domination characterizing different patriarchies may vary by women's class, race, ethnicity, and sexual orientation, just as various patriarchies may require substantively different political solutions for the liberation of all women. As Audre Lorde points out, recognition of these "many varied tools of patriarchy" will also entail an increased awareness of the many varied differences among women.[109] By recognizing this diversity and the grounds for unity within this diversity, we can take an important step toward restoring women to history and restoring our history to women.

NOTES

This essay is based on work completed as a part of the "Southern Women: The Intersection of Race, Class, and Gender" working paper series cosponsored by the centers for research on women at Memphis State University, Duke University, University of North Carolina, and Spelman College. I thank E. Higginbotham, L. Coleman, S. Coverman, M. Heung, C. Greene, L. Weber Cannon, M. Sartisky, G. Welty, H. Benenson, H. Hayes, and two anonymous reviewers for their useful comments and critical insights. I am also grateful to the National Endowment for the Humanities 1985 summer stipend program for funding this research.

1. Joan Kelly, *Women, History and Theory: The Essays of Joan Kelly* (Chicago: University of Chicago Press, 1984), 1.
2. *Ibid.*, 9. Kelly uses the term "mode of production," rather than form of production, in her discussion of social change and sexual inequality. Yet, she incorrectly equates changes in the mode of production with less significant economic changes wrought by events like the American Revolution. To be more precise, this paper analytically distinguishes between the mode of production—which represents the dominant form of production in a given historical era—and other specific forms of production which can coexist alongside the dominant mode within a given social formation.
3. The term "Black women" is sometimes used in this article interchangeably with "slave" and "sharecropping women." However, not all Black women were slaves since there were also free people of Color living in the southern states during the antebellum era.
4. For the classical Marxist discussion of the origins of patriarchy, see Frederick Engels, *The Origin of the Family, Private Property, and the State* (New York: International Publishers, 1974). For a modern socialist feminist analysis, see Heidi I. Hartmann, "The Unhappy Marriage of Marxism and Feminism: Towards a More Progressive Union," in *Women and Revolution*, ed. Lydia Sargent (Boston: South End Press, 1981), 1-41.
5. Trudier Harris, "On *The Color Purple*, Stereotypes, and Silence," *Black American Literature Forum*, 18, no. 4 (1984): 155-61; Mel Watkins, "Sexism, Racism and Black Women Writers," *New York Times Book Review* (June 1986), 1 and 35-37. While the film *The Color Purple* had a number of virtues, it also did much to reinforce racist stereotypes, a problem exacerbated by the juxtaposition of slapstick comedy with the serious issues of racist terror and domestic violence. Thus, I am not praising this film but merely recognizing its role in bringing the controversies over oppression by the oppressed to a much larger audience.
6. Judith Hole and Ellen Levine, "The First Feminists," and Jo Freeman, "The Women's Liberation Movement: Its Origins, Structure, Activities, and Ideas," both in *Women: A Feminist Perspective*, ed. Jo Freeman, rev. ed. (Palo Alto, Calif.: Mayfield, 1984), 533-42, 543-56.
7. This quote is a paraphrase of the title of Annett Kolodny's article, "Dancing through the Minefield: Some Observations on the Theory, Practice, and Politics

of a Feminist Literary Criticism," in *The New Feminist Criticism: Essays on Women, Literature, and Theory*, ed. Elaine Showalter (New York: Pantheon, 1985), 144-67. For a discussion of some of these political dilemmas, see Angela Y. Davis, *Women, Race and Class* (New York: Monthly Review Press, 1981).

8. Combahee River Collective, "A Black Feminist Statement," in *Capitalist Patriarchy and the Case for Socialist Feminism*, ed. Zillah R. Eisenstein (New York: Monthly Review Press, 1979), 362-72.

9. Ann Petry, "Like a Winding Sheet," in *Women and Fiction: Short Stories By and About Women*, ed. Susan Cahill (New York: New American Library, 1975), 132-42.

10. Kelly, *Women, History and Theory*, 1-15; Nancy Woloch, *Women and the American Experience* (New York: Knopf, 1984), 83.

11. Gerald David Jaynes, *Branches without Roots: Genesis of the Black Working Class in the American South, 1862-1882* (New York: Oxford University Press, 1986), 141-223.

12. Jonathan M. Wiener, *Social Origins of the New South: Alabama, 1860-1885* (Baton Rouge: Louisiana State University Press, 1978), 70-73; Susan A. Mann, "Sharecropping in the Cotton South: A Case of Uneven Capitalist Development in Agriculture," *Rural Sociology* 39, no. 3 (1984): 412-29.

13. R. Ransom and R. Sutch, *One Kind of Freedom: The Economic Consequences of Emancipation* (New York: Cambridge University Press, 1977), 1-39.

14. Slaves and sharecroppers may not have made these conceptual distinctions between public and private spheres of life. As Lawrence Levine argues, slaves did not subjectively compartmentalize their lives like people do in the modern era. See Lawrence W. Levine, *Black Culture and Black Consciousness: Afro-American Folk Thought from Slavery to Freedom* (Oxford: Oxford University Press, 1977), 157-58. Nevertheless, I have maintained these distinctions because this category scheme is objectively meaningful in terms of power relations arising from the difference between production for use and production for exchange.

15. Kelly, *Women, History and Theory*, 12-13.

16. Whether domestic labor constitutes production for use or production for exchange has been subject of long-standing debates in the feminist literature. Indeed, in a previous article I argued that, under certain historical conditions, domestic labor can entail production for exchange, such as when this domestic labor is directed toward reproducing the commodities of labor power or wage labor. See Emily Blumenfeld and Susan Mann, "Domestic Labour and the Reproduction of Labour Power: Towards an Analysis of Women, the Family, and Class," in *Hidden in the Household: Women's Domestic Labour under Capitalism*, ed. Bonnie Fox (Toronto: Women's Press, 1980), 267-307.

17. Ruth Allen, *The Labor of Women in the Production of Cotton* (Austin: University of Texas Press, 1931), 147; Carolyn E. Sachs, *The Invisible Farmers: Women in Agricultural Production* (Totowa, N.J.: Rowman & Allanheld, 1983), 26.

18. Kelly, *Women, History and Theory*, 20. Kelly also suggests an analysis of changes in women's cultural roles, their political roles, and ideologies about women.

19. Considering the many ways in which Blacks were excluded from economic and political power during these eras, cultural roles might prove extremely important for reassessing sexual inequality in future research. See, e.g., Deborah Gray White's *Ar'n't I a Woman? Female Slaves in the Plantation South* (New York: Norton, 1985) for a discussion of some of the cultural roles of slave women.

20. This study relies heavily on a few notable exceptions to the scarcity of research on sharecropping women. These exceptions include the following works: Jacqueline

Jones, *Labor of Love, Labor of Sorrow: Black Women, Work, and the Family from Slavery to the Present* (New York: Basic, 1985); Jaynes, *Branches without Roots;* Jack Temple Kirby, *Rural Worlds Lost: The American South, 1920-1960* (Baton Rouge: Louisiana State University Press, 1987).

21. Although oral histories present problems in terms of the representativeness of such historical evidence, they do provide a more valid means of empathetically under-standing the subjects of one's research in keeping with the sociological method of *verstehen.* Moreover, in this particular study, oral histories help to reduce the inherent problems of a social researcher like myself, studying men and women of a different race and class, who also lived in a different historical era.

22. An abolitionist sympathizer quoted in Jones, *Labor of Love*, 15.

23. *Ibid.*, 15; Ransom and Sutch, *One Kind of Freedom*, 233.

24. White, *Ar'n't I a Woman?*, 114.

25. Jones, *Labor of Love*, 15 and 17.

26. Robert William Fogel and Stanley L. Engerman, *Time on the Cross: The Economics of American Negro Slavery* (Boston: Little, Brown, 1974), 141-42; bell hooks, *Ain't I a Woman: Black Women and Feminism* (Boston: South End Press, 1981), 23; Jones, *Labor of Love*, 18-19.

27. Eugene Genovese, *Roll, Jordan, Roll: The World the Slaves Made* (New York: Vintage, 1976), 490; hooks, *Ain't I a Woman*, 21-22; Jones, *Labor of Love*, 42.

28. Leslie H. Owens, *The Species of Property: Slave Life and Culture in the Old South* (New York: Oxford University Press, 1976), 195.

29. An observer quoted in Christie Farnham, "Sapphire? The Issue of Dominance in the Slave Family, 1830-1865," in *"To Toil the Livelong Day": America's Women at Work, 1780-1980*, ed. Carol Groneman and Mary Beth Norton (Ithaca, N.Y.: Cornell University Press, 1987), 68-83, esp. 79-80. Farnham notes various authors' discussion of men's work within slave households. She concludes that such male domestic labor tended to be an occasional activity.

30. Jones, *Labor of Love*, 29. For a discussion of how the slave's own domestic labor provided one of the few spheres of autonomy and meaningful work in the slave community, see Angela Y. Davis, "The Black Woman's Role in the Community of Slaves," *Black Scholar* 3 (December 1971): 3-14.

31. Genovese, *Roll, Jordan, Roll*, 494-95; White, *Ar'n't I a Woman?*, 122.

32. John W. Blassingame, *The Slave Community: Plantation Life in the Antebellum South* (New York: Oxford University Press, 1972), 94.

33. *Ibid.*, 94; Jones, *Labor of Love*, 29; White, *Ar'n't I a Woman?*, 113.

34. Jones, *Labor of Love*, 29; Genovese, *Roll, Jordan, Roll*, 544.

35. There are numerous discussions of this in Fox, ed., *Hidden in the Household*.

36. Jaynes, *Branches without Roots*.

37. *Ibid.*, 230-32; Ransom and Sutch, *One Kind of Freedom*, 232-36; Wiener, *Social Origins*, 46; Jones, *Labor of Love*, 60.

38. A landowner quoted in Jaynes, *Branches without Roots*, 187.

39. *Ibid.*, 185-87.

40. An observer quoted *ibid.*, 185.

41. Thomas Ferguson's contract quoted *ibid.*

42. Jones, *Labor of Love*, 46.

43. Elizabeth Rauh Bethel, *Promiseland: A Century of Life in a Negro Community* (Philadelphia: Temple University Press, 1981), 45-50.

44. Kirby, *Rural Worlds Lost,* 157 and 159; Jones, *Labor of Love,* 63; Theodore Rosengarten, *All God's Dangers: The Life of Nate Shaw* (New York: Knopf, 1975), 120-21.

45. Sharecropper Ned Cobb quoted in Rosengarten, *All God's Dangers,* 120.

46. Jones, *Labor of Love,* 63.

47. Dolores Janiewski, "Sisters under Their Skins: Southern Working Women, 1880-1950," in *Sex, Race, and the Role of Women in the South,* ed. Joanne V. Hawks and Sheila L. Skemp (Jackson: University Press of Mississippi, 1983), 13-35, esp. 16.

48. Allen, *Labor of Women,* 174; see also Sachs, *Invisible Farmers,* 26.

49. Fred A. Shannon, *The Farmer's Last Frontier: Agriculture, 1860-1933* (New York: Farrar & Rinehart, 1945), 88.

50. Kirby, *Rural Worlds Lost,* 157; Jones, *Labor of Love,* 63; Rosengarten, *All God's Dangers,* 59.

51. Zora Neale Hurston, *Jonah's Gourd Vine* (New York: Lippincott, 1971), 16-17.

52. Joan M. Jensen, *With These Hands: Women Working the Land* (Old Westbury, N.Y.: Feminist Press, 1981), 164-65; Jones, *Labor of Love,* 86-88. For a description of the living conditions of many southern sharecroppers, see Kirby, *Rural Worlds Lost,* 174-77.

53. A freedwoman quoted anonymously in Jones, *Labor of Love,* 60; see also 78.

54. Bethel, *Promiseland,* 47-48; Jaynes, *Branches without Roots,* 231-32.

55. Blassingame, *Slave Community,* 80 and 92; Fogel and Engerman, *Time on the Cross,* 141-42; Genovese, *Roll, Jordan, Roll,* 489; Jones, *Labor of Love,* 82.

56. Quoted in Herbert G. Gutman, "Marital and Sexual Norms among Slave Women," in *A Heritage of Her Own: Toward a New Social History of American Women,* ed. Nancy F. Cott and Elizabeth H. Pleck (New York: Simon & Schuster, 1979), 298-310, esp. 304.

57. *Ibid.,* 304; see also John Hope Franklin, *From Slavery to Freedom: A History of Negro Americans,* 3d ed. (New York: Random House, 1967), 200.

58. Levine, *Black Culture,* 96-97.

59. Numerous cases where Black women resisted the domination and violence perpetrated by both Black and white males can be found in Gerda Lerner, ed., *Black Women in White America: A Documentary History* (New York: Pantheon, 1972); see also Gutman, "Marital and Sexual Norms," 306-7; and White, *Ar'n't I a Woman?,* 151-52.

60. Genovese, *Roll, Jordan, Roll,* 500-501; hooks, *Ain't I a Woman,* 44 and 47; Jones, *Labor of Love,* 104; Rosengarten, *All God's Dangers,* 14; Woloch, *Women and the American Experience,* 226.

61. Letty Cottin Pogrebin, *Family Politics: Love and Power on an Intimate Frontier* (New York: McGraw-Hill, 1984), 96.

62. Jones, *Labor of Love,* 82.

63. Rosengarten, *All God's Dangers,* 32.

64. Genovese, *Roll, Jordan, Roll,* 473.

65. Woloch, *Women and the American Experience,* 191. As Kirby, *Rural Worlds Lost,* 173, points out, divorce was also a luxury few southern sharecroppers could afford. Moreover, he argues that, because these people viewed marriage as sacred, traditional morality and poverty "conspired" to bind these people together.

66. Blassingame, *Slave Community,* 83; Genovese, *Roll, Jordan, Roll,* 460-61. For a contrasting view on sexual abuse, see Fogel and Engerman, *Time on the Cross,* 130-34.

67. Davis, "Black Woman's Role," 8; Jones, *Labor of Love*, 20; Lerner, ed., *Black Women in White America*, 15; hooks, *Ain't I a Woman*, 23 and 37.

68. White, *Ar'n't I a Woman?*, 164. For a more lengthy discussion of violence against Black men and women during the Reconstruction Era, see W.E.B. Du Bois, *Black Reconstruction in America, 1860-1880* (New York: Atheneum, 1975), 670-728.

69. A Black landowner's daughter quoted in Janiewski, "Sisters under Their Skins," 15.

70. A Black servant quoted in Lerner, ed., *Black Women in White America*, 156; see also Janiewski, "Sisters under Their Skins," 18; and Jones, *Labor of Love*, 73, 114, and 127-34. The absence of information on whether these women controlled the income they received from domestic service precludes a complete analysis of the implications of this aspect of sharecropping women's work for Kelly's theses.

71. Blassingame, *Slave Community*, 91; Genovese, *Roll, Jordan, Roll*, 483, hooks, *Ain't I a Woman*, 35-36; Jones, *Labor of Love*, 103; Rosengarten, *All God's Dangers*, 10 and 273; White, *Ar'n't I a Woman?*, 151-52.

72. A Black woman quoted anonymously in Lerner, ed., *Black Women in White America*, 157.

73. Sharecropper Ned Cobb quoted in Rosengarten, *All God's Dangers*, 10.

74. Genovese, *Roll, Jordan, Roll*, 484. For a discussion of the role of isolation in domestic violence, see David Finkelhor, "Common Features of Family Abuse," in *Marriage and the Family in a Changing Society*, ed. James M. Henslin (New York: Free Press, 1985), 500-507, esp. 504.

75. Kirby, *Rural Worlds Lost*, 169-70; my emphasis. Another researcher found a "bitterness towards men as a class" among the young Black women sharecroppers she interviewed, while older Black women did not express this same "bitterness" as noted in Janiewski, "Sisters under Their Skins," 19.

76. For a discussion of issues often covered under the rubric of reproductive freedom, see Nadean Bishop, "Abortion: The Controversial Choice," in *Women: A Feminist Perspective*, ed. Jo Freeman (Palo Alto, Calif.: Mayfield, 1979), pp. 64-79.

77. Gutman, "Marital and Sexual Norms," 307; Kirby, *Rural Worlds Lost*, 162-63; White, *Ar'n't I a Woman?*, 84.

78. Fogel and Engerman, *Time on the Cross*, 78-86; Herbert G. Gutman, *The Black Family in Slavery and Freedom, 1750-1925* (New York: Pantheon, 1976), 273-77; Blassingame, *Slave Community*, 87 and 89-92; Jones, *Labor of Love*, 34-35.

79. Blassingame, *Slave Community*, 86; Genovese, *Roll, Jordan, Roll*, 473.

80. Blassingame, *Slave Community*, 80-83 and 89-92; Fogel and Engerman, *Time on the Cross*; Gutman, *The Black Family*, 318; Genovese, *Roll, Jordan, Roll*, 452-57.

81. White, *Ar'n't I a Woman?*, 70; see also Gutman, *The Black Family*, 80 and 265.

82. Blassingame, *Slave Community*, 93; Fogel and Engerman, *Time on the Cross*, 122-23; White, *Ar'n't I a Woman?*, 68.

83. White, *Ar'n't I a Woman?*, 69, 111-12, and 124; Jones, *Labor of Love*, 19 and 35.

84. Jones, *Labor of Love*, 85.

85. Quoted in Kirby, *Rural Worlds Lost*, 164. As Kirby points out, many of the interviews with southern farm families funded by the New Deal's Federal Writers' Project included questions on birth control. For a discussion of these interviews and various attempts by private and public agencies to distribute birth control information and devices in the 1930s, see 162-69.

86. James C. Mohr, *Abortion in America: The Origins and Evolution of National Policy* (New York: Oxford University Press, 1978), 256-57. It is debatable whether, prior to the Civil War, professional medical practice was any more successful in

improving health care than was the lay medical practice of midwives. However, as Mohr points out, the Civil War is often viewed as a transition point for advances in professional medicine, despite the fact that professional medical care for women has been criticized up until the present day. For discussions of the role of wives and midwives in medical care for sharecropping and slave households, see Jones, *Labor of Love*, 56 and 80-81; Federal Writers' Project, *These Are Our Lives* (New York: Norton, 1975), 26; Rosengarten, *All God's Dangers*, 118-19; White, *Ar'n't I a Woman?*, 111-12.

87. Franklin, *From Slavery to Freedom*, 308.

88. Jones, *Labor of Love*, 91; Bethel, *Promiseland*, 41; Federal Writers' Project, *These Are Our Lives*, 19-29; Kirby, *Rural Worlds Lost*, 156.

89. Jones, *Labor of Love*, 64, 76-78, 90, and 96-99; Rosengarten, *All God's Dangers*, 19. According to these sources, it appears that fathers had the last word in deciding the allocation of their children's labor between farm and school. Apparently, this decision generated conflict between sharecropping mothers and fathers, with mothers emphasizing school work and fathers emphasizing farm work.

90. In eleven southern states, the average expenditure in 1930 for each white child was $44.31 as compared with $12.57 for each Black child. For more information on the quality of education, see Arthur F. Raper and Ira De A. Reid, *Sharecroppers All* (Chapel Hill: University of North Carolina Press, 1941), 110-12.

91. Druzilla Cary Kent, *A Study of the Results of Planning for Home Economics Education in the Southern States* (New York: Columbia University, Teachers College, Bureau of Publications, 1936), 11.

92. Woloch, *Women and the American Experience*, 226. There are conflicting views in the literature regarding the role that male and female Afro-American leaders played in fostering female subservience and domesticity. Here distinctions should be made between leaders who advocated traditional, patriarchal roles for men and subservient roles for women, those who advocated equal political rights for men and women, and those who included, along with demands for equal political rights, demands for equal social rights and roles. For different views on this subject, see hooks, *Ain't I a Woman*, 89-102 and 161-84, as contrasted to Elmer P. Martin and Joanne Mitchell Martin, "The Black Woman: Perspectives on Her Role in the Family," in *Ethnicity and Women* (Madison: University of Wisconsin Press, 1986), 184-205, esp. 197-99.

93. Franklin, *From Slavery to Freedom*, 202; see also Blassingame, *Slave Community*, 91; Genovese, *Roll, Jordan, Roll*, 502; Jensen, *With These Hands*, 71-75.

94. These findings call into question Kelly's second thesis, since the position of women improved despite the reduction of women's work outside of the home. Other research provides further anomalous cases. For example, in fascist Germany during the 1930s and 1940s, the increase in women working outside of the home was substantial, in large part as a result of wartime demands. Yet this increase in women's production for exchange, which Kelly predicted would improve women's position, was in fact accompanied by an extensive antifeminist movement which campaigned against women smoking and wearing trousers, closed down birth control centers, and exacted heavy punishments for abortion. See Richard Grunberger, *The 12-Year Reich: A Social History of Nazi Germany, 1933-1945* (New York: Ballantine, 1971), 133, 256-58, 261-62, 278-81, and 288-89. These anomalies would suggest that along with economic roles, the political structures within a given mode of production need to be examined since the extent to which forms

of political organization are more democratic or more authoritarian than one another can greatly affect the position of women.

95. White, *Ar'n't I a Woman?*, 158-59.

96. *Ibid.*, 122, 151, and 152. In addition, on pp. 20-22 White notes that her conclusion about equal relations differs from that of many other writers on American slavery whom she claims too often exaggerated male slave masculinity in an effort to negate the derogatory male "Sambo" myth.

97. See Martin and Martin, "The Black Woman"; and Davis, "The Black Woman's Role." Angela Davis's discussion of relations within slave households is particularly interesting because she grounds her analysis in the Hegelian master-slave dialectic, pointing out on pp. 7-8 how the fact that slave women performed both male and female work roles provided these women with "proof of their ability to transform things" as well as a "practical awareness of the oppressor's utter dependence on her"—thus serving to "unharness an immense potential in the black woman." Davis is also careful not to romanticize Black gender relations; she refers to them as a "deformed equality."

98. Martin and Martin, "The Black Woman," 193.

99. Farnham, "Sapphire"; hooks, *Ain't I a Woman*. If an analysis of American slavery also takes into account the influence of African culture and heritage, the patriarchal features of traditional African family lives would increase the likelihood that American slave households were patriarchal. For a discussion of the relationship between American slavery and the subjugation of women in traditional African cultures, see Martin and Martin, "The Black Woman," 188-89, or hooks, 16-20.

100. hooks, *Ain't I a Woman*, 88.

101. Jones, *Labor of Love*, 104-5.

102. Hartmann, "The Unhappy Marriage."

103. Freeman, *Women*, 536-39.

104. Alison M. Jaggar and Paula S. Rothenberg, *Feminist Frameworks: Alternative Theoretical Accounts of the Relations between Women and Men*, 2d ed. (New York: McGraw-Hill, 1984).

105. Christiana Greene has suggested that the findings of this study would support, rather than critique, Kelly's thesis, if public and domestic spheres were viewed as less differentiated under sharecropping because of the integral and complementary nature of work inside and outside of the home. I thank Ms. Greene for bringing this different interpretation to my attention. However, in my view, this interpretation ignores the importance of the sexual division of labor for determining patriarchal control within family labor enterprises. In this regard, see also Susan A. Mann, review of *Farm Women: Work, Farm and Family in the United States* by Rachel Ann Rosenfeld, in *American Journal of Sociology* 93, no. 1 (July 1987): 243-45.

106. Janiewski, "Sisters under Their Skins," 15.

107. See the introduction or any of the essays in Fox, ed., *Hidden in the Household*.

108. Harriet Friedmann, "Patriarchal Commodity Production," *Social Analysis* 20 (December 1986): 47-55; Susan George, *How the Other Half Dies: The Real Reasons for World Hunger* (Montclair, N.J.: Allanheld, Osmun, 1981), 20-21.

109. Audre Lorde, "An Open letter to Mary Daly," in *Sister Outsider: Essays and Speeches by Audre Lorde*, ed. Audre Lorde (New York: Crossing, 1984), 66-71, esp. 67.

18

"A Career to Build, a People to Serve, a Purpose to Accomplish":
Race, Class, Gender, and Detroit's First Black Women Teachers, 1865-1916

John B. Reid

The period before World War I comprises an important era in the history of Detroit's black community. Prior to the large-scale migration of blacks that transformed the city, Detroit's small black community formed a significant part of the city's population. Although a few historians have examined this part of Detroit's history, most of their studies do not discuss black women in any depth.[1] The emerging study of black women's history illustrates that the history of cities like Detroit cannot be understood without an examination of the black women within them.[2] In Detroit black women schoolteachers had a dramatic impact on the community. These teachers worked inside and outside of the classroom to elevate the race and to fight negative perceptions of black womanhood. Yet in spite of their significant achievements, their legacy remains ambiguous because of the limitations imposed by the Detroit educational system and the stereotypes that continued to confine black women.[3]

The identities of Detroit's black women teachers are difficult to uncover because the public school system did not record the race of its employees. In addition, information in manuscript sources, city directories, and census material is often unclear or contradictory. The 1910 United States Census lists eight female and three male black teachers in Detroit; another source refers to 17 black teachers in Detroit in 1915, although both of these sources probably include teachers in private schools.[4] I have identified ten of Detroit's black women public schoolteachers before the Great Migration of the World War I era (in alphabetical order): Florence Cole, J. Cook, Lola Gregory, Azalia Smith Hackley, Etta Edna Lee, Meta Pelham, Fannie M. Richards, Clara Shewcraft, Theresa Smith, and Sarah Webb.[5] One woman, Delia Pelham Barriers, worked with Richards in one of the segregated public schools, but apparently as an assistant and not formally as a teacher. We know more about some of these women than others, but the little we know nonetheless points to this group as a prominent and important part of Detroit's black community.[6]

These women had remarkably similar backgrounds. Nearly all of Detroit's early teachers came from relatively prosperous families; in fact, all but one were from families a Detroit paper called the "Cultured Colored

Forty"—families that boasted some education and/or material stability that separated them from laboring black people.[7] Two of the four women mentioned in the news item were Detroit teachers—Fannie Richards and Lola Gregory. The Pelhams of Detroit, whose members included Delia Pelham Barriers and Meta Pelham, were arguably the most elite family in Detroit between the Civil War and the Great Migration of the World War I era. A Detroit newspaper referred to the Pelham women as "among our most cultured and highly respected ladies in [the black] community."[8] Florence Cole's father, James H. Cole, was Detroit's richest black until his death in 1907.[9]

Several of these teachers also shared a mixed racial heritage or at least a light complexion, suggesting that a light complexion aided one's entrance into the black elite and into the public school system. A 1915 survey of Detroit blacks owning real estate or among the city's professionals and business people supports this contention. Only 239 of 1496 of these people were deemed "full-blooded Negroes."[10] Richards and Shewcraft definitely had white grandparents. Hackley's appearance in photographs shows her light complexion. The fact that Theresa Smith was twice singled out for her dark complexion suggests it was unusual for a woman of her standing.[11]

In addition, several of these teachers—Richards, the Pelhams, Lee, Cook—shared roots in the free black communities of Virginia, a fact that has significance for the history of black education in Detroit. The Fredricksburg, Virginia, free black community had a history of agitating for the right to educate their children well before the Civil War. However, in the 1830s, the Virginia legislature passed legislation severely restricting the activities of free blacks. One of the most important provisions prohibited the education of blacks, slave or free. In 1838, the free black residents of Fredricksburg petitioned the state legislature to allow the education of their children out-of-state, but the state refused.[12] The Richards family, along with several other prominent black families who left Fredricksburg in the 1850s for Detroit in response to these restrictions, believed the denial of education was one of the most important of these restrictions. The Pelham family migrated at about the same time from Petersburg, Virginia.[13] The resulting Detroit community contained several middle-class[14] blacks with a history of a strong desire for education and a willingness to agitate for it. This may partially explain this community's later commitment and success in desegregating the city's schools.

These newly arriving families found an educational system in Detroit that provided a public school for black children beginning in 1842. Before 1840, black Detroiters had provided their own education as did most Northern free black communities.[15] In 1836, Detroit's blacks opened a private school in the Fort Street East building and appointed James Field, a black, as teacher. Two white men took over in 1838, but they were soon replaced by the Reverend William Monroe, a leading member of the black community and an emigrant from Indiana. When free public schools began in Detroit in 1842, the Detroit Board fired Monroe and replaced him with a white person, demonstrating the Board's initial preference for white teachers. Monroe taught a private class for four more years in the Second Baptist Church.[16] In 1851, Monroe again became the teacher of the colored school, first in St. Matthew's Episcopal Church and later in the Fourth Ward School Building, formerly a white school. Monroe retired in 1856, and white teachers took over the school, with a white male, John Whitbeck, becoming principal in 1860.[17] The resulting school system left children without black teachers, and left educated blacks, especially black women, without an important career opportunity.

Unfortunately, this educational system functioned as social control that did not uplift black citizens.[18] The Detroit system, like other urban educational systems of the era, largely attempted to control the new urban population, and black children were a small but important part of this population.[19] The Detroit Board of Education's first report bears this out: Detroit's public schools were to be aimed at the "hundreds of youth treading the pathway of vice and misery." The report addressed these youth again in the report: "The committee will not here dwell upon the evils of so large a mass of youth loose upon society in a city like ours—evils which are not only visited upon the authors of their being, upon themselves, but upon the morals, reputations, and the purse of the public."[20] The association between urban development and public education becomes stronger when looking at public education in rural Michigan—rural Michiganders did not have public schools until 1869.

Apparently, the system accomplished its goals. In 1843, the *Detroit Gazette* commented on public schools:

> The primary schools were open for six months in the six several wards for the younger class of scholars, and the immediate consequences was the clearing of our avenues, streets and lanes of ragged, filthy children, engaged in every species of mischief, and growing up the pupils of depravity and crime. The second view presented the same children cleanly clad, inmates of school rooms, and the third exhibited them in connection with children of what is termed the better classes of society, contending for superiority, and finally the schools of the summer closed with universal satisfaction.[21]

Even though Michigan was one of the first Midwestern states to provide for the teaching of black students, it cannot be attributed completely to its relatively liberal attitudes.[22] Considering the attitudes expressed in the *Gazette*, the fact that the Board created a school for black youngsters, even though funds were already stretched thin, isn't surprising. Here the consideration of a class threat from the new urban residents crossed racial, ethnic, and gender lines. However, race did mandate the creation of a separate school for black children. The small size of the black community in the 1840s and the proximity of their residences made one school sufficient to educate the city's black children—88 students were enrolled in 1840.[23]

The very function of education in Detroit limited the amount of change black teachers could instigate. The system's discrimination against women also limited change. From its beginnings in 1842, Detroit's public education system placed women on the bottom of the occupational hierarchy. The Detroit

Board of Education's first report in 1842 described the school system in the following way:

> There should be at once established two grades of schools in each ward, and one or more high schools in the city. The first, primary schools, to be taught by females, and composed of the youngest class of children; the second, middle schools, to be taught by masters, and composed of the older and more advanced scholars. . . .[24]

Of course masters meant men; in November 1842 two middle schools opened, staffed exclusively by men.[25] No one on the Board challenged the idea of women as appropriate only for primary teaching.[26]

The lower wages one could pay women workers motivated the Detroit school system to hire mostly women as teachers. From the beginning, the Detroit schools had limited funds. In 1842, the Board could afford to establish only one school in each ward to be operated six months of the year, resulting in crowded classes. In 1865 Detroit teachers averaged fifty-six students, while Chicago teachers averaged fifty-three and Cleveland's averaged forty-seven.[27] When the Board sought to reduce costs in 1864, it decided to hire as few male teachers as possible. In the words of Mr. O'Rourke, president of the Board, "women are good and cheaper."[28] Because female schoolteachers could not be married before the 1930s, administrators rationalized lower salaries for women because these women presumably did not have to provide for dependents. Detroit's first colored school, established in 1842, paid men $30 a month to $18 a month for women. In 1865, the average male teacher earned $993, while the average woman earned $383. In 1912, the mostly female schoolteacher's average salary was $1158—the average janitor earned $1382.[29]

Adding race to this situation made it worse. Black men and women of all classes faced considerable employment discrimination in Detroit before World War I, but black women fared the worst. Detroit's factories did not welcome most black men. Census records indicate that in 1870, 43.4% of black men were employed in service occupations and another 28% worked as laborers; in 1910, 49.6% remained in service jobs. But the numbers were much worse for black females. In 1870, 98.8% of employed black women worked in service occupations. But by 1910 the native-white percentage in domestic work dropped to 22.7%, and 43% for foreign-born white women, while 86.8% of black women remained in domestic work. In addition, both black men and black women often had the most difficult and unpleasant domestic tasks.[30] Clearly, Detroit's black women bore the brunt of both racial and gender discrimination, which justified their economic exploitation.

The class and race factors made the position of black teachers even worse. Employment discrimination against black people placed them among the laboring classes in grossly disproportionate numbers, making education a luxury for the fortunate few of middle-class status. And although black women received the same pay as white women for similar teaching positions, white female teachers were able to gradually move into more prestigious and higher paying positions in the last three decades of the nineteenth century. Black women were restricted to primary teaching well into the twentieth century, confining them to the lowest paying and least prestigious teaching jobs in the system. However, these issues should not be oversimplified. The ideas of virtuous womanhood and women's separate sphere also buttressed the exploitation of white women's labor by male administrators. Black women were similarly exploited, but the prestige rewards for them in their own communities were higher. Helping to advance the race was a noble goal, and the economic exploitation of black people made teaching a respected profession whose members could be considered some of the black community's most fortunate members.

The decreasing autonomy of teachers in the nineteenth century also limited Detroit's black women teachers. Bureaucratization took place throughout late nineteenth-century school systems as a means of making administration more efficient. Men, especially those of Anglo-Saxon descent, monopolized the newly created administrative positions.[31] Their manipulation of socially constructed ideas of gender rationalized this dominance. The corresponding and interrelated processes of bureaucratization of administration and feminization of the teaching forces greatly reduced the teachers' autonomy in the classroom and their power in the system. The late nineteenth-century male image illustrated the abilities necessary for administration: men were thought to have problem-solving, analytical minds, more overall intelligence, and the ability to set aside emotions when making decisions.[32] They also obtained exclusive access to the sanctioned expertise of higher education, a barrier white women just started to break through in the latter part of the nineteenth century and black women even later, allowing men to monopolize competence. The expertise these administrators gained was invested with scientific authority, and as science, bureaucracy, and efficiency became inextricably linked, the teacher in the classroom became a dependent arm of the educational system. The authority the teacher possessed in early nineteenth-century schoolrooms was gradually transferred to expert curriculum developers.[33] Supervisory officers who observed teachers to make sure they conformed to the dictates of the school administrators maintained the control of the central administration. The number of these officers in Detroit increased from 31 in 1890 to 329 in 1920.[34]

Detroit's first black women teachers accomplished much despite these limitations. The achievements of Fannie Richards,[35] the city's first black teacher, are rather well-known, especially her involvement in the struggle to desegregate Detroit's public schools.[36] Detroit's black community had protested inequality since the 1840s because according to the State Colored Convention in 1843, the Detroit educational system allowed blacks only "a scanty and inadequate participation in the privileges of education."[37] But the changing conditions of the 1850s and 1860s exacerbated the problems with Detroit's separate and unequal system. The growth of Detroit's black population made one school insufficient. Between 1840 and 1860, Detroit's black population grew from 193 to 1402, effectively excluding large numbers of black children from attending the one separate school.[38] An additional factor contributing to the tension may have been improper treatment of students in the separate school. At least one student was unable to attend the colored school because of the cruelty of the teachers.[39] These factors combined with the nationwide movement for black rights that accompanied the rhetoric of the Civil War. Throughout the Midwest in 1864-5, blacks petitioned legislatures to integrate schools.[40] A mixed school law was even debated in Congress between 1867 and 1875, but Southern legislators eventually defeated the bill.[41]

The Detroit Board of Education created a second public school for black children and appointed Richards its first and only teacher in 1865. However, this did not resolve the problems inherent in separate schooling. Soon after Richards' appointment, the movement for desegregation in Michigan accelerated, and Richards played an important role. The Michigan legislature outlawed school segregation in the state in 1869. When the Detroit Board of Education refused to comply, a group of prominent black Detroiters including Fannie Richards and her brother, John D. Richards, helped initiate and financially support a lawsuit against the Board. The Michigan Supreme Court ruled against the Detroit Board that year, but the Board did not comply until 1871 after pressure from the black community, a clear demonstration of the Board's opposition to integrated schools.

The exact extent of Richards' involvement in this struggle remains unclear.[42] We know that her brother was Detroit's leading black speaker and politician at the time. We also know that she knew John J. Bagley, a wealthy white industrialist, a financial supporter of the 1869 lawsuit, and Michigan's fifteenth governor, although we do not know the extent of this relationship. Richards' prominence as Detroit's first black female teacher and her association with these two important figures in the movement suggest she had influence in the movement. At the time, she would have been the only black Detroiter with intimate knowledge of the public school system, and could have served as an important advisor to those making public arguments. She certainly served the movement as a symbol of black competence and of the injustice of the Detroit educational system.

This desegregation struggle demonstrates the intersections of race, class, and gender in the black Detroit of the 1860s. The black middle class, along with liberal whites, conceived and financed this struggle. Laboring blacks simply did not have the money or connections to engage in this kind of organized protest. Furthermore, the goals of poor and working-class blacks of this period tended to place more concrete economic issues ahead of civil rights and equal education issues.[43] The Richards family, with its education and financial stability, could guide the community's efforts in directions that benefited the black middle class. However Richards herself exercised her influence behind the scenes, she was sure to remain within the boundaries dictated by the proscriptions of women's separate sphere that cut across the boundaries of race and class.

Regardless of Richards' efforts in the desegregation struggle, her historical significance can't be limited to this one issue. The temptation to view Richards as a "great black woman" mimics the "great white man" school of historical scholarship that excluded so many people from the nation's history.[44] Although Richards may be the most prominent of these women, in reality she was just one of a group of women whose work for advancement of the race, and particularly black womanhood, has remained largely invisible. This group of teachers were among the most dedicated and productive participants in black community self-help efforts in Detroit in the era before the Great Migration.

The careers and contributions of these teachers cannot be understood without looking at the larger context of black self-help and the particular role black women and black women educators played in it. Because of exclusion from institutions and organizations that serve the needs of the white community, black Americans have been forced to create their own institutions and organizations. Education has been one of the most important parts of black self-help, because it has promised to raise the educated above the limits of race and class. The earliest black self-help organizations—black churches, social organizations, philanthropic groups—created parallel educational institutions as part of their program for aiding the black community.[45] In addition, both organizations and individuals have taken it upon themselves to create educational institutions that educate young people and train the next generation of black teachers and black leaders. An examination of the careers of early Detroit teachers—even those who quit teaching in public schools—demonstrates that the urge to lift the race through service in the schools cannot be separated from the desire to advance the race generally, and that these efforts were not confined to the crowded nineteenth-century classrooms.

Detroit's black women teachers actively worked inside the classroom to aid and advance the race. This motivated these women to enter teaching. Black people, especially black women, believed that education of the whole black community was the answer to black people's troubles. Furthermore they believed women to be best suited for the instruction of young children in accordance with the Victorian ideal of womanhood.[46] Unfortunately, historians know little about the daily activities in these classrooms, but the available evidence suggests that black teachers were probably more sensitive to issues of race and class than whites. After all, the act of becoming educated and seeking employment in the public schools required at least an internal denial of popular racist theories. In 1915, a local newspaper interviewed Fannie Richards, and she said: "The mixture was interesting to watch in the classroom, for while the Jewish children led in arithmetic, and the German children were the best thinkers, the colored children were the best readers, almost orators, I might say."[47] At this time, few others in the Detroit educational system would have had such positive attitudes about the ability of black students. In fact, intelligence testing had just begun systematically defining large percentages of black students as retarded.[48] Azalia Smith Hackley also took special interest in the "culturally and materially" deprived students.[49] Her case suggests that the experience of race discrimination combined with the gender roles assigned women could translate into a concern for the disadvantaged of all races.

In addition to bringing an oppositional consciousness to the classroom, this first generation of teachers broke critical barriers to the advancement of blacks and particularly black women. As a group, these women pioneered in many endeavors, paving the way for future blacks in the Detroit educational system. Fannie Richards has received a certain amount of attention for being the first black to teach in Detroit's mixed schools.[50] Yet at least two other early black teachers broke educational barriers. Meta Pelham was the first black woman to graduate from Detroit's mostly white Central High School, a remarkable achievement considering the school's failure rate in this era was 90 percent.[51] Azalia Smith Hackley was also among Central High's first black graduates, and later was the first black graduate of Denver University School of Music.[52]

These teachers also broke a barrier every time one became the first black to teach in a particular school or neighborhood. Before the Great Migration changed the racial configuration of the city, nearly all blacks lived on the near east side of Detroit but never comprised more than 65 percent of residents in that particular area. Most often, blacks formed less than 50 percent of the residents on a block, even on the near east side.[53] As a result, black teachers usually entered schoolrooms in neighborhoods with mostly white residents, although after 1870 most of the white students in these neighborhoods were increasingly non-Anglo-Saxon immigrants, and no black teacher taught in the white Anglo-Saxon west side. The interactions between black teachers and white parents were not always harmonious. One white parent removed her child from Lincoln School on Theresa Smith's first day because "colored people are all right in their place, but they never ought to be placed as teachers in our public schools."[54]

Evidence suggests the school administration attempted to keep racial conflict to a minimum. A study of the schools where black teachers taught shows that all taught in the near east side where nearly all of Detroit's blacks resided. Clara Shewcraft was the only exception, having taught in Hamtramck after 1918, but she spent her first eleven years in schools in the near east neighborhood.[55] And although only eleven black teachers can be found before 1871, several taught at the same schools in near east Detroit, although in only one case did they teach at the same time.[56] This suggests that the Detroit school administrators considered race when hiring and placing Detroit's black teachers. They most likely intended these hires to placate the black community that had consistently challenged inequality in education.

After breaking the barriers, these teachers contradicted existing racial and sexual stereotypes by serving as symbols of black female competence at a time when the abilities of all black Americans were being called into question. The nineteenth century witnessed the progressive growth of scientific racism which declared blacks inherently and permanently inferior.[57] Theresa Smith's experience confirms that some whites considered black teachers to be inconsistent with their place in the racial hierarchy of the time. In this context, the act of teaching, especially the teaching of white students, contradicted assumptions about the intellectual ability of black people.

Black women teachers, however, had to overcome more than just negative images of black competence. As Patricia Morton has demonstrated, black women were represented in unique ways that demonstrate the convergence of gender and race.[58] Dominant culture discourse had divided black womanhood into good and bad stereotypes: the Mammy stereotype exemplifying the good, the sexually promiscuous and mean Jezebel exemplifying the bad. These images correspond to the symbolic representations of women in Western culture which are defined by the binary opposition of Eve and Mary as symbols of womanhood.[59] Adding race changed the images. The image of Mary became the happily servile Mammy. The supposed hypersexuality of African blood transformed Eve into the oversexed and mean image of Jezebel.[60] In this context, Detroit's black women teachers worked to dispute the bad stereotype. The role of the chaste teacher, the moral equivalent to the preacher, served this purpose well. The communities policed the moral behavior of nineteenth century teachers, insuring that students were exposed to high ethical image. The prohibition of marriage was designed to maintain their pure image.[61] The combination served the black women teachers well, for it provided them with just the image they needed to contradict the stigma of the evil and promiscuous black woman. Ironically, these restrictions offered more to black women teachers than to their white counterparts.

But denial of the Jezebel image wasn't enough. The Mammy image could also constrict black women teachers. This non-sexual, masculine figure—happy in her subservience, dedicated in her care for white children—was probably applied to Detroit's early black teachers. For example, the *Detroit Free Press* described Fannie Richards as having the "eyes of a devoted mammy."[62] This image of black women as strong, loyal, and subservient may help explain the willingness of Detroit Board members to allow these women to teach in the public schools at all. Teaching, then, despite its attempt to confront negative stereotypes of black womanhood, could not always overcome these alternating images.

Detroit's black women teachers engaged in a complex of resistance activities geared towards black people in general and black women in particular outside the classroom. The work of these teachers discussed above was part of these resistance activities. But Detroit's black women teachers did not confine their influence on behalf of black people, and in particular black women, to the classroom. Their participation and leadership in the black women's clubs extended their efforts into the community.

Black women's clubs have a long history, and they have played an important role in providing education and aid to black communities. The organization of black women to serve their communities dates back to the earliest days of the black presence in America, but black women's clubs began forming in large numbers in the 1830s. Spurred by the increasingly large free communities in urban areas, the growing number of educated black women with some free time, and the urgent needs of the black community's poor, black women began forming groups around specific educational, philanthropic, and welfare activities.[63] This movement accelerated in the 1890s when self-help activities began to take precedence over civil rights agitation in an increasingly hostile racial climate. In that decade these clubs began to organize on state and national levels. The National Association of Colored Women's Clubs (NACWC) was organized in 1896, and the Michigan State Federation of Colored Women's Clubs was organized 1898 at a meeting of the NACWC.[64]

These clubs developed alongside similar organizations in the white community that did not welcome black participants. Like these white women's clubs, and in keeping with the Victorian belief that men and women should live their lives in separate spheres, black women's club work usually involved nurturing activities expected of those in the women's sphere. Caring for social inferiors, children, and the aged required moral superiority and nurturing ability—the natural abilities of the ideal Victorian woman.[65] Black women's work in clubs differed from white women's in its commitment to more universal programs instead of individual relief and its commitment to protecting women from sexual exploitation.[66]

Some of the first new clubs formed in the 1890s to care for the elderly as the need became crucial.[67] Black clubwomen built hundreds of homes for the aged all over the country between 1890 and 1913.[68] However, young children became the primary interest of black clubwomen because they believed the best way to reform society was to instruct and care for the young.[69] Generally, providing child-care facilities and kindergartens were two of the primary functions of colored women's clubs throughout the country.[70]

The Detroit Study Club provides an example of one of these clubs. Organized in 1898, this club included several of Detroit's early black teachers: Fanny Richards, Lola Gregory, Clara Shewcraft, Meta Pelham, Theresa Smith, and former assistant Delia Pelham Barriers. This club heard members deliver lectures, invited dignitaries such as Booker T. Washington to speak to the community, and used its monies to help needy students attend school.[71] That W.E.B. DuBois wrote and asked for information about institutions maintained by blacks is evidence of their importance to the black community.[72]

Detroit's black women teachers influenced this club and others by comprising a disproportionate number of both members and leaders.[73] Their numbers allowed them to shape the direction of the clubs more than any other occupational group. In addition, their influence almost certainly went beyond their numbers because of their possession of culturally admired education and speaking experience. This may partially explain their disproportionate representation among presidents of the Michigan federation of black women's clubs: three of the first eleven presidents of the Michigan Federation of Colored Women's Clubs, organized in 1898, were Detroit teachers—Fanny Richards, Meta Pelham, and Lola Gregory.[74] Delia Pelham Barrier, Richards' assistant during her first teaching years, was also one of the first presidents of this organization. The power and authority of teachers in the clubs may have contributed to the division of the MFCWC into two factions—mothers and teachers. At the 1913 meeting, these two groups formally debated ways in which women's clubs could attract young members. Fanny Richards and Lola Gregory argued the teacher's position, Delia Pelham Barrier and another women the mother's, with Meta Pelham moderating. Unfortunately, the club did not record the content and outcome of this debate.[75]

The Detroit home for elderly black women and kindergartens in Detroit public schools further demonstrate the significance of teachers' work in the clubs. Detroit teacher Fannie Richards initiated and served as first president of Detroit's Phillis Wheatley Home for Aged Colored Ladies in 1897, the most significant relief effort for Detroit elderly of the era. As for aiding the young, Detroit's teachers acted on this belief through their choice of careers, and usually they brought their conviction and their knowledge to the clubs. But in at least one case, the club experience of a teacher may have provided the impetus for reform of the public schools. Fannie Richards convinced the Detroit school administration to experiment with kindergarten in 1872, making Detroit one of the first United States cities to provide kindergarten education.[76] This demonstrates not only Richards' influence with the Board, but also shows the interrelation of the work of black Detroit teachers in public education and their work in black women's clubs.

Their work, however, reflected the middle-class prejudices of the time. They often imposed middle-class standards on the lower classes, and they tended to treat those they aided in a condescending manner.[77] Clearly these black clubwomen adopted middle-class dress, demeanor, and attitudes.[78] And although black women's clubs allowed working-class women to join, unlike their white counterparts, middle-class women still monopolized the leadership.

In addition, by their middle-class values and behaviors they attempted to separate themselves from the poor masses to some extent. Nevertheless, the adoption of these middle-class standards and values did more than separate and self-aggrandize: middle-class values became part of a wider resistance and confrontation to the unique racial and sexual stereotypes imposed on black women.[79] Sociologist Mary Taylor Blauvelt, after attending a meeting of the Michigan Federation of Colored Women's Clubs in the first decade of the twentieth century, confirms this. She found that a desire to redeem black womanhood separated these clubs from those of white women.[80] Here race mandated the creation of the clubs, and race mandated a modification of their functions and membership to serve the needs of the black community and black women particularly.

In addition to their work in black women's clubs, nearly all of those who left teaching remained active in some form of self-help activity, demonstrating the extent of Detroit's black women teachers' commitment to advancement of the race. At least one teacher—Etta Edna Lee—married and was forced to leave teaching but continued active participation in clubs. Theresa Smith left primary school teaching for her university teaching positions, continuing her interest in educating young blacks. She was listed as an honorary member of the Detroit Study Club during her absence.[81] Azalia Smith Hackley earned a degree in music, and started a club in Denver, Colorado, committed to the "education and the promotion of our colored women and the promotion of their interests." She also became nationally known for her work to preserve and teach black folk music all over the United States.[82]

Detroit's black women teachers were an astonishingly committed group. In her biography of Azalia Smith Hackley, M. Marguerite Davenport writes that Hackley "had a career to build, a people to serve, a purpose to accomplish," and would never "betray her race" by abandoning her commitment to her work.[83] This quotation could be applied to the rest of Detroit's early black women teachers as well. Together, they advocated change both inside and outside the classroom. Working for racial advancement in an inhospitable system, these teachers broke racial barriers and stood as examples of black women's competence to the thousands of young people who passed through their classrooms. They did so despite the fact that a combination of racial and sexual discrimination placed them on the bottom of the school system's career ladder. They also led the black women's clubs, where they continued their work to advance the race and to obliterate negative stereotypes of black womanhood. Certainly, they were not immune to the operations of class, and these operations in public education and in society at large limited the extent to which they could create change. But one thing is certain—they created positive change for the black community, and particularly black women, that belied their small numbers.

NOTES

1. David Katzman, *Before the Ghetto: Black Detroit in the Nineteenth Century* (Urbana: University of Illinois Press, 1973). Darlene Clark Hine, "Black Women in the Middle West: The Michigan Experience," lecture published by the Historical Society of Michigan, 1990, 24.

2. Historians are just beginning to look at the lives and activities of black women, and very little has been written about black women in Michigan. Darlene Clark Hine, "Lifting the Veil, Shattering the Silence: Black Women's History in Slavery and Freedom," in Darlene Clark Hine, ed., *The State of Afro-American History: Past, Present, and Future* (Baton Rouge: Louisiana State University Press, 1986), and Darlene Clark Hine, "Black Women in the Middle West." The first studies to emerge in this field were Angela Davis, "Reflections on the Black Women's Role in the Community of Slaves," *Black Scholar*, III (1971), 2-15. Sharon Harley and Rosalyn Terborg-Penn edited *The Afro-American Woman: Struggles and Images* (Port Washington, N.Y.: National University Publications, 1978), a pioneering work on black women's history. However, scholarly historical works on black women did not emerge in large numbers until the decade of the 1980s. Two of the most significant of these are Deborah Gray White's *Ar'n't I A Woman?: Female Slaves in the Plantation South* (New York: W.W. Norton & Co., 1985) and

Jacqueline Jones' *Labor of Love, Labor of Sorrow: Black Women, Work, and the Family from Slavery to the Present* (New York: Vintage Books, 1985). Both emphasize the unique slave and work experience of African-American women in the South. In 1990, black women's history received a tremendous boost with the publication of the sixteen volume series *Black Women in United States History*, edited by Darlene Clark Hine et al., and published by Carlson Publishing, Brooklyn, N.Y.

3. To date, very little has been written specifically on black teachers, and nearly all of the scholarship concerns teachers in the segregated schools of the South. See for example Sharon Harley, "Beyond the Classroom: The Organizational Lives of Black Female Educators in the District of Columbia, 1890-1930," *Journal of Negro Education*, 51 (1982), 254-65; Melinda Chateauvert, "The Third Step: Anna Julia Cooper and Black Education in the District of Columbia, 1910-1960," *Sage: A Scholarly Journal on Black Women* (student supplement 1988), 7-13; Sandra N. Smith, "Charlotte Hawkins Brown," *Journal of Negro Education*, 51 (1982), 191-206.

4. U.S. Bureau of the Census, *Negro Population, 1790-1915*, tables 17 and 18, 518, 521. Frances H. Warren, *Michigan Manual of Freedmen's Progress* (Detroit, 1915), 270, 293-5, 310, 313.

5. The methods I used to identify these women as teachers varied. Well-known sources such as David Katzman, *Before the Ghetto: Black Detroit in the Nineteenth Century* (Urbana: University of Illinois Press, 1973), identified Fannie Richards, Meta Pelham, Azalia Smith Hackley, Florence Cole, and Lola Gregory as teachers. Warren, *The Michigan Manual of Freedmen's Progress*, identified Sarah Webb and Mrs. J. Cook as teachers. I located Clara Shewcraft and Etta Edna Lee in the records of the Michigan Federation of Colored Women's Clubs, State Archives, State Library of Michigan, Lansing, Michigan. I stumbled upon Theresa Smith in an article in the Parson Scrapbooks in the Detroit Public Library. I then confirmed their employment as teachers by consulting the records of the Detroit School System and Detroit City Directories. All of the teachers in this article worked for public institutions because their employment as teachers can be established with some certainty. However, some black women and men probably worked as teachers in private schools, while others undoubtedly worked in the public schools before World War I but cannot be identified as black. For all these reasons, this paper does not include all of the black women teachers of the era. It attempts to discuss them as an important group, and the above sampling is sufficient for that purpose.

6. The following is the basic biographical information this researcher has thus far unearthed:

Fannie M. Richards (1841-1922). Born on October 1, 1841 in Fredricksburg, Virginia. Her parents were Maria Louise Moore, a free person of color born in Toronto to black and white parents, and Adolphe Richards, a British-educated Hispanic with some African ancestry. Moore moved her family to Detroit in 1851. Fannie Richards was educated first in the clandestine schools of antebellum Fredricksburg, and after the age of ten in the segregated public schools of Detroit. Richards moved to Toronto to attend high school. She taught in Detroit's Colored School Number 2 between 1865-71, and in Everett School between 1871-1915. She died in Detroit in 1922 and is buried in Elmwood Cemetery.

Delia Pelham Barriers and Meta Pelham (1864-1941). Although apparently not a full-fledged teacher, Delia Pelham Barriers was hired to assist Richards in Colored School Number 2 in 1865. Meta Elizabeth Pelham entered Detroit's teaching ranks as well. After teaching fifteen years in Hannibal, Missouri, Meta

315

Pelham returned to Detroit to write for the *Plaindealer*, and eventually replaced Fannie Richards at Everett School in 1916. She taught there until 1923, and at Russell School until her retirement in 1935. Benjamin Pelham's daughter Frances N. Pelham and Joseph H. Pelham's daughters Mabel Pelham and Gladys Pelham also taught in the public schools, though all three taught after 1916.

E. Azalia Smith Hackley (1867-1922) is one of the most well-known of Detroit's early teachers, but not for her teaching. The daughter of a teacher in Murfreesboro, Tennessee, and the granddaughter of Wilson Beard, a prosperous Detroit laundry owner, Hackley became nationally known for her work in teaching black folksongs to individuals and groups all over the United States. Hackley attended Detroit public schools, graduated from Washington Normal School in 1886, and taught in Detroit's Clinton School for eight years (1886-1894).

Theresa Smith (b. ca. 1876) began teaching in Detroit schools in 1894 (not related to Azalia Smith Hackley). Originally from Windsor, Canada, Smith and her sister Pauline came to Detroit for an education. Because Pauline Smith was unable to get stenographic work, she opened her own stenographic office, which became quite successful. Smith taught at Lincoln School in Detroit for one year (1894) before accepting a position as head of the Model Training Department of the State Normal and Industrial College in Tallahassee, Florida. She later went on to a similar position at Fisk University, and eventually became Professor of English and History at Lincoln Institute.

Florence Frances Cole (d. 1907) is another member of a prosperous family who pursued a career in teaching. Cole's father, James Henry Cole, was one of the few Detroit black elite born in the Deep South. He migrated to rural Michigan and worked on a farm as a stable boy until the Civil War, when he was able acquire a grain store and livery that supplied the army. He took these profits and bought into Detroit real estate, amassing over $200,000 of property before his death in 1907, making him Detroit's wealthiest black. Cole taught in Detroit's schools until her marriage in 1897 to Dr. James W. Amers. She died in 1907.

Clara Shewcraft (1876-1944) was also a member of a prosperous family. Richard Turner Shewcraft, the son of mixed parents from Gilford County, North Carolina, became a prominent black artist. His daughter, Clara Shewcraft, worked as a milliner after graduation from Detroit Central High in 1902. In 1905 she moved to Ypsilanti, Michigan, to attend the State Normal School, and in 1907 she was hired to teach in Detroit, first at Bishop School and then at Parke and several others until 1937.

Lola B. Gregory (1869-1940), Etta Edna Lee, Sarah Webb, Mrs. J. Cook were four other members of elite families who joined the public teaching ranks of Detroit. Unfortunately, little is known about them. Gregory taught at Johnston School from 1892 until 1921, and then at Norvell School until her resignation in 1939. Etta Edna Lee, a member of the Lee family from Fredericksburg, taught at Clinton School from 1895 to 1899, when she married and left the system. Sarah Webb taught at Colored School Number 3 from 1869 until the integration of schools in 1871. Mrs. J. Cook was most likely Sarah Ann Cook. Cook operated a private school until 1870 when she joined the staff of Colored School Number 3. Her husband apparently died before she took this position.

7. A *Detroit News-Tribune* article about "Detroit's Most Exclusive Social Clique, the Cultured Colored '40' " named forty heads of families and eleven individuals. The Cole, Cook, Pelham, Shewcraft, Smith, and Webb families are listed. Fannie

Richards and Lola (a.k.a. Lulu) Gregory are listed among the individuals. Only Etta Edna Lee can't be connected to this group. *Detroit News-Tribune*, April 27, 1902.

8. *Detroit Advocate*, May 18, 1901.

9. *Detroit News-Tribune*, April 27, 1902.

10. Warren, *Michigan Manual of Freedmen's Progress*, 36.

11. Fuller and Williams describe her as being "of pure African blood." Fuller and Williams, biography of the Smith sisters in "Detroit Heritage." Her dark complexion was also noted in a newspaper article describing her conflict with a white parent. The article was not dated, nor was the newspaper named, but it most likely came from the *Detroit Journal* in August or September 1894. The Parson Scrapbooks, Burton Historical Collection, Detroit Public Library, Detroit, Michigan.

12. Luther Porter Jackson, *Free Negro Labor and Property Holding* (New York: D. Appleton-Century Co., 1942), 154. John Hope Franklin and Alfred Moss, Jr., *From Slavery to Freedom: A History of Negro Americans* (New York: Alfred Knopf, 1988), 148. W.B. Hartgrove, "The Story of Maria Louise Moore and Fannie M. Richards," *Journal of Negro History* 1 (1916), 25-6.

13. The Pelham Family Papers, Burton Historical Collection, Detroit Public Library, Detroit, Michigan.

14. The term middle-class in this paper is applied in the same way to both black and white people in order to emphasize how developments that caused the transformation of the middle class in the late nineteenth century affected black teachers. Economic exploitation of black people in this era combined with racism left the black community without an upper class comparable to the white ruling class. Therefore, the middle-class black community was to some degree the most prosperous and powerful part of that community, and historians often refer to this class as the elite of the black community.

15. Carter G. Woodson, *The Education of the Negro Prior to 1861* (New York: Arno Press, 1968).

16. Katzman, *Before the Ghetto*, 23-4. Arthur B. Moehlman, *Public Education in Detroit* (Bloomington, IL: Public School Publishing Co., 1925), 99-100.

17. Katzman, *Before the Ghetto*, 23-4. Moehlman, *Public Education*, 99-100; Moehlman incorrectly claims that John Whitbeck ran the school between 1850 and 1870. He also does not discuss the many moves and personnel changes in the school. These inconsistencies suggest he relied on the incorrect history of the colored schools printed in the *Detroit Advertiser & Tribune* of April 19, 1867.

18. For a discussion of class and education, see Andy Green, *Education and State Formation: The Rise of Education Systems in England, France, and the U.S.A.* (New York: St. Martin's Press, 1990), 36. For race and education, see Leonard P. Curry, *The Free Black in Urban America 1800-1850: The Shadow of the Dream* (Chicago: the University of Chicago Press, 1981), 147.

19. Michael B. Katz, *Reconstructing Education* (Cambridge: Harvard University Press, 1987), Chapter One.

20. Detroit Board of Education, "Annual Report of the Board of Education of Detroit 1842."

21. *Detroit Gazette*, December 1842.

22. The Northern tier of Midwestern states was considerably less racist than the Southern tier, perhaps due to their distance from large centers of black population. Illinois and Indiana had not yet provided for the education of black children in

1861. V. Jacque Voegeli, *Free But Not Equal: The Midwest and the Negro During the Civil War* (Chicago: University of Chicago Press, 1967), 2, 170.

23. Moehlman, *Public Education in Detroit*, 68.

24. *Ibid.*, 82.

25. *Ibid.*, 86.

26. These barriers were not absolute. In 1860 an eighteen-year-old woman with a reputation as a disciplinarian was given a middle school class that had driven away two male teachers. The majority of the Board opposed her, but she successfully tamed the class. She left teaching after that year for unknown reasons. *Ibid.*, 101.

27. *Ibid.*, 108.

28. *Ibid.*, 115.

29. *Ibid.*, 193.

30. Katzman, *Before the Ghetto*, 110

31. As late as 1930, 98 percent of school superintendents nationwide were native born, and 90 percent were of Anglo-Saxon descent. David Tyack, *The One Best System: A History of American Urban Education* (Cambridge: Harvard University Press, 1974), 233.

32. Joel Spring, *The American School, 1642-1985: Varieties of Historical Interpretation of the Foundations and Development of American Education* (New York: Longman, 1986), 137.

33. Stephen J. Ball, *Foucault and Education: Disciplines and Knowledge* (London: Routledge, 1990), 73.

34. Tyack, *The One Best System*, 185. Some of this increase is due to population growth, but the rate of supervisor expansion was still double that of the rate of population growth.

35. One can find short biographies of Fannie Richards in several sources, including Rayford Logan and Michael Winston, eds., *Dictionary of American Negro Biography* (1982) and Jessie Carnie Smith, *Notable Black American Women* (1991). Perhaps the best biographical source is Hartgrove, "The Story of Marie Louise Moore and Fannie M. Richards."

36. Although two men—James Field and William Monroe—taught in schools under the direction of the city, Richards is considered the first black teacher because she was the first to be hired on a permanent basis. See *Detroit Schools*, vol. 31, no. 2 (October 20, 1970), 1. This is a questionable distinction, but either way does not diminish Richards' career or importance.

37. Katzman, *Before the Ghetto*, 24-5.

38. These numbers are approximate due to the tendency of census takers of the period to undercount black residents. *Ibid.*, 13, 62.

39. The student was future prominent clubwoman Frances Preston. "Pioneer women of Afro-American Descent," 3, unpublished manuscript, in Federation of Colored Women's Clubs Collection, State Archives of Michigan, Lansing, Michigan, 60-14-A, B1, F2.

40. Voegeli, *Free But Not Equal*, 165.

41. Alfred H. Kelly, "The Congressional Controversy over School Segregation, 1867-1875," *American Historical Review* LXIV, no. 3 (April 1959), 537-63.

42. One article has been written about Richards' role in the desegregation struggle, but the author could only confirm that Richards was one of several financial supporters of the 1869 lawsuit. Robin S. Peebles, "Fannie Richards and the Integration of the Detroit Public Schools," *Michigan History* 65 (1981), 30-1.

43. August Meier, *Negro Thought in America 1880-1915* (Ann Arbor: University of Michigan Press, 1963), 10-11.

44. For a discussion of these issues, see Gloria T. Hull, Patricia Bell Scott, and Barbara Smith, eds., *All the Women Are White, All the Blacks Are Men, But Some of Us Are Brave* (Old Westbury, N.Y.: Feminist Press, 1982).

45. Woodson, *Education of the Negro Prior to 1861*.

46. Cynthia Neverdon-Morton, *Afro-American Women and the Advancement of the Race* (Knoxville: University of Tennessee Press, 1989), 5-6.

47. Peebles, "Fannie Richards," 31.

48. Detroit was among the nation's leaders in using intelligence tests to separate students and thereby make the educational process more efficient. Tyack, *The One Best System*, 208-9. Estimates vary from 17 percent to 53 percent as to how many black students were declared retarded by their performance on these tests. However, all agree that the percentage was much higher for black students, especially those born in the Southern states. Conot, *American Odyssey*, 141. Forrester B. Washington, "The Negro in Detroit: A Survey of the Conditions of a Negro Group in a Northern Industrial Center During the War Prosperity Period," unpublished, Burton Historical Collection, Detroit Public Library, Detroit, Michigan.

49. M. Marguerite Davenport, *Azalia: the Life of Madame E. Azalia Hackley* (Boston, 1947), 44.

50. Richards was rather well-known in Detroit at the end of her career. Her retirement warranted an article in the *Detroit News-Tribune*, and her death was front page news in 1922. *Detroit News-Tribune*, June 20, 1915. *Detroit News*, February 16, 1922. A book of pioneering black women listed Richards as one of five successful black teachers in white schools that were "establishing the ability of Afro-American women," indicating that Richards' reputation extended beyond the borders of Detroit. M. A. Majors, *Noted Negro Women—Their Triumphs and Activities* (Chicago, 1893), 171. Today she is still remembered for her pioneering role; her portrait hangs in the Detroit Public Library and a city school bears her name.

51. Federation of Colored Women's Clubs Records, 60-14-A, B1, F38. Pelham graduated in 1881. M. Pelham personnel record, Detroit Public Schools, Detroit, Michigan. Of the class that entered in 1881, only 16 of 160 students graduated. Moehlman, *Public Education in Detroit*, 145.

52. Davenport, *Azalia*, 41, 86.

53. Katzman, *Before the Ghetto*, 69.

54. Newspaper clipping, from the *Detroit Journal*, undated but probably from 1894. Found in the Parson Scrapbook, Burton Historical Collection, Detroit Public Library, Detroit, Michigan.

55. Clara Shewcraft personnel file, Detroit Public Schools, Detroit, Michigan.

56. Meta Pelham taught at Everett School after Fannie Richards retired in 1915. Azalia Smith and Etta Edna Lee both taught at Clinton School, though not at the same time.

57. George Fredrickson, *The Black Image in the White Mind* (New York: Harper Row, 1971).

58. Patricia Morton, *Disfigured Images* (Westport, CT: Praeger, 1990), xii.

59. Joan Wallach Scott, *Gender and the Politics of History* (New York: Columbia University Press, 1988), 43.

60. From the earliest contacts, Europeans associated Africans with the animal world and its corresponding unbridled sexual lust. Winthrop Jordan, *Black Over White:*

American Attitudes toward the Negro 1550-1812 (Chapel Hill, NC: University of North Carolina Press, 1968).

61. Like ministers, teacher's lives were subject to scrutiny. David Riesman, *Constraint and Variety in American Education* (Garden City, NY: Doubleday and Company, Inc., 1956), 125.

62. *Detroit Free Press*, June 20, 1915.

63. Gerda Lerner, *Black Women in White America: A Documentary History* (New York: Vintage Books, 1973), 436.

64. Robin S. Peebles, "Detroit's Black Women's Clubs," *Michigan History*, 48.

65. Dorothy Salem, *To Better Our World: Black Women in Organized Reform, 1890-1920* (Brooklyn: Carlson Publishing, Inc., 1990), 30.

66. Linda Gordon, "Black and White Visions of Welfare: Women's Welfare Activism, 1890-1945," *Journal of American History* 78 (September 1991), 559-90.

67. Salem, *To Better Our World*, 68.

68. Over 100 of these homes were created between 1890 and 1913. Meier, *Negro Thought*, 134.

69. Salem, *To Better Our World*, 78.

70. Meier, *Negro Thought*, 135.

71. See minutes of the meetings of the Detroit Study Club for December 11, 1886; March 2, 1887; and April 14, 1910. Records of the Detroit Study Club, Burton Historical Collection, Detroit Public Library, Detroit, Michigan. Box 4, Folder 2.

72. Minutes for the May 7, 1909 meeting of the club. The actual DuBois letter is not in the collection. Records of the Detroit Study Club, Box 3, Folder 2, 5.

73. 12 of the 75 members of the Michigan Federation of Colored Women's Clubs were teachers at one time. MFCWC, 60-14-A, B1. In 1910, 0.003 percent of black Michigan women worked as teachers. This group was 0.009 percent of employed black women. U. S. Bureau of the Census, *Negro Population, 1790-1915*, 518, 521.

74. Peebles, "Detroit's Black Women's Clubs," 48.

75. Lucy Johnson, "History of the Detroit Study Club," unpublished manuscript in the Records of the Detroit Study Club.

76. Moehlman, *Public Education in Detroit*, 111.

77. Salem, *To Better Our World*, 30. Lynda F. Dickson, "Toward a Broader Angle of Vision in Uncovering Women's History: Black Women's Clubs Revisited," in Darlene Clark Hine, ed., *Black Women in United States History* (Brooklyn: Carlson Publishing, Inc., 1990), 117.

78. Mary Taylor Blauvelt, "The Race Problem as Discussed by Negro Women," *American Journal of Sociology* VI (1911), 662-672. Blauvelt attended a meeting of the MFCWC, and that is the basis for her article.

79. Darlene Clark Hine, "Black Women's History, White Women's History: the Juncture of Race and Class," *Journal of Women's History*, Vol. 4, No. 2 (Fall 1992), 125-133.

80. Blauvelt, "The Race Problem," 665.

81. Records of the Detroit Study Club, Burton Historical Collection, Detroit Public Library, Detroit, Michigan. Box 3, Folder 1.

82. Davenport, *Azalia*, 93, 148, 157. A building at Hampton University was named after Azalia Smith Hackley for her contributions to the race.

83. *Ibid.*, 50.

19

Still in Chains:

Black Women in Western Prisons, 1865-1910

Anne M. Butler

> ... the said Sarah King was one of a number of contraband Negroes brought
> to St. Louis from Alabama, who were all huddled together in some miserable
> hut ... and the child of this woman was found with a ten dollar gold piece in
> its possession ... and upon the testimony of the child ... being found with
> such a piece of money, she [Sarah King] was convicted and sentenced to two
> years.[1]

So wrote a petitioner seeking a pardon for Sarah King, an Alabama mulatto
woman, whose legal difficulties in Missouri began sometime in the spring of
1864. The petitioner, Mrs. Lavina P. Jorden, who wanted King released to her
for domestic service, assured Governor Thomas Fletcher that the former slave
had a husband away with the federal army, had a child who needed motherly
attention, was a "good ... trusty ... patient and faithful" black woman, and
that "the whole affair" was just a "kind of Negro fuss."[2]

Actually, "the whole affair" is suggestive of much more than a simple
fuss. Nowhere in the country did opportunity seem more alluring after the
Civil War than in the most promising of natural regions—the American West.
It has been well documented that displaced persons—black and white, male
and female—turned to the expanses of the frontier with hope for a more
promising future.[3] The Far West beckoned as the "new" region, where Americans could put aside the antiblack, antislave preoccupations that had obsessed
the cultures of North and South. In this emerging society, migrating blacks
must have anticipated that the lingering vestiges of a slave society would dissi-
pate in the face of a frontier tradition that allegedly judged people less by their
color and more by their pluck and hard work.[4]

However, the Sarah King episode casts a shadow across such easy notions, so cherished in the nation's stereotypical vision of the West. The blatantly
circumstantial evidence under which the Missouri court sent King to the state
penitentiary raises the possibility that black women, especially within the context of their incarceration in western prisons, faced a frontier more hostile than
expansive, more oppressive than egalitarian. These frontier penitentiaries have
drawn their share of scholarly attention, but most accounts contain only a
passing general reference to female prisoners and rarely give details about
black women convicts as a group.[5] Yet records drawn from several state penal

systems indicate that the freedom, the justice, the opportunity so often associated, however mythically, with the American frontier continued to elude black women long after the official demise of slavery. This paper does not suggest that black male prisoners enjoyed elements of freedom and justice while women did not. Prison registers and investigative reports give ample contrary documentation. Sample evidence can be found in any register or report cited in this paper that black men endured inhumane assaults on their dignity and the obliteration of their legal rights. However, an underlying thrust of this article rests on the notion that the significant dynamics of black womanhood have been ignored or de-emphasized in the process of suggesting that the most important result of slavery concerns its demoralizing impact on black men.[6] Whether part of a large Texas population or a small Montana group, black women found that racism, which had earlier been an energizing force of institutional slavery, retained its most powerful forms inside the penal system.

This article focuses, with only limited comparative pretenses, on the experiences of black women in western prisons. It does so in an effort to recapture one aspect of the black frontier, which deserves its own consideration as a western process. Racial comparisons in the saga of western development cannot be entirely appreciated until the black frontier assumes its own identity. Black westerners should not be expected to stand forever in the shadow of the white experience. Although the women here were few in number and scattered about the West, the fundamental commonality of their incarceration suggests that the full scope of frontier life for blacks has yet to be unraveled.

Although the punishment of slaves rested with owners before the end of the Civil War, occasionally blacks were turned over to the local courts. For example, in 1846 a fifteen-year-old mentally retarded slave, Nelly, was indicted for the murder of her infant. White citizens of the community, Warrenton, Missouri, petitioned on her behalf and asked for her release. They cited Nelly's youth, her mental limitations, the possibility that the child was stillborn, and emphasized that a public trial would be a social embarrassment to the widow and ten children of Nelly's recently deceased owner, the apparent father of her infant. Supported by a white community distressed for its own reputation, Nelly was pardoned 14 October 1846.[7]

By 1866, prison registers, in border and former slave states, began to show a dramatic rise in the number of blacks incarcerated, and, among them, more and more women. This was particularly true in Louisiana where, after 1869, the decentralized state penal system fell under the private control of a former Confederate officer, Major Samuel Jones. Dissatisfied with the loose structure of the penitentiary, Jones began to phase out convict leasing from Baton Rouge to levees, farms, and railroad labor camps around the state. He preferred to concentrate the prisoners at is isolated 18,000 acre plantation, Angola, located on the eastern bank of the Mississippi River; Jones initiated his plan, transferring the Louisiana women convicts to that location in 1881.[8]

Louisiana's intimate economic and cultural bonding of blacks and whites, coupled with the state's extensive lands in the trans-Mississippi, make this particular "Gateway to the West" a sound base from which to cast a profile of the nineteenth century black female prisoner. Between 1866 and 1872, sixty-seven women entered the Louisiana state prison system. Black and mulatto women accounted for sixty-four of those women. They ranged in age from thirteen to seventy-seven, and, but for one, all had been born in slave states. The convictions listed three murderers, one kidnapper, one leader of a riot, and three women committed without any criminal charges against them, apparently on the whim of officers in their home counties. The remaining fifty-six black women—including the girl of thirteen and the elderly woman of seventy-seven—faced sentences of three to twenty-four months for charges in some way connected to robbery or larceny.[9] Only one entry in the register identifies the stolen property, and its scant value indicates that in Louisiana a misdemeanor could mean a lengthy term at hard labor; a forty-eight-year-old mulatto woman found herself sentenced to three months in state penitentiary, rather than the country jail, for stealing a shirt.[10]

Other aspects of these former slaves' lives can be extrapolated from the register data. Of the sixty-four black women remanded to state officials for this period, only five could read; of those five, one could write. In addition to their cultural deprivation, these women came to prison literally bearing the physical scars of their earlier lives. Generations of dietary deficiency told in their heights: only eight stood taller than five feet four inches, more than thirty measured five fee two inches or below. On these diminutive frames, the women carried weights that averaged between 120 and 140 pounds. Young women, many not yet twenty-five years old, had already sustained massive injuries. Blindness in one eye, the absence of all teeth, disfigurement from burns, disease, and wounds were the prisoners' usual distinguishing characteristics.[11]

The register listed the occupation of most women to be "common laborer," and the work they did, whether inside the prison or outside for a local citizen, was a continuation of the domestic labor and field drudgery of their slave days.[12] Those who thought to escape this dreary existence might have been deterred by the story of Alice Dunbar. In 1868, Dunbar bolted from the superintendent's office after serving almost a full year of an eighteen-month sentence. The authorities did not apprehend her until 1871, when she was returned to the state prison system.[13] Upon completion of her outstanding six months, Dunbar received her discharge; officials added no extension to her sentence, for, just as during slavery days, this fifty-one-year-old black woman had paid for her escape attempt—stripped to the waist and flogged with a cat-o-nine tails.[14]

This picture of black women of all ages—poor, abused, illiterate, and unjustly imprisoned—blended easily with other historical data about the most extreme treatment inflicted on former slaves in cultures of the Deep South, regardless of Louisiana's hefty territorial tilt into the Far West.[15] Yet Louisiana provided a foundation from which to assess the power of southern racial attitudes in the development of western communities, the tolerance of northerners for antiblack sentiment, and the transference of societal standards and values into frontier communities. Accordingly, more may be explained about the impact of the South on the ultimate regional identity of the trans-Mississippi West. Certainly, in relation to the subject of penal institutions, it seems clear that the experiences of Louisiana black convict women set a tone for the patterns found on the far frontier.

In Texas, for example, penal authorities consulted more than once with their Louisiana neighbors about prison management, and in the Lone Star State freed black women faced a judicial system not one bit friendlier.[16] In 1867, William Sinclair, an inspector for the Bureau of Refugees, Freedman, and Abandoned Lands, sought executive clemency for former slaves detained at the Huntsville penitentiary.[17] Among the 220 blacks that Sinclair hoped to assist, he listed fourteen women, all of whom had been slaves. In a passionate letter to his superiors, Sinclair called the convicts "the innocent and unfortunate victims of their [former owners'] wrath and disappointment."[18] Convinced that the prisoners were guilty of little or no crime and outraged that most of them had been held in a county jail for at least six months prior to trial, Sinclair determined to document the injustices through interviews with each black convict.[19] Other than Elvira Mays, who had given her jailed husband a home-baked pie, the filling of which included an inedible axe, all these Texas black women were in prison for some type of thievery charge. Their thefts included stealing a hog, a nightgown, a pair of drapes, a petticoat, a pair of stockings, and $1.00. Sinclair found these women incarcerated in the state penitentiary for terms that ranged from two to five years at hard labor.[20]

By 1874, interested parties like Sinclair had retreated from Texas, and the control of the Huntsville penitentiary had passed into the hands of a private contractor. Any semblance of human decency inside the prison collapsed. Local Texans complained about the screams and groans that came from the prison or its surrounding rural labor camps; outside the state, prison reformers held the facility in low regard.[21] The charges of corruption had become so widespread that businessmen who retained a fifteen-year contract on Texas convict labor felt compelled to address the 1874 National Prison Congress at St. Louis, Missouri.

The speaker, Colonel A.J. Ward, who served as prison manager, assured the St. Louis delegates that by his presence he wanted the Texas penitentiary to be brought, "into more . . . understood relations with the . . . workers in the cause of the prisons . . . ."[22] He then outlined the Texas system. He declared it differed from any in the East because his prisoners were drawn from the "ignorant masses" and lacked "cleverness and intelligence." Ward attempted to soften his thinly disguised racial slurs by insisting that the prison operated on a plan for the reformation of the convicts. This included an appeal to self-respect, coupled with religious and educational opportunities, all supplemented by peaceful and cheery visits from family and friends. In an astonishing gesture, Ward invited members of the Prison Congress to visit Huntsville and make a first hand inspection of its effective management.[23]

Ward's boldness and stupidity are indeed surprising in the wake of subsequent testimony leveled against him later in the same year. Granted, he had not inherited a penitentiary system in mint condition, but under his management the abuses toward prisoners reached new extremes.[24] The contours of Ward's administration became public knowledge when the U.S. Army decided to transfer into the Kansas State Penitentiary two groups of military prisoners found near death at Huntsville. Late in 1874, these prisoners, the barely living repudiation of Ward's earlier assertions about reformation and self-respect, provided some eye-witness accounts of how women fared with Colonel Ward as the overseer at Huntsville.[25]

For years officials had known that Huntsville conditions violated state laws that required segregation of the sexes in both living and work arrangements. Routinely, women and men shared a common bunkhouse or had adjacent cells and worked together in the cotton factory. These infractions seemed almost mild amidst the grisly reports of filth and brutality volunteered by the rescued military prisoners. They recounted a bleak tale of the fourteen women prisoners, at least twelve of whom were black; none had been extricated from Huntsville by the government inspector.[26]

According to the reports given in Kansas, Texas inmates of both sexes mingled without constraints during both work and leisure hours. Women convicts roamed the yard, carrying the infants conceived and born inside the penitentiary. Apparently, guards or male prisoners fathered these children, although inmates could be severely punished if sexual liaisons were discovered by the administration.[27]

The prison doctor, a white convict, repeatedly bragged of his coercive sexual relations with a black female prisoner, "Old Jane." During her imprisonment, Jane gave birth to a child of black and white parentage. The prisoners thought the convict doctor to be the father, although he received no punishment for the infraction. Perhaps his prison status as the doctor excused him. Jane had no privileges to save her from punishment for this pregnancy.

Immediately after the birth, the authorities separated the mother and newborn infant and closed Jane in the dungeon. Before she entered the isolation cell, Jane endured that special humiliation so often inflicted on women "offenders" through time: officials shaved her head.[28] The postponement of these penalties until after the child's arrival is without explanation, for certainly either could have been carried out during the pregnancy. There is the twisted possibility that, even in an environment as devoid of human dignity as a nineteenth century rural prison, the aura generated by pregnancy might grant to women a temporary modicum of "protection" and "respect." That prison officials should find violence toward women so tolerable, but decree it to be suspended because of pregnancy, highlights the distorted race and gender dynamics, not only on the frontier, but throughout American society.

If pregnancy abated the worst abuses, it was the only time that women prisoners could expect the slightest relief. Generally the system spared women convicts no form of punishment. Guards hung women in the stocks so that the tips of their toes barely touched the ground. Women were beaten, raped, and forced to "ride" the wooden horse. Prisoners regarded this device, a pick-handle that had been embedded into an upright post, as the most brutal torture at Huntsville. A convict forced to straddle this apparatus had to dangle in space without moving. The inmates reported they felt a creeping paralysis spread through the genitalia, legs, and arms before they passed out.[29]

Through a parade of prison managers at Huntsville, women convicts found that very little changed over the next several years. In 1909 a committee investigating abuses in the penitentiary system visited a female camp a few miles from the Huntsville prison. In that camp, the committee found seventy-one women prisoners.[30] Of these, sixty-seven were black women. The four non-black convicts—three white women and one Hispanic—lived in quarters apart from the black women and performed the lighter domestic chores about the facility. Black women inmates toiled at all types of heavy field cultivation. The evidence of sexual misconduct by state employees working at the women's camp was so severe that the committee considered it too shocking for publication and refused to include the information in the final report.[31]

The Texas prison system, a rural agricultural operation, fashioned somewhat intentionally along the lines of the Louisiana penitentiary, had not much improved since the horrified government inspector, William Sinclair, made his report in 1867. Black women continued to outnumber whites, they still did the heavy labor of field hands, and they had little or no protection against physical and sexual assaults by male inmates and overseers.

Although in 1874 the Kansas authorities had publicized the Texas abuses with some degree of smugness, even a cursory look at the penal system in the former state suggests that it paralleled Huntsville more than officials wanted to acknowledge.[32] The 1874 happy boast of "point[ing] in triumph to the condition of our Kansas penitentiary" might not have been echoed by black women who served time in that prison.[33]

Between 1865 and 1906 the Kansas penitentiary received approximately 200 women; of these at least 150 were black or mulatto females.[34] From the prisoner data, regularly recorded only after 1883, two items suggest some cultural changes for black women. First, these Kansas black women were generally taller than their Louisiana counterparts of two decades earlier, with the new average heights falling between five feet four inches and five feet six inches. Body scars from cuts and burns remained about the same. Perhaps more important, the literacy statistics of an earlier era had been almost reversed. From among approximately 125 women prisoners, 109 could read and write, an apparent affirmation of the oft made claim that blacks eagerly sought educational opportunities after the Civil War.[35] Other aspects of their experiences, however, had not changed that much.

Of the fifty women who entered the Kansas system between 31 December 1901 and 7 January 1906, thirty-two were black. Three of these women were older than thirty, twenty-four of them were between the ages of seventeen and twenty-five; only one had served a previous prison term in Kansas or elsewhere. Nine women were imprisoned for violent crimes such as arson or manslaughter; one woman was sentenced for bigamy. However, the majority of black women entered the Kansas penitentiary for a conviction related to robbery or larceny. Most received sentences of from one to five years, although one woman faced a term of eleven years. With the exception of two laborers and one seamstress, all these black women gave some form of housework—cooking, washing, cleaning—as their occupation.[36]

The black women imprisoned in Kansas more than thirty-five years after the close of the Civil War continued to reflect the patterns prevalent among the Louisiana and Texas convicts. Most were young, poor women charged with crimes connected to the domestic services they performed. Although the Kansas recorder identified none of the missing property, it seems likely that white employers charged black domestics with thievery of items comparable to the stolen goods listed in the Texas register some years before.

The physical conditions in the prison also paralleled standards common in Louisiana and Texas. During an investigation into punishments at the Kansas State Penitentiary, matrons of the female ward testified that as late as 1910 strait jackets, handcuffs, and gags were routinely used to restrain female prisoners.[37] One warden had "rings . . . placed in the wall . . . of the female ward, for the purpose of extending the arms of prisoners for punishment, the . . . arms being fastened to a ring and extended above the prisoner's head."[38]

In 1905, Florence Akers, a twenty-year-old mulatto cook from Texas, received a sentence of from five to twenty-one years in the Kansas penitentiary on a charge of manslaughter.[39] The county attorney declared Akers to have "associates . . . of the worst class . . . their principle business [is] holding up and robbing people," and insisted she had operated with this gang in several Kansas and Missouri towns.[40] Akers conceded that everything in her past was not perfect, but denied her connection to the gang and hoped that, as this charge represented her first trouble with the law, she might be released to assist in the care of her insane sister, Lulu.[41] Other officials involved in the case tended to agree that Akers's main crime had been to be caught in a house of "tough women," who proceeded to testify against her. Over a period of five and one-half years, the arresting sheriff, the local jailer, a prison guard, and her lawyer all petitioned for her pardon. In 1910 the sheriff declared to Governor Walter Stubbs that Florence Akers had "served long enough for another's crime."[42] J.B. Bowers, a black guard at the penitentiary, wrote that he and his wife believed the young woman innocent and offered help after her release. That did not come until Akers had served more than five years for a murder she apparently did not commit.[43] The local jailer summed it up bluntly when he wrote to the governor, "Florence Akers was Railroaded."[44]

If so, she was not alone in Kansas, or in other states, some of which may appear remote from the most odious aspects of southern race relations. Linked to the national slavery debates by the Kansas-Nebraska Act, the latter state, overshadowed in history by the dramatic events that occurred in the former, always seemed peripheral to frontier race issues. Additionally, the preponderance of Scandinavian immigrants who plunged into farming on the Nebraska plains cast a European tone to area demographics that further distanced the state from border regions where black-white interaction might be expected.

Yet within the Nebraska penitentiary the patterns of incarceration for black women mirrored those of the deep southern frontier states in startling ways. Between 1869 and 1910, Nebraska imprisoned ninety women.[45] Of these, there were fifty-one black women, nine white women, a single native American, and one Hispanic. The records leave the racial identity of the remaining twenty-eight women unclear, although it seems certain that given the disproportionate number of blacks, some of these prisoners should be counted in that group.[46]

Among the black women, eleven had been convicted of a violent crime and had received sentences ranging from one to seven years. None of these women secured a gubernatorial pardon, and all, with one exception, served from one-half to three-fourths of her time before parole.[47] One prisoner, convicted of procuring, served two months in the state penitentiary for a crime usually penalized at the county level. The remaining thirty-nine black women went to the penitentiary for a charge of robbery or larceny. All of these convicts served the full amount of time before parole eligibility or a "good time" release. The governor interceded for only one black woman, serving four years for robbery. He commuted her sentence so that she could be transferred to the insane asylum.[48]

Statistics for white women prisoners are difficult to compare since only nine can be identified with certainty in a forty-one-year period. That small group included two convicted as bigamists, two sentenced for grand larceny, and five imprisoned for murder, manslaughter, or assault. These last five included two women with no occupations, one housekeeper, one dressmaker, and one prostitute. The two bigamists—one a nineteen-year-old chambermaid, the other a twenty-eight-year-old seamstress—entered guilty pleas and served until eligible for discharge. Of the two women convicted for grand larceny, one served her time and one received a pardon from the governor. Of the white women imprisoned for crimes of violence, one served until released for "good time," one died in prison, one shunted back and forth to the insane asylum, and two received gubernatorial pardons.[49]

Although the pool for comparison is small, the experiences of black and white women prisoners seem to have varied in Nebraska. In the first instance, white women simply did not enter the state penal system in numbers comparable to black women. This suggests that white women who broke the law, with the exception of some extremely poor ones who offended sexual social conventions, served their sentences at the local level. Generally, white women did not face the grand larceny and robbery convictions that included imprisonment in the state penitentiary, as did black women. Furthermore, although gubernatorial intervention remained limited, white women convicted of violent crimes appear to have had a better chance for executive pardon than black women.

Indeed, great distance from the pervasiveness of southern culture did not seem to enhance the situation for black women. Even in the face of the most flimsy evidence, juries did not hesitate to send black women to the state penitentiary. Such was the rueful discovery of Bessie Fisher, a black prostitute who moved to Butte, Montana, in 1901. Fisher shot and killed "Big Eva" Smith when the larger woman lunged forward with threats of a beating. Despite the testimony of an eyewitness that Fisher fired in self-defense, the corroboration from the coroner's inquest, and the expectation of the prosecutor that the defendant would be acquitted, the jury returned a verdict of second degree murder.[50] Nineteen-year-old Bessie Fisher entered the Montana State Penitentiary where she became one of the twenty-three black women from among sixty female prisoners (ten white, twenty-seven not identified) incarcerated from 1888-1910.[51] There, despite her attorney's promise to secure a new trial, she languished for more than one-half of her twenty year sentence without the benefit of parole or pardon.[52]

From Louisiana to Montana, black women, burdened both by race and gender, juggled an uneasy relationship with western society. Most commonly, those who were arrested and convicted were young, uneducated women with negligible resources. When apprehended by the law, black women found a series of injustices set into motion; their crimes were often minor or nonexistent, serious charges materialized around the most questionable or circumstantial evidence, the issue of guilt or innocence became unimportant, a prison sentence tended to exceed the seriousness of the crime, parole and pardon procedures favored white female prisoners, and treatment inside the prisons emphasized brutality. If imprisoned wrongfully, a black woman's main hope for assistance lay with concern of a good-spirited attorney, the efforts of a devoted family, or the desire of a local resident for cheap, docile labor. Without one of these sources, black women who entered state penitentiaries became forgotten citizens on the American frontier.

The experiences of black women in western prisons demand that historians ask more finely turned questions about the concepts of justice and equality in frontier communities, as well as the way in which social values were transmitted from region to region. Although black female prison populations never assumed large numbers, the constraints these women faced hardly varied from state to state. While all prisoners faced extreme treatment in nineteenth-century institutions, black women in the states surveyed were more likely to be sent to the state penitentiary, serve their full sentence, and be excluded from pardon procedures than white women who committed comparable crimes. The apparent indifference with which officials and private citizens tolerated questionable court procedures and prison atrocities points to the power of racial discrimination in the burgeoning West, regardless of a state's geographical location.

The evidence here suggests that southern antiblack attitudes permeated western communities close to and beyond the confines of Dixie. Within these five states there are indications that southern racial values remained a powerful force, regardless of the size of the black population. Whether there were many or few blacks in a state, authorities applied the penal code with haste and vigor against offenders. Racism, invincible as ever after the death of slavery, shaped the quality of life for blacks more than community regard for frontier pluck and individual hard work.

This serves to remind Americans that, once again, the meaning of opportunity in the West demands a reassessment to determine where, for whom, and under what conditions such a happy status existed. As for the black women listed in the prison registers of Louisiana, Texas, Kansas, Nebraska, and Montana, the West appears to have offered an uncertain freedom and little justice. Rather, these black women found that, in the West, a forge of racism reshaped the chains of slavery into the bars of a penitentiary.

NOTES

The author thanks the Research Division of Gallaudet University for funding.

1. Mrs. Lavina P. Jorden to Governor Thomas Fletcher, February 1865, Sara King File, State of Missouri: Pardon Papers, Record Group [Hereafter RG] 5, Box 19, Missouri State Archives, Jefferson City, Missouri [Hereafter MSA].

2. *Ibid.*

3. For general treatment, see Richard A. Bartlett, *The New Country: A Social History of the American Frontier, 1776-1890.* (New York, 1974); Norman Crockett, *The Black Towns* (Lawrence, 1979); Gerald McFarland, *A Scattered People: An American Family Moves West* (New York, 1987), esp. 175-245; Sandra L. Myres, *Westering Women and the Frontier Experience: 1800-1915* (Albuquerque, 1982), esp. 238-70; Randall Bennett Woods, *A Black Odyssey: John Lewis Waller and the Promise of American Life, 1878-1900* (Lawrence, 1981). Black migration to the frontier was, at least partially, impelled by a general feeling of optimism that, according to Benjamin Quarles, characterized the feelings of former slaves in the immediate postwar era. *The Negro in the Making of America* (New York, 1964), 126. Harold Hyman's assertion that in the first flush of Reconstruction, Republican politicians believed that, "States would no longer impose on individuals the desperate disabilities that slavery represented . . . ," may further explain why black men and women turned to the West for social and political freedoms they suspected would be grudgingly offered in the Old South. See *A More Perfect Union: The Impact of the Civil War and Reconstruction on the Constitution* (Boston, 1975), 283.

4. With the emergence of black history in the 1960s, it became clear that the frontier experience of Afro-Americans had been largely ignored. Some of the first attempts to redress that neglect tended to simply affirm the presence of blacks on the frontier. For example, Philip Durham and Everett L. Jones, *The Negro Cowboys* (New York, 1965), and William Loren Katz, *The Black West* (Garden City, 1971). These authors

did not entirely ignore western discrimination, but their goals seem to have been to document the black experience as a reality. Their works were followed by scholars who questioned more closely the quality of frontier justice for blacks. For example, Robert G. Athearn, *In Search of Canaan: Black Migration to Kansas, 1879-1880* (Lawrence, 1978); Thomas C. Cox, *Blacks in Topeka, Kansas, 1865-1915: A Social History* (Baton Rouge, 1982); Randall Bennet Woods, "Integration, Exclusion, or Segregation? The 'Color Line' in Kansas: 1878-1900," *Western Historical Quarterly*, 14 (April 1983), 181-98.

5. For examples see Garland E. Bayliss, "The Arkansas State Penitentiary Under Democratic Control, 1874-1896," *Arkansas Historical Quarterly*, 34 (Autumn 1975), 195-213; Gary R. Kremer and Thomas E. Gage, "The Prison Against the Town: Jefferson City and the Penitentiary in the 19th Century," *Missouri Historical Review*, 74 (July 1980), 414-32; Harvey R. Hougen, "The Impact of Politics and Prison Industry on the General Management of the Kansas State Penitentiary, 1883-1909," *Kansas Historical Quarterly*, 43 (Autumn 1977), 297-318; Paul G. Hubbard, "Life in the Arizona Territorial Prison, 1876-1910," *Arizona and the West*, 1 (Winter 1959), 317-30; William C. Nesheim, "A History of the Missouri State Penitentiary: 1833-1875" (master's thesis, University of Missouri-Kansas City, 1970); Gordon L. Olson, "'I Felt Like I Must Be Entering . . . Another World': The Anonymous Memoirs of an Early Inmate of the Wyoming Penitentiary," *Annals of Wyoming*, 47 (Fall 1975), 152-90; James A. Wilson, "Frontier in the Shadows: Prisons in the Far Southwest, 1850-1917," *Arizona and the West*, 22 (Winter 1980), 323-42. Material about gender, race, and American prisons is found in Nicole Hahn Rafter, "Gender, Prisons, and Prison History," *Social Science History*, 9 (Summer 1985), 233-47, and by the same author, *Partial Justice: Women in State Prisons, 1800-1935* (Boston, 1985).

6. See also John Vodicka's "Prison Plantation: The Story of Angola," *Southern Exposure*, 6 (Number 4, 1978), 32-38. Vodicka claims that between 1870-1901 more than 3,000 Louisiana convicts, almost all black men, died under the lease system. For black womanhood, see bell hooks, *Ain't I a Woman: Black Women and Feminism* (Boston, 1981), and Pauli Murray, "The Liberation of Black Women," in *Our American Sisters: Women in American Life and Thought*, 4th ed., ed. Jean E. Friedman et al. (Lexington, MA, 1987), 557-59.

7. Citizens' Petitions, Nelly ——— File, State of Missouri: Pardon and Parole Papers, RG 5, Box 3, MSA. For a general discussion see Herman Lee Crow, "A Political History of the Texas Penal System: 1829-1951" (doctoral dissertation, University of Texas, 1964), 85-86.

8. The process by which the Louisiana penitentiary came to be located at the Angola plantation stretched across a broad expanse of time. In 1835 the state moved its convicts from New Orleans to Baton Rouge. Under Jones's administration the relocation of prisoners to Angola was accomplished before his death in 1894. Assistant Warden Roger S. Thomas, Interview with author, Louisiana State Penitentiary, Angola, Louisiana [Hereafter LSP], 22 June 1987. See also, Assistant Warden Roger S. Thomas to Warden Frank C. Blackburn, Unpublished Reports, "The History of Angola Series," 24 September, 23 October, 27 December 1985, and 7 January 1986, Office of the Warden, LSP. See also, Vodicka, "Prison Plantation."

9. All data drawn from Louisiana State Penitentiary Register of Convicts Received: 13 February 1866-29 December 1889, Prisoners #1-9073, Office of the Warden,

LSP. These years were summarized since it was an era when the Unionist government wanted to exert a strong hand in Louisiana, and it might be expected that blacks enjoyed some measure of legal protection from arbitrary arrest and imprisonment. Actually, by 1873 there was ample evidence that any such protection was rapidly collapsing. See William S. McFeely, *Grant: A Biography* (New York, 1982), 417-18.

10. Eugenie Comes, Prisoner #183, Louisiana State Penitentiary, Register of Convicts Received: 13 February 1866-29 December 1899, Prisoners #1-9073, Office of the Warden, LSP.

11. *Ibid.*, passim. See especially entries for Prisoners #61, 94, 150, 217, 300, 301, 460, 726, 954, 1074, 1549, 1716, 2261, 2265, 2288, and 2289.

12. Assistant Warden Roger S. Thomas, Interview with the author, 22 June 1987. Also see Assistant Warden Roger S. Thomas to Warden Frank C. Blackburn, Unpublished Reports, "The History of Angola Series," 12 December 1985, Office of the Warden, LSP. Domestic use of black female convicts was common in other states, as well. By 1865, ten black women inmates staffed the penitentiary kitchen at the Texas prison. See Crow, "A Political History, 85. Also, parole requests for black women most commonly stemmed from the desire of a local white woman to secure domestic help. See samples from records of the following states: Prisoner Files #1391, 3337, 948, and 21695, Arkansas Department of Corrections, Pine Bluff, Arkansas; Pardon and Parole Papers, State of Missouri, RG 5; Box 22, Folder 2; Box 23, Folders 7 and 17; Box 25, Folders 10 and 26; Box 31, Folder 10; MSA; and Pardon and Parole Files, Governor's Office, Kansas State Penitentiary, Box 1, Florence Akers; Box 2, Ella Anderson; Box 13, Ella Bradfield; Box 20, Annie Carmack; Box 36, Bertha Draper; Kansas State Historical Society, Topeka, Kansas [Hereafter KSHS].

13. Alice Dunbar, Prisoner #529, Louisiana State Penitentiary, Register of Convicts Received: 13 February 1866-29 December 1899, Prisoners #1-9073, Office of the Warden, LSP.

14. Assistant Warden Roger S. Thomas, Interview with author, 22 June 1987. Assistant Warden S. Thomas to Warden Frank C. Blackburn, Unpublished Reports, "The History of Angola Series," 13 June 1986, Office of the Warden, LSP. By *de facto* policy this became a punishment reserved for black women, since officials almost never held white women inside the prison walls. Brutal physical punishments were not unknown in most nineteenth-century prisons. Nonetheless, black women often caught the greater brunt of such treatment. See Rafter, *Partial Justice*, 150-51.

15. For general treatment see, John Hope Franklin, *Reconstruction: After the Civil War* (Chicago, 1961); Rayford W. Logan, *The Betrayal of the Negro: From Rutherford B. Hayes to Woodrow Wilson* (New York, 1965); August Meier and Elliott Rudwick, *From Plantation to Ghetto* (New York, 1970); and McFeely, *Grant*.

16. Crow, "A Political History," 47, 69.

17. William H. Sinclair to Lt. J.F. Kirkman, 26 February 1867, Records of the Bureau of Refugees, Freedmen, and Abandoned Lands, RG 105, Texas, Assistant Commissioner, Letters Received Register, vol. 1, 1866-67, Box 4, N-S, National Archives, Washington, D.C. The author thanks Barry A. Crouch of Gallaudet University for this research material.

18. *Ibid.*, 3.

19. *Ibid.*, 23.

20. *Ibid.*, 8. Sinclair apparently failed in his efforts to correct this situation. A Reconstruction committee that convened in June 1868 recommended that most of the 160 convicts at the Texas penitentiary should be granted executive clemency. See Crow, "A Political History," 47, 69.

21. *Ibid.*, 101-103; *Public Institutions, Second Annual Report of the Board of Commissioners: Kansas State Penitentiary* (Topeka, 1875), 294; Michael A. Kroll, "The Prison Experiment: A Circular History," *Southern Exposure*, 6 (Number 4, 1978), 9; Blake McKelvey, "A Half Century of Southern Penal Exploitation," *Social Forces*, 13 (Number 1, 1934-35), 113-16.

22. Ward, Dewey, and Company Lessees, "The Texas State Penitentiary," from the *Transactions of the Prison Congress, 1874*, repr. *Public Institutions*, 339.

23. *Ibid.*, 340-42.

24. Crow, "A Political History," 77, 96.

25. *Public Institutions*, 343, 351.

26. One prisoner's testimony seems to suggest that two of the women prisoners were white. *Ibid.*, 346.

27. *Ibid.*, 346-49.

28. *Ibid.*, 349, 351.

29. *Ibid.*, 346-47.

30. The efforts of Texas officials to correct abuses by placing women in a separate female facility failed to produce the desired reform. None of several plans, for example, in 1895, 1907, or 1909, brought any real change. See Crow, "A Political History," 178, 197-98. See also Rafter, *Partial Justice*, 88-89.

31. Crow, "A Political History," 178.

32. Selection of Lansing, Kansas, as the site for the state penitentiary dated to 1867. Penal institutions dominated the history of Lansing and its neighbor, Leavenworth. The presence of federal, state, and military authorities shaped the economic and social direction of the people of both communities. It was not uncommon for local citizens to escort visitors on a guided tour through the Leavenworth prison, as late as 1908. See Sister Mary Celestia Letters, Prison Ministry File, 1908-1915, Archives, Sisters of Charity, Leavenworth, Kansas. Also, Sister M. Seraphine, D.C., Interview with author, 3 July 1987, Leavenworth, Kansas.

33. *Public Institutions*, 352. Harvey R. Hougen argues that Warden Henry Hopkins' administration from 1867-1883 was marked by a generally progressive spirit that faltered under later managements. In "The Impact of Politics," Hougen does not discuss women in the Kansas prison.

34. Prison records in Kansas were not always consistently maintained. Racial designations did not become a regular entry until after 1883. Therefore, the actual number of black female prisoners received may have been somewhat higher than noted here. See those prison registers after 1880, especially Statement of Convicts, Prison Ledger A, 1864-1919, KSHS. In the same agency, Pardon and Parole Files, 1863-1919 and photographs from the state penitentiary are useful in compiling prisoner information.

35. Failure to record all data for all prisoners makes an accurate reading of this material difficult. Sufficient information does appear to suggest patterns of change. See State Penitentiary, Statement of Convicts, Prison Ledgers, 1864-1906, *passim*, KSHS.

36. Kansas State Penitentiary Records, Prisoner Ledger I, Number 1-1953 (Series II), 1901-1906, *passim*, KSHS.

37. Affidavits of Mary Fitzpatrick and Elizabeth Simpson, 22 May 1914, Governor George Hodges Papers, Correspondence, 1913-1915, Board of Corrections: Investigations of Punishments, Box 33, KSHS.

38. Affidavit of Mary Fitzpatrick, 22 May 1914, Governor George Hodges Papers, KSHS.

39. Kansas State Penitentiary Records, Prisoner Ledger I, Number 1-1953 (Series II), 1901-1906, Prisoner #1629, KSHS.

40. Undated brief with remarks of Deputy County Attorney Dawson and Judge Stilwell, Florence Akers Parole File, Governor's Office; State Penitentiary, Pardon and Parole Files, Box 1, KSHS.

41. *Ibid.*, Undated statement of Florence Akers.

42. *Ibid.*, M.L. Ogg to Governor Walter Stubbs, 24 February 1910.

43. *Ibid.*, J.B. Bowers to Governor Stubbs, 18 March 1910.

44. *Ibid.*, O.M. Johnson to Governor Walter Stubbs, 22 February 1910.

45. Nebraska began construction of a state penitentiary at Lincoln in 1870. Prior to that time only inferior local jails were available. Aaron M. Boom, "History of Nebraska Penal Institutions: 1856-1940" (master's thesis, University of Nebraska, 1951), 84. A separate prison for women was opened at York in 1920, although inmates could be returned to the male facility at Lincoln for disciplinary purposes. Mary R. Norquest, "Nebraska Center for Women: History," Unpublished report, n.d., Office of Records Management, Nebraska Center for Women, York, Nebraska.

46. All information about Nebraska prisoners drawn from Inmate Record Jackets; Inactive File, Project #3087, Microfilm box 77, 18-22, Nebraska State Penitentiary, Nebraska State Penal Complex, Lincoln, Nebraska, and Nebraska State Penitentiary Descriptive Record, vol. 1-3, RG 86, Rolls 1 and 2, Nebraska State Archives, Lincoln, Nebraska [Hereafter NSA].

47. Prisoner Case #1075, 2082, 2359, 2433, 2806, 3116, 3475, 4026, 4165, 4583, 5308, Nebraska State Penitentiary Descriptive Records, vol. 1-3, RG 86, Rolls 1 and 2, NSA.

48. Prisoner #4630, Nebraska State Penitentiary Descriptive Record, vol. 3, RG 86, Roll 2, NSA.

49. Data drawn from Prisoner #164, 187, 327, 1797, 2029, 3769, 3938, 4376, 5175, Nebraska State Penitentiary, Descriptive Records, vol. 1-3, RG 86, Rolls 1 and 2, NSA.

50. *Butte Miner*, 13, 16, 17 May 1901.

51. State of Montana, State Prison Convict Register, 1879-1920; State of Montana, Description of Prisoners, vol. 6-8, 1885-1911, Old Montana Prison, Deer Lodge, Montana [Hereafter OMP].

52. State of Montana, State Prisoner Convict Register, 60; State of Montana, Description of Prisoners, vol. 7, 1901-1908, Case #1185, 537, OMP.

20

The Southern Side of "Glory":

Mississippi African-American Women During the Civil War

Noralee Frankel

On the Clark plantation in Hinds Co., until the battle of Vicksburg ended in [July] 1863, which was the first time we knew we were free, all the slaves in the surrounding county was gathered into a camp on a plantation about five miles from Vicksburg. We remained in this camp until October 1863. My husband with others were sent up to Vicksburg to enlist. I went with him; he was examined, pronounced sound and was accepted and went immediately into camp with the troops, he was made a cook for the company. I followed and for several week I assisted him in cooking. . . . [from Maria Clark's widow's pension testimony. Maria Clark was a slave and the wife of Henry Clark, also a former slave, who served in the Third Calvary, United States Colored Troops][1]

The movie *Glory* depicts the Civil War experiences of the Fifty-fourth Massachusetts Regiment of African-American soldiers. For most Americans, the movie represents their first exposure to the fact that thousands of Black troops fought and died in the Civil War. Unlike the Fifty-fourth, most of these soldiers were not born in the North, but lived as slaves in the South. Initially resistant, the federal government finally allowed African-American men to become soldiers in 1862, and slave men throughout the South enlisted. In Mississippi, for example, they formed the core of six regiments exceeding seventeen thousand men. African-American women such as Maria Clark joined their men in their quest for freedom. The impact of army life on African-American women in the South has yet to be told.

Each Northern victory in Mississippi, particularly the capture of Vicksburg, Jackson, and Natchez in 1863, encouraged increasing numbers of slave men and women to flee their enslavement. While Black young men went into the army, the women, both single and married, followed the soldiers. John Eaton, a military chaplain in the Mississippi Valley, saw slave women after the fall of Vicksburg, "following the army, carrying all their possessions on their heads, great feather beds tied up in sheets and holding their few belongings."[2] When William Tecumseh Sherman advanced through the state of Mississippi in 1863-64, behind his army were "10 miles of negroes . . . a string of ox wagons, negro women and children behind each brigade that equalled in length the brigade itself."[3]

These former slave women and children migrated to areas, usually cities, where the army stationed the soldiers. As exslave Frances Brown recalled, "The soldiers came through there [Hinds Co.] and I came away with them. I did not know one regiment from another; all I knew was that they were Yankee soldiers. I came right here to Vicksburg, Miss. with them. I don't know what year that was but I guess it was after Vicksburg surrendered for they were mustering in colored soldiers when I got here."[4]

Upon arrival, the women sometimes lived in army tents.[5] Gradually, though, the majority of women, including family members of Black soldiers, moved into other residences outside of the barracks. They lived as near to the enlisted men as the army officers permitted. Accommodations ranged from boarding houses to shanties, although to a soldier even the poorest housing looked better than army barracks. One soldier recalled that a fellow comrade, when not on duty, stayed with his wife, "who lived but a short distance from the barracks" in a shanty. "This house was covered with boards . . . I have been in the house. It was a comfortable house. The house was more comfortable than a tent."[6] Still, Northern philanthropists journeying South to help the newly freed slaves were greatly distressed over the women's living conditions. According to one observer, the exslaves in Natchez, mainly women and children, "live in a community by themselves in the outskirts of the town, a cabin is built . . . say 12 feet wide with walls, 7 feet in height and divided off into compartments . . .and each one is appropriated to a family."[7] One army officer bluntly stated that "soldiers' wives and children are living in wretchedness and miserable hovels. . . ."[8]

Located near the army, some of the African-American women obtained employment as nurses, cooks, laundresses, as well as personal servants to white officers.[9] For example, the woman living in the shanty "more comfortable than a tent" worked as a washerwoman for thirty men in the Fifth Heavy Artillery, soldiers of which built her that house. The soldiers probably ensured housing for her because she provided a necessary domestic service for them. While both Black soldiers and Black women served as cooks and nurses, the army only hired women as laundresses. Washing and ironing clothes for the same men over a period of months, they kept close contact with the soldiers, especially if they had known them during slavery.

Unmarried women performing domestic work in the army camp found willing mates among the soldiers. Having left her slave master to come to Vicksburg with her sister and brother, Ellen Creevy became a soldier's bride. A laundress for several Black soldiers, she met her future husband while visiting the army camp.[10] As with other slave women, Anna Roberts also followed the Union soldiers to Vicksburg. Once there, she moved in with a woman who baked for the soldiers. Roberts later remembered that the "the Fifth Heavy Artillery was camped right up on the hill above where we lived and I would go there every morning and sell the pies about all out." Anna felt quite comfortable in camp since she had known several of the soldiers before the war. One soldier, who had lived on the same plantation with Anna, recalled that during one of her visits, "she met Richard Roberson and she got stuck on him and told me that she and Roberson were going to get married."[11] Similarly, Lucinda Westbrooks, who married Frank Morris during the war, recalled that she "had been washing for Morris and we decided to marry and so we did."[12]

Unlike Anna Roberson and Lucinda Westbrooks who met their mates during the war, many former slave women were actually remarrying their slave husbands while these men served in the army. Even though slave marriages possessed no legal standing, couples took these unions seriously. While enslaved, men and women considered themselves married when they lived together with consent of their master, often following a small wedding ceremony performed by the slave owner or slave preacher. During the war, some of the slave couples legally remarried. While slaves, Eliza Foreman and Nathaniel Foreman wed in 1858. When Eliza Foreman came to Vicksburg as a domestic servant for a Yankee officer, she remarried her soldier husband. Their marriage certificate stated that:

> This certifies, that I have this day joined in lawful marriage, Nathaniel Foreman . . . and Eliza Todd . . . in compliance with the ordinance of God, and by authority of the United States of America, vested in me, in accordance with No. 15, special Order of the Secretary of War . . . signed Joseph Warren, chaplain 25, Inf. assistant in charge of freedmen. . . ."[13]

African-Americans kept army chaplains busy performing marriage ceremonies. Former slave Lucinda Westbrooks recalled being "married by a white man preacher Miller—who came there with the first Yankees and went around marrying the soldiers. He married lots of other soldiers the same day."[14] Chaplains also held weddings for several couples simultaneously. One army wife recalled that "there were about a dozen married at the same time and stood right around in a row. . . ."[15] Soldiers invited their comrades to these festivities. While in the Fifth Heavy Artillery, John Dollins attended the marriage of his pre-war companion and fellow slave, Louis Caston.[16] Women friends, known since slavery or met during the war, also came to the ceremonies.[17]

While the army gave former slaves the first access to legal marriages, army officials used legalized marriage of African-Americans as a means to restrict civilian interaction with soldiers. In order to control the numbers of women entering army camps, Samuel Thomas, an officer in Vicksburg, decided to forbid any nonlegally married couples from living together. After Emily Fulgert joined her slave husband Gordon Fulgert's "regiment, . . . orders [were] enforced that soldiers should remarry under the laws and flag then Gordon Fulgert . . . remarrie[d] [Emily] again this being the second marriage once by the owner and once by Provost Marshal Samuel Thomas at Vicksburg."[18] The army applied the new orders to women living inside and outside of the barracks. One exsoldier, when explaining how he knew a couple was married so that the widow could obtain her husband's military pension, emphatically stated that "I have personal knowledge that said parties lived and cohabited as man and wife in the camp and [as she was] so treated by the officers and all others, and if she had not been recognized by the officers as his lawful wife she would not have been allowed to remain in the camp as such."[19] The army forcefully encouraged couples such as Private Benjamin Lee and Winne Moore to wed. Having known Benjamin Lee before the war, Moore moved in with Lee when she came to Vicksburg. While living together, "there was a law passed by the officers that no man should live with a woman unless he married her and then Ben and Winnie went up to [Samuel Thomas' headquarters] . . . and were married or they said they married any how. Most all the boys were living with women and went up and were married."[20]

Besides encouraging legal marriages, white officers such as Samuel Thomas used more extreme methods for dealing with the large numbers of former slave women and children in the army lines. They banned women from army quarters and sent them to deserted plantations to raise cotton for the Northern government to sell. Overcrowding of the areas where soldiers were stationed and sexual activity between African-American women and soldiers, both white and Black, became rationales for moving African-American women out of the cities. The army officers considered the women disruptive to military procedure. Samuel Thomas complained that "the Regiments are crowded with women of bad character and soldiers' wives and children are living in wretchedness and miserable hovels, when land can be furnished in safe localities where they can build good houses and support themselves by cultivating it."[21] A few officers even worried about the white soldiers' sexual exploitation of former slave women, but most perceived any African-American women consorting with Union soldiers as corrupting the troops.[22]

In Natchez, General Tuttle at the suggestion of chief health officer A.W. Kelley decided to rid the city of large numbers of civilian African-American residents. They ordered every Black man and woman "to present a paper certifying that he or she was living on the premises of some responsible white person and was *employed* by them." While allowing African-American women who worked for the military such as laundresses to remain, the army forcibly began to remove other former slave women from the city. The military only modified the policy when Black soldiers marched into the office of one of the Union officers and informed him that "they could no longer endure the trial of seeing their wives and children driven in to the streets and if he would not at once interfere and protect them they should *positively* do it themselves."[23]

The military, however, continued to initiate civilian removal plans. A year later, Lieutenant L.W. Brobet grew concerned as more former slaves arrived in Natchez. Brobet, as with military officers elsewhere, believed that exslave women should be rounded up and taken to Union-held plantations. Another military commander in Natchez thwarted Brobet by allowing the wives and children of African-American soldiers to stay, even though Brobet considered the soldiers' families the "main cause" of the congestion in Natchez.[24]

In spite of the soldiers' protests, the army moved hundreds of African-American women onto land abandoned by Southern planters.

Soldiers acted individually as well as in groups against the army's insistence on relocating the soldiers' families. When Samuel Williams's wife was "taken to a government farm . . . he came after her and she came to Vicksburg to her husband."[25] Similarly, when another soldier found his family on federally controlled land, "he hired a wagon and carried [his wife] and the children . . . here to Vicksburg."[26] One of slavery's worst horrors had been the threat of a family member being sold and sent away to work elsewhere. Since insuring a stable family life motivated slave men to enlist, African-American soldiers were unwilling to tolerate the army's breaking up of Black families.

Northern officers failed to appreciate the emotional ties formed during slave marriages nor did they approve of any relationship other than legalized marriage. Certainly, some of the Black women visiting the army camps of Black soldiers engaged in sexuality activity, but few of the women sleeping with these men were paid prostitutes. Occasionally, soldiers lied by falsely indicating that the women with whom they were intimate were their legal wives.[27] These exceptions, however, failed to negate the devotion shown by African-American couples.

African-American soldiers and wives displayed their mutual affection by seeing each other whenever possible. When their wives lived outside the barracks, soldiers obtained passes to see them. Couples enjoyed their conjugal visits. Richard Roberts's bunk mate recalled that "whenever [Richard] could get away at night he was with [his wife, Anna]."[28] Benjamin Lee's passion for his new wife caused him to obtain "a pass to come from home whenever he wanted to and often ran in home without a pass."[29] Moses Wilson's wife recalled "I was there near my husband in the camps and he came often to see me of nights."[30] Soldiers, like Allen Alexander, whose spouses stayed on the plantation, even sent for their wives to join them.[31] When their husbands became unable to visit them, wives, when able, came to camp to visit or nurse their husbands staying in hospitals from war related injuries and illnesses.[32]

Former slaves maintained their family life as best they could throughout the war. They remained committed whenever possible to their extended family as well as to their spouses and children. For example, washerwoman Ellen Creevy met her husband while visiting her brothers in the army. The army also gave African-Americans the opportunity to meet former slaves from outside their plantation neighborhood, greatly expanding exslaves' physical and social geography, although the exslaves continued to value older landmarks such as the slave family and the plantation community. Slave women ran to the Union lines to gain liberation from enslavement. They discovered during the war that freedom and even legal marriage failed to provide family autonomy removed from white interference. As they fought for family stability, during Reconstruction, they continued to learn that their Northern liberators would often play a confusing and contradictory part in their struggle. Due to the movie *Glory*, African-American soldiers' contributions to the Northern victory are finally receiving recognition. Black women's experiences during the Civil War also deserve attention and continued study.

NOTES

1. Widow's Pension File, Henry Clark, United States Colored Troops, Cavalry, A Company, 3rd. Regiment, National Archives and Records Administration (NARA), Washington, DC.

2. John Eaton, *Grant, Lincoln, and the Freedmen: Reminiscences of the Civil War* (New York: Longmans, Green, and Co., 1907), p. 83.

3. W.T. Sherman to Major General Halleck, 29 February 1864, letter in *The War of the Rebellion: A Compilation of the Official Records of the Union and Confederate Armies* (Washington, DC: Government Printing Office, 1880-1901), Series I, Vol. 58, p. 498.

4. Widow's Pension File, John Brown, Heavy Artillery (USCHA), G, 5, Regiment, 387.412, NARA, Washington, DC.

5. Widow's Pension File, Richard Roberts (USCHA), A, 5, 317.426, NARA, Washington, DC.

6. Widow's Pension File, Richard Sled (USCHA), I, 5, 394.755, 389.853, NARA, Washington, DC.

7. William Thirds to Mr. Whipple, 19 November 1863, American Missionary Association, Mississippi, 71576.

8. Samuel Thomas, letter, Register of Letters, Office of the General Superintendent of Freedmen, Mississippi, BRFAL, Record Group, 105, NARA, Washington, DC and Samuel Thomas, letter, Register of Letters Received, Office of the General Superintendent of Freedmen, Mississippi, BRFAL, Record Group, 105, NARA, Washington, DC.

9. Widow's Pension File, John Brown.

10. Widow's Pension File, Hubbard Reynolds (USCHA), G, 5, 163.950, 741.430, NARA, Washington, DC.

11. Widow's Pension File, Richard Roberts.

12. Widow's Pension File, Elick Westbrooks (USCHA), F, 5, 171.128, 309.238, NARA, Washington, DC.

13. Widow's Pension File, Nathaniel Foreman (USCHA), C, 5, 1211.340, 177.645, NARA, Washington, DC.

14. Widow's Pension File, Elick Westbrooks.

15. Widow's Pension File, Richard Sled.

16. Widow's Pension File, Louis Caston (USCHA), K, 5, 388.190, 384.190, NARA, Washington, DC.

17. Widow's Pension File, Tod Weldome (USCHA), I, 5, 397.384, 440.081; Samuel Taylor (USCHA) H 5, 210.144, NARA, Washington, DC.

18. Widow's Pension File, Gordon Fulgert (USCINF), E, 53, 320.012, 266.793, NARA, Washington, DC.

19. Widow's Pension File, Hannibal Wallace (USCHA), K, 5, 375.899, NARA, Washington, DC.

20. Widow's Pension File, Benjamin Lee (USCHA), L, 5, 380.960, NARA, Washington, DC.

21. Samuel Thomas, letter, Register of Letters Received, Office of the General Superintendent of Freedmen, Mississippi, BRFAL, Record Group 105, NARA, Washington, DC, M826-14.

22. Leon F. Litwack, *Been In the Storm So Long: The Aftermath of Slavery* (New York: A. Knopf, 1979) p. 129; Jacqueline Jones, *Labor of Love, Labor of Sorrow: Black Women, Work and the Family from Slavery to the Present* (New York: Vintage Books, 1986), pp. 50-51; and Joseph T. Glatthaar, *Forged in Battle: The Civil War Alliance of Black Soldiers and White Officers* (New York: The Free Press, 1990), p. 91.

23. S.G. Wright to Rev. George Whipple, 7 April 1864, American Missionary Association, Mississippi, 71635; Herbert G. Gutman, *The Black Family in Slavery and Freedom, 1750-1925* (New York: Vintage Books, 1977), pp. 23-24.

24. L.W. Brobet to A.S. Mitchell, 18 March 1865, Natchez: Unregistered Letters Received, Office of the Assistant Commissioner, Mississippi, BRFAL, Record Group 195, NARA, Washington, DC.

25. Widow's Pension File, Samuel Williams (USCHA), G, 5, 168.903, 175.358, NARA, Washington, DC.

26. Widow's Pension File, Gordon Fulgert.

27. Widow's Pension File, William Washington (USCHA), I, 5, 687.674, J 512.928, NARA, Washington, DC.

28. Widow's Pension File, Richard Roberts; also Widow's Pension File; Hubbard McReynolds (USCHA), G, 5, 163.950, 741.430, NARA, Washington, DC.

29. Widow's Pension File, Benjamin Lee.

30. Widow's Pension File, Moses Wilson (USCHA), G, 5, 315.778, 273.769, NARA, Washington, DC.

31. Widow's Pension File, Allen Alexander (USCINF) A, 58, 145.205, 97.533, NARA, Washington, DC.

32. Widow's Pension File, Richard Roberts; Widow's Pension File, Richard Sled.

21

Domination and Resistance:

The Politics of Wage Household Labor in New South Atlanta

Tera W. Hunter

> Relations of domination are, at the same time, relations of resistance. Once established, domination does not persist of its own momentum. Inasmuch as it involves the use of power to extract work, production, services, taxes against the will of the dominated, it generates considerable friction and can be sustained only by continuous efforts at reinforcement, maintenance, and adjustment.
>
> James C. Scott, *Domination and the Art of Resistance: Hidden Transcripts* (1990)

Washerwomen in Atlanta organized a massive strike in the summer of 1881. Over the course of a two week period in July they summoned 3000 supporters through the neighborhood networks they had been building since emancipation. The strike articulated economic as well as political grievances: the women demanded higher fees for their services and fought to maintain the distinctive autonomy of their trade. When city officials threatened the "washing amazons" with the possibility of levying an exorbitant tax on each individual member of the Washing Society (the group responsible for the strike), the women issued a warning of their own: "We, the members of our society, are determined to stand our pledge . . . we mean business this week or no washing."[1]

Southern household workers, who are often stereotyped as passive victims of racial, sexual, and class oppression, displayed a profound sense of political consciousness through the organization of this strike. Moreover, they initiated it at the dawn of the New South movement, an effort by ambitious businessmen to change the course and fortunes of regional economic development. In order to promote the goals of industrial capitalism and to attract northern capital below the Mason-Dixon Line, proponents of the New South heralded an image of all Southern workers as artless by nature and indifferent to class struggle. But these working-class women stridently scorned this agenda.

The protest in Atlanta was not unique in the post-slavery era. Washerwomen in Jackson, Mississippi, struck in 1866. And on the heels of the Great Strike of 1877, laundresses and other household workers in Galveston stopped work as well.[2] Both of these boycotts articulated goals for a living wage and autonomy, yet neither matched the proportions and the affront the Atlanta women posed to the emergent New South ideology. The Atlanta strike was unusual; domestic workers rarely organized strikes. But they did find a multitude of other ways to oppose oppression, usually in the form of surreptitious and quotidian resistance.[3]

Household workers often resorted to covert tactics of resistance because they were frequently the only options available within a system of severe constraints. The magnitude of seemingly unassuming gestures looms large if we realize that workers sometimes transformed them into collective dissent or used them as building blocks for the occasional large-scale outburst. Nonetheless, it is a testament to the potency of the forces dominating women workers in the South that defiance would assume this form and that these forces were powerful enough to cover up the expression of opposition. The importance of strikes such as that by the Atlanta washerwomen in part is that they have generated a precious few documents straight from the mouths of working-class women in the form of letters and petitions to municipal officials and reports from journalists who witnessed mass meeting and rallies. In the main little direct testimony exists from household workers about their activities and the motivations that prompted them. But there is another way to scout out working-class women's discontent and dissent. Evidence from employers and their proxies in public authority positions unwittingly expose the resilience and creativity of African-American household workers' efforts to counter domination.

This article is an effort to understand resistance by looking at the character of domination and the attempts to counter it from Reconstruction to World War I. Domination is defined here as the process of exercising power over the dispossessed by whatever means necessary, but without overt conflict where possible. Conversely, resistance is defined as any act, individual or collective, symbolic or literal, intended by subordinates to deny claims, to refuse compliance with impositions made by superordinates, or to advance claims of their own.[4] This essay outlines examples of African-American women domestics combatting injustice, and it analyzes the responses of employers and public officials. As household workers struggled to negate conditions of abject servitude, their employers worked even harder to repress and contain these workers. The subsequent contests reveal how structures of inequality were reproduced and challenged in daily interactions; their public airing suggests that wage household labor had broader social and political implications beyond its significance to private homes. Atlanta is a fitting place to begin exploring the larger ramifications of wage household labor. Young, white, upwardly mobile businessmen in the years after the Civil War began cultivating an image of the city as the vanguard of a "New South." As the ideas of these urban boosters were instituted, it became all too clear that "modernization" of the social, political, and economic order included racial segregation and political disfranchisement. From this perspective, Atlanta did not simply embody the contradictions of life under Jim Crow; the conscious leadership role it assumed in the region also made it instrumental in creating and perpetuating them.[5]

This self-proclaimed model of the New South held the distinction of employing one of the highest per capita numbers of domestic workers in the nation during the period of this study.[6] Such a repute was not coincidental to the seeming contradiction between the goals of modernization and the advocacy of a retrogressive system such as segregation. One might expect that a modernizing economy would shirk old fashioned manual household labor in favor of up to date mechanized and commercial production. Yet manual household work furthered the goals of the advocates of the New South in restricting black workers' social and economic opportunities. African-American women who migrated to Atlanta following Emancipation were segregated into household labor. Virtually no other options were available to them, yet wage work was essential to the sustenance of their livelihoods from childhood to death. And in Atlanta, as in other Southern cities, the disproportionate sex ratio among blacks made wage work all the more imperative for women, especially for single, divorced, or widowed mothers saddled with the sole responsibility for taking care of their families. And the low wages paid to black men meant that even married women could rarely escape outside employment and worked in far greater numbers than their white counterparts.[7]

Yet despite this occupational confinement, black women managed to assert some preferences for the particular kind of domestic labor they performed. Single and younger women accepted positions as general maids or child-nurses more often, for example, while married women usually chose positions as laundresses. Washerwomen represented the largest single category of waged household workers in Atlanta, and by 1900 their total numbers exceeded all other domestics combined.[8] Laundresses picked up loads of dirty clothes from their patrons on Monday; washed, dried and ironed throughout the week; and returned the finished garments on Saturday. This labor process encumbered their already cramped living quarters with the accoutrements of the trade, but it exempted workers from employer supervision, yielded a day "off," allowed workers to care for their children and to perform other duties intermittently, incorporated family members into the work routine, and facilitated communal work among adult women.[9]

Regardless of the specific domestic job black women chose, the majority insisted on living in their own homes rather than with their employers. Elsewhere in the country, where immigrant European and native-born white women were more numerous, live-in domestic work predominated; but for recently freed slaves, living with their own families was foremost to approximating independence.[10] Above all, living on their own meant for the former slaves breaking the physical chains of bondage and reestablishing the kinship ties scattered and torn asunder by the caprice of fluctuating fortunes or the ill will of owners. It also meant preventing employers from exercising unmitigated control over their entire lives. Some employers accepted a live-out arrangement, perhaps, because it coincided with their own ambivalence about continuing the intimacy that prevailed between master and slaves. But many employers resented the loss of control that resulted.[11]

Black women's priorities in the post-Civil War years demonstrated that economic motivations alone did not influence their decisions about wage labor. They sought instead to balance wage-earning activities with other needs and obligations. Consequently they moved in and out of the labor market as circumstances in their personal lives demanded and switched jobs frequently. Domestic workers quit in order to buy time off for a variety of reasons, among them participation in special functions, such as religious revivals, or taking care of family members who became ill. The workers also resorted to quitting to make clear their discontent over unfair practices when other efforts to obtain satisfactory redress failed. Quitting did not necessarily guarantee a better situation elsewhere (and often did not), but it reinforced workers' desire for self-determination and deprived employers of the ascendancy to which they were accustomed as slaveholders.

Consequently, quitting made it difficult for employers to find "good" servants and, especially, to keep them—the single most oft-repeated complaint from Reconstruction onward.[12] Quitting violated employers' expectations of the ideal worker: one who conformed to relentless hours of labor, made herself available at beck and call, and showed devoted loyalty throughout her entire life. In 1866, as the clamor among employers demanding relief quickly rose to a high pitch, the Atlanta City Council interceded on their behalf by passing a law to nullify free labor's most fundamental principle. To obstruct the liberties essential to authentic independence, to hinder the ease and frequency of workers changing jobs, the law required employers of domestics to obtain recommendations from the previous employer before hiring them.[13]

The 1866 law is instructive of the general crisis of free labor in the South following the Civil War. As African-Americans showed a marked determination to make their new status live up to their needs and expectations, planters and urban employers rejected the ideals of the free labor system that conflicted with the safekeeping of white supremacy. In 1865, during the brief reign of Presidential Reconstruction under Andrew Johnson, Democrats in state legislatures in the South instituted the Black Codes, laws designed, among other things, to diminish blacks' rights in labor contracts.[14] The 1866 law was strongly reminiscent of this mechanism and its passage signalled the increasing role of the state in relationships formerly governed entirely by individual masters. Black women workers would still be vulnerable to arbitrary personal power although its exercise would be tempered by the 13th Amendment. Nonetheless employers would try to coerce workers with the aid of the state. The enactment of the law in 1866 provided concrete evidence that household workers' refusals to acquiesce to unrelenting physical exertion forced employers to procure outside intervention.

Employers' augmentation of their authority with municipal power, however, proved ineffective in part because of their ambivalent attitude towards the law. Frustrated employers were often willing to employ almost any black woman in their ever illusive search for individuals whose personal characteristics and occupational behavior coincided with the traits of "good" servants. Despite the employers' dissatisfaction with the way the system worked, and in defiance of the law passed for their own protection, they preferred to hire workers without the requisite nod from former bosses rather than face the unthinkable possibility of no servants at all.

Black women's active opposition to the law also helped to defeat it as they continued to quit work at will. Quitting was an effective strategy of resistance precisely because it could not be quelled outside a system of bound labor. Though some women workers may have openly confronted their employer before departing, quitting as a tactic thrived because it did not require such direct antagonism. Workers who had the advantage of living in their own homes could easily make up excuses for leaving, or leave without notice at all—permitting small and fleeting victories for individuals to accumulate into bigger results as domestics throughout Atlanta and the urban South repeated these actions over and over again. The instability created in the labor market strengthened the bargaining position of domestic workers since employers persisted in thinking of the pool as scarce, though, in absolute numbers, the supply of domestic workers available to the employing population in Atlanta was virtually endless. The incongruence between the perception of a dearth and the reality of an abundance suggests that black women's self-assertion had indeed created a shortage of workers with the attributes employers preferred.[15]

Quitting and other forms of everyday struggle continued for many decades long after Reconstruction. In 1912 an Atlanta mayoral candidate offered an extreme, if novel, solution to the menacing problem of restraining domestic workers' self-assertions. George Brown, a physician, supported a public health reform that encompassed the concerns of white employers. The candidate promised pure drinking water, free bathing facilities, improved sanitary provisions at railroad stations, and a (white) citizenry protected from exposure to contagious germs.[16] The latter proposal had direct implications for black domestics whom employers and health officials accused of spreading tuberculosis through the food they cooked, the houses they cleaned, and the clothes they washed. Laundry workers were the most vociferously attacked objects of scorn. The freedom they enjoyed from direct white supervision permitted them to operate more as contractors than as typical wage workers, which made them vulnerable to scrutiny of their labor and personal lives.[17]

Brown and like-minded individuals heightened the fear that domestic workers were the primary emissaries of physical contagions and impressed upon white minds that black women were also the harbingers of social disease as well. The attribution of pestilence to domestics unveils deeper frictions that lay bare a central paradox about Jim Crow, which by then was firmly in place. The social and political geography of Atlanta bolstered the exploitation and containment of black bodies and their spatial separation from upper-class whites. African-Americans were segregated in the worst areas of the city and had the least access to the municipal resources essential to good health, services such as street pavings, proper waste disposal, and potable water were provided to Atlantans on the basis of both racial and class privileges. By the late 19th century upper-class whites in large numbers had moved out to ostentatious suburbs and had begun to escape regular interaction with the unattractive sites that the inequitable distribution of city resources typically bred.[18] Yet these white suburbanites continued to hire black household workers from such malodorous neighborhoods. White anxieties about the contaminating touch of black women reflected the ambivalence of a tension between revulsion and attraction to the worker who performed the most intimate labor, taking care, for example, of children.

Brown proposed to wipe out the public health problem and to diminish the ubiquitous "servant problem" in one sweeping measure. He proposed the creation of a city-run servant bureau invested with broad discretionary judiciary powers that would require domestics to submit to rigorous physical examination and to offer detailed personal and employment histories before obtaining prerequisite licenses for work. Brown sought to reinstitute "absolute control" of servants and to relieve white fears by criminalizing presumed carriers of disease; he promised to punish domestics who impeded efforts to keep the scourge away from the door steps of their white bosses.

And the mayoral hopeful went further: he called for disciplinary measures to be used against workers who exercised the conventional liberties of wage work. Quitting for reasons employers did not consider "just" or displaying other forms of recalcitrance would constitute sufficient grounds for arrest, fines, incarceration, or labor on the chain gang.[19] As a candidate outside the inner circle of New South politicos, Brown hardly had a chance to win the election, but his campaign is noteworthy for its dissemination of pejorative images of domestics that further legitimized their subordination as a source of cheap labor.

The Brown campaign is also suggestive about the changing constitution of domination in response to household workers' agency. The prominence of the disease issue, even beyond the mayoral campaign, showed signs of a shift in the "servant problem" discourse from an emphasis on so-called inherent deficiencies of black women, such as laziness and the lack of a proper work ethic, to a more powerful critique of domestic workers as the bearers of deadly organisms.[20] Worker mobility and other acts of defiance undoubtedly took their toll on employers' patience, but the prospects of contracting tuberculosis or other communicable diseases provided new and greater rationalizations for establishing comprehensive mechanisms of control over black females. The ostensible concern with public health, however, falters as an adequate explanation for these exacerbated prejudices, if we consider that proposals like Brown's were based on the faulty assumption that disease traveled solely on one-way tickets from blacks to whites. The servant bureau of Brown's imagination would not have alleviated the propagation of germs, but it would have stripped household workers of important rights. Carried to their logical conclusion, the punitive measures could have conveniently led to a convict labor system for domestic workers, forcing them to work at the behest of employers without compensation and under the threat of physical brutality.

Several of the issues raised in George Brown's run for mayor reverberated in another infamous campaign. Joseph M. Brown, son of the former Confederate governor and unrelated to George, ran for the U.S. Senate against the incumbent Hoke Smith in 1914. The two Brown men shared the view that domestic workers' defiance posed an ample threat to social stability in the New South that justified state intervention. Both men berated the large numbers of household workers who participated in benevolent and mutual aid associations, also known as secret societies, and both believed that it was imperative to dismantle the workers' capacity to bolster clandestine resistance through such institutions.[21]

From Reconstruction onward, black women led and joined secret societies to pool their meager resources to aid the sick, orphaned, widowed, or unemployed, and to create opportunities for personal enrichment as well as broader race advancement. The number of such organizations with explicit labor-related goals were few, but groups that brought working-class women together for other expressed purposes were known to transform themselves on the spur of the moment and operate as quasi-trade unions when necessary.[22]

George Brown had entreated white men to put him in the mayor's seat so that he could direct the cleansing mission of his servant bureau toward eradicating these organizations that debilitated "helpless" white housewives.[23] "Little Joe" Brown followed suit in his bid for the Senate two years later by rebuking African-American domestics for devising "blacklists" in secret societies that deprived errant employers. This tactic was especially unnerving to him (and others) because it shrouded a collective act by relying on individuals to quietly refuse to work, leaving behind perplexed housewives with the sudden misfortune of not being able to find willing workers. Joe Brown preyed on white Southern fears to dramatize the urgent need to eliminate these quasi-union activities and he tried to race-bait his opponent Hoke Smith, no stranger to this ploy himself. Brown accused the black mutual aid groups of conspiring with white labor unions in an interracial syndicate, a charge which white labor leaders quickly rebutted.[24] Brown forewarned the voters against choosing Smith and of the consequences of failing to elect him and neglecting to outlaw the institutional basis of African-American women's dissent: "Every white lady in whose home negro servants are hired then becomes subservient to these negroes," he stated.[25] Brown lost the Senate race, yet his devotion to assailing household workers' resistance had unintended consequences, it acknowledged its effect.

Schemes designed to thwart household workers' agency reached a peak as the Great Migration intensified during World War I. In May 1918, Enoch Crowder, the Selective Service Director, issued a "work or fight" order aimed at drafting unemployed men into the armed forces. The order stressed the nation's need for labor's cooperation in contributing to the war effort through steady gainful work or military service. Trade unions immediately protested the potential abuses that could result from such a directive, having heard of abuses perpetrated against striking British workers under a similar law. Newton D. Baker, the Secretary of War, made assurances to the contrary, but striking machinists in Bridgeport, Connecticut, were threatened with Crowder's order.[26] Southern legislatures and city councils deliberately designed their own "work or fight" laws to break the will of black workers in order to maintain white supremacy in a time of rapid change and uncertainty. Similar to the logic used by white Progressives in anti-vagrancy campaigns during the same period, "work or fight" laws were rationalized as a solution to alleged crime and moral depravity that resulted when blacks filled all or part of their day with pursuits other than gainful work. Atlanta had one of the highest per capita arrest records in the country in the early 20th century, largely because of vagrancy and other misdemeanor convictions; the individuals apprehended were often gainfully employed and always disproportionately black.[27] The relative scarcity of labor produced by the war prompted Southern lawmakers to manipulate Crowder's order and use it to clamp down on African-Americans at the very moment when the war opened new opportunities for employment and increased their bargaining positions in existing jobs.

White Southerners abandoned the original intention of the Federal measure to fill the army with able-bodied men by making the conscription of *women* central to its provisions.[28] As opportunities for black women expanded in the sewing trades, commercial laundries, and less rapidly, small manufacturing plants, the number available for household work declined, giving an edge to those who remained in negotiating for better terms.[29] Employers of domestics resented this new mobility and sought to contain it by using "work or fight" laws to punish black women who vacated traditional jobs.

Individuals arrested under the laws' provisions included black housewives, defined as "idle" and unproductive, and other self-employed black women such as hairdressers. A group of self-described "friends" of the Negro race in Macon, Georgia, iterated some of the assumptions behind such enforcement. Black women should not withdraw from wage work in general and household labor in particular, no matter what the circumstances; the Macon group argued that patriotic duty required that black women not "sit at home and hold their hands, refusing to do the labor for which they are specially trained and otherwise adapted." Black women's domestic work was essential to the war effort, insisted the Macon group, because it exempted white women "from the routine of housework in order that they may do the work which negro women cannot do."[30] In Atlanta, two 17-year-old girls experienced the encroachment of this notion of patriotism first-hand. "You can not make us work," Nellie Atkins and Ruth Warf protested upon arrest and proceeded to break windows to vent their anger at the injustice, which doubled the sentence to 60 days each in the prison laundry.[31] Warf and Atkins were relatively fortunate, however; other women were tarred and feathered and violently attacked by vigilantes.[32]

African-Americans in Atlanta took the lead in organizing what eventually became a regional assault against racist and sexist implementation of "work or fight" laws. They enlisted the national office of the NAACP, which in turn launched an investigation and supported local chapters in the South in order to stop the passage of the abusive laws. The NAACP discovered that employers not only used the laws to conscript non-domestics; the employers also used the laws against employed household workers who demanded higher wages to meet the rising costs of living, organized protests, quit work because of unfair treatment, or took time out for other activities.[33] Over a half-century after the Jackson washerwomen's strike, for example, all the household workers in the city organized and established a six-day work week, with Sundays off. But employers launched a counter-offensive, forcing the workers to return to an unforgiving seven-day schedule or face prosecution.[34]

Blacks in Atlanta successfully lobbied Governor Hugh Dorsey to veto discriminatory "work or fight" legislation passed by the Georgia House and Senate. Fearing the intensification of the Great Migration and the loss of black laborers, Dorsey responded to their demands. The Atlanta branch of NAACP similarly appealed to the city council and managed to preempt legislation at the local level, and eliminated de jure discrimination through a war time measure. Police and vigilantes, however, found other methods of abusing black women with impunity.[35]

The blatantly unjust harassment of household workers during World War I revealed another variation on a familiar theme—the New South's unabashed disdain for the privileges of free labor. Yet the physical brutality and legal coercion rationalized by state "work or fight" laws also signalled the breakdown of the authority of the elite in controlling a work force whose hallmark was supposedly servility. Like similar proposals to regulate domestic workers in previous years, "work or fight" laws uncovered an effort by employers to eliminate black women's ongoing resistance. The abusive legislation also uncloaked the impact of the Great Migration. As African-Americans left the South en masse to pursue freedom in Northern industrial towns, white Southern employers struggled to maintain power over those who stayed.

"Work or fight" laws and the other efforts to control domestic workers are interesting in part because they evidence struggle and contestation that till now had been obscured. While in many of the instances noted above, the household workers' collective consciousness may have been out of sight, it was not out of mind. The washerwomen's strike in the summer of 1881 reveals how working-class women's resistance could and did take a different form, as they openly proclaimed the usually "hidden transcript" of opposition in a profound way.[36] The strike displayed an astute political consciousness among black working-class women who made so-called private labor a public issue and insisted on autonomy and a living wage.[37]

The communal character and self-organization of laundry work proved critical to this mobilization as it facilitated the creation of a relatively autonomous space that had already nurtured the foundation of working-class women's solidarity. The Atlanta laundresses built on this tightly knit system, extended it through an intensive door to door recruitment of adherents to their cause, and sustained it through mass or decentralized ward meetings held nightly. Their capacity to rise to this occasion demonstrates why washerwomen were the most outspoken leaders in domestic workers' strikes documented in the South. It is no accident that, as incidents in later years would indicate, employers often combined forces to repress this particular group.

White city leaders put their full weight behind employers' attempts to annihilate a strike. At least one landlord threatened to raise the rent of his washerwoman if she raised the fees for her work. A businessman scoffed "at the colored people's stupidity in not seeing that they were working their own ruin" and warned that if they persisted they would be faced with a harsh winter without white charity.[38] The police arrested several street organizers for "disorderly conduct," charging them with disruptive and violent behavior as they canvassed their neighborhoods. Leading capitalists raised funds for a state-of-the-art steam laundry and offered to employ "smart Yankee girls" to buttress the counter-offensive and requested a tax exemption from the city council to subsidize the costs. Meanwhile, municipal authorities proposed a scheme to regulate the trade and destroy the workers' independence: councilmen suggested that each member of any washerwomen's organization pay an exorbitant business tax of $25.00.[39] In the end, however, the City Council rejected the license fee; the councilmen may have been daunted by the continued determination of women who refused to buckle under to threats and who vowed to reappropriate the license fee and city regulation to gain the benefits of private enterprise. As the women themselves stated in an open letter to the mayor, "We have agreed, and are willing to pay $25 or $50 for licenses as a protection so we can control the washing for the city."[40]

Not only did the washerwomen's spirit of rebellion frustrate the actions of their opponents, it set an example for other black workers. Waiters at the National Hotel followed on the women's coat tails and won demands for better wages and working conditions previously rejected by management. Cooks, maids, and child nurses also were inspired to begin organizing for better wages. Even the *Atlanta Constitution*, ardent ally of the employers, begrudgingly admitted that the "amazons" had shown remarkable organization.[41]

The most telling piece of evidence about the strike's impact appeared several weeks after the event had apparently subsided, when an unidentified source divulged to the newspaper that the washerwomen were threatening to call a second potentially more perilous general strike of all domestics during the upcoming International Cotton Exposition. While there were no further reports to suggest that this rumor ever came to fruition, the mere threat of a second strike at such a critical moment is quite telling. The laundry workers were clearly conscious of the significance of this event which had been touted as the debut of the New South movement and as a showcase for Atlanta, an upstart metropolis eager to be emulated. A strike held at that particular time not only would have spoiled the image of docile labor that New Southerners were carefully projecting to attract northern capital, it would have wreaked havoc on a city already anxious about its capacity to host the thousands of visitors who would require the services of cooks, maids, child-nurses, and laundresses. The newspaper forewarned white housewives: "prepare for the attack before it is made," and they did.[42]

The actual outcome of the washerwomen's strike is inconclusive, though it is curious that reports on the protest petered out in the medium that had openly flaunted its partisanship against it. Whether or not some or all of the washerwomen were able to gain higher wages we may never know; however, they continued to maintain a modicum of independence in their labor not enjoyed by other domestics. The strike speaks volumes symbolically about African-American working-class women's consciousness of their racial, class, and gender position. Domestic work was synonymous with black women in freedom as it was in slavery, and the active efforts by whites to exploit labor clearly circumscribed black lives. Yet black women fought for dignity, to be treated with respect, and for a fair chance to earn the necessary resources for making a decent living. The women identified autonomy as vital to freedom and to making decisions about wage work most commensurate with their non-wage responsibilities as mothers, sisters, daughters, and wives.

The employers could not fathom the motivations that inspired domestic workers to act in these ways. But employers knew they could not afford to take a pacified work force for granted. They used coercion, repression, and violence and sought support from the state to extract compliance to their wishes, which helped to determine the form that resistance would take. Domination and resistance were always defined in dynamic relationship to one another, thus it is not surprising that strikes were atypical events. Domestic workers developed other ways to articulate their grievances and assert their own demands, however, and in return their actions influenced the character of domination itself. The illusive quality of the black women's surreptitious actions made them difficult to control by individual employers and kept them vigilant. Domination was not a project that could be erected in full form and left to operate on its own momentum; it required ongoing efforts of surveillance and reconstitution in order to guarantee its effect.[43] At times this meant that domestic workers won small gains and moments of relief, as when they quit work. At other times their resistance led to greater repression, as during the period of World War I with the implementation of "work or fight" laws.

The contested character of wage household labor between Reconstruction and World War I also highlights another important point. Far from functioning as "separate spheres," the so-called public sphere of politics and business and the private sphere of family and home infiltrated one another in complex ways. It should be noted, however, that employers sometimes displayed an ambivalence about the relationship between their prerogatives as managers of labor and the intervention of public authorities, literally, on their home turfs. Municipalities and legislatures often stopped short of imposing legislation; recall, for example, that the Atlanta City Council failed to impose the business tax on individual laundry workers during the 1881 strike. African-American women's opposition may have thwarted employers' efforts to subdue them, but other factors may have also hindered employers from realizing the optimal balance between compulsion and free labor. In an economy moving toward modernization, even in the constrained version of Southern capitalism, the issue of state power versus individual employer authority was never consistently resolved. Waged household labor played an important role in the economic, social, and political life of the New South. The women who performed the labor, the women and men who employed them were consummate political actors all. Further theoretical speculation and empirical research of the issues raised in this essay will advance our understanding of the development of New South capitalism beyond what we already know about social relations in agriculture and industry.

NOTES

An earlier version of this paper was first presented at the Annual Meeting of the Organization of American Historians, Louisville, Kentucky, April 1991. Thanks to Stephanie Shaw and Robin D. G. Kelley for their generous comments. Kelley along with Elsa Barkley Brown, Leon Fink, Jacquelyn Hall, and Elizabeth Faue provided incisive critiques of the latest version. I am also grateful to Julius Scott, III, David Montgomery, and Nancy Cott for their insightful readings of the many incarnations of the larger project that this essay is drawn from. The writing was supported by a grant from the Institute for Research in Social Science of the University of North Carolina, Chapel Hill.

1. *Atlanta Constitution*, Aug. 3, 1881.
2. See *Jackson Daily Clarion*, June 24, 1866, reprinted in Philip S. Foner and Ronald Lewis, eds., *The Black Worker: A Documentary History from Colonial Times to the Present* (Philadelphia, 1978-84), II, 345; *Galveston Daily News*, 1, 2, 5, 7, and 16 Aug. 1877. For a full account of all the strikes, see Tera W. Hunter, "Household Workers in the Making: Afro-American Women in Atlanta and the New South, 1861 to 1920," unpublished Ph.D. diss. Yale Univ., 1990.
3. This essay relies on the following works on resistance: James C. Scott, *Weapons of the Weak: Everyday Forms of Peasant Rebellion* (New Haven, 1985); *Domination and the Arts of Resistance: The Hidden Transcripts* (New Haven, 1990); Rosalind O'Hanlon, "Recovering the Subject: *Subaltern Studies* and Histories of Resistance in Colonial South Asia," *Modern Asian Studies*, 22 (1988), 189-224; John Fiske, *Understanding Popular Culture* (Boston, 1989).
4. See O'Hanlon, "Recovering the Subject," 199-200; and Scott, *Weapons of the Weak*, 289-303.
5. On Atlanta as a leading city in the New South see James Michael Russell, *Atlanta, 1847-1890: City Building in the Old South and the New* (Baton Rouge, 1988), *passim;* Don H. Doyle, *New Men, New Cities, New South: Atlanta, Nashville, Charleston, Mobile, 1860-1910* (Chapel Hill, 1990), *passim;* Howard N. Rabinowitz, *Race Relations in the Urban South, 1865-1890* (NY, 1978), *passim;* C. Vann Woodward, *Origins of the New South, 1877-1913* (Baton Rouge, 1951), 124.
6. For a comparison of rates of employment of domestic workers in various cities, see David Katzman, *Seven Days a Week: Women and Domestic Service and Industrializing America* (NY, 1978), 61, 286.

7. On rates of married women in the work force, see Joseph A. Hill, *Women in Gainful Occupations 1870 to 1920* (Washington, DC, 1929), 334-336.

8. U.S., Dept. of Commerce and Labor, Bureau of the Census, *Special Reports: Occupations at the Twelfth Census* (Washington, DC, 1904), 486-489.

9. On laundry work, see Sarah Hill, "Bea, the Washerwoman," Federal Writer's Project Papers, Southern Historical Collection, Univ. of North Carolina, Chapel Hill; Jasper Battle, "Wash Day in Slavery," in George P. Rawick, ed., *The American Slave: A Composite Autobiography* (Westport, CT, 1972-1978), II, pt. 1, 70; Katzman, *Seven Days a Week*, 72, 82, 124; Daniel Sutherland, *Americans and Their Servants: Domestic Service in the United States from 1800 to 1920* (Baton Rouge, 1981), 92; Faye E. Dudden, *Serving Women: Household Service in Nineteenth Century America* (Middletown, CT, 1983), 224-225; Patricia E. Malcolmson, *English Laundresses: A Social History, 1850-1930* (Urbana, 1986), 11-43.

10. On live-out arrangements see Katzman, *Seven Days a Week*, 87-91.

11. See, for example, testimony of Albert C. Danner, U.S. Senate, Committee on Education and Labor, *Report Upon the Relations Between Labor and Capital* (Washington, DC, 1885), 105 (hereafter cited *Labor and Capital*).

12. See Myrta Lockett Avary, *Dixie After the War: An Exposition of Social Conditions Existing in the South during the Twelve Years Succeeding the Fall of Richmond* (Boston, 1906; reprint ed., 1937), 192; entries for 17 June through 2 Dec., 1866, Samuel P. Richards Diary, Atlanta Historical Society; entries for May 1865, Ella Gertrude Clanton Thomas Journal, Duke University Archives; Emma J. S. Prescott, "Reminiscences of the War," 49-55, Atlanta Historical Society.

13. Alexa Wynell Benson, "Race Relations in Atlanta, As Seen in a Critical Analysis of the City Council Proceedings and Other Related Works, 1865-1877" (unpublished MA essay, Atlanta Univ., 1966), 43-44.

14. On the crisis of free labor see Eric Foner, *Politics and Ideology in the Age of the Civil War* (NY, 1978), 97-125. On Black Codes see Eric Foner, *Reconstruction: America's Unfinished Business, 1863-1877* (NY, 1988), 109-202.

15. David Katzman speculates on the basis of the ratio of workers to employers that there were enough laundresses in Atlanta for every white household and even some black. See Katzman, *Seven Days a Week*, 91-92 and table 2-6.

16. On George Brown's campaign see *Atlanta Constitution*, 8, 15, 28, 29 Sept. 1912.

17. For example see H. McHatton, "Our House and Our Servant," *Atlanta Journal-Record of Medicine*, 5 (July 1903), 212-219; *Atlanta Constitution*, Dec. 19, 1909; William Northen, "Tuberculosis among Negroes," *Journal of the Southern Medical Association*, 6 (Oct. 1909), 415; H. L. Sutherland, "Health Conditions of the Negro in the South: With Special Reference to Tuberculosis," *Journal of the Southern Medical Association*, 6 (Oct. 1909), 399-407; *Daily Times*, n.p., Sept. 7, 1912, in Tuskegee Institute News Clip file (hereinafter TINF).

18. On the social and political implications of Atlanta's geography see James M. Russell, "Politics, Municipal Services, and the Working Class in Atlanta, 1865 to 1890," *Georgia Historical Quarterly*, 66 (1982), 467-491; Jerry Thornbery, "The Development of Black Atlanta, 1865-1885" (unpublished Ph.D. diss., Univ. of Maryland, 1977); Dana F. White, "The Black Sides of Atlanta: A Geography of Expansion and Containment, 1870-1970," *Atlanta Historical Journal*, 26 (Summer/Fall 1982), 199-225.

19. *Atlanta Constitution*, Sept. 15, 1912.

20. For other discussions associating domestic workers with disease and proposals to regulate them, see *Atlanta Constitution*, Feb. 11, Mar. 11, 12, 25, 1910, Oct. 2, 1912; and *Atlanta Independent*, Feb. 19, 1910.

21. *Atlanta Constitution*, Sept, 15, 1912; 1914 campaign literature, Joseph M. Brown Papers, Atlanta Historical Society.

22. For example see *Atlanta Constitution*, Mar. 31, 1910; Ruth Reed, *Negro Women of Gainsville, Georgia* (Athens, GA, 1921), 46. Canadian working-class women's mutual aid organizations operated similarly: see Varpu Lindström-Best, *Defiant Sisters: A Social History of Finnish Immigrant Women in Canada* (Toronto, 1988), 56-60.

23. *Atlanta Constitution*, Sept. 15, 1912.

24. 1914 campaign literature, Joseph M. Brown Papers, Atlanta Historical Society. Also see *Atlanta Constitution*, Mar. 31, 1910. The white trade unionists vehemently denied the charges by reminding their supporters that "the 'nigger' question is generally the last and most desperate resort of demagogues to win votes." While they admitted the importance of black workers organizing in separate unions to prevent undercutting white workers, they opposed integration and social equality. "'Little Joe' knows that there is not a single white labor unionist in Georgia, or the South, who would stand for that sort of thing," they insisted. *Journal of Labor*, July 24, 1914.

25. 1914 campaign literature, Joseph M. Brown Papers, Atlanta Historical Society; Dewey Grantham, *Hoke Smith and the Politics of the New South* (Baton Rogue, 1958), 270-273.

26. David M. Kennedy, *Over Here: The First World War and American Society* (NY, 1980), 269; David Montgomery, *Workers' Control in America* (Cambridge, 1979), 127-134.

27. Charles Crowe, "Racial Violence and Social Reform: Origins of the Atlanta Riot of 1906," *Journal of Negro History*, 52 (1968), 247; John Dittmer, *Black Georgia in the Progressive Era 1900-1920* (Urbana, IL, 1977), 87-88.

28. Walter F. White, "'Work or Fight' in the South," *The New Republic*, 18 (Mar. 1, 1919), 144-146.

29. See U.S. Dept. of the Interior, Bureau of the Census, *Report of the Population of the United States at the Eleventh Census: 1890* (Washington, DC, 1897), pt. II, 634-635; U.S. Dept. of Commerce and Labor, Bureau of the Census, *Special Reports: Occupations at the Twelfth Census* (Washington, DC, 1904), 486-489; idem, *Thirteenth Census of the United States Taken in the Year 1910*, vol. IV, "Population Occupational Statistics" (Washington, DC, 1914), 536-537; idem, *Fourteenth Census of the United States Taken in the Year 1920*, vol. IV, "Population, Occupations" (Washington, DC, 1923), 1053-1055.

30. Macon *News*, Oct. 18, 1918, in TINF. The federal government also made similar appeals to black women through war propaganda. See, for example, the Portsmouth, Virginia, *Star*, Oct. 21, 1918, in TINF.

31. Quoted in *Baltimore Daily Herald*, Sept. 10, 1918, Group 1, Series C, Administrative Files, Box 417, National Association for the Advancement of Colored People Papers, Library of Congress (hereinafter NAACP, LC).

32. For instances of violence against women, see Walter F. White, "Report of Conditions Found in Investigation of 'Work or Fight' Laws in Southern States," Group 1, Series C, Administrative Files, Box 417, NAACP, LC.

33. Walter F. White, "Report of Conditions Found in Investigation of 'Work or Fight' Laws in Southern States," NAACP, LC; Chicago *Defender*, July 13, 1918, and *New York Age*, Nov. 19, 1918, in TINF.

34. *New York Age*, Nov. 19, 1918, in TINF.

35. One outcome of the NAACP's involvement in this campaigning was that it increased the interests of black Southerners in joining the organization. Thus, "work or fight" laws became a critical galvanizing issue for the growth of local NAACP chapters in the South. See for example, *Atlanta Constitution*, July 10-Aug. 25, 1918; Rev. P. J. Bryant, Remarks to the 10th Annual Conference of the NAACP, June 24, 1919, Group 1, Series B, Annual Conference Files, Box 2, NAACP, LC.

36. On "hidden transcripts" see Scott, *Domination of the Arts of Resistance, passim.*

37. See Rabinowitz, *Race Relations in the Urban South*, 74-76; Katzman, *Seven Days a Week*, 196-197; William H. Harris, *The Harder We Run: Black Workers Since the Civil War* (1982), 37; Dudden, *Serving Women*, 232; Dorothy Sterling, *We Are Your Sisters: Black Women in the Nineteenth Century* (NY, 1984), 357-358; Jacqueline Jones, *Labor of Love, Labor of Sorrow: Black Women, Work and the Family from Slavery to Freedom* (NY, 1985), 148-149; Donna Van Raaphorst, *Union Maids Not Wanted: Organizing Domestic Workers, 1870-1940* (NY, 1988), 200. My own interpretation is closest to the only other study that considers most of the available evidence: Thornbery, "Development of Black Atlanta," 215-220. Rabinowitz's account has prevailed as the definitive one, often cited uncritically by other historians. But in the haste to force the event to conform to a thesis that emphasizes white attitudes and black inefficacy in the face of white power, he ignores significant evidence and overstates the known reprisals made against the women.

38. *Atlanta Constitution*, Aug. 3, 1881.

39. *Atlanta Constitution*, July 24, 1881.

40. *Atlanta Constitution*, Aug. 3, 1881. The women may have been counting on resources from individual savings and mutual aid organizations to help defray the costs of the fees. Nonetheless, the cost still would have been exorbitant.

41. *Atlanta Constitution*, July 21, 1881.

42. *Atlanta Constitution*, Sept. 6, 1881.

43. See Scott, *Domination*, 45.

22

Sojourner Truth
in Life and Memory:
Writing the Biography of an American Exotic[1]

Nell Irvin Painter

Sojourner Truth has been listed among great African-Americans since early in this century. You can buy postcards that show her portrait on one side and her words on the other and a button with her picture for your lapel to display your feminist credentials. Most North Americans, particularly those who are black and/or feminist, recognize her name. Her words inspire us, we say, but rarely do we know her deeds. Even so, her name is weighted with meaning while most of her contemporaries' have been forgotten. Although few white women's, black men's, or black women's reputations have survived from the nineteenth century (particularly if they belonged to people who were poor and uneducated), Truth's memory endures. Considering that she was illiterate, it is remarkable that her words, recorded by others, constitute her power and her fame. Solidly rooted in the evangelical culture of the antebellum northern United States, she nevertheless represents a phenomenon that we usually associate with the twentieth century: being famous for being famous. But what did she do? A brief biography will help define the historical figure, as opposed to the legend, to which I will return.

Sojourner Truth in Life

Isabella the Slave

Sojourner Truth, born Isabella in 1797, was the daughter of James and Elizabeth (Betsy) Bomefree, slaves in Ulster County, New York, and she appeared to be of unmixed African ancestry. As a child she received from her mother minimal religious instruction that included teaching Isabella the 'Lord's Prayer' in Dutch. In 1810 Isabella moved to New Paltz, New York, to become the slave of John Dumont, with whom she remained for seventeen years. As Dumont's Isabella she gained a reputation for working hard and considering herself apart from and above the general run of slaves. In her 1850 *Narrative* she disdains her peers, whose thoughts, she says, 'are no longer than my finger.'[2] At some point during her stay in New Paltz she married a man known only as Thomas, who was also enslaved, with whom she had five children. Thomas did not figure in her life after New Paltz.

Isabella's first act as a public person took place approximately a year before she was emancipated by New York state law in 1827. One of her younger children, Peter, had been sold into perpetual slavery in Alabama, which was illegal under New York state law. Isabella appealed to local Quakers, who helped her find a lawyer and recover her son. At about the same time she became a Christian after seeing a blinding light that she identified with Jesus, whom she saw as an intercessor. She also initiated a change of owners and spent her last year in slavery in Kingston with a Quaker couple, the Van Wagenens. There she met a Miss Greer (or Grear), a fervent Methodist, who took the newly emancipated Isabella with her to New York City in 1828 or 1829.

Isabella in New York City

In New York, Isabella attended the predominantly white John Street Methodist Church (the oldest Methodist church in the United States, founded in 1766) and the black African Methodist Episcopal Zion Church (founded in 1796, when blacks withdrew from the John Street Church because of racial discrimination). She also began to forge her own reputation as a gifted Methodist preacher and visionary at the camp meetings that were frequently held around New York City during the Second Great Awakening, that massive religious upheaval that stretched from Kentucky to Maine, and from the 1790s through the 1830s.

In New York City Miss Greer introduced Isabella to Elijah Pierson, who was involved with the Magdalene Asylum, a mission of middle-class New Yorkers, mostly women, to prostitutes on Bowery Hill.[3] Isabella soon found the Magdalene Asylum too raucous for her taste, but she continued as a household worker with Pierson for several years. In Pierson's house Isabella met Robert Matthews, an American of Scottish descent, who called himself Matthias, and she converted to his views in 1832. Matthews had been an itinerant preacher in and around Rochester in the late 1820s. In 1830 he declared himself a prophet and Jew and took the name Matthias. With Pierson's support he established a "kingdom," a sort of religious commune, first in New York City, then up the Hudson River in Sing Sing.

In Matthias's kingdom Isabella occupied an anomalous position. She, like the white members, had contributed her material resources to the commune. Yet she functioned as a domestic worker as much as a full-fledged member. The white women in the commune did some housework, but the brunt of the hardest and dirtiest labor fell on Isabella. Nonetheless she was clearly far more integral a member of the commune than a mere domestic drudge. She had joined the kingdom out of religious conviction and stuck with it as a conscious decision. Though not a leader of the commune—the leaders were male—her opinion mattered.

The kingdom disintegrated in 1835, after spouse swapping at Matthias's behest and Pierson's death in questionable circumstances. Considering that Isabella remained in the kingdom until it fell apart, she probably shared many of Matthias's religious tenets. It is not possible to know exactly what she believed at this point, for neither Isabella nor Matthias recorded their beliefs. After the commune's demise, however, journalists reported that Matthias thought that women were the fount of all evil, that eating pork was wrong, that heaven would be achieved only on earth, that the world would soon burn up, and that God was angry with people.[4]

Sojourner Truth

After the break-up of the Matthias kingdom, Isabella continued to do household work in New York City until divine revelation changed the direction of her life. As so often happened in the United States in the early nineteenth century, God spoke to her directly. In 1843 she took the name Sojourner Truth and set out to preach love and brotherhood on the roads and camp meetings to the east of New York. As an itinerant female preacher, she belonged to an established tradition of women evangelists, Quakers and Methodists, in which her closest peers were black women like Jarena Lee and Zilpha Elaw.[5] Prohibited by church discipline to head established churches, these female prophets heeded the divine calling to preach and reached wide, heterogeneous audiences.

Preaching as she went, Sojourner Truth traveled through Brooklyn, Long Island, and Connecticut and into Massachusetts, where she encountered the Northampton Association of Education and Industry, a labor commune along the lines of Brook Farm. Established in 1841 and headed by George W. Benson (William Lloyd Garrison's brother-in-law), the Northampton Association brought together middle-class reformers who prized honest labor, peace, and racial and gender equality. Prominent abolitionists such as Frederick Douglass, William Lloyd Garrison, and an anti-slavery Member of the British Parliament, George Thompson, were frequent visitors.

In Northampton as in New York and Sing Sing, Truth belonged to a commune whose other members were well-educated whites. But where the Matthias Kingdom had stood for an uncodified, personal religion, the Northampton Association represented contemporary transcendentalism and Fourierist socialism, which were far less insular and more sophisticated philosophies. In Northampton Sojourner Truth came into contact with prominent Garrisonians under whose influence she honed her preaching gift and developed into the bearer of the antislavery and feminist messages that her late twentieth-century audience remembers. Although the Northampton Association dissolved in 1846, Truth remained with the Bensons, to whom she contributed household labor.

By the late 1840s she had acquired a reputation as a powerful speaker, so that by the time she went to Ohio and Indiana in the early 1850s she was already well known. Never able to accumulate much personal wealth or income, she supported herself through donations and the sale of *The Narrative of Sojourner Truth*, recorded by Oliver Gilbert and originally published in Boston in 1850. In the 1850s she was often one of the several speakers at antislavery meetings where Frederick Douglass and William Lloyd Garrison also appeared. She was never the featured speaker at abolitionist and women's rights meetings, perhaps because, in contrast to Frederick Douglass and others who commented in an informed manner on current political topics, she was considered a speaker who could be relied upon to be brief, idiosyncratic, and highly entertaining. Her remarks were often omitted from newspaper summaries or mentioned only briefly, as though her message were already well known. She does not appear in the official proceedings of the women's rights meeting in Akron, Ohio, in 1851, for instance, at which she uttered what is now her most famous line: 'Ar'n't I a Woman?'[6]

In 1856 Truth moved to Battle Creek, Michigan, which served as her permanent base, although she spent long periods on the road. Continuing to lecture on the antislavery and women's rights circuit, she bared her breast to prove that she was a woman in 1858 and the following year answered Frederick Douglass's admonition to southern slaves to seize their freedom forcibly by asking Douglass whether God were dead.

As was the case with other abolitionists, the Civil War changed Sojourner Truth's priorities. She became concerned with the plight of fugitive slave refugees in Washington, DC, who were known as 'contrabands,' and between 1864 and 1870 spent much of her time there working on their behalf. Volunteering alongside other abolitionists like Josephine Griffing, Harriett Jacobs and Laura S. Haviland, she visited hospitals and homes, preaching 'order, cleanliness and virtue.'[7] As a small-scale effort to place freedpeople with prospective northern employers came to an end, Truth became convinced that the freedpeople needed land and their own state in the West. Nine years before the black Exodus to Kansas of 1879, she presented President Ulysses S. Grant with a petition calling for the settlement of the freedpeople on public lands. She visited Kansas in 1871-72, advocating black migration to the West. Truth's itinerant ministry and freedmen's aid campaign ended in 1875, when her grandson and amanuensis, Sammy Banks, fell ill and died, forcing her return to Battle Creek. The historian Saunders Redding writes that her funeral in 1883 in the Congregational and Presbyterian churches in Battle Creek was the town's largest ever.[8]

In most general phrasing, Sojourner Truth's deeds were three-fold: she had been an enslaved worker, an experience she called upon regularly to authenticate her views; she was an inspired, moving preacher with a style that combined the power of her African heritage and the rhetoric of Second Great Awakening evangelism; and she was a forceful advocate for the rights of blacks (enslaved and emancipated) and women (black and white). In the era of the self-made man, Sojourner Truth, the poor, uneducated former slave, created the persona of the prophet.

The Legend of Sojourner Truth

Truth had begun to forge a reputation as a speaker at antislavery and women's rights meetings in the 1840s, and by 1850 she was famous enough to merit the recording of her life in the *Narrative of Sojourner Truth*. This account contains all the material that is widely known about Truth, which has reappeared countless times in subsequent biographies. The now famous 'Ar'n't I a woman' speech to the 1851 Ohio women's convention did not become emblematic of her rhetoric until the late 1870s, for contemporary newspapers accounts, while capturing the gist of her remarks—that women deserved equal rights with men and that black women who had worked all their lives and enjoyed no privileges were just as much women as pampered ladies—did not appear in the form in which we know them.[9] In the mid-nineteenth century, Truth's more famous line was 'Frederick, is God dead?,' the second clause of which was carved on her grave stone.

During her lifetime, Truth's reputation within and beyond abolitionist and women's rights circles was greatly enhanced in an essay by Harriet Beecher Stowe, 'Sojourner Truth, The Libyan Sibyl.' After the publication of Stowe's article, Truth was often called the 'Libyan Sibyl,' as in newspaper accounts of her speeches and in the caption of the frontispiece illustration of the 1878 edition of the *Narrative of Sojourner Truth*. This single essay is so important an ingredient of the Sojourner Truth legend and is so useful in explicating Truth's nineteenth-century persona that it deserves closer examination.

The 'Libyan Sibyl'

When Harriet Beecher Stowe wrote 'Sojourner Truth, The Libyan Sibyl' for the *Atlantic Monthly* of 1863 she had not seen Truth for several years.[10] Stowe was writing a great deal rather quickly, perhaps carelessly, when she penned 'The Libyan Sibyl.' Stowe's Sojourner Truth, based on memory, cursory research in Truth's and Gilbert's *Narrative* and anti-slavery newspaper coverage from the late 1850s, presents Truth's characteristics, genuine or not, that were most useful to this hurried author. According to Stowe, Truth was born in Africa and had already died. Hence the essay is far more valuable as an indication of how Truth was seen by her audiences than as a source of information about her life. Considering that much reportage on Truth was inaccurate, perhaps Stowe becomes all the more valuable as a reflection of Truth's mid-nineteenth-century persona.[11]

Stowe describes a singular character who had visited her home and staged an amusing performance before several prominent preacher guests. Writing at length and in dialect, as though she is quoting Truth, Stowe has Truth present a short slave narrative, sing hymns and mention her preaching frequently. Stowe's Truth is more an ex-slave than an abolitionist (though Stowe says that she is known only in radical abolitionist circles) and not a very enthusiastic supporter of women's rights. One of Truth's two comments on women's rights is deprecatory, ridiculing the idea of wearing bloomers. The other paraphrases part of an 1851 version of Truth's remarks before the Ohio women's rights convention. To round out her description, Stowe quotes Wendell Phillips quoting Truth asking 'Frederick, is God Dead?' Through Phillips, Stowe records Truth's ability to move an audience with a few well-chosen words. As Stowe presents her, Truth sees herself primarily as a preacher whose main text is her conversion experience. In her description, Truth is depicted as a charismatic figure with what Stowe, the spiritualist, terms 'a strong sphere.'[12]

In this sketch, Truth appears first and foremost as an exotic; she is so far outside the cultured mainstream that she had never heard of the most prominent preacher of mid-nineteenth-century America, Stowe's brother, Henry Ward Beecher. When Stowe introduces Beecher, Truth, with the temerity of the ignorant, compares herself to him. Stowe's Truth is an African, a native, a character who embodies the 'fervor of Ethiopia, wild, savage, hunted of all nations, but burning after God in her tropic heart...'[13] In an essay that is about 5250 words long, Stowe uses the words Africa or African eleven times, adding several other phrases that include 'tropics,' 'Libyan,' 'Ethiopian,' 'Egypt,' and 'native.' While she compares Truth to a strange and foreign work of art, Stowe draws upon a domestic stereotype, that of the pickaninny, to characterize Truth's nine-year-old grandson, James Caldwell. In Stowe's hands, Caldwell becomes 'the fattest, jolliest woolly-headed little specimen of Africa that one can imagine.'[14] As in her description of Uncle Tom's and Aunt Chloe's children in Uncle Tom's Cabin, this black child becomes a grinning example of thoughtless mirth, a figure that belongs to the panorama of American racist caricature.

The immense cultural distance between the naive Truth, on the one hand, and Stowe and the 'eminent clergymen' on the other is emphasized as Stowe quotes one of her educated guests as requesting, more than once, that Truth come entertain them because they are feeling 'dull.' As though she were a sideshow, Truth (who is ostensibly a house guest for a few days) is summoned to spice up a boring evening. Indeed, Stowe says that 'an audience was what she wanted.' Truth in this setting plays a part reminiscent of one of P.T. Barnum's antebellum performers, Joice Heth, who claimed to be a 161-year-old slave who had nursed George Washington.[15]

The Sojourner Truth that emerges from Stowe's essay is an ideal nineteenth-century type—the pastoral, which is primitive, exotic, and utterly unlike civilized people. Pioneers in American studies like Henry Nash Smith and Leo Marx long ago pointed out the attractiveness of the pastoral in nineteenth-century American imaginations.[16] As the northern United States industrialized and urbanized, educated white Americans caught up in a complex and alienating urban reality sought out the pastoral, figures of pristine purity, unspoiled by education and civilization. Whereas cultivated folk were enervated by the complex realities with which they grappled daily in offices and factories, exotics supposedly represented an older, or at least a simpler reality, isolated from the complicated facts of conflict and responsibility.[17] In the 'Libyan Sibyl,' Stowe marks off the boundaries between herself and Truth and her grandson by stressing their otherness—Truth as 'the' African, uneducated, divinely inspired, and charismatic—her grandson as a figure of fun. Stowe's approach, which stresses Truth's ethnic and racial heritage as the source of her genius, represents what historian George M. Fredrickson calls the 'romantic racialism' so prevalent among abolitionists.[18]

Current scholarship identifies this nineteenth-century primitivism and romantic racialism with imperialist literature which, employing the singular—as in phrases like Stowe's 'the African seems to seize on the tropical fervor and luxuriance of Scripture imagery as something native' and 'the African nature'—stresses disparities of power and distinctions between European and Euro-Americans and natives, domestic and foreign.[19] This sort of characterization leads easily to racial generalizations, whether favorable (as in Stowe's portrait of Truth) or vicious, as in late-nineteenth and twentieth century racism. Recent literary scholarship terms generalizations such as Stowe's 'orientalism' as 'essentialist metonymy' that tends to deny the individuality of the native/colored subject.[20]

For all her fondness for Truth, or what she makes of her memory, Stowe reduces her to the status of a primitive whose observations might be witty, divinely inspired, but valuable only as entertainment.

Valuable she was and familiar as a type that did not force her white audiences to adjust their preconceptions about race and sex. The very familiarity of the pastoral as a genre may well explain the resilience of Truth's legend while her more educated black female counterparts in abolition and women's rights remained largely unknown until quite recently. Truth's naive persona did not force her white audiences to reevaluate their stereotypes about black women, as did educated black spokeswomen like Mary Ann Shadd Cary, Grace and Sarah Douglass, Maria Stewart, and Frances Ellen Watkins Harper. In a society in which most white Americans assumed that black women were subjects to be instructed and patronized, these better-educated and less picturesque figures were hard for many of their white colleagues to stomach. Women like Harper and Stewart, who did not capture the popular imagination as did those closer to the pastoral, were quickly forgotten by all but specialists in Afro-American history. For a century or more the two most famous nineteenth-century black women were both untutored ex-slaves: Harriet Tubman and Sojourner Truth. Until just now, at least, the naive, rather than the educated persona seems to have better facilitated black women's entry into American memory.[21]

Stowe's portrait of Truth, though far better fleshed out than shorter descriptions that appeared in the newspapers, has much in common with them, in part because the latter often drew on the influential 'Libyan Sibyl' portrait. Every article mentions Truth's powerful personality and eloquence. But at the same time, Truth's function as an amusing performer is also noted, even before black audiences.[22] The 1878 edition of the *Narrative* contains reprints from newspapers (undated, but from the late 1860s and early 1870s) that reinforce this impression:

From the Fall River, Massachusetts, papers: (p. 201) 'Sojourner Truth—the colored American Sibyl—will speak in the vestry of the Franklin Street Church, on Monday evening. Come and hear an *original*.'

From the New Jersey papers: (p. 204) 'Springfield, Union County, New Jersey, and its Presbyterian Church were honored on Wednesday night by the presence of that lively old negro mummy, whose age ranges among the hundreds—Sojourner Truth—who fifty years ago was considered a crazy woman. . .'

From the Detroit papers: (p. 237) 'This remarkable woman, born a slave in the State of New York more than eighty years ago, and emancipated in 1827, will speak in the lecture room of the Unitarian Church, corner of Shelby Street and Lafayette Avenue, on Monday evening, to any who will choose to hear her. Her lecture will be highly entertaining and impressive. She is a woman of strong religious nature, with an entirely original eloquence and humor, possessed of a weird imagination, of most grotesque but strong, clear mind, and one who, without the aid of reading or writing, is strangely susceptible to all that in thought and action is now current in the world. . . .'

Mid-nineteenth-century audiences and readers would have seen a Sojourner Truth that was different from her late twentieth-century characterization. Only after the Civil War did her image change somewhat, though not entirely, in the direction of the twentieth-century persona.

Before the Civil War, Truth spoke for women's rights and abolition in general terms. If she had a concrete aim, it was to sell copies of her *Narrative* and illustrated calling cards, which were her main source of income. But once she went to Washington during the war and discovered the pressing needs of the southern refugees, her speeches took on a pointed edge. She spoke to collect monetary aid for the freedpeople and to gain signatures on her petition for their relocation in the West. By the late 1860s, then, her coverage grew more serious as she represented needs that were readily apparent. With her virtual retirement from the lecture circuit in the late 1870s her coverage improved again, particularly as Frances Gage's version of Truth's 1851 speech gained currency. This version, which first appeared in the 1870s, quotes Truth's lines as they are known today: Truth speaks of her work and her sufferings, repeating three times the rhetorical question, 'ar'n't I a woman?' Although she did not die until 1883, by the late 1870s Truth had been off the lecture circuit long enough for her actual performances, with the amusing naivete that obscured the sharpness of her intellect, to fade from memory. Increasingly this speech, along with her question to Frederick Douglass, established her reputation as a great black American.

Sojourner Truth in American Memory

The desuetude of American feminism at the turn of the century readjusted Truth's status, and her memory slipped away from white feminist and into the hands of blacks. In the early twentieth century, Truth's legend depended mainly on black compilers, who, remembering her value to white reformers as an exotic, recast the Stowe-inflected version of Truth's contributions to reform. Whereas white antislavery and women's rights advocates had found Truth's naive persona charming and attractive, twentieth-century blacks were ambivalent about her antebellum success as a representative, before white audiences, of the American pastoral.

The very otherness that had made Truth so appealing to Harriet Beecher Stowe diminished her in the eyes of educated, forward-looking African Americans. Frederick Douglass mentioned her only briefly in the 1892 version of his autobiography, *The Life and Times of Frederick Douglass, Written by Himself*, and the scholar known as the father of Negro History, Carter G. Woodson, saw Truth as a minor figure. In a book that originally appeared in the 1920s, Woodson spoke of Truth as 'an illiterate woman' who, accompanying serious antislavery lecturers such as Frederick Douglass and Charles Lenox Remond, would 'stir audiences with her heavy voice, quaint language, and homely illustrations.'[23]

Hallie Q. Brown, the president of the National Association of Colored Women, published *Homespun Heroines and Other Women of Distinction* in 1926, in which a neutral, six-page profile of Truth paraphrased material from Truth's *Narrative* and featured a photo of her with President Abraham Lincoln.[24] Another pioneer black historian, Benjamin Brawley of Howard University, included Truth in his *Negro Builders and Heroes* published in 1937 by the University of North Carolina Press, which also published Arthur Huff Fauset's touching, perceptive, full-length biography of Truth in 1938, the first since Gilbert's *Narrative*.

Not surprisingly, Truth's story acquired renewed attractiveness during the 1960s, when she appeared in collective biographies, such as Sylvia G.L. Dannett's *Profiles of Negro Womanhood*, New York, 1964, and in full-length biographies for young readers such as Jacqueline Bernard's *Journey Toward Freedom*, New York, 1967. These accounts lack both the amusement of nineteenth-century witnesses of an exotic and the ambivalence of early twentieth-century black scholars toward an illiterate who charmed white audiences.

By the late twentieth century, Sojourner Truth emerges as an admirable figure who is not at all to be patronized or dismissed. With her words unencumbered by her ambiguous personal presence, Truth has by now been distilled into an essence of her nineteenth-century strength: an ability to delve to the heart of a controversial matter with a few, well-chosen words. Her genius no longer complicated by a presentation that played into the hands of romantic racists, Sojourner Truth today symbolizes a self-made woman of extraordinary perception. She serves the interests of African Americans and feminists by demanding that feminist thought—so long the preserve of middle- and upper-class northern whites—include black women and poor women who have worked for other people all their days. Today Sojourner Truth is the embodiment of the need to reconstruct an American history that is sensitive simultaneously to race, class, and gender.

A Scholarly Biography?

For all this attention, however, no historian has yet published a scholarly biography of Sojourner Truth, doubtless for reasons that I have encountered in my own work on this formidable character. This first difficulty concerns the virtual lack of autobiographical documents. Although Truth has a narrative, it is built of materials that had already been stylized and sanitized. The 128-page section of her slave narrative represents stories that she told countless times on the lecture circuit and out of which she had by 1850 distilled much nuance and affect. As an illiterate all her days, she left only a handful of letters that were dictated to her grandson or others and that again provide few glimpses into her thought or feelings.[25] While it is a commonplace that every biography has an autobiography at its heart, it is also true that without autobiography, biography remains a hollow undertaking. In Sojourner Truth's case, the lack of personal materials has meant that each of her biographies retraces the familiar ground of her *Narrative* and other published sources.

Truth was powerful, poignant, and entertaining on the lecture circuit, but the illiteracy that authenticated her naive persona entails serious drawbacks for her biographer. Illiterate as she was and more influenced by divine (rather than institutional) realities, Truth stayed outside the organizational loops of antislavery and feminist circles. Not having filled regular organizational roles, she attracted and generated very few documents. No letters to or from her detail her position in these movements, and principals, such as Frederick Douglass, William Lloyd Garrison, and Harriet Beecher Stowe, barely comment upon her in their correspondence. The lack of documents from Truth might not be so crippling if she had played a less peripheral part in the movements upon whose platforms she spoke. Almost nothing remains from her about events, experiences, and people, almost nothing about her in other people's correspondence. Yet documents (that do not exist from or about Sojourner Truth) are a biographer's essential raw material. As well-known as she is today, Truth remains the phantom of the abolitionist movement, unheard of in biographies of abolitionists and feminists and missing almost entirely from histories of their movements.

Faced with insurmountable barriers to the composition of a scholarly biography, why do I not simply give up and call this an impossible task? When it comes to producing a conventional biography, this must be the response. But as a historian of people who have been termed inarticulate, I cannot stop there. The obstructions in the way of Sojourner Truth's biography are commonplace and lie between the biographer and most of her female, poor, and/or non-white subjects. If Sojourner Truth, who is at least very famous, poses such challenges to biographers, there are scores—hundreds?—of other, less-known but worthy subjects who pose exactly the same problems. The Sojourner Truth biographical problem becomes a larger question of how to deal with people who are in History but who have not left the kinds of sources to which historians and biographers ordinarily turn.[26] In order not to cede biography to subjects who had resources enough to secure the educations that would allow them to leave the usual sources for the usual kind of biographies, we need to construct new biographical approaches. In this case, I begin—here in the most preliminary and tentative way—by attempting to understand what made Sojourner Truth a historical phenomenon, for that is what the sources permit.

NOTES

1. I would like to acknowledge the support of the Center for Advanced Study in the Behavioral Sciences, Stanford, California, National Endowment for the Humanities grant #FC-20060-85, and the Andrew W. Mellon Foundation and the assistance of Philip Lapsansky of the Library Company of Philadelphia, Bettye Collier-Thomas of Temple University, Dorothy Sterling of Wellfleet, Massachusetts, Carleton Mabee of the State University of New York, New Paltz, Joan D. Hedrick of Trinity College, Lynn Hudson of the University of North Carolina at Chapel Hill, and Leen-Kiat Soh of the University of Kansas School of Business.

2. Written down by Olive Gilbert, a Connecticut abolitionist who is now known only as the author of the *Narrative of Sojourner Truth*. The *Narrative* originally appeared in 1850. Subsequent editions included additional material. I have used Gilbert's *Narrative of Sojourner Truth: A Bondswoman of Olden Time, Emancipated by the New York Legislature in the Early Part of the Present Century With a History of her Labors and Correspondence Drawn from her "Book of Life"* (Battle Creek, Michigan, 1878). The quote is from page 24.

3. See Carroll Smith Rosenberg, 'Beauty, the Beast, and the Militant Woman: A Case Study in Sex Roles and Social Stress in Jacksonian America,' in *Disorderly Conduct: Visions of Gender in Victorian America* (Harper & Row, New York, 1985), pp. 109-28. Smith Rosenberg was not aware of Sojourner Truth's association with the Magdalene Asylum.

4. G. Vale, *Fanaticism: Its Source and Influence, Illustrated by the Simple Narrative of Isabella, in the Case of Matthias, Mr. and Mrs. B. Folger, Mr. Pierson, Mr. Mills, Catherine, Isabella, &c. &c. A Reply to W.L. Stone, With Descriptive Portraits of All the Parties, While at Sing-Sing and at Third Street.—Containing the Whole Truth—and Nothing but the Truth* (New York, 1835), part I, pp. 45-46.

5. See William L. Andrews, ed., *Sisters of the Spirit: Three Black Women's Autobiographies of the Nineteenth Century* (Indiana University Press, Bloomington, Indiana, 1986).

6. *The Proceedings of the Woman's Rights Convention. Held at Akron, Ohio. May 28 and 29, 1851* (Bert Franklin, New York, 1851). These proceedings contain an apology for omitting some material for lack of space, but what was considered most important, such as letters from important persons who did not attend, was included.

7. Quote in Dorothy Sterling, ed., *We Are Your Sisters: Black Women in the Nineteenth Century*. (Norton, New York, 1984), p. 255. This collection contains the most interesting extant letters from Sojourner Truth. Others are in the 1878 edition of Truth's *Narrative*. Harriet Jacobs is currently the object of considerable scholarly interest, though until the mid-1980s, she was less well-known than Truth.

8. Saunders Redding, 'Sojourner Truth,' in Edward T. James, ed., *Notable American Women*, Vol. III (Harvard University Press, Cambridge, Mass., 1971), p. 481.

9. The now-standard account (by novelist and poet Frances Dana Gage, president of the women's convention of 1851) of what has become known as the 'Ar'n't I a woman?' speech first appeared in an article, probably in the Boston *Woman's Journal* in the late 1870s, that I have not yet been able to locate. This account was reprinted in the 1878 edition of *The Narrative of Sojourner Truth*, reprinted again in the *Woman's Journal* of 1 December 1883, and again for the first volume of Elizabeth Cady Staton, Susan B. Anthony, and Matilda Joslyn Gage's *History of Woman Suffrage* (Fowler & Wells, New York, 1881), the source that most quotes cite.

   I have seen two 1851 accounts of Truth's remarks. The report in the Boston *Liberator* (13 June 1851) says of Truth, in its entirety: 'Sojourner Truth spoke in her own peculiar style, showing that she was a match for most men. She had ploughed, hoed, dug, and could *eat* as much, if she could get it. The power and wit of this remarkable woman convulsed the audience with laughter. I wish I could report every word she said, but I cannot.' The report in the Ohio *Anti-Slavery Bugle*, collected in the Black Abolitionist Papers, goes into more detail, but as in the *Liberator*, does not mention the 'Ar'n't I a woman?' refrain that has come to characterize this speech.

10. 'Libyan Sibyl', *Atlantic Monthly* XI, no. 66 (April 1863), pp. 473-81.

11. Reporters often made mistakes, and Truth was not exempt as a subject. In 1861 the Boston *Liberator* (21 June 1861) carried a story by Josephine Griffing that described her as half Indian. In 1876, seven years before her actual death, the Boston *Woman's Journal* (5 August 1876) reported that she had died and named Harriet Beecher Stowe rather than Olive Gilbert as the compiler of her narrative. When the *Woman's Journal* (1 December 1883) correctly reported her death, it gave her age as 110.

12. Stowe, 'Libyan Sibyl,' pp. 473, 477.

13. *Ibid.*, p. 477.

14. *Ibid.*, p. 474. See also Jacqueline Bernard, *Journey Toward Freedom: The Story of Sojourner Truth* (Norton, New York, 1967), p. 178.

15. Leo Braudy, *The Frenzy of Renown: Fame and Its History* (Oxford University Press, New York, 1986), p. 501. According to an undated Philadelphia newspaper reprinted in the 1878 edition of the *Narrative of Sojourner Truth*: 'Sojourner Truth jocularly denies that she ever nursed General Washington, but she says she "has done quit" telling people how old she is.' (page 224)

16. Henry Nash Smith, *Virgin Land: The American West as Symbol and Myth* (Harvard University Press, Cambridge, Mass., 1950), pp. 49-52, 84, and Leo Marx, *The Machine in the Garden: Technology and the Pastoral Ideal in America* (Oxford University Press, New York, 1964), pp. 5-11.

17. See Richard Poirier, *The Performing Self* (Oxford University Press, New York, 1971), p. 163.

18. George M. Fredrickson, *The Black Image in the White Mind: The Debate on Afro-American Character and Destiny, 1817-1914* (Harper & Row, New York, 1971), pp. 97-117.

19. Stowe, 'Libyan Sibyl,' p. 480.

20. See Abdul R. JanMohammed, 'The Economy of Manichean Allegory: The Function of Racial Difference in Colonialist Literature', and Mary Louis Pratt, 'Scratches on the Face of the Country' or, 'What Mr. Barrow Saw in the Land of the Bushmen,'

in Henry Louis Gates, Jr., ed., *'Race,' Writing and Difference* (University of Chicago Press, Chicago, 1986), pp. 87, 139, and Edward W. Said, *Orientalism* (Pantheon, New York, 1978), pp. 40-49, 72-73, 206-207, 232-235.

21. The lives of educated nineteenth-century black women are the subjects of the following partial list of published and forthcoming works: Gerda Lerner, ed., *Black Women in White America* (Random House, New York, 1972); Rosalyn Terborg-Penn and Sharon Harley, eds., *The Afro-American Woman* (Kennikat Press, Port Washington, NY, 1978); Paula Giddings, *"When and Where I Enter . . .": The Impact of Black Women on Race and Sex in America* (William Morrow & Co., New York, 1984); Dorothy Sterling, ed., *We Are Your Sisters: Black Women in the Nineteenth Century* (Norton, New York, 1984); Marilyn Richardson, ed., *Maria W. Stewart, America's First Black Woman Political Writer: Essays and Speeches* (University of Indiana Press, Bloomington, 1987); Bettye Collier-Thomas, *Frances Ellen Watkins Harper: Abolitionist and Feminist Reformer* (University of North Carolina Press, Chapel Hill, forthcoming).

22. E.g., a report of a Truth speech at the Anthony Street Church, whose congregation was African-American, is studded with the notation '[Laughter].' (New York *Anti-Slavery Standard*, 10 December 1853).

23. Carter G. Woodson and Charles H. Wesley, *Negro Makers of History*, 6th ed. (Associated Publishers, Washington, DC, 1968), pp. 201-2; Frederick Douglass, *The Life and Times of Frederick Douglass, Written by Himself* (New York, 1892, reprinted 1972); Arthur Farset, *Sojourner Truth: God's Faithful Pilgrim* (University of North Carolina Press, Chapel Hill, 1938).

24. The photograph that appears opposite page 16 in *Homespun Heroines* is a composite image.

25. Carleton Mabee's 'Sojourner Truth, Bold Prophet: Why Did She Never Learn to Read?' *New York History* (January 1988), pp. 55-57, provides a thoughtful, sustained inquiry into Truth's life-long illiteracy.

26. Two recent biographers, Robert Hill on Marcus Garvey and Martin Bauml Duberman on Paul Robeson, have faced this problem. Hill, whose biography is forthcoming, is relying on the Garvey papers, which collected every extant document about Garvey. Duberman, is his *Paul Robeson: A Biography* (Knopf, New York, 1989), relied heavily on the journal and correspondence of Robeson's wife Eslanda.

23

Black Womanhood in Nineteenth-Century America:

Subversion and Self-Construction in Two Women's Autobiographies

Beth Maclay Doriani

In recent years both feminist and Afro-American literary studies have challenged us to consider the dynamics of self among excluded people and to question the assumption that the American self can be adequately represented by the solitary white male. These critics have begun to recover the voices of women and Afro-Americans in treatments of American history and literature, decisively changing the way we approach American Studies. In exploring the beginnings of a black, female literary tradition, Frances Smith Foster, Mary Helen Washington, Valerie Smith, Henry Louis Gates, Jr., Hazel Carby, and others have questioned the idea that white men's experiences are representative of American culture.[1] These and other scholars collectively have begun to show us the coherence of a black women's literary tradition.

The importance of black women's experience has only begun to be considered by autobiographical critics. Estelle C. Jelinek, Donna C. Stanton, and Shari Benstock recently pointed out the exclusion of women's works from analyses of the autobiographical self and then began to fill that gap with their studies on the theory and practice of women's autobiography.[2] Yet in focusing on women's experiences, even these fine critics have only marginally included discussions of autobiographies written by *black* women.[3] Regina Blackburn, Frances Smith Foster, Elizabeth Fox-Genovese, and, most recently—in the only book-length study of its kind—Joanne M. Braxton have begun the study in greater depth, yet there remains much room to explore the black female autobiographical self. In Braxton's words, feminist critics have "been almost as guilty of overlooking black women's autobiographical writings as have the critics of the so-called mainstream of Afro-American literature."[4] Autobiographical critics would do well to explore the self-portraitures of women, including black women, to develop our understanding of American selfhood.

Following Braxton's methods, we need to focus on the individual texts of black women in relation to each other in close readings. We must refuse to conflate black women's voices into depersonalized, generalized abstractions if we are to read their texts well and fully as Fox-Genovese urges.[5] While Braxton helpfully focuses on the voice, forms, and themes in black women's autobiography in the writers' quest for identity, the self-definitions of the autobiographers as they express their identity still need to be analyzed. In two nineteenth-century autobiographical works, Harriet Jacobs's *Incidents in the Life of a Slave Girl: Written by Herself* (1861) and Harriet Wilson's *Our Nig: or, Sketches from the Life of a Free Black* (1859)—a text Braxton does not treat—we see two early attempts by black women to define themselves. When juxtaposed in close readings, the works reveal surprisingly similar definitions of the black female self. These definitions defy the social constraints on the writers' identities as women and as blacks, as well as the reproduction of those constraints in the genre conventions that the writers manipulate. A close comparison of the works also reveals similar rhetorical strategies. Both women achieve a creation of self through subversive interplay with readers' expectations, as they draw on and reshape popular female genres—the seduction novel and the domestic novel—as well as an Afro-American genre, the slave narrative. In Jacobs and Wilson we see the beginnings of an autobiographical practice that revises the understandings of personhood developed by black male and white female literary traditions.

Despite the difference in genre—one is a slave narrative; the other, a novel—critics agree that both *Incidents* and *Our Nig* are the life-stories of their writers. Jean Fagan Yellin first documented the authenticity of Jacobs's *Incidents* and published an annotated edition of the narrative that establishes the real names of the people.[6] Similarly, Henry Louis Gates, Jr. has shown that events of *Our Nig* parallel closely the documented events of Wilson's life. Wilson's book tells the story of her life as a legally free Northern mulatto woman who lives in the household of a white family that serves as her guardian. Gates has documented the authorship of, and events surrounding, her narrative in his recent edition of *Our Nig*.[7] The recovery of the narratives and the documentation of their autobiographical authenticity make possible a deeper understanding of Afro-American women's history and literary quest for identity.

Harriet Jacobs published her *Incidents* twenty years after her flight from slavery. She had fled to the North in 1842 after nearly seven years in hiding, eventually making her way to Rochester where she began working in 1849 in an antislavery reading room, office, and bookstore. There, she read her way through the abolitionists' library of books and papers and met abolitionist Amy Post, who urged her to make her personal history public. Not until 1852, when she was freed legally with her "purchase" by a white friend, Cornelia Grinnell Willis, did Jacobs seriously consider writing her autobiography. She initially planned to dictate her story to best-selling author Harriet Beecher Stowe. But upon suffering a racial insult from Stowe, Jacobs eventually decided to write it herself.[8] Convinced that Mrs. Willis's husband, well-known magazinist Nathaniel Parker Willis, was proslavery, she secretly worked at her narrative at night while employed as a nursemaid for the Willis family.

In 1853, Jacobs began sending sample pieces to newspapers in the form of letters from a fugitive slave, eventually completing the entire narrative privately in the autobiographical genre of her people. Like other slave narratives, the work was an account of her personal history, written in part to aid the abolitionist cause. Jacobs was unable initially to find a publisher. Finally, a publisher agreed to take her manuscript, provided that she include an introduction by Lydia Maria Child. In addition to her introduction, the abolitionist Child also provided some editorial assistance. Despite the bankruptcy of her publisher, Jacobs's story finally appeared in print when she bought the plates and had a Boston printer publish the narrative. Her book was visible for a time and then forgotten. Finally, in 1981, her letters to Amy Post became accessible and her authorship was authenticated. Jacobs's achievement is at last beginning to be recognized. With Yellin's documentation of the events of the narrative, the work stands as Jacobs's autobiography—her story "written by herself," as the narrative's subtitle accurately indicates.

Similarly, Harriet Wilson's story received little attention in her own time and remained in obscurity for over a century. Working as a dressmaker in Boston in the late 1850s, Wilson wrote *Our Nig*, as she indicates in her preface, so that she might retrieve her son, George Mason Wilson, from his foster home. His father, Thomas Wilson, ran away to sea in 1852 shortly before the birth of the child. Unable to care for her son, Harriet Wilson was forced to relinquish George to the "County House" for the destitute at Goffstown, New Hampshire. Eventually, because of her own rapidly deteriorating health and inability to pay George's board, she gave her son as a foster child to "a kindly gentleman and lady" in New Hampshire. Wilson moved to Boston in 1855, remaining there until 1863, after which her name disappeared from public documents. Published in 1859, *Our Nig* was printed in a small run by the George C. Rand and Avery Company. Ironically, Wilson wrote the work so that she could be reunited with her son, but he died six months after its publication. After 1859 her book received almost no commentary until 1983, when it was republished by Random House. As Gates has shown, the work stands as her account of her life—her "autobiography."

In recent years critics have begun to explore *Incidents* and *Our Nig* with respect to women's and Afro-American literary traditions. Yellin, Carby, and Smith have demonstrated Jacobs's struggle to resist the ideological implications of the sentimental novel and the "cult of true womanhood";[9] Gates has seen a similar struggle in Wilson through her narrator, Frado, in *Our Nig*.[10] Washington and Foster also briefly consider *Incidents* and *Our Nig*, respectively, as works standing in the tradition of the slave narrative.[11] Yet none of these critics extensively explores Jacobs's and Wilson's works within the tradition of autobiography and the autobiographical shaping of the self; none provides sustained close readings, which are necessary to discover these black women's self-definitions. While most of the current criticism and analysis of *Incidents* focuses on its relationship to slave narratives written by men and Jacobs's frank treatment of sexuality (peculiar to her work as a woman's narrative), no one has illuminated the self that Jacobs defines and then compared it to that of another Afro-American, female writer. When we juxtapose Jacobs's slave narrative and the autobiographical novel of the free black woman Wilson, we see the limitations placed on black women and the surprisingly similar ways that two women in different circumstances overcame them. We also discover a shared definition of personhood, one that portrays black women as shapers of their own identities and destinies, and as individuals who need not meet the standards of whites and males to achieve their own personhood.

In writing their autobiographical narratives, Jacobs and Wilson reshaped the conventions of personhood expressed in a dominant Afro-American genre: the male slave narrative. In this genre, the narrator traditionally built his story around a presentation of himself that emphasized, for the most part, the qualities valued and respected by white men: courage, mobility, rationality, and physical strength. As in the case of Frederick Douglass, the male slave's story tended to focus on the isolated heroism of the subject, the slave portraying himself as self-initiating, self-propelling, and self-sustaining. His story highlighted his individualism as he resisted overseers and escaped to the North. As Washington and Smith have each argued, by representing themselves as isolated heroic subjects, male slave narrators defined their humanity in terms of prevailing concepts of American male identity, "mythologizing rugged individuality, physical strength, and geographical mobility."[12] Self-reliance remained central to the black man's conception of manhood: the slave man expressed it in his emphasis on the solitariness of the journey North. He also expressed it in his description of freedom in terms of the acquisition of literacy and the physical mastery over the slaveholder or overseer, as both Douglass and William Wells Brown do. Learning to read makes the slave a man, Douglass says about himself; being beaten makes him a slave. The acquisition of literacy meant for the slave man a degree of self-sufficiency. By overpowering his overseer, the slave man—like Douglass—also gains a kind of symbolic freedom, upon which his physical and geographical liberation are predicated, as Smith points out. Independence, self-sufficiency, and mobility remained so central to the male slave narrator's conception of his own personhood that, in Smith's words, "the journey from slavery to freedom—from bondage to independence—was also the journey from slavery to manhood."[13]

As black women, Jacobs and Wilson could not adopt these conventions of personhood as they were reproduced in the male slave narrative. Neither could they wholeheartedly embrace the definitions of womanhood that the popular genres of women carried to the American reading public in the 1830s, 1840s, and 1850s. The literary conventions of the women's genres, the seduction novel and the domestic novel, reproduced the version of womanhood that the white middle-class women's magazines, gift annuals, and religious literature expressed. As *Godey's Lady's Book* and other women's magazines described her, the "true" American woman was pious, pure, submissive, and domestic.[14] These were standards by which white women apparently judged themselves, and were judged by, forming the core of a womanhood valued by the prosperous and growing middle class. This version of womanhood undergirded the popular genres of white women, shaping their literary conventions.

Seduction novels such as Susanna Rowson's *Charlotte Temple* (1791) and Hannah Foster's *The Coquette* (1707), both of which enjoyed enormous popularity for decades, suggested that American womanhood meant female innocence and helplessness. The plot of *Charlotte Temple*, for example, involved an innocent maiden's susceptibility to seduction and abandonment by the predatory males of the upper class. As in this novel, the popular seduction tales customarily portrayed women as victims and sexual prey; the central female character falls victim to an unscrupulous man and dies as a result. Passive, subservient, and ultimately silenced by their death, these characters suggest a version of womanhood that portrays women as men's inevitable dupes. The woman's expression of sexual passion earned her the author's condemnation and punishment by death. Thus the novels also portrayed a reality that had little moral ambiguity; "good" and "evil" were easily identifiable bipolar categories. For white middle-class women, the novels seemed to serve an important social and educational function by exploring the dangers of unsuitable relationships and the consequences of sexual transgression, as Cathy N. Davidson points out.[15] For black women such as Jacobs and Wilson, however, the literary conventions proved inadequate in their presentation of a reality far from the experience of women of Jacobs's and Wilson's race and class.

The domestic novel also reproduced a cultural definition of womanhood in Jacobs's and Wilson's day. Through the novels of authors such as Susan Warner, Maria Cummins, and E. D. E. N. Southworth, female readers saw an enhanced version of womanhood, one that did not present women as helpless victims the way that seduction novels of the earlier generation did. Domestic novels such as Warner's *The Wide, Wide World* (1851), Cummins's *The Lamplighter* (1854), and Southworth's eighteen novels (1849-1860) were built around the story of a young girl who, as Nina Baym describes, "is deprived of the supports she had rightly or wrongly depended on to sustain her throughout life and is faced with the necessity of winning her own way in the world." As in the seduction novel, the domestic novel presented clear moral categories of good and evil, as it paired the heroine with a villainess or with another heroine. It differed from the seduction novel in its portrayal of the heroine who developed the capacity to survive and surmount her own troubles; her success was a function and reflection of her own efforts and character. Helped occasionally by people in her community, the heroine also called on God for strength as she mustered her own internal resources.[16]

The domestic novels typically ended happily, the heroine finding fulfillment in marriage, family, and her home. Certainly, as Baym has shown in detail, the genre endorsed a "cult of domesticity," the happy home presented as the pinnacle of human bliss. According to Baym, "domesticity is set forth as a value scheme for ordering all of life, in competition with the ethos of money and exploitation that is perceived to prevail in American society."[17] The domestic ideal placed the woman in the home sequestered away from the marketplace and political arena, the woman finding her greatest happiness in domestic relations—the warmth and love of human attachments. The literary conventions of the women's genre thus carried to the female reading public the personification of the "ideal woman" who was pious, pure, domestic, and submissive, a formula that Jacobs and Wilson would have to confront in writing their own narratives.

The formulation of womanhood was so powerful in nineteenth-century America that not only did white, middle-class women aspire to this standard but so did many black women, at least publicly, as seen in early Afro-American novels and other sources, according to Foster. The idealized black woman was partly white: she was the "tragic mulatta"—"the earliest and most pervasive image of the female protagonist in Afro-American literature," according to Foster. She was pious, pure, domestic, and frail; she was also beautiful and more refined than most white-skinned women.[18] Patterned after the "true woman" as whites described her, the "tragic mulatta" remained an ideal unreachable by most black women in antebellum America, given their oppressive conditions.

Yet it was a standard preferable to many white women's view of their female slaves. As Fox-Genovese points out, although slaveholding women lived in close relationship to many of their female slaves—and sometimes even had some affection for them, especially the house servants—white plantation mistresses consistently saw their slaves as property and themselves as privileged "ladies" of the ruling class. Women, to be ladies, had to have servants, according to the white southern ideal—thus slave women could never hope to reach the ideal.[19] Even in homes with the best mistress-slave relationships, mistresses tended to see their slaves as a necessary nuisance, interpreting any sign of independence as obstinacy, impertinence, impudence. At worst, as Hazel Carby and Gerda Lerner have argued, many white southern mistresses (and others) saw their female slaves as breeders, existing only for the master's profit, incapable of sexual purity.[20] Their very ability to survive abuse meant that they could not hope to meet white women's ideal of womanhood, since fragility—even death—were associated by whites with innocence, purity, and femininity. The self-definitions of Jacobs and Wilson are even more striking when we consider the degree to which they challenged these conventions, both literary and social, of blacks and whites.[21]

As the autobiographical manuscripts of black females, *Incidents* and *Our Nig* had to adhere to certain nineteenth-century conventions in order to attract a white publisher, if not a predominantly white audience. White autobiography was sanctioned; its authenticity was assumed. The writers of black autobiography, on the other hand, had to prove themselves. As William Andrews argues, black autobiographers in the nineteenth century faced the challenge of inventing devices and strategies that would endow their stories with the appearance of authenticity, knowing that their works would be received with skepticism and resistance.[22] Especially in the antebellum period, enslaved blacks in the South as well as free blacks in the North were seen as recognizably depraved, vicious, and, for the most part, incorrigible, alien people. Only the perfectly free autobiographer was thought to be perfectly truthful. Thus, by

1865, black autobiography had evolved into a complex oratorical mode, the genre distinguished by its rhetorical aims: to "reach into the hearts of men" and to bear witness to the truth, Andrews explains, whether it was produced by an ex-slave or not. In the case of the slave narrative, experienced abolitionists realized that the first-person narrative, with its promise of intimate glimpses into the mind and heart, would be more compelling to the uncommitted mass of readers than the oratory and polemics of the antislavery press. Yet the public did not read to become familiar with the individual slave but to get a firsthand look at the institution of slavery. Ex-slaves knew from their abolitionist sponsors that the skeptical white public would believe nothing but documentable "facts" in a slave narrative; the most reliable slave narrative therefore "would be the one that seemed purely mimetic, one in which the self is at the periphery instead of the center of attention, . . . transcribing rather than interpreting a set of objective facts."[23]

Aiming to prevent their voices—and their self-definitions—from being subsumed by the generic conventions of black autobiography, Jacobs and Wilson adopt different strategies in their subversions of the conventions of the slave narrative, the primary form of nineteenth-century black autobiography. Jacobs adopts the strategy that the best slave writers adopt: she assumes the stance of dispassionate observer of her own life, endowing her narrative with the appearance of objectivity yet controlling the events with artistic subjectivity. Wilson, on the other hand, changes the rules of the literary game by writing a novel—an ostensibly fictionalized account of her life—instead of the traditional autobiographical genre of her race, the slave narrative. Equally important, both Jacobs and Wilson revise the conventions of white women's genres, the seduction novel and the domestic novel. They express as their goals not only the security of their children and a home but economic independence and political justice. They also defy the understandings of sexual morality found in the white women's genres, challenging readers to think about the complexity of morality and virtue. In doing so, they bend the conventions to their other purpose, the creation of selves consistent with their own experience as black women. They show that the world of the black woman—as a person inextricably bound up with others yet responsible for her own survival, emotionally, economically, and politically—demands a revised definition of true womanhood, a revision of the nineteenth-century white woman's social and literary stereotype as well as that of the black woman, the "tragic mulatta." Such a definition must be flexible enough to address issues of race, economic level, and social status. Jacobs and Wilson advance such a definition as they develop their own creations of identity, expressing a new vision of the American self.

Jacobs, in her *Incidents of the Life of a Slave Girl*, at the outset seems the demure, "objective" slave girl that her audience expects, yet she subtly comes to exercise her control. She opens her preface with an assertion of the truthfulness of her account and her objectivity as a narrator:

> Reader, be assured this narrative is no fiction. I am aware that some of my adventures may seem incredible; but they are, nevertheless, strictly true. I have not exaggerated the wrongs inflicted by Slavery; on the contrary, my descriptions fall far short of the facts.[24]

Her writing is a "testimony," she says, intended to "convince the people of the Free States what Slavery really is" (2). Jacobs "properly" assumes a stance of humility, denigrating her own ability as an ex-slave writer: "I wish I were more competent to the task I have undertaken. But I trust my readers will excuse deficiencies. . . . I was born and reared in Slavery . . . " (1).

In explaining her reason for writing, Jacobs indicates that she will conform to her white audience's expectation of placing herself on the periphery of the action. She also properly presents herself as a representative type of enslaved women in the South:

> I have not written my experiences in order to attract attention to myself; on the contrary, it would have been more pleasant to me to have been silent about my own history. Neither do I care to excite sympathy for my own sufferings. But I do earnestly desire to arouse the women of the North to a realizing sense of the condition of two millions of women at the South, still in bondage, suffering what I suffered, and most of them far worse. (1)

Apparently she will not advance her individual self or assert her own identity; she indicates that she will merely report the facts.

Even in this brief preface we see her authorial control when she baldly declares her choosing to conceal the names of places and to give people fictitious names. Even her title indicates her control: this is not "a narrative of the life of a slave" but a presentation of "incidents," carefully selected and shaped. Moreover, the brevity and small number of the appended materials themselves—the editor's introduction and two short letters from white advocates—testify to her high degree of authorial control compared with such apparatus in other narratives, according to Robert Stepto's framework of the Afro-American narrative.[25] Jacobs does not need appended materials to establish her as a reliable, individual self.

In shaping the role and character of her narrator Linda Brent, Jacobs asserts her identity as a black woman. Although Brent often takes the stance of a reporter, she more frequently assumes the role of an engaged participant, placing herself in the center of the action as she describes her feelings and reactions to the events of her life. She even directly addresses the reader, giving voice to her emotions—her anger, embarrassment, or indignation.

This strategy, along with the seduction plot, draws on the genre of the popular seduction novel, but Jacobs's narrative proves to be a revision of the conventions of that genre. As Yellin argues, Jacobs uses the pattern of the seduction novel for her own purposes.[26] Unlike the narrators of that fiction or the female domestic novel, when Brent addresses the reader it is not to flatter the audience with a favorable image of itself; she does not implicitly congratulate readers for their sympathy.[27] Rather, in all but one instance Jacobs challenges her audience to liberate itself from its wrongheadedness. At one time she chides,

> If you want to be fully convinced of the abominations of slavery, go on a southern plantation, and call yourself a negro trader. Then there will be no concealment; and you will see and hear things that will seem to you impossible among human beings with immortal souls. (52)

Defiant and aggressive in her tone, she does not placate a fictive reader who is a product of the conventions of the time. Her readers are reasonable, thinking adults, open to the standards of justice and morality that are part of the structure of self-concept she creates; she, however, is superior to her audience, who is completely ignorant of the black female experience.

The one situation in which she comes closest to the popular female genres occurs when she tells the reader of her master's attempts to possess her sexually. Although Brent's reluctance to be frank about her sexual harassment may suggest the conventions of domestic fiction (in which the author is above offering a frank discussion about sexuality),[28] her response to the harassment stands in stark contrast to that of white women in their genres. As Foster has suggested, slave women in their narratives seem to minimize the details of their sexual exploitation because they refuse to present themselves as utter victims.[29] Likewise, the way Brent responds to the sexual oppression suggests Jacobs's unwillingness to characterize herself as powerless and passive. As Yellin explains, "Jacobs's narrator does not characterize herself conventionally as a passive female victim, but asserts that—even when young and a slave—she was an effective moral agent. She takes full responsibility for her actions."[30] Brent agrees to become Mr. Sands's mistress, defying her master Flint's demand that she become his concubine. "I will not try to screen myself behind the plea of compulsion from a master; for it was not so," she says. "Neither can I plead ignorance or thoughtlessness . . . I knew what I did, and I did it with calculation" (54). Harassed by Flint, Brent retaliates by showing preference for another.

In agreeing to become Mr. Sands's mistress, the narrator "relinquished 'purity' in an effort to maintain her 'self-respect,' . . . to avoid being 'entirely subject to the will of another,'" Yellin points out.[31] Linda Brent thus foils her master, refusing to submit and thereby become an utter victim. In Brent's words, "I knew nothing would enrage Dr. Flint so much as to know that I favored another" (55). That Brent herself chooses her sexual partner, refusing to take the stance of a passively selected woman, undermines images of the slave—and the woman, as the seduction novel portrays her—as a powerless, submissive sexual toy. By her own account Brent is not totally defenseless. She has some part in shaping her destiny, gaining through Mr. Sands two well-loved children, a lover, and protection from the advances of her master. Although she may seem merely conventional when she calls her sexual involvement a "headlong plunge" or a "great sin," ultimately Jacobs challenges the sexual ideology of the white world, asserting the complex morality of her world in defiance of whites' easy definitions of the virtuous female self: "The condition of the slave confuses all principles of morality and, in fact, renders the practice of them impossible," she declares (55).

Jacobs's is a world in which black females are not only prevented from conforming to the white sexual standard of female "purity," but are forced to adopt its opposite. In a particularly bold move, she defies her white readers to condemn her:

> You never knew what it is to be a slave; to be entirely unprotected by law or custom; to have the laws reduce you to the condition of a chattel, entirely subject to the will of another. I know I did wrong. . . . I feel that the slave woman ought not to be judged by the same standard as others. (55-56)

In issuing such a challenge, Jacobs asserts herself through her narrator as a virtuous woman, one conforming to a more complex standard of morality than that of the white world. Her world of the "demon Slavery" precludes easy pronouncements of right and wrong.

In addition to sexual values, Jacobs inverts readers' values of submission, motherhood, and beauty. She shows that her refusal to submit—to her master and the slave system as a whole—is the crime for which she must imprison herself for seven years. She indicates that the bearing of children does not define the slave as a true woman, since children are merely commodities—the property of the slaveowner—who can be taken away at any time. And she points out that beauty, an asset to the self-concept of the white woman, is to be dreaded in the world of the slave woman. As her narrator discovers, it is the greatest curse for the female slave. Thus Jacobs modifies white definitions of the "true woman" and challenges the black analogue, the "tragic mulatta"—the pure, beautiful, piously submissive black woman.

The feminine values that Jacobs *can* affirm—as Baym has found them in women's fiction of this period—are the qualities of intelligence, will, resource-fulness, and courage which allow women to overcome their hardships.[32] Hiding out in her attic home, Jacobs displays these qualities—and her power over her master—in the tricks she plays on Flint: Brent sends false letters to him from the North, arranges for the sale of her children to their father, and spies on her angry master, getting the trickster's "last laugh" by making him think that she is far away and powerless.[33] Brent agrees to such an existence, of course, not only to save herself but her children as well. Her ultimate goals are true freedom and a good home for her children and herself. Like the white women fiction-writers of the nineteenth century, Jacobs defines herself in terms of her home and her children; in pursuit of these, she reveals her will and strength of character. Freedom for Jacobs—and many other women of her time, as Baym implies—involves a relationship to others, interdependence; Jacobs is not an Emersonian lone hero but is inextricably bound to others, her extended family and her children.

Yet Jacobs goes beyond the conception of freedom found in white woman's fiction, broadening the definition of woman as homemaker and mother to include economic and political dimensions. In a pointed challenge to the values of domestic fiction, the narrator closes her story by stating, "Reader, my story ends with freedom; not in the usual way with marriage" (201). Economic independence, not marital dependence, is what she strives for as well as a home and the company of her children. For her, true freedom entails economic freedom. Unlike the heroine of the nineteenth-century cult of domesticity, Jacobs does not shun the public sphere of the marketplace, which many women saw as corruptive. Nor does she shun the political arena, citing in her preface her desire to move women to political action.

Jacobs's broadening of the definition of freedom to include the economic and political spheres reveals an understanding of freedom not found in white woman's fiction. She suggests that an accurate definition of womanhood for her time includes not only domesticity, relationships with her children and others, and the qualities of resourcefulness and personal strength, but also the ability to survive on her own—emotionally, economically, and politically. Implicitly revealing the limitations of the Emersonian self-reliant man, she shows that resourcefulness, will, courage, and self-reliance need not be opposed to interdependence and sacrificial love.

Selecting a different genre and writing as a free northern black, Harriet Wilson in *Our Nig* presents a strikingly similar definition of herself as a black woman, in some ways going beyond Jacobs in her challenge to nineteenth-century generic conventions. She shows her cleverness and will immediately in her choice of title and pseudonym: *Our Nig; or, Sketches from the Life of a Free Black in a Two-Story White House, North. Showing that Slavery's Shadows Fall Even There*, by "Our Nig." As Jacobs acknowledged in her title, Wilson identifies her work not as a traditional "narrative of the life," but asserts authorial control in her decision to write selected "sketches." Titling her work to exhibit power in the tradition of Afro-American signification, Wilson identifies these sketches as those of a "free black," when her life shows little more freedom than that of an enslaved southern woman.[34]

Exercising authorial power by signifying again, she loads the word "white" with extra meaning, using it to describe the color of both the house and its inhabitants. Wilson's choice of "our nig" for title and pseudonym shows her at her most parodic. Her placing quotation marks around the name that her white family gave her questions the validity of the label—a sarcastic, comic retaliation at the culture which would deprive her of a true identity. To include "our" challenges the idea of her belonging to someone; to call herself "nig" challenges the idea that her identity is defined only by her skin color and labels used by whites.

In her preface, Wilson indicates that she will present only those events appropriate to her purpose; she ironically and ostentatiously establishes her readers' expectations and conventions of objectivity that will shape her self-presentation: "I do not pretend to divulge every transaction of my own life . . . I have purposely omitted what would provoke shame in out good anti-slavery friends at home."[35] She states that her purpose is to provide economic support for herself and her children; she does not write to satisfy some white patron's ends but her own ends as she asks for compassion: "Deserted by kindred, disabled by failing health, I am forced to some experiment which shall aid in maintaining myself and child without extinguishing this feeble life" (3). In stating such a purpose, she shows her understanding that economic independence is vital to freedom as America defines it, and challenges the cult of domesticity in her fearless entry into the marketplace.

When she appeals to her "colored brethren" to "rally around me a faithful band of supporters and defenders," she places herself squarely in the political arena acting as a spokesperson for her people, implicitly urging her readers to join her in condemning northern racism. Linking the domestic—"Life . . . In A . . . House"—with the political by means of her subtitle, "Showing that Slavery's Shadows Fall Even There," Wilson subverts readers' expectations of a novel about the home.[36] Her subject matter is domestic life, but instead of a predictable sentimental novel, Wilson exposes racism and the truth about one woman's sufferings.

Wilson further undermines readers' expectations by her conscious selection of an audience: she excludes white readers from the outset, appealing to her "colored brethren universally for patronage" and asserting that it is not for "the refined and the cultivated" that "these crude narrations appear" (3). She defies the white establishment through her omission of a white editor's preface and assistance. She needs no white patron to introduce her; neither does she need one to revise, condense, or arrange any words of her text, as Lydia Maria Child admits doing for Jacobs.[37] Not one of the three letters appended to Wilson's text questions that Harriet Wilson wrote and ordered every word of *Our Nig*.

In choosing the genre of the novel instead of a genre similar to the slave narrative, Wilson goes beyond Jacobs in asserting her control and shaping her identity. She makes a daring move in her decision to create a text exclusively the property of whites, the novel. Relinquishing the opportunities of the generic autobiography, she also foregoes a first-person narrator and tells her tale through a selectively omniscient third-person narrator. She shows that she can submerge her voice under the third-person point of view yet present herself through other, more subtle means. Yet her preface and chapter titles make it clear that she is indeed telling her own life-story, albeit a fictionalized representation. Autobiography and fiction overlap in many of her chapter titles: for example, she calls chapter 1 "Mag Smith, My Mother" yet relies on a third-person narrator to tell the story. Similar examples of the shift in person include chapter 2, "My Father's Death," and chapter 3, "A New Home for Me." And in chapter 7 the narrator lapses into the first person in the initial sentence.

These inconsistencies narrow the gap between autobiography and fiction, as the reader hears Wilson's own voice in these lapses into the first person. The author and the protagonist become more closely connected as the novel approaches its conclusion, which in its lack of closure flows into the appended letters.[38] As Gates explains, "the fiction, or *guise* of her fictional account of her life, tends to fall away the nearer her novel approaches its own ending, and the ending of her text, the composite biography written by Mrs. Wilson's friends."[39] Fiction and autobiography become one discourse, heightening Wilson's control over her self-presentation as she manipulates the genre constraints.

The story of seduction and the trials of an orphan girl against a villainess in *Our Nig* parallels the typical plot of nineteenth-century white women's novels, according to Baym's formulation.[40] Like Jacobs, Wilson manipulates this plot and shows the complexity of moral issues. In her case, she challenges the traditional identification of black with evil and white with goodness, as Gates points out; she refuses to separate neatly good and evil by color, socioeconomic status, or gender. White characters of the same family and the same socioeconomic status fall into both categories of good and evil; so do black characters. White, genteel Mrs. Bellmont and her daughter are clearly evil, but so is the black man—a fugitive slave—who seduces Frado and then abandons her, leaving her pregnant. Conversely, Jack and (especially) James Bellmont show kindness to Frado, aiding her in the struggle against their mother. White Aunt Abby similarly gives aid. And Frado's father, Jim, is "a kind-hearted African" (19), a man who describes himself as "black outside" with "a white heart inside" (12).

In Mag, Frado's white mother, we find Wilson's most complex treatment of good and evil. A poor white woman orphaned early in life and seduced as a young woman, Mag gives birth to a child out of wedlock and becomes a public disgrace. Yet the narrator's treatment of her in these early chapters is gentle and sympathetic, not judgmental as it is in, for example, Susanna Rowson's *Charlotte Temple* or Hannah Foster's *The Coquette*. In both of these novels the authors offer the experience of the female character in part as a moral lesson, showing the dire consequences of sexual passion, as Davidson suggests.[41] In contrast, Wilson in *Our Nig* portrays Mag as a victim of "a sneering world," not her own sexuality (7). Even her marriage to the kind-hearted Jim and her subsequent motherhood through him—in what is perhaps the most abhorrent configuration of miscegenation for the nineteenth century—is not portrayed as evil.

Mag becomes, however, more and more selfish, willful, and irresponsible after Jim's death. The narrator connects her descent into "perpetual infamy" (16) not with her interracial marriage but with her giving herself up to the evil of her oppressive existence:

> Mag had lived an outcast for years. She had ceased to feel the gushings of penitence; she had crushed the sharp agonies of an awakened conscience. She had no longings for a purer heart, a better life. Far easier to descend lower. (16)

Mag's evil, for the narrator, is the result of both her oppressive environment and, more important, her own embracing of evil. Unlike the moral stereotypes of the domestic or seduction novel, Wilson develops plot situations and characters with realistic ambiguities.

Wilson explores the issue of morality further in another subversion of the domestic novel, and in so doing she presents herself, through Frado, as a virtuous woman by nonwhite standards. Frado is piously innocent—yet she ultimately repudiates Christianity, in contrast to the piously Christian women of the domestic novel. She shows her virtue in her long-suffering, compassionate sacrifice as she toils beside the dying James's bedside. She remains outside the respectability of the church; although at first she shows interest in Christianity so that she can share heaven with James. Frado eventually resolves "to give over all thought of a future world" because "she did not wish to go" to a heaven that would permit entry to Mrs. Bellmont (104). When the evil daughter, Mary, dies, "Frado's innocent joy signifies her ironic rejection of Christian religion," despite all of Aunt Abby's and James's efforts to convert her.[42] In a pointed inversion of white and black, good and evil, Frado suggests to Aunt Abby the possibility of Mary's going to hell and being blacker than she. Citing Mary as her mother's idol (another criticism of hypocritical Christianity), she exclaims, "'Wouldn n't [sic] mistress be mad to see her a nigger!'" (107). Frado's own virtue is suggested by her consistent lack of hypocrisy.

In a further modification of women's genres, Wilson departs from stereotypical images of the "true woman" and the "tragic mulatta." Her heroine, Frado, is not piously submissive. The first description of Frado, given when she is six years old as her parents decide where to place her, presents her as one with eyes "sparkling with an exuberance of spirit almost beyond restraint" (17). Even at this early age we see a glimmer of her independence and self-reliance, qualities necessary for the black female's survival in white America. Her (new) quarters at the Bellmont home consist of an attic room, cramped and dimly lit, strangely parallel to Linda Brent's attic home and metaphorically suggestive of the constricted existence of antebellum black women in general. Yet Frado's "willful, determined nature" (28) enables her to survive, and, like Brent, Frado's cleverness and trickery allow her some degree of mastery over her oppressive white world. At school she is said to be "ever at some sly prank when unseen by her teacher, in school hours; not unfrequently [sic] some outburst of merriment, of which she was the original, was charged upon some innocent male, and punishment inflicted which she merited" (38). In fact, she has such control over her white classmates that "any of them would suffer wrongfully to keep open the avenues of mirth" (38). Clever trickery of a willful sheep that repeatedly provokes her further suggests attempts at mastering a white world which would have *her* behave as a sheep (53-55).

In contrast to the image of the "tragic mulatta," Frado as a young woman discovers her voice and the power of her will, as in the slave narrative. Although Mrs. Bellmont continues physically and emotionally to abuse her, Frado shows that her spirit cannot be broken. In a key scene Frado, standing "like one who feels the stirring of free and independent thoughts" (105), defies Mrs. Bellmont to strike her. "Strike me, and I'll never work a mite more for you," Frado shouts. Stunned, Mrs. Bellmont drops her weapon and, "desisting from her purpose of chastisement," follows Frado into the house, carrying Frado's wood. Like Linda Brent who frustrated Flint's lust, Frado here has a "last laugh": "Her triumph in seeing [Mrs. Bellmont] enter the door with her burden, repaid her for much of her former suffering" (105).

Frado's tough-spiritedness and sense of initiative persist even when she is physically incapacitated. As a young woman she becomes ill and is removed to the home of two spinsters, but soon she comes "to the old resolution to take care of herself, to cast off the unpleasant charities of the public" (124). She perfects her sewing, a gesture towards her own economic independence. She marries and has a child but, like Brent, Frado is eventually left without a husband. She must resort to her "self-dependence" (127). The final picture that we have of Frado suggests her sense of dignity and resourcefulness:

> And thus, to the present time, may you see her busily employed in preparing her merchandise; then sallying forth to encounter many frowns, but some kind friends and purchasers. Nothing turns her from her steadfast purpose of elevating herself. (130)

Frado works for herself and her child, the narrator points out (128), even giving up the child to "a kind gentleman and lady" (136) who could provide him a good home until she can recover from her sickness and abject poverty, as the novel and letters together indicate. Like Jacobs, Wilson suggests a new definition of motherhood: loyalty and self-sacrificial love to the point of separating oneself from one's children so that they may benefit.

The novel, like Jacobs's narrative, ends with a series of appended letters as do many slave narratives, but Wilson defies the stereotype of the "heroic slave." In her narrative, the writers of the letters—"Allida," Margaret Thorne, and "C. D. S."—do not stop at testifying to the truth of the author's assertions or the goodness of her character. Unlike most slave narratives, these letters have a purpose beyond that of testimony: they appeal to the reader to buy the book, thereby aiding the author in her quest for economic independence. "I hope those who call themselves friends of our dark-skinned brethren," writes Thorne, "will lend a helping hand, and assist our sister not in giving, but in buying a book; the expense is trifling, and the reward of doing good is great" (140). Of course, even at the outset of her narrative Wilson has revised slave narrative conventions by beginning with an account of her parentage, not her own birth. Unlike the "heroic slave," she has a clear and definite knowledge of her heritage and her role in society: she is an individual and not a type. She does not move "up" from slavery or oppression—as in the pattern of ascension that Stepto describes for Afro-American narrative—but moves "within" the oppressive community, struggling for independence and selfhood within the confines of racism.[43]

Her awareness of this role is most apparent in the way she concludes the novel. The lack of closure, an indicting revision of the white domestic novel, also challenges stereotypes of women. Like Jacobs—and unlike the "tragic mulatta"—she desires financial independence, but the lack of closure at the end of the novel indicates an ambiguity about her own success. Whether she will completely achieve that success depends upon the number of books the people of her racist world will buy. The narrator explicitly appeals to the reader in the novel's closing lines: "[S]he asks your sympathy, gentle reader. Refuse not. . . . Enough has been unrolled to demand your sympathy and aid" (130). It is the poverty and oppression Wilson faces as a black woman that force her to "experiment," first by writing, and then by attempting to sell her story. Her novel lacks closure because her ultimate success is uncertain given the confines of racism. Having no guarantee of a house and home, Wilson must revise the sentimental convention of the happy ending. As an autobiographical act of a black woman, *Our Nig* can end only in uncertainty, if it is to have integrity.

Given the popularity of slave narratives and the lesser popularity of black fiction—and her own admission of her need for financial gain—Wilson's decision to write a novel can be read as a bold move toward self-definition.[44] She draws on the literary conventions of her contemporary white female novelists, yet abandons those conventions when they fail to satisfy her needs as an author. Gates points out that Harriet Wilson "revised significantly the white woman's novel, and thereby made the form her own. By this act of formal revision she *created* the black woman's novel. . ."[45] Her rhetorical decision stands as a daring assertion of herself as a black author and her autonomy as a black woman. She shows that she need not conform to all the conventions of slaves *or* of white women. In adopting the genre of the novel and exploiting its flexibility for her own ends, she asserts the right of and the necessity for self-definition, one that will meet the demands of both her race and her gender.

Harriet Jacobs and Harriet Wilson both create identities that defy nineteenth-century stereotypes and exploit autobiographical forms to teach their readers about the black female self. They define a womanhood different from the definitions advanced by the white world, and they demonstrate that autobiography can have as its aim historical messages as well as the creation of identity. Like the white heroine of women's fiction, they show their sense of communal identity, portraying themselves as bound to their children and extended families. Resourceful and intelligent, they take responsibility for the welfare of their children, and like the white, male, Emersonian hero, they show themselves to be self-reliant—shapers of their own destinies and responsible for their own survival. Jacobs and Wilson defy simple and effortless formulations of womanhood. These women must sacrifice what the white culture connects with self-respect precisely in order to gain that self-respect: sexual "purity" and, for both of them, their role as mothers as they sacrificially separate themselves from their children for the welfare of the children. They suggest new definitions of virtue as they illustrate the moral complexity of their worlds. They show a new domesticity as they provide their *own* homes for themselves and their children, and both women are bold enough to enter the marketplace and the political arena. Moreover, contrary to views of whites and, as Foster suggests, of black men, neither woman sees herself as an utter victim. Jacobs and Wilson define themselves through their protagonists as women with will, courage, cleverness, and self-reliance; able to gain economic independence, and thus, freedom as America defines it. They assert their control and their power of self-definition in their handling of genre, revising the conventions of literary form and the identity that whites and males impose on them as nineteenth-century black women.

NOTES

1. See, for example, Frances Smith Foster, *Witnessing Slavery: The Development of the Ante-Bellum Slave Narratives* (Westport, Conn., 1979); Mary Helen Washington, *Invented Lives: Narratives of Black Women 1860-1960* (Garden City, N.Y., 1987); Valerie Smith, *Self-Discovery and Authority in Afro-American Narrative* (Cambridge, Mass., 1987); Henry Louis Gates, Jr., "Parallel Discursive Universes: Fictions of the Self in Harriet E. Wilson's *Our Nig*," in *Figures in Black: Words, Signs, and the "Racial" Self*, ed. Gates (New York, 1987), 125-63; Hazel Carby, *Reconstructing Womanhood: The Emergence of the Afro-American Woman Novelist* (New York, 1987).

2. Estelle C. Jelinek arrives at her conclusion in her overview of autobiographical criticism in *The Tradition of Women's Autobiography: From Antiquity to the Present* (Boston, 1986), 1-8. Donna C. Stanton discusses the problem of women's exclusion in "Autogynography: Is the Subject Different?" in *The Female Autograph: Theory and Practice of Autobiography from the Tenth to the Twentieth Century*, ed. Stanton (Chicago, 1987), 3-20. Shari Benstock has discussed the reigning attitudes towards autobiography in theories and practices that often do not take women into account as writers of autobiography in "Authorizing the Autobiographical," in *The Private Self: Theory and Practice of Women's Autobiographical Writings*, ed. Benstock (Chapel Hill, 1988), 10-33.

3. Mary Helen Washington, *Invented Lives*, 7, among others, has pointed out that black women wrote about 12 percent of the total number of extant slave narratives, but none of these is as well-known as the narratives by men. The result has been that the life of the male slave has come to be representative. Jelinek, *The Tradition of Women's Autobiography*, includes ex-slave Harriet Jacobs's autobiography in her discussion of nineteenth-century slave narratives but does not discuss her rhetorical strategies and the shaping of her identity.

4. Joanne M. Braxton, *Black Women Writing Autobiography: A Tradition within a Tradition* (Philadelphia, 1989), 8. See also Regina Blackburn, "In Search of the Black Female Self: African-American Women's Autobiographies and Ethnicity," in *Women's Autobiography: Essays in Criticism*, ed. Estelle C. Jelinek (Bloomington, 1980), 133-48; Frances Smith Foster, "Adding Color and Contour to Early American Self-Portraitures: Autobiographical Writings of Afro-American Women," in *Conjuring: Black Women, Fiction, and Literary Tradition*, ed. Marjorie Pryse and Hortense J. Spillers (Bloomington, 1985), 25-38; Elizabeth Fox-Genovese, "My Statue, My Self: Autobiographical Writings of Afro-American Women," in Benstock, *The Private Self*, 63-89; and William L. Andrews, *To Tell a Free Story: The First Century of Afro-American Autobiography, 1760-1865* (Urbana, Ill., 1986), which is one of the most gender-balanced treatments of the subject.

5. Fox-Genovese, "My Statue, My Self," 67.

6. Jean Fagan Yellin, "Written by Herself: Harriet Jacobs' Slave Narrative," *American Literature* 53 (Nov. 1981): 479-86. Yellin's annotated edition of Harriet A. Jacobs's

Incidents in the Life of a Slave Girl Written by Herself (1861; reprint, Cambridge, Mass., 1987) further documents the authenticity of Jacobs's autobiography.

7. Harriet E. Wilson, *Our Nig; or, Sketches in The Life of a Free Black, in a Two-Story White House, North, Showing that Slavery's Shadows Fall Even There. By "Our Nig,"* ed. Henry Louis Gates, Jr. (1859; reprint, New York, 1983). See also Gates, "Parallel Discursive Universes," 125-63.

8. Yellin, Introduction to *Incidents*, xix.

9. Jean Fagan Yellin, "Texts and Contexts of Harriet Jacobs's *Incidents in the Life of a Slave Girl: Written by Herself*," in *The Slave's Narrative*, ed. Charles T. Davis and Henry Louis Gates, Jr. (New York, 1985), 262-82; Carby, *Reconstructing Womanhood*; and Valerie Smith, *Self-Discovery and Authority in Afro-American Narrative* (Cambridge, Mass., 1987). Barbara Welter discusses the nineteenth-century notion of true womanhood in her essay, "The Cult of True Womanhood," in *Dimity Convictions: The American Woman in the Nineteenth Century*, ed. Welter (Athens, Ohio, 1977), 21-41.

10. Gates, Introduction to *Our Nig*, xi-lv.

11. Washington, *Invented Lives*, 10-12; Foster, "Adding Color and Contour," 25-38. Foster discusses the protagonist of Wilson and those of two other black women writers, Jarena Lee and Nancy Prince, as transcending the image of the victimized slave woman and the white "true woman," but she does so only briefly.

12. Smith, *Self-Discovery and Authority*, 34. Washington, *Invented Lives*, 8, incisively points out that Frederick Douglass's eldest daughter tells a story different from Douglass's, one that emphasizes the help of one Anna Murray, a free black woman of Baltimore. Douglass makes no mention of her.

13. Smith, *Self-Discovery and Authority*, xxix, 34.

14. Welter, "The Cult of True Womanhood," 21-41.

15. Cathy N. Davidson, *Revolution and the Word: The Rise of the Novel in America* (New York, 1986), 125-26.

16. Nina Baym, *Woman's Fiction: A Guide to Novels by and about Women in America, 1820-1870* (Ithaca, 1978), 11, 35, 38, 41-43.

17. *Ibid.*, 27.

18. Foster, "Adding Color and Contour," 34.

19. Elizabeth Fox-Genovese, *Within the Plantation Household: Black and White Women of the Old South* (Chapel Hill, 1988), 129-45. Fox-Genovese elaborates on the differences in practice that southern and northern white women associated with the ideal of the lady, given the southerners' context of slavery, but she agrees that the ideals of the white southern lady included female delicacy and frailty, piety, purity, chastity, and motherhood. See 196-241.

20. Carby, "Slave and Mistress: Ideologies of Womanhood under Slavery," in *Reconstructing Womanhood*, 20-39; Gerda Lerner, *Black Women in White America: A Documentary History* (New York, 1972), 45. Foster also notes whites' views of the black woman are closely identified with illicit sex, in *Witnessing Slavery*, 131.

21. Even in the Reconstruction period, when black intellectuals sought to recreate the "public face" of the race, the black woman was pictured as conforming to standards of womanhood similar to those of whites, not having her own self-definition: she was portrayed as domestic and kind, with the added attributes of being schooled and an admirer of fine arts, as the genteel white ladies of the period were. See Henry Louis Gates, Jr., "The Trope of a New Negro and the Reconstruction of the Image of the Black," *Representations* 24 (Fall 1988): 129-55.

22. William L. Andrews, "The First Century of Afro-American Autobiography: Theory and Explication," in *Studies in Black American Literature: Black American Prose Theory*, ed. Joe Weixlmann and Chester J. Fontenot (Greenwood, Fla., 1983), 4. James Olney supports the point, citing it as the reason that even in the best known slave narratives (with the exception of Douglass's) the conventions of content, theme, form, and style remained conventions, "untransformed and unredeemed." See his " 'I Was Born': Slave Narratives, Their Status as Autobiography and as Literature," in *The Slave's Narrative*, ed. Charles T. Davis and Henry Louis Gates, Jr. (New York, 1985), 158.

23. Andrews, "First Century," 5, 8-9, 9-10. Douglass retains control over his text by keeping his voice central and makes his *Narrative of the Life of Frederick Douglass* (1845; reprint, Cambridge, Mass., 1979) seem "a remarkable literary achievement," in Robert Burns Stepto's view. For a summary of the relationship between appended documents and the slave's narrative, see Stepto's " 'I Rose and Found My Voice': Narration, Authentication, and Authorial Control in Four Slave Narratives," in Davis and Gates, *The Slave's Narrative*, 225-41.

24. Jacobs, *Incidents*, 1.

25. Robert Burns Stepto, *From Behind the Veil: A Study of Afro-American Narrative* (Urbana, Ill., 1979).

26. Yellin, Introduction, *Incidents*, xxx.

27. For readings of *Incidents* as a work conforming to the conventions of woman's fiction, see Raymond Hedin, "Strategies of Form in the American Slave Narrative," in *The Art of Slave Narrative: Original Essays in Criticism and Theory*, ed. John Sekora and Darwin T. Turner (Macomb, Ill., 1982), 27-28; and Annette Niemtzow, "The Problematic of Self in Autobiography: The Example of the Slave Narrative," in Sekora and Turner, 105-7. Neither considers Jacobs's revision of the female genres.

28. Niemtzow, "The Problematic of Self in Autobiography," 106.

29. Frances Smith Foster, " 'In Respect to Females': Differences in the Portrayals of Women by Male and Female Narrators," *Black American Literature Forum* 15 (Summer 1981): 67.

30. Yellin, Introduction, *Incidents*, xxx.

31. *Ibid.*

32. Baym, *Woman's Fiction*, 22.

33. Keith Byerman, "We Wear the Mask: Deceit as Theme and Style in Slave Narrative," in Sekora and Turner, *Art of Slave Narrative*, 70-82, sees deceit and the trickster motif not as secondary but central to the design of the slave narratives. Lucinda H. MacKethan, "Metaphors of Mastery in the Slave Narratives," *ibid.*, 55-69, also sees as central the metaphor of the trick, adding two others: the metaphor of the word and language to be used as a trap and weapon, and the metaphor of narrative order itself as a "design" with which to overpower the master. Such an emphasis enhances Jacobs's (and Wilson's) self-definitions.

34. For a discussion of the received definitions of signification as a play of language, see Roger D. Abrahams, *Deep Down in the Jungle: Negro Narrative Folk-lore from the Streets of Philadelphia*, rev. ed. (Chicago, 1970); and Henry Louis Gates, Jr., " 'The Blackness of Blackness': A Critique of the Sign and the Signifying Monkey," in Sekora and Turner, *Art of Slave Narrative*, 129-39.

35. Wilson, *Our Nig*, preface.

36. Motivated by abolitionism, Harriet Beecher Stowe had done this earlier in *Uncle Tom's Cabin*. Wilson's strategy is striking for the self-definition she advances.

37. Lydia Maria Child, "Introduction by the Editor," in *Incidents*, 3.

38. Gates indicates that the latter chapters of *Our Nig* parallel closely the events of Wilson's life he and others have been able to document; curiously, scholars have not been able and "probably shall not be able" to document the events of the early chapters, he indicates in his introduction (xxxii). He suggests that the first-person presences in the early chapters

> perhaps reveal the author's anxiety about identifying with events in the text that she cannot claim to recollect clearly. . . . In later chapters Mrs. Wilson had no need to demonstrate or claim the direct relation between author and protagonist, since, as our research reveals, these two sets of events, the fictional and the biographical, overlap nicely. (xxxvii)

Whatever the reason for Wilson's shifts, it is clear that, as the appended letter by Allida indicates, the novel is a kind of "Autobiography."

39. Gates, Introduction, *Our Nig*, xxxvi.

40. Baym, *Woman's Fiction*, 35-44.

41. Davidson, *Revolution and the Word*, 110-47.

42. Gates, Introduction, *Our Nig*, xlix.

43. Stepto, *From Behind the Veil*.

44. Gates, Introduction, *Our Nig*, xxx.

45. *Ibid.*, xlvi.

24

Clothing as an Expression of History:

The Dress of African-American Women in Georgia, 1880-1915

Patricia K. Hunt

"Her head [was] closely wrapped in a dark bandana. She was clad in a black and white flowered print dress and a dark gray sweater, from which a white ruffle was apparent at the neck. Only two buttons of the sweater were fastened and it fell away at the waist displaying her green striped apron. From beneath the long dress, her feet were visible encased in men's black shoes laced with white

This woman wears a headcloth which she has intricately wrapped and folded around her head. The portion hanging down at the back and sides may have been used to shield the neck from the sun. For ease of working in the fields, her skirt is shortened by a cord tied around her hips. *Courtesy of Georgia Department of Archives and History.*

strings. Her ornaments consisted of a ring on her third finger, earrings, and tortoise-rimmed glasses."[1] This is how a Federal Writers Project interviewer described Julia Bunch's appearance. Yet another stated that Ryna Bryant's "outfit consisted of a dull gray waist with a turban to match and a faded blue skirt. Large brass earrings dangled from her ears."[2] Both women were former slaves interviewed in the early 1930s and provide intriguing insights about the clothing worn by African-American women after the Civil War.

Clothes make statements about economic status, occupational roles, affiliations with other people, differentiation from others, and individual expression. As economist Thorstein Veblen stated in *The Theory of the Leisure Class* in 1899, "Apparel . . . is always in evidence and affords an indication of our pecuniary standing to all observers at the first glance."[3] Studies of clothing can indicate whether individuals or groups of people adhered to prevailing styles or wore out-of-date or cultural items of dress. By studying the clothing worn by African-American women in Georgia in the late nineteenth and early

An African-American woman churning butter on the front porch of the Jesse Middleton Hunt farm, located between Round Oak and Waxside. Her headcloth is draped and folded. The small round collar and flange over the shoulder of the bodice represent a typical style for 1910. *Courtesy of Georgia Department of Archives and History.*

This unidentified woman's mob cap and bib apron symbolize her occupation as a domestic servant. *Courtesy of Georgia Department of Archives and History.*

twentieth centuries, we learn not only about these women but also about what they wore.

Few clothing history studies exist about minority groups in the United States. This is particularly true of African-American women, due in part to the lack of their extant garments either before and after the Civil War. Since most of these women were slaves or otherwise disadvantaged, their clothing was worn out and discarded, made into children's clothing, used to repair other clothing or to make quilts. Lewis Favor, a former slave, stated that "heavier cover such as quilts, etc. were made from the dresses and the other clothing that was no longer fit for wear."[4] Lina Hunter, also a former slave, indicated that her old balmoral petticoat was used to patch a quilt.[5]

Though little clothing has survived, other primary sources such as photographs serve as records of the past. Photographs that have good clear images

Although blind, Leah Pitts of Jones County was known to be an efficient seamstress. Photographed in 1905, she wears the pouter pigeon bodice, long skirt and pompadour hairstyle typical of the period. A popular neckband and broach accentuate the neckline. *Courtesy of Georgia Department of Archives and History.*

give specific details of black women's clothing. They also provide context by revealing whether the women participated in the wearing of occupational, fashionable, or cultural items of dress, and depicting how the women wore the garments and accessories.

Some of the clothing items worn by African-American women symbolized their occupations as nursery nurses, cooks, or maids. Two such items were the mob cap and apron. The mob cap was a white linen or cotton fabric hat with a ruffled brim. Such hats have been worn by domestic servants in England and America since the late eighteenth century.[6] Aprons were usually three-quarters in length or longer, worn with or without a bib.

A typical assumption is that African-American women in the late nineteenth and early twentieth centuries wore out-of-style or worn-out clothing, which led to the conclusion that they could not afford current styles or that they had no interest in wearing fashionable attire. This was not the case at all, for many African-American women in Georgia wore fashionable styles of dress.

Clothing styles changed rapidly in the late nineteenth and early twentieth centuries. African-American women in Georgia who could afford to wear the current styles of dress followed these changes as closely as white women in the state, indicated by the following photographs. In so doing they were participating in the social function of fashion, which Mary Ellen Roach and Kathleen Musa have defined as "a form of human behavior and a product of human behavior, which is widely accepted for a limited time and is replaceable by another fashion that is an acceptable substitute."[7] Their adoption of current fashions in their dress was one way in which some African-American women both asserted their affluence and assimilated into mainstream American society.

At the same time many other black women had neither the opportunities nor the economic resources to wear the latest styles in clothing. These women wore the clothing they had, whether worn-out and patched or out-of-fashion. Nevertheless, many of them participated in aesthetic and artistic expression that had nothing to do with following the latest fashion. Their artistry is particularly evident in their headcloths. African-American women used plain and patterned fabric to construct these headwraps, including paisley and plaid patterns, as well as solid light and dark colors. English actress Frances Kemble, while living on her husband's plantation in Georgia during the late 1830s,

The full pompadour hairstyle, pouter pigeon bodice with high standing band collar and full, long sleeves were popular in 1904. This Spelman student's long skirt trimmed with two bands of ribbon at the bottom was also fashionable at that time. *Courtesy of Spelman College.*

This unidentified Thomas County woman, photographed in 1895, used paisley patterned fabric to construct her headcloth. Paisley was a favorite motif in the early to mid-nineteenth century. *Courtesy of Georgia Department of Archives and History.*

made the observation that "the deepest possible shades [of color] blended in fierce companionship round one dusky visage; head handkerchiefs, that put one's very eyes out from a mile off; chintzes with sprawling patterns, that might be seen if the clouds were printed with them."[8] Having long been worn by Africans and continued to be worn by early slaves, such headwear served as a symbolic link to later generations of Georgia black women and to their cultural heritage on both sides of the Atlantic.

The following photographs provide visual evidence of the variety of clothing worn by African-American Georgia women over the course of three and a half decades and suggest the context, meaning, and socio-economic function their dress reflected.

NOTES

1. George P. Rawick, ed., *The American Slave: A Composite Autobiography* (Westport, Conn., 1972), Vol. 12: *Georgia Narratives*, Part 1, Series 2, 156.
2. Malcolm and Muriel Bell, *Drums and Shadows: Survival Studies Among the Georgia Costal Negroes* (Athens, 1940), 40.
3. Thorstein Veblen, *The Theory of the Leisure Class* (New York, 1899), 119.
4. Lewis Favor quoted in Rawick, *The American Slave*, Vol. 12, Part 2, 321.
5. Lina Hunter quoted *ibid.*, Part 1, Supplement Series 1, 258.
6. Georgine De Courtais, *Women's Headdress and Hairstyles* (London, 1986), 174.
7. Mary Ellen Roach and Kathleen E. Musa, "Fashion," in *New Perspectives on the History of Western Dress* (New York, 1980), 19-26.
8. Frances A. Kemble, *Journal of a Residence on a Georgia Plantation in 1838-1839* (Athens, 1984), 93.

The thirteen women in this 1892 class photograph from Spelman College wear fitted bodices with high necklines and long fitted sleeves which are slightly fuller at the top, known as "kickups." Their hairstyles with fullness over the brow are probably arranged in a chignon at the back. *Courtesy of Spelman College Archives.*

Spelman College students dressed fashionably for the 1883-1889 period. The close fitting bodices have high standing band collars and close fitting sleeves. The floor-length skirts have draped fronts and probably have bustles to hold out fullness in the upper back. *Courtesy of Spelman College.*

Mama Jo Hunt, a Gordon County nurse, wears the mob cap and bib apron, customary attire for nurses in this 1908 photograph. *Courtesy of Georgia Department of Archives and History.*

These two women, photographed in Baker County, Georgia, in 1912, are wearing dresses representative of the 1909-1915 period. Dresses featured high waistlines and round or vee necklines. Skirts were long and narrow. *Courtesy of Georgia Department of Archives and History.*

This unidentified couple wears fashionable attire for the 1880s. The woman is wearing a gable hat with peaked crown, bodice with high collar, and full-length skirt. *Courtesy of the Herndon Home, Atlanta.*

These women wear typical daytime dresses of the 1883-1889 period. Both feature close fitting bodices, standing band collars, and long fitted sleeves. The skirts have draped fronts and high shelf bustles (a basket or pillow-like structure worn underneath the skirt). Left, *courtesy of the Herndon Home, Atlanta*; right, *courtesy of Spelman College.*

In this portrait of Mr. and Mrs. Frank Butler Black, Mrs. Black is wearing the pouter pigeon bodice with full pouched front and high standing band collar. Her long, plain skirt is also characteristic of the period as is her upswept hairstyle. *Courtesy of Georgia Department of Archives and History.*

This nurse combined fashion with occupation in this 1907 photograph. She wears an apron with a fashionable pouter pigeon bodice and full-length skirt. Her hat features a wide brim and shallow crown also characteristic of the period. *Courtesy of Georgia Department of Archives and History.*

This unidentified woman wears a dark colored scarf over her head. Her fitted bodice with asymmetrical trim, long fitted sleeves, and high standing band collar were stylish in the early 1890s. Her scarf may represent mourning or possibly indicate that she was a nurse, since some nineteenth-century nursing orders wore such scarfs over their hair. *Courtesy of Georgia Department of Archives and History.*

Adrienne McNeil Herndon was the wife of Alonzo Herndon, a former slave. Herndon learned to barber and eventually owned three barber shops in Atlanta. In 1905 he founded the Atlanta Life Insurance Company, and in 1910 the historic Herndon Home was built. The enormous sleeves, popular in the mid-1890s, can be seen in this photograph of his first wife, who died in 1910. The high standing band collar is also characteristic of the period, as well as her hairstyle. *Courtesy of the Herndon Home.*

This 1898 photograph provides an excellent demonstration of 1890s bodices with large sleeves, wide lapels, and plastron fronts. One woman holds a hat, another a fan. Both are typical accessories for the period. *Courtesy of Spelman College.*

Fashions of the Edwardian period (1900-1908) are in evidence in this photograph of the Mother's Club of Grady County, Georgia. Bodices have high, boned collars and the pouter pigeon, full-pouched front. Floor-length skirts hugged the hips and flared out to a trumpet shape at the bottom. Hair was full in front and pinned high in the back. *Courtesy of Georgia Department of Archives and History.*

Part VI

United States—
Twentieth Century

25

"Civilization," the Decline of Middle-Class Manliness, and Ida B. Wells's Antilynching Campaign (1892-94)

Gail Bederman

For, if civilization means anything, it means self-restraint; casting away self-restraint the white man becomes as savage as the negro.
—Ray Stannard Baker, "What is a Lynching?"[1]

It is the white man's civilization and the white man's government which are on trial.
—Ida B. Wells, *A Red Record*[2]

All England's congenital meddlers and busybodies are forming societies for civilizing us, and express themselves about our social state in language which Samoan natives would resent.
—*New York Times*, 19 August 1894[3]

In March 1894, Ida B. Wells sailed to England in order to agitate against the rise of racial violence in the United States. She left a country where lynching was rarely mentioned in the white Northern press, where she herself was unknown to most whites. In June 1894, she returned a celebrity, vilified as a "slanderous and nasty-minded mulatress"[4] by some papers and lauded by others. Above all, she returned to an America where lynching was widely discussed as a stain on American civilization.

Wells's success in bringing lynching to the attention of the Northern middle class was due, in large part, to her ingenious manipulations of the Northern middle class's widespread fears about declining male power. By playing on Americans' anxiety about gender dominance, she was able to raise the stakes among middle-class Northern whites, who had previously tolerated lynching as a colorful, if somewhat old-fashioned, Southern regional custom (e.g., the *New York Times* humorously editorialized in 1891, "the friends of order [in Alabama] have been in pursuit of a negro. . . . If they catch him they will lynch him, but this incident will not be likely to add to the prevailing excitement" of the more "serious" moonshining problem[5]). Historians have long recognized Wells's successful debunking of the myth of the black rapist, but this was only part of her larger strategy of playing on the 1890s' gender tensions.[6] As the epigraphs suggest, Wells brilliantly and subversively manipulated dominant middle-class ideas about race, manhood, and civilization in order to force white Americans to address lynching. Wells, in short, convinced nervous whites that lynching imperiled American manhood.

To understand how Wells played upon white Northerners' fears about dwindling manhood, we need to understand the centrality of Victorian manliness in 1890s middle-class identity. From the time the middle class had begun to form itself as a class, gender had been a crucial constitutive element of middle-class self-definition.[7] Between 1820 and 1860, as increasing numbers of men had begun to earn comfortable livings as entrepreneurs, professionals, and managers, the middle class had become increasingly conscious of itself as a class, with interests, tastes, and life-styles different from both the very rich and from those who performed manual labor. In large cities as well as smaller towns, they and their families began to differentiate themselves from other social elements by stressing their gentility, respectability and adherence to evangelical Christian values.[8]

Gender was central to this self-definition.[9] Indeed, according to Mary Ryan, "the American middle class molded its distinctive identity around domestic values and family practices," especially as elaborated and instituted by evangelical Protestant women.[10] The middle class celebrated true women as pious, maternal guardians of virtue and domesticity, and contrasted pure, domestic middle-class women with working-class women, whose evident willingness to neglect domestic duties made them appear un-Christian and morally deficient.[11]

Manhood was equally crucial to middle-class identity. Middle-class constructions of both manliness and womanliness centered around willful control of sin.[12] Yet the middle class believed that men, unlike "naturally good" women, were beset by powerful gusts of sinful desires.[13] This passionate masculine nature was considered simultaneously the source of men's greatest danger and of men's greatest power. Succumbing to overwhelming emotion or sexual passion would sap a man's force, rendering him weak and degenerate.[14] Therefore, middle-class parents taught their sons to build a strong, manly "character" as they would build a muscle, through repetitive exercises of control over impulse.[15] The middle class saw this ability to control powerful masculine passions through strong character and a powerful will as a primary source of men's strength and authority. By gaining the manly strength to control *himself*, a man gained the strength, as well as the duty, to protect and direct those weaker than himself: his wife, his children, or his employees. The mingled honor, high-mindedness, and strength stemming from this powerful self-mastery were encapsulated in the term *manliness*.[16]

Middle-class men invoked ideals of manliness in business and domestic practices throughout the nineteenth century. In the context of the market economy's unpredictability, a strong character built on high-minded self-restraint was seen as the rock on which middle-class men could build their fortunes. Middle-class men were awarded—or denied—credit based on others' assessment of the manly strength of their characters, and credit raters like *Dun and Bradstreet* reported on businessmen's honesty, probity, and family life.[17] Manly control over impulse also helped the middle class develop its distinctive family practices. Celebrations of manly self-restraint encouraged young men to work hard and live abstemiously, so that they could amass the capital to go into business for themselves, and to postpone marriage until they could support a family in proper middle-class style.[18] In short, by the end of the century, a discourse of manliness stressing self-mastery and restraint expressed and shaped middle-class identity.

By the 1890s, however, both manliness and middle-class identity seemed to falter. Middle-class manliness had been created in the context of a small-scale, competitive capitalism, which had all but disappeared by the 1890s. In the context of a bureaucratic, interdependent society, the manly codes of self-restraint began to seem less relevant. For example, with the growth of large-scale corporate enterprises, the proportion of middle-class men who could aspire to independent entrepreneurship dwindled. At the same time, the rapid expansion of low-level clerical work in stores and offices meant that young men beginning their careers as clerks were unlikely to gain promotion to responsible, well-paid management positions, as had clerks in their fathers' generation.[19] Under these conditions, manly self-denial grew increasingly unprofitable. Concurrent with middle-class men's narrowing career opportunities came new opportunities for commercial leisure. The growth of a consumer culture encouraged many middle-class men, faced with lowered career expectations, to find identity in leisure instead of work.[20] Yet codes of manliness dictated they must work hard and become economically independent. The consumer culture's ethos of pleasure and frivolity clashed with ideals of manly self-restraint, further undermining the potency of middle-class manliness.[21]

Although cultural and economic changes had taken their toll, middle-class men continued to uphold manliness, for abandoning it would mean abandoning male power itself. Discourses of manliness were embedded in their very identities. They formed their sons into men by teaching them manliness. Especially in the context of challenges from the Gilded Age woman's movement, abandoning familiar constructs of manliness was an unimaginable option.

Instead, middle-class men, uncomfortably confused about the nature and sources of male power, began to cast about for new ways to fortify their shaky constructions of manliness. They adopted a variety of strategies, from growing crazes for body building and college football, to warnings of neurasthenic breakdowns among overworked middle-class men.[22] A new rhetoric about maleness appeared. Contemporaries coined the new epithets "sissy," "pussyfoot," and "stuffed shirt"[23] and began to speak approvingly about something they called "masculinity." The noun "masculinity," although rarely used until the late 1890s, would soon come into frequent parlance—precisely because it could convey new connotations about maleness different from the more usual "manliness." These reformulations frequently were fragmented and contradictory. For example, increasing numbers of middle-class men frequented urban red-light districts, yet many remained confused and ambivalent about the meaning of their illicit sexual activity. Was it an inevitable outcropping of naturally explosive masculine passions? Or was it a sordid loss of manly self-control and a sign of moral weakness?[24] In short, by the time Ida B. Wells sailed for England in 1893, middle-class manliness had taken on the character of a beloved but fragile friend, whose weakness must at all costs remain unacknowledged.

To recoup their losses and explain what made them powerful as men, many middle-class men began to focus on race, and the qualities which made them powerful as "the *white* man." The 1890s were a period of virulent racism and racially conceived nativism.[25] The primarily native-born middle-class gazed with distaste upon increasing crowds of Eastern and Southern European immigrants, and saw masses of unassimilable "races," whose unfamiliar customs and tendency to vote for "machine" Democrats challenged middle-class control of American cities. Anglo-Saxonism provided one powerful explanation of middle-class men's supremacy by rooting white manhood in racial traits purportedly developed long ago in the forests of Germany.[26] White Americans believed the Anglo-Saxon race, as Francis Parkman put it, was "peculiarly masculine." Anglo-Saxons were described as independent, adventurous, strong of will, tenacious of purpose—as manly.[27]

The trope "the white man" also linked powerful manhood to race. When 1890s whites spoke of "the white man," they usually paired him with "the negro" or "the Indian." Referring to "the black man" or "the red man," the logical parallel construction, would mean conceding that black and red men were equally manly—thus undercutting the ideological work of the phrase "the white man." For example, in 1905 Ray Stannard Baker argued that lynching was unworthy of "the white man," because it rendered him as unmanly as "the negro": "For if civilization means anything, it means self-restraint; casting away self-restraint the white man becomes as savage as the negro."[28] But perhaps the most important thing about "the white man"—as the Baker quote also suggests—was the way it worked as a synecdoche. By referring to "the white man," contemporaries simultaneously invoked the manly white males who were "civilized" and "civilization" itself.

Affirming the manly power of the white man's "civilization" was one of the most powerful ways middle-class men found to assert their interwoven racial, class, and gender dominance. "Civilization" kept the weakness of manliness hidden by repeatedly interweaving manhood and race, and affirming that white racial superiority proved white men the most manly in the world. Since Wells built her entire English antilynching tour around resistance to this discourse of "civilization," we need to spend some time examining it.

In the Darwinist 1890s, "civilization" had become a racial concept. Rather than simply meaning "the west" or "industrially advanced societies," "civilization" denoted a precise stage in human evolution—the one following the more primitive stages of "savagery" and "barbarism." Human races progressed in historical steps from simple and less valuable "savagery," through "barbarism," to advanced and more valuable "civilization." But only whites had, as yet, advanced to the civilized stage. In fact, people believed "civilization" was itself a *racial* trait, *inherited* by all Anglo-Saxons and other "advanced" white races.[29]

Gender was an essential component of civilization, for extreme sexual difference was seen as a hallmark of civilization's advancement. Savage (that is, nonwhite) men and women were almost identical, but civilized races had evolved the pronounced sexual differences celebrated in the middle class's doctrine of "separate spheres." Civilized women were "womanly"—spiritual, motherly, dedicated to the home. And civilized white men were the most manly ever evolved—firm of character, self-controlled, protectors of women and children.[30]

But the power of "civilization" stemmed from the way it *interwove* middle-class beliefs about racial and gender hierarchy. "Civilization" *naturalized* white male power by linking male dominance and white supremacy to human evolutionary development. Harnessing manliness to white supremacy, and celebrating both as essential to human progress, "civilization" temporarily revitalized middle-class Victorian manliness.

To understand how the discourse of civilization reinforced the power of manliness, let's consider a familiar example: Chicago's 1893 Columbian Exposition. In authorizing the exposition, Congress had called for "an exhibition of the progress of civilization in the New World."[31] In order to exhibit "the progress of civilization," the organizers divided the world's fair into two areas.[32] The civilized section, known as "The White City," celebrated advanced, masculine technology. Its focal point was the majestic "Court of Honor," a formal basin almost a half-mile long, surrounded by massive white *beaux arts* buildings. "Honorable," according to an 1890 dictionary, was a synonym for "manly," and contemporaries would not have missed the Court of Honor's association with manhood.[33] The seven huge buildings framing the Court of Honor represented seven aspects of the highest civilized advancement (Manufactures, Mines, Agriculture, Art, Administrations, Machinery, and Electricity), all presented as the domain of civilized white *men*. These buildings housed thousands of enormous engines, warships, trains, machines, and armaments. The White City also glorified middle-class men's familiar world of commerce, exhibiting the most advanced products and manufacturing processes—"dynamos and rock drills, looms and wallpaper"—and housing these exhibits in magnificent white temples.[34] In short, by celebrating "civilization," the White City celebrated the power and perfection of Victorian manhood, and poets hailed it as "A Vision of Strong Manhood and Perfection of Society."[35]

Woman's place in the "advancement of civilization" was represented in the White City by the smaller, much less formidable Woman's Building. Despite the feminist intentions of its board of Lady Managers, visitors were impressed mostly by the Woman's Building's softness, compared to the masculine dynamos and technological marvels of the rest of the White City. Said the *New York Times*, "the achievements of man [are] in iron, steel, wood, and the baser and cruder products . . . [while] in the Woman's Building one can note . . . more refined avenues of effort which culminate in the home, the hospital, the church, and in personal adornment."[36] Its location underlined women's marginality: Not only was the Woman's Building located at the very edge of the manly White City, it was also situated immediately opposite the White City's only exit to the uncivilized Midway. On the border between civilized and savage (as befit women, who according to modern science, were more primitive than men) the Woman's Building underlined the manliness of the white man's civilization.[37]

In contrast, the Midway, the exposition's uncivilized section, provided spectacles of barbarism—"authentic" villages of Samoans, Egyptians, Dahomans, Turks, and other exotic races.[38] Guidebooks advised visitors to visit the Midway only after visiting the White City, in order to fully appreciate the contrast between the civilized White City and the uncivilized native villages.[39] Where the White City spread out in all directions from the Court of Honor, emphasizing the complexity of manly civilization, the Midway's attractions were organized linearly down a broad avenue, providing a lesson in racial hierarchy. Visitors entering the Midway from the White City would first pass the German and Irish villages, proceed past the barbarous Turkish, Arabic, and Chinese villages, and finish by viewing the savage American Indians and Dahomans. "What an opportunity was here afforded to the scientific mind to descend the spiral of evolution," enthused the *Chicago Tribune*, "tracing humanity in its highest phases down almost to its animalistic origins."[40]

Where the White City stressed the manliness of the white man's civilization, the Midway's villages depicted the absence of manliness among uncivilized, nonwhite races. In the Persian, Algerian, Turkish, and Egyptian villages, for example, unmanly dark-skinned men cajoled customers to shed manly restraint and savor their countrywomen's sensuous dancing.[41] Male audiences ogling scantily clad belly dancers could have it both ways, simultaneously relishing the dances' suggestiveness and basking in their own sense of civilized superiority to the swarthy men hawking tickets outside, unashamedly vending their countrywomen's charms.[42] Those who had just visited the White City would be especially conscious of their own racially superior manliness.

Least manly of all the Midway's denizens, according to many commentators, were the savage Dahomans, who seemed to lack gender differences entirely. The *New York Times* described "The Dahomey gentleman (or perhaps it is a Dahomey lady, for the distinction is not obvious), who may be seen at almost any hour . . . clad mainly in a brief grass skirt and capering nimbly to the lascivious pleasings of an unseen tom-tom pounded within. . . . There are several dozen of them of assorted sexes, as one gradually makes out. . . ." The columnist then ridiculed African-American spectators for imagining themselves more civilized than the Dahomans.[43] In short, the Columbian Exposition demonstrated, in a variety of ways, that "nonwhite" and "uncivilized" denoted "unmanly"; and conversely, that whiteness and civilization denoted powerful manhood.

The bifurcation of the Columbian Exposition between civilized White City and uncivilized Midway worked only if the darkest races were always represented as insurmountably savage. Therefore, organizers rebuffed the many African Americans who worked tirelessly to gain representation on the White City's organizing bodies. The exposition's logic of constructing manly white civilization in opposition to savage swarthy barbarism made it impossible for the white organizers to recognize the existence of fully civilized African Americans. Black men and women objected vociferously to their exclusion and agitated to be included in the exhibits and planning committees, but to no avail.[44]

Ida B. Wells, like most educated African Americans, was outraged by this racist exclusiveness. Always attuned to the cultural dynamics behind whites' racism, in her counterattack she pinpointed the key discourse: the exposition's celebrations of manly white American "civilization." Along with Frederick Douglass, she called for black Americans to fund a pamphlet, printed in English, French, German, and Spanish, in which civilized African Americans could explain to the rest of the civilized world why the less-than-civilized exposition organizers had excluded them. Warning that "[t]he absence of colored citizens from participating therein will be construed to their disadvantage by the representatives of the civilized world there assembled," Wells promised her pamphlet would set forth "the past and present condition of our people and their relation to American civilization."[45]

And it did. Entitled *The Reason Why the Colored American Is Not in the World's Columbian Exposition*, the pamphlet inverted the white organizers' depiction of manly civilization as the opposite of Negro savagery. Instead, Wells argued, the best illustration of America's "moral grandeur" and civilization would have been to exhibit the phenomenal progress African Americans had made after only twenty-five years of freedom. For centuries, American blacks had "contributed a large share to American prosperity and civilization."[46] Why, then, was the colored American not in the Columbian Exposition?

The pamphlet's answer, left implicit to avoid excessive confrontation, was that the *white* American was not the manly civilized being he pretended to be. Wells's coauthor Frederick Douglass made this argument, lamenting the unfortunate necessity of speaking plainly of wrongs and outrages endured "in flagrant contradiction to boasted American Republican liberty and civilization."[47] Indeed, far from embodying high civilization, white Americans still embraced "barbarism and race hate."[48] Yet the Negro was "manfully resisting" this oppression, and "is now by industry, economy and education wisely raising himself to conditions of civilization and comparative well being."[49] Douglass concluded his chapter by insisting upon black manliness: "We are men and our aim is perfect manhood, to be men among men. Our situation demands faith in ourselves, faith in the power of truth, faith in work and faith in the influence of manly character."[50]

The balance of the pamphlet, compiled and partly written by Ida B. Well, documented Douglass's assertion of black manhood. Since emancipation, African Americans had demonstrated manly character, making phenomenal strides in education, the professions, the accumulation of wealth, and literature. Nonetheless, white Americans had perversely attacked this youthful black manliness—through oppressive legislation, disfranchisement, the convict lease system, and the "barbarism" of lynch law. Finally, the pamphlet documented the exposition organizers' deliberate exclusion of blacks—except, Douglass sniffed, "as if to shame the Negro, the Dahomians [sic] are also here to exhibit the Negro as a repulsive savage."[51] In short, the pamphlet demonstrated that excluding the colored American from the Columbian Exposition, far from glorifying American civilization, demonstrated American barbarism.

Wells and Douglass, headquartered in the White City's small Haitian Building, distributed 10,000 copies of *The Reason Why* during the three months before the fair closed. (Debarred from representing his own nation, Douglass had been named Haiti's representative to the exposition.) Wells received responses from England, Germany, France, Russia, and India.[52] Yet Wells's greatest success in turning the claims of "manly civilization" against white racism lay not in her world's fair agitation, but in her 1892-94 campaigns against lynching.

In 1892, Wells had been forced into Northern exile by her agitation against lynching. At thirty, she was already an experienced journalist and agitator. Since March 1892, she had spearheaded black Memphis's protest against the heinous lynching of three respected local businessmen, one of whom had been a close personal friend. Finally, in May, she wrote her famous editorial: "Nobody in this section of the country believes the old thread bare lie that Negro men rape white women. If Southern white men are not careful, they will overreach themselves and public sentiment will have a reaction; a conclusion will then be reached which will be very damaging to the moral reputation of their women."[53] White Memphis's violent response shocked Wells: editorialists threatened her with mutilation and hanging; her presses were seized and sold; and white men watched her home, vowing to kill her on sight.

Exiled to the North, she framed new tactics for her new circumstances. While she continued to urge black Americans to boycott, vote, and agitate against white oppressors,[54] she knew these methods alone could not stop lynching. Instead, as she later recalled, she focused her efforts on "the white press, since it was the medium through which I hoped to reach the white people of the country, who alone could mold public sentiment."[55] Yet the white Northern press excluded most African-American writers. To gain a hearing in the white press, Wells was forced to create effective new arguments and tactics. To this end, she began to work to counter the middle-class's interweavings of manly authority and white racial dominance.[56]

One month after arriving in the North, the *New York Age*, a major black newspaper, published Wells's attack on Southern lynching, later reprinted as *Southern Horrors*.[57] This pamphlet, addressed to the American people, black and white, described dozens of gruesome, horrific Southern lynchings, each appalling enough to convince any open-minded reader that lynching must be stopped. Yet Wells had long lost faith that white Americans would be open-minded where racial justice was concerned.[58] Aware that whites would shrug off tales of tortured black men, Wells chose to invoke an issue that she knew would affect white men more viscerally: their fears of declining manliness.

Wells recognized that inherent in the "lynching for rape" scenario was a symbolic celebration of the power of Victorian manliness. Like the White City—which demanded that black men be represented as unmanly rapists so that white men could embody powerful, manly civilization—the lynching for rape scenario represented black men as unmanly savages so that white men could embody powerful, manly self-restraint. As Jacquelyn Dowd Hall argued, by constructing black men as "natural" rapists and by resolutely and bravely avenging the (alleged) rape of pure white womanhood, Southern white men constructed themselves as ideal men: "patriarchs, avengers, righteous protectors."[59]

This lynching for rape scenario stirred *Northern* white men too, because it dramatized the potency of traditional manliness. In this dramatization, upright character and powerful manliness (embodied in the white lynch mobs) restrained uncontrolled, unmanly, sexual passion (embodied in the Negro rapist). These noxious images permeated Northern press reports of Southern lynchings. The *Providence Journal*, reporting a Louisiana lynching in 1893, celebrated the mob's manly restraint. "Three Negroes were lynched in a quiet, determined manner by a mob of white men on Friday night. . . . The lynching was one of the coolest that has taken place in this section."[60] And the *New York Times*, describing the Memphis lynching of Wells's friends, stressed what it called the "quick and quiet" demeanor of the white men in the mob, contrasting their stern and firm behavior with that of the "shivering negroes" whom they murdered.[61] In these depictions, the black victims represented weak, unmanly passion—whether fear or lechery—while the lynch mob represented the strength of manly self-control.

In *Southern Horrors*, Wells refuted the lynching scenario by inversion. Where whites' scenario depicted black men as unmanly passion incarnate, Wells depicted black men as manliness personified. In Wells's framework, black men lynched for "rape," far from embodying uncontrolled lust, were innocent victims, seduced into having consensual sex with carnal white women. As Wells put it, they were "poor blind Afro-American Samsons who suffer themselves to be betrayed by white Delilahs."[62] Like the Biblical Samson, these black men had been manly towers of strength until they were ensnared and destroyed by the wiles of a wicked woman. The white Delilahs who falsely cried "rape" were the real embodiments of lust, not the innocent lynch victims. To prove white women, and not black men, instigated these liaisons, Wells listed thirteen white women who willingly had sexual relationships with black men. Only upon discovery were these liaisons called "rapes." Several of these white women were prostitutes, and Wells joked bitterly, " 'The leading citizens' of Memphis are defending the 'honor' of *all* white women, *demi-monde* included."[63]

Where whites' lynching scenario depicted lynch mobs as disciplined, manly, and restrained, Wells depicted them as vile, unmanly cowards, hiding their own rampant lusts with sanctimonious calls for chastity and excusing their brutal murders by invoking the honor of harlots. Wells argued that white Southern men, including those who formed the lynch mobs, were enthusiastic *supporters* of rape and sexual abuse—as long as the victims were *black*. Far from suppressing lust, "the white man" gloried in it. His miscegenation laws, Wells wrote, "only operate against the legitimate union of the races: they leave the white man free to seduce all the colored girls he can," knowing he need neither marry nor support the victims of his lust.[64] Furthermore, Wells charged, Southern white men were "not so desirous of punishing rapists as they pretend." If they truly reviled *rape*, they would not so readily forgive the many *white* men who raped *black* women. Again, Wells named names and gave dates, overwhelming the reader with cases of black women and little girls brutally raped by white men, with no objections from their white neighbors. Yet these solid white citizens of the South—rapists and accessories to rape—murdered black men who slept with willing white women, and proclaimed themselves defenders of chastity![65] Hypocrisy, licentiousness, and unrestrained passion—sexual lust and blood lust—characterized Southern white men, as Wells depicted them. Thus, in her account, the Southern lynch mob did not embody white manliness *restraining* black lust—it embodied white men's lust running amok, *destroying* true black manliness.

Finally, Wells attacked the idea that lynching showed the continuing power of manliness. Instead, she argued, Northern men could only regain their manliness by stopping the lynching. These ideas echoed old antislavery arguments: just as antislavery activists had warned that the slave power would spread North and contaminate free labor, so Wells warned that Southern men's unrestrained lust had spread north and corrupted Northern men's manliness. Northern white men had abrogated their manly duty to restrain vice. They had allowed white Southerners to rape, butcher, and burn black Americans alive, and this tolerance of vice had rotted their manliness. Throughout America, Wells wrote, "Men who stand high in the esteem of the public for Christian character, for moral and physical courage, for devotion to the principles of equal and exact justice to all, and for great sagacity, stand as cowards who fear to open their mouths before this great outrage."[66]

More was at stake in these tactics than mere rhetoric. In refuting this discourse of civilization, Wells was trying to stop lynching by producing an alternative discourse of race and manhood. "Civilization" positioned black men as unmanly savages, unable to control their passions through manly will. Northern whites, accepting the linkage of white civilization and manhood, believed black men were savage rapists; therefore, they tolerated the brutal actions of Southern lynch mobs. As Hazel Carby insightfully argued, black women, including Wells, reconstructed the sexual ideologies of the nineteenth century to produce an alternative discourse of womanhood.[67] Similarly, Wells's antilynching propaganda constructed an alternative discourse of manhood, remaking and redefining the "truths" that whites deployed to define and limit black men's place in the world, and to construct white men as powerful and manly.

In 1892, however, most whites ignored Wells's pamphlet. A few scattered antilynching articles in white periodicals borrowed Wells's arguments. For example, in 1892 Albion Tourgée, the period's most forthright antiracist white, wrote in the *Chicago Daily Inter-Ocean*, "[W]ithin a year half a score of colored men have been lynched for the crime of having white mistresses, while it does not seem to be thought necessary to hang or burn the white woman, nor is the white man who keeps a colored mistress in any danger of violence at the hands of his fellow citizens. . . . "[68] George C. Rowe, the sole black contributor to an 1894 symposium on lynching in the *Independent*, made a similar case.[69] But such articles were exceptional. Wells, like most blacks, could only get her articles published in the black press, which few whites read. Despite the eloquence of *Southern Horrors*, Wells's objective of reaching white Northerners remained frustrated.

By 1893, after a year of writing and speaking in the North, Wells still had no access to the white American press. When offered the opportunity to tour England, she jumped at it, recognizing that although the white American press ignored *her*, they might not ignore the British.[70] Although her first tour—in 1893—got very little American press coverage, it laid the foundation for her 1894 tour, which got all the publicity she desired. When Wells returned, she had become notorious; and white Americans had discovered that, due to their tolerance and practice of lynching, the rest of the world's Anglo-Saxons doubted whether white Americans were either manly or civilized.

Wells shaped both tours in terms of "civilization."[71] Her speeches, her writings, and even her demeanor framed her mission as an appeal from one civilized race to another for protection from violent white barbarians. As she told one British journalist, if Britain told America "the roasting of men alive on unproved charges and by a furious mob was a disgrace to the civilisation of the United States, then every criminal in America, white or black, would soon be assured of a trial under the proper form of law."[72] Wells spoke to British audiences, but her goal was to convince Americans that their tolerance of lynching rendered them unmanly savages in the eyes of the civilized world.

Wells knew that many Americans felt a pleasurable sense of racial kinship with the English—as fellow anglo-Saxons, the most manly and civilized of all races. By forming an alliance with British reformers, Wells attacked this smug racial empathy. As she told an audience in Birmingham (England), "America cannot and will not ignore the voice of a nation that is her superior in civilisation . . . I believe that the silent indifference with which [Great Britain] has received the intelligence that human beings are burned alive in a Christian (?) country, and by civilised (?) Anglo-Saxon communities is born of ignorance of the true situation; and that if she really knew she would make the protest long and loud."[73] American Anglo-Saxons were unmanly and uncivilized and needed direction from their civilized British superiors.

Similarly, Wells's newspaper columns from abroad, published in the white *Chicago Daily Inter-Ocean*, described the massive support she received from the most prominent, civilized British dignitaries.[74] Wells detailed dinners given in her honor by prominent members of Parliament and intimate gatherings organized by titled aristocrats. In all her columns, these celebrities expressed shock at lynching's barbarity. Often she included stories of loutish white Americans whose incivility further convinced the British of American barbarism. For example, a "swell reception" was given for her at Princess Christian's Writer's Club, Wells wrote, and "[t]he ubiquitous and (so far as I am concerned) almost invariably rude American was on evidence there. In a strident voice she pronounced my statements false. I found she had never been in the South and was a victim to her own imagination. I heard an Englishwoman remark after the encounter was over that she had seen a side of Mrs. ———'s character which she never knew before."[75] In contrast, Wells always carried herself with restraint, dignity, and refinement, and Britons clearly appreciated her as a true lady.[76] By presenting herself and her mission as embodying civilized values, Wells highlighted the barbarism of white Americans.

Throughout, Wells hammered away at the myth of the black rapist. In the context of "civilization," though, her old arguments from *Southern Horrors* took on new weight. Since civilization, by definition, entailed pure womanliness and upright manliness, Wells could now show that white Americans' lasciviousness proved them uncivilized. Barbarous white American men burned innocent black men alive for the "crime" of sleeping with willing white women, while they themselves brutally and boldly raped black women. Wells also added statistics, culled from the white *Chicago Tribune*, to prove that fewer than one-third of all lynch victims had even been *accused* of rape. The unchaste white women, who took black lovers, then watched them burn, were also uncivilized; but, Wells claimed, unchastity was endemic to the white South: "Why should it be impossible to believe white women guilty of the same crime for which southern white men are notorious?"[77] Why should it be hard to imagine that depraved white men, whose crimes had peopled the South with mulattoes, had depraved white daughters?

Most unmanly of all, however, were the bloodthirsty lynch mobs. Wells argued passionately that by refusing to try accused African Americans in a court of law, and by engaging the most horrific of tortures, lynch mobs and the Americans who tolerated them exposed themselves as barbarians.

> Make your laws as terrible as you like against that class of crime [rape]; devise what tortures you choose; go back to the most barbarous methods of the most barbarous ages; and then my case is just as strong. Prove your man guilty, first; hang him, shoot him, pour coal oil over him and roast him, if you have concluded that civilization demands this; but be sure the man has committed the crime first.[78]

No one but a brute, of course, could conclude that "civilization demands" an accused criminal be burned alive, without benefit of trial.

Similarly, in describing an Alabama lynching, Wells ironically interwove references to race and gender, invoking "civilization" in order to condemn Americans as manifestly uncivilized. Bitterly she wrote, "the civilization which defends itself against the barbarisms of Lynch Law by stating that it lynches human beings only when they are guilty of awful attacks upon women and children" might have been expected to give these alleged *arsonists* a fair trial, especially since "one of the prisoners charged was a woman, and if the Nineteenth Century has shown any advancement upon any lines of human action, it is preeminently shown in its reverence, respect and protection of its womanhood." But, Wells argued, these uncivilized white men were entirely unmanly—anxious not to protect womanhood, but to butcher it. The victims, Wells wrote, "were caged in their cells, helpless and defenseless; they were at the mercy of civilized white Americans, who, armed with shotguns, were there to maintain the majesty of American law." And these "brave and honorable white southerners . . . lined themselves up in the most effective manner and poured volley after volley into the bodies of their helpless, pleading victims, who in their bolted prison cells could do nothing but suffer and die."[79] Manliness and civilization, which stood for the rule of law, the defense of the weak, and the protection of womanhood, did not exist in the American South.

Wells's powerful tactics mobilized the British press and reformers, who turned lynching into that season's *cause célèbre*. A *Westminster Gazette* writer said he could no longer "regard our American cousins as a civilised nation."[80] The *Christian World* thought American lynch law "would disgrace a nation of cannibals."[81] The *Birmingham Daily Gazette* editorialized, "The American citizen in the South is at heart more a barbarian than the negro whom he regards as a savage. . . . Lynch law is fiendishly resorted to as a sort of sport on every possible opportunity, and the negroes are butchered to make a Yankee holiday. . . . Either they mistrust their legal institutions or they murder in wantonness and for mere lust of blood."[82] Murdering in "wantonness," "lusting" for blood—Americans had degenerated past any claim to manliness or civilization.

Having convinced a large segment of the British public of American barbarism, Wells called upon the moral forces of Britain to stop it. She convinced the gatherings she addressed to pass resolutions condemning lynching as uncivilized, and warning the United States that its tolerance of lynch law was lowering it in the estimation of civilized countries. She got the national conventions of major religious denominations—Baptists, Methodists, Quakers, Unitarians—to send resolutions to their counterparts in America condemning lynching as uncivilized, and ask what they were doing to stop it. Individual churches and reform organizations followed suit, sending resolutions to American organizations, politicians, and publications, warning that the civilized world held all Americans—Northern or Southern—responsible for these "barbarisms."[83] For example, Liverpool's Unitarian church wrote to the *Christian Register*, American's leading Unitarian periodical, expressing its "grief and horror" upon learning of "the barbarities of Lynch Law as carried out by white men on some of the coloured citizens of the United States." They demanded to know why American Unitarians did not stop such horrific torture and brutality, which instilled into white American children the "lust of cruelty and callousness of murder." The American Unitarians were forced to agree that lynching made "the dark deeds of the dark ages seem light in comparison," and the magazine sent letters of protest to three Southern mayors and Governor W.T. Northen of Georgia.[84]

Wells ultimately convinced British reformers that they bore the responsibility of civilizing the United States. As Sir Edward Russell wrote in the *Liverpool Daily Post* (and as Wells quoted to her American readers), Americans were "horrifying the whole of the civilized world," and needed British uplift, for "when one reflects that [such things] still happen while we in this country are sending missions to the South Sea Islands and other places, they strike to our hearts much more forcibly, and we turn over in our minds whether it were not better to leave the heathen alone for a time and to send the gospel of common humanity across the Atlantic. . . ."[85] Moreover, the British were preparing to send such "missionaries." By the end of her tour, prominent British reformers were organizing antilynching societies and planning to send representatives to the United States to investigate these atrocities first hand.[86] Such societies had been formed previously to protest Turkish and other exotic atrocities, but never to investigate fellow Anglo-Saxons.

All this British fervor finally got Wells her hearing in the white American press. Wells could be ignored; but the British were considered fellow Anglo-Saxons, racial equals qualified to pronounce upon civilized manliness. Thus, American men felt obligated to reply to their accusations.

The *Memphis Daily Commercial* attempted to discredit Wells by libeling her character. Playing on longstanding racist discourses depicting black women as especially licentious—thus unwomanly and uncivilized—it flooded England with newspapers accusing Wells of being a "negro adventuress" with an unsavory past. Yet Wells skillfully turned these insults to her advantage by using them to prove American barbarity. Her rebuttal, circulated to newspapers throughout Great Britain, noted "so hardened is the Southern public mind (white) that it does not object to the coarsest language and most obscene vulgarity in its leading journals so long as it is directed against a negro," and pointed out that since the *Daily Commercial* could not deny the barbarity of the South's frequent lynchings, they were reduced to smearing her character. British papers were as shocked as Wells intended. The *Liverpool Daily Post* described the articles as "very coarse in tone, and some of the language is such as could not possibly be reproduced in an English journal." Since it was neither manly nor civilized to libel a lady's character, the episode served to reinforce British opinions of American barbarism.[87]

Southern newspapers typically insisted that rape justified lynching and that "the negro" was uncivilized. The Atlanta *Constitution* argued that British agitation was futile, since "the negroes themselves are the only people who can suppress the evil, and the way for them to get rid of it is to cease committing" rape.[88] The New Orleans *Times-Democrat* opined that once Wells left Britain, she would no longer be believed, for Americans "know well that the Negro is not a model of virtue and the white man a cruel, bloodthirsty tyrant, as the Wells woman pretends . . ."[89] A Southern educator complained that "stigmatizing [Southern men] as savages and barbarians" did no good—the real problem lay with the Negro, who was "still a semi-savage far below the white man in the science and practice of civilization."[90]

Other critics accused the British of hypocrisy, arguing that British colonists abused blacks more brutally than white southerners did. The Democratic *Philadelphia Daily Record*, for example, countered the British and Foreign Unitarian Association's condemnations by alleging, "John Bull looks at America with one eye and Africa with the other. His hands are bloody with recent African butcheries. . . ."[91] While plausible, these criticisms stemmed not from concern for Africans, but from resentment of meddlesome British "civilizers."

Many Northern Democrats and Southerners complained that American lynch law was none of Britain's business.[92] In this they echoed British conservatives, like the *London Times*, which accused the antilynchers of having a "fanatical anxiety to impose our own canons of civilization upon people differently circumstanced." The *New York Times* cited the column as the sentiment of "a big majority of sensible Englishmen, who resent the meddlesome antics of a little and noisy minority," and approvingly reprinted it.[93] Governor Northen of Georgia accused Wells of being funded by a syndicate of British and American capitalists who wanted to stop British immigration to the South.[94]

The last straw for those upset about British "meddling" came in early September 1894, when the London Anti-Lynching Committee sent a small fact-finding delegation to tour the South.[95] Governor O'Ferrall of Virginia complained, "Things have come to a pretty pass in this country when we are to have a lot of English moralists sticking their noses into our national affairs," and fourteen other governors, Northern and Southern, concurred. Governor Northen accused the British of unmanly hypocrisy, suggesting the antilynching committee return to England and "prevent by law the inhuman sale of virtuous girls to lustful men in high places. Hang all such demons as 'Jack, the Ripper'; punish as it deserves the barbarous, wholesale slaughter of negroes in Africa by Englishmen who go there to steal their gold. . . ." Governor Turney of Tennessee agreed: "I think they had better purify their own morals before coming among a better people."[96]

Governor Turney was embarrassed, however, when several days later six black men accused of arson were lynched near Memphis; he condemned the murders and offered a reward of $5,000 for the lynchers' capture. Jeered the Northern editors of the *Independent*, "It is very unfortunate . . . that just after Miss Wells's charges had been loudly pronounced false other such atrocious cases should have occurred, as if to justify all that she had said. . . ."[97] But in Memphis, Wells's campaign had borne fruit. Although two years before, Memphis's civil leaders had destroyed Wells's presses and driven her north for protesting the three businessmen's murders, now they piously proclaimed their horror of lynch law. The *Memphis Scimitar*—the same paper that two years earlier had demanded that Wells herself be lynched—editorialized, "Every one of us is touched with blood-guiltiness in this matter, unless we prove ourselves ready to do our duty as civilized men and citizens who love their country and are jealous of its good name."[98] White Memphis merchants even demonstrated their civilized manliness by holding an indignation meeting, and raising $1,000 for the murdered men's widows and orphans![99] Thirteen white men were indicted, although never convicted, for the lynchings. According to historian David Tucker, the Memphis press never again condoned lynch law; and no new lynchings occurred until 1917.[100]

Wells's campaign also inspired many white Northerners to object more vocally to lynching. In Chicago, Brooklyn, and Santa Cruz, whites were reported to have formed antilynching societies, although these organizations seem to have been ephemeral.[101] While some Northern papers still defended lynching as necessary to deter rape, many others agreed with the *Cleveland Leader* that "[a]cts of barbarism have been committed in this country within the last twenty years by people claiming to be civilized which would scarcely have been credited to the cruelest and most bloodthirsty savages in Africa."[102]

In sum, Wells's British agitation had hit a nerve. White Americans, the cheers for the Columbian Exposition still ringing in their ears, were chagrined to discover prominent British reformers calling them unmanly barbarians. The United States—the glory of the civilized world, the epitome of evolutionary progress—was the object of "missionaries"! Finally, Wells had the attention of the white American public. Her campaign, by enlisting the aid of British reformers, had forced indifferent American whites to address lynching. The *Indianapolis Freeman*, like most of the African-American press, proclaimed that Wells's campaign had put an end to white complacency. "For the first time since the commencement of its long debauch of crime, the South has been jerked up to a sudden standstill; it is on the defensive. . . . The North has at last realized that the so-called race problem is a matter that concerns not only the South, but the nation . . ."[103] Wells could not force white Americans to *oppose* lynching, but in 1894, they could no longer *ignore* lynching.

How effective was Wells's agitation in the long run? Wells did not stop lynching. Although lynching did decline after 1892, most historians credit factors other than Wells's efforts.[104] The British antilynching committees, faced with white Americans' vehement complaints about the London committee's visit, canceled further fact-finding tours and restricted their activities to outraged letter-writing campaigns.[105] Southern lynchings continued, and Wells continued to agitate against them.

But even if Wells could not put an end to the violence, her success in putting American whites on the defensive did force some long-lasting, if subtle, shifts in whites' approaches to lynch law. White Americans had no stomach for being called unmanly and uncivilized by the British. After 1894, most Northern periodicals stopped treating lynching as a colorful Southern folkway. They dropped their jokey tones and piously condemned lynching as "barbarous"—although they still implied one could do little to stop it. It became a truism that lynching hurt America in the eyes of the "civilized world."[106] At the same time, Wells's statistics forced the Northern press to acknowledge that most lynch victims had *not* been accused of rape—although the lynching for rape scenario retrained its appeal as a dramatization of white male power, and the myth of the Negro rapist remained almost as strong as ever. Southern states began to pass antilynching laws—which, unfortunately, were almost never enforced.[107] While it is impossible to know whether these small changes actually deterred any prospective lynchers, in the context of the nation's overwhelming climate of racist violence, they must be seen as modest but definite victories.

To appreciate how skillfully Ida B. Wells conducted her antilynching campaign, one needs to understand, as Wells did, the subtle ways race, gender, and class were interwoven in the 1890s. With social and cultural change threatening middle-class dominance, middle-class men had become fearful that their manhood was at risk. In order to strengthen faltering constructs of traditional manly power, they turned to race. By envisioning themselves as "the white man," whose superior manliness set them apart from more primitive dark-skinned races, middle-class men reassured themselves that their manliness remained as strong as ever. "Civilization" naturalized this combined manly/racial dominance by tying it to human evolutionary progress. By celebrating "civilization," as they did at the 1893 Columbian Exposition, middle-class white men reassured themselves that they were the most powerful beings ever evolved.

Wells inverted these linkages between manhood and white supremacy. Where white Northerners imagined lynching proved white men's superior manliness, Wells argued the reverse: lynching proved black men were far more manly than whites who tolerated lynching. Where white Americans constructed elaborate pageants like the Columbian Exposition to dramatize that white men were more manly and civilized than savage dark-skinned races, Wells mobilized "civilization" to demonstrate the opposite: white Americans were despicably unmanly and uncivilized.

Wells's manipulation of manliness and civilization can be seen as one example of a tactic oppressed groups have frequently adopted: mobilizing dominant discourses in subversive ways. Women's and labor historians have written about many such cases—from Cleveland unionists who turned their employers' calls for "law and order" into a potent rationale for a citywide strike,[108] to working girls in turn-of-the-century New York who parodied upper-class fashions in order to publicly assert their own working-class identities,[109] to labor activists and woman's activists who found in Protestantism a potent rationale for their own liberatory projects.[110] Similarly, Ida B. Wells inverted discourses in manly civilization, which made lynching tolerable to many whites, in order to show that manliness could only be saved, and civilization advanced, by stamping out lynch law.

Unlike Cleveland's law-and-order unionists or New York's stylish working girls, who were synthesizing beliefs and identities for themselves, however, Wells was consciously working to propagandize her *oppressor*. Her effectiveness stemmed from the skill with which she manipulated cherished middle-class ideologies. Her strategy of playing on middle-class men's fears about the fragility of traditional manliness succeeded brilliantly. Working with constructs so crucial to her audience's own shaky self-image made Wells's propaganda especially effective; her accusations, especially devastating.

By inverting "civilization" and challenging the links between white supremacy and manliness, Wells produced an antiracist construction of manhood. Wells recognized that behind middle-class gender lay a fundamental assumption that pure women and manly men were *white*. To attack that one point, as Wells and many of her contemporaries did, was to attack the entire edifice of middle-class identity and middle-class gender. Victorian ideologies of womanhood marginalized black women by depicting them as unwomanly harlots and contrasting them with white women, who were depicted as "real" women, high-minded and sexually pure. By resisting these ideas and insisting on black women's pure womanliness, black women in effect produced an alternative discourse of womanhood, as shown by Hazel Carby.[111] In the same way, middle-class formulations of manliness marginalized black men by depicting them as unmanly rapists, whose uncontrolled sexuality contrasted with the restrained self-mastery and manliness of "the white man." By arguing that it was "the white man," and not the black man, who was lustful and uncivilized, Wells produced a less damaging formulation of gender.

Middle-class gender's racial underpinnings may seem merely ideological, but as Wells recognized, they had dire material repercussions. They legitimized both the sexual victimization of black women and the brutal murders of black men. Wells's insistence upon the womanliness of black women and the manliness of black men was meant to dismantle the ideological structure that facilitated whites' oppressive practices. By subverting whites' raced discourses of gender, Wells hoped to force an end to racial violence.

For Wells, critiquing middle-class gender was a *tactic*, not an objective. More than a theorist, Wells was a skilled journalist, a gifted publicist, a consummate activist. As such, she understood—and was gifted at—practical propaganda. Above all else, she passionately desired to end the terror black Americans faced at the hands of "Judge Lynch." She analyzed the complexities of middle-class Americans' race/class/gender system in order to forge an effective weapon for social change. Cognizant of the subtle dynamics of these discourses, she was able to manipulate them to her political ends. She shook middle-class whites out of their complacency and forced them to pay attention to racial violence. By adeptly reading and manipulating interwoven discourses of class, race, and gender Wells made her antilynching campaign a success. Her example suggests that the ability to deconstruct the discourses of race, gender, and class, more than merely an academic exercise, is an inherently *practical* political skill for those interested in effectively motivating social movements.

NOTES

For helpful criticisms of earlier drafts, many thanks to Mari Jo Buhle, Ruth Feldstein, Elizabeth Francis, Kevin Gaines, Suzanne Kolm, Louise Newman, Mary Lou Roberts, Joan Scott, the audience at my Berkshire Conference panel, and Barbara Melosh and the *RHR* readers.

1. Ray Stannard Baker, "What is a Lynching? A Study of Mob Justice, South and North," *McClure's Magazine* 24 (February 1905): 429.
2. Ida B. Wells. *A Red Record*, reprinted in *On Lynchings* ([1895] Salem NH, 1987), 98.
3. "China Cares Not to Borrow. . . . If They Believe All That They Read, It Is Not Surprising English Busybodies Talk of Forming Societies to Civilize Us," *New York Times*, 19 August 1894, 1.
4. "British Anti-Lynchers," *New York Times*, 2 August 1894, 4.
5. "An Idyll of Alabama," *New York Times*, 30 December 1891, 4. See also "The Cartwright Avengers," *New York Times*, 19 July 1893, 4.
6. Paula Giddings, *When and Where I Enter: The Impact of Black Women on Race and Sex in America* (New York: Bantam Books, 1984), 27-29.
7. Mary P. Ryan, *Cradle of the Middle Class: The Family in Oneida County, New York, 1790-1865* (Cambridge: Cambridge University Press, 1981); Leonore Davidoff and Catherine Hall, *Family Fortunes: Men and Women of the English Middle Class, 1780-1850* (Chicago: University of Chicago Press, 1987). Although *Family Fortunes* discussed English, and not American, middle-class formation, many of the observations, especially about the importance of manliness in class formation, are applicable to the United States.
8. Stuart M. Blumin, *The Emergence of the Middle Class: Social Experience in the American City, 1760-1900* (Cambridge: Cambridge University Press, 1989), 138-191, 298-310; Paul E. Johnson, *A Shopkeeper's Millennium: Society and Revivals in Rochester, New York 1815-1837* (New York: Hill and Wang, 1978).
9. Ryan, *Cradle of the Middle Class*, 83-151; Davidoff and Hall, *Family Fortunes*, 71-192.
10. Ryan, *Cradle of the Middle Class*, 15.
11. Nancy F. Cott, *The Bonds of Womanhood: "Woman's Sphere" in New England, 1780-1835* (New Haven: Yale University Press, 1977); Christine Stansell, *City of Women: Sex and Class in New York 1789-1860* (New York: Alfred A. Knopf, 1986), 63-75, 163-65.
12. Norman Vance, *The Sinews of the Spirit: The Ideal of Christian Manliness in Victorian Literature and Religious Thought* (Cambridge: Cambridge University Press, 1985), 8-10; E. Anthony Rotundo, "Learning about Manhood: Gender Ideals and the Middle-Class Family in Nineteenth-Century America," in *Manliness and Morality: Middle-Class Masculinity in Britain and America 1800-1940*, eds. J.A. Mangan and James Walvin (New York: St. Martin's Press, 1987), 37-40, 43-46.
13. John D'Emilio and Estelle B. Freedman, *Intimate Matters: A History of Sexuality in America* (New York: Harper and Row, 1988), 178-82.
14. *Ibid.*, 68-69; John S. Haller, Jr., and Robin M. Haller, *The Physician and Sexuality in Victorian America* (Urbana: University of Illinois Press, 1974), 191-234; Cynthia

Eagle Russett, *Sexual Science: The Victorian Construction of Womanhood* (Cambridge, Mass.: Harvard University Press, 1989), 112-16.

15. On character, see Warren I. Susman, "Personality and the Making of Twentieth-Century Culture," in *Culture as History* (New York: Pantheon, 1984), 273-77; David I. Macleod, *Building Character in the American Boy* (Madison: University of Wisconsin Press, 1983).

16. On "manliness" see Davidoff and Hall, *Family Fortunes*, 108-13; Peter G. Filene, *Him/Her/Self*, 2d ed. (Baltimore: Johns Hopkins University Press, 1986), 70-71; Mangan and Walvin, eds., *Manliness and Morality*; and Vance, *The Sinews of the Spirit*.

17. Davidoff and Hall, *Family Fortunes*, 207-8; Ryan, *Cradle of the Middle Class*, 140-2.

18. Ryan, *Cradle of the Middle Class*, 165-85.

19. Blumin, *Emergence of the Middle Class*, 290-95; Filene, *Him/Her/Self*, 70-73.

20. Lewis A. Erenberg, *Stepping Out: New York Nightlife and the Transformation of American Culture, 1890-1930* (Chicago: University of Chicago Press, 1981), 33-59; John F. Kasson, *Amusing the Million: Coney Island at the Turn of the Century* (New York: Hill and Wang, 1978).

21. Gail Bederman, "The Women Have Had Charge of the Church Work Long Enough," *American Quarterly* 41 (September 1989): 435-40.

22. On middle-class men's confusion about the meaning of manhood, see Bederman, "Church Work," 432-65; Filene, *Him/Her/Self*, 69-93; Elliott J. Gorn, *The Manly Art: Bare Knuckle Prizefighting in America* (Ithaca: Cornell University Press, 1986), 179-206; John Higham, "The Reorientation of American Culture in the 1890s," in *Writing American History: Essays on Modern Scholarship* (Bloomington: Indiana University Press, 1978), 73-102; Michael S. Kimmel, "The Contemporary 'Crisis' of Masculinity in Historical Perspective," in *The Making of Masculinities*, ed. Harry Brod (Boston: Allen & Unwin, 1987), 121-54; Joe L. Dubbert, "Progressivism and the Masculinity Crisis," in *The American Man*, eds. Elizabeth H. Pleck and Joseph H. Pleck (Englewood Cliffs, NJ: Prentice-Hall, 1980). For an opposing view, see Margaret Marsh, "Suburban Men and Masculine Domesticity," *American Quarterly* 40 (June 1988): 165-86.

23. Higham, "Reorientation," 78-79.

24. D'Emilio and Freedman, *Intimate Matters*, 178-82.

25. Thomas F. Gossett, *Race: The History of an Idea in America* (Dallas: Southern Methodist University Press, 1963), 287-309; John Higham, *Strangers in the Land: Patterns of American Nativism 1860-1925* (New York: Atheneum, 1971), 131-57.

26. On Anglo-Saxonism, see Stuart Anderson, *Race and Rapprochement: Anglo-Saxonism and Anglo-American Relations, 1895-1904* (Rutherford, NJ: Fairleigh Dickinson University Press, 1981); Gossett, *Race*, 84-123, 310-38; Nell Irvin Painter, *Standing at Armageddon: The United States, 1877-1919* (New York: W.W. Norton & Company, 1987), 149-52.

27. Anderson, *Race and Rapprochement*, 20-21; Parkman quoted in Gossett, *Race*, 95.

28. Baker, "What is a Lynching?," 429.

29. George W. Stocking, Jr., "The Dark Skinned Savage," in *Race, Culture, and Evolution* (New York: The Free Press, 1968), 112-32, esp. 114, 121-22. For an excellent and exhaustive analysis of the history and development of the discourse of "civilization," see George W. Stocking, *Victorian Anthropology* (New York: The Free Press, 1987).

30. Russett, *Sexual Science*, 144-48.

31. Quoted in Virginia C. Meredith, "Woman's Part at the World's Fair," *Review of Reviews* 7 (May 1893): 417.

32. Robert W. Rydell, *All The World's a Fair: Visions of Empire at American International Expositions, 1876-1916* (Chicago: University of Chicago Press, 1984), 38-71. My discussion of the racial aspect of the fair draws heavily upon Rydell's excellent analysis. On the cultural meaning of the Columbian Exposition, see also Kasson, *Amusing the Million*, 17-28; and Alan Trachtenberg, *The Incorporation of America: Culture and Society in the Gilded Age* (New York: Hill and Wang, 1982), 208-34.

33. *The Century Dictionary: An Encyclopedic Lexicon of the English Language* (New York: The Century Company, 1890), s.v. "manly."

34. "The World's Columbian Exposition—A View from the Ferris Wheel," *Scientific American* 69 (9 September 1893): 169.

35. *Chicago Daily Inter-Ocean*, 26 April 1893, Supplement Cited in Rydell, *All the World's a Fair*, 249, n. 19.

36. "Exhibits Which Prove That the Sex Is Fast Overhauling Man," *New York Times*, 25 June 1893, quoted in Jeanne Madeline Weimann, *The Fair Women* (Chicago: Academy Chicago, 1981), 427. For a similar assessment, somewhat more humorously patronizing, see M.A. Lane, "The Woman's Building, World's Fair," *Harper's Weekly* 36 (9 January 1892): 40.

37. Russett, *Sexual Science*, 54-77.

38. For lists of Midway attractions, see map in "Opening of the World's Columbian Exposition, Chicago, 1 May 1893," *Scientific American* 68 (6 May 1893): 274-5; "Notes from the World's Columbian Exposition Chicago 1893," *Scientific American* 68 (27 May 1893): 323.

39. Rydell, *All the World's a Fair*, 61-62.

40. *Ibid.*, 65.

41. "Sights at the Fair," *Century Magazine* 46 (5 September 1893): 653.

42. For contemporary commentary on this dynamic, see "The World's Columbian Exposition—A View from the Ferris Wheel," 169; and Frederic Remington, "A Gallop Through the Midway," *Harper's Weekly* 37 (7 October 1893): 996.

43. "Wonderful Place for Fun," *New York Times*, 19 June 1893, 9. On Dahomans as popularly seen as the most primitive savages at the fair, see Rydell, *All the World's a Fair*, 66.

44. Elliot M. Rudwick and August Meier, "'Black Man in the 'White City': Negroes and the Columbian Exposition, 1893," *Phylon* 26 (Winter 1965): 354-55; Ann Massa, "Black Women in the 'White City'," *Journal of American Studies* 8 (December 1974): 319-37.

45. Wells and Douglass's letter is reprinted in "No 'Nigger Day,' No 'Nigger Pamphlet'!" *Indianapolis Freeman*, 25 March 1893, 4. The *Freeman*'s editor, who was involved in a long-standing feud with Wells, accused her of washing American dirty laundry (i.e., bringing up slavery) in public, for foreign guests. Unfortunately, Wells and Douglass were unable to raise funds to cover printing full translations into four languages. Only the introduction was translated, into French and German.

46. [Ida B. Wells], "Preface," in *The Reason Why the Colored American Is Not in the World's Columbian Exposition* [ed. Ida B. Wells] (Chicago, 1892), no page number.

47. Frederick Douglass, "Introduction," *The Reason Why*, 2.

48. *Ibid.*, 3.

49. *Ibid.*, 10-11.

50. *Ibid.*, 12.

51. *Ibid.*, 9. Lest this sound like Douglass lacks respect for Dahomans, note that American cartoonists leapt to draw unflattering depictions of impossibly thick-

lipped Dahoman men, clad (like women) only in brief grass skirts, necklaces, bracelets, and earrings. See Rydell *All the Worlds' a Fair*, 53, 54, 70.

52. Alfreda M. Duster, ed., *Crusade for Justice: The Autobiography of Ida B. Wells* (Chicago: University of Chicago Press, 1970), 117.

53. Ida B. Wells, *Southern Horrors: Lynch Law in All Its Phases*, reprinted in *On Lynchings* ([1892]; Salem, NH: Ayer Company, 1987), 4.

54. See, for example, Iola [Ida B. Wells], "Iola's Southern Field—Save the Pennies," *New York Age*, 19 November 1892, 2; *idem*, "The Reign of Mob Law: Iola's Opinion of Doings in Southern Field," *New York Age*, 18 February 1893 (typescript in Ida B. Wells Papers, University of Chicago); Wells, *Southern Horrors*, 22-23.

55. Duster, ed., *Crusade for Justice*, 86, 219.

56. More complete biographical information on Wells's campaign and her beginnings as an antilynching activist may be found in: Duster, ed., *Crusade for Justice*; Bettina Aptheker, "Woman Suffrage and the Crusade against Lynching, 1890-1920," in *Woman's Legacy: Essays on Race, Sex, and Class in American History* (Amherst: University of Massachusetts Press, 1982), 53-76; Paula Giddings, "Ida Wells-Barnett 1862-1931," in *Portraits of American Women from Settlement to the Present*, eds. G.J. Barker-Benfield and Catherine Clinton (New York: St. Martin's Press, 1991), 366-85; Giddings, *When and Where I Enter*, 19-31, 89-93; Thomas C. Holt, "The Lonely Warrior: Ida B. Wells-Barnett and the Struggle for Black Leadership," in *Black Leaders of the Twentieth Century*, eds. John Hope Franklin and August Meier (Urbana: University of Illinois Press, 1982), 39-50; Mary Magdelene Boone Hutton, "The Rhetoric of Ida B. Wells: The Genesis of the Anti-Lynch Movement" (Ph.D. diss., University of Indiana, 1975); Dorothy Sterling, *Black Foremothers: Three Lives* (New York: The Feminist Press, 1988), 61-117; Mildred Thompson, "Ida B. Wells-Barnett: An Exploratory Study of an American Black Woman 1893-1930: (Ph.D. diss., George Washington University, 1979), 20-125; David M. Tucker, "Miss Ida B. Wells and Memphis Lynching," *Phylon* 32 (Summer 1971): 112-22. Hazel V. Carby deftly analyzed Wells's antilynching pamphlets in the context of the 1890s black women's movement in *Reconstructing Womanhood* (New York: Oxford University Press, 1987), 95-120, and in "'On the Threshold of Woman's Era': Lynching, Empire and Sexuality in Black Feminist Theory," in *"Race," Writing, and Difference*, ed. Henry Louis Gates, Jr. (Chicago: University of Chicago Press, 1985), 301-16.

57. Wells, "Preface," *Southern Horrors*, no page number.

58. For Wells's lack of faith in appealing to whites for justice, see Iola [Ida B. Wells], "Freedom of Political Action—A Woman's Magnificent Definition of the Political Situation," *New York Freeman*, 7 November 1885, 2; Ida B. Wells Diary 1884-1887, entry for 11 April 1887 (Ida B. Wells Papers, University of Chicago), 183.

59. Jacquelyn Dowd Hall, "'The Mind that Burns in Each Body': Women, Rape and Racial Violence," in *Powers of Desire: The Politics of Sexuality*, eds. Ann Snitow, Christine Stansell, and Sharon Thompson (New York: Monthly Review Press, 1983), 328-49, esp. 335. On the myth of the black rapist, see Angela Davis, "Rape, Racism, and the Myth of the Black Rapist," *Women, Race, and Class* (New York: Vintage Books, 1981), 172-201. On Southern white men's projecting repressed sexuality onto black men, see also Jacquelyn Dowd Hall, *Revolt Against Chivalry: Jessie Daniel Ames and the Women's Campaign Against Lynching* (New York: Columbia University Press, 1979), 148; and Trudier Harris, *Exorcising Blackness: Historical*

and Literary Lynching and Burning Rituals (Bloomington: Indiana University Press, 1984), 1-28.

60. "Negro Lynching," *Providence Journal*, 2 February 1893, 5.

61. "Negroes Lynched by a Mob," *New York Times*, 10 March 1892, 1.

62. Wells, *Southern Horrors*, "Preface" (no page number), and 5.

63. *Ibid.*, 7-10, quotation on 8. Italics in original.

64. *Ibid.*, 6.

65. *Ibid.*, 11-12.

66. *Ibid.*, 14.

67. Carby, *Reconstructing Womanhood*, 6; and "On the Threshold," 303-4.

68. Albion Tourgée, "A Bystander's Notes," *Chicago Daily Inter-Ocean*, 24 September 1892, 4.

69. George C. Rowe, "How to Prevent Lynching," *The Independent* 46 (1 February 1894): 131-2.

70. Duster, ed., *Crusade for Justice*, 77-78, 82, 85-86. Also see Wells's comments in "Idol of her People," *Chicago Daily Inter-Ocean*, 8 August 1894, 2.

71. *Note on sources*: Although Wells's speeches were covered extensively by the English press, they are mostly not obtainable in this country. Hutton's dissertation, "The Rhetoric of Ida B. Wells," used British press reports extensively to document both tours. The excerpts Hutton cited are similar in tone to interviews Wells gave to American papers immediately after returning and to Wells's book, *A Red Record*, published early in 1895. Thus, I am using these sources, in addition to a few available English sources, to reconstruct what Wells said.

72. "A Sermon on Ibsen—A Coloured Woman In the Pulpit," *Christian World* 38 (14 march 1894): 187; quoted in Hutton, "Rhetoric," 127.

73. Ida B. Wells, "Lynch Law in the United States" (letter), *Birmingham Daily Post* (England, photocopy, n.d. [16 May 1893]), in Ida B. Wells Papers, University of Chicago. The article is reprinted and dated in Duster, ed., *Crusade for Justice*, 101, but is not accurately transcribed.

74. Significantly, Wells never explicitly discussed incidents of lynching in these columns, evidently believing that British censure would upset Northern whites far more than African-American suffering. Similarly, Wells rarely discussed the economic causes of lynching to white audiences during these years, although she regularly raised economic issues in her writings for African-American newspapers. She had a sophisticated analysis of the economic causes of lynching, catalyzed by her realization that the three Memphis grocers had been lynched in order to stop them from competing with white merchants. Yet she nearly always stressed issues of "civilization" and downplayed economic factors for white audiences during the years of her British tours. This was probably because she did not believe most white Americans would *care* that blacks were being murdered for economic reasons, while she knew it would rankle them to be called uncivilized.

75. Ida B. Wells, "Ida B. Wells Abroad," *Chicago Daily Inter-Ocean*, 25 June 1894, 10. Also in Duster, ed., *Crusade for Justice*, 179.

76. "Ida B. Wells Abroad—The Bishop of Manchester on American Lynching," *Chicago Daily Inter-Ocean*, 23 April 1894, 10; "Against Lynching—Ida B. Wells and Her Recent Mission in England," *Chicago Daily Inter-Ocean*, 4 August 1894, 9.

77. Quoted in "An Anti-Lynching Crusade in America Begun," *Literary Digest* 9 (11 August 1894): 421.

78. Ida B. Wells, *London Daily Chronicle*, 28 April 1894, 3; quoted in Hutton, "Rhetoric," 135.

79. Wells, *A Red Record,* 74-5.

80. "The Bitter Cry of Black America—A New 'Uncle Toms [*sic*] Cabin'," *Westminister Gazette* 3 (10 May 1894): 2; quoted in Hutton, "Rhetoric," 146.

81. "Lynch Law in America," *Christian World* 38 (April 19, 1894): 287, quoted in Hutton, "Rhetoric," 156.

82. From a photocopy in the Ida B. Wells Papers, marked "The *Birmingham Daily Gazette*, May 18th [1893]."

83. Ida B. Wells, "Ida B. Wells Abroad," *Chicago Daily Inter-Ocean*, 25 June 1894, 10; Hutton, "Rhetoric," 156-59, 170-71; Duster, ed. *Crusade for Justice*, 176, 190-97; "English Feeling upon America's Lynchings," *Literary Digest* 9 (14 July 1894): 308; "That Irish Begging Letter," *New York Times*, 9 September 1894, 12; "The Sneer of a Good Natured Democrat" *Indianapolis Freeman*, 16 June 1894, 4.

84. Hutton, "Rhetoric," 157-58. Quotations from Richard Acland Armstrong, "Lynching in the United States" (letter), *Liverpool Mercury*, 3 April 1894, 3; and "Lynch Law in the South," *Christian Register* 83 (12 April 1894): 225-26; both as cited in Hutton, "Rhetoric."

85. Quoted in Ida B. Wells, "Ida B. Wells Abroad," *Chicago Daily Inter-Ocean*, 19 May 1894, 16. A version is also in Duster, ed., *Crusade for Justice*, 157-58, but it is not transcribed precisely.

86. Duster, ed., *Crusade for Justice*, 215-17; Hutton, "Rhetoric," 68-69.

87. Ida B. Wells, "Ida B. Wells Abroad," *Chicago Daily Inter-Ocean*, 7 July 1894, 18; also in Duster, ed., *Crusade for Justice*, 183-86. For other evidence of attempts to smear Wells, see "Editor Flemming's Denial," *Indianapolis Freeman*, 28 July 1894, 4; and "Is it Necessary?" *Indianapolis Freeman*, 4 August 1894, 4.

88. Quoted in "How Miss Wells' Crusade is Regarded in America," *Literary Digest* 9 (28 July 1894): 366.

89. Quoted in "The Anti-Lynching Crusade," *Literary Digest* 9 (8 September 1894): 544.

90. Edward C. Gordon, "Mob Violence: "The 'National Crime,'" *Independent* 46 (1 November 1894): 1400.

91. Quoted in "The Sneer of a Good Natured Democrat," *Indianapolis Freeman*, 16 June 1894, 4. See also "British Treatment of Negroes," *New York Times*, 20 August 1894, 8; and "How Miss Wells' Crusade is Regarded in America," 367.

92. Since the South was solidly Democratic, Northern Democratic newspapers were more likely to defend Southern practices and politicians, while Republican newspapers were more likely to attack them. See, for instance, "An Anti-Lynching Crusade in America Begun," *Literary Digest* 9 (11 August 1894): 421-22; Editorial, *New York Times*, 16 March 1894, 4.

93. Reprinted as "Lessons for Busybodies," *New York Times*, 15 October 1894, 9; "London Week of Excitement," *New York Times*, 7 October 1894, 1. See also "English Criticism of the English Anti-Lynching Committee," *Literary Digest* 9 (27 October 1894): 757; and "British Anti-Lynchers," *New York Times*, 2 August 1894, 4. In the London *Spectator*, a debate on lynching raged in the Letters to the Editor column, while the editors simultaneously condemned lynching and called on Britons to stop interfering in American internal affairs. See Editorial, *Spectator* 72 (16 June 1894): 810; W. McKay, "Lynching in Georgia: A Correction" (letter), *Spectator* 73 (28 July 1894): 111; S. Alfred Steinthal, "Lynching in America" (letter), *Spectator* 73 (4 August 1894): 142; Chas. S. Butler, "The Lynching of Negroes in America"

(letter), *Spectator* 73 (25 August 1894): 240; "Lynch Law in the United States" (letter), *Spectator* 73 (8 September 1894): 303; and "Lynching in America and English Interference," *Spectator* 73 (11 August 1894): 1669-70.

94. "An Anti-Lynching Crusade in America Begun," 421.

95. Although some historians have suggested that no delegations of British antilynching committees ever came to the United States, contemporary press reports suggest that Sir John Gorst—and perhaps a small committee—came as a representative of the London committee. See "Sir John Gorst's Report," *New York Times*, 10 September 1894, 8; "Governor Northen is Aroused," *New York Times*, 11 September 1894, 2; "Southern Governors on English Critics," *Literary Digest* 9 (22 September 1894): 601-2; and Peter Stanford, "Serious Complications—The Anti-Lynch Sentiment in England Being Cooled," *Indianapolis Freeman*, 1 December 1894, 1.

96. "Governor Northen is Aroused," 2; "Southern Governors on English Critics," 601-2.

97. "A Bad Week for the Lynchers," *Independent* 46 (18 September 1894): 1187.

98. Quoted in "The Latest Lynching Case," *Literary Digest* 9 (15 September 1894): 577; Wells, *Southern Horrors*, 5.

99. "Killing of the Six Tennessee Negroes," *New York Times*, 9 September 1894, 12.

100. Tucker, "Miss Ida B.Wells," 121-22.

101. "How Miss Wells' Crusade Is Regarded in America," 366; "Helping Miss Wells's Crusade," *New York Times*, 11 December 1894, 6.

102. Quotation in "The Anti-Lynching Crusade," *Literary Digest*, 545. For a selection of Northern newspaper editorials in favor of and against the antilynch agitation, see in addition, *ibid*. (11 August 1894): 421-22; and "Remedies for Lynch Law: A Case in Point," *Indianapolis Freeman*, 4 August 1894, 4.

103. "His 'Opinion' No Good," *Indianapolis Freeman*, 29 September 1894, 4. See also "Remedies for Lynch Law: A Case in Point"; and Thompson, "An Exploratory Study," 116-22.

104. Edward L. Ayers, *Vengeance and Justice* (New York: Oxford University Press, 1984), 237-55; Joel Williamson, *The Crucible of Race: Black-White Relations in the American South Since Emancipation* (New York: Oxford University Press, 1984), 117-18. Tucker credits Wells's campaign with curtailing lynchings in Memphis, however; see Tucker, "Miss Ida B. Wells," 121-22.

105. James Elbert Cutler, *Lynch-Law* (New York: Longmans, Green and Co, 1905), 229-30; Peter Stanford, "Serious Complications—The Anti-Lynch Sentiment in England Being Cooled," *Indianapolis Freeman*, 1 December 1894, 1.

106. See, for example, "Lynching," *New York Times*, 8 December 1895, 5; "Lynching in the South," *New York Times*, 14 January 1896, 4; compare these to "The Cartwright Avengers," *New York Times*, 19 July 1893, 4.

107. "Public Sentiment Against Lynching," *New York Times*, 8 December 1895, 32; Cutler, *Lynch Law*, 233-45.

108. Steven J. Ross, *Workers on the Edge: Work, Leisure, and Politics in Industrializing Cincinnati* (New York: Columbia University Press, 1985), 270-93.

109. Kathy Peiss, *Cheap Amusements: Working Women and Leisure in Turn-of-the Century New York* (Philadelphia: Temple University Press, 1986), 62-67. Christine Stansell made a similar argument in *City of Women*, 164-65.

110. Herbert G. Gutman, "Protestantism and the American Labor Movement," in *Work, Culture & Society in Industrializing America* (New York: Vintage Books, 1976), 79-117; Elizabeth and Kenneth Fones-Wolf, "Trade-Union Evangelism: Religion and

the AFL in the Labor Forward Movement, 1912-16," in *Working Class America*, eds. Michael H. Frish and Daniel J. Walkowitz (Urbana: University of Illinois Press, 1983), 153-84; Elizabeth Cady Stanton, ed., *The Woman's Bible* (New York: European Publishing Company, 1895); and Kathryn Kish Sklar, *Catharine Beecher: A Study in American Domesticity* (New York: W.W. Norton & Company, 1973).

111. Carby, *Reconstructing Womanhood*, 6, 20-61; Giddings, *When and Where*, 82-89.

26

Black Club Women and the Creation of the National Association of Colored Women

Stephanie J. Shaw

Much of what we know about black club women has been explained in the context of the creation of the National Association of Colored Women (NACW).[1] This scholarship often links black club women's activities to the most immediate and most obvious stimuli—the rising tide of Jim Crowism, the increase in lynching and other acts of mob violence, the vile verbal and literary attacks on the character of black women, and the general deterioration of race relations throughout the nation.[2] Historian Rayford Logan referred to these decades at the end of the nineteenth century as "the Nadir" in the history of American race relations.[3]

Club women themselves spoke out and wrote enough to suggest that those problems were important catalysts for their activism. Late-nineteenth-century journalist, community activist, and club leader Ida B. Wells-Barnett launched her antilynching crusade not simply after the brutal killing of her good friend, Thomas Moss, but also after her thorough investigation of lynching incidents concluded that the recent increase in lynching was carefully and deliberately orchestrated in response to black economic gains and political potential. Mary Church Terrell added the abuse of vagrancy laws, the convict lease system, and peonage to the increasing threats to black life and security. Prominent turn-of-the-century Virginia club woman Janie Porter Barrett summarized the feelings of sympathetic contemporary observers (and recent scholars) when she wrote: "No one can deny that the Negro race is going through the most trying period of its history. Truly these are days when we are 'being tried as by fire.'"[4]

Considering the evidence that black club women left, it is not difficult to see why current-day scholars interpret the organization of the NACW as a response to these bad conditions. But such a conclusion ignores considerable evidence that reveals the obvious flaw in the interpretation. According to historian Willie Mae Coleman, the Colored Women's League, formed in Washington, D.C., in 1892, was a coalition of 113 organizations. The more nationally oriented National Federation of Afro-American Women, formed in 1895, represented the combination of 85 organizations.[5] When these two federations combined in 1896 to form the NACW, the impetus and inclination for black women to form a collective was more than a few years old. In fact, it predated the so-called nadir of African-American history by generations.

The purpose of this article is to formulate a new interpretation of the creation of the national black women's club coalition of the 1890s—one that points to the internal traditions of the African-American community rather than activities in the white community. Numerous factors suggest the need for the alternative view. First, the history of "voluntary associations" among African-Americans indicates a historical legacy of collective consciousness and mutual associations. Second, individual histories of diverse club women reveal early lessons in racial consciousness and community commitment. And third, the work of organized black women before the formation of the NACW was no different from the activities of club women after the creation of the NACW. Altogether, the founding of the NACW did not mark the beginning of the important organized work of black women against racism, sexism, and their effects, as earlier studies imply. Instead, the creation of the national organization represents another step in an internal historical process of encouraging and supporting self-determination, self-improvement, and community development.

At least as early as the advent of American slavery, African-Americans consistently demonstrated inclinations toward community consciousness and collective activity. Historians of the antebellum South, slavery, and slave culture inform us that even under slavery, black men and women operated as a community within a community in which both personal and social identities developed and helped to ameliorate the harsh conditions of their enforced bondage.[6] Slaves often acted together in rebellion, or colluded afterwards to protect those implicated in acts of resistance.[7] Plantation childcare situations, the forced secrecy surrounding organized religious ceremonies, and the potential for and actual loss of blood family members continually encouraged the development of group consciousness.[8] Folk tales provided lessons in group survival and examples of community ethics.[9] Historian Lawrence Levine writes that the most enduring characteristic of slave songs was their group nature. While they often functioned to set the pace of work for slaves, in improvised verses, one gang member might chastise another for not carrying his/her burden of the work. Structurally, through lining-out and call-and-response forms, the songs allowed a slave "at one and the same time to preserve his voice as a distinct entity and to blend it with those of his fellows."[10] Slaves in All Saints Parish, South Carolina, even imposed "a cooperative work ethos upon the highly individualist task system" of work which their owners used in an attempt to regulate their labor. Slaves adapted the labor system proposed by their masters and overseers "to their own sense of appropriateness" as they worked the crop in a row, hoeing and moving across the field synchronously to the rhythm of a work song.[11] Historian Deborah Gray White notes that slave women developed a network within the slave community that was supportive, empowering, and instrumental to their survival.[12]

Within the non-slave population of the antebellum period, the associations of individuals could take on more structure. They abounded in the North and South as benevolent and beneficial societies and intellectual and community uplift groups, among others. The Free African Society, formed in Philadelphia in 1787 by Richard Allen and Absolom Jones, is best known for the creation of the African Methodist Episcopal Church. From its inception, however, The Free African Society was also a mutual-aid society. The Female Benevolent Society of St. Thomas took over the organization in 1793, and two years later the all-male African Friendly Society of St. Thomas joined the women. The Daughters of Africa, which existed as early as 1821, was a mutual-aid organization of approximately 200 black working-class women. Members bought groceries and supplies for the needy, paid sick benefits, and lent money to society members in emergency situations. One scholar estimates that by 1850 there were at least 200 black mutual-aid societies in the country's major cities, with a total of 13,000 to 15,000 members.[13] This estimate is undoubtedly conservative, for 1838 there were 119 such organizations with 7,372 members in Philadelphia alone.[14]

African-American women worked for self-improvement and racial advancement in a variety of settings during the antebellum period. Historian Linda Perkins writes that "the threads that held together the organizational as well as individual pursuits . . . were those of 'duty' and 'obligation' to the race. The concept of racial obligation was intimately linked with the concept of racial 'uplift' and 'elevation.'" Perkins notes the efforts of the Colored Female Produce Society, formed in 1831, to boycott slave-made products. Members of the Boston-based Afri-American Female Intelligence Society used their collected dues to buy newspapers and books and to rent a reading room. Also, members of at least one year were eligible for illness benefits. One reporter claimed that the Ohio Ladies Education Society had, by 1840, done "more towards the establishment of schools for the education of colored people . . . in Ohio than any other organized group."[15]

When slavery ended, African-Americans had considerable experience operating mutual associations, and carrying those practices through the Reconstruction period ensured future survival. Greater physical mobility, the tremendously unstable economy, and a determination to be free and independent of whites continued to encourage mutual associations. Historian Armstead Robinson writes that during the Reconstruction period, black men and women began to develop "their communal infrastructure."[16] To that end, among the many associations created during this period were agricultural societies concerned with planting, harvesting, contracting labor, and homesteading; savings and loan associations; insurance companies; trade unions; fire departments; burial, literary, social, educational, and business societies; and many others.[17] Even the educational institutions developed among former slaves during this period focused not simply on schooling the individual but on the educational needs and interests of the group in tandem.[18] Taken to the extreme, all-black towns formed in the south and west during and immediately after the Reconstruction period were radical and ultimate examples of mutual associations.[19]

Although Federal Reconstruction organizations and institutions eventually collapsed, black self-help groups continued to thrive, and black women's activities were prominent. The Daughters of Zion, founded in 1867 in Memphis, Tennessee, was a church-affiliated group that served the same purpose that the earlier associations and later women's clubs served—individual and community self-help and uplift. With over 300 members at one time, the group organized relief efforts after the war, employed a physician to care for congregation members, and worked in various other public health and education activities.[20] Mary Prout founded The Independent Order of St. Luke (IOSL) in 1867. The Order began as a traditional beneficial society for women, and later admitted men. Under the subsequent leadership of Maggie Lena Walker, the organization flourished financially and grew to 100,000 members in 28 states. Walker also devised the plans for the St. Luke Penny Savings Bank, a major financial institution that came about as a result of community cooperation. And once in place, the bank fostered that tradition by becoming a symbol of accomplishment, a source of pride, and a facilitator of community development. Walker credited her success not simply to her own abilities but also to "the strength of the St. Luke collective as a whole and . . . the special strengths and talents of the inner core of the St. Luke women in particular." She linked black women as individuals to the advancement of the group by encouraging them to work to improve conditions of the home, community, and race.[21]

The details of Elsa Barkley Brown's study of Maggie Lena Walker indicate that the development of community consciousness and social responsibility was not accidental but a consequence of deliberate processes. Among black women in general, a variety of individuals participated in those processes. For example, if Clara Jones, a prominent Detroit librarian and club woman, had not heard it before, when she was preparing to leave home to attend college in the late 1920s, her grandfather, a former slave, reminder her: "you're going to get your education, and it's not yours. You're doing it for your people."[22] Jones later characterized her family as "a fiercely education-conscious family." And she added that "it was accepted that my four brothers and sisters and . . . [I] would all go to college to help our race. That was the way everyone thought in those days."[23]

Janie Porter Barrett's community activism is well known, but rarely do we get a glimpse of aspects of her early life that might help to explain her activism. Born in 1870, Barrett founded the Locust Street Settlement House in Hampton, Virginia, and the Peak Turnout, Virginia, Home for Delinquent Girls (later called the Girls' Industrial School). Her mother worked as a nurse for a wealthy white family, and she reared Janie in their home. Janie's mother apparently accepted her employer's educating Janie along with the white children of the family, but she left her position when the white woman of the house announced that she wanted to become Janie's legal guardian and send her to a northern white school for more education. Historian Tullia Brown Hamilton notes that the employer expected Janie to pass for white while attending the school. After quitting her job, Janie's mother sent her daughter to Hampton Institute instead. Obviously, Barrett's mother wanted to have control over her daughter's education, but we can also speculate about Barrett's mother's race consciousness. That is, it was not only unacceptable for her child to pass for white, but it was also important for Barrett to go to a black school. Not surprisingly, because of her upbringing in the comfortable white household, Barrett found the living conditions at Hampton in the 1880s to be very disappointing. After all, she had always enjoyed having a room that "was daintily furnished, and . . . surroundings [that] bespoke refinement and ease." Evidently, the white household did not foster the development of any realistic racial identity either. But Hampton could and did remedy that. Barrett wrote that when she first arrived at Hampton, she got tired of being drilled on her "duties to the race." She noted that she always woke up happy on Sundays, because on Sundays, she said, "I didn't have to do single thing for my race." But students and faculty at Hampton succeeded at making Barrett more socially responsible and racially conscious. And when she created the Locust Street Settlement House in 1890—six years before the formation of the NACW and 18 years before the creation of the Virginia Federation of Colored Women's Clubs (VFCWC)—she used money that she and her husband had intended to use to install indoor plumbing in their home.[24]

Twenty-five years later, Barrett, a well-seasoned community activist, had held offices in the NACW and the VFCWC and was launching her project to create a home for delinquent black girls in Virginia. When Margaret Murray Washington, a principal at Tuskegee Institute and the wife of Booker T. Washington, offered her a principalship at Tuskegee Institute, Barrett wrote to Hollis Frissell (then president of Hampton Institute) that "Washington's letter makes me wish that I could be in two places at once. I should be glad to serve at Tuskegee, but I know I am going where I am needed [most?] and though this undertaking is most difficult, it isn't impossible, and if the friends will stand by me, this Home School will be, in time, a tremendous power for good." In fact, the home school became a model program set up on the cottage plan and the honor system, with the VFCWC as one of its major financial supporters.[25]

Ida B. Wells (Barnett) was born a slave in Holly Springs, Mississippi, in 1862, of parents who insisted on educating their children, and some of Wells's first teachers were individuals who came to Holly Springs specifically to aid the recently freed men and women. Wells eventually left her hometown to continue her education, but after her parents died during the yellow fever epidemic of 1878, she and her surviving siblings immediately came under the guardianship of the Masons, a fraternal society of which her father was a member. Such fraternal societies traditionally assumed the responsibility for the surviving dependents of deceased members. While it is unlikely that this incident alone caused Wells to become an activist, surely the lesson in social responsibility was not lost. Within a short time, she became very active in civil rights causes. In 1884 she successfully sued the Chesapeake and Ohio Railroad for not allowing her to ride in a first-class car for which she had a ticket, but a higher court overturned the decision. Before the reversal occurred, railroad company lawyers offered Wells money to settle the case out of court, but she turned down their offers, dismissing the possibility of an individual payoff while pushing for a larger victory for the race. By the 1890s her articles on educational conditions for black residents in Memphis resulted in her being fired from her teaching position. More scathing pieces on lynching resulted in her fleeing for her life.[26] While she lived in exile, other black club women helped to support and protect her.[27] Wells wrote that most of the trouble she encountered with whites resulted from her actions on behalf of the race. But she said she owed it to herself and her race to tell the truth about white racism.[28]

Jane Edna Hunter, born in 1882 on a South Carolina plantation, grew up in a household with her parents that at one time also enjoyed the presence of her grandmother and great-grandmother, both of whom were former slaves. Her parents appreciated the value of formal education but apparently could neither assume the right nor afford the privilege; Hunter worked her way through school. At the end of one summer of employment, because she needed all of her earnings to obtain school necessities, a friend agreed to purchase her return train ticket. When at the last minute it became apparent that the person who had offered to purchase the ticket would not follow through, the 20 or so proud friends and neighbors who gathered at the train station to see her off began to put together their change, ultimately collecting enough money for her ticket and fifty cents to spare.[29]

Hunter eventually finished secondary and nursing school, but when she relocated to Cleveland in 1905, she did not easily find housing or work. She had no family and few friends in that city, and the first place she lived turned out to be a residence for prostitutes. As soon as she established herself favorably in housing and in work, she and a few friends met to form the Working Girl's Home Association to build a home for "the poor motherless daughters of the race." The women who formed this voluntary association pledged to contribute five cents a week and committed themselves to recruiting new members. The first home opened in 1911. After the second facility opened in 1917, Hunter tried to explain her motivation:

> There was something . . . [that] kept urging and making me less content with what I was doing and calling me into a broader service. . . . Then the thought came to me that there were other girls who had come to Cleveland, perhaps under similar circumstances as myself and were strangers and alone and were meeting with the same difficulties and hardships in trying to establish themselves in a large city.

The Working Girl's Home Association proved to be a successful venture and its residence grew from a 23-room facility to a 72-room facility in 1917. By

1928 the institution had 135 bedrooms, 4 parlors, 6 clubrooms, a cafeteria, and a beauty salon.[30]

The creation of the Working Girl's Home Association represented a traditional response to a particular problem in that the black community historically turned to voluntary associations to resolve internal problems. But Jane Edna Hunter's organization also represented what was new about many of the black women's associations (more often called leagues or clubs after 1890) formed around this time. It was a voluntary association, but the women who came together to form the association did not share the common local history that the earlier church and/or community society members shared. Hunter and many of her colleagues were relative newcomers to Cleveland. In general, the origins of the membership of the late-nineteenth- to early-twentieth-century women's clubs were often different in this substantial way. These women were not necessarily total strangers to one another, but they were quite often newcomers to the geographic locales where they became prominently associated with club work.

Records of the Federation of Colored Women's Clubs of Colorado, for example, indicate that many of its members were not natives of Colorado. Gertrude Ross, who held numerous offices beginning in 1911, was from Illinois. Ruth Howard, one of Denver's most active residents, came to Colorado from Texas. Elizabeth Ensley, the founder of the Federation in 1903, came from Massachusetts by way of Washington, D.C., and Mississippi. Among the many other examples, Bettey Wilkins, a member of several federated clubs in Colorado, came from Ohio.[31]

The few published accounts of black women's clubs suggest the same. Elizabeth Lindsay Davis provides brief biographical sketches of 71 Illinois club women in her book on the state federation. She notes the birth place and location of the club work for 39 of the women (54%). Only one of the women was active in club work in the place where she was born.[32] Delilah Beasley's 1919 work on black pioneers in California explicitly identifies 19 women who were members of clubs, at least 14 of whom were migrants to California.[33]

Tullia Brown Hamilton studied the leadership of the NACW and detailed similar statistics. Out of 108 women, Hamilton determined the birth places of 70. Approximately half of that number were born in the antebellum slave states (while over 90% of the general population was born and still lived there in the 1890s), and of that number born in the south, 65% settled in the north or west after some migration within the south. Hamilton also concluded that even among northern club women, "in all likelihood [they] migrated to other areas of the North, West, or even the South before settling down."[34]

To be sure, because of turn-of-the-century migration patterns, many African-Americans in the urban areas where clubs proliferated had migrated there.[35] More important, the clubs allowed women who had left their original communities to continue to associate with one another for individual and collective advancement as earlier mutual associations had. Significantly, the diverse geographic origins of the residents now meant that "the community" was no longer local; it had national roots. And so to effectively address the concerns of the members, the club network and many club activities became national.[36]

The 25 members of the Willing Worker's Club of Stamford, Connecticut, gave $2,000 to "needy causes throughout the city" between 1901 and 1907. The Art and Study Club of Moline, Illinois, enumerated among its functions visiting the sick and clothing the poor. Members of the Adelphi Club of St. Paul, Minnesota, read race literature, supported two elderly women, took fruit and magazines to city hospitals, gave food baskets to the needy on Easter and Thanksgiving, took clothes to a local orphanage, and supported a South Carolina kindergarten. Black club women in Boston supported a kindergarten in Atlanta, Georgia. Although charters, bylaws, and objectives are not available for most turn-of-the-century clubs, the actions of members of many of them suggest that they also believed in a stated aim of the Neighborhood Union of Atlanta, Georgia: "to develop group consciousness and mass movements."[37]

Supporting the less able and improving standards of living meant providing services normally supported by local governments through public taxes. But providing these services pushed the activities of these women beyond traditional "charity work" and, in fact, represented community development. Charleston, South Carolina, club woman Susan Dart Butler operated a library for African-Americans in a building owned by her father and stocked primarily with his books. Local black club women helped to maintain the facility until it became too expensive for them to operate. At that point, Butler leased it to the city for one dollar a year on the condition that public officials maintain it as a black library. Black club women in Atlanta, Georgia, helped the Neighborhood Union to establish and maintain a public health clinic for black residents. They eventually leased it to the city, also, and thereby forced the public support that similar clinics in the white community always enjoyed. In both instances, the women ultimately donated the facilities to the city.[38]

In Delaware, Texas, Arkansas, West Virginia, Florida, Virginia, and Alabama the state federations of colored women's clubs created institutions for sheltering black juvenile delinquents who would otherwise have suffered incarceration with adult prison populations. In Missouri, Texas, North Carolina, Mississippi, Florida, Virginia, Alabama, Georgia, South Carolina, and Louisiana, black club women funded, built, and maintained public health clinics and/or hospitals.[39] Club women also created homes for black working women in such urban areas as Cleveland, Chicago, New York, Newark, Boston, Little Rock, and Kansas City (Missouri). The Neighborhood Union House was a model settlement house that groups throughout the country sought to emulate. Other prominent settlements created by club women included the Locust Street Settlement in Hampton, Virginia, the Phillis Wheatley in Cleveland, and the Russell Plantation Settlement and the Calhoun Settlement in rural Alabama. In all of the former confederate states, in midwestern states including Kansas, Indiana, Ohio, Illinois, Minnesota, and in numerous northern and western states, black club women built, supported, and/or managed nursery schools and kindergartens, orphanages, and homes for the black elderly. The White Rose Home in New York gained a national reputation for its work to protect black women migrants from the south. Altogether, the work of black club women on behalf of the race involved a broad range of activities. And even when their activities seemed explicitly directed to the benefit of women—as with the effort for women's suffrage and work with the YWCA movement—or some other less race-specific topic, they understood the consequences of all such work in terms of improving conditions for the race.[40]

The activities of NACW affiliates did not differ dramatically from earlier association activities. Club women provided aid to people in the community at large and therefore worked as the old benevolent societies worked. They provided emergency support for members and therefore functioned as the old mutual-aid/beneficial associations functioned. And they worked for self-improvement and community uplift as both benevolent and beneficial societies of an earlier period had. But the NACW was different from those earlier associations not only in that it was a national black women's collective, but also it was the country's leading national race organization—predating the creation of the NAACP by 15 years. Even after founding of the NAACP, the NACW remained, for some time, the leading black national organization working for the individual and collective advancement of African Americans, because the NAACP remained controlled by whites for many years.

Self-help and racial uplift were always important objectives of black women's public activism, but the focal points of the activism did change over time. In earlier decades, the shared conditions of slavery and the limited mobility that slaves enjoyed restricted their associations to groups that included but went beyond the "family" to embrace the whole slave community. Except for the anti-slavery societies, associations of free blacks in the antebellum period maintained a local orientation as well. In the post-emancipation period, black women's organizations abounded, and many, like the IOSL, eventually had national connections. But the voluntary associations formed by club women around the turn of the century embraced local women with shared traditions and outlooks who were often no longer from the same families, churches, neighborhoods, or even regions. And not only did that aspect of diversity not preclude their organizing, but it encouraged the creation of a national structure to perpetuate the historical traditions of self-help, community development, and racial uplift despite the demographic shifts in progress.

If the formation of black women's clubs represents but one phase in a long history of group identification and mutual association, then the formation of the NACW represents not only the broadening base, vision, and abilities of black club women, but also another logical step in the effort to maintain and/ or improve important historical mechanisms for racial self-help. Through this newly rationalized and nationalized structure, black women could speak more profoundly about problems specific to them as black women and problems that affected them as they affected the race. There is no need to defend black club women against charges of imitating white women (the General Federation of Women's Clubs) or compensating for exclusion by the white women. African-American women's tradition of mutual association predated the GFWC by many years. And black women were reformers long before the Progressive Era. It is equally inappropriate to interpret the creation of the national coalition of African-American women's clubs as a response to the contemporary attacks on black female morality. Such attacks undoubtedly gave the organizers an important "cause" that could evoke an immediate response from the black community. But those attacks rested on a historical tradition, too, and at best the attacks only became more public and more frequent at this time. White society had always maintained that black people were immoral and evil; black slavery itself had been rationalized through this explanation.[41] The formation of the NACW represented no psycho-social shift in the women's personal identities or in their social, political, and economic agendas. Rather, it was simply a new national voice through which black club women could continue the struggle to improve their personal lives and the general standard of life in the ever-broadening communities of which they were a part.

NOTES

An earlier version of this article was presented at the August 1988 meeting of the Pacific Coast Branch of the American Historical Association in San Francisco. Robin D.G. Kelley, Gary W. Reichard, and William Toll provided useful comments on earlier drafts of this paper. And Elsa Barkley Brown was extremely helpful in the preparation of the original conference paper and in the revisions.

1. See for examples, Ruby M. Kendricks, "'They Also Serve': The National Association of Colored Women, Inc.," *Negro History Bulletin* 42 (March 1954): 171-75; Tullia Kay Brown Hamilton, "The National Association of Colored Women, 1896-1920" (Ph.D. diss., Emory University, 1978); Angela Y. Davis, *Women, Race and Class* (New York: Random House, 1983), 127-36. Activities of church and civil groups not associated with the NACW are included in Gerda Lerner's "Early Community Work of Black Club Women," *Journal of Negro History* 59 (April 1974): 158-62; and throughout Dorothy C. Salem's "To Better Our World: Black Women in Organized Reform, 1890-1920" (Ph.D. diss., Kent State University, 1986). The most recent treatment of black women's organized self-help efforts is Anne Firor Scott, "Most Invisible of All: Black Women's Voluntary Associations," *Journal of Southern History* 56 (February 1990): 3-22.

2. See Cynthia Neverdon-Morton, *Afro-American Women of the South and the Advancement of the Race, 1895-1925* (Knoxville: University of Tennessee Press, 1989), 191-201. And see local and state studies, including Darlene Clark Hine, *When the Truth is Told: A History of Black Women's Culture and Community in Indiana, 1875-1950* (Indianapolis: National Council of Negro Women, 1981); Marilyn Dell Brady, "Kansas Federation of Colored Women's Clubs: 1900-1930," *Kansas History: A Journal of the Central Plains* 9 (Spring 1986): 19-30; Erlene Stetson, "Black Feminism in Indiana, 1893-1933," *Phylon* 64 (December 1983): 292-98; Earline

Rae Ferguson, "The Woman's Improvement Club of Indianapolis: Black Women Pioneers in Tuberculosis Work, 1903-1933," *Indiana Magazine of History* 84 (September 1988): 237-61; Wilson Jeremiah Moses, "Domestic Feminism, Conservativism, Sex Roles, and Black Women's Clubs, 1893-1896," *Journal of Social and Behavioral Sciences* 24 (Fall 1987): 166-177. When historians discuss the attacks on black female morality as the most important reason for organizing the NACW, they usually point to the infamous James Jacks letter, in which he charged that all black women were prostitutes, liars, and thieves. Maude Thomas Jenkins, in "The History of the Black Woman's Club Movement in America" (Ed.D. diss., Columbia University Teachers College, 1984), does explore the complex range of issues that crystallized and encouraged the formation of the NACW. She also links black women's associations in general to an African tradition of mutual aid.

3. See Rayford Logan, *The Negro in American Life and Thought: The Nadir, 1877-1901* (New York: Dial Press, 1954). The revised version of this book was published with the title *The Betrayal of the Negro*.

4. Alfreda E. Duster, ed., *Crusade for Justice: The Autobiography of Ida B. Wells-Barnett* (Chicago: University of Chicago Press, 1968), 47-52; Ida B. Wells, *Southern Horrors: Lynch Law in all its Phases* (New York: New York Age Print, 1892); and *A Red Record: Tabulated Statistics and Alleged Causes of Lynchings in the United States, 1892-1893-1894* (Chicago: Donohue and Henneberry Press, 1895); Mary Church Terrell, "Lynching From a Negro's Point of View," *North American Review* 178 (June 1904): 853-68; Janie Porter Barrett, *Locust Street Social Settlement: Founded and Managed by Colored* (Hampton, Va.: Hampton Normal and Agricultural Institute, 1912), 19, in the Harris and Janie Porter Barrett Collection, Huntington Library Archives, Hampton University, Hampton, Va.

5. Willie Mae Coleman, "Keeping the Faith and Disturbing the Peace: Black Women From Anti-Slavery to Women's Suffrage" (Ph.D. diss., University of California-Irvine, 1982), 75.

6. See, for examples, Sterling Stuckey, "Through the Prism of Folklore: The Black Ethos in Slavery," *The Massachusetts Review* 9 (Summer 1968): 417-37; John Blassingame, *The Slave Community* (New York: Oxford University Press, 1972); George Rawick, *From Sundown to Sun Up* (Westport, Conn.: Greenwood Publishing Co., 1972); Eugene Genovese, *Roll, Jordan, Roll: The World the Slaves Made* (New York: Pantheon Books, 1974); Herbert G. Gutman, *The Black Family in Slavery and Freedom, 1750-1925* (New York: Vintage Books, 1976).

7. See Angela Davis, "Reflections on the Black Woman's Role in the Community of Slaves," *The Black Scholar* 2 (December 1971): 2-15; Allan Kulikoff, *Tobacco and Slaves: The Development of Southern Cultures in the Chesapeake, 1680-1800* (Chapel Hill: University of North Carolina Press, 1986), 343-44; Herbert Aptheker, *American Negro Slave Revolts* (New York: Columbia University Press, 1943); and see note 6 above.

8. Orville Vernon Burton, *"In my Father's House are Many Mansions:" Family and Community in Edgeville, S.C.* (Chapel Hill: University of North Carolina Press, 1985), 164-65; Kulikoff, *Tobacco and Slaves*, 345-51; Albert J. Raboteau, *Slave Religion: The "Invisible Institution" in the Antebellum South* (Oxford: Oxford University Press, 1978); Norrece T. Jones, Jr., *Born a Child of Freedom Yet a Slave: Mechanisms of Control and Strategies of Resistance in Antebellum South Carolina* (Hanover: University Press of New England, 1990).

9. Stuckey, "Through the Prism of Folklore": Lawrence Levine, *Black Culture and Black Consciousness: Afro-American Folk Thought From Slavery to Freedom* (New York: Oxford University Press, 1977), 81-135; Blassingame, *The Slave Community*, 127-30.

10. Levine, *Black Culture and Black Consciousness*, 6, 7, 10, 33-34; Raboteau, *Slave Religion*, 243-45.

11. Charles Joyner, *Down by the Riverside; A South Carolina Slave Community* (Urbana: University of Illinois Press, 1984), 58-59.

12. Deborah Gray White, *Ar'n't I a Woman?: Female Slaves in the Plantation South* (New York: W.W. Norton & Co., 1985), 119-141.

13. Leonard P. Curry, *The Free Black in Urban America, 1800-1850* (Chicago: University of Chicago Press, 1981), 197-214; Dorothy Sterling, Ed., *We Are Your Sisters: Black Women in the Nineteenth Century* (New York: W.W. Norton & Co., 1984), 104-07. See also Philip S. Foner, *History of Black Americans: From Africa to the Emergence of the Cotton Kingdom* (Westport, Conn.: Greenwood Press, 1975), 555-78; Herbert Aptheker, *A Documentary History of the Negro People in the U.S.*, 3 vols. (New York: Citadel Press, 1951, 1973, 1974), *passim*; Dorothy Porter, "The Organized Educational Activities of Negro Literary Societies, 1828-1846," *Journal of Negro Education* 6 (October 1936): 555-576; Julie Winch, *Philadelphia's Black Elite: Activism, Accommodation, and the Struggle for Autonomy, 1787-1848* (Philadelphia: Temple University Press, 1988), 5-15.

14. Curry, *The Free Black in Urban America*, 202. An 1835 issue of *Niles Register* estimated that Baltimore had 34-40 black mutual-aid societies. Curry's estimate of 200 groups is baffling considering that he cites the individual statistics for Baltimore and Philadelphia.

15. Linda Perkins, "Black Women and Racial 'Uplift' Prior to Emancipation," in *The Black Woman Cross Culturally*, ed. Filomina Chioma Steady (Cambridge: Schenkman Publishing Co., 1981), 317-334.

16. Armstead Robinson, "Plans Dat Comed From God: Institution Building and the Emergence of Black Leadership in Reconstruction Memphis," in *Towards a New South? Studies in Post-Civil War Southern Communities*, ed. Orville Burton and Robert G. McMath (Westport, Conn.: Greenwood Press, 1982), 71-102.

17. See W.E.B. DuBois, ed., *Some Efforts of American Negroes for their Own Social Betterment* (Atlanta: Atlanta University Press, 1898); Guy B. Johnson, "Some Factors in the Development of Negro Social Institutions in the United States," *American Journal of Sociology* 30 (November 1934): 329-337; Inabel Burns Lindsay, "Some Contributions of Negroes to Welfare Services, 1865-1900," *Journal of Negro Education* 25 (Winter 1956): 18; Joel Williamson, *After Slavery: The Negro in South Carolina During Reconstruction, 1861-1877* (Chapel Hill: University of North Carolina Press, 1965), 321-23; Vernon Lane Wharton, *The Negro in Mississippi, 1865-1890* (Chapel Hill: University of North Carolina Press, 1947; reprint, New York: Harper & Row, 1965), 270-73; Peter Rachleff, *Black Labor in Richmond, 1865-1890* (Urbana: University of Illinois Press, 1989), *passim*; Elsa Barkley Brown, "Womanist Consciousness: Maggie Lena Walker and the Independent Order of St. Luke," *Signs: Journal of Women in Culture and Society* 14 (Spring 1989): 610-633. A Scrap of paper dated 1898 in the Harris and Janie Porter Barrett collection at Hampton notes the creation of The People's Building and Loan Association of Hampton, Virginia in 1889. The note claims that by 1898, the organization had loaned over $140,000 to members, earned over $30,000 in dividends, and helped stockholders purchase 250 houses.

18. See James D. Anderson, *The Education of Blacks in the South, 1860-1935* (Chapel Hill: University of North Carolina Press, 1988).

19. For examples of studies on black towns, see Nell Irvin Painter, *The Exodusters: Black Migration to Kansas After Reconstruction* (New York: Alfred A. Knopf, 1977); Kenneth M. Hamilton, *Black Towns and Profit: Promotion and Early Development in the Trans-Appalachian West* (Urbana: University of Illinois Press, 1990).

20. Kathleen C. Berkeley, "'Colored Ladies also Contributed': Black Women's Activities from Benevolence to Social Welfare, 1866-1896," *The Web Southern Social Relations: Women, Family and Education*, ed. Walter J. Fraser, Jr., R. Frank Saunders, Jr., and Jon L. Wakelyn (Athens: University of Georgia Press, 1985), 180-82.

21. Benjamin [Griffith] Brawley, *Negro Builders and Heroes* (Chapel Hill: University of North Carolina Press, 1937), 267-70; Brown, "Womanist Consciousness," 616-17.

22. See Mary Brinkerhoff, "Books, Blacks Beautiful to Her," *Dallas Morning News*, July 23, 1971, in vertical files, Biographical-women, "Clara Jones," Walter P. Reuther Archives of Labor History and Urban Affairs, Wayne State University, Detroit. (Hereafter cited as Labor Archives).

23. Robert Kraus, "Black Library Chief Bears No Scars After Squabble," Detroit *Free Press*, February 18, 1971 in vertical files, Labor Archives; Maggie Kennedy, "A Librarian Who Speaks Her Mind," *Dallas Times Herald*, October 21, 1976, in 1970-76 Clippings box, Clara Jones Papers, Black Librarians' Archives, North Carolina Central University School of Library Science, Durham. Interestingly, when Jones read Joel Chandler Harris's Uncle Remus stories as an adult, she recognized them as stories she had heard all her life, but she was appalled by what she characterized as the "injected" racism. In their original form, the stories often included themes of collective consciousness.

24. Florence Lattimore, *A Palace of Delight (The Locust Street Settlement for Negroes at Hampton, Virginia)* (Hampton, Va: Hampton Normal and Agricultural Institute, 1915), 4-8; Sadie Iola Daniel, *Women Builders* (Washington, D.C.: Associated Publishers, 1970), 54-61; Hamilton, "The National Association of Colored Women," 140.

25. "Virginia State Federation of Colored Women's Clubs: Its Origin and Objectives," and Edna M. Colson, "The Petersburg Women's Council," typescripts, Virginia Federation of Colored Women's Clubs Papers, Johnson Memorial Library Special Collections, Virginia State University, Petersburg, VA; William Anthony Aery, "Helping Wayward Girls: Virginia's Pioneer Work," *Southern Workman* 44 (November 1915): 598-604; Esther F. Brown, "Social Settlement Work in Hampton," *Southern Workman* 33 (July 1904): 393-96; Janie Porter Barrett to Dr. [Hollis P.] Frissell, December 25, 1915, Harris and Janie Porter Barrett Collection.

26. Duster, *Crusade for Justice*, xiv-xix, 5, 15-20.

27. See Salem, "To Better Our World," 24-25.

28. Duster, *Crusade for Justice*, 69, 93. Wells-Barnett dedicated her autobiography to "our youth [who] are entitled to the facts of race history which only the participants can give." *Ibid.*, 5.

29. Adrienne Lash Jones, "Jane Edna Hunter: A Case Study of Black Leadership, 1910-1950" (Ph.D. diss., Case Western Reserve University, 1983), 49-64. Also note that black community residents of Norfolk, Virginia, were so proud of Lula McNeil and so optimistic about her potential for the community that, after she graduated at the

top of the first graduating class of the first black high school in that city, they all contributed money for educating her further at the state normal school. After graduation, she taught school for awhile and later returned to nursing school and became a public health nurse. See Lula Catherine McNeil interview transcript, Black Nurses Archives, Hampton, University, Hampton, Va.

30. Jones, "Jane Edna Hunter," 93-100; Mayme V. Holmes, "The Story of the Phillis Wheatley Association of Cleveland," *Southern Workman* 57 (October 1928): 399-401; Jane E. Hunter, "Phyllis Wheatley Association of Cleveland: An Institution Devoted to Better, Brighter Girls, Happier, Heartier Women," *The Competitor* 1 (March 1920): 52-54.

31. Minutes of the Federation of Colored Women's Clubs of Colorado, June 28, 1911; June 13, 1917; June 9, 1920; June 14-17, 1932; June 11-13, 1946; "Autobiography of Mrs. Hattie Taylor"; "Biography of Mrs. Elizabeth Ensley, Founder of the State Federation of Colored Women's Clubs"; and "Biography of Bettey Wilkins," in the Records of the Federation of Colored Women's Clubs of Colorado, Western History Division, Denver Public Library, Denver.

32. Elizabeth L. Davis, *The Story of the Illinois Federation of Colored Women's Clubs* (n.p., n.d.) esp. chapter 6, "Who's Who," in the Henry P. Slaughter Collection, Woodruff Library, Atlanta University Center Archives, Atlanta.

33. Delilah L. Beasley, *The Negro Trail Blazers of California* (Los Angeles: Times Mirror Printing, 1919), esp. chapter 13, "Distinguished Women."

34. See Hamilton, "The National Association of Colored Women," 39-53.

35. Hamilton notes that 42 of the 59 clubs represented at the first NACW Convention in Nashville in 1897 were from urban areas. *Ibid.*, 55.

36. This is not to suggest that the "communications revolution" under way at the time had no impact on these women's efforts to create a national organization.

37. DuBois, *Efforts at Social Betterment*, 45-50; Davis, *The Story of the Illinois Federation of Colored Women Clubs*, 6-10; Salem, "To Better Our World," 155; "Neighborhood Union's Aim Granted By the Laws of Georgia Under the Charter of the State of Georgia," box 3, f. 1931, Neighborhood Union Collection, Atlanta University Center Archives, Atlanta.

38. Ethel Evangeline Martin Bolden, "Susan Dart Butler: Pioneer Librarian" (M.A. thesis, Atlanta University, 1959); Jacqueline Anne Rouse, *Lugenia Burns Hope: Black Southern Reformer* (Athens: University of Georgia Press, 1989), 71-73; Neverdon-Morton, *Afro-American Women of the South*, 159-161. Janie Porter Barrett also eventually turner over the Industrial School to the State of Virginia.

39. Untitled typescript [a history of the Virginia State Federation of Colored Women's Clubs], 2-3, and Edna M. Colson, "The Petersburg Women's Council," typescript, The Virginia Federation of Colored Women's Clubs Papers; Frances Reynolds Keyser, "Florida Federation of Colored Women's Clubs Establish a Home for Delinquent Girls," *The Competitor* 3 (May 1921): 34; Salem, "To Better Our World," 124-209; Hamilton, "The National Association of Colored Women," 72, 76.

40. Salem, "To Better Our World"; Paula Giddings, *When and Where I Enter: The Impact of Black Women on Race and Sex in America* (New York: William Morrow & Co., 1984), 135; isolated papers of the Kansas City, Mo., Federation of Colored Women's Clubs, b. 28-4, f. 96, Frederick Douglass Collection, Moorland-Spingarn Research Center, Howard University, Washington, D.C.; "The History of the Cincinnati Federation of Colored Women's Clubs (1904-1952)," typescript,

Mirriam Hamilton Spotts Papers, Amistad Research Center, Tulane University, New Orleans; Aery, "Helping Wayward Girls"; Pitt Dillingham, "Black Belt Settlement Work," *Southern Workman* 31 (July 1902): 383-388 and (August 1902): 437-444; Hunter, "Phyllis Wheatley Association of Cleveland"; Mrs. Laurence C. Jones, "Mississippi's Bright Club Fields," *The Competitor* 3 (May 1921): 27-28; Holmes, "The Story of the Phillis Wheatley Association of Cleveland, Ohio." Almost every issue of *Woman's Era* and *National Notes* includes details of similar activities for NACW affiliates throughout the country. On suffrage and interracial cooperation, see Jane Olcott, *The Work of Colored Women* (New York: War Work Council, National Board of the YWCA, 1919), issued by the Colored Work Committee; Cynthia Neverdon-Morton, "The Black Women's Struggle for Equality in the South, 1895-1925," in *The Afro-American Woman: Struggles and Images*, ed. Sharon Harley and Rosalyn Terborg-Penn (Port Washington, N.Y.: Kennikat Press, 1978), 43-57; and Rosalyn Terborg-Penn, "Discontented Black Feminist: Prelude and Postscript to the Passage of the Nineteenth Amendment," in *Decades of Discontent: The Women's Movement, 1920-1940*, ed. Lois Scharf and Joan M. Jenson (Westport, Conn: Greenwood Press, 1983), 261-78.

41. See discussions on origins of American racism in Winthrop Jordan, *White Over Black: American Attitudes Toward the Negro, 1550-1812* (New York: Oxford University Press, 1974).

27

Black and White Visions of Welfare:
Women's Welfare Activism, 1890-1945

Linda Gordon

One of the pleasures of historical scholarship is that it may lead into unexpected paths, and what begins as a frustration—say, from an apparent shortage of sources—may end as a new opening. This essay began as an attempt to examine gender differences in visions of public welfare among reformers. Having compiled material about women welfare activists who were mainly white, I found I could not distinguish the influence of gender from that of race in their perspectives. (Indeed, to many white historians, the racial characteristics of the white people we studied were invisible until we began to learn from minority historians to ask the right questions.) So I set up a comparison between black and white women welfare activists, with results that were illuminating about both groups. Three major areas of difference between black and white women's ideas emerged: first, about the nature of entitlement, between a black orientation toward universal programs, and a white orientation toward supervised, means-tested ones; second, in attitude toward mothers' employment; third, in strategies for protecting women from sexual exploitation. In what follows I want both to show how those differences were manifest and to suggest their roots in historical experience.[1]

Several historians have recently studied black women's civic contributions, but black women's reform campaigns have not usually been seen as part of welfare history. How many discussions of settlement houses include Victoria Earle Matthews's White Rose Mission of New York City, or Margaret Murray Washington's Elizabeth Russell Settlement at Tuskegee, Alabama, or Janie Porter Barrett's Locust Street Social Settlement in Hampton, Virginia, or Lugenia Burns Hope's Neighborhood Union in Atlanta, Georgia (or many others)? In examining this activism from a welfare history perspective, I came to understand how the standard welfare histories had been by definition white-centered. It was possible to make the widespread welfare reform activity of minority women visible only by changing the definition of the topic and its periodization.[2]

The white experience has defined the very boundaries of what we mean by welfare. Whites were by 1890 campaigning for *government programs* of cash relief and of regulation such as the Pure Food and Drugs Act and anti-child labor laws. These welfare programs had racial content, not only in the perspectives of the reformers (white) but also in the identification of their objects (largely the immigrant working class, which, although white, was perceived as racially different by turn-of-the-century reformers). The programs also had class content, visible, for example, in their rejection of traditional working-class cooperative benevolent societies. Moreover, because of these orientations, welfare in the late nineteenth century was increasingly conceived as an *urban* reform activity.[3]

By contrast African Americans, still concentrated in the South and in rural communities, had been largely disfranchised by this time, and even in the North had much less power than whites, certainly less than elite whites, to influence government. Southern states had smaller administrative capacities and were more paltry in their provision of public services even to whites. African Americans did campaign for governmental programs and had some success; at the federal level, they had won an Office of Negro Health Work in the United States Public Health Service, and they had gotten some resources from the extension programs of the United States Department of Agriculture. Nevertheless, black welfare activity, especially before the New Deal, consisted to a great extent of *building private institutions*. Black women welfare reformers created schools, old people's homes, medical services, community centers. Attempting to provide for their people what the white state would not, they even raised private money for public institutions. For example, an Atlanta University study of 1901 found that in at least three southern states (Virginia, North Carolina, and Georgia) the private contribution to the Negro public schools was greater than that from tax moneys.[4] For example, a teacher in Lowndes County, Alabama, appealed for funds in 1912.

> Where I am now working there are 27,000 colored people. . . . In my school district there are nearly 400 children. I carry on this work eight months in the year and receive for it $290, out of which I pay three teachers and two extra teachers. The State provides for three months' schooling . . . I have been trying desperately to put up an adequate school building for the hundreds of children clamoring to get an education. To complete it . . . I need about $800.[5]

Thus a large proportion of their political energy went to raising money, and under the most difficult circumstances—trying to collect from the poor and the limited middle class to help the poor. White women raised money, of course, but they also lobbied aldermen and congressmen, attended White House conferences, and corresponded with Supreme Court justices; black women had less access to such powerful men and spent proportionally more of their time organizing bake sales, rummage sales, and church dinners. One detailed example may illustrate this: the Gate City Kindergartens, established in Atlanta in 1905.

> Another method of raising funds was through working circles throughout the city. . . . From Bazaars held at Thanksgiving time, lasting as long as a week, when every circle was responsible for a day, one day of which a turkey dinner was served. Money was made by sales in items of fancy work, aprons, etc.,

canned fruit, cakes and whatever could be begged. The association realized as much as $250.00 at a Bazaar. From track meets sponsored by colleges, and participated in by the children of the public school, $100.00 gate receipts were cleared. Food and cake sales brought at times $50.00. April sales brought $50.00, and one time the women realized as much as $100.00 from the sale of aprons. Sales of papers, magazines and tin foil brought as much as $50.00. A baby contest brought $50.00. Intercollegiate contest brought $100. Post-season baseball games realized as much as $25.00. Sales of soap wrappers, soap powder wrappers, saved and collected from housewives, and baking powder coupons brought $25.00. . . . [The list is twice this long.]

It cost $1,200 in cash to maintain the kindergartens each year. In addition donations in kind were vital: all five kindergartens were housed in donated locations; clothes were constantly solicited for the needy children; for several years Procter & Gamble gave five boxes of Ivory soap annually.[6] Some black welfare activist were adept at raising white money but had to accept sometimes galling strings, and even the most successful tried to shift their economic dependence to their own people.[7] No doubt some of these money-raising activities were also pleasurable and community-building social occasions, but often they were just drudgery, and those doing the work hated it. Jane Hunter, a Cleveland black activist, wrote that "this money getting business destroys so much of ones real self, that we cannot do our best."[8]

This essay uses a limited comparison—between black and white women reformers—to alter somewhat our understanding of what welfare *is* and to bring into better visibility gender and race (and class) influences on welfare thinking. The essay uses two kinds of data: written and oral history records of the thought of these activists, and a rudimentary collective biography of 145 black and white women who were national leaders in campaigns for public welfare between 1890 and 1945.[9] This method emerges from the premise expressed by the feminist slogan, "The personal is political": that political views and activities are related not only to macroeconomic and social conditions but also to personal circumstances—such as family experiences and occupational histories.

My approach uses a broad definition of welfare. I include reformers who sought regulatory laws, such as the Pure Food and Drugs Act, compulsory education, and anti-child labor regulations. I do not include reformers who worked mainly on labor relations, civil rights, women's rights, or a myriad of other reform issues not centrally related to welfare.[10] In categorizing many different activists, I had to ignore many differences in order to make broad generalization possible. This method inevitably obscures context and some fascinating personalities. Many more monographs are necessary, but I notice that historical thinking develops through a constant interplay between monographs and syntheses; I hope that this essay, because of its very breadth, will stimulate more monographs.

I did not form this sample according to a random or other formal selection principle. Instead I identified members of my sample gradually during several years of research on welfare campaigns and then tracked down biographical information. The process is a historian's form of snowball sampling, because often tracking down one activist produces references to another. Naturally, there are many bits of missing information because biographical facts are difficult to find for many women, especially minority women. I make no claim to having created a representative sample or an exhaustive list. But, on the methodological principle of saturation, I doubt that my generalizations would be much altered by the addition of more individuals.

To bound my sample, I included only those who were national leaders—officers of national organizations campaigning for welfare provision or builders of nationally important institutions, such as hospitals, schools, or asylums. (For more on the sample, see the Appendix.) These leaders were not typical welfare activists; more typical were those who worked exclusively locally, and their personal profiles might be quite different. But the national leaders had a great deal of influence on the thinking of other women. I included only activists prominent chiefly after 1890 because it was in the 1890s that such key national organizations as the National Association of Colored Women began and that white women welfare activists began a marked emphasis on *public* provision. I followed welfare activism until 1945 because I wanted to look at broad patterns of ideas across a long period of policy debate; I ended in 1945 because after that date, among white women, there was a marked decline in such agitation and among blacks a shift in emphasis to civil rights.

My approach sacrifices, of course, change over time. Substantial generational as well as individual differences among women had to be put aside. For example, the early black activists were, on average, more focused on race uplift and the later more on integration; during this period the mass northward migration of blacks shifted reformers' concerns not only away from the South but also increasingly toward urban problems. The white women welfare activists of the 1890s tended to divide between Charity Organization Society devotees and settlement advocates; by the 1930s, they were more united in promoting professionalism in public assistance. Nevertheless, I am convinced that there are enough continuities to justify this periodization, continuities that will emerge in the discussion below.

The two groups thus formed were in many ways not parallel. For example, the white women were mainly from the Northeast or Midwest, and there were few southern white women—only 16 percent of the group were either born or active in the South, whereas a majority of the black women were born in the South. For another example, many of the black women were educators by occupation, while white women who were educators were few. But these divergences are part of what I am trying to identify, part of the differences in black and white women's perspectives. Among whites, northerners contributed more to national welfare models than did southerners. And education had particular meanings for African Americans and was integrated into campaigns for the welfare of the race in a distinctive way. Generalizing among a variety of women of several generations, the comparison naturally eclipses some important distinctions, but it does so to illuminate others that are also important.[11] I identified sixty-nine black women as national leaders in welfare reform. Separating the white from the black women was not my decision: the networks were almost completely segregated. First, the national women's organizations were segregated; those that included blacks, such as the Young Women's Christian Association (YWCA), had separate white and black locals. Second, since black women rarely held government positions, they rarely interacted with white women officially. Third, the national network of white women reformers usually excluded black women even when they could have been included.[12] The exclusion of black women from the white women's clubs and ignoring or trivializing of life-and-death black issues, such as lynching, have been amply documented.[13] To cite but one example, one of the most important women in the New Deal—Mary McLeod Bethune—was not a part of the tight, if informal, caucus that the white New Deal women formed.[14] There were important counterexamples, interracial efforts of significant impact, particularly local ones: in Chicago, for instance, white settlement and charity workers joined black reformers in campaigning for public services for dependent children, establishing the Chicago Urban League, and responding to the 1919 race riot. In the South interracial efforts arose from evangelical religious activity. Some white members of this sample group worked with the Commission of Interracial Cooperation, forming its Women's Council, which had 805 county-level groups by 1929.[15] The national YWCA became a forum for communication between black and white women. But these efforts were marked by serious and sometimes crippling white prejudice, and the core networks of women remained segregated.

While the black group was created in part by white racism, it was also created from the inside, so to speak, by personal friendships. Often these relationships were born in schools and colleges and continued thereafter, strengthened by the development of black sororities after 1908. The creation of national organizations and networks extended relationships and ideas among these black women leaders across regional boundaries. For example, the Phillis Wheatley Home for the protection of single black urban women, established by Jane Hunter in Cleveland in 1911, spurred the opening of similar homes in Denver, Atlanta, Seattle, Boston, Detroit, Chicago, Greenville, Winston-Salem, Toledo, and Minneapolis by 1934. When Fannie Barrier Williams spoke in Memphis in 1896, she had never been in the South before, having grown up in upstate New York and settled in Chicago.[16] More and more the women began to travel widely, despite the difficult and humiliating conditions of travel for black women. Friendships could be intense, despite distance; black women early in the twentieth century, like white women, sometimes spoke openly of their strong emotional bonds. Darlene Clark Hine quotes Jane Hunter writing Nannie Burroughs, "It was so nice to see you and to know your real sweet self. Surely we will . . . cultivate a lasting friendship. I want to be your devoted sister in kindred thought and love." At other times Hunter wrote to Burroughs of her loneliness "for want of a friend."[17] Mutual support was strong. When in the 1930s the president and trustees of Howard University, led by Abraham Flexner, tried to force Howard's dean of women, Lucy D. Slowe, to live on campus with her girls (something the dean of men was not, of course, required to do) and she refused to comply, a whole network of women interceded on her behalf. A group of five asked for a meeting with Flexner, which he refused. Another group of women interviewed trustees in New York and reported to Slowe their perceptions of the situation. Mary McLeod Bethune urged her to be "steadfast" and campaigned for her among sympathetic Howard faculty.[18] The network was divided by cliques and encompassed conflicts and even feuds. Yet it had a "bottom line" of loyalty. Even those who criticized Bethune for insufficient militance understood her to be absolutely committed to the network of black women.[19]

The black women's network was made more coherent by its members' common experience as educators and builders of educational institutions. Education was the single most important area of activism for black women. The majority of women in this sample taught at one time or another, and 38 percent were educators by profession. For many, reform activism centered around establishing schools, from kindergartens through colleges, such as Nannie Burroughs's National Training School for Women and Girls in Washington, D.C., or Lucy Laney's Haines Institute in Augusta, Georgia, or Arenia Mallory's Saints Industrial and Literary Training School in Mississippi. In his 1907 report on economic cooperation among Negro Americans, for example, W. E. B. Du Bois counted 151 church-connected and 161 nonsectarian private Negro schools. Although he did not discuss the labor of founding and maintaining these institutions, we can guess that women contributed disproportionately.[20]

Another black welfare priority was establishment of old people's homes, considered by Du Bois the "most characteristic Negro charity." These too, according to the early findings of Du Bois, were predominately organized by women.[21] But if we were to take the period 1890-1945 as a whole, the cause second to education was health. Black hospitals, while primarily initiated by black and white men, depended on crucial support from black women. Between 1890 and 1930, African Americans created approximately 200 hospitals and nurse-training schools, and women often took charge of the community organizing and fund-raising labor. Over time black women's health work changed its emphasis, from providing for the sick in the 1890s to preventive health projects after about 1910. Yet even in the first decade of the century, Du Bois found that most locations with considerable black populations had beneficial and insurance societies that paid sickness as well as burial benefits; these can be traced back a century before Du Bois studied them. In several cities the societies also paid for medicines and actually created their own health maintenance organizations. With the dues of their members they hired physicians, annually or on a quarterly basis, to provide health care for the entire group.[22]

Many women's clubs made health work their priority. The Washington, D.C., Colored YWCA built a program around visiting the sick. The Indianapolis Woman's Improvement Club focused on tuberculosis, attempted to make up for the denial of service to blacks by the Indianapolis board of health, the city hospital, and the Marion County tuberculosis society. The preventative health emphasis was stimulated in part by educational work. For example, Atlanta's Neighborhood Union did a survey of conditions in the black schools in 1912-1913 that revealed major health problems; in 1916 this led the Neighborhood Union to establish a clinic that offered both health education and free medical treatment. Possibly the most extraordinary individual in black women's public health work was Modjeska Simkins, who used her position as director of Negro work for the antituberculosis association of South Carolina to inaugurate a program dealing with the entire range of black health problems, including maternal and infant mortality, venereal disease, and malnutrition as well as tuberculosis. Perhaps the most ingenious women's program was Alpha Kappa Alpha's Mississippi Health Project. These black sorority women brought health care to sharecroppers in Holmes County, Mississippi, for several weeks every summer from 1935 to 1942. Unable to rent space for a clinic because of plantation owners' opposition, they turned cars into mobile health vans, immunizing over 15,000 children and providing services such as dentistry and treatment for malaria and VD to 2,500–4,000 people each summer.[23]

These reformers were united also through their churches, which were centers of networking and of activism, in the North as well as the South. Indeed, more locally active, less elite black women reformers were probably even more connected to churches; the national leadership was moving toward more secular organization, while remaining more church-centered than white women welfare leaders. Black churches played a large role in raising money, serving in particular as a conduit for appeals for white money, through missionary projects.[24]

The YWCA also drew many of these women together. Victoria Matthews's White Rose Mission influenced the YWCA, through its leader Grace Dodge, to bring black women onto its staff, which experience groomed many black women leaders.[25]

And despite the fact that these were national leaders, they shared a regional experience. At least 57 percent were born in the South. More important, perhaps, two-thirds of these migrated to the northeast, midwest, and mid-Atlantic regions, thus literally spreading their network as they fled Jim Crow and sought wider opportunity.[26]

Most members of this network were married—85 percent. More than half of the married women had prominent men as spouses, and their marriages sometimes promoted their leadership positions.[27] Lugenia Burns Hope was the wife of John Hope, first black president of Atlanta University; Irene Gaines was the wife of an Illinois state legislator. Ida Wells-Barnett's husband published Chicago's leading black newspaper. George Edmund Haynes, husband of Elizabeth, was a Columbia Ph.D., a professor at Fisk, an assistant to the secretary of labor from 1918 to 1921, and a founder of the Urban League. George Ruffin, husband of Josephine, was a Harvard Law graduate, a member of the Boston City Council, and Boston's first black judge. Most of the women, however, had been activists before marriage, and many led lives quite independent of their husbands. (Of these married women, 20 percent were widowed, divorced, or separated.)

Their fertility pattern was probably related to their independence. Of the whole group, 43 percent had no children; and of the married women, 34 percent had no children (there were no unmarried mothers).[28] (In comparison, 31 percent of the white married women in the sample were childless.) It thus seems likely that these women welfare activists used birth control, although long physical separations from their husbands may have contributed to their low fertility.[29] In their contraceptive practices these women may have been as modern as contemporary white women of comparable class position.

For most African-American women a major reason for being in the public sphere after marriage was employment, due to economic necessity; but for this group of women, economic need was not a driving pressure. A remarkable number had prosperous parents.[30] Crystal Fauset's father, although born a slave, was principal of a black academy in Maryland. Elizabeth Ross Haynes's father went from slavery to ownership of a fifteen-hundred-acre plantation. Addie Hunton's father was a substantial businessman and founder of the Negro Elks. Mary Church Terrell's mother *and* father were successful in business. Most black women in the sample had husbands who could support them; 51 percent of the married women had high-professional husbands—lawyers, physicians, ministers, educators.[31] The women of this network were also often very class-conscious, and many of the clubs that built their collective identity were exclusive, such as the sororities, the Chautauqua Circle, and the Twelve in Atlanta. The fact that about 40 percent were born outside the South provides further evidence of their high status, since the evidence suggests that the earlier northward migrants were the more upwardly mobile.[32] In all these respects, this group probably differed from typical local activists, who were less privileged. Yet even among this elite group only a tiny minority—12 percent—were not employed.[33] To be sure, this economic privilege was only relative to the whole black population; on average, the black women's network was less wealthy than the white women's. Even those who were born to middle-class status were usually newly middle-class, perhaps a generation away from slavery and without much cushion against economic misfortune. Still, among many whites the first and most important emblem of middle-class status was a woman's domesticity. One can safely conclude that one meaning of these women's combining of public and family lives was the greater acceptance among African Americans, for many historical reasons, of the public life of married women.

The black women's national network was made more homogeneous by educational attainment, high social status, and a sense of superiority to the masses that brought with it obligations of service. Of the black women, 83 percent had a higher education, comparable to the proportion of white women, and 35 percent had attended graduate school. These figures may surprise those unfamiliar with the high professional achievement patterns of black women between 1890 and 1945. The full meaning of the statistics emerges when one compares them with the average educational opportunities for blacks in the United States at this time. In the earliest year for which we have figures, 1940, only 1 percent of Afro-Americans, male and female, had four or more years of college. Moreover, only 41 percent of the women in this sample attended black colleges, whereas those colleges conferred 86 percent of all black undergraduate degrees in the period from 1914 to 1936.[34] Several women in this sample who were born into the middle class described learning for the first time in adulthood of the conditions of poverty in which most African Americans lived—an ignorance characteristic of prosperous whites but rarer among blacks. As Alfreda Duster, Ida Wells-Barnett's daughter, recalled, "It was difficult for me to really empathize with people who had come from nothing, where they had lived in cottages, huts in the South, with no floor and no windows and had suffered the consequences of the discrimination and the hardships of the South."[35] Many black women joined Du Bois in emphasizing the importance of building an intellectual and professional elite, calling upon the "leading" or "intelligent" or "better class of" Negroes to take initiatives for their people. Class and status inequalities, measured by such markers as money, occupation, and skin color, created tensions in this network, as comparable inequalities did in the white network.[36] Some thought of their obligations in the eugenic terms that were so fashionable in the first three decades of this study. "I was going to multiply my ability and my husband's by six," Alfreda Duster said in describing her decision to have six children.[37] Such thinking had somewhat different meanings for blacks than for whites, however, reflecting their awareness that race prejudice made it difficult for educated, prosperous blacks to escape the discrimination and pejorative stereotyping that held back all African Americans. As Ferdinand Barnett, later to become the husband of Ida B. Wells, put it in 1879, "One vicious, ignorant Negro is readily conceded to be a type of all the rest, but a Negro educated and refined is said to be an exception. We must labor to reverse this rule; education and moral excellence must become general and characteristic, with ignorance and depravity the exception."[38]

Indeed, the high social status and prosperity common in this group should not lead us to forget the discrimination and humiliation that they faced. Their high levels of skills and education were frustrated by lack of career opportunity. Sadie Alexander, from one of the most prominent black families in the United States, was the first black woman Ph.D., with a degree from the University of Pennsylvania. But she could not get an appropriate job because of her color and was forced to work as an assistant actuary for a black insurance company. Anna Arnold Hedgeman, one of the youngest women in this sample, from a small Minnesota town where she had attended integrated schools and churches, graduated from Hamline University in St. Paul and then discovered that she could not get a teaching job in any white institution. Instead she went to work in Holly Springs, Mississippi, until she found the Jim Crow intolerable. Despite the relatively large black middle class in Washington, D.C.,

African-American women there could not generally get clerical jobs in the federal government until the 1940s.[39]

Moreover, this black activism was born in an era of radically worsening conditions for most Afro-American women, in contrast to the improving conditions for white women. The older women in this network had felt segregation intensify in their adult lifetimes; there was widespread immiserization and denial of what political power they had accumulated after the emancipation. In the 1920s the second Ku Klux Klan attracted as many as 6 million members. These experiences, so rarely understood by whites, further reinforced the bonds uniting black women and influenced their welfare visions.[40]

The seventy-six white women, like the blacks, constituted a coherent network. Most of them knew each other, and their compatibility was cemented by a homogeneous class, religious, and ethnic base. Most had prosperous, many even prominent parents; virtually all were of north European, Protestant backgrounds, from the Northeast or Midwest. The nine Jewish members were hardly representative of Jewish immigrants: five had wealthy German-Jewish parents (Elizabeth Brandeis Raushenbush, Hannah Einstein, Josephine and Pauline Goldmark, and Lillian Wald). There were three Catholics (Josephine Brown, Jane Hoey, and Agnes Regan), but they were hardly typical of Catholics in the United States in the period: they were all native-born of prosperous parents. The shared Protestantism of the others was more a sign of similar ethnic background than of avid religious commitment, for few were churchgoers or intense believers, and churches did not organize their welfare activities.

The great majority (86 percent) were college-educated, and 66 percent attended graduate school. By contrast, in 1920 fewer than 1 percent of all American women held college degrees. It is worth recalling, however, that 83 percent of the black women were college-educated, and their disproportion to the black population as a whole was even greater. The white women had attended more expensive, elite schools; 37 percent had graduated from one of the New England women's colleges.

The white women had even more occupational commonality than the blacks. The great majority were social workers.[41] To understand this correctly we must appreciate the changing historical meanings of *social work*. Prior to the Progressive Era, the term did not refer to a profession but to a range of helping and reform activity; the word *social* originally emphasized the reform, rather than the charity, component. Here it is relevant that many had mothers active in social reform.[42] The early twentieth-century professionalization of social work has often been conceptualized as creating a rather sharp break both with amateur friendly visiting and with political activism. The experience of the women I am studying suggests otherwise: well into the 1930s they considered casework, charity, and reform politics as "social work." By contrast to the Afro-American women, very few were educators, a pattern that suggests that creating new educational institutions was no longer a reform priority for white women and that other professional jobs, especially governmental, were open to them.[43]

The whites had at least as much geographical togetherness as the black women. Sixty-eight percent worked primarily in the New England and mid-Atlantic states—hardly surprising since the national headquarters of the organizations they worked for were usually located there. Moreover, 57 percent had worked in New York City during the Progressive Era or the 1920s. New York City played a vanguard role in the development of public services and regulation in the public interest, and women in the network were influential in that city's welfare programs. New York City settlement houses specialized in demonstration projects, beginning programs on a small, private scale and then getting them publicly funded. The settlements initiated vocational guidance programs, later adopted by the public schools; they initiated use of public schools for after-hours recreation programs and public health nursing. Lillian Wald, head of the Henry Street Settlement, coordinated the city's response to the 1919 influenza epidemic. The settlements lobbied for municipal legislation regulating tenements and landlord-tenant relations and milk purity and prices. In 1917 the Women's City Club of New York City opened a Maternity Center in Hell's Kitchen, where they provided prenatal nursing care and education and housekeeping services for new mothers. Expanded to ten locations in Manhattan, this effort served as a model for the bill that eventually became the Sheppard-Towner Act. The Women's City Club provided an important meeting place for many of these women, and it can serve as an indicator of their prosperity: members had to pay substantial dues and an initiation fee, and the club purchased a mansion on Thirty-fifth Street and Park Avenue for $160,000 in 1917.[44]

Some of these white women had been active in party politics even before they had the vote. Some had been in the Socialist party, and many were active in the 1912 Progressive party campaign. Most, however, preferred nonpartisan public activism. During the late 1920s and 1930s they became more active in political parties and transferred their allegiances to the Democratic party. Here too New York was important, because the political figure who most attracted these women to the Democrats was Franklin D. Roosevelt, in his governorship and then his presidency. Several women who had been active in reform in the city, notably Belle Moskowitz, Rose Schneiderman, and Eleanor Roosevelt, took on statewide roles. The Al Smith campaign of 1928 promoted more division than unity, however, because most women social workers were critical of his "wet" positions and his association with machine politics. The reassuring presence of his aide Moskowitz and Franklin Roosevelt's "aide" Eleanor Roosevelt was critical in bringing their network into the Democratic party.[45]

The black network also underwent a political realignment from Republican to Democratic, but with different meanings, largely associated with migration northward, because the southern Democratic party was essentially closed to blacks. Ironically, this transition was also in part effectuated by Eleanor Roosevelt, who became the symbol of those few white political leaders willing to take stands on racial equality.[46] Nevertheless Eleanor Roosevelt did not create an integrated network, nor was she able to swing the white network to support the leading black demand during the Roosevelt administration: a federal antilynching law.

Women in both networks taught, mentored, even self-consciously trained each other. Among blacks this occurred in colleges, in white-run organizations such as the YWCAs, and in black organizations such as sororities, the National Association of Colored Women (NACW), and many local groups. A higher proportion of the white than of the black women worked in settlement houses—probably partly because so many of the white women were single. That experience strongly encouraged intergenerational connections and intimacy, because the younger or newer volunteers actually lived with their elders, seeing them in action. In the civic organizations, leaders groomed, protected, and promoted their protégés: Jane Addams did this with Alice Hamilton, Lillian Wald, and Florence Kelley; Sophonisba Breckinridge launched her student Grace Abbott's career by placing her at the head of the newly formed Immigrants' Protective League; the whole network campaigned for Abbott and then for Frances Perkins to become secretary of labor.[47] Such involvements continued when network members became federal or state officials, with other members as their employees. The chiefs of the Children's and Women's bureaus—the two key federal agencies run by women—exercised extraordinary involvement in the personal lives of their employees. Mary Anderson, for example, head of the Women's Bureau, corresponded frequently with her employees in other parts of the country about their family lives, advising them, for example, about the care of aging parents.[48]

It is quite possible that black women's personal and profession support networks were just as strong; there is less evidence because, as several historians of African-American women have suggested, black women left fewer private papers than did white.[49] Given this caveat, the white women's network does appear to differ in one measure of mutual dependence. The great majority of the white women were single—only 34 percent had ever been married, and only 18 percent remained married during their peak political activity (42 percent of those who ever married were divorced, separated, or widowed). Only 28 percent had children. In this respect they are probably quite different from many local welfare activists, a group that included less elite and more married women. Moreover, 28 percent were in relationships with other women that might have been called "Boston marriages" a few decades before.[50] (My figure is a conservative one since I counted only those women for whom I could identify a specific partner. It does not include such women as Edith Rockwood who lived until her death in 1953 with Marjorie Heseltine of the Children's Bureau and Louise Griffith of the Social Security Agency and who built and owned a summer house jointly with Marion Crane of the Children's Bureau.[51]) At the time these relationships were mainly not named at all, although Mary ("Molly") Dewson referred to her mate as "partner." Contemporaries usually perceived them as celibate.[52] Today some of these women might be called lesbian, but there is much controversy among historians as to whether it is ahistorical to apply the word to that generation, a controversy I wish to avoid here since it is not relevant to my argument. What is relevant is not their sexual activity but their dependence on other women economically, for jobs; for care in grief, illness, and old age; for vacation companionship; for every conceivable kind of help. Despite their singleness, their efforts were very much directed to family and child welfare. It is remarkable to contemplate that so many women who became symbols of matronly respectability and asexual "social motherhood" led such unconventional private lives.

Moreover, they turned this mutual dependency into a political caucus. When lesbian history was first being written, these relationships between women were seen, first, in exclusively private and individual terms, and second, as a life-style that isolated them from the heterosexual social and cultural mainstream. Recently, Estelle Freedman and Blanche Wiesen Cook have helped change that paradigm.[53] The women's female bonding did not disadvantage them but brought them political power, and they got it without making the sacrifices of personal intimacy that men so often did. Privileged women that they were, several of them had country homes, and groups would often weekend together; we can be sure that their conversation erased distinctions between the personal and political, between the gossip and tactics.

In truth we do not know how different these white women's relationships were from black women's. Many black married women, such as Bethune and Charlotte Hawkins Brown, lived apart from their husbands (but so did several white women counted here as married, such as Perkins); and a few black women, such as Dean Lucy Slowe of Howard, lived in Boston marriages. Many blacks in this sample spoke critically not only of men but of marriage and feared its potential to demobilize women. Dorothy Height lamented that the "over-emphasis on marriage has destroyed so many people."[54]

Both white and black women, if single, experienced a sense of betrayal when a friend married; and both, if about to marry, feared telling their single comrades.[55] In time, particularly from the 1930s on, the white women's sense that marriage and activity in the public sphere were incompatible choices diminished, and more married activists appeared.[56] This change, however, only makes it the more evident that throughout the period, black women had greater willingness, necessity, or ability to combine marriage and public activism, through coping strategies that may have included informal marital separations.

The white women's friendship network was particularly visible among the most prominent women because they took it with them to their prominent and well-documented jobs. Their friendships transcended boundaries between the public and private sectors, between government and civic organization. In this way they created what several historians have begun calling a "women's political culture"—but again we must remember that this concept has referred primarily to white women. The powerful settlement houses, Hull House and the Henry Street Settlement, for example, became virtually a part of municipal government and were able to command the use of tax money when necessary. When women gained governmental positions, there was as much extraagency as intraagency consultation and direction. In its first project, collecting data on infant mortality, the Children's Bureau used hundreds of volunteers from this organizational network to help. In 1920, Florence Kelley of the National Consumers' League (NCL) listed investigations the Women's Bureau should undertake, and these were done. Mary Anderson of the Women's Bureau arranged for the NCL to draft a bill for protection of female employees for the state of Indiana, and Anderson herself wrote comments on the draft. In 1922 Anderson wrote Mary Dewson of the NCL asking her to tone down her critical language about the National Women's Party, and Dewson complied; in 1923 Dewson asked Anderson to help her draft a response to the National Women's Party that was to appear in the *Nation* under Dewson's name.

Such cooperation continued throughout the New Deal. A good example was the Women's Charter, an attempt made in 1936, in response to the increased intensity of the campaign for the Equal Rights Amendment (ERA), to negotiate a settlement between the two sides of the women's movement. An initial meeting was attended by representatives of the usual white women's network civic organizations—YWCA, League of Women Voters, Women's Trade Union League, American Association of University Women, Federation of Business and Professional Women—as well as several state and federal government women. The first draft of the charter was written by Anderson, still head of the Women's Bureau; Frieda Miller, then head of the women's section of the New York State Department of Labor; Rose Schneiderman, formerly of the National Recovery Administration (until the Supreme Court overruled it) and soon to become head of the New York State Department of Labor; and Mary Van Kleeck. The drafting of the charter exemplifies two of the findings regarding this network: the importance of New York and the predominance of single women.[57]

Singleness did not keep these women from useful connections with men, however. These connections came with kinship and class, if not with marriage. Clara Beyer got her "in" to the network because Felix Frankfurter recommended her to administer the 1918 District of Columbia minimum wage law. She then brought in Elizabeth Brandeis, the daughter of Louis Brandeis, to share the job with her. Brandeis's two sisters-in-law, Josephine and Pauline Goldmark, were also active in this network. Sophonisba Breckinridge, Florence Kelley, Julia Lathrop, and Katherine Lenroot were daughters of senators or congressmen. Loula Dunn's father and two grandfathers had been in the Alabama legislature. Susan Ware computed, about a different but overlapping group of New Deal women, that almost 50 percent (13 of 28) were from political families.[58] These women often learned politics in their households and knew where to get introductions and referrals to politically influential people when they needed them. When Beyer said, "It was my contacts that made [me] so valuable, that I could go to these people," she was speaking about both her women's network and her male connections.[59]

With these group characteristics in mind, I want to examine the welfare ideas of these two networks.

One major difference in the orientation of the two groups was that the whites, well into the Great Depression, more strongly saw themselves as helping others—people who were "other" not only socially but often also ethnically and religiously. The perspective of the white network had been affected particularly by large-scale immigration, the reconstitution of the urban working class by people of non-WASP origin, and residential segregation, which grouped the immigrants in ghettos not often seen by the white middle class. Much has been written about the arrogance and condescension these privileged social workers showed their immigrant clients. Little has been done to discover the impact of the immigrant population on the reformers' own ideas. The black/white comparison suggests that ethnic difference between the white poor and white reformers not only discouraged identification but also slowed the reformers' development of a structural understanding of the origins of poverty, as opposed to one that blamed individual character defects, however environmentally caused. Thus into the 1940s, the great majority of the white women in this sample supported welfare programs that were not only means-tested but also "morals-tested," continuing a distinction between the worthy and the unworthy poor. They believed that aid should always be accompanied by expert supervision and rehabilitation so as to inculcate into the poor work habits and morals that they so often (or so the reformers believed) lacked. (And, one might add, they did not mind the fact that this set up a sexual double standard in which women aid recipients would be treated differently and more severely than men recipients.)[60]

In comparison, black women were more focused on their own kind. Despite the *relative* privilege of most of them, and there was criticism from blacks of the snobbery of some of these network members, there was less distance between helper and helped than among white reformers. There was less chronological distance, for all their privileges were so recent and so tenuous. There was less geographical distance, for residential segregation did not allow the black middle class much insulation from the black poor. Concentrating their efforts more on education and health, and proportionally less on charity or relief, meant that they dealt more often with universal needs than with those of the particularly unfortunate and sought to provide universal, not means-tested, services.

These were differences of degree and should not be overstated. Most of the white women in this sample favored environmental analyses of the sources of poverty. Many black women's groups engaged in classic charity activity. In the 1890s Washington, D.C., black women volunteered to work with the Associated Charities in its "stamp work," a program designed to inculcate thrift and saving among the poor. In the depression of 1893 these relatively prosperous black "friendly visitors" donated supplies of coal and food staples. The Kansas Federation of Women's Clubs, Marilyn Brady found, clung to all the tenets of the "cult of true womanhood" except, perhaps, for fragility. As Ena Farley wrote of the Boston League of Women for Community Service, "Their patronage roles toward others less fortunate than themselves not only dramatized their relative superiority within the minority structure, but also gave them the claim to leadership and power positions." But these programs must be understood in a context in which the needy were far more numerous, and the prosperous far fewer, than among whites.[61]

This does not mean that there was no condescension among black women. Black leaders shared with white ones the conviction that the poor needed training, to develop not only skills but also moral and spiritual capacities. Mary Church Terrell could sound remarkably like a white clubwoman.

> To our poor, benighted sisters in the Black Belt of Alabama we have gone and we have been both a comfort and a help to these women, through the darkness of whose ignorance of everything that makes life sweet or worth the living, no ray of light would have penetrated but for us. We have taught them the A B C of living by showing them how to make their huts more habitable and decent with the small means at their command and how to care for themselves and their families.[62]

Like the Progressive Era white female reformers, the blacks emphasized the need to improve the sexual morals of their people.[63] Fannie Barrier Williams declared that the colored people's greatest need was a better and purer home life—that slavery had destroyed home ties, the sanctity of marriage, and the instincts of motherhood.[64]

Concern for sexual respectability by no means represented one class or stratum imposing its values on another; for black as for white women it grew also from a feminist, or womanist, desire to protect women from exploitation, a desire shared across class lines. But this priority had profoundly different meanings for black women reformers. Not only were black women more severely sexually victimized, but combatting sexual exploitation was for blacks inseparable from race uplift in general, as white sexual assaults against black women had long been a fundamental part of slavery and racial oppression. Indeed, black activists were far in advance of white feminists in their campaigns against rape and their identification of that crime as part of a system of power relations, and they did not assume that only *white* men were sexual aggressors. The historian Darlene Clark Hine suggests that efforts to build recreational programs for boys also reflected women's strategies for protecting girls from assault. Nevertheless, given the difficulties of effecting change in the aggressors, many black welfare reformers focused on protecting potential victims. Many of the earliest black urban institutions were homes designed to protect working women. Black women's considerable contribution to the founding and development of the Urban League had such motives. Just as the efforts by white welfare reformers to protect girls and women contained condescending and victim-blaming aspects, particularly inasmuch as they were directed at different social groups (immigrants, the poor), so victim blaming was present among black reformers too. The problem of sex exploitation could not be removed from intrarace class differences that left some black women much more vulnerable than others, not only to assault but also to having their reputations smeared; black, like white, women defined their middle-class status in part by their sexual respectability. But their sexual protection efforts were so connected to uplift for the whole race, without which the reformers could not enjoy any class privileges, that the victim blaming was a smaller part of their message than among whites.[65]

Moreover, despite the sense of superiority among some, the black women reformers could not easily separate their welfare from their civil rights agitation.[66] As Deborah White puts it, "The race problem . . . inherently included the problems of poverty."[67] Race uplift work was usually welfare work by definition, and it was always conceived as a path to racial equality. And black poverty could not be ameliorated without challenges to white domination. A nice example: in 1894 Gertrude Mossell, in a tribute to black women's uplift activity, referred to Ida Wells's antilynching campaign as "philanthropy." Several of these women, notably Terrell and Anna J. Cooper, were among the first rebels against Booker T. Washington's domination because of their attraction both to academic educational goals for their people and to challenges to segregation.[68] Those who considered themselves women's rights activists, such as Burroughs, Terrell, and Cooper, particularly protested the hypocrisy in the white feminists' coupling of the language of sisterhood with the practice of black exclusion—as in Terrell's principled struggle, as an elderly woman, to gain admission to the District of Columbia chapter of the American Association of University Women.

To be sure, there was a shift in emphasis from race uplift and thus institution building in the first part of this long period of study to the struggle against segregation in the second. But the shift was only visible in overview, because many women activists had been challenging racism from early in their careers. Williams, for example, as early as 1896, insisted that white women needed to learn from blacks.[69] YWCA women such as Eva Bowles, Lugenia Burns Hope, and Addie Hunton struggled against discrimination in the YWCA soon after the first colored branch opened in 1911. Charlotte Hawkins Brown, who was noted and sometimes criticized for her snobbery and insistence on "respectability," nevertheless "made it a practice, whenever insulted in a train or forced to leave a pullman coach and enter the Jim Crow car, to bring suit." At least one lawyer, in 1921, tried to get her to accept a small settlement, but she made it clear that her purpose was not financial compensation but justice.[70] Cooper, whose flowery and sentimental prose style might lead one to mistake her for a "soft," accommodating, spirit, rarely let a slur against Negroes go unprotested. She wrote to the Oberlin Committee against Al Smith in 1928 that she could not "warm up very enthusiastically with religious fervor for Bible 'fundamentalists' who have nothing to say about lynching Negroes or reducing whole sections of them to a state of peonage."[71]

The many women who had always challenged racism made a relatively smooth transition to a civil rights emphasis in their welfare work. There were conflicts about separatist versus integrationist strategies from the beginning of this period, not only in women's participation in leading black discourse but also in women's own projects. For example, Jane Hunter's establishment of a black YWCA in Cleveland evoked much black criticism, especially from those who thought her success in raising white money sprang from her decision not to challenge the white YWCA. Yet most black women in this network used separate institution-building and anti-segregation tactics at the same time. Nannie Burroughs, noted for her work as an educator promoting black Christian and vocational education, urged a boycott of the segregated public transportation system of Washington, D.C., in 1915.[72] (And Burroughs was Hunter's model.) In the 1930s Burroughs denounced the Baptist leadership and resisted its control so strongly that that church almost cut off financial support for the National Training School for Girls that she had worked so hard and long to build. " 'Don't wait for deliverers,' she admonished her listeners. . . . 'There are no deliverers. They're all dead. . . . The Negro must serve notice . . . that he is ready to die for justice.' " The Baptists relented, but Burroughs was still provoking white churchmen a decade later. In 1941 she canceled an engagement to speak for the National Christian Mission because the hierarchy insisted on precensoring her speech.[73] "The Negro is oppressed not because he is a Negro—but because he'll take it."[74] Bethune, who began her career as founder of a black college and was criticized by some for her apologias for segregated New Deal programs, was walking a picket line in front of Peoples Drugs in the District of Columbia, demanding jobs for colored youth, in 1939 even while still at the National Youth Administration.[75]

Moreover, the greater emphasis on civil rights never eclipsed uplift strategies. From the New Deal on, black government leaders were simultaneously trying to get more black women hired, protesting the passing over of qualified black applicants, and working to improve the qualifications and performance of black individuals. In 1943 Corinne Robinson of the Federal Public Housing Authority organized a skit, entitled *Lazy Daisy*, which called upon black government workers to shed slothful habits.[76] Nannie Burroughs in 1950 complained that the average Negro "gets up on the installment plan—never gets dressed fully until night, and by then he is completely disorganized." But that is because, she explained, "He really has nothing to get up to." To repeat: there was for these women no inherent contradiction between race uplift and antidiscrimination thinking.[77]

These black welfare activists were also militant in their critique of male supremacy, that militance, too, arising from their work for the welfare of the race. Deborah White has argued that the black women's clubs, more than the white, claimed leadership of the race for women. Charlotte Hawkins Brown declared her own work and thoughts were just as important as Booker T. Washington's.[78] Moreover, their ambitions were just as great as those of the white women: Afro-Americans spoke of uplifting their race; white women described themselves as promoting the general welfare, but only because their focus on their own race was silent and understood. Whether or not these women should be called feminists (and they certainly did not call themselves that), they shared characteristics of the white group that has been called "social feminists"; their activism arose from efforts to advance the welfare of the whole public, not just women, in a context where, they believed, men did not or could not adequately meet the needs.[79]

Black and white women welfare reformers also differed in their thinking about women's economic role. The white women, with few exceptions, tended to view married women's economic dependence on men as desirable, and their employment as a misfortune; they accepted the family wage system and rarely expressed doubts about its effectiveness, let alone its justice. There was substantial variation within this network and change over time in its members' views of the family wage. There was also substantial contradiction. Beginning in the 1890s, women social investigators repeatedly demonstrated that the family wage did not work, because most men did not earn enough, because some men became disabled, and because others were irresponsible toward their families. Sybil Lipschultz has shown that between two key Supreme Court briefs written by women in the white network—for *Muller v. Oregon* in 1908, and for *Adkins v. Children's Hospital* in 1923—the grounds for protective legislation changed considerably. The brief for *Muller* privileged sacred motherhood and treated women's wage labor as an anomaly that should be prevented; the brief for *Adkins* argued from women's weaker position in the labor market and the need for government to intervene because it was not an anomaly.[80] Yet when the women's welfare network moved away from protective labor legislation toward public assistance or family policy, its recommendations presupposed that the desirable position for women was as domestic wives and mothers dependent on male earnings. The many unmarried women in the network viewed their own singleness as a class privilege and a natural condition for women active in the public sphere and felt that remaining childless was an acceptable price for it. They were convinced that single motherhood and employment among mothers meant danger. They feared relief to single mothers offered without counseling or employment offered to mothers other than temporarily, because they resisted establishing single-mother families as durable institutions.[81]

This is where the social work legacy is felt. The white reformers were accustomed to, and felt comfortable with, supervising. Long after Jane Addams with her environmentalist, democratic orientation became their hero, they continued to identify with the Charity Organization Society fear of "pauperizing" aid recipients by making it too easy for them and destroying their work incentive—and they feared that too much help to deserted women, for example, would do just this, let men off the hook. They did not share the belief of many contemporary European socialists that aid to single mothers should be a matter of right, of entitlement. Even Florence Kelley, herself a product of a European socialist education, defended the family wage as the appropriate goal of reform legislation. A divorced mother herself, she nevertheless lauded "the American tradition that men support their families, the wives throughout life," and lamented the "retrograde movement" that made the man no longer the breadwinner. The U.S. supporters of mothers' pensions envisioned aid as a gift

467

to the deserving and felt an unshakable responsibility to supervise single mothers and restore marriages and wives' dependency on husbands whenever possible. This "white" view was clearly a class perspective as well. A troubling question is unavoidable: Did these elite white women believe that independence was a privilege of wealth to which poor women ought not aspire?[82]

The black woman reformers also held up breadwinner husbands and nonemployed wives as an ideal; black and white women spoke very similarly about the appropriate "spheres" of the two sexes, equally emphasizing motherhood.[83] The difference I am describing here is not diametric. Lucy D. Slowe, dean of women at Howard, believed that working mothers caused urban juvenile delinquency, and she called for campaigns to "build up public sentiment for paying heads of families wages sufficient to reduce the number of Negro women who must be employed away from home to the detriment of their children and of the community in general."[84] Personally, many of the married black activists had trouble prevailing upon their husbands to accept their activities, and some were persuaded to stay home. Ardie Halyard, recollecting the year 1920, described the process:

> Interviewer: How did your husband feel about you working?
> Halyard: At first, he thought it was very necessary. But, afterwards, when he became able to support us, it was day in and day out, "When are you going to quit?"[85]

Dorothy Ferebee's husband could not tolerate her higher professional status. Inabel Lindsay promised her husband not to work for a year and then slid into a lifelong career by taking a job that she promised was only temporary.[86]

Mixed as it was, acceptance of married women's employment as a long-term and widespread necessity was much greater among blacks than among whites. Fanny Jackson Coppin had argued in the 1860s for women's economic independence from men, and women were active in creating employment bureaus. We see the greater black acknowledgment of single mothers in the high priority black women reformers gave to organizing kindergartens, then usually called day nurseries. In Chicago, Cleveland, Atlanta, Washington, and many other locations, daytime child care facilities were among the earliest projects of women's groups. Terrell called establishing them her first goal, and her first publication was the printed version of a speech she had delivered at a National American Woman Suffrage Association convention, which she sold for twenty-five cents a copy to help fund a kindergarten.[87] In poor urban white neighborhoods the need for child care may have been nearly as great, and some white activists created kindergartens, but proportionally far fewer. Virtually no northern white welfare reformers endorsed such programs as long-term or permanent services until the 1930s and 1940s; until then even the most progressive, such as Kelley, opposed them even as temporary solutions, fearing they would encourage the exploitation of women through low-wage labor.[88]

Black women decried the effects of the "double day" on poor women as much as did white reformers. They were outspoken in their criticism of men who failed to support families. Burroughs wrote, "Black men sing too much 'I Can't Give You Anything But Love, Baby.' "[89] But their solutions were different. From the beginning of her career, Burroughs understood that the great majority of black women would work all their lives, and she had to struggle against continuing resistance to accepting that fact to get her National Training School funded. And most black women activists projected a favorable view of working women and women's professional aspirations. Elizabeth Ross Haynes wrote with praise in 1922 of "the hope of an economic independence that will some day enable them [Negro women] to take their places in the ranks with other working women."[90] Sadie Alexander directly attacked the view that a married woman's ideal should be domesticity. She saw that in an industrial society the work of the housewife would be increasingly seen as "valueless consumption" and the women should "place themselves again among the producers of the world."[91]

This high regard for women's economic independence is also reflected in the important and prestigious role played by businesswomen in black welfare activity. One of the best-known and most revered women of this network was Maggie Lena Walker, the first woman bank president in the United States. Beginning work at age fourteen in the Independent Order of St. Luke, a mutual benefit society in Richmond, Virginia, that provided illness and burial insurance as well as social activity for blacks, in 1903 she established the St. Luke Penny Savings Bank. Walker became a very wealthy woman. She devoted a great deal of her money and energy to welfare activity, working in the National Association for the Advancement of Colored People, the National Association of Wage Earners, and local Richmond groups. In the context of Afro-American experience, Walker's business was itself a civil rights and community welfare activity; many reformers, including prominently Bethune and Du Bois, believed that economic power was a key to black progress. The St. Luke enterprises stimulated black ownership and employment. They opened a black-owned department store in Richmond, thus threatening white economic power, and met intense opposition from white businessmen; indeed, a white Retail Dealers' Association was formed to crush the store. Several noteworthy businesswomen-activists got rich manufacturing cosmetics for blacks: the mother-daughter team, C. J. Walker and A'Lelia Walker (not related to Maggie Walker) of Pittsburgh and Indianapolis, and Annie Turnbo Malone of St. Louis. Reformer Jane Hunter was respected not only because of her welfare contributions but also because, once penniless, she left an estate of over $400,000 at her death; as was Sallie Wyatt Stewart, who left over $100,000 in real estate.[92]

These factors suggest considerable differences in orientation (among the numerous similarities) between white and black women activists, although the preliminary stage of research on this topic requires us to consider the differences more as hypotheses than as conclusions. First, black women claimed leadership in looking after the welfare of their whole people more than did comparable whites. Because of this assumption of race responsibility, and because for blacks welfare was so indistinguishable from equal rights, black women emphasized programs for the unusually needy less, and universal provision more, than did white women. Perhaps in part because education was so important a part of the black women's program, and because education developed for whites in the United States as a universal public service, blacks' vision of welfare provision followed that model. Among whites, a relatively large middle class encouraged reformers to focus their helping efforts on others and kept alive and relatively uncriticized the use of means and morals testing as a way of distributing help, continuing the division of the "deserving" from the "undeserving" poor. Among the black reformers, despite their relatively elite position, welfare appeared more closely connected with legal entitlements, not so different from the right to vote or to ride the public transportation system.[93] Had their ideas been integrated into the white women's thinking, one might ask, would means testing and humiliating invasions of privacy have been so uniformly accepted in programs such as Aid for Families with Dependent Children (AFDC), over which the white women's network had substantial influence?

Another difference is the black women's different attitude toward married women's employment. Most of the white women welfare reformers retained, until World War II, a distinctly head-in-the-sand and even somewhat contradictory attitude toward it; it was a misfortune, not good for women, children, or men; helping working mothers too much would tend to encourage it. Thus they were more concerned to help—sometimes to force—single mothers to stay home than to provide services that would help working mothers, such as child care or maternity leave. Black women were much more positive about women's employment. Despite their agreement that a male family wage was the most desirable arrangement, they doubted that married women's employment would soon disappear or that it could be discouraged by making women and children suffer for it. In relation to this race difference, it is hard to ignore the different marital status of the majority of the women in the two groups: Most of the black women had themselves had the experience of combining public-sphere activism with marriage, if less often with children.[94] Perhaps the fact that most of the white women had dispensed with marriage and family, probably largely by choice, made them see the choice between family and work as an acceptable one, oblivious to the different conditions of such "choice" among poorer women.

Third, black and white welfare reformers differed considerably about how to protect women from sexual exploitation. Black welfare reformers were more concerned to combine the development of protective institutions for women with an antirape discourse. Among whites, rape was not an important topic of discussion during this period, and in protective work for women and girls, male sexuality was treated as natural and irrepressible. It is not clear how the black activists would have translated antirape consciousness into welfare policy, had they had the power to do so, but it seems likely that they would have tried.

There were also substantial areas of shared emphases between white and black women. Both groups oriented much of their welfarist thinking to children, rarely questioning the unique responsibility of women for children's welfare. Neither group questioned sexual "purity" as an appropriate goal for unmarried women. Both groups used women's organizations as their main political and social channels. Both emphasized the promotion of other women into positions of leadership and jobs, confident that increasing the numbers of women at the "top" would benefit the public welfare. Both believed that improving the status of women was essential to advancing the community as a whole. At the same time, both groups, in the 1920s, were moving away from explicitly feminist discourse and muting their public criticisms of what we would today call sexism. Moreover they shared many personal characteristics: low fertility, relatively high economic and social status, very high educational attainment.

These impressions raise more questions than they answer. I wonder, for example, what was the relation between the national leaders and local rank-and-file activists: Were the leaders "representative" of "constituencies"? One might hypothesize that local activists were more often married and less elite, since singleness and prosperity were probably among the factors that allowed women to travel and to function nationally. To what extent were the black/white differences functions of chronology? White reformers were, for instance, active in building educational institutions in the nineteenth century; by the early twentieth century the institutions they needed were in place. Further research might also make it possible to identify historical circumstances that contributed to these race differences, circumstances such as migration, changing demand for labor, immigration, and its closure.

I approached this evidence as part of a general inquiry into welfare thinking in the United States in this century. In this project I found, as have several other historians, that the white women's reform network—but not the black—had some influence on welfare policy, particularly in public assistance programs. I have tried to show here that his influence was as much colored by race as by gender. The white women's influence supported the legacies in our welfare programs of means testing, distinguishing the deserving from the undeserving, moral supervision of female welfare recipients, failing to criticize men's sexual behavior, and discouraging women's employment. Black women's influence on federal welfare programs was negligible in this period; indeed, the leading federal programs—old-age insurance, unemployment compensation, workmen's compensation, and the various forms of public assistance such as AFDC—were expressly constructed to exclude blacks. It is not too late now, however, to benefit from a review of black women's welfare thought as we reconsider the kind of welfare state we want.[95]

APPENDIX

The women in these samples were selected because they were the leaders of national organizations that lobbied for welfare programs (such as the National Consumers' League, the National Child Labor Committee, the National Association of Colored Women, or the National Council of Negro Women), or government officials responsible for welfare programs who were also important advocates of such programs, or builders of private welfare institutions. Women who were simply employees of welfare programs or institutions were not included; for example, educators were only included when they were builders of educational institutions. For the blacks, this sample of welfare activists overlaps extensively with a sample one might construct of clubwomen and political activists, but not exactly; for example, Ida Wells-Barnett is not here because she must be categorized as primarily a civil rights, not a welfare, campaigner. Among the whites this sample overlaps somewhat with "social feminists," but those who were primarily labor organizers, for example, are not included.

Some of what appear to be race differences are differences of historical time and circumstance. Thus a study of women between, say, 1840 and 1890 would have included more white women educators (because white women were then working to build educational institutions as black women were later) and more white married women (because the dip in the marriage rate among college-educated white women occurred later). Regional differences are also produced by this definition of the samples: a focus on local or state, as opposed to national, activity would have led to the inclusion of more western and southern women, for example; women in the Northeast and mid-Atlantic were more likely to be important in national politics because New York and Washington D.C., were so often the headquarters of national activities.

In order to simplify this list, only a single, general, major area of welfare activism is given for each woman. Because many women were active in several areas, the identifications given here do not necessarily conform to some figures in the text, for example, how many women were social workers or educators. The categories for the white and black women are not the same. Among the whites I gave more specific identifications to indicate the importance of several key arenas, such as the National Consumers' League and the United States Children's Bureau. To use such specific identifications among the black women would have been uninformative, since virtually all were, for example, active in the National Association of Colored Women. Furthermore, a few black women participated in such a variety of welfarist activity organized through the NACW, sororities, or other women's organizations that I could define their major sphere as simply club work.

Table 1
Selected Black Women Welfare Activists

Name	Main Reform	Name	Main Reform
Alexander, Sadie Tanner Mossell	Civil rights	Jones, Verina Morton	Social work
Anthony, Lucille	Health	Laney, Lucy Craft	Education
Ayer, G. Elsie	Education	Lawton, Maria Coles Perkins	Education
Barnes, Margaret E.	Education	Lindsay, Inabel Burns	Education
Barrett, Janie Porter	Education	Lyle, Ethel Hedgeman	Club
Bearden, Bessye	Civil rights	Mallory, Arenia Cornelia	Education
Bethune, Mary McLeod	Education	Malone, Annie M. Turnbo	Education
Bowles, Eva Del Vakia	Social work	Marsh, Vivian Osborne	Club
Brawley, Ruth Merrill	Social work	Matthews, Victoria Earle	Social work
Brown, Charlotte Hawkins	Education	Mays, Sadie Gray	Social work
Brown, Sue M.	Education	McCrorey, Mary Jackson	Social work
Burroughs, Nannie Helen	Education	McDougald, G. Elsie Johnson	Education
Callis, Myra Colson	Employment	McKane, Alice Woodby	Health
Carter, Ezella	Education	Merritt, Emma Frances Grayson	Education
Cary, Alice Dugged	Child welfare	Nelson, Alice Ruth Dunbar	Social work
Cook, Coralie Franklin	Education	Pickens, Minnie McAlpin	Civil rights
Cooper, Anna Julia Haywood	Education	Randolph, Florence	Club
Davis, Belle	Health	Ridley, Florida Ruffin	Club
Davis, Elizabeth Lindsey	Club	Ruffin, Josephine St. Pierre	Club
Dickerson, Addie W.	Club	Rush, Gertrude E.	Social work
Faulkner, Georgia M. DeBaptiste	Social work	Saddler, Juanita Jane	Civil rights
Fauset, Crystal Bird	Civil rights	Snowden, Joanna Cecilia	Social work
Ferebee, Dorothy Boulding	Health	Stewart, Sallie Wyatt	Social work
Gaines, Irene McCoy	Civil rights	Talbert, Mary Barnett	Civil rights
Harris, Judia C. Jackson	Social work	Taylor, Isabelle Rachel	Social work
Haynes, Elizabeth Ross	Civil rights	Terrell, Mary Eliza Church	Civil rights
Hedgeman, Anna Arnold	Civil rights	Walker, A'Lelia	Social work
Height, Dorothy I.	Civil rights	Walker, Maggie Lena	Social work
Hope, Lugenia Burns	Social work	Warren, Sadie	Social work
Hunter, Jane Edna Harris	Social work	Washington, Margaret Murray	Education
Hunton, Addie D. Waites	Civil rights	Wells, Eva Thornton	Social work
Jackson, Juanita Elizabeth	Civil rights	Wheatley, Laura Frances	Education
Jeffries, Christina Armistead	Civil rights	Williams, Fannie Barrier	Social work
Johnson, Bertha La Branche	Education	Young, Mattie Dover	Social work
Johnson, Kathryn Magnolia	Civil rights		

Table 2
Selected White Women Welfare Activists

Name	Main Reform	Name	Main Reform
Abbott, Edith	Social work	Kelley, Florence Molthrop	Consumers' League
Abbott, Grace	Children's Bureau	Kellor, Frances (Alice)	Immigrant welfare
Addams, Jane	Settlement	Lathrop, Julia Clifford	Children's Bureau
Amidon, Beulah Elizabeth	Social work	Lenroot, Katherine Frederica	Children's Bureau
Anderson, Mary	Women's Bureau	Loeb, Sophie Irene Simon	Mothers' pension
Armstrong,	Social Security	Lundberg, Emma Octavia	Children's Bureau
Barbara Nachtrieb		Maher, Amy	Social Security
Armstrong, Florence Arzelia	Social Security	Mason, Lucy Randolph	Consumers' League
Beyer, Clara Mortenson	Children's Bureau	McDowell, Mary Eliza	Settlement
Blair, Emily Newell	Democratic party	McMain, Eleanor Laura	Settlement
Bradford, Cornelia Foster	Settlement	Miller, Frieda Segelke	Women's Bureau
Breckinridge,	Social work	Moskowitz, Belle Israels	Democratic party
Sophonisba Preston		Newman, Pauline	Women's Bureau
Brown, Josephine Chapin	Social work	Perkins, Frances	Social Security
Burns, Eveline Mabel	Social Security	Peterson, Agnes L.	Women's Bureau
Cannon, Ida Maud	Medical social work	Pidgeon, Mary Elizabeth	Women's Bureau
Colcord, Joanna	Social work	Rankin, Jeannette Pickering	Congresswoman
Coyle, Grace Longwood	Social work	Raushenbush,	Unemployment
Crane, Caroline Bartlett	Sanitation reform	Elizabeth Brandeis	
Deardorff, Neva Ruth	Social work	Regan, Agnes Gertrude	Social work
Dewson, Mary W. (Molly)	Democratic party	Richmond, Mary Ellen	Social work
Dinwiddie, Emily Wayland	Housing reform	Roche, Josephine Aspinall	Consumers' League
Dudley, Helena Stuart	Settlement	Roosevelt, (Anna) Eleanor	Social work
Dunn, Loula Friend	Social work	Schneiderman, Rose	Labor
Eastman, Crystal (Catherine)	Industrial health	Sherwin, Belle	Club
Einstein, Hannah Bachman	Mother's pensions	Simkhovitch, Mary Kingsbury	Settlement
Eliot, Martha May	Children's Bureau	Springer, Gertrude Hill	Social work
Ellickson, Katherine Pollak	Social Security	Switzer, Mary Elizabeth	Social work
Elliott, Harriet Wiseman	Democratic party	Taft, (Julia) Jessie	Social work
Engle, Lavinia Margaret	Social Security	Thomas, M. Carey	Education
Evans, Elizabeth Glendower	Consumers' League	Towle, Charlotte Helen	Social work
Fuller, Minnie Ursala	Child welfare		(academic)
Goldmark, Josephine Clara	Consumers' League	Vaile, Gertrude	Social work
Goldmark, Pauline Dorothea	Consumers' League	Van Kleeck, Mary Abby	Women's Bureau
Gordon, Jean Margaret	Consumers' League	Wald, Lillian D.	Settlement
Hall, Helen	Settlement	White, Sue Shelton	Democratic party
Hamilton, (Amy) Gordon	Social work	Wood, Edith Elmer	Housing reform
Hamilton, Alice	Industrial health	Woodbury,	Children's Bureau
Hoey, Jane Margueretta	Social Security	Helen Laura Sumner	
Iams, Lucy Virginia Dorsey	Housing reform	Woodward, Ellen Sullivan	Social work
Keller, Helen	Health reform		

NOTES

For critical readings of this article in draft I am indebted to Lisa D. Brush, Nancy Cott, Elizabeth Higginbotham, Evelyn Brooks Higginbotham, Jacquelyn D. Hall, Stanlie James, Judith Walzer Leavitt, Gerda Lerner, Adolph Reed, Jr., Anne Firor Scott, Kathryn Kish Sklar, Susan Smith, David Thelen, Susan Traverso, Bill Van Deburg, Deborah Gray White, and anonymous reviewers. I could not meet all the high standards of these scholars, many of whom took a great deal of time and care with this sprawling essay, but several of them not only offered valuable insights but also saved me from some errors resulting from my venture into a new field, and I am extremely grateful.

1. For a critique of gender bias in existing welfare scholarship and an explanation of the need for further research about the influence of gender, see the introduction to Linda Gordon, ed., *Women, the State, and Welfare* (Madison, 1990), 9-35.
2. One of the subjects of this study, Inabel Burns Lindsay, former dean of the Howard University School of Social Work, wrote a dissertation on this topic at the University of Pittsburgh in 1952, and published Inabel Burns Lindsay, "Some Contributions of Negroes to Welfare Services, 1865-1900," *Journal of Negro Education*, 25 (Winter 1956), 15-24. Her publication did not spark others, however. A valuable collection of documents is Edyth L. Ross, ed., *Black Heritage in Social Welfare, 1860-1930* (Metuchen, 1978). Neither publication considers the particular role of women. For suggestions that black women participated more in organized activity than did white women, see Anne Firor Scott, "Most Invisible of All: Black Women's Voluntary Associations," *Journal of Southern History*, 56 (Feb. 1990), 5; and Ena L. Farley, "Caring and Sharing since World War I: The League of Women for Community Service—A Black Volunteer Organization in Boston," *Umoja*, 1 (Summer 1977), 1-12. Victoria Earle Matthews's surname is sometimes spelled "Mathews." Ralph E. Luker, "Missions, Institutional Churches, and Settlement Houses: The Black Experience, 1885-1910," *Journal of Negro History*, 69 (Summer/Fall 1984), 101-13; Dorothy C. Salem, *To Better Our World: Black Women in Organized Reform, 1890-1920* (Brooklyn, 1990), 44-45; Sharon Harley, "Beyond the Classroom: The Organizational Lives of Black Female Educators in the District of Columbia, 1890-1930," *Journal of Negro Education*, 51 (Summer 1982), 262; Jacqueline Anne Rouse, *Lugenia Burns Hope: Black Southern Reformer* (Athens, Ga., 1989); Elizabeth Lasch, "Female Vanguard in Race Relations: 'Mother Power' and Blacks in the American Settlement House Movement," paper delivered at the Berkshire Conference on the History of Women, Rutgers University, June 1990 (in Linda Gordon's possession). Since the black settlements were often called missions and were often more religious than typical white settlements, historians have not clearly recognized the broad range of services they provided and the organizational/agitational centers they became.
3. On public social welfare programs attacking working-class self-help programs in England, see Stephen Yeo, "Working-Class Association, Private Capital, Welfare, and the State in the Late Nineteenth and Twentieth Centuries," in *Social Work, Welfare, and the State*, ed. Noel Parry et al. (London, 1979). Self-help associations of the poor were probably as common in the United States as in England.
4. Charles L. Coon, "Public Taxation and Negro Schools," quoted in W. E. B. Du Bois, ed., *Efforts for Social Betterment among Negro Americans* (Atlanta, 1909), 29. The tax

tax money spent on black schools was, of course, proportionally and absolutely far less than that spent on white.

5. Cynthia Neverdon-Morton, *Afro-American Women of the South and the Advancement of the Race, 1895-1925* (Knoxville, 1989), 79.

6. Louie D. Shivery, "The History of the Gate City Free Kindergarten Association" (from a 1936 Atlanta University M.A. thesis), in *Black Heritage in Social Welfare*, ed. Ross, 261-62.

7. Tera Hunter, "'The Correct Thing': Charlotte Hawkins Brown and the Palmer Institute," *Southern Exposure*, 11 (Sept./Oct. 1983), 37-43; Sandra N. Smith and Earle H. West, "Charlotte Hawkins Brown," *Journal of Negro Education*, 51 (Summer 1982), 191-206.

8. Darlene Clark Hine, "'We Specialize in the Wholly Impossible': The Philanthropic Work of Black Women," in *Lady Bountiful Revisited: Women, Philanthropy, and Power*, ed. Kathleen D. McCarthy (New Brunswick, 1990), 84.

9. For help in gathering and analyzing biographical data, I am indebted to Lisa Brush, Bob Buchanan, Nancy Isenberg, Nancy MacLean, and Susan Traverso.

10. For a discussion of the definition of welfare, see Gordon, ed., *Women, the State, and Welfare*, 19-35; and Linda Gordon, "What Does Welfare Regulate?" *Social Research*, 55 (Winter 1988), 609-30. Child labor is both a welfare and labor reform issue. I have included it here because, for so many women active in this cause, it seemed a logical, even inevitable, continuation of other child welfare activity; opposition to child labor was a much-used argument for mothers' pensions and Aid to Families with Dependent Children.

11. Although my focus is on welfare, a similar predominance of northern whites and southern blacks occurred among the national women's organizations. For example, Margaret (Mrs. Booker T.) Washington was the first southerner to be head of any national secular women's group—in her case, the National Association of Colored Women (NACW). See Darlene Rebecca Roth, "Matronage: Patterns in Women's Organizations, Atlanta, Georgia, 1890-1940" (Ph.D. diss., George Washington University, 1978), 81. On the integration of education into campaigns for welfare by African Americans, see, for example, Elizabeth Higginbotham, "Too Much to Ask: The Costs of Black Female Success," ch. 3, "Socialized for Survival" (in Elizabeth Higginbotham's possession).

12. Of the 69 black women, 5 held governmental positions: Mary McLeod Bethune was director of the Division of Negro Affairs at the National Youth Administration under Franklin D. Roosevelt; Alice Cary was a traveling advisor to the Department of Labor during World War I; Crystal Fauset was a state legislator from Philadelphia and race relations advisor to the Works Progress Administration during the New Deal; Anna Hedgeman was assistant to the New York City commissioner of welfare in 1934. By contrast, 53% of the white women held federal government positions and 58% held state positions.

13. Neverdon-Morton, *Afro-American Women of the South*, 191-236; Rosalyn Terborg-Penn, "Discrimination against Afro-American Women in the Women's Movement, 1830-1920," in *The Afro-American Woman: Struggles and Images*, ed. Sharon Harley and Rosalyn Terborg-Penn (Port Washington, 1978), 17-27.

14. These white reformers were not more racist than the men engaged in similar activity and often less. Eight white women from this sample were among the founding members of the National Association for the Advancement of Colored People

(NAACP): Jane Addams, Florence Kelley, Julia Lathrop, Sophonisba Breckinridge, Mary McDowell, Lillian Wald, and Edith and Grace Abbott.

15. Steven J. Diner, "Chicago Social Workers and Blacks in the Progressive Era," *Social Service Review*, 44 (Dec. 1970), 393-410; Sandra M. Stehno, "Public Responsibility for Dependent Black Children: The Advocacy of Edith Abbott and Sophonisba Breckinridge," *Social Service Review*, 62 (Sept. 1988), 485-503; Gerda Lerner, *Black Women in White America: A Documentary History* (New York, 1972), 459; Salem, *To Better Our World*, 248-50; Jacquelyn Dowd Hall, *Revolt against Chivalry: Jessie Daniel Ames and the Women's Campaign against Lynching* (New York, 1979), 66.

16. Jacqueline Rouse, biographer of Lugenia Burns Hope of Atlanta, lists ten other black activists who, with Hope, formed a close southern network by about 1910: Bethune in Florida, Nettie Napier and M. L. Crosthwait in Tennessee, Jennie Moton and Margaret Washington in Alabama, Maggie Lena Walker in Virginia, Charlotte Hawkins Brown and Mary Jackson McCrorey in North Carolina, and Lucy Laney and Florence Hunt also in Georgia. Rouse, *Lugenia Burns Hope*, 5. Rouse also identifies an overlapping group of black southern women educators—Hope, Hunt, McCrorey, Washington, Moton, Bethune, with the addition of Marion B. Wilkinson of South Carolina State College; Julia A. Fountain of Morris Brown College in Atlanta; and A. Vera Davage of Clark College in Atlanta. *Ibid.*, 55. Paula Giddings, *In Search of Sisterhood: Delta Sigma Theta and the Challenge of the Black Sorority Movement* (New York, 1988). Darlene Rebecca Roth found that black clubwomen retained closer ties with their schools than did white clubwomen. Roth, "Matronage," 183. Hine, "'We Specialize in the Wholly Impossible,'" 70-93; Fannie Barrier Williams, "Opportunities and Responsibilities of Colored Women," in *Afro-America Encyclopaedia; or, the Thoughts, Doings, and Sayings of the Race*, ed. James T. Haley (Nashville, 1896), 146-61.

17. Hine, "'We Specialize in the Wholly Impossible,'" 83.

18. On the attempt to force Lucy D. Slowe to live in the women's dormitory, see the letters in folder 59, box 90-3, and folder 100, box 90-4, Lucy D. Slowe Papers (Moorland-Spingarn Research Center, Howard University, Washington, D.C.), esp. Coralie Franklin Cook et al. to Lucy D. Slowe, June 9, 1933, folder 9, box 90-2, *ibid.*; Clayda J. Williams to Slowe, Aug. 23, 1933, *ibid.*; Mary McLeod Bethune to Slowe, Nov. 23, 1933, folder 28, *ibid.* Howard University was notorious for its discriminatory treatment of women, backward even in relation to other colleges at the time. On Howard, see Giddings, *In Search of Sisterhood*, 43.

19. For remarks made about Bethune at the 1938 National Conference of Negro Women White House Conference, praising her for not being satisfied to be the token black but struggling to increase black representation in the New Deal, see folder 4, box 1, series 4, pp. 27-28, National Council of Negro Women Papers (Mary McLeod Bethune Museum and Archives, Washington, D.C.).

20. Tullia Brown Hamilton also found this focus on education predominant among the black women reformers she studied. Tullia Brown Hamilton, "The National Association of Colored Women, 1896-1920" (Ph.D. diss., Emory University, 1978), 45-46. Similarly Roth found that even among Atlanta's most elite organization of black women, the Chautauqua Circle, all had been employed as teachers; Roth, "Matronage," 181. Melinda Chateauvert found that women graduates of Washington, D.C.'s elite black Dunbar High School (who outnumbered males 2 to 1 around 1910) were overwhelmingly likely to go on to the district's free Miner Teacher's College to become teachers; Melinda Chateauvert, "The Third Step:

Anna Julia Cooper and Black Education in the District of Columbia," *Sage*, 5 (Student Supplement 1988), 7-13. For the same conclusion, see Carol O. Perkins, "The Pragmatic Idealism of Mary McLeod Bethune," *ibid.* (Fall 1988), 30-36. W. E. B. Du Bois, ed., *Economic Cooperation among Negro Americans* (Atlanta, 1907), 80-88.

21. Du Bois, ed., *Efforts for Social Betterment among Negro Americans*, 65-77. For a northern local example, see Russell H. Davis, *Black Americans in Cleveland: From George Peake to Carl B. Stokes, 1796-1969* (Cleveland, 1972), 192.

22. Darlene Clark Hine, *Black Women in White: Racial Conflict and Cooperation in the Nursing Profession, 1890-1950* (Bloomington, 1989), xvii; Edward H. Beardsley, *A History of Neglect: Health Care for Blacks and Mill Workers in the Twentieth-Century South* (Knoxville, 1987), 101; Susan L. Smith, "The Black Women's Club Movement: Self-Improvement and Sisterhood, 1890-1915" (M.A. thesis, University of Wisconsin, Madison, 1986); Susan L. Smith, "Black Activism in Health Care, 1890-1950," paper delivered at the conference "Black Health: Historical Perspectives and Current Issues," University of Wisconsin, Madison, April 1990 (in Gordon's possession); Salem, *To Better Our World*, 74; Du Bois, *Economic Cooperation among Negro Americans*, 92-103; Du Bois, *Efforts for Social Betterment among Negro Americans*, 17-22; Scott, "Most Invisible of All," 6; Claude F. Jacobs, "Benevolent Societies of New Orleans Blacks during the Late Nineteenth and Early Twentieth Centuries," *Louisiana History*, 29 (Winter 1988), 21-33; Kathleen C. Berkeley, "'Colored Ladies Also Contributed': Black Women's Activities from Benevolence to Social Welfare, 1866-1896," in *The Web of Southern Social Relations: Women, Family, and Education*, ed. Walter J. Fraser, Jr., R. Frank Saunders, Jr., and Jon L. Wakelyn (Athens, Ga., 1985), 181-203.

23. Colored YWCA, *Fifth and Sixth Years Report, May 1909-May 1911* (Washington, n.d.), 10-11 (Library, State Historical Society of Wisconsin, Madison); I am indebted to Bob Buchanan for this reference. Earline Rae Ferguson, "The Woman's Improvement Club of Indianapolis: Black Women Pioneers in Tuberculosis Work, 1903-1938," *Indiana Magazine of History*, 84 (Sept. 1988), 237-61; Darlene Clark Hine, *When the Truth Is Told: A History of Black Women's Culture and Community in Indiana, 1875-1950* (Indianapolis, 1981). The Atlanta Neighborhood Union also worked against tuberculosis. Cynthia Neverdon-Morton, "Self-Help Programs as Educative Activities of Black Women in the South, 1895-1925: Focus on Four Key Areas," *Journal of Negro Education*, 51 (Summer 1982), 207-21; Walter R. Chivers, "Neighborhood Union: An Effort of Community Organization," *Opportunity*, 3 (June 1925), 178-79. Modjeska Simkins's work is briefly summarized in Beardsley, *History of Neglect*, 108-12. Smith, "Black Women's Club Movement"; Smith, "Black Activism in Health Care."

24. Fannie Barrier Williams, "Social Bonds in the 'Black Belt' of Chicago: Negro Organizations and the New Spirit Pervading Them," *Charities*, Oct. 7, 1905, pp. 40-44; Scott, "Most Invisible of All," 8.

25. The Young Women's Christian Association was segregated, and these activists fought that segregation. Nevertheless, as Dorothy Height points out forcefully in her interview, "It was unmatched by any other major group drawn from the major white population" in the opportunities it offered to black women; Dorothy Height interview by Polly Cowan, Feb. 11, 1974-Nov. 6, 1976, 173, Black Women Oral History Project (Schlesinger Library, Radcliffe College, Cambridge, Mass.). See also descriptions of YWCA opportunities in Frankie V. Adams interview by Gay

Francine Banks, April 26, 28, 1977, transcript, p. 9, *ibid.*; Salem, *To Better Our World*, 46.

26. I could not identify birthplaces for all the women, and those with missing information include some likely to have been southern-born.

27. Others have reached similar conclusions. See Marilyn Dell Brady, "Kansas Federation of Colored Women's Clubs, 1900-1930," *Kansas History*, 9 (Spring 1986), 19-30; Linda Marie Perkins, *Black Feminism and "Race Uplift," 1890-1900* (Cambridge, Mass., 1981), Bunting Institute Working Paper (ERIC microfiche ED 221445), 4; Salem, *To Better Our World*, 67.

28. In the black population in general, 7% of all married women born 1840-1859 were childless, and 28% of those born 1900-1919 were childless. U.S. Department of Commerce, Bureau of the Census, *Historical Statistics of the United States: Colonial Times to 1970* (2 vols., Washington, 1975), I, 53.

29. Black women's overall fertility was declining rapidly in this period, falling by one-third between 1880 and 1910, and southern black women had fewer children than southern white women. Some of this low fertility was attributable to poor health and nutrition. Moreover, the women in this network were virtually all urban, and the fertility of urban black women was only half that of rural black women. See Jacqueline Jones, *Labor of Love, Labor of Sorrow: Black Women, Work, and the Family from Slavery to the Present* (New York, 1985), 122-23. Supporting my view of black women's use of birth control, see Jessie M. Rodrique, "The Black Community and the Birth-Control Movement," in *Passion and Power: Sexuality in History*, ed. Kathy Peiss and Christina Simmons (Philadelphia, 1989), 138-54. This article offers a convincing criticism of my own earlier work, which overstated black hostility to birth control campaigns because of their genocidal implications. I also learned from Elizabeth Lasch's unpublished paper that Margaret Murray Washington's settlement at Tuskegee offered a course of study on sex hygiene that included birth control; this suggests the need for further research on black women's advocacy of birth control. Lasch, "Female Vanguard in Race Relations," 4.

30. I was able to identify 25% (17) with prosperous parents.

31. Marilyn Dell Brady found the same marital patterns for black women reformers in her study of Kansas. Brady, "Kansas Federation of Colored Women's Clubs, 1900-1930," 19-30. The major figures she studied were married and supported by their husbands.

32. Anna Arnold Hedgeman, *The Trumpet Sounds: A Memoir of Negro Leadership* (New York, 1964), 25, 74; Farley, "Caring and Sharing since World War I," 317-27. Hamilton, "National Association of Colored Women," 41; Paula Giddings, *When and Where I Enter: The Impact of Black Women on Race and Sex in America* (New York, 1984), 108; Berkeley, "'Colored Ladies Also Contributed,'" 185-86.

33. For corroboration on the employment of well-to-do black women, see Roth, "Matronage," 180-81. On black women's socialization toward employment, see Inabel Burns Lindsay interview by Marcia Greenlee, May 20-June 7, 1977, transcript, pp. 4, 40, Black Women Oral History Project.

34. Charles S. Johnson, *The Negro College Graduate* (Chapel Hill, 1938), 18-20; U.S. Department of Commerce, Bureau of the Census, *The Social and Economic Status of the Black Population in the United States: An Historical View, 1790-1978* (Washington, 1979), 93.

35. Alfreda Duster interview by Greenlee, March 8-9, 1978, transcript, p. 9, Black Women Oral History Project; Hedgeman, *Trumpet Sounds*, 3-28.

36. In my comments on the class attitudes of black women welfare reformers, I am mainly indebted to the interpretations of Deborah Gray White, especially in Deborah Gray White, "Fettered Sisterhood: Class and Classism in Early Twentieth Century Black Women's History," paper delivered at the annual meeting of the American Studies Association, Toronto, Nov. 1989 (in Gordon's possession). See also Williams, "Social Bonds in the 'Black Belt' of Chicago." On black discrimination against relatively dark skinned women, see, for example, Nannie Burroughs, "Not Color But Character," *Voice of the Negro*, 1 (July 1904), 277-79; Duster interview, 52; Giddings, *In Search of Sisterhood*, 105; Perkins, *Black Feminism and "Race Uplift,"* 4; and Nancy Weiss, *Farewell to the Party of Lincoln: Black Politics in the Age of FDR* (Princeton, 1983), 139. Berkeley argues against the importance of class differences in the NACW, but I found them substantial. See Berkeley, "'Colored Ladies Also Contributed.'" On class development among blacks, see August Meier and David Lewis, "History of the Negro Upper Class in Atlanta, Georgia, 1890-1958," *Journal of Negro Education*, 28 (Spring 1959), 128-39.

37. Duster interview, 37.

38. Philip S. Foner, ed., *The Voice of Black America: Major Speeches by Negroes in the United States, 1797-1971* (New York, 1972), 462.

39. Hedgeman, *Trumpet Sounds*, 1-28; Chateauvert, "The Third Step"; Height interview, 40; Caroline Ware interview by Susan Ware, Jan. 27-29, 1982, transcript, p. 94, Women in Federal Government Oral Histories (Schlesinger Library).

40. Robert Alan Goldberg, *Hooded Empire: The Ku Klux Klan in Colorado* (Urbana, 1981), vii.

41. Of the white women reformers, 78% had been social workers at some time; 68% had social work as their major reform area. I checked to see if the social work background could have been a characteristic of the less prominent women, but this was not the case. The most prominent two-thirds of the group were even more frequently social workers (84%).

42. Stanley Wenocur and Michael Reisch, *From Charity to Enterprise: The Development of American Social Work in a Market Economy* (Urbana, 1989), 33.

43. Of the white women, 18% had held academic jobs at one time; 9% were mainly employed as educators. For only 1% was education their major reform area.

44. Lillian Wald, *Windows on Henry Street* (Boston, 1934); Mary Kingsbury Simkhovitch, *Neighborhood: My Story of Greenwich House* (New York, 1938); William W. Bremer, *Depression Winters: New York Social Workers and the New Deal* (Philadelphia, 1984); George Martin, *Madame Secretary: Frances Perkins* (Boston, 1976), 134-35; Elisabeth Israels Perry, "Training for Public Life: ER and Women's Political Networks in the 1920s," in *Without Precedent: The Life and Career of Eleanor Roosevelt*, ed. Joan Hoff-Wilson and Marjorie Lightman (Bloomington, 1984), 30.

45. Elisabeth Israels Perry, *Belle Moskowitz: Feminine Politics and the Exercise of Power in the Age of Alfred E. Smith* (New York, 1987), 76-77; Walter Trattner, "Theodore Roosevelt, Social Workers, and the Election of 1912: A Note," *Mid-America*, 50 (Jan. 1968), 64-69. On pre-woman suffrage women's electoral participation, see, for example, S. Sara Monoson, "The Lady and the Tiger: Women's Electoral Activism in New York City before Suffrage," *Journal of Women's History*, 2 (Fall 1990), 100-135.

46. I thank Anne Firor Scott for pointing out this similarity to me.

47. On settlement house relationships, see Virginia Kemp Fish, "The Hull House Circle: Women's Friendships and Achievements," in *Gender, Ideology, and Action:*

Historical Perspectives on Women's Public Lives, ed. Janet Sharistanian (Westport, 1986); and Kathryn Kish Sklar, "Hull House in the 1890s: A Community of Women Reformers," *Signs*, 10 (Summer 1985), 658-77. Lela B. Costin, *Two Sisters for Social Justice: A Biography of Grace and Edith Abbott* (Urbana, 1983), 38-40; Martin, *Madame Secretary*, 233.

48. See, for example, Ethel Erickson to Mary Anderson, July 14, 1938, box 1263, Women's Bureau Papers, RG 86 (National Archives); Anderson to Erickson, Aug. 4, 1938, *ibid.*; Erickson to Anderson, July 29, 1942, *ibid.*; Anderson to Erickson, Aug. 1, 1942, *ibid.*

49. Darlene Clark Hine, "Rape and the Inner Lives of Black Women in the Middle West: Preliminary Thoughts on the Culture of Dissemblance," in *Unequal Sisters: A Multicultural Reader in U.S. Women's History*, ed. Ellen Carol DuBois and Vicki L. Ruiz (New York, 1990), 292-97; Deborah Gray White, "Mining the Forgotten: Manuscript Sources for Black Women's History," *Journal of American History*, 74 (June 1987), 237-42; Elsa Barkley Brown, comment at Berkshire Conference on the History of Women, 1990.

50. The singleness of the white women reformers was characteristic of other women of their race, class, and education in this period. In 1890, for example, over half of all women doctors were single. Of women earning Ph.D.'s between 1877 and 1924, three-fourths remained single. As late as 1920, only 12% of all professional women were married. See, for example, Carl N. Degler, *At Odds: Women and the Family in America from the Revolution to the Present* (New York, 1980), 385. Roth corroborates the significance of martial breaks in the lives of activists, finding that civically active white women in Atlanta in this period were more likely to be widows. Roth, "Matronage," 182. On Boston marriages, see Micaela di Leonardo, "Warrior Virgins and Boston Marriages: Spinsterhood in History and Culture," *Feminist Issues*, 5 (Fall 1985), 47-68.

51. Mrs. Tilden Frank Phillips, memoir, Feb. 22, Feb. 26, 1953, folder 22, Edith Rockwood Papers (Schlesinger Library); will of Edith Rockwood, folder 20, *ibid.*

52. Blanche Wiesen Cook, "The Historical Denial of Lesbianism," *Radical History Review*, 20 (Spring/Summer 1979), 60-65. For quotations from a (hostile) contemporary source, see James Johnson, "The Role of Women in the Founding of the United States Children's Bureau," in *"Remember the Ladies": New Perspectives on Women in American History: Essays In Honor of Nelson Manfred Blake*, ed. Carol V.R. George (Syracuse, 1975), 191.

53. Cook, "Historical Denial of Lesbianism"; Blanche Wiesen Cook, "Female Support Networks and Political Activism: Lillian Wald, Crystal Eastman, Emma Goldman," in *A Heritage of Her Own*, ed. Nancy F. Cott and Elizabeth H. Pleck (New York, 1979), 412-44; Estelle B. Freedman, "Separatism as Strategy," *Feminist Studies*, 5 (Fall 1979), 512-29.

54. Slowe lived with Mary Burrill, who is treated as a partner in letters to and from Slowe and in letters of condolence to Burrill after Slowe's death in 1937. See letters in box 90-1, Slowe Papers. Height interview, 52.

55. Duster interview, 11; Wendy Beth Posner, "Charlotte Towle: A Biography" (Ph.D. diss., University of Chicago School of Social Service Administration, 1986), 47, 77-78.

56. Mary Dewson to Clara Beyer, Oct. 12, 1931, folder 40, box 2, Clara Beyer Papers (Schlesinger Library); Ware interview, 40-42; Janice Andrews, "Role of Female Social Workers in the Second Generation: Leaders or Followers," 1989 (in

Gordon's possession). The possibility of combining marriage and career had been debated intensely starting in the 1920s, but it was in the 1930s that the change began to be evident, See Lois Scharf, *To Work and to Wed: Female Employment, Feminism, and the Great Depression* (Westport, 1980).

57. Florence Kelley to Anderson, June 28, 1920, box 843, Women's Bureau Papers; Anderson to Dewson, Aug. 23, 1920, *ibid.*; Anderson to Dewson, Oct. 23, 1922, *ibid.*; Dewson to Anderson, June 1, 1923, *ibid.* Anderson to Mary Van Kleeck, Jan. 8, 1937, folder 22, box 1, Mary Anderson Papers (Schlesinger Library); Judith Sealander, "Feminist against Feminist: The First Phase of the Equal Rights Amendment Debate, 1923-1963," *South Atlantic Quarterly*, 81 (Spring 1982), 154-56. Mary R. Beard participated in the early meeting to draft the charter but did not, ultimately, sign it. I thank Nancy Cott for clarification on this point.

58. Susan Ware, *Beyond Suffrage: Women in the New Deal* (Cambridge, Mass., 1981), 156-57.

59. Vivien Hart, "Watch What We Do: Women Administrators and the Implementation of Minimum Wage Policy, Washington, D.C., 1918-1923," paper delivered at the Berkshire Conference on the History of Women, 1990, p. 31 (in Gordon's possession).

60. Gordon, "What Does Welfare Regulate?"; Barbara Nelson, "The Origins of the Two-Channel Welfare State: Workmen's Compensation and Mothers' Aid," in *Women, the State, and Welfare*, ed. Gordon, 123-57.

61. Brady, "Kansas Federation of Colored Women's Clubs"; Lindsay, "Some Contributions of Negroes to Welfare Services," 15-24; Constance Greene, *The Secret City: A History of Race Relations in the Nation's Capital* (Princeton, 1967), 144-46; Neverdon-Morton, *Afro-American Women of the South*; Neverdon-Morton, "Self-Help Programs as Educative Activities of Black Women in the South"; Farley, "Caring and Sharing since World War I," esp. 4.

62. Mary Church Terrell, "Club Work among Women," *New York Age*, Jan. 4, 1900, p. 1. Although this speech was given in 1900, another given in 1928 uses virtually the same rhetoric. See Mary Church Terrell, "Progress and Problems of Colored Women," *Boston Evening Transcript*, Dec. 15, 1928, folder 132, box 102-4, Mary Church Terrell Papers (Moorland-Spingarn Research Collection).

63. For just a few examples, see Elise Johnson McDougald, "The Task of Negro Womanhood," in *The New Negro: An Interpretation*, ed. Alain Locke (New York, 1925), 369-84; Mary Church Terrell, "Up-To-Date," *Norfolk Journal and Guide*, Nov. 3, 1927, folder W, box 102-2, Terrell Papers; Williams, "Opportunities and Responsibilities of Colored Women"; and many speeches by Slowe, box 90-6, Slowe Papers. See also Perkins, *Black Feminism and "Race Uplift."*

64. Williams, "Opportunities and Responsibilities of Colored Women," 150.

65. White, "Fettered Sisterhood"; Hine, "Rape and the Inner Lives of Black Women in the Middle West." White reformers' rhetoric about protecting women named prostitution, not rape, as the problem. See Ellen DuBois and Linda Gordon, "Seeking Ecstasy on the Battlefield: Nineteenth-Century Feminist Views of Sexuality," *Feminist Studies*, 9 (Spring 1983), 7-25; Lillian Wald, "The Immigrant Young Girl," in *Proceedings of the National Conference of Charities and Correction at the Thirty-sixth Annual Session Held in the City of Buffalo, N.Y., June 9th to 16th, 1909* (Fort Wayne, n.d.), 264. Jane Edna Hunter, *A Nickel and a Prayer* (Cleveland, 1940); Marilyn Dell Brady, "Organizing Afro-American Girls' Clubs in Kansas in the 1920s," *Frontiers*, 9 (no. 2, 1987), 69-73; Greene, *Secret City*, 144-46; Salem, *To*

Better Our World, 44-46; Scott, "Most Invisible of All," 15; Monroe N. Work, "Problem of Negro Urban Welfare" (from *Southern Workman*, Jan. 1924) in *Black Heritage in Social Welfare*, ed. Ross, 383-84; "Foreword" (from *Bulletin of National League on Urban Conditions among Negroes*, Report 1912-13), *ibid.*, 241; Guichard Parris and Lester Brooks, *Blacks in the City: A History of the National Urban League* (Boston, 1971), 3-10; Hine, "'We Specialize in the Wholly Impossible,'" 73.

66. Evelyn Brooks, "Religion, Politics, and Gender: The Leadership of Nannie Helen Burroughs," *Journal of Religious Thought*, 44 (Winter/Spring 1988), 7-22; Cheryl Townsend Gilkes, "Building in Many Places: Multiple Commitments and Ideologies in Black Women's Community Work," in *Work and the Politics of Empowerment*, ed. Ann Bookman and Sandra Morgen (Philadelphia, 1988), 53-76.

67. White, "Fettered Sisterhood," 5.

68. Mrs. N. F. Mossell, *The Work of the Afro-American Woman* (1894; reprint, Freeport, 1971), 32. Ida Wells-Barnett is the woman most associated with this challenge to Booker T. Washington, but she was not included in this sample because she was primarily a civil rights, rather than a welfare, activist. On Anna J. Cooper, see Sharon Harley, "Anna J. Cooper: A Voice for Black Women," in *Afro-American Woman*, ed. Harley and Terborg-Penn, 87-96; and Louise Daniel Hutchinson, *Anna J. Cooper: A Voice from the South* (Washington, 1981). On Mary Church Terrell, see Dorothy Sterling, *Black Foremothers* (New York, 1979); and Elliott Rudwick, *W. E. B. Du Bois: Voice of the Black Protest Movement* (Urbana, 1982), 129-30.

69. Williams, "Opportunities and Responsibilities of Colored Women," 157.

70. Story told in Lerner, *Black Women*, 375-76. On the complexity of Brown's attitudes, see Tera Hunter, "'The Correct Thing'"; and Smith and West, "Charlotte Hawkins Brown."

71. Anna J. Cooper to A. G. Comings, Oct 1, 1928, folder 5, box 32-1, Anna J. Cooper Papers (Moorland-Spingarn Research Collection). Cooper was another one of those figures who tirelessly challenged racism even in its apparently small or accidental varieties. For example, she wrote to the *Atlantic Monthly* complaining about an article mentioning a poor Negro with lice. *Atlantic Monthly* editors to Cooper, Jan. 31, 1935, folder 5, box 23-1, *ibid.*

72. Hine, "'We Specialize in the Wholly Impossible'"; Evelyn Brooks Barnett, "Nannie Burroughs and the Education of Black Women," in *Afro-American Woman*, ed. Harley and Terborg-Penn, 97-108; Brooks, "Religion, Politics, and Gender," 12.

73. Burroughs, speech at Bethel AME Church in Baltimore, reported in "Baptists May Oust Nannie H. Burroughs," *Chicago Defender*, Sept. 9, 1939; "Nannie Burroughs Refuses to Speak on National Christian Mission," *Pittsburgh Courier*, Feb. 1, 1941, Burroughs Vertical File (Moorland-Spingarn Research Collection).

74. Burroughs's 1943 remark is quoted in Lerner, *Black Women*, 552.

75. On criticism of Bethune, see B. Joyce Ross, "Mary McLeod Bethune and the National Youth Administration: A Case Study of Power Relationships in the Black Cabinet of Franklin D. Roosevelt," *Journal of Negro History*, 60 (Jan. 1975), 1-28. On her defense of the New Deal, see Mary McLeod Bethune, "'I'll Never Turn Back No More!'" *Opportunity*, 16 (Nov. 1938), 324-26; "Mrs. Bethune Praises NYA Courses as 'Bright Ray of Hope for Rural Negroes,'" *Black Dispatch*, May 1, 1937, Bethune Vertical File (Moorland-Spingarn Research Collection); "Mrs. Bethune Hails Achievements of the New Deal," *Washington Tribune*, Nov. 12, 1935, *ibid.*;

"55,000 Aided by the NYA Program, Says Dr. Bethune," *Washington Tribune*, April 23, 1938, *ibid.* On her picketing, see photo and caption, "Give US More Jobs," *Washington Afro-American*, Aug. 12, 1939, *ibid.*

76. Corrinne Robinson to Jeanetta Welch Brown, with script of *Lazy Daisy* enclosed, Sept. 22, 1943, folder 274, box 17, series 5, National Council of Negro Women Papers.

77. Era Bell Thompson, "A Message from a Mahogany Blond," *Negro Digest*, 9 (July 1950), 31.

78. White, "Fettered Sisterhood"; Smith and West, "Charlotte Hawkins Brown," 199.

79. I am in sympathy with Cott's critique of the use of the concept "social feminism," but it remains descriptive of a widely understood phenomenon, and we have as yet no term to substitute. Nancy F. Cott, "What's in a Name? The Limits of 'Social Feminism'; or Expanding the Vocabulary of Women's History," *Journal of American History*, 76 (Dec. 1989), 809-29.

80. Sybil Lipschultz, "Social Feminism and Legal Discourse: 1908-1923," *Yale Journal of Law and Feminism*, 2 (Fall 1989), 131-60.

81. Linda Gordon, *Heroes of Their Own Lives: The Politics and History of Family Violence, Boston, 1880-1960* (New York, 1988), 82-115.

82. Florence Kelley, "Minimum-Wage Laws," *Journal of Political Economy*, 20 (Dec. 1912), 1003.

83. See, for examples, Roth, "Matronage," 87; Brady, "Kansas Federation of Colored Women's Clubs," 19-31; and Marilyn Dell Brady, "Organizing Afro-American Girls' Clubs in Kansas in the 1920s," *Frontiers*, 9 (no. 2, 1987), 69-73.

84. Lucy D. Slowe, "Some Problems of Colored Women and Girls in the Urban Process" [probably 1930s], folder 143, box 90-6, Slowe Papers.

85. Ardie Clark Halyard interview by Greenlee, Aug. 24, 25, 1978, transcript, p. 15, Black Women Oral History Project.

86. Dorothy Boulding Ferebee interview by Merze Tate, Dec. 28-31, 1979, transcript, p. 9, *ibid.*; Lindsay interview, 4-5.

87. Sharon Harley, "For the Good of Family and Race: Gender, Work, and Domestic Roles in the Black Community, 1880-1930," *Signs*, 15 (Winter 1990), 336-49; Helen A. Cook, "The Work of the Woman's League, Washington D.C.," in *Some Efforts of American Negroes for Their Own Social Betterment*, ed. W. E. B. Du Bois (Atlanta, 1898), 57; Du Bois, ed., *Efforts for Social Betterment Among Negro Americans*, 119-20, 126-27; Giddings, *When and Where I Enter*, 100-101; Hine, *When the Truth Is Told*, 52-54; Ross, ed., *Black Heritage in Social Welfare*, 233-34; Perkins, *Black Feminism and "Race Uplift,"* 7-8; Allan Spear, *Black Chicago: The Making of a Ghetto, 1890-1920* (Chicago, 1967), 102; Stehno, "Public Responsibility for Dependent Black Children"; Harley, "Beyond the Classroom," 254-65; Rouse, *Lugenia Burns Hope*, 28; Davis, *Black Americans in Cleveland*, 195; Stetson, "Black Feminism in Indiana"; Green, *Secret City*, 144-46; Mary Church Terrell, *A Colored Woman in a White World* (Washington, 1940), 153.

88. The white reformers in the first decades of the twentieth century were campaigning hard for mothers' pensions and feared that daytime child care would be used as an alternative, forcing mothers into poor jobs. But they continued to see mothers' employment as a misfortune. For example, Florence Kelley in 1909 argued that day nurseries should be acceptable only for temporary emergencies and that the social cost of mothers' employment was always too high. "A friend of mine has conceived the monstrous idea of having a night nursery to which women so employed might

send their children. And this idea was seriously described in so modern a publication as Charities and the Commons . . . without a word of editorial denunciation." Florence Kelley, "The Family and the Woman's Wage," *Proceedings of the National Conference of Charities and Correction . . . 1909*, pp. 118-21.

89. Giddings, *When and Where I Enter*, 205.

90. Barnett, "Nannie Burroughs and the Education of Black Women." For Elizabeth Ross Haynes's statement of 1922, see Lerner, *Black Women*, 260.

91. Giddings, *When and Where I Enter*, 196.

92. My discussion of Walker is based on Elsa Barkley Brown, "Womanist Consciousness: Maggie Lena Walker and the Independent Order of Saint Luke," *Signs*, 14 (Spring 1989), 610-33. On the significance of black banks and other businesses, see also Du Bois, *Economic Cooperation among Negro Americans*, 103-81. Hedgeman, *Trumpet Sounds*, 47-48; *Who's Who in Colored America* (New York, 1927), 209; Hine, "'We Specialize in the Wholly Impossible,'" 86; Hine, *When the Truth Is Told*, 51.

93. This orientation toward entitlement was evident *despite* the southern state governments' relatively smaller size, and it casts some doubt on state capacity explanations for reformers' strategies.

94. Although many of the Afro-American women leaders were legally married, it does not necessarily follow that they lived their daily lives in close partnerships with their husbands or carried much domestic labor responsibility.

95. Gordon, "What Does Welfare Regulate?"

28

Discontented Black Feminists:

Prelude and Postscript to the Passage of the Nineteenth Amendment

Rosalyn Terborg-Penn

A significant number of black women and black women's organizations not only supported woman suffrage on the eve of the passage of the Nineteenth Amendment but attempted to exercise their rights to vote immediately after the amendment's passage in 1920. Unfortunately for them, black women confronted racial discrimination in their efforts to support the amendment and to win the vote. Consequently, discontented black feminists anticipated the disillusionment that their white counterparts encountered after 1920. An examination of the problems black women faced on the eve of the passage of the woman suffrage amendment and the hostility black women voters endured after the amendment passed serves as a preview of their political status from 1920 to 1945.

The way in which black women leaders dealt with these problems reveals the unique nature of feminism among Afro-American women. Black feminists could not overlook the reality of racism and class conflict as determining factors in the lives of women of their race. Hence, black feminists of the post-World War I era exhibited characteristics similar to those of black feminists of the woman suffrage era and of the late nineteenth-century black women's club movement. During each era, these feminists could not afford to dismiss class or race in favor of sex as the major cause of oppression among black women.

Prelude to Passage of the Nineteenth Amendment

On the eve of the passage of the Nineteenth Amendment, black women leaders could be counted among other groups of women who had worked diligently for woman suffrage. At least ninety black women leaders endorsed woman suffrage, with two-thirds of these women giving support during the decade immediately before passage of the amendment. Afro-American women organized suffrage clubs, participated in rallies and demonstrations, spoke on behalf of the amendment, and wrote essays in support of the cause. These things they had done since the inception of the nineteenth-century woman's rights movement. However, the largest woman suffrage effort among black women's groups occurred during the second decade of the twentieth century. Organizations such as the National Federation of Afro-American Women, the National Association of Colored Women (NACW), the Northeastern Federation of Colored Women's Clubs, the Alpha Kappa Alpha Sorority, and the Delta Sigma Theta Sorority actively supported woman suffrage. These organizations were national or regional in scope and represented thousands of Afro-American women. Some of the women were from the working class, but most of them were of middle-class status. Across the nation, at least twenty black woman suffrage organizations or groups that strongly endorsed woman suffrage existed during the period.[1]

Three examples provide an indication of the diversity in types of woman suffrage activities among black women's organizations. In 1915 the Poughkeepsie, New York, chapter of the Household of Ruth, a working-class, black women's group, endorsed woman suffrage by sending a resolution to the New York branch of the National Woman's Party (NWP) in support of the pending state referendum on woman suffrage. With the need for an intelligent female electorate in mind, black women of Texas organized voter leagues in 1917, the year Texas women won the right to vote. Among these was the Negro Women Voters' League of Galveston. Furthermore, in 1919, the Northeastern Federation of Colored Women's Clubs, representing thousands of women from Montreal to Baltimore, petitioned the National American Woman Suffrage Association (NAWSA) for membership.[2]

The enthusiastic responses of black women to woman suffrage may seem astonishing when one realizes that woman suffrage was a predominately middle-class movement among native born white women and that the black middle class was very small during the early twentieth century. Furthermore, the heyday of the woman suffrage movement embraced an era that historian Rayford Logan called "the nadir" in Afro-American history, characterized by racial segregation, defamation of the character of black women, and lynching of black Americans, both men and women. It is a wonder that Afro-American women dared to dream a white man's dream—the right to enfranchisement—especially at a time when white women attempted to exclude them from that dream.[3]

The existence of a double standard for black and white women among white woman suffragists was apparent to black women on the eve of Nineteenth Amendment passage. Apprehensions from discontented black leaders about the inclusion of black women as voters, especially in the South, were evident throughout the second decade of the twentieth century. During the early years of the decade, black suffragists such as Adella Hunt Logan, a club leader and suffragist from Tuskegee, Alabama; Mary B. Talbert, president of the National Association of Colored Women; and Josephine St. Pierre Ruffin, a suffragist since the 1880s from Boston and the editor of the *Woman's Era*, a black women's newspaper, complained about the double standard in the woman suffrage movement and insisted that white suffragists set aside their prejudices to allow black women, burdened by both sexism and racism, to gain political equality.[4]

Unfortunately, with little influence among white women, the black suffragists were powerless and their words went unheeded. By 1916 Carrie Catt, president of the NAWSA, concluded that the South had to be conciliated if woman suffrage was to become a reality. Thus, in order to avoid antagonizing southern white women who resented participating in the association with black women, she urged southern white delegates not to attend the NAWSA convention in Chicago that year because the Chicago delegation would be mostly black.[5]

The trend to discriminate against black women as voters continued, and in 1917 the *Crisis*, the official organ of the National Association for the Advancement of Colored People (NAACP), noted that blacks feared white female voters because of their antiblack woman suffrage and antiblack male sentiments. Afro-American fears went beyond misgivings about white women. In 1918 the editors of the *Houston Observer* responded to black disillusionment when they called upon the men and women of the race to register to vote in spite of the poll tax, which was designed especially to exclude black voters.[6]

Skepticism about equality of woman suffrage among blacks continued. Mrs. A. W. Blackwell, an African Methodist Episcopal church leader in Atlanta, estimated that about 3 million black women were of voting age. She warned, however, that a "grandmother clause" would be introduced after passage of a suffrage amendment to prevent black women, 90 percent of whom lived in the South, from voting.[7]

Disillusionment among black suffragists became so apparent that several national suffrage leaders attempted to appease them with reassurances about their commitment to black woman suffrage. In 1917 Carrie Catt and Anna Shaw wooed black female support through the pages of the *Crisis*. In the District of Columbia, the same year, Congresswoman Jeannette Rankin of Montana addressed an enthusiastic group of Alpha Kappa Alpha Sorority women at Howard University. There she assured the group that she wanted all women to be given the ballot regardless of race.[8]

However, in 1917 while the New York state woman suffrage referendum was pending in the legislature, black suffragists in the state complained of discrimination against their organizations by white suffragists during the statewide woman suffrage convention at Saratoga. White leaders assured black women that they were welcomed by the movement. Although the majority of the black delegates were conciliated, a vocal minority remained disillusioned.[9]

By 1919, the year before the Nineteenth Amendment was adopted by Congress, antiblack woman suffrage sentiments continued to plague the movement. Shortly before the amendment was adopted, several incidents occurred to further disillusion black feminists. Mary Church Terrell, a Washington, D.C., educator and national leader among black club women, reported that white suffragists in Florida discriminated against black women in their attempts to recruit support for the campaign. In addition, the NAACP, whose policy officially endorsed woman suffrage, clashed with Alice Paul, president of the NWP, because she allegedly said, "that all this talk of Negro women voting in South Carolina was nonsense."[10] Later, Walter White, the NAACP's assistant to the executive secretary, complained to Mary Church Terrell about Alice Paul and agreed with Terrell that white suffrage leaders would be willing to accept the suffrage amendment even if it did not enfranchise black women.[11]

Within a week after receiving Walter White's letter, Mary Church Terrell received a letter from Ida Husted Harper, a leader in the suffrage movement and the editor of the last two volumes of *The History of Woman Suffrage*, asking Terrell to use her influence to persuade the Northeastern Federation of Colored Women's Clubs to withdraw their application seeking cooperative membership in the NAWSA. Echoing sentiments expressed earlier by NAWSA president Carrie Catt, Harper explained that accepting the membership of a black organization was inexpedient for NAWSA at a time when white suffragists sought the cooperation of white southern women. Harper noted that the major obstacle to the amendment in the South was fear among whites of the black woman's vote. She therefore asked federation president Elizabeth Carter to resubmit the membership application after the passage of the Nineteenth Amendment.[12]

At its Jubilee Convention in Saint Louis in March 1919, the NAWSA officially catered to the fears of their southern white members. In response to a proposal by Kentucky suffragist Laura Clay that sections of the so-called Susan B. Anthony amendment that would permit the enfranchisement of black women be changed, the convention delegates agreed that the amendment should be worded so as to allow the South to determine its own position on the black female vote.[13]

During the last months before the passage of the Susan B. Anthony amendment, black suffragists had been rebuffed by both the conservative wing of the suffrage movement, the NAWSA, and by the more radical wing, the NWP. Why then did Afro-American women continue to push for woman suffrage? Since the 1880s, most black women who supported woman suffrage did so because they believed that political equality among the races would raise the status of blacks, both male and female. Increasing the black electorate, they felt, would not only uplift the women of the race, but help the children and the men as well. The majority of the black suffragists were not radical feminists. They were reformers, or what William H. Chafe calls social feminists, who believed that the system could be amended to work for them. Like their white counterparts, these black suffragists assumed that the enfranchised held the key to ameliorating social ills. But unlike white social feminists, many black suffragists called for social and political measures that were specifically tied to race issues. Among these issues were antimiscegenation legislation, jim crow legislation, and "lynch law." Prominent black feminists combined the fight against sexism with the fight against racism by continuously calling the public's attention to these issues. Ida B. Wells-Barnett, Angelina Weld Grimké, and Mary Church Terrell spoke out against lynching. Josephine St. Pierre Ruffin and Lottie Wilson Jackson, as well as Terrell and Wells-Barnett took steps to challenge jim crow facilities in public accommodations, and antimiscegenation legislation was impugned by Terrell, Grimké, and Wells-Barnett.[14]

Blacks understood the potential political influence, if not political power, that they could harness with woman suffrage, especially in the South. White supremacists realized it too. Although there were several reasons for southern opposition to the Nineteenth Amendment, the one common to all states was fear of black female suffrage. This fear had been stimulated by the way in which Afro-American women responded to suffrage in states that had achieved woman suffrage before the passage of the federal amendment. In northern states with large black populations, such as Illinois and New York, the black female electorate was significant. Chicago elected its first black alderman, Oscar De Priest, in 1915, the year after women won the right to vote. In 1917, the year the woman suffrage referendum passed the New York state legislature, New York City elected its first black state assemblyperson, Edward A. Johnson. In both cities the black female vote was decisive in the election. In the South, Texas Afro-American women mobilized in 1918 to effectively educate the women of their race in order to combat white opposition to their voting.[15]

By 1920 white southern apprehensions of a viable black female electorate were not illusionary. "Colored women voter's leagues" were growing throughout the South, where the task of the leagues was to give black women seeking to qualify to vote instructions for countering white opposition. Leagues could be found in Alabama, Georgia, Tennessee, and Texas. These groups were feared also by white supremacists because the women sought to qualify black men as voters as well.[16]

Whites widely believed that black women wanted the ballot more than white women in the South. Black women were expected to register and to vote in larger numbers than white women. If this happened, the ballot would soon be returned to black men. Black suffrage, it was believed, would also result in the return of the two-party system in the South, because blacks would consistently vote Republican. These apprehensions were realized in Florida after the passage of the Nineteenth Amendment. Black women in Jacksonville registered in greater numbers than white women. In reaction, the Woman Suffrage League of Jacksonville was reorganized into the Duval County League of Democratic Women Voters. The members were dedicated to maintain white supremacy and pledged to register white women voters.[17]

In Texas, where women could vote before the passage of the Nineteenth Amendment, black women, nevertheless, were discriminated against. In 1918 six black women had been refused the right to register at Forth Worth on the ground that the primaries were open to white Democrats only. Efforts to disfranchise black women in Houston failed, however, when the women took legal action against the registrars who attempted to apply the Texas woman suffrage law to white women only. A similar attempt to disqualify Afro-American women in Waxahachie, Texas, failed also.[18]

Subterfuge and trickery such as the kind used in Texas were being used throughout the South by 1920. In North Carolina, the predictions of Mrs. A. W. Blackwell came true when the state legislature introduced a bill known as the "grandmother clause" for women voters. The bill attempted to protect illiterate white women from disfranchisement, but the legislators had not taken into account that "grandfather clauses" had been nullified by the Supreme Court. Nonetheless, black leaders called to the women of the race to stand up and fight. This they did.[19]

In 1920 black women registered in large numbers throughout the South, especially in Georgia and Louisiana, despite major obstacles placed against them by the white supremacists. In defense, Afro-American women often turned to the NAACP for assistance. Field Secretary William Pickens was sent to investigate the numerous charges and recorded several incidents which he either witnessed personally or about which he received reports. In Columbia, South Carolina, during the first day of registration black women apparently took the registrars by surprise. No plan to disqualify them had been put into effect. Many black women reported to the office and had to wait for hours while the white women were registered first. Some women waited up to twelve hours to register. The next day, a $300 tax requirement was made mandatory for black women. If they passed that test, the women were required to read from and to interpret the state or the federal constitutions. No such tests were required of white women. In addition, white lawyers were on hand to quiz and harass black women. Although the *Columbia State*, a local newspaper, reported disinterest in registering among black women, Pickens testified to the contrary. By the end of the registration period, twenty Columbia black women had signed an affidavit against the registrars who had disqualified them. In the surrounding Richland County, Afro-American women were disqualified when they attempted to register to vote. As a result, several of them made plans to appeal the ruling.[20]

Similar reports came from Richmond, Virginia, where registrars attempted to deny or successfully denied black women the right to register. A black woman of Newburn, North Carolina, signed an affidavit testifying to the difficulty she had in attempting to register. First she was asked to read and to write the entire state constitution. After successfully reading the document, she was informed that no matter what else she did, the registrar would disqualify her because she was black. Many cases like this one were handled by the NAACP, and after the registration periods ended in the South, its board of directors presented the evidence to Congress. NAACP officials and others testified at a congressional hearing in support of the proposed enactment of the Tinkham Bill to reduce representation in Congress from states where there was restriction of woman suffrage. White supremacy prevailed, however, as southern congressmen successfully claimed that blacks were not disfranchised, just disinterested in voting. Hence, despite the massive evidence produced by the NAACP, the Tinkham Bill failed to pass.[21]

The inability of the NAACP to protect the rights of black women voters led the women to seek help from national woman suffrage leaders. However, these attempts failed also. The NWP leadership felt that since black women were discriminated against in the same ways as black men, their problems were not woman's rights issues, but race issues. Therefore, the woman's party felt no obligation to defend the rights of black women.[22]

That they would be abandoned by white female suffragists in 1920 came as no surprise to most black women leaders. The preceding decade of woman suffrage politics had reminded them of the assertions of black woman suffrage supporters of the past. Frederick Douglass declared in 1868 that black women were victimized mainly because they were blacks, not because they were women. Frances Ellen Watkins Harper answered in 1869 that for white women the priorities in the struggle for human rights were sex, not race. By 1920 the situation had changed very little, and many black suffragists had been thoroughly disillusioned by the machinations of the white feminists they had encountered.[23]

Postscript—Black Feminists, 1920-1945

Afro-American Women continued to be involved in local and national politics during the post-World War I years. However, few organized feminist activities were apparent among the disillusioned black feminists of the period. Afro-American women leaders and their organizations began to focus on issues that continued to plague both the men and the women of the race, rather than upon issues that concerned white feminists. The economic plight of black women kept most of them in poverty and among the lowest of the working classes. Middle-class black women were still relatively few in number. They were more concerned about uplifting the downtrodden of the race or in representing people of color throughout the world than in issues that were limited to middle-class feminists. Hence, during the 1920s there was little concern among black women over the Equal Rights Amendment debate between the more conservative League of Women Voters (LWV) and the more radical NWP. Although the economic roles of many white American women were expanding, the status of black women remained basically static between the wars. As a result, black feminists identified more with the plight of Third World people who found themselves in similar oppressed situations. Former black suffragists were more likely to participate in the Women's International League for Peace and Freedom (WILPF) or the International Council of Women of the Darker Races than in the LWV or the NWP.

In 1920 Howard University professor Benjamin Brawley examined the economic status of black women. He found that there were over 1 million black females in the United States work force in 1910. Fifty-two percent of them worked as farmers or farm laborers, and 28 percent worked as cooks or washerwomen. In essence, 80 percent of black women workers were doing arduous, menial work. Brawley speculated that conditions had not changed much by 1920.[24] In 1922 black social worker Elizabeth Ross Haynes found that 2 million black women in the nation worked in three types of occupations: domestic and personal service, agriculture, and manufacturing and mechanical industries. Of the 2 million, 50 percent were found in domestic service. Only 20,000 were found in semiskilled jobs in manufacturing and mechanical industries. Haynes's findings in 1922 were in keeping with Brawley's speculations.[25]

Unfortunately, by 1945 the position of black women in the work force had not changed significantly. Black women ranked lowest on the economic scale among men and women, black and white.

Geographically, during the period, the black population was shifting from the rural South to the urban North and West. Nearly 90 percent of the adult black female population lived in the South in 1920. By 1930 less than 80 percent of that population did. In 1940 the percentage had dropped to nearly 75 percent.[26] Even with this drop, however, three-fourths of the adult black women of the nation remained in the South, where they were virtually disfranchised. The black women who found their way north and west lacked the political influence necessary to change the status of black women because of their economic powerlessness. What temporary gains black women made in World War I industry quickly faded away during the postwar years.

In 1935 the average weekly wage for a black domestic worker was $3.00 and washerwomen received a mere 75 cents a week. Working conditions, as well as wages, were substandard, and black women were exploited by white women as well as by white men. In observing the working conditions of New York City domestic workers, Louise Mitchell found that standards had not changed much by 1940. Some women worked for as little as $2.00 a week and as long as 80 hours a week. Mitchell noted Women's Bureau findings that indicated that women took domestic work only as a last resort. She concluded that black women were the most oppressed of the working classes.[27]

As the United States entered World War II, black women found more opportunities in industry. However, jobs available to black women were the ones for which white workers were not available. War industry jobs were often found in urban centers outside of the South. Consequently, the majority remained outside of the mainstream of feminist consciousness because feminist interests were not their interest, and those black feminists of the woman suffrage era found little comfort from white feminists. Several of the black feminists of the woman suffrage era remained in leadership positions during the 1920s and the 1930s, while others faded from the scene. In addition, new faces became associated with black female leadership. Among these were Amy Jacques Garvey and Mary McLeod Bethune. Although all of these women either identified themselves or have been identified as feminists, their major concerns between the world wars were racial issues, with the status of black women as a major priority.

A look at the 1920s reveals that most of the black women's organizations that were prominent during the woman suffrage era remained so. Nonetheless, new groups were organized as well. Elizabeth Carter remained president of the Northeastern Federation of Colored Women's Clubs, which celebrated its twenty-fifth anniversary in 1921. The leadership of the NACW was in transition during the 1920s. Mary B. Talbert retired as president and was succeeded by a former suffragist, Hallie Q. Brown, in 1922. In the middle of the decade Mary McLeod Bethune assumed the presidency. In 1922 several NACW leaders organized the International Council of Women of the Darker Races.

Margaret Murray Washington, the wife of the late Booker T. Washington and the first president of the National Federation of Afro-American Women, was elected president.[28]

In addition to these established black women's organizations, there was the women's arm of Marcus Garvey's United Negro Improvement Association (UNIA). At its peak, in 1925, the UNIA had an estimated membership of 2 million and can be considered the first mass movement among working-class black people in the nation. Amy Jacques Garvey, Marcus Garvey's wife, was the articulate leader of the women's division and the editor of the women's department of the UNIA official newspaper, *Negro World*. A feminist in the international sense, Amy Jacques Garvey's feminist views embraced the class struggle as well as the problems of Third World women. A black nationalist, Garvey encouraged women of color throughout the world to organize for the benefit of themselves as well as their own people. Although she gave credit to the old-line black women's clubs, Garvey felt their approach to the problems of Third World women was limited. A Jamaican by birth, she called for revolutionary strategies that did not merely reflect the reform ideas of white middle-class women. Instead Garvey called upon the masses of black women in the United States to acknowledge that they were the "burden bearers of their race" and to take the lead in fighting for black independence from white oppression. Amy Jacques Garvey combined the UNIA belief in the power of the black urban working class with the feminist belief that women could think and do for themselves. The revolutionary implications of her ideas are reflected in the theme of the women's pages of *Negro World*—"Our Women and What They Think." Garvey called for black women's dedication to social justice and to national liberation, abroad as well as at home.[29]

Garvey was a radical who happened to be a feminist as well. Her views were ahead of her time; thus, she would have fit in well with the mid-twentieth century radical feminists. However, the demise of the UNIA and the deportation of Marcus Garvey in 1927 shattered much of Amy Jacques Garvey's influence in the United States and she returned to Jamaica. In the meantime, the majority of black feminists of the 1920s either joined the white social feminists, such as Jane Addams and the WILPF, or bypassed the feminists altogether to deal with race issues within black organizations.

The leadership of the WILPF was old-line and can be characterized as former progressives, woman suffragists, and social feminists. Jane Addams presided over the organization before U.S. entry into World War I and brought black women such as Mary Church Terrell, Mary B. Talbert, Charlotte Atwood, Mary F. Waring, and Addie W. Hunton into the fold. Terrell had been a member of the executive committee since 1915. As a league representative, she was elected a delegate to the International Congress of Women held in Paris in 1919. Upon her arrival, Terrell was impressed with the conference delegates but noticed that there were none from non-western countries and that she was the only delegate of color in the group. As a result, she felt obligated to represent the women of all the nonwhite countries in the world, and this she attempted to do. At the conference meeting in Zurich, Switzerland, Terrell agreed to represent the American delegation and did so by speaking in German before the largely German-speaking audience. In addition, she submitted her own personal resolution to the conference, despite attempts by American committee members to change her wording. "We believe no human being should be deprived of an education, prevented from earning a living, debarred from any legitimate pursuit in which he wishes to engage or be subjected to humiliations of various kinds on account of race, color or creed."[30] Terrell's position and thinking were in keeping with the growing awareness among black women leaders in the United States that Third World people needed to fight oppression together.

Although Mary Church Terrell remained an active social feminist, her public as well as private views reflected the disillusionment of black feminists of the woman suffrage era. In 1921 she was asked by members of the WILPF executive committee to sign a petition requesting the removal of black troops from occupied German territory, where they were alleged to be violating German women. Terrell refused to sign the petition because she felt the motives behind it were racist. In a long letter to Jane Addams, the executive committee chairman, Terrell explained why she would not sign the petition. She noted that Carrie Catt had investigated the charges against the black troops and found them to be unfounded. The troops, from French colonies in Africa, were victims, Terrell contended, of American propaganda against black people. Making a dramatic choice between the feminist organization position and her own loyalty to her race, Terrell offered to resign from the executive committee. Addams wrote her back, agreeing with Terrell's position and asking her not to resign.[31] In this case, when given the choice between the politics of feminism and the race pride, Terrell felt that her energies were needed to combat racism, and she chose to take a national position in the controversy.

Several other attempts were made at interracial cooperation among women's groups during the early 1920s, but most of these efforts were white-dominated and short-lived. An exception was the Cooperative Women's League of Baltimore, founded in 1913 by Sarah C. Fernandis. This group maintained relations with white women's civic leagues in connection with local health and sanitation, home economics, art, and education projects. In 1925 the league initiated its twelfth annual program.[32] This organization was quite conventional, a far cry from feminist—black or white. However, the activities were, like most black women's group activities of the times, geared to strengthen local black communities.

Other black-white cooperative ventures on a grander scale included the Commission on Inter-Racial Cooperation of the Women's Council of the Methodist Episcopal Church South. In October 1920 the commission held a conference on race relations. Only four black women were invited and they were selected because of their husbands' prominence, rather than for their feminist views. The conference pledged a responsibility to uplift the status of black women in the South, calling for a reform of the conditions under which black domestics worked in white homes. The delegates passed resolutions supporting improved sanitation and housing for blacks, fair treatment of blacks in public accommodations, the prevention of lynching, and justice in the courts. Significantly, no mention of protecting black women's suffrage was made. Several months later, the National Federation of Colored Women's Clubs met at Tuskegee, Alabama, and issued a statement that seemed to remind the Methodist Episcopal women of their pledge and called for increased cooperation and understanding from southern white women. Interestingly, the black women included suffrage in their resolution.[33]

Nothing came of this attempt at interracial cooperation, for neither the social nor the economic status of black women improved in the South during the 1920s. The trend toward interracial cooperation continued nevertheless, and in 1922 the YWCA appointed a joint committee of black and white women to study race problems. Once, again, only four black women were invited to participate. Principles were declared, but little came of the gathering.[34]

In the meantime, most black women's organizations had turned from attempts to establish coalitions with white women's groups to concentrate upon pressing race problems. Lynching was one of the major American problems, and black women organized to fight it. On the national front, black women's groups used political strategies and concentrated their efforts toward passage of the Dyer Anti-Lynching Bill. In 1922 the Northeastern Federation of Colored Women's Clubs appointed a delegation to call on Senator Lodge of Massachusetts to urge passage of the Dyer bill. In addition, the Alpha Kappa Alpha Sorority held its national convention in Indianapolis and sent a telegram to President Warren Harding urging the support of his administration in the passage of the bill. Also that year, the NACW met in Richmond and appointed an antilynching delegation to make contact with key states needed for the passage of the Dyer bill in Congress. In addition, the delegation was authorized to meet with President Harding. Among the black women in the delegation were veteran antilynching crusader Ida B. Wells-Barnett, NACW president Hallie Q. Brown, and Rhode Island suffragist Mary B. Jackson.[35]

Perhaps the most renowned antilynching crusader of the 1920s was Spingarn Medal winner Mary B. Talbert. In 1922 she organized an executive committee of 15 black women, who supervised over 700 state workers across the nation in what Talbert called the Anti-Lynching Crusade. Her aim was to "unite a million women to stop lynching," by arousing the consciences of both black and white women. One of Talbert's strategies was to provide statistics that showed that victims of lynching were not what propagandists called sex-hungry black men who preyed upon innocent white women. The crusaders revealed that eighty-three women had been lynched in the United States since Ida B. Wells-Barnett had compiled the first comprehensive report in 1892. The Anti-Lynching Crusade was truly an example of woman power, for the crusaders believed that they could not wait for the men of America to stop the problem. It was perhaps the most influential link in the drive for interracial cooperation among women's groups. As a result of its efforts, the 1922 National Council of Women, representing 13 million American women, resolved to "endorse the Anti-Lynching Crusade recently launched by colored women of this country."[36]

Although the Dyer bill was defeated, it was revised by the NAACP and introduced again in the House of Representatives by Congressman Leonidas C. Dyer of Missouri and in the Senate by William B. McKinley of Illinois in 1926. That year the bill failed again, as did similar bills in 1935, 1940, and 1942. However, it was the effort of blacks and white women organized against lynching that pressed for legislation throughout the period. Without a doubt, it was the leadership of black women, many of whom had been active in the late nineteenth-century women's club movement and in the woman suffrage movement, who motivated white women in 1930 to organize the Association of Southern Women for the Prevention of Lynching. Although a federal antilynching bill never passed the Congress, by the end of the 1940s public opinion had been sufficiently convinced by the efforts of various women's groups that lynching was barbarous and criminal. Recorded incidents of lynching ceased by 1950.

Even though interracial cooperation in the antilynching campaign was a positive factor among black and white women, discrimination against black women by white women continued to plague feminists. In 1925, for example, the Quinquennial of the International Council of Women met at the Washington Auditorium in the District of Columbia. The council sought the cooperation of NACW president Mary McLeod Bethune and arrangements were made to have a mass choir of black women perform. The night of the concert, black guests were placed in a segregated section of the auditorium. Mary Church Terrell reported that when the singers learned of what was happening, they refused to perform. Foreign women delegates were in the audience, as well as white women from throughout the nation. Many of them were angry because the concert had to be cancelled. Terrell felt that this was one of the most unfortunate incidents of discrimination against black women in the club movement. However, she agreed with the decision of her black sisters not to sing.[37]

National recognition of black women did not really come until 1936, when Mary McLeod Bethune was appointed director of the Division of Negro Affairs, National Youth Administration, under the Franklin D. Roosevelt administration. The founder of Bethune-Cookman Institute in Daytona, Florida, Bethune had been a leader in the black women's club movement since the early 1920s. NACW president from 1924 to 1928, she founded the National Council of Negro Women (NCNW) in 1935. What feminist consciousness Bethune acquired was thrust upon her in the mid-1930s because for the first time, a black woman had the ear of the president of the United States and the cooperation of the first lady, who was concerned not only about women's issues, but about black issues. In 1936 Bethune took advantage of her new status and presented the concerns of the NCNW to Eleanor Roosevelt. As a result, sixty-five black women leaders attended a meeting with Eleanor Roosevelt to argue the case for their greater representation and appointments to federal bureaus. They called for appointments of professional black women to the Children's Bureau, the Women's Bureau, and each department of the Bureau of Education that dealt with the welfare of women and children. The NCNW also wanted the appointment of black women to administrative positions in the Federal Housing Administration and Social Security Board. In addition, they called for enlarging the black staff of the Bureau of Public Health and for President Roosevelt to suggest to the American Red Cross that they hire a black administrator.[38]

The NCNW requests reflect two trends among middle-class women in the mid-1930s. First, they were calling for positions that black women had never held, nor would achieve until a generation later; consequently, their ideas were revolutionary ones in terms of federal policies. Second, they were calling for policies to benefit not only their sex, but their race; hence, the NCNW reflected the position established by black feminists a generation before.

Mary McLeod Bethune's leadership was acknowledged by black women's groups throughout the nation, and she accepted the responsibility by referring to herself as the representative of "Negro womanhood." In 1937 she visited the Flanner House, a black settlement house in Indianapolis whose black woman superintendent, Clio Blackburn, said the institution's aim was to help black people help themselves. If no other person represented this standard to black women at this time, Mary McLeod Bethune did. The following year she met with the Alpha Kappa Alpha Sorority in Boston to assist them in a benefit for the Mississippi Health Project, a project to help black people in that region which was sponsored by the national sorority.[39]

Middle-class black women clearly reflected their dedication to uplifting the race at a time when most Afro-Americans were thwarted not only by race prejudice but also by economic depression. Although activities that involved race uplift were not feminist in orientation, many black feminists took an active role in them. In an interview with Mary McLeod Bethune in 1939, Lillian B. Huff of the *New Jersey Herald News* asked her about the role of black women leaders and how Bethune related to her leadership position. Bethune, who had come from humble origins, felt that black women had room in their lives to be wives and mothers as well as to have careers. But most importantly, she thought, black women should think of their duty to the race.[40]

Bethune's feelings were not unique to black women, for most black feminists and leaders had been wives and mothers who worked yet found time not only to struggle for the good of their sex, but for their race. Until the 1970s, however, this threefold commitment—to family and to career and to one or more social movements—was not common among white women. The key to the uniqueness among black feminists of this period appears to be their link with the past. The generation of the woman suffrage era had learned from their late nineteenth-century foremothers in the black women's club movement, just as the generation of the post-World War I era had learned and accepted the experiences of the preceding generation. Theirs was a sense of continuity, a sense of group consciousness that transcended class. Racial uplift, fighting segregation and mob violence, contending with poverty, as well as demanding rights for black women were long-standing issues of concern to black feminists.

The meeting of the National Conference on Problems of the Negro and Youth at Washington, D.C., in 1939 was a good example of this phenomenon among black women. Bethune called the meeting and invited a range of black leaders from Mary Church Terrell and feminist Nannie Burroughs, who were both in their seventies, to Juanita Jackson Mitchell, the conference youth coordinator. The young Mitchell had been a leader among black civil rights activists in the City-Wide Young People's Forum in Baltimore a few years before. Bethune noted the success of the meeting of young and old, all of whom had a common interest in civil rights for Afro-Americans.[41]

By 1940 March Church Terrell had written her autobiography. At the age of seventy-seven, she was one of the few living links with three generations of black feminists. In her introduction, Terrell established her own interpretation of her life story, which in many ways reflected the lives of other black feminists. "This is the story of a colored woman living in a white world. It cannot possibly be like a story written by a white woman. A white woman has only one handicap to overcome—that of sex. I have two—both sex and race. I belong to the only group in this country which has two such huge obstacles to surmount. Colored men have only one—that of race."[42]

Terrell's reference to her status as an Afro-American woman applied throughout United States history to most black women, regardless of class. In view of this, it is not surprising that black women struggled, often in vain, to keep the right to vote from 1920 to 1940. A brief reference to this struggle, a story in itself, reveals that they fought to keep the little influence they had although black feminists anticipated that many of them would lose. Nonetheless, black female enthusiasm was great immediately following the passage of the Nineteenth Amendment. In Baltimore alone, the black electorate increased from 16,800 to over 37,400 in 1921, indicating that the number of black women voters surpassed the number of black men registered to vote. By 1922, however, attempts to thwart the influence of black women voters were spreading across the South. As a result, the NACW recommended that all of its clubs lobby for the enforcement of the Nineteenth Amendment.[43]

By 1924 feminist Nannie Burroughs had assessed the status of black women of voting age and their relationship to white feminists. Burroughs noted that white women continued to overlook or to undervalue the worth of black women as a political force in the nation. She warned white female politicians to tap the potential black female electorate before white men exploited it.[44] With the exception of Ruth Hanna McCormick, who recruited Mary Church Terrell to head her 1929 Illinois campaign for the United States Senate, warnings such as Burroughs's did not seem to influence white female leaders. For example, disillusioned members of the Republican Colored Women

State Committee of Wilmington, Delaware, protested unsuccessfully when they lost their representation on the state Republican committee. A merger of the Women's Advisory Committee, a white group, with the State Central Committee had caused the elimination of black women representatives. The decline in black women's participation in Republican party politics was evident by 1928, when only 8 out of 104 black delegates to the Republican National Convention were women. The same year, the NACW program did not even bother to include suffrage among its priorities for women of the race.[45]

Although President Roosevelt made good his promise to Mary McLeod Bethune, so that by 1945 four black women had received outstanding federal appointments, the political viability of black women in the early 1940s was bleak. The list of black elected officials from 1940 to 1946 included no women.[46] Agents of white supremacy continued to subvert what vestiges of political influence blacks held. For example, in 1942 Congressman Martin Dies, chairman of the congressional committee investigating un-American activities, attempted to link several national black leaders to the Communist party. Among the group was Mary McLeod Bethune, who remained the only black woman prominent in national politics.[47]

Hence, over twenty years after the passage of the Nineteenth Amendment racial discrimination festered in most areas of American life, even among feminists and women in political life. Prejudice did not distinguish between middle-class and working-class black women, nor between feminists and nonfeminists who were black. Although black women continued to use what political rights they maintained, the small number of those politically viable made little impact upon public policies.

NOTES

1. See Rosalyn Terborg-Penn, "Nineteenth Century Black Women and Woman Suffrage," *Potomac Review* 7 (Spring-Summer 1977): 13-24; and Rosalyn M. Terborg-Penn, "Afro-Americans in the Struggle for Woman Suffrage" (Ph.D. dissertation, Howard University, 1977), pp. 180-85.

2. *Indianapolis Freeman*, 28 August 1915; Monroe N. Work, ed., *The Negro Year Book, 1918-1919* (Tuskegee Institute, Ala.: The Negro Year Book Publishing Co., 1919), pp. 57-59 (hereafter cited as *Negro Year Book*, by year); Rosalyn Terborg-Penn, "Discrimination Against Afro-American Women in the Woman's Movement, 1830-1920," *The Afro-American Woman: Struggles and Images*, edited by Sharon Harley and Rosalyn Terborg-Penn (Port Washington, N.Y.: Kennikat Press, 1978), p. 26.

3. See Rayford W. Logan, *The Negro in the United States* (Princeton, N.J.: Van Nostrand, 1957); and Terborg-Penn, "Discrimination Against Afro-American Women," pp. 17-27.

4. Terborg-Penn, "Afro-Americans in the Struggle for Woman Suffrage," chapter 4.

5. David Morgan, *Suffragists and Democrats: The Politics of Woman Suffrage in America* (East Lansing, Mich.: Michigan State University Press, 1972), pp. 106-07.

6. *Crisis* 15 (November 1917): 18; *Negro Year Book, 1918-1919*, p. 60.

7. Mrs. A. W. Blackwell, *The Responsibility and Opportunity of the Twentieth Century Woman* (n.p., n.d.), pp. 1-5. This pamphlet is housed in the Trevor Arnett Library, Atlanta University.

8. *The Crisis* 15 (November 1917): 19-20; *New York Age*, 10 May 1917.

9. *New York Age*, September 20, 1917.

10. Walter White to Mary Church Terrell, 14 March 1919, Mary Church Terrell Papers, Box no. 3, Library of Congress, Washington D.C. (hereafter cited as MCT Papers); Charles Flint Kellogg, *NAACP: A History of the National Association for the Advancement of Colored People, 1909-1920* (Baltimore: Johns Hopkins Press, 1967), p. 208.

11. Walter White to Mary Church Terrell, 14 March 1919, MCT Papers, Box no. 3.

12. Ida Husted Harper to Mary Church Terrell, 18 March 1919, and Ida Harper to Elizabeth Carter, 18 March 1919, MCT Papers, Box no. 3.

13. Aileen Kraditor, *The Ideas of the Woman Suffrage Movement, 1890-1920* (Garden City, N.Y.: Anchor Books, Doubleday and Co., 1971), pp. 168-69; *Crisis* 17 (June 1919): 103; Ida Husted Harper, ed., *The History of Woman Suffrage, 1900-1920* (New York: J. J. Little and Ives Co., 1922), pp. 580-81.

14. Terborg-Penn, "Afro-American in the Struggle for Woman Suffrage," chapters 4 and 5.

15. *Ibid.*, pp. 207, 217-18, 225.

16. *Crisis* 19 (November 1920): 23-25; *Negro Year Book, 1921*, p. 40.

17. Kenneth R. Johnson, "White Racial Attitudes as a Factor in the Arguments Against the Nineteenth Amendment," *Phylon* 31 (Spring 1970): 31-32, 35-37.

18. Terborg-Penn, "Afro-American in the Struggle for Woman Suffrage," pp. 301-02.

19. *Ibid.*, pp. 303-04.

20. William Pickens, "The Woman Voter Hits the Color Line," *Nation* 3 (October 6, 1920): 372-73.

21. *Ibid.*, p. 373; NAACP, *Eleventh Annual Report of the NAACP for the Year 1920* (New York: NAACP, 1921), pp. 15, 25-30.

22. William L. O'Neill, *Everybody Was Brave* (Chicago: Quadrangle Press, 1969), p. 275.

23. Terborg-Penn, "Afro-Americans in the Struggle for Woman Suffrage," p. 311.

24. Benjamin Brawley, *Women of Achievement: Written for the Fireside Schools* (Nashville, Tenn.: Woman's American Baptist Home Mission Society, 1919), pp. 14-17.

25. Elizabeth Ross Haynes, "Two Million Negro Women at Work," *Southern Workman* 15 (February 1922): 64-66.

26. Unites States Department of Commerce, Bureau of Census, *Population Trends in the United States, 1900-1960* (Washington, D.C.: U.S. Government Printing Office, 1964), pp. 231, 234.

27. Gerda Lerner, ed., *Black Women in White America: A Documentary History* (New York: Random House, Pantheon Books, 1972), pp. 226-27; Louise Mitchell, "Slave Markets Typify Exploitation of Domestics," *Daily Worker*, 5 May 1940.

28. *Negro Year Book, 1922-24*, p. 37.

29. *The Negro World*, 24 October 1925, 5 March 1927. See Mark D. Matthews, "'Our Women and What They Think,' Amy Jacques Garvey and *The Negro World*," *Black Scholar* 10 (May-June 1979): 2-13.

30. Mary Church Terrell, *A Colored Woman in a White World* (Washington D.C.: Randsdell, Inc., 1940), pp. 330-33.

31. *Ibid.*, pp. 360-64.

32. *Crisis* 30 (June 1925): 81.
33. *Negro Year Book, 1921-22*, pp. 6-9.
34. *Negro Year Book, 1922-24*, pp. 18-19.
35. *Ibid.*, pp. 37-38; *Crisis* 23 (March 1922): 218; *Crisis* 24 (October 1922): 260.
36. *Crisis* 24 (November 1922): 8.
37. Terrell, *A Colored Woman in a White World*, pp. 370-71.
38. Mary McLeod Bethune, Vertical File, Howard University, Washington D.C., Clippings Folder, 1930, *Black Dispatch*, April 16, 1936 (hereafter cited as Bethune Vertical File and the source).
39. Bethune Vertical File, *Indianapolis Recorder*, 14 December 1937, *Boston Guardian*, 18 October 1938.
40. Bethune Vertical File, *New Jersey Herald News*, 14 October 1939.
41. Bethune Vertical File, *Black Dispatch*, 28 January 1939.
42. Terrell, *A Colored Woman in a White World*, first page of the introduction.
43. *Crisis* 23 (December 1921): 83; *Negro Year Book, 1922-24*, p. 37.
44. *Negro Year Book, 1922-24*, p. 70.
45. Terrell, *A Colored Woman in a White World*, pp. 355-56; *Negro Year Book, 1922-24*, p. 70; *Negro Year Book, 1931-32*, pp. 13, 92-93. Blacks did not vote the Democratic party on a large scale until the second Franklin D. Roosevelt administration.
46. *Negro Year Book, 1947*, pp. 286-87, 289-91.
47. Bethune Vertical File, *Black Dispatch*, 10 October 1942.

29

The Black Community and the Birth Control Movement

Jessie M. Rodrique

The decline in black fertility rates from the late nineteenth century to World War II has been well documented. In these years the growth rate of the black population was more than cut in half. By 1945 the average number of children per woman was 2.5, and the degree of childlessness, especially among urban blacks, had reached unprecedented proportions. Researchers who explain this phenomenon insist that contraception played a minimum role, believing that blacks had no interest in the control of their own fertility. This belief also affects the interpretation of blacks' involvement in the birth control movement, which has been understood as a movement that was thrust upon an unwilling black population.

This essay seeks to understand these two related issues differently. First, I maintain that black women were, in fact, interested in controlling their fertility and that the low birth rates reflect in part a conscious use of birth control. Second, by exploring the birth control movement among blacks at the grassroots level, I show that despite the racist ideology that operated at the national level, blacks were active and effective participants in the establishment of local clinics and in the birth control debate, as they related birth control to issues of race and gender. Third, I show that despite black cooperation with white birth control groups, blacks maintained a degree of independence that allowed the organization for birth control in their communities to take a qualitatively different form.

Demographers in the post-World War I years accounted for the remarkable decline in black fertility in terms of biological factors. Fears of "dysgenic" population trends coupled with low birth rates among native, white Americans underlay their investigations of black fertility. Population scholars ignored contraception as a factor in the birth decline even as late as 1938. Instead, they focused upon the "health hypothesis," arguing that the fertility drop resulted from general poor health, especially sterility caused by venereal disease. While health conditions seem likely to have had some effect, there is no reason to exclude contraceptive use as an additional cause, especially when evidence of contraceptive knowledge and practice is abundant.[1]

In drawing their conclusions, researchers also made many questionable and unfounded assumptions about the sexuality of blacks. In one large study of family limitation, for example, black women's lower contraceptive use was attributed to the belief that "the negro generally exercises less prudence and foresight than white people do in all sexual matters."[2] Nor is the entire black population represented in many of these studies. Typically their sample consists of women whose economic status is defined as either poor or very poor and who are either illiterate or who have had very little education. Population experts' ideological bias and research design have tended to foreclose the possibility of Afro-American agency, and thus conscious use of contraception.[3]

Historians who have chronicled the birth control movement have focused largely on the activities and evolution of the major birth control organizations and leading birth control figures, usually at the national level. None have interpreted the interests of the movement as particularly beneficial to blacks. Linda Gordon, in her pathbreaking book, *Woman's Body, Woman's Right*, focused on the 1939 "Negro Project," established by the Birth Control Federation of America (BCFA) as a conservative, elitist effort designed "to stabilize existing social relations." Gordon claims that the birth control movement in the south was removed from socially progressive politics and unconnected to any analysis of women's rights, civil rights, or poverty, exemplifying the movement's male domination and professionalization over the course of the twentieth century. Other historians concur, asserting that birth control was "genocidal" and "anathema" to black women's interests, and that the movement degenerated into a campaign to "keep the unfit from reproducing themselves." Those who note its presence within the black community in a slightly more positive light, qualify their statements by adding the disclaimer that support and information for its dissemination came only from the black elite and were not part of a grassroots movement.[4]

There is however, an ample body of evidence that suggests the importance of birth control use among blacks. Contraceptive methods and customs among Africans as well as nineteenth-century slaves have been well documented. For example, folklorists and others have discovered "alum water" as one of many birth control measures in early twentieth-century southern rural communities. The author of a study of two rural counties of Georgia noted the use of birth control practices there and linked it to a growing race pride. In urban areas a "very common" and distinctive practice among blacks was to place Vaseline and quinine over the mouth of the uterus. It was widely available and purchased very cheaply in drugstores.[5]

The black press was also an abundant source of birth control information. The *Pittsburgh Courier*, for example, carried numerous mail order advertisements for douche powder, suppositories, preventative antiseptics, and vaginal jellies that "destroyed foreign germs."[6] A particularly interesting mail order ad was for a product called "Puf," a medicated douche powder and applicator that claimed to be a "new guaranteed method of administering marriage hygiene." It had a sketch of a calendar with the words "End Calendar Worries Now!" written across it and a similar sketch that read "Tear-Up Your Calendar, Do Not Worry, Use Puf." The instructions for its use indicate euphemistically that Puf should be used "first," meaning before intercourse, and that it was good for hours, leaving little doubt that this product was fully intended to be used as a birth control device.[7]

Advertisements for mail order douches are significant since they appear to reflect a practice that was widespread and well documented among black women. Studies conducted in the mid-thirties overwhelmingly concluded that douching was the preferred method of contraception used by black couples. Yet contemporary researchers neglected to integrate this observation into their understanding of the fertility decline since they insisted that douching was an "ineffective contraceptive." However ineffective the means, the desire for birth control in the black community was readily apparent, as George Schuyler, editor of the *National Negro News*, explained: "If anyone should doubt the desire on the part of Negro women and men to limit their families it is only necessary to note the large sale of preventative devices sold in every drug store in various Black Belts."[8]

Within the black community the practice of abortion was commonly cited by black leaders and professionals as contributing to the low birth rates. Throughout the twenties and thirties the black press reported many cases of abortions that had ended in death or the arrest of doctors who had performed them. Abortion was discussed in the *Pittsburgh Courier* in 1930 in a fictionalized series entitled "Bad Girl," which dealt with a range of attitudes toward childbearing among Harlem blacks. When Dot, the main character, discovers she is pregnant, she goes to a friend who works in a drugstore. The author writes:

> Pat's wonderful remedy didn't help. Religiously Dot took it and each night when Eddie came home she sadly admitted that success had not crowned her efforts. "All that rotten tasting stuff just to keep a little crib out of the bedroom." After a week she was tired of medicine and of baths so hot that they burned her skin.[9]

Next, she sought the advice of a friend who told her that she would have to have "an operation" and knew of a doctor who would do it for fifty dollars.

The *Baltimore Afro-American* observed that pencils, nails, and hat pins were the instruments commonly used for self-induced abortions and the *Birth Control Review* wrote in 1936 that rural black women in Georgia drank turpentine for the same purpose. The use of turpentine as an abortifacient is significant since it is derived from evergreens, a source similar to rue and camphor, both of which were reported by a medical authority in 1860 to have been used with some success by southern slaves. Although statistics for abortions among black women are scarce, a 1938 medical study reported that twenty-eight percent or 211 of 730 black women interviewed said that they had one or more abortions. A black doctor from Nashville in 1940 asserted in the *Baltimore Afro-American* that abortions among black women were deliberate, not only the result of syphilis and other diseases: "In the majority of cases it is used as a means of getting rid of unwanted children."[10]

These data, while somewhat impressionistic, indicate that a number of contraceptive methods were available to blacks. Many were, and still are, discounted as ineffective "folk methods."[11] There was, however, a discernible consciousness that guided the fertility decline. A discourse on birth control emerged in the years from 1915 to 1945. As blacks migrated within and out of the south to northern cities, they began to articulate the reasons for limiting fertility. It is here that one begins to see how interconnected the issue of birth control was to many facets of black life. For women, it was linked to changes in their status, gender roles within the family, attitudes toward motherhood and sexuality, and, at times, feminism. Birth control was also integral to issues of economics, health, race relations, and racial progress.

In these years blacks contributed to the "official" nationwide debate concerning birth control while also voicing their particular concerns. Frequent coverage was given to birth control in the black press. Newspapers championed the cause of birth control when doctors were arrested for performing abortions. They also carried editorials in favor of birth control, speeches of noted personalities who favored its use, and occasionally sensationalized stories on the desperate need for birth control. Often, the topic of birth control as well as explicit birth control information was transmitted orally, through public lectures and debates. It was also explored in fiction, black periodicals, and several issues of the *Birth Control Review* dedicated to blacks.[12]

Economic themes emerged in the birth control discourse as it related to issues of black family survival. Contraceptive use was one of a few economic strategies available to blacks, providing a degree of control within the context of the family economy. Migrating families who left behind the economy of the rural south used birth control to "preserve their new economic independence," as did poor families who were "compelled" to limit their numbers of children. A 1935 study of Harlem reiterated this same point, adding that the low birth rates of urban blacks reflected a "deliberate limitation of families." Another strategy used by black couples for the same purpose was postponing marriage. Especially in the years of the Depression, birth control was seen as a way to improve general living conditions by allowing more opportunities for economic gain.[13]

Birth control was also linked to the changing status of black women and the role they were expected to play in the survival of the race. On this issue a degree of opposition to birth control surfaced. Some, most notably black nationalist leader Marcus Garvey, believed that the future of the black race was contingent upon increasing numbers and warned that birth control would lead to racial extinction. Both Garveyites and Catholic church officials warned that birth control interfered with the "course of nature" and God's will.[14]

These issues were evident in an exchange between the journalist J. A. Rogers and Dean Kelly Miller of Howard University in 1925. Writing in *The Messenger*, Rogers took Miller to task for his statements concerning the emancipation of black women. Miller is quoted as saying that black women had strayed too far from children, kitchen, clothes, and the church. Miller, very aware that black women had been having fewer children, cautioned against race suicide. Using the "nature" argument of Garvey and the Catholic church, he argued that the biological function of women was to bear and rear children. He stated, "The liberalization of women must always be kept within the boundary fixed by nature." Rogers strongly disagreed with Miller, saying that the move of black women away from domesticity and childbearing was a positive sign. Rogers wrote, "I give the Negro woman credit if she endeavors to be something other than a mere breeding machine. Having children is by no means the sole reason for being."[15]

Other black leaders supported this progressive viewpoint. In his 1919 essay "The Damnation of Women," W. E. B. Du Bois wrote that "the future woman must have a life work and future independence.... She must have knowledge ... and she must have the right of motherhood at her own discretion."[16] In a later essay he described those who would confine women to childbearing as "reactionary barbarians."[17] Doctor Charles Garvin, writing in 1932, believed that it was the "inalienable right of every married woman to use any physiologically sound precaution against reproduction she deems justifiable."[18]

Black women also expressed the need for contraception as they articulated their feelings about motherhood and sexuality. Black women's fiction and poetry in the years from 1916 to the early thirties frequently depicted women who refused to bring children into a racist world and expressed their outrage at laws that prevented access to birth control information. Nella Larsen, for example, in her 1928 novella *Quicksand*, explored the debilitating physical and emotional problems resulting from excessive childbearing in a society that demanded that women's sexual expression be inextricably linked to marriage and procreation.[19]

Others spoke of the right not to have children in terms that were distinctly feminist. For example, a character in the *Courier* serial "Bad Girl" put it this way: "The hospitals are wide open to the woman who wants to have a baby, but to the woman who doesn't want one—that's a different thing. High prices, fresh doctors. It's a man's world, Dot. The woman who wants to keep her body from pain and her mind from worry is an object of contempt."[20] The changing status of women and its relation to childbearing were also addressed in Jessie Fauset's 1931 novel, *The Chinaberry Tree*. Fauset's male characters asserted the need for large families and a "definite place" for women in the home. The female character, however, remained unconvinced by this opinion. She had "the modern girl's own clear ideas on birth control."[21]

Other writers stressed the need for birth control in terms of racial issues and how birth control could be used to alleviate the oppressive circumstances of the black community. For example, Chandler Owen, editor of *The Messenger*, wrote a piece for the 1919 edition of the *Birth Control Review* entitled "Women and Children of the South." He advocated birth control because he believed that general improvements in material conditions would follow from fewer children. Observing that young black women in peonage camps were frequently raped and impregnated by their white overseers, Owen also linked involuntary maternity to racial crimes.[22]

The advocacy of birth control for racial progress occurred most frequently during the Depression, and it helped to mobilize community support for clinics. Newell Sims of Oberlin College, for example, urged that birth control for blacks would be a "step toward independence and greater power" in his 1931 essay "A New Technique in Race Relations." In his opinion a controlled birth rate would free more resources for advancement. The black press hailed the essay as "revolutionary."[23] Other advocates insisted that all blacks, but especially poor blacks, become involved in the legislative process to legalize birth control. It was imperative that the poor be included in the movement since they were the ones most injured by its prohibition. One black newspaper, the *San Francisco Spokesman*, promoted a very direct and activist role for blacks on this issue. "To legalize birth control, you and I should make expressed attitudes on this question a test of every candidate's fitness for legislative office," it argued in 1934. "And those who refuse or express a reactionary opinion should be flatly and uncompromisingly rejected."[24]

For many blacks birth control was not a panacea but one aspect of a larger political agenda. Unlike some members of the white community who myopically looked to birth control as a cure-all for the problems of blacks, most blacks instead described it as a program that would "modify one cause of their unfavorable situation."[25] They stressed that true improvement could come only through the "equalization of economic and social opportunities."[26] Newell L. Sims summed up this position most eloquently in his 1932 essay "Hostages to the White Man." It was a viewpoint stressed well into the forties by numerous and leading members of the black community. He wrote:

> The negro in American is a suppressed class and as such must struggle for existence under every disadvantage and handicap. Although in three generations since slavery he has in many ways greatly improved his condition, his economic, social and political status still remain that of a dominated exploited minority. His problem is, therefore, just what it has been for three quarters of a century, i.e., how to better his position in the social order. Naturally in all his strivings he has found no panacea for his difficulties, for there is none. The remedies must be as numerous and varied as the problem is complex. Obviously he needs to employ every device that will advance his cause. I wish briefly to urge the merits of birth control as one means.[27]

Many also insisted that birth control be integrated into other health care provisions and not be treated as a separate "problem." E. S. Jamison, for example, writing in the *Birth Control Review* in 1938 on "The Future of Negro Health," exhorted blacks to "present an organized front" so that birth control and other needed health services could be made available to them. Yet he too, like Sims, emphasized independence from the white community. He wrote that "the Negro must do for himself. Charity will not better his condition in the long run."[28]

Blacks also took an important stand against sterilization, especially in the thirties. Scholars have not sufficiently recognized this point: that blacks could endorse a program of birth control but reject the extreme view of eugenicists, whose programs for birth control and sterilization often did not distinguish between the two. The *Pittsburgh Courier*, for example, whose editorial policy clearly favored birth control, was also active in the anti-sterilization movement. It asserted in several editorials that blacks should oppose the sterilization programs being advanced by eugenicists and so-called scientists because they were being waged against the weak, the oppressed, and the disfranchised. Candidates for sterilization were likely to be those on relief, the unemployed, and the homeless, all victims of a vicious system of economic exploitation. Du Bois shared this viewpoint. In his column in the *Courier* in 1936 he wrote, "the thing we want to watch is the so-called eugenic sterilization." He added that the burden of such programs would "fall upon colored people and it behooves us to watch the law and the courts and stop the spread of the habit." The *San Francisco Spokesman* in 1934 called upon black clubwomen to become active in the anti-sterilization movement.[29]

Participation in the birth control debate was only one aspect of the black community's involvement; black women and men also were active in the establishment of birth control clinics. From 1925 to 1945 clinics for blacks appeared nationwide, many of which were at least partly directed and sponsored by local black community organizations. Many of the organizations had a prior concern with health matters, creating an established network of social welfare centers, health councils, and agencies. Thus, birth control services were often integrated into a community through familiar channels.[30]

In Harlem the black community showed an early and sustained interest in the debate over birth control, taking a vanguard role in agitation for birth control clinics. In 1918 the Women's Political Association of Harlem, calling upon black women to "assume the reins of leadership in the political, social and economic life of their people," announced that its lecture series would include birth control among the topics for discussion.[31] In March of 1923 the Harlem Community Forum invited Margaret Sanger to speak to them at the Library Building in the Bronx, and in 1925 the Urban League made a request to the American Birth Control League that a clinic be established in the Columbus Hill section of the city.

Although this clinic proved unsuccessful, another clinic, supported by the Urban League and the Birth Control Clinical Research Bureau, opened a Harlem branch in 1929. This particular clinic, affiliated with Margaret Sanger, had an advisory board of approximately fifteen members, including Harlem-based journalists, physicians, social workers, and ministers. There was apparently very little opposition to the work of this clinic, even among the clergy. One minister on the advisory board, William Lloyd Imes of the St. James Presbyterian Church, reported that he had held discussions on birth control at his church; at another meeting he announced that if a birth control pamphlet were printed, he would place it in the church vestibule. Another clergyman, the

Reverend Shelton Hale Bishop, wrote to Sanger in 1931 that he believed birth control to be "one of the boons of the age to human welfare."[32] The Reverend Adam Clayton Powell of the Abyssinian Baptist Church both endorsed birth control and spoke at pubic meetings where he denounced the "false modesty" surrounding questions of sex. Ignorance, he believed, led to unwanted pregnancies among young girls.[33]

Support for birth control clinics by black community organizations was also apparent in other locations throughout the country. Their activism took various forms. In Baltimore, for example, a white birth control clinic had begun to see blacks in 1928. In 1935 the black community began organizing and by 1938 the Northwest Health center was established, sponsored and staffed by blacks. The Baltimore Urban League played a key role in its initial organization, and the sponsoring committee of the clinic was composed of numerous members of Baltimore's black community, including ministers, physicians, nurses, social workers, teachers, housewives, and labor leaders.[34]

In Richmond, Fredericksburg, and Lynchburg, Virginia, local maternal welfare groups raised funds for expenses and supplies for the birth control clinics at the Virginia Medical College and the Hampton Institute, and publicized birth control services at city health departments. And in West Virginia, the Maternal and Child Health Council, formed in 1938, was the first state-wide birth control organization sponsored by blacks.[35]

Local clubs and women's organizations often took part in either sponsoring birth control clinics or bringing the topic to the attention of the local community. In New York these included the Inter-Racial Forum of Brooklyn, the Women's Business and Professional Club of Harlem, the Social Workers Club of Harlem, the Harlem branch of the National Organization of Colored Graduate Nurses, the Harlem YWCA, and the Harlem Economic Forum. In Oklahoma City fourteen black women's clubs sponsored a birth control clinic for black women, directed by two black physicians and one black clubwoman. The Mother's Health Association of the District of Columbia reported to the *Birth Control Review* in 1938 that they were cooperating with black organizations that wanted to start a clinic of their own.[36]

Clinics in other cities were located in black community centers and churches. For example, the Kentucky Birth Control League in 1936 reported that one of the clinics in Louisville was located in the Episcopal Church for Colored People and was operated by a Negro staff. The Cincinnati Committee on Maternal Health reported in 1939 the opening of a second black clinic where a black physician and nurse would work.[37]

Community centers and settlement houses were also part of the referral network directing blacks to birth control services. The Mother's Health Office in Boston received clients from the Urban League, the Robert Gould Shaw House, and the Harriet Tubman House. The Henry Street Settlement sent women to the Harlem clinic, and the Booker T. Washington Community Center in San Francisco directed black women to the birth control clinic in that city. In 1935 the Indiana Birth Control League reported that black clients were directed to them from the Flanner House Settlement for Colored People.[38]

In 1939 the Birth Control Federation of America (BCFA) established a Division of Negro Service and sponsored pilot clinics in Nashville, Tennessee, and Berkeley County, South Carolina. The Division consisted of a national advisory council of thirty-five black leaders, a national sponsoring committee of 500 members who coordinated state and local efforts, and administrative and field personnel. The project in Nashville was integrated into the public health services and located in the Bethlehem center, a black social service settlement, and the Fisk University Settlement House. Both clinics were under the direction of black doctors and nurses. The program was also supplemented by nine black public health nurses who made home visits and performed general health services including birth control. The home visits served the large numbers of women who worked as domestics and could not attend the clinics during the day; 5,000 home visits were made in Nashville in a two-year period. In South Carolina, clinic sessions providing both medical care and birth control services were held eleven times each month at different locations in the county for rural women, seventy percent of whom were black.[39]

Simultaneously with the development of these two projects, the BCFA launched an educational campaign to inform and enlist the services of black health professionals, civic groups, and women's clubs. While professional groups are often credited with being the sole source of birth control agitation, the minutes and newsletters of the Division of Negro Service reveal an enthusiastic desire among a broad cross-section of the black community to lend its support for birth control. In fact, black professional groups often worked closely with community groups and other "non-professionals" to make birth control information widely available. For example, the National Medical Association, an organization of black physicians, held public lectures on birth control in conjunction with local groups beginning in 1929, and when birth control was discussed at annual meetings their otherwise private sessions were opened up to social workers, nurses, and teachers. The National Association of Colored Graduate Nurses, under the direction of Mabel Staupers, was especially active in birth control work. Cooperation was offered by several state and local nursing, hospital, and dental associations. One nurse responded to Staupers' request for help with the distribution of birth control information by writing, "I shall pass the material out, we will discuss it in our meetings and I will distribute exhibits at pre-natal clinics at four health centers and through Negro Home Demonstration Clubs."

The participation of Negro Home Demonstration Clubs in birth control work is significant because it is an entirely overlooked and potentially rich source for the grassroots spread of birth control information in the rural South. Home Demonstration Clubs grew out of the provisions of the Smith-Lever Cooperative Extension Act of 1914 and had, by the early twenties, evolved into clubs whose programs stressed health and sanitation. The newsletter of the Division of Negro Service in 1941 reported that five rural State Negro Agricultural and Home Demonstration Agents offered full cooperation with the division. The newsletter included the response of H. C. Ray of Little Rock, Arkansas. He wrote, "We have more than 13,000 rural women working in home demonstration clubs . . . it is in this connection that I feel our organization might work hand in hand with you in bringing about some very definite and desirable results in your phase of community improvement work. We will be glad to distribute any literature." Also involved with rural birth control education were several tuberculosis associations and the Jeanes Teachers, educators funded by the Anna T. Jeanes foundation for improving rural black schools.[40]

Other groups showed interest in the programs of the Division of Negro Service either by requesting birth control speakers for their conventions or by distributing literature to their members. Similar activities were conducted by the Virginia Federation of Colored Women's Clubs, which represented 400 women's clubs, the Negro Organization Society of Virginia, the National Negro Business League, the National Negro Housewives League, the Pullman Porters, the Elks, the Harlem Citizens City-Wide Committee, and the Social Action Committee of Boston's South End. In 1944, for example, the NAACP and a black boilermakers' union distributed Planned Parenthood clinic cards in their mailings to their California members. Twenty-one Urban Leagues in sixteen states as of 1943 actively cooperated with the BCFA in the display of exhibits, distribution of literature, the promotion of local clinical service, and adult community education programs. These national and local black organizations advocated birth control as one aspect of a general program of health, education, and economic development in the late thirties and early forties.[41]

Even in their cooperation with the BCFA, leading members of the black community stressed their own concerns and disagreements with the overall structure of the birth control movement. Their comments reveal important differences in orientation. At a meeting of the National Advisory Council of the Division of Negro Service in 1942, members of the council made it clear that birth control services and information must be distributed to the community *as* a community. Their goal was one of inclusion; members stated that they were disturbed at the emphasis on doctors, and that teachers, ministers, and other community members must be utilized in birth control work. Even the black physicians on the council stressed the need for keeping midwives, volunteers, and especially women practitioners involved in the movement and suggested that mobile clinics traveling throughout the rural South distribute birth control and other needed health services. This approach to birth control diverged significantly from the conservative strategy of the white BCFA leadership, which insisted that birth control services be dispensed by private, individual physicians. Black physicians, it seems, were more sensitive to the general health needs of their population and more willing to experiment with the delivery of birth control services. They favored the integration of birth control into public health services while many white physicians were opposed.[42]

Others on the council stated that black women could be reached only through community organizations that they trusted, and they stressed again the necessity of not isolating birth control as a special interest to the neglect of other important health needs. Still others pointed to the need for birth control representatives who recognized social differences among urban blacks.

At the level of clinic attendance, clinicians also observed a difference between white and black patrons. Black women, they noted, were much more likely to spread the word about birth control services and bring their relatives and friends to the clinics. Some rural women even thought of "joining" the clinic as they might join a community organization. A white woman, however, was more likely to keep the information to herself and attend the clinic alone. A statistician from the Census Bureau supported this observation when he speculated in 1931 that "grapevine dissemination" of birth control information contributed to low black birth rates. These reports are a testimony to the effectiveness of working-class black women's networks.[43]

Moreover, many local birth control groups were often able to maintain independence from the Planned Parenthood Federation of America even though they accepted and used PPFA's display and educational materials. This situation was evident at the Booker T. Washington community center in San Francisco. A representative from PPFA had sent this center materials and then did not hear from anyone for some time. After almost one year the director of the Washington center wrote back to PPFA, informing the staff that birth control programs were flourishing in the center's area. In fact, the group had used the Federation's materials extensively at community centers and civic clubs, and the local black sorority, Alpha Kappa Alpha, had accepted sponsorship of a mothers' health clinic. The PPFA representative described this situation as typical of many black groups. They would not respond to PPFA communications, but would use PPFA materials and be actively engaged in their own form of community birth control work.[44]

In a speech delivered to PPFA in 1942 Dr. Dorothy Ferebee, a black physician and leader, stated, "It is well for this organization to realize that the Negro at his present advanced stage of development is increasingly interested more in programs that are worked out with him and by him than in those worked out for him."[45] This statement reveals a fundamental difference in the goals and strategies of the black and white communities. In the past scholars have interpreted the birth control movement as a racist and elitist set of programs imposed on the black population. While this may describe the intentions of the national white leadership, it is important to recognize that the black community had its own agenda in the creation of programs to include and reach wide segments of the black population.

As this essay demonstrates, black women used their knowledge of "folk methods" and other available methods to limit their childbearing. The dramatic fertility decline from 1880 to 1945 is evidence of their success. Moreover, the use of birth control was pivotal to many pressing issues within the black community. The right to control one's own fertility emerged simultaneously with changing attitudes toward women in both the black and white communities that recognized their rights as individuals and not only their roles as mothers. And these changing attitudes contributed to the dialogue within the black community about the future of the family and strategies for black survival. Birth control also emerged as part of a growing race consciousness, as blacks saw birth control as one means of freeing themselves from the oppression and exploitation of white society through the improvement of their health and their economic and social status. Birth control was also part of a growing process of politicization. Blacks sought to make it a legislative issue, they opposed the sterilization movement, and they took an active and often independent role in supporting their clinics, educating their communities, and tailoring programs to fit their own needs. In their ideology and practice blacks were indeed a vital and assertive part of the larger birth control movement. What appears to some scholars of the birth control movement as the waning of the movement's original purposes during the 1920s and 1930s was within the black community a period of growing ferment and support for birth control. The history of the birth control movement, and the participation of black Americans in it, must be reexamined in this light.

NOTES

1. Reynolds Farley, *Growth of the Black Population* (Chicago: 1970), 3, 75; Stanley Engerman, "Changes in Black Fertility, 1880-1940," in *Family and Population in Nineteenth Century America*, ed. Tamara K. Hareven and Maris A. Vinovskis (Princeton: 1978), ch. 3. For an excellent review of the demographic literature, see Joseph McFalls and George Masnick, "Birth Control and the Fertility of the U.S. Black Population, 1880 to 1980," *Journal of Family History* 6 (1981): 89-106; Peter Uhlenberg, "Negro Fertility Patterns in the United States," *Berkeley Journal of Sociology* 11 (1966): 56; James Reed, *From Private Vice to Public Virtue* (New York: 1978), ch. 14.

2. Raymond Pearl, "Contraception and Fertility in 2,000 Women," *Human Biology* 4 (1932): 395.

3. McFalls and Masnick, "Birth Control," 90.

4. Linda Gordon, *Woman's Body, Woman's Right* (New York: 1976), 332-35; Paula Giddings, *When and Where I Enter: The Impact of Black Women on Race and Sex in America* (New York: 1984), 183; Robert G. Weisbord, *Genocide? Birth Control and the Black American* (Westport, Conn.: 1975); William G. Harris, "Family Planning, Socio-Political Ideology and Black Americans: A Comparative Study of Leaders and a General Population Sample" (Ph.D. dissertation, University of Massachusetts, 1980), 69.

   A brief chronology of early birth control organizations is as follows: the American Birth Control League was founded in 1921 and operated by Margaret Sanger until 1927. In 1923 Sanger had organized the Clinical Research Bureau and after 1927 controlled only that facility. In 1939 the Clinical Research Bureau and the American Birth Control League merged to form the Birth Control Federation of America. In 1942 the name was changed to the Planned Parenthood Federation of America (hereafter cited as ABCL, BCFA, and PPFA).

5. For contraceptive use among Africans, see Norman E. Himes, *Medical History of Contraception* (New York: 1936). For statements concerning birth control use among black Americans, see W. E. B. Du Bois, "Black Folks and Birth Control," *Birth Control Review* 16 (June 1932): 166-67 (hereafter cited as *BCR*); Herbert Gutman, *The Black Family in Slavery and Freedom, 1750-1925* (New York: 1976). Du Bois had first observed the trend toward a steadily decreasing birth rate in *The*

Philadelphia Negro: A Social Study (Philadelphia: 1899). For folk methods see Elizabeth Rauh Bethel, *Promiseland: A Century of Life in a Negro Community* (Philadelphia: 1981), 156-57; Newbell Niles Puckett, *Folk Beliefs of the Southern Negro* (New York: 1926); Arthur Raper, *Preface to Peasantry: A Tale of Two Black Belt Counties* (Chapel Hill, N.C.: 1936), 71; "Report of the Special Evening Medical Session of the First American Birth Control Conference" (1921), Box 99, Folder 1017, Margaret Sanger Papers, Sophia Smith Collection, Smith College, Northampton, Mass.

6. *Pittsburgh Courier*, 25 April 1931, n.p. (hereafter cited as *Courier*).

7. *Courier*, 1 December 1934, 7.

8. McFalls and Masnick, "Birth Control," 103; George Schuyler, "Quantity or Quality," *BCR* 16 (June 1932): 165-66.

9. See, for example, *Courier*, 9 March 1935, 2; and *San Francisco Spokesman*, 1 March 1934, 1 (hereafter cited as *Spokesman*); Vina Delmar, "Bad Girl," *Courier*, 3 January 1931, 2.

10. *Baltimore Afro-American*, 3 August 1940, n.p. (hereafter cited as *Afro-American*); "A Clinic for Tobacco Road," *BCR* 3 [New Series] (January 1936): 6; Gutman, *The Black Family*, 80-85; John Gaston, "A Review of 2,422 Cases of Contraception," *Texas State Journal of Medicine* 35 (September 1938): 365-68; *Afro-American*, 3 August 1940, n.p. On abortion see also "Birth Control: The Case for the State," *Reader's Digest* (November 1939).

11. McFalls and Masnick, "Birth Control," 103.

12. "Magazine Publishes Negro Number on Birth Control," *San Francisco Spokesman*, 11 June 1932, 3; "Birth Control Slayer Held Without Bail," *Courier*, 11 January 1936, 4.

13. Alice Dunbar Nelson, "Woman's Most Serious Problem," *The Messenger* (March 1927): 73; Clyde Kiser, "Fertility of Harlem Negroes," *Milbank Memorial Fund Quarterly* 13 (1935): 273-85; Caroline Robinson, *Seventy Birth Control Clinics* (Baltimore, 1930), 246-51.

14. Weisbord, *Genocide?*, 43.

15. J. A. Rogers, "The Critic," *The Messenger* (April 1925).

16. W. E. B. Du Bois, "The Damnation of Women," in *Darkwater: Voices from Within the Veil*, ed. Herbert Aptheker (1921; rpt. Millwood, N.Y.: 1975).

17. W. E. B. Du Bois, "Birth," *The Crisis* 24 (October 1922): 248-50.

18. Charles H. Garvin, "The Negro's Doctor's Task," *BCR* 16 (November 1932): 269-70.

19. For an excellent discussion of the theme of sexuality in black women's fiction, see the introduction to Nella Larsen, *Quicksand and Passing*, ed. Deborah E. McDowell (New Brunswick, N.J.: 1986). See also Mary Burrill, "They That Sit in Darkness," and Angelina Grimké, "The Closing Door," *BCR* 3 (September 1919); Jessie Fauset, *The Chinaberry Tree* (New York: 1931); Angelina Grimké, *Rachel* (n.p., 1920); Georgia Douglas Johnson, *Bronze: A Book of Verse* (1922; rpt. Freeport, N.Y.: 1971).

20. Delmar, "Bad Girl," *Courier*, 3 January 1931, 2.

21. Fauset, *The Chinaberry Tree*, 131-32, 187.

22. Chandler Owen, "Women and Children of the South," *BCR* 3 (September 1919): 9, 20.

23. Quoted in *Courier*, 28 March 1931, 3, and *Norfolk Journal and Guide*, 28 March 1931, 1.

24. J. A. Ghent, "Urges Legalization of Birth Control: Law Against Contraception Unjust to the Poor," *Spokesman*, 9 July 1932, 3; "The Case of Dr. Devaughn, or Anti-Birth Control on Trial," *Spokesman*, 22 February 1934, 6.

25. W. G. Alexander, "Birth Control for the Negro: Fad or Necessity?" *Journal of the National Medical Association* 24 (August 1932): 39.

26. Charles S. Johnson, "A Question of Negro Health," *BCR* 16 (June 1932): 167-69.

27. Newell L. Sims, "Hostages to the White Man," *BCR* 16 (July-August 1932): 214-15.

28. E. S. Jamison, "The Future of Negro Health," *BCR* 22 (May 1938): 94-95.

29. "Sterilization," *Courier*, 30 March 1935, 10; "The Sterilization Menace," *Courier*, 18 Jan. 1936, 10; W. E. B. Du Bois, "Sterilization," *Courier*, 27 June 1936, 1; "Are Women Interested Only in Meet and Eat Kind of Club?" *Spokesman*, 29 March 1934, 4.

30. For examples of black social welfare organizations see, for example, William L. Pollard, *A Study of Black Self-Help* (San Francisco: 1978); Edyth L. Ross, *Black Heritage in Social Welfare, 1860-1930* (London: 1978); Lenwood G. Davis, "The Politics of Black Self-Help in the United States: A Historical Overview," in *Black Organizations: Issues on Survival Techniques*, ed. Lennox S. Yearwood (Lanham, Md.: 1980). This statement is also based on extensive reading of the *Pittsburgh Courier*, *Norfolk Journal and Guide*, *Baltimore Afro-American*, *San Francisco Spokesman*, and *New York Age* for the 1920s and 1930s.

31. *The Messenger* (July 1918): n.p.

32. "Report of executive secretary" (March 1923), Series I, Box 4, Planned Parenthood Federation of America Papers, American Birth Control League Records, Sophia Smith Collection, Smith College, Northampton, Mass.; Hannah Stone, "Report of the Clinical Research Department of the ABCL" (1925), Series I, Box 4, PPFA Papers; "Urban League Real Asset, Clinic an Example of How it Assists," *Courier*, 2 November 1935, 1; William Lloyd Imes to Margaret Sanger, 16 May 1931 and 23 November 1932, Box 122b, Folders 1333 and 1336, Sanger Papers. Shelton Hale Bishop to Margaret Sanger, 18 May 1931, Box 122b, Folder 1333, Sanger Papers.

33. "Minutes of the first meeting of 1932, Board of Managers, Harlem Branch" (25 March 1932), Box 122b, Folder 1336, Sanger Papers; "Companionate Marriage Discussed at Forum," *New York Age*, 12 May 1928, n.p.

34. E. S. Lewis and N. Louise Young, "Baltimore's Negro Maternal Health Center: How It Was Organized," *BCR* 22 (May 1938): 93-94.

35. "West Virginia," *BCR* 23 (October 1938): 121, "Birth Control for the Negro," Report of Hazel Moore (1937), Box 22, Folder 10, Florence Rose Papers, Sophia Smith Collection, Smith College; "Negro Demonstration Project Possibilities" (1 December 1939), Box 121, Folder 1309, Sanger Papers.

36. For information on black organizations, see Box 122b, Sanger Papers, especially 25 March 1932; "Minutes of the regular meeting of the Board of Directors of the ABCL," December 1922, Series I, Box 1, PPFA Papers; "Report of the executive secretary" (11 November 1930), Series I, Box 4, PPFA Papers; "ABCL Treasurer's annual reports for the year 1936," Series I, Box 4, PPFA Papers; "Harlem Economic Forum Plans Fine Lecture Series," *Courier*, 14 November 1936, 9; "Birth Control Clinic Set Up for Negroes; Sponsored by Clubs," *Oklahoma City Times*, 28 February and 4 March 1938; "Illinois Birth Control League," *BCR* 22 (March 1938): 64. By 1931 many black organizations in Pittsburgh supported the use of

birth control; see "Pittsburgh Joins Nation-Wide League for Birth Control," *Courier*, 21 February 1931, 1.

37. "Annual Reports of the State Member Leagues for 1936, the Kentucky Birth Control League," Series I, Box 4, PPFA Papers; "Annual Report 1938-39, Cincinnati Committee on Maternal Health," Box 119A, Folder 1256, Sanger Papers.

38. "Mother's Health Office Referrals" (5 January 1933), Massachusetts Mother's Health Office, Central Administrative Records, Box 35 and 36, Planned Parenthood League of Massachusetts, Sophia Smith Collection, Smith College; "PPFA field report for California, 1944," Box 119, Folder 1215, Sanger Papers; "Annual Meeting of the BCFA, Indiana Birth Control League, 1935," Series I, Box 4, PPFA Papers.

39. "Chart of the Special Negro Project Demonstration Project," Box 22, Folders 8 and 2, Rose Papers; John Overton and Ivah Uffelman, "A Birth Control Service Among Urban Negroes," *Human Fertility* 7 (August 1942): 97-101; E. Mae McCarroll, "A Condensed Report on the Two Year Negro Demonstration Health Program of PPFA, Inc.," presented at the Annual Convention of the National Medical Association, Cleveland, 17 August 1942, Box 22, Folder 11, Rose Papers; Mabel K. Staupers, "Family Planning and Negro Health," *National News Bulletin of the National Association of Colored Graduate Nurses* 14 (May 1941): 1-10.

40. "Preliminary Annual Report, Division of Negro Service" (7 January 1942), Box 121, Folder 1309, Sanger Papers; "Doctors' Annual Meeting Marked by Fine Program; Local Committee Involved in Planning Meeting," *New York Age*, 7 September 1929, 8; "National Medical Association Meeting Held in Washington," *New York Age*, 27 August 1932, 4. For information on the Smith-Lever Extension Act, see Alfred True, *A History of Agricultural Extension Work in the United States 1785-1923* (Washington, D.C.: 1928). Information on home demonstration clubs also appears in T. J. Woofter, Jr., "Organization of Rural Negroes for Public Health Work," *Proceedings of the National Conference of Social Work* (Chicago: 1923), 72-75; "Activities Report, Birth Control Negro Service," 21 June-21 July 1941, Box 22, Rose Papers; "Progress Outline 1940-42" and "Activities Report, Birth Control Negro Service," 16 June-21 June 1941, Box 22, Rose Papers. For information on Jeanes Teachers see, for example, Ross, *Black Heritage*, 211.

41. Information on organizations is based on numerous reports and newsletters from the years 1940-42, in Box 22, Rose Papers; see also "Newsletter from Division of Negro Service, December, 1941," Box 121, Folder 1309, and "PPFA Field Report for California, 1944," Box 119, Folder 1215, Sanger Papers.

42. "Activities Report, January 1, 1942-February 6, 1942" and "Progress Outline 1940-42," Box 22, Folder 4, Rose Papers; *Family Guardian* (Massachusetts Mother's Health Council) 5 (December 1939): 3, and 10 (July 1940): 3; "Minutes of the National Advisory Council Meeting, Division of Negro Service," 11 December 1942, Box 121, Folder 1310, Sanger Papers; Peter Murray, *BCR* 16 (July-August 1932): 216; M. O. Bousefield, *BCR* 22 (May 1938): 92. James Reed notes the opposition of the American Medical Association to alternative forms of health care systems in *From Private Vice to Public Virtue*, Part IV and 254.

43. "Notes on the Mother's Clinic, Tucson, Arizona," Box 119, Folder 1212, Sanger Papers; "A Clinic for Tobacco Road," *BCR* 3 [New Series] (January 1936): 6-7; Leonore G. Guttmacher, "Securing Patients for a Rural Center," *BCR* 23 (November 1938): 130-31; "Chas E. Hall [*sic*] Census Bureau Expert, Gives Figures for Ten

States in Which Number of Children Under Five Shows Decrease," *New York Age*, 7 November 1931, 1.

44. "Activities Report, Birth Control Negro Service," 21 November 1942, Box 22, Rose Papers.

45. "Project Reports," *The Aframerican* (Summer and Fall 1942): 9-24.

30

And Still I Rise:

Black Women and Reform, Buffalo, New York, 1900-1940

Lillian S. Williams

No Negro woman can afford to be an indifferent spectator of the social, moral, religious, economic, and uplift problems that are agitated around [her].[1]

Mary Burnett Talbert

Mary Burnett Talbert, Oberlin College graduate and Buffalo social activist, in her vice presidential address to the biennial convention of the National Association of Colored Women (NACW) in 1916 in Baltimore, told assembled delegates that they should "take an active personal interest in everything that concerns the welfare of home, church, community, state, . . . [and] country, for once [they] have struck out in this great work [they] are doing the work of God."[2] Black women engaged in a persistent struggle for change. Yet these reformers embodied a protest tradition that had manifested itself in the secular and religious organizations of Buffalo's black community during the nineteenth century.[3] The private sphere for these women was inextricably intertwined with the public sphere. Indeed, they felt that their activism was "ordained" by God. They thus held offices in their churches as well as in political and social clubs. They sometimes operated in gender-exclusive organizations and at other times in mixed groups. These reformers were womanists.[4] They embraced an ideology somewhat like that articulated by contemporary black feminists, such as Barbara Smith, who contend that black women confront daily a "simultaneity of oppressions."[5] Yet most of these women's reform activities addressed the subordinate status to which blacks, especially women and children, had been consigned and so they worked with black men to redress their grievances as blacks and women. These women saw themselves as critical links in a social movement designed to liberate the black community from second-class citizenship. Their participation in community liberation struggles was a means of empowerment for them as individuals.[6]

This study examines the extent to which Buffalo black women were involved in the process of social, political, and economic change and the extent to which they were successful. It also explores the social and economic characteristics of these reformers and their relationship to black men. In the process it explores the nature of black women's culture and suggests that such an analysis is a viable way to address the historical experiences of all women. Such a study can best be conducted in the local setting, examining the individual players and their relationship to larger social movements. Moreover, there is still a need for selected case studies of women's clubs that address their impact.[7] Such an analysis is a critical first step in writing the history of black women and reform in the United States.

On the eve of the twentieth century, Buffalo blacks had well-established ties to the city, for they had resided there long before its incorporation in 1832. The African-American population, however, remained small through the first decade of the twentieth century when it hovered around 1,000.[8] Despite its small size, the community was a driving force in the nineteenth-century movements to abolish slavery, to improve public education, and to eradicate Jim Crow in the city.

Buffalo had been an important center of reform during the nineteenth century. The Free Soil Party held its convention there and the religious revival movement was important. In addition, the National Negro Convention movement met at the Vine Street AME Church in 1843, and the Niagara Movement, the forerunner of the National Association for the Advancement of Colored People (NAACP), was organized at the home of William and Mary Talbert in 1905.[9]

By the twentieth century, Buffalo's prominence as a great commercial center, the result of the opening of the Erie Canal in 1825, had given way to the new industrial city. Buffalo remained a major transportation hub, second only to Chicago; its cattle industry rivaled that of Kansas City and Chicago; and it was the world's leading flour-milling center. The steel mills and the canneries were also major economic forces. Such an industrial base should have offered blacks secure, well-paying jobs. In actuality the economic status of black men and women was circumscribed by race and class, with most blacks employed in the service sector as domestic workers, chauffeurs, porters, bellhops, and cooks. Only a few found jobs in the industrial sector of the city before the outbreak of World War I caused factories to offer significantly broadened employment opportunities both for local blacks and newly arrived southern immigrants.[10]

The economic and social circumstances of their community affected black women and their perceptions of the world. The informal networks of kin and fictive kin that undergirded their nineteenth-century reform efforts remained important. But just as the increase in the black population compelled Buffalo blacks in general to reassess their programs and goals, so too did it prod black women to organize into formal, structured groups designed to improve their status as blacks and as women. They were influenced both by the reformist ethos of the Progressive Era and their own tradition of self-help and mutuality. Black women perceived their involvement in reform movements as a means of achieving self-actualization. Mary Talbert expressed their beliefs when she said, "We cannot get out of sympathetic touch with our fellowmen, for our daily association with men and women teaches us to know our limitations, our weaknesses and it enables us to improve our own individuality into a richer and nobler character."[11] These women confronted head-on the dilemmas facing their communities as a result of geographic mobility, racism, technological change, and urban growth. Many of their clubs were affiliated with the newly established National Association of Colored Women founded in Washington, D.C. in 1896. This organization resulted from the merger of two rival groups, the National Federation of Afro-American Women led by Josephine St. Pierre Ruffin of Boston and the National League of Colored Women headed by Mary Church Terrell of Washington.[12]

Mary Burnett Talbert was the most widely known activist in Buffalo. Mary Burnett was born in 1866 in Oberlin, Ohio, where she was educated, graduating from Oberlin College in 1886 at the age of nineteen. Upon graduation she began her teaching career at Bethel University in Little Rock, Arkansas, and in 1887 she became assistant principal of the Little Rock High School. After her marriage to William H. Talbert in 1891, she moved to Buffalo.[13]

Nineteenth-century forces shaped Mary Burnett Talbert's values and philosophy. In Oberlin, she attended the Congregational Church, a church involved in several reform movements that impacted upon the lives of African Americans. The politics of the post-Reconstruction era and her father's involvement in the Ohio Republican Party also influenced her, as did her mother's business pursuits. Furthermore, her liberal arts training at Oberlin introduced her to some of the most eminent intellectuals in the United States. Oberlin also brought her into contact with other young, progressive black women, such as Mary Church (Terrell) and Anna Julia Cooper, who later helped lead the struggle against racism, sexism, and colonial domination. All of these women were prominent in black women's reform efforts and they became leaders of the National Association of Colored Women, a major forum for their causes. They staunchly adhered to the contemporary black ideology of self-help and racial solidarity as expounded by Booker T. Washington, W.E.B. DuBois, and T. Thomas Fortune. Yet they succeeded in perfecting a delicate balancing act that permitted them to be independent of these apparently divergent camps.[14]

Talbert was active in both sacred and secular women's organizations in Buffalo. The Buffalo Phyllis Wheatley Club, founded in 1899 and affiliated with the NACW, kept its members abreast of contemporary issues. Talbert later served as president of this organization, and during her administration the Phyllis Wheatley Club invited the NAACP to organize in Buffalo. Mary Talbert was an ardent supporter of her husband's church, the Michigan Avenue Baptist Church, which had been at the forefront of black leadership in Buffalo for nearly a century. She also was a member of the Naomi Chapter of the Order of the Eastern Stars, a benevolent association, and was its first Worthy Matron or chief administrative officer. Mary Talbert's approach to the uplift of blacks in Buffalo was to do whatever was necessary to liberate her community from second-class citizenship. Thus, on some occasions she took individual action, while on others she affiliated with organizations to implement her programs.[15]

523

Less prominent but equally important in the black women's club move-ment was Clara Payne, a member of an old, established Buffalo family. In 1905, at the age of 45, Payne worked as a domestic. But she fared better than most domestics in Buffalo, for she lived with her parents on Laurel Street, an area of the city where successful blacks had access to better housing. Indeed, her father was a clerk in the Buffalo municipal government, a measure of middle-class status in the black community. Payne experienced significant so-cial mobility. In 1915, she was a caterer, and by 1925 she had become a social worker. She held several administrative posts in the NAACP and the National Urban League.[16]

Other women leaders were newcomers to the Queen City, but with a previous history of social activism. Bessie Williams arrived in Buffalo in 1921 still feeling a sense of pride and victory stemming from her Garveyite activities. She and her husband, Daniel, settled in Buffalo to seek employment in the Bethlehem Steel Mill following his firing by the Jones and Laughlin Steel Company in Aliquippa, Pennsylvania, after the Williamses' refusal to repudiate Marcus Garvey and his Universal Negro Improvement Association (UNIA) and to resign their positions in the organization. In protest of his dismissal from the company, thirty-eight of his co-workers walked off their jobs and migrated to Buffalo with Daniel and Bessie Williams. Williams continued her involvement in the UNIA in Buffalo. She was also active in the establishment of the Michigan Avenue Branch of the Young Men's Christian Association (YMCA), and she participated in local Republican Party politics. Williams worked as a domestic.[17]

Several activists had attended college or normal school, like Dora Needham Lee, a 1921 graduate of the Buffalo Normal School, and Amelia Anderson, a Syracuse University graduate. Both taught school in Buffalo and wanted to use the NAACP and several of the NACW affiliated organizations as forums to attack the social disorders they observed around them. Anderson and Lee were presidents of the Empire State Federation of Colored Women's Clubs. Susan Evans had attended college in Chicago and had trained at a settlement house there. She founded the Phyllis Wheatley Club in Buffalo in 1899 and was its first president; Evans also was elected national recording secretary of the NACW in 1901, in recognition of her exceptional skills and her commitment to black women's reform activities. She later directed the settlement house that the Phyllis Wheatley Club founded in Buffalo in 1905. Mrs. C. H. Banks, also of the Phyllis Wheatley Club, was a graduate of Hampton Institute in Virginia.[18] Most educated black women in Buffalo were teachers, but they were forced to abandon their careers upon marriage. These women were left few options outside of volunteerism.

Buffalo black women's reform efforts were not restricted solely to college graduates and to the middle class.[19] First, too few women fitted into this category. Second, all black women were limited by their oppression as blacks and women and perceived their fates as one. Further, the neighborhoods in which most Buffalo blacks resided were heterogeneous and allowed blacks an opportunity to interact with people from different class as well as ethnic backgrounds. Eva Coles, a housewife, houseworker Anna Davis, waitress Ella Martin, and Helen Smith, an undertaker, were participants in the club movement of black women in the self-styled "City of Good Neighbors."[20] These women's involvement in the club movement opened new vistas for them.

Most clubwomen in the Buffalo black community were young, ranging from 25 years to 35 years of age. However, women in their sixties and seventies joined these organizations, especially religious-oriented groups such as the Women's Mite Missionary Society (WMMS) of Bethel African Methodist Episcopal Church. These women also were influenced by the times during which they lived. The pre-World War I era was one of progressive change. If a composite picture can be painted of the black female reformer in Buffalo at the time, it is one of a woman sensitive to her community's needs, aggressive in her approach to finding solutions to its problems, and committed to eradicating them. Most were involved in several reform organizations. These women also enjoyed the support of their male kin, some of whom were also business, social or political activists in their own right.[21]

Women's public activities were perceived as an extension of their household responsibilities. The tenet underlying their public involvement was the belief that women possessed unusual moral qualities that could benefit society at large. Black women equated family with community. M. S. Pearson of Durham, North Carolina, explained NACW sentiments:

> ... the caring of [a woman's] children is simply extending the family housekeeping into community housekeeping. The education of the city's children are [sic] reaching out from her own. The work of beautifying parks, vacant lots ... , keeping clean the streets and alleys, is supplying the art and sanitation which she studies at home to the city's educational influence.[22]

During the latter part of the nineteenth century and the early twentieth century, African-American women organized local and national clubs to implement their reform proposals for their communities. Journalist Frances Ellen Watkins Harper observed, "The nineteenth century is discovering woman herself. The world cannot move without woman's sharing in that movement."[23] Educator Anna J. Cooper concurred, noting that women, by daring to move and speak, were merely completing the circle of the world's vision.[24] Fanny Barrier Williams, lecturer and clubwoman, summed it up thus: "In our day and in this country, a woman's sphere is just as large as she can make it and still be true to her finer qualities of soul."[25] Mary Burnett Talbert had no reservations about women's place in the social order. On the eve of World War I she argued that black women were on the dawn of a better day and maintained that woman's sphere is not limited: "she has the right to enter any sphere where she can do the most good."[26] Talbert also believed that black women possessed a unique quality and that it was incumbent upon them to help black men "free themselves from the yokes of moral and political [bondage]."[27] Such sentiment fostered womanist ideas.

This posture of turn-of-the-century black women spokespersons was predicated upon their historical and cultural experiences. Historian Deborah Gray White documented the nature of bonded woman's culture.

> If [slave women] seemed exceptionally strong it was partly because they often functioned in groups and derived their strength from numbers. Slave women developed their own female culture, a way of doing things and a way of assigning value that flowed from the perspective they had [on their lives].[28]

This was the legacy that these women carried into freedom and passed down to their daughters. The nineteenth-century notion of the "cult of true womanhood" held little meaning for African-American women who were one generation removed from chattel slavery, or if a legacy of freedom was theirs, had never been accorded a special status because of their gender. Also, the black community was more tolerant of women's participation in the public sphere than its white counterpart and subsequently black women had a long history of political activism. Finally, a disproportionate number of black women worked outside their homes in an effort to supplement their family income.[29] Therefore, they may have had greater expectations of themselves and their community.

Black women in Buffalo, like those nationwide, united to combat the negative stereotypes perpetrated by the press and some white feminists.[30] But they especially deplored the plight of black women and children. They wanted to protect them and at the same time uplift them, for they believed that only opportunity and environment separated them from the masses. Their task, then, was to provide the circumstances by which black children and women could advance intellectually, spiritually, and economically. Fanny Barrier Williams observed among colored women that "the club is the effort of a few competent on behalf of the more incompetent."[31] Talbert concluded that it took love of woman for woman for the average clubwoman to engage in these endeavors. Mary Church Terrell shared this view, too and noted that the black woman since emancipation had been moving ahead, educating herself and dedicating her life to the advancement of the race. This was the special mission of black women—"to lift as they climbed." By 1914 nationwide the NACW had more than 50,000 members in some 1,000 clubs.[32]

Soon after Susan Evans, a social worker, founded the Buffalo Phyllis Wheatley Club it sought affiliation with the NACW. In her letter of application to the parent organization, club secretary Mary Talbert wrote that it was established solely for the purpose of uplifting our "fallen" women in Buffalo and protecting the children.[33] The Phyllis Wheatley Club symbolized the nature of black women's reform in the Queen City at the turn of the century, but it was only one of many groups that black women organized.

Most Buffalo black women's clubs sought political, social, and economic change in their communities. The energizing force for Buffalo black women's reform efforts was the harsh reality of black people's lives in the city. They saw a community whose opportunities for economic and political advancement were limited by racism. Furthermore, they saw the need for improvement in health delivery services and an education program predicated on African-American values. They also held institutions, as well as individuals, accountable for moral development. To assure that they were, clubwomen created special projects that addressed these issues.

At the turn of the century, black women's clubs nationwide focused on the moral development of their communities. In part their actions reflected the widespread negative stereotypes of blacks, particularly women, that the media and others depicted. But these women also believed that an impeccable moral code was the sine qua non for sound mental and physical development.[34] In Buffalo, the Phyllis Wheatley Club, the brainchild of Susan Evans, represented the new thrust of Progressive Era urban institutions, bent on pursuing scientific approaches to effecting social change. Its organizing efforts were successful, and membership grew from the original eleven to 100 in 1900, its first year in operation.[35] The club immediately made its presence felt by addressing issues of personal and institutional morality and self-improvement for all segments of the Buffalo community.

It was not unusual for the police to tolerate vice in black neighborhoods. Buffalo's black community, like others across the nation, was plagued by charges of immorality, and the police force was exceedingly lax in enforcing city ordinances governing crime in black areas. So although the vice squad cracked down on illicit activities, it had reached a tacit agreement with white underworld figures, permitting them to ply their trades within a five-block area that encompassed the homes of middle-class blacks and two of their most important churches, the Vine Street African Methodist Episcopal Church and the Michigan Avenue Baptist Church. The Phyllis Wheatley Club was not about to sit idly by and permit this effrontery to the race. Members called a special meeting and demanded "that the police do their duty in carrying out the laws forbidding the licensing of immoral places."[36] They won the support of white temperance advocate Mrs. A. B. Wilson. Mary Talbert received an invitation to join the citywide Committee of Fifteen to monitor police enforcement of city ordinances.[37] Club members' actions were a catalyst for other organizations to protest the laxity with which the public safety forces protected black interests.

Buffalo black women also conducted a moral crusade aimed at the black community itself. During the early decades twentieth century, Buffalo blacks experienced mortality rates that were twice as high as those of whites.[38] Black clubwomen's emphasis on morality was a remnant from the Victorian Era, but these Progressive Era women saw a direct connection between their community's health and morality. They felt that one had to learn to "regard the physical body with the utmost reverence as a beautiful, sacred temple, to be kept pure, sweet and clean, that the soul may find a fitting means of expression."[39] Women's church groups, such as the missionary societies, and their secular counterparts offered public programs predicated on biblical scriptures that emphasized moral development. Clubwomen considered these teachings so important that they became an integral part of the structure of all of their youth programs. The National Association of Colored Girls' Clubs, affiliates of the NACW, were vehicles for them to inculcate members with an acceptable code of behavior. Black women organized several affiliates in Buffalo. Mary Talbert conducted in her home weekly sessions for teenage girls that addressed morality and self-improvement, political ideology, and community uplift as well as wholesome recreation. In 1920, Talbert called upon women from the community to organize a junior YWCA and to help her "direct and assist" the girls. Several new advisers joined her and used their homes as sites for the Y meetings.[40] In the 1930s, the Women's Guild of the Buffalo Cooperative Economic Society offered similar programs for children.[41]

Dr. Mary F. Waring, NACW Health Department chair, in 1929 urged women to sponsor preventative health care measures in their communities.[42] Buffalo black clubwomen shared this concern. They either sponsored or played significant roles in a number of community health forums, including well-baby clinics and education programs that disseminated information on hygiene, nutrition, and disease prevention.[43] The Phyllis Wheatley Club sponsored mothers' clubs that taught women the proper ways to raise the children of their community for sound physical, emotional, and moral development. It also worked among the "fallen" women of the community, offering counseling, job information, and companionship.

Most African-American women's clubs engaged in some form of charity work. Their organized benevolence provided crucial resources to indigent community members. The Phyllis Wheatley Club joined forces with other groups affiliated with the Empire State Federation of Women's Clubs and provided a monthly "pension" for Harriet Tubman, the Civil War veteran and Auburn nursing home resident, who symbolized their own quest for freedom and self-determination.[44] Committed to humanitarian causes, the Phyllis Wheatley Club also attacked the problems of housing and food shortages and inadequate clothing. Club members either purchased, made, or mended clothes to distribute to the needy. They donated food baskets to the poor and on holidays provided special meals for them. They did not allow racial barriers or other divisive factors to interfere with their benevolent activities and on Christmas Day, 1901, club members served meals to 500 people, most of whom were white. These women also established a home for aged African Americans in Buffalo and on one occasion interceded to prevent the eviction of an elderly woman from her home.[45]

Other black women's groups joined the Phyllis Wheatley Club in its organized benevolence. The Lit-Mus Club, a literary club founded in 1922, assumed responsibility for helping to feed and clothe the poor.[46] The Booklovers, another literary society, made sizable contributions of food and clothing to needy Buffalonians.[47] While most African-American clubwomen in Buffalo felt a commitment to their less fortunate brothers and sisters, the premier benevolent organization was the African American church. Women's missionary societies, standing auxiliaries in most churches, were organized to help alleviate pain and suffering wherever they found them. Predicated on the Christian notion of brotherly love, they incorporated visitation, consultation, and instruction to implement their programmatic goals. The Josephine Hurd Women's Mite Missionary Society of the Bethel AME Church, founded in 1915, was one of these groups. During harsh economic times, such as the Depression of 1929, WMMS increased its benevolent efforts. It provided appliances, fuel and shelter, as well as food and clothing for constituents. It also donated taxi fares to the elderly to permit them to attend the Sunday worship services.[48] All of these women's contributions played an important role in their community.

On the eve of the twentieth century, Buffalo's African-American women had been involved in activities designed to eliminate race and gender oppression for nearly a century. Black women found that racism lurked at every corner in the Queen City. No one was immune to its clutches. In some instances they had personal racial encounters in areas of employment, politics, housing, and public accommodations. Some had encountered it vicariously through the experiences of their families and friends in Buffalo and across the nation. The Lit-Mus Club in 1931 contracted with a catering company to hold a luncheon in its facilities. When owners discovered that the club was composed of black women, they broke the contract.[49] Such incidents and the fear that pervasive racism would destroy their children compelled black women to attack racism head-on. Their tireless efforts to eradicate racism were important in publicizing its inimical effects on blacks and winning white support.

Buffalo blacks hailed the announcement that the city was to be the site of the 1901 Pan-American Exposition, for they perceived this event as an opportunity to advertise worldwide the progress that African Americans had made since slavery ended. However, their enthusiasm waned when they learned that the planning commission had decided not to appoint a black to its board. This was the first time in recent history that a planning board had failed to appoint an African-American representative. Its decision virtually assured that the African-American experience would be absent from the exhibit.[50]

Spearheaded by the Phyllis Wheatley Club, blacks protested this action. The club invited Buffalo residents to attend a forum at the Michigan Avenue Baptist Church to discuss this issue and to decide on a course of action to win the support of intransigent commissioners. Speaking before an interracial audience of more than 200, Mary Talbert cogently argued for the inclusion of blacks in this twentieth-century exhibition. In her address, "Why the American Negro Should Be Represented at the Pan-American Exposition," Talbert noted that the exhibit should represent the cultural diversity of the hemisphere. She also told her audience that previous exhibitions on African peoples at world fairs had been quite successful. Moreover, she argued that the 1901 Pan-American Exposition planning committee was turning back the hands of time, for every other major planning committee included a black commissioner. Black politicians like James A. Ross, and white reformers such as Mrs. A. B. Wilson, pledged their support for black representation at the Exposition. The assembled group adopted resolutions declaring that "the Negroes of Buffalo were unanimous in their desire to have a Negro exhibit" at the Pan-American Exhibition and that planning officials should appoint a black commissioner immediately.[51] Many of those present believed that Mary Talbert could best represent blacks because of her educational background and her experience. The Phyllis Wheatley Club's challenge to the power structure represented a pyrrhic victory. Although Pan-American Exposition officials capitulated to the black community's wishes by including an exhibit on African Americans, it focused on slavery and minstrelsy and depicted blacks in stereotyped images.[52] Commissioners, however, refused to appoint a black representative, even of the stature of Mary B. Talbert.[53]

The Phyllis Wheatley Club's fight against racism was to be a long and protracted one, with limited victories. It and the black community continued to be plagued by the negative images that the press depicted.[54] In 1910, the club sought outside help to address this issue and invited the National Association for the Advancement of Colored People to organize a local chapter. Their actions received widespread support from black men and women as well as sympathetic whites. Several black women's clubs joined the struggle to mitigate the harmful effects of racism. They believed that education was a viable means to change people's attitudes. Therefore, they specifically targeted public institutions such as schools and libraries for their crusade. The Phyllis Wheatley Club donated the works of Phyllis Wheatley and other leading black writers to the public library in 1901.[55] Organized to "improve [its] community and provide socialibility [sic] among members," the Lit-Mus Club also provided avenues for Buffalonians to learn about black life and culture. It introduced Negro History Week to Buffalo, and annually beginning in 1928 it made arrangements for the public library to set up special exhibits during its observance.[56] Black women's organizations invited prominent speakers such as educators Charlotte Hawkins Brown and Mary Church Terrell, historian J. A. Rogers, and poet Countee Cullen to discuss contemporary issues that the race confronted.[57] The presence of these eminent intellectuals boosted morale among blacks and acted as a catalyst in gaining some white support for black causes in the city.

Buffalo black women understood the importance of political action to help effect social change and they had long participated in organizations established to shape public policy. Earlier they had been involved in abolitionism, the ratification movement for support of the Fifteenth Amendment to the Constitution, and the school integration movement in the city. Although black women organized suffrage groups and participated in suffrage demonstrations, their lack of the vote did not deter them from "mature" political action. They could rely on their ability to influence black men's political views. After all, black men adhered to the same folkways and mores and frequently supported the implementation of black women's social programs. This was their guarantee that their voices would be heard in the policy-making halls of the city, state, and country.[58] They also perceived the NAACP, with its branches across the nation, as an effective tool for addressing the critical issues that the Buffalo community experienced. Such a network, dedicated to the eradication of racism and human rights violations, meant that communities with small black populations, like Buffalo, could draw on that network to avoid isolation and political suicide.

With the exception of disparate speeches and writings of Mary Talbert, firsthand accounts of Buffalo black women's political beliefs are thin. But their involvement in community groups, like the NAACP, the National Urban League and the Buffalo Cooperative Economic Society, and national women's clubs provides a clear indication of their political views. Their activities in the NAACP, especially, demonstrate their beliefs regarding race and gender. Black women not only began the organizational activities of the NAACP, but they always comprised a significant proportion of its membership.[59] As officers, executive directors, and members of their own auxiliary, black women were in a position to influence the direction of the organization. Their philosophy was grounded in their experiences. Although they were well represented in the organization from the beginning, it was 1917 before the body elected a woman officer. In that year, Amelia Anderson assumed the position of secretary. Three years later black women held the two most important executive positions in the local branch: C. J. Jones was president and Clara Payne was vice president. Jones stated that she had accepted the presidency after Dr. Marion Allen's resignation rather than "see our branch go to pieces and the Cause fail here in Buffalo."[60] But President Amelia Anderson at the annual membership drive of 1928 captured black women's sentiments regarding the organization's significant political role when she told her audience of 500:

> We [the local Association] must play [our part] so well that we will be a valuable asset to the National Office in becoming so strong, so powerful, so active and so effective that no government north or south, no party, in fact no individual will dare to commit any indignity against any member of the race without realizing that he will be defended by every legitimate and constitutional means.[61]

She continued:

> . . . newly gained members for the Buffalo Branch means the awakening on the part of the Colored people to the need of organization; it means the awakening to a sense of citizenship denied, and the responsibility and obligation in bringing to themselves, the children, and in fact, to America, herself, the realization of a fuller blessing on the part of the Colored people in the participation of the nation's political, economic and community life.[62]

Anderson's speech drew upon her community's self-help and religious values and black women's culture to effect social change. Liberation for blacks, that is, self-determination, could result only from their collective actions. Moreover, the choice for blacks was obvious. They had to set aside class differences and act out of love for their children. They had to create for them a nurturing environment that would allow them to pursue the American Dream. Black children had to be imbued with religious values that stressed mutuality and commitment to struggle. Black women moved with what at times seemed like a messianic fervor in their efforts to transform society. The new world order they sought would transform America to the benefit of all of its citizens.

Women established their own auxiliary to the NAACP. Operating through committees on education, fund-raising, and entertainment, these women sponsored plays and concerts featuring African American artists. They hosted "interracial" teas to promote racial harmony and drew upon a network of sympathetic white women to carry their cause back to their own organizations. The monies that the auxiliary raised were crucial in keeping the branch viable.[63] The women's auxiliary to the NAACP succeeded because members formed an important connection with other advancement organizations in the black community. They also represented an intricate network with women in other social uplift groups in the black community and they relied on their cooperation and interdependence. Mrs. T. J. Holcolm was active in the Michigan Avenue YMCA; Elizabeth Talbert in the Friendship Home for African American Girls; Alberta Nelson, the Buffalo Cooperative Economic Society; and Otis Davenport Jackson was a member of the Board of Directors of the National Urban League. Ruth Scruggs and Frances Nash were active in the federated women's clubs of the city.[64] All of the members of the auxiliary were involved in their churches and could depend on their congregations to help promote their causes. Each brought to her committee assignments a wealth of skills in public relations and fund-raising techniques as well as her important networks. Their presence in the organization facilitated the implementation of NAACP programs and was instrumental in bringing into the Association diverse individuals from the community. Until Buffalo black women gained the right to vote in federal elections in 1920, the NAACP was the most important vehicle for their political activities.[65]

In the 1920s the Negro Women's Civic and Research Club met frequently at its headquarters in the heart of the growing black community. Organized to study "thoroughly vital points pertaining to our government and the Negro race," the club hoped to guide and teach "self-independence" as it pursued equality of opportunities for African Americans. Members conducted seminars on such topics as "The Value of the Vote," the speeches of local and national political figures, and blacks' struggles for self-determination.[66] For these women the denial of justice for black men was a feminist issue. In the 1930s black women joined forces with other local and national groups in support of the defense of the Scottsboro Boys.[67] Women's participation in such forums provided them with the prerequisite skills to assume roles in politics. After the ratification of the Nineteenth Amendment, Buffalo black women began to organize Republican clubs. Support for Marcus Garvey's Universal Negro Improvement Association was also strong among women. By the middle of the decade their participation in politics had evolved to a new stage in the political maturation process, for they formed Democratic women's clubs and held office in united political groups, too.[68]

Gender issues and race issues were often the same for black women. World war and the migration and depression years were particularly difficult for black women and provided them an impetus for action predicated on their consciousness of their identity as women. The protection of black women, especially the young who came to the city in search of economic opportunities, was a major issue for many black women's organizations. Clubwomen knew from their own experiences that these women were vulnerable to exploitation, and tales of the slavelike conditions under which some young black women domestics lived in the North were widespread. The Douglass Club, a group of progressive black women, uncovered a case in Buffalo. A young black woman had been brought to the city as a child and had been forced to work for a white attorney's family for eighteen years. In addition to stealing her labor, this family denied her the opportunity for schooling beyond sixth grade and prevented her from attending church or communicating with outsiders. The Douglass Club, with the aid of Cornelius Ford, a prominent black businessman, found the young woman a new home and a job that paid wages.[69] It was because of the need to inform young, single black women about work conditions and employee rights that black women helped found and operated the Friendship Home for Girls. Moreover, Buffalo offered a paucity of housing, recreational, and educational facilities for these young women.

Increasingly, Buffalo black women found themselves the victims of physical and verbal attacks if they were on the streets after dark.[70] Black women were especially vulnerable to exploitation because of the widely disseminated negative stereotypes about their character and the belief that blacks should work in subordinate positions. Elizabeth Talbert, Otis Davenport Jackson, Viola Wheeler, and others, cognizant of the wide range of issues confronting young women, took the initiative in operating the Friendship Home that community churches financed. This center provided the services traditionally offered by the YWCA—safe, sanitary housing accommodations and education. A resident matron was always available for consultation, and Friendship House provided "a place where issues relating to the moral, social, religious, and ethical welfare of the [black] people are correlated and put into execution."[71] Viola Wheeler supervised a curriculum consisting of sewing, first aid, music, and English. The academic year concluded in June with a literary and musical program highlighting the accomplishments of the residents during the year.[72] The Friendship Home provided alternatives for black women and helped many to make a smooth transition into their new community.

Black women in Buffalo carried out their reform activities in a labyrinth of independent as well as auxiliary units. The establishment of black women's auxiliaries was the result of both the marginalization that women frequently experienced in mixed gender groups as well as their desire to maintain vehicles through which to exercise a ritual of solidarity. These forums, like black women's independent clubs, provided a laboratory for them to pursue social engineering policies. It also offered them a nurturing environment in which to receive leadership training.

The Women's Mite Missionary Society of the Bethel African Methodist Episcopal Church gave black women an opportunity to mingle with young and old. Women's involvement in this religious organization illustrates the nature of their subordinate culture and the ways it benefited them. The Women's Mite Missionary Society grew out of the sentiment expressed by James H. A. Johnson in his essay "Women's Exalted Station" that appeared in the *AME Church Review* in 1892. He contended that every "true woman" was to be a "helpmeet" for man and drew the line between man's constitution and her own. He further stated that woman "realized man's adaptability to a different sphere, and did not seek entry into it." Johnson wrote:

> The woman who claims admission to every position occupied by man, and is willing to shoulder her musket and fight for it, is a monstrous outgrowth of the coarser elements of female nature.[73]

Although Johnson's views defied the historical relations between African-American men and women, women responded by forming their own auxiliary, for they perceived it as an effective means to implement church dogma. WMMS also assured them that their voices would be heard in the church hierarchy. But WMMS offered women more. In the confines of their own organization they were guaranteed a forum for self-expression.

The Bethel AME chapter held weekly meetings at the homes of its members. The site of its meetings alone changed the dynamics of women's experience in the church and promoted egalitarian relations. Sessions consisted of brief worship services, committee reports, and activity periods that were used to make quilts or to repair clothing for rummage sales, and to socialize. From its founding in 1915 through the 1940s, the format of their meetings remained virtually unchanged. They had found their niche. Members never discussed issues of autonomy or their role in the church body. They were more concerned about self-help and the promotion of church activities than church politics.[74]

WMMS activities reflected a distinct woman's culture characterized by benevolence, mutuality, and nurturance. Sisterhood was important and members addressed each other as such, a symbolic gesture, indicating that they believed that they were bound by ties of consanguinity based on their historical experience. Class and age barriers were bridged as day workers and professionals in their twenties to seventies mingled amicably in WMMS. The missionary meetings strengthened their feelings of sisterhood and their devotion to their community. Every member of WMMS engaged in the ongoing assignment of making quilts that were sold to help finance many of the organization's projects. This task reinforced the fact that their combined efforts could produce a beautiful work of art that served a practical purpose, whereas individually they had useless scraps of material. The quilts, like the women themselves, represented a shared historical experience and taught women that they could effect change by pooling their resources.

The sisters of WMMS affiliated with other women in local and state missionary societies where their benevolence had an even broader impact. Through activities generally considered women's work, they aided and comforted the indigent. These women felt a kinship and commitment to blacks in Africa and other parts of the diaspora. They therefore extended their missionary activities to West Africa and Haiti. WMMS fund-raising activities also provided crucial support to the Bethel AME Church.[75]

In addition to providing essential services to their church and community, membership in the Women's Mite Missionary Society was an important vehicle for black women to secure organizational and leadership skills that could be used in the formation of secular organizations later. Moreover, women who joined WMMS were given an opportunity to work on collective projects, to worship together, and to socialize informally. At the same time their gatherings provided a forum to exchange information on jobs, child care, health care, and other social and political concerns. In this forum, too, older women had an opportunity to pass on their traditions, customs, and values to younger women. Women's membership in WMMS reinforced their communal spirit and afforded many members an opportunity to escape the monotony that often presented itself in their lives.

The Buffalo data clearly show that black women articulated community concerns, galvanized their collective power, and seized the opportunity to provide leadership. Throughout a forty-year period, black women designed projects to uplift their communities through education, benevolence, self-improvement, and the amelioration of race relations. Their successes resulted from their ability to mobilize resources such as their collective organizational and management skills and their effective fund-raising techniques.[76] Moreover, they utilized their knowledge of African Americans' historical experiences and their national network of women as weapons to effect social change. They worked with black men and gained their respect. Buffalo black women's organized activities indicate their continued awareness of their community's greatest social concerns and a firm commitment to reform.

The study of Buffalo black women and reform also elucidates our understanding of the structure of the organizations within which women operated. Both autonomous and auxiliary units provided women the opportunity to design and implement reform programs within the context of their African-American woman's culture. The auxiliary, juxtaposed with the parent body, allowed women the opportunity to utilize their informal networks to achieve the formal, structured programmatic goals of the parent organization. Yet their involvement did not preclude their playing a meaningful role in the parent organization itself. The auxiliary often became the lifeblood of the organization. The Buffalo Urban League auxiliary's chief function was to study community social problems. It also assumed responsibility for raising the balance of the black community's financial assessment that the National Urban

League mandated before authorizing the establishment of a chapter.[77] Robert Bagnall, field secretary of the NAACP branches, observed that women's auxiliaries "have become the dominant factor in keeping the branches alive."[78] These auxiliaries frequently were responsible for community educational and cultural programs. All of these activities were significant in carrying out the mandate of the institutions to which African-American women belonged, and their separate units afforded them the opportunity to expand their power within the parent organization and to seek self-actualization. Black women used their dual status as both outsider and insider not only to function effectively but also to manipulate two worlds—one dominated by racism, the other sexism. Their clear understanding of their status as women and blacks and their keen perceptions enabled them to play key roles in improving living conditions for African Americans in Buffalo. Their organized activities indicate a clearly articulated definition of black womanhood that was linked to the black community's interest and was characterized by self-help, racial solidarity and community uplift.

NOTES

The research for this essay was supported in part by a grant from the New York African American Institute. The author wishes to acknowledge the special assistance of Francine Frank, Dean of the College of Humanities and Fine Arts at SUNY Albany, and Daniel Williams, Archivist, Frissell Library, Tuskegee University. She also appreciates the comments that Allen Ballard, Mary Frances Berry, Florence Bonner and Bonnie Spanier made on an earlier draft of this essay.

1. *National Association Notes*, 19 (October 1916), p. 3, Frissell Library, Tuskegee University, Tuskegee Alabama, hereafter cited as *National Association Notes*.
2. *Ibid.*
3. "Proceedings, National Convention of Colored Citizens held in Buffalo, New York, in 1843," Schomburg Research Center, New York Public Library; Dorothy Porter, "The Organized Educational Activities of Negro Literary Societies, 1828-1846," in August Meier and Elliott Rudwick, eds., *The Making of Black America*, Vol. 1 (New York: Atheneum, 1969), p. 277; Arthur White, "The Black Movement Against Jim Crow Education in Buffalo, New York, 1800-1900," *Phylon* xxx (Winter 1969), pp. 375-95; *Buffalo Courier*, January 4, 1897, p. 4; *Buffalo Courier*, April 4, 1897, p. 6.
4. Alice Walker coined "womanist" to describe a black feminist or feminist of color. She defines it as "wanting to know more and in greater depth than is considered 'good' for one; committed to survival and wholeness of entire people, male and female; traditionally universalist." Alice Walker, *In Search of Our Mothers' Gardens* (New York: Harcourt Brace Jovanovich, 1983), p. xi. I use "feminist" and "womanist" interchangeably, but it is this definition that I employ in reference to black women. Other works on womanist theory are Elsa Barkley Brown, "Womanist Consciousness: Maggie Lena Walker and the Independent Order of St. Luke," in *Signs*, 14, no. 3 (March 1989), pp. 610-33; Patricia Hill Collins, "The Social Construction of Black Feminist Thought," in *Signs*, 14, no. 4 (Summer 1989); Angela Davis, *Women,*

Race and Class (New York: Vintage, 1983); bell hooks, *Ain't I a Woman: black women and feminism* (Boston: South End Press, 1981); Barbara Smith, *Home Girls* (New York: Kitchen Table Women of Color Press, 1983).

5. Smith, *Home Girls*, pp. xix-lvi.

6. For a discussion of black women's culture and self-help in the black community, see Deborah Gray White, *Ar'n't I a Woman?* (New York: Norton, 1985), pp. 119-141; Edward Magdol, "Against the Gentry: An Inquiry into a Southern Lower-Class Community and Culture," in Edward Magdol and Jon Wakelyn, eds., *The Southern Common People* (Westport: Greenwood, 1980), pp. 191-210.

7. For additional studies of black women's organized activities, see Darlene Clark Hine, *When the Truth Is Told* (Indianapolis: National Council of Negro Women, 1983); Cynthia Neverdon-Morton, *Afro-American Women of the South and the Advancement of the Race* (Knoxville: University of Tennessee, 1989); Paula Giddings, *When and Where I Enter* (New York: Morrow, 1984), pp. 95-118; Gerda Lerner, *The Majority Finds Its Past* (New York: Oxford University Press, 1979), pp. 83-93; Charles Wesley, *The History of the National Association of Colored Women's Clubs, Inc.: A Legacy of Service* (Washington, D.C.: National Association of Colored Women's Clubs, Inc., 1985), hereafter cited as *NACWC, Inc.*; Earline Rae Ferguson, "The Woman's Improvement Club of Indianapolis: Black Women Pioneers in Tuberculosis Work, 1903-1938," *Indiana Magazine of History* 84 (September 1988), pp. 237-61; Marilyn Dell Brady, "Kansas Federation of Colored Women's Clubs, 1900-1930," *Kansas History* 9 (Spring 1986), pp. 19-30.

8. The New York State Manuscript Census recorded 1,200 blacks in Buffalo in 1905, 1,600 in 1915, and 9,000 in 1925; Lockwood Library, State University of New York at Buffalo (microfilmed).

9. Proceedings, National Convention of Colored Citizens, 1843; *Buffalo Morning Express*, July 12, 1905, p. 6; *Buffalo Courier*, July 12, 1905, p. 7; John Mayfield, *Rehearsal for Republicanism: Free Soil and the Politics of Antislavery* (Port Washington, NY: Kennikat Press, 1979).

10. The growth and development of Buffalo is discussed in Robert Holder, *Beginnings of Buffalo Industry* (Buffalo: Buffalo and Erie County Historical Society, 1960); Robert Bingham, *Cradle of the Queen City* (Buffalo: Buffalo Historical Society, 1931). For a discussion on the conditions of black laborers, see Lillian S. Williams, "Afro-Americans in Buffalo, 1900-1930: A Study in Community Formation," *Afro-Americans in New York Life and History*, 8, No 2 (July 1984), pp. 3-35.

11. *National Association Notes*, 19 (October 1916), p. 5.

12. "A History of the Club Movement Among Colored Women of the United States of America, 1902, as contained in the minutes of the conventions, held in Boston, July 19-31, 1895 and of the National Federation of Afro-American Women held in Washington, D. C., July 20-22, 1896," Moorland-Spingarn Research Center, Howard University, Washington, D.C.; Charles Wesley, *NACWC, Inc.*, pp. 24-39; Elizabeth Lindsay Davis, *Lifting as We Climb* (Washington, D.C.: National Association of Colored Women's Clubs, 1933).

13. There is no scholarly biography of Mary Burnett Talbert. Her most comprehensive biographical sketch is Lillian S. Williams, "Mary Morris Burnett Talbert (1866-1923)," in David Eggenberger, ed., *Encyclopedia of World Biography*, Vol. 15 (Palatine, Illinois: Jack Heraty McGraw Hill, 1988), pp. 396-98. Other useful sketches appear in *The Crisis*, 27 (December 1923), p. 77; Hallie Q. Brown, *Homespun*

Heroines and Other Women of Distinction (Xenia, Ohio: Aldine Publishing, 1926), pp. 216-19; Rayford Logan and Michael Winston, eds., *Dictionary of American Negro Biography* (New York: Norton, 1985), pp. 576-77.

14. *Buffalo Daily Courier*, July 9, 1901, p. 6; *ibid.*, July 12, 1901, p. 9; *Buffalo Morning Express*, July 11, 1901, p. 3; *Buffalo Evening News*, July 9, 1901, p. 5; International Council of Women of the Darker Races (ICWDR) History (carbon), in Mary Church Terrell Papers, Box 21, Manuscript Division, Library of Congress; ICWDR, Treasurer's Report, Mary Church Terrell Papers, Box 102-12, folder 240, Moorland-Spingarn Research Center.

15. Wesley, *NACWC, Inc.*, pp. 78, 83-87; *National Association Notes* 25 (May 1923), p. 3; *National Association Notes* 26 (November 1923), p. 3.

16. Minutes, Organizational Committee, October 1, 1926, Urban League Papers, Series IV, Box 28, Manuscript Division, Library of Congress. Employment information on Clara Payne was taken from the New York State Manuscript Census, 1905, 1915, 1925.

17. Interview, Bessie Williams, February 26, 1976.

18. *Buffalo Courier*, March 3, 1901; *Fiftieth Anniversary Banquet Program, Lit-Mus Club, 1922-1972*, in possession of author, hereafter cited as *Fiftieth Anniversary*; interview, Dr. Shirley Harrington, member, Booklovers, June 7, 1979; Wesley, *NACWC, Inc.*, pp. 59, 209; *Buffalo Morning Express*, July 12, 1905; Dora Needham Lee, "History of the Empire Federation of Women's Clubs," pp. 7-8 (carbon), in Maria C. Lawton Club Papers, Albany, New York; I am grateful to Mrs. Virginia Poyer for bringing the Lee history to my attention.

19. Standard socioeconomic indicators frequently do not explain adequately social class in the African-American community during the first half of the twentieth century. Respectability and other values have to be included among the salient variables. Hence, domestics, officers in benevolent organizations, and others who worked in semiskilled and skilled positions could comprise the black middle class. For a discussion of class in the black community, see St. Clair Drake and Horace Cayton, *Black Metropolis* (New York: Harper, 1962), pp. 379-754; E. Franklin Frazier, *The Negro in the United States* (New York: Macmillan, 1957); David Gordon, *Segmented Work, Divided Workers: The Historical Transformation of Labor in the U.S.* (New York: Cambridge, 1982), pp. 165-227; Bart Landry, *The New Black Middle Class* (Berkeley: University of California Press, 1987); William J. Wilson, *The Declining Significance of Race: Blacks and Changing American Institutions* (Chicago: University of Chicago Press, 1978).

20. Economic opportunities for black women in Buffalo were extremely limited, as they were across the country. Of 100 women placed by a black employment agency in Buffalo in 1923, 91 were placed in domestic service, 2 in factories, and 7 in hotels and restaurants. Niles Carpenter, *Nationality, Color and Economic Opportunity* (Buffalo: University of Buffalo, 1927), p. 166.

21. Livestock dealer Cornelius Ford served on the Board of Managers of the Michigan Avenue YMCA and was treasurer of the *Buffalo American*. William Jackson was executive secretary of the Michigan Avenue YMCA, a position that gave him high visibility in Buffalo. Dr. Ivorite Scruggs was a member of the Board of Managers of the Michigan Avenue YMCA. William H. Talbert, a wealthy city clerk and real estate dealer, was an organizer of the Niagara Movement and was president of the Buffalo Colored Republican Club. *Buffalo Courier Express*, April 20, 1951; Abbreviated History, "Memorabilia, 1926-1936," and "Recognition Week Programs,

April 21-27, 1947," Michigan Avenue YMCA Papers; these records are located in the Archives of the Afro-American Historical Society of the Niagara Frontier, North Jefferson Branch, Buffalo and Erie County Library, Buffalo, New York; hereafter cited as MAYMCA; *Buffalo Courier Express*, March 17, 1955; W.E.B. DuBois Papers, reel 3, frame 284, University of Massachusetts, Amherst; Frank Lincoln Mather, *Who's Who of the Colored Race*, Vol. I (Detroit: Gale Research Company, 1976, orig., 1915), p. 258.

22. *National Association Notes*, 19 (January 1917), p. 12.

23. Giddings, *When and Where I Enter*, p. 96.

24. *Ibid.*

25. *Ibid.*

26. Mary Church Terrell Papers, reel 17, frame 257, Lockwood Library, State University of New York at Buffalo.

27. *Ibid.*

28. White, *Ar'n't I a Woman?*, pp. 119, 121.

29. Between 1900 and 1930 married black women were twice as likely to be employed outside of their homes as their white counterparts. U. S. Bureau of the Census, *Historical Statistics of the United States: Colonial Times to 1957* (Washington, D. C.: U. S. Bureau of the Census, 1960), pp. D 26-45. Other sources on black women and employment are Mary White Ovington, *Half a Man: The Status of the Negro in New York* (New York: Hill and Wang, 1969), pp. 76-92; Jacqueline Jones, *Labor of Love, Labor of Sorrow* (New York: Basic Books, 1985), pp. 196-231.

30. Black women constantly had to prove their respectability. See Darlene Clark Hine, "Lifting the Veil, Shattering the Silence: Black Women's History in Slavery and Freedom," Darlene Clark Hine, ed., *The State of Afro-American History* (Baton Rouge: Louisiana State University Press, 1986), pp. 223-49; Darlene Clark Hine, "Rape and the Inner Lives of Black Women in the Middle West: Preliminary Thoughts of the culture of Dissemblance," in *Signs* 14, No.4 (Summer 1989), pp. 912-20; Lerner, *The Majority Finds Its Past*, pp. 94-111; Rosalyn Terborg-Penn, "Discrimination Against Afro-American Women in the Woman's Movement, 1830-1920," in Sharon Harley and Rosalyn Terborg-Penn, eds., *The African American Woman: Struggles and Images* (Port Washington, N. Y.: Kennikat Press, 1978), pp. 17-27.

31. Giddings, *When and Where I Enter*, p. 98.

32. *Ibid.*, p. 95.

33. *National Notes* (January 1901), Mary Church Terrell Papers, Box 102-12, Folder 244, Moorland-Spingarn Research Center.

34. *National Association Notes* 12 (October 1908); *ibid.*, 23 (January-March 1921), pp. 12-14; Giddings, *When and Where I Enter*, pp. 98-100.

35. *Buffalo Courier*, March 3, 1901.

36. *Ibid.*, March 11, 1902.

37. *Ibid.*

38. First Annual Report, Buffalo Urban League, 1928, Urban League Headquarters, Buffalo, N.Y.

39. *National Association Notes*, 19 (January 1917), p. 12.

40. *Buffalo American*, November 11, 1920; *ibid.*, November 25, 1920.

41. The records of the Buffalo Cooperative Economic Society are located in the Archives of the Afro-American Historical Association of the Niagara Frontier, North Jefferson Branch, Buffalo and Erie County Library. For a history of the

organization see Monroe Fordham, "BCES, Inc., 1928-1961: A Self-Help Organization," in *Niagara Frontier* (Summer 1976), pp. 41-49.

42. *National Notes*, 31 (February 1929), p. 16, Box 41, Mary Church Terrell Papers, Library of Congress.

43. "Scrapbook, Memorabilia, 1926-1936," MAYMCA.

44. *National Association Notes*, 15 (November 1911), p. 4.

45. *Buffalo Commercial Advertiser*, November 12, 1900; *Buffalo Courier*, March 3, 1901; *ibid.*, March 11, 1902.

46. "Fiftieth Anniversary Program."

47. Interview, Dr. Shirley Harrington, member, Booklovers, June 7, 1979.

48. Minutes WMMS, October 7, 1926, in the Bethel AME Church records in the Archives of the Afro-American Historical Association of the Niagara Frontier, North Jefferson Branch, Buffalo and Erie County Library.

49. Fourth Annual Report, Buffalo Urban League, 1931, Buffalo Urban League Headquarters.

50. *National Association Notes* (January 1901), in Mary Church Terrell Papers, Box 102-13, folder 244; Moorland-Spingarn Research Center.

51. *Ibid.*

52. "Old Plantation Exhibit," *Official Catalogue and Guide to the Pan-American Exposition* (Buffalo: Charles Ahrhart, 1901); Richard H. Barry, *Snapshots on the Midway of the Pan-American Exposition* (Buffalo: Robert Allen Reid, 1901).

53. *National Association Notes*, January, 1901.

54. John Brent to May Child Nerney, April 16, 1915, NAACP Administrative Files, Films and Plays, Box C 299; M. Clark to John Brent, December 10, 1920, Box G 130, NAACP Branch Files, Manuscript Division, Library of Congress.

55. *Buffalo Courier*, March 3, 1901.

56. "Fiftieth Anniversary; Lit-Mus Meeting Agenda, 1944-1945." I am grateful to Robin Hicks for sharing the Lit-Mus Club agenda with me.

57. Report for 20th Annual Conference, 1929, NAACP Branch Files, Box G 130, Manuscript Division, Library of Congress; *Buffalo Evening Times*, November 17, 1930, National Urban League, Series V, Box 13, Manuscript Division, Library of Congress; "Fiftieth Anniversary."

58. Martin Kilson describes the evolutionary stages in the political maturation of African American communities in Martin Kilson, "The Political Status of American Negroes in the Twentieth Century," in Martin Kilson and Robert Rotberg, eds., *The African Diaspora: Interpretive Essays* (Cambridge: Harvard University Press, 1976), pp. 459-84. Black women's political activities and their exercise of the franchise through black men's vote is discussed in Bettye Collier-Thomas and Ann Gordon, eds., *Black Women and the Vote, 1837-1965*, forthcoming.

59. Membership lists for the Buffalo NAACP Branch for the years 1920 to 1940 indicate that the percentage of women was upward of 50 percent, except for 1930 when they comprised their low, 28 percent. Buffalo NAACP Branch Files, Box G 130, Library of Congress.

60. C. J. Jones to James Weldon Johnson, June 22, 1925, NAACP Papers, Box G 130, Manuscript Division, Library of Congress.

61. *Buffalo American*, April 28, 1928.

62. *Ibid.*

63. Report to the Annual Conference, prepared by Ameila Anderson, July 2, 1929, NAACP Papers, Box G 130, Manuscript Division, Library of Congress.

64. Minutes, Buffalo Cooperative Economic Society, April 6, 1939; *Buffalo American*, April 30, 1925; First Annual Report, Buffalo Urban League, 1928; interview, Teresa Evans, Secretary, Buffalo Urban League, 1926-1961, February, 1977; Report of the 20th Annual Conference, NAACP, 1929.

65. The New York State Legislature ratified an amendment to the Constitution that granted the franchise to women in the State in 1917. David M. Ellis et al., *History of New York State* (Ithaca: Cornell University, 1967), pp. 391-92.

66. *Buffalo American*, August 12, 1920.

67. C.I. Claflin to Morris Shapiro, April 1, 1936; Mrs. A. Kennedy to Morris Shapiro, n.d., NAACP Papers, H Addenda, Box 6, Manuscript Division, Library of Congress.

68. *Buffalo American*, October 7, 1920, November 25, 1920, September 22, 1921, and October 13, 1921; Talbert Family Papers, Folder A80-14, Buffalo and Erie County Historical Society, Buffalo, New York.

69. *Buffalo American*, December 9, 1920; *ibid.*, December 16, 1920.

70. Charles Johnson, "The Negro in Buffalo," p. 107, The National Urban League, 1923 (mimeographed), State University of New York at Buffalo Archives.

71. *Buffalo American*, April 30, 1925.

72. *Ibid.*

73. *AME Church Review*, 8 (April 1892), pp. 403-04. For a discussion of the origin of WMMS, see the "AME Philadelphia Conference Branch, 1874," Moorland-Spingarn Research Center. Also Lewellyn Longfellow Berry, *A Century of Missions of the AME Church, 1840-1940* (New York: Gutenberg Printing Company, 1942), pp. 101-03.

74. Minutes, WMMS, October 7, 1926-December 8, 1945. In the 1940s Amelia Anderson introduced book discussions into the regular agenda of WMMS meetings.

75. Minutes, WMMS, December 2, 1926, April 27, 1927, June 30, 1927, September 5, 1940.

76. For a discussion of the impact of such resources on grassroots organizations and reform movements, see Aldon Morris, *Origins of the Civil Rights Movement: Organizing for Change* (New York: The Free Press, 1984).

77. First Annual Report, Buffalo Urban League, 1928.

78. Robert Bagnall to Antoinette Ford, April 11, 1929, NAACP Branch Files, Box G 130, Manuscript Division, Library of Congress.

31

"We All Seem Like Brothers and Sisters":

The African-American Community in Manhattan, Kansas, 1865-1940

Nupur Chaudhuri

African-Americans communities in Kansas have been the subject of a number of scholarly investigations conducted over several decades. Black migration to Kansas, participation of black troops from Kansas in the Spanish-American War, and education of African-Americans in nineteenth-century Kansas are the foci of these studies.[1] Yet, except for the establishment of Nicodemus as a black colony, our knowledge of communities in Kansas where black experiences, cultures, and institutions evolved has remained rather limited.

Thomas Cox's study of the African-American community in Topeka and his history of the blacks in Wyandotte County have laid the groundwork for further research on the growth of black neighborhoods during the nineteenth and twentieth centuries.[2] Though social processes generally occur throughout a society at a given time, they almost always vary in shape, content, and consequence from place to place and community to community within that society.[3] Because many communities collectively determined to contour of black society in general, accounts of other black settlements as well as the three already mentioned are needed to create an understanding of the evolution and contribution of African-American communities in nineteenth-century Kansas. By studying individual black communities in several towns and cities, one can gain a comprehensive view of the African-American culture in Kansas and acquire an insight into what is specifically and uniquely local to a particular town.

This study of an African-American community between 1865-1940 is an effort to reconstruct the unfolding process of community development among the blacks in Manhattan. It focuses on patterns of early residence and employment, education of the African-American children, and religious, social, cultural and political activities. Neighborhoods provide a framework to study social processes, affording us the opportunity to use the "little" picture as a means to achieve empathy and to discover the "big" picture.[4] Experiences of the African-American community during the latter part of the nineteenth century also offer a unique lens through which we can view Manhattan's past.

Social, economic, political, and institutional experiences of African-American communities are examined from such sources as census data, newspaper articles, church records, official records on marriage, and from the narratives of different community activities. But these sources provide only part of the necessary information for reconstructing the black experience. Accounts of the growth and development of many African-American communities, especially those in small-town Kansas, are often the experiences of ordinary people whose lives, activities, and feelings are commonly overlooked and unrecorded. Because oral history—recording private feelings, priorities, and values—is an important means of recapturing responses of the common people in a community, interviews of twenty-three elderly African-American citizens in Manhattan also served as a source of information for this article.[5]

The 1855 territorial census of Kansas recorded that thirteen blacks and mulattoes lived in Riley County and the adjacent counties of Pottawatomie, Clay, Marshall, and Washington.[6] Whether any one of them lived in Manhattan is not clear, but the U.S. census of 1860 showed no blacks residing in Manhattan.

The 1865 state census provides us with the first concrete evidence of blacks living in Manhattan. That year Manhattan's total population of 328 included nine African-Americans. The black population was apparently smaller in Manhattan than in some of the adjacent areas such as St. George Township in Pottawatomie County which had a black population of sixteen. According to the 1865 census, two black families resided in Manhattan: the Simmses and the Thomases. Oliver Simms (age thirty-two) came from Georgia and his wife, Eliza (age thirty-six), was from Kentucky. Edom Thomas (age thirty-six) also came from Kentucky. Records of marriage certificates in Manhattan indicate that Edom Thomas married Amanda on November 9, 1865.[7] The Thomas family consisted of thirteen-year-old M. Thomas, twelve-year-old B. Thomas, and two-year-old Abraham Lincoln Thomas. A Sixteen-year-old male, J.S. Thomas from Massachusetts, and unrelated to the Edom Thomas family, lived in Manhattan Township and worked for R.H. Kimball, a prominent early settler in Manhattan.[8]

The subsequent years until about the mid-1880s can be seen as a period of marked increase in the growth of the black community. Whereas in 1865 the African-American population constituted about 2.7 percent of the total population, in 1870 the black population made up 5.9 percent of the total population. The federal census noted an interracial marriage between Charles Mathews, a thirty-three-year-old black farmer from Georgia, and Mary Mathews, a thirty-two-year-old white woman from Indiana. The same census also revealed that the majority of the black population of sixty-five, of which forty-four were males and twenty-one females, came from Missouri, Kentucky, Tennessee, Texas, Virginia, Georgia, Arizona, North Carolina, Indiana, and Illinois. Some blacks like Sally Breakbill, living in adjoining areas, also moved to Manhattan in the period between 1865 and 1870. Forty-one-year-old Sally Breakbill and her family were living in St. George Township in 1865. She had been sold away from her first husband before the Civil War, and later she married William Breakbill, a black farmer in St. George Township. Sally had four children, two of whom were from her first marriage. William Breakbill, soon after the birth of her third child, left Sally.[9] She then moved to Manhattan sometime before 1870.

The state census of 1875 noted that the black population rose to about one hundred of which sixty-four were males and thirty-six were females. The percentage of the population that was black nearly doubled in the next five years. The increase in the population was due to both an influx of arrivals from other states and resettlements of blacks within the state of Kansas. The Griggsbys from Tennessee and the Mitchells from eastern Kansas are examples of the new immigrants. With about one hundred people, Manhattan had a visible black ethnic community before the 1879 Exodus.

In 1879, the black migration to Kansas, including Manhattan, took a sharp upward turn. In a few months in 1879, some six thousand blacks from Louisiana, Mississippi, and Texas immigrated to Kansas. Their movements were unplanned and unorganized. This migration to Kansas is known as the Exodus of 1879 in reference to the perception of these African-Americans that they were going to the "Promised Land."[10]

Many black refugees, coming by boat, landed at Wyandotte, first stop inside the Kansas border, which they considered to be a sanctuary. This river town with about five thousand residents was totally unprepared to receive such a large influx of destitute black migrants. Tension mounted and on April 18, 1879, the mayor of the city issued a proclamation prohibiting any steamboat line or transportation company "importing destitute persons to our shore." By now 1,700 to 2,000 destitute blacks were already in Wyandotte. On April 21, the steamboat *Durfee* arrived in Wyandotte with another 240 black passengers. When the captain of the boat was told not to unload any passengers at Wyandotte, he anchored his boat near the Plankington and Armour packing plant in Kansas City, Missouri. Lacking any municipal ordinance prohibiting the entry of black immigrants, the authorities in Kansas City, Missouri, were forced to accept this group of 240 passengers. A money-raising campaign was quickly launched, and within a few days all but one family were shipped to Manhattan.[11]

The *Manhattan Enterprise* on May 2, 1879, gave an account of the arrival of these African-American immigrants:

> As soon as it became known last Thursday that two carloads of Exodites had reached this place, they were visited by a large number of citizens of both sexes, all ages and colors. Being entirely destitute, active measures were at once taken for their relief. The whole number were removed to the old paper mill, where they are at present. The accommodations are not great, but there is good shelter from the weather.

According to the newspaper report, 104 persons were put off in Manhattan and one of them died shortly after his arrival. The whereabouts of the other passengers are not known. The *Manhattan Enterprise* further reported that 70 persons from this group immediately began to work as farm laborers, and the rest, mothers with children, had to be taken care of for food and shelter. The city had to find accommodations for the helpless refugees. The newspaper noted that

> many of our farmers need cheap hands yet do not feel able to build a shanty to accommodate the mother and children. The first few days after the arrival of the Exodites it costs some $15 per day to feed [all of] them. This has dwindled down until now it costs only $5 per day.[12]

On April 25, 1897, a meeting was held in the office of a local merchant, George W. Higginbothom, "to consider what steps should be taken in reference to colored refugees from the South now seeking homes in Kansas."[13] An executive committee of George W. Higginbothom, L.R. Elliot, E.L. Patee, S.M. Ferguson, J.T. Ritchie, George S. Gree, and J.T. Ellicot was created to look after the interests of the black refugees.[14] Dr. E.L. Patee volunteered the service of free medical treatment for sick refugees and even extended the offer to furnish the needed medicine without charge, if no offer of relief came from local druggists.

Table 1
Exodusters Receiving Aid, 1880

Name	Amount	Donor
Lewis Henderson	$3.15	E. B. Purcell
Lewis Holly	7.15	—
—	2.95	Stingly & Huntress
Norman Robinson	2.50	E. B. Purcell
A. Jackson	3.57	—
—	4.21	Stingly & Huntress
A. Cooper	1.88	—
Mrs. Green	4.37	—
Mr. Rodgers	1.55	—
Lucy Collins & four children	3.50	(rent for two rooms of Limboker)
Lucy Collins & three children	3.65	E. B. Purcell
Lucy Collins & family		(rent for two rooms of Limboker)
Lucy Collins & four children	4.15	(fuel and provisions)
Lisie Barlow	2.60	E. B. Purcell
Lisie Barlow	8.18	Stingly & Huntress
—	3.90	Stingly & Huntress
Lisie Doyl	1.25	—
—	2.20	E. B. Purcell
E. Johnson	7.75	—
—	1.05	Stingly & Huntress
Sam Jackson	6.30	E. B. Purcell
Albert Porvel	2.30	—
—	1.00	Stingly & Huntress
Melisa E. Davis	2.40	—
—	1.25	—

Source: Manhattan Township Trustee Book, RCHS Archives, #2909, pp. 71-72.

The official record of J.P. Peckham, township trustee of Manhattan Township, included the names of all refugees who were unable to provide for themselves. The records from April 1879 to July 1880 recorded the names of the black refugees and the amount of help these individuals received from various citizens of the town. Peckham listed the names of the exodusters separately from the names of the longtime African-American residents of Manhattan. The records reveal that by May 24, 1879, $65.35 had been spent for provisions and fuel for the exodusters, as well as $9.30 for cooking utensils.

The Exodus significantly increased the black population of Manhattan. The 1880 census lists its total population as 2,105. The number of black men, women, and children was 315, or 15 percent of the total population. But this was to be the peak in relative size of the black community. Although the population of blacks increased slightly during the next five years, the total population in Manhattan increased even more, so that when compared with the overall population, the black community actually decreased from 15 percent to about 12 percent by 1885. The census data from 1880 to 1940 clearly indicate that in Manhattan the black population progressively decreased from the highest figure of 15 percent in 1880 to slightly more than 2 percent in 1940, although the absolute number of the black citizens randomly fluctuated in the years 1920 and 1940.

Table 2
Manhattan Population

Year	Black Population	Total Population
1865	9	328
1870	66	1,108
1875	100	1,753
1880	315	2,105
1885	357	3,030
1890	307	3,014
1895	312	3,110
1900	314	4,684
1910	303	5,722
1915	315	7,186
1920	289	7,989
1925	344	10,072
1930	332	10,136
1940	270	11,659

While demography can say something about the vitality of a black community and its impact on the private lives and experiences of these early African-American settlers, other sources can aid in piecing together a comprehensive view. From the interviews of senior citizens and from newspaper accounts, one can attempt to form a picture of the black experience in Manhattan. Among the twenty-three African-American senior citizens interviewed, five traced their roots in Manhattan as far back as 1880 and 1910. They were aware of their heritage in American slavery. Lena Wilson indicated that her mother was a slave in Mississippi before she came to live in Manhattan. Deola Bennett stated, "my grandpa on my mama's side, he was a slave. . . . It took them a whole year to come through Illinois"; and Dorothy Elaine Brown Fulghem stated that her grandmother from her mother's side was a slave. She believed that most of her family came from Tennessee "during the slavery time." Helen Christian Baker reported that her grandfather and his family came to Manhattan in a covered wagon. Ruth Bayard informed us that her great-grandmother, a slave in Kentucky, came here with her family "during the time slaves became free." George Giles stated that his grandmother came to Manhattan in early 1900.

As to why her ancestors chose to come to Kansas, Deola Bennett acknowledged, "They [her grandparents] did not know where they were going to camp. They finally said, 'Just go to Kansas.' So they made it to Kansas." Dorothy Fulghem explained:

> They were white people that brought them up here to Kansas. That's the way I understood Grandma. And it seemed like they worked for people, but yet and still they had their independence. . . . The folks just brought her. [Mrs. Fulghem asked herself] Were they sharecroppers? I believe they were and they brought my grandmother.

Where the black pioneers established their first homes in Manhattan is not clear. The first black church in Manhattan, known as the Second Methodist Episcopal Church, was built in 1866 at the corner of Sixth and El Paso on the south side of the town. The establishment of this church suggests that a number of black families lived in the vicinity of the church, but others apparently settled elsewhere away from the church so that no specific neighborhood existed in the beginning.

Segregation was a later development. Mrs. Fulghem recalled hearing from her grandmother about living on Bluemont Hill on the north side of the town. When the exodusters arrived in Manhattan, some of them apparently sought homes in the northern part of the town.[15] But by 1880, a large black population had settled in the southwest part of the town. The *Nationalist* in January 1880 reported that "at the rate the colored people are building in the southwest part of town, they will soon have to have a separate city government. New houses are going up all the time."[16] This tended to homogenize the black community around the residential center established by the pioneers. No apparent reason for the move towards the south side has been found in any contemporary documents, but some of those interviewed had their own thoughts on the subject. Mrs. Fulghem noted, "Segregation. They [whites] got all the black people and they got this land together and we are all pushed back over here, so that is why this is our part of town." She further amplified, "That is where everyone was, every family, they each had so much land, and that was just where all the black people were, and families. We had our own churches, we had our own school." On this southward move Ruth Bayard remarked, "They [whites] just wanted blacks south of Poyntz [Avenue], kind of like in a little settlement."

According to the interviewees, the black neighborhood was confined between Second and Tenth streets and between Pottawatomie and Colorado streets. Deola Bennett forcefully stated, "That's where the Negroes live. Well, we couldn't go farther than Colorado [Street], that's where the Negroes could buy. You couldn't go up there. Oh. no. My God, no. they didn't want you up there."

Over and over again interviewees emphasized that the African-Americans could hardly establish residence outside of their neighborhood in other parts of Manhattan.[17] Mrs. Fulghem described how white families tried to stop them from buying a house on Colorado Street. Even though they paid half the price of the house in cash, the banks refused to lend them the rest of the money. But they bought "the house under the assumption of the same name that it was in and on the thing, under the quota that if you miss one payment, you leave everything you ever put in this place." Finally, by borrowing money from Mrs. Arthur Peine, who had been raised by Mrs. Fulghem's grandmother, they paid back the bank.

The forced segregation promoted endogamous relationships in the black community. Roberta Starnes described her neighborhood on Yuma Street, "Everybody was kin around us . . . my grandmother's sister lived next door to us." The segregated African-American families depended on each other for help and mutual support in their struggles for a decent and respectable living. Rosa Louise Hickman said, "In those days everybody looked after everybody's children. You didn't do anything that you got away with. Somebody told your parents. They could correct you and they would tell on you. . . . We are sort of like one family, we just all stuck together." Responding to the feeling of oneness, Ruth Bayard reported, "We all seem like brothers and sisters, more like a family, and we just didn't have nothing to choose from because we was around each other all the time in school and, you know, just kind of around together in a cluster."

In the segregated south side, a few white families lived in the midst of the predominantly black community. Clara Elizabeth Irving Settler remarked:

> Next door to us was a white family on the left, on the right was also a white family, and the next door down was a black family. Across the street was a white family. I would say in the block that we lived was integrated . . . but the street itself was mostly black.

Although the African-Americans had limited mobility and opportunity in this white dominated society and their resentment of such treatment ran deep, they apparently harbored a feeling of good will toward white families who lived south of Yuma. Mrs. Settler commented, "We got along fine. We were all in about the same economic level, so they couldn't say anything. All poor people."

Among early African-American settlers, Sally Breakbill apparently created a strong impression at least in the mind of one person in the white community. Ellen Ellsworth-Martin, daughter of Josiah Pillsbury, a prominent early white settler in Manhattan, wrote, "I remember seeing Aunt Sallie come into the Baptist Church with her little brood every Sunday morning. They sat in the part of the church which was called 'Amen corner.' They were always starched and clean. Aunt Sallie was a fine Christian woman."[18] Another black woman widely respected by whites was Clarinda Craig who began to work as a midwife in the late 1870s. Ellen Ellsworth-Martin noted that "a good many of Manhattan's early citizens owe their lives to Auntie Craig for the wonderful care she gave them."[19]

These women were exceptions because they had more contact with the whites. Although the blacks found empathy from some members in the white community, the African-Americans generally lived under fear of ridicule and hostility from members of the dominant race. In two instances black women were physically attacked by white teenagers:

> Most of the exodites are unusually polite persons. Not long ago, one of the women was coming from Dr. Stillman's with a pail of milk on her head, and some brutal boys stoned her, not only knocking the pail from her head, but considerably bruising her face and arms. The same boys, whose name we withhold this time, stoned another woman, cutting a large gash in her face. This in return for the politeness of these strangers in a strange land! We trust that if this ever happens again, the young outlaws will be arrested and punished severely.[20]

Obviously, some citizens condemned such violent acts, but these acts served as reminders to blacks that generally greater safety was to be found within the confines of their own community.

Since the 1880s, African-Americans have become actively involved in opposing discrimination. The Afro-American League, among several organizations in Topeka, was a pioneer group in maintaining opposition to any form of racial discrimination. Some African-Americans from Manhattan such as A. Cooper and W.H. Hamilton joined the Afro-American State League and worked for civil liberties.[21]

These efforts, however, had only very limited effect in cultivating positive relations between social groups. Interviews with the black senior citizens describe the extent to which social interaction was limited between the black and the white communities. Usually, once a year on Emancipation Day, August 2, the black community was allowed to share space with the white community in the white neighborhood. According to Mr. and Mrs. Fulghem:

> On this day the white folks would feed us the food. And it was election day, or it was close to election day....That was when somebody from downtown wanted to be elected. Oh, you know, for county attorney, sheriff, or mayor. Yes, we would go up there and have somebody to barbecue it and fix it.

Only on that day could black families have their own picnics and social gatherings at the city park and swim at the city swimming pool. However, even then the two groups were not really integrated. Although the whites allowed the blacks to share their space in the city park, they maintained their distance from the African-Americans.

Among the various festive occasions, Emancipation Day was an especially important day for African-American. A "procession formed at colored Methodist church, and, headed by the Band, marched through Poyntz Avenue to the grove across the Kansas, making a good showing. On the grounds, a speaker's stand had been erected, long tables arranged and several [band] stands were in full blast." After listening to several pieces of band music, at about noon, the president of the group called the people to order and "prayer was offered by a reverend colored gentleman from abroad." The principal speaker, a Reverend Lynch of Topeka, directed his comments towards the "new comers" and to their "present situation." After the program at the grove was carried out, they repaired to the County hall, where they danced till morning."[22] The interviews of the elderly blacks reveal that the black community celebrated Emancipation Day until the celebration was discontinued after 1930. This was explained with the comment that "those things just faded out, and July 4 replaced the day for all."

Distinct separation between the two races persisted through the turn of the century. Like many centers of social activities, the theater hall was segregated. The African-Americans attending shows at the Wareham Opera House were allowed to sit only in the balcony. Around 1908, the owner of this opera house wrote in his diary:

> The largest audience that has convened in the opera house this session came together last Friday night to hear the music rendered by the Reminye concert company, in fact it was a jam for pit to gallery [sic]. "Nigger heaven" was gay with new Easter bonnets and the bald headed [men] row was occupied by modesty and decorum.[23]

All public places except the hospitals were segregated. Public accommodations like restaurants and hotels and even the single dormitory (now Van Zile Hall) of the Kansas State Agricultural College practiced discrimination. Black students who attended the college lived on the south side of the town. Mrs. Starnes mentioned that her mother rented rooms to four black college students. Mrs. Hickman and Mrs. Alexander listed the names of the black families who rented rooms to black students. Iva Benjamin, one of the interviewees, stated:

> In the late thirties and forties I used to cook for the students, and the biggest I ever had was twelve students. The annex [Douglass Center Annex] where I would serve evening meals, because years ago where they [black students] lived, they did not have cooking privileges, and you could not go in any of these eating places and eat unless you ate in the kitchen. Even at the bus station you ate in the kitchen.

Leaders of the white community further strengthened the isolation of blacks by promulgating a law which prohibited unescorted white women from entering restaurants operated by the blacks.[24]

Even the local churches maintained the color barrier by requiring African-Americans to sit in the back. Although blacks attended these churches, they really were not part of the congregation. Perhaps this desire to belong led many of them to establish their own church which would then be their place for cultural expression and social bonding. One church had been built before the Exodus, and three more churches were constructed thereafter. The first black church in Manhattan, Second Methodist Episcopal Church, was organized as a mission church in 1866. It was a wooden frame building with a seating capacity of one hundred. The Freedmen's Aid Society of the Annual Conference provided this church with aid for many years, and additional help came from the white First Methodist Episcopal Church. In the 1880s, the Second Methodist Episcopal Church was located on Fifth Street between Rock Island and the Union Pacific tracks. Alfred Griggsby, Edom William, John Williams, William Davis, Thomas Bula, Brother Logan, and Edom Thomas were some of the trustees during the 1870s and 1880s. From 1866 to 1881, Reverend Griffing served as minister, and after Reverend Griffing's death, Reverend William became the pastor. During this time two services were held on Sundays with prayer meeting on Wednesdays. After the morning service, Sunday School was held. In 1881, the congregation had fifteen members, and the number rose to thirty-five in 1883. In the early 1900s, the Second Methodist Episcopal moved to Tenth and Yuma, and a stone church building, called Shepard Chapel in honor of Bishop W.O. Shepard who dedicated the church, replaced the frame structure in 1916. Shepard was a minister of the Methodist Episcopal Church from the Wichita area.[25] Around this time approximately forty-six people attended the Shepard Church.

Reminiscing about erecting the stone building, Deola Bennett stated, "Oh, yes, when they broke the line, they had a plow and everybody in there paid a dollar and you pull the plow across the line." George Giles remembered, "My mother bought a window, had her name on one of those windows. [It] was a painted window."

The Bethel African Methodist Episcopal Church was organized in October 1879, and a wooden frame building which could seat about one hundred people was erected at 401 Yuma Street in 1900. Reverend Oscar Haskins was the first pastor and Reverend Mathew Jones succeeded him in October 1880. Some of the trustees of this church in the 1880s were Ed Williams, George Wesley, George Barney, John Anderson, and Nick Holbert. Two services were held on Sundays, and Sunday Schools were held after the morning services. In the 1880s, the superintendents of the Sunday School were Mary Inman, Smith Burdett, A.H. Haywood, Caroline Berry, B.G. Gilbert, and Edmonia Alexander. Usually, two teachers taught the Sunday School, which began with ten students. By 1892, the number of students had increased to sixty-five.[26]

In March 1880, a group of blacks began conducting worship services in Avenue School, located at the present site of the middle school on Poyntz Avenue. This congregation was organized by the First Baptist Church and was named the Second or Colored Baptist Church. It is not clear, however, from the church records or the interviews why the First Baptist Church organized the Colored Baptist Church. In 1882, the congregation obtained a frame building at Ninth and Yuma, and about forty adults and seventy-five children attended the Sunday School. Reverend Abraham Cooper was the pastor and Lewis Call was the superintendent. In 1920, the Second Baptist merged with Mount Zion Baptist Church, and the reorganized church was named Pilgrim Baptist Church.[27] Little is known about the Mount Zion Baptist Church. It was organized around 1890 at the corner of Juliette and El Paso streets, with seventy members, and Reverend W.H. White of Topeka served as a pastor. Emma Parks, one of the interviewees, reported that her father started the Church of God in Christ around 1933, and meetings were held at his home at 1020 Colorado.

Besides fulfilling the religious needs of Manhattan's black community, the churches played an important role in promoting close-knit social bonds. The black ministers took turns in organizing the church services so that the entire African-American community could attend the same church on a particular Sunday. The churches were the center for social activities. Interviews of the African-American senior citizens explain how the early pastors of these churches organized their programs: for a number of years, Bethel A.M.E. Church had its program on the first Sunday of the month; Shepard Church held its program on the second Sunday of the month; Pilgrim Baptist Church on the third Sunday of the month; and the Church of God on the fourth Sunday of the month.

Recollecting her childhood, Helen Baker stated:

> I think we hardly ever went out of our block, and that's where we would go would be church. We went to church quite often. There was always something going on for the kids in our church. We would go to different houses and gather food and go back to church and eat it.

Churches became their second home in their limited world, as evidenced by Rosa Hickman's response:

> Well, as children you had to go in them days, you know. You may go in the morning, you didn't get back until like it was night. And then, if you get sleepy like at night, well, then you straightened out in them pews and go to sleep, because, you know, no need to say "I want to go home" or something, because in those days you know the mother and father was the head of the household and not the children.

In their interviews the senior citizens repeatedly emphasized that the church had many important roles in shaping the course of their lives. Mrs. Fulghem noted, "We were raised in the church, and the church was just full, and just active and everything. We had our league, we had our regular meetings and everything."

In the 1960s, the Shepard Church merged with the First Methodist Church. Explaining this merger, Mr. Fulghem remarked, "Most of the older people died out, and it wasn't enough members to keep the church going and to pay ministers. . . . It was one of the things I really hated to see go down. It was our church." Mrs. Bennett expressed her feelings by stating, "We lost it and white folks took it over and we have to go there."

Little is known about the education of black children in Manhattan before 1879. Many blacks in Kansas believed that only through education would they be able to achieve economic prosperity and improve their social status. In the absence of any written records, we can only presume that during the 1860s and 1870s the blacks in this town shared those feelings. Many whites also believed that only thorough education would blacks become productive and responsible citizens.[28]

During the early 1860s, the only schools open to blacks in Kansas were privately supported Freedmen's schools or evening schools. Later in the decade, with the rise of the African-American population, charity schools could not accommodate all the black children. Consequently, public schools were under pressure to provide education for African-American children, although many white citizens, fearing that "mixed education" implied the eradication of social differentiation, did not wish to integrate the public school system. In 1867, the Kansas Legislature passed a law that supported separate but equal education for both black and white children. The statute made the school districts responsible for the "education of white and colored children, separately or otherwise, securing to them equal educational advantages."[29] The implementation of separate schools came about in two phases, the legislature first allowing separate schools only in first-class cities, and by 1868, allowing the same for second-class cities.[30]

In the early 1860s, however, a small minority of white Kansans had voiced opposition to the system of separate schools either on moral grounds or because of economic considerations. The factions for and against the system soon were embroiled in a major political issue. The citizens of Manhattan were also divided. In his editorial in the *Nationalist*, Albert Griffin asked every citizen to work against the increasing prejudices "which prohibited colored brethren and sisters' from obtaining an equal education."[31] Voicing opposition to this attitude of integrated school systems, one subscriber wrote, "Compel us to associate with the negro, and we become a slave in turn."[32] Because their numbers were few in Manhattan in the 1860s and early 1870s, it is likely that the black children attended the same school as the white children. Ellen Ellsworth-Martin attended school with black children, and in her reminiscences she wrote about the funeral of a black classmate—eleven-year-old Tom, son of Kate Noris. Tom's funeral was held in the Methodist Church, and the entire class under the supervision of Libby Hoyt attended. The children laid flowers on the casket, and Ellen recalled, "That was the tragedy that came into our young lives and I never forgot it."[33] Unlike their parents, the white and the black children and some of the teachers were not self-conscious about integrated education.

After the 1879 Exodus, the number of black children in Manhattan increased considerably, and the question of an integrated school system became a greater issue. When the school board met in August 1879, the *Manhattan Enterprise* reported, "The annual school [board] meeting was held at the new school house last Thursday. There was a very small attendance. Among the questions which came up was whether the colored scholars should have separate apartments from the whites. It was decided not."[34] The debate on totally segregated schools continued in the press and in the school board meetings for the next few years, and the promoters of such philosophy apparently achieved a partial victory in 1884 when black children began attending separate classes from the white children but in the same building.

Both the black and white population of Manhattan perceived Selina Wilson as the principal of the black students and Eli Freeman as the second teacher. Wilson was teaching first grade with twenty-seven students, whereas Freeman was teaching second grade with thirty-four students.[35] In 1896, among fifteen students that graduated from Manhattan's ninth grade, one was a black student, Sarah E. Thomas, daughter of Edwin Thomas a laborer and Emma Thomas a homemaker.[36] In 1901, the number of black students in Manhattan's school was 137. This number dropped to 111 in 1902 and to 107 the following year. In this last group of 107, 51 were female students.[37]

The first reference to a completely separate school for Manhattan's black children can be found in the minutes of the board of education meeting on July 6, 1903.[38] It recorded that "Eli C. Freeman and Eli Cruise representing the Americus Club were present and presented views of that club regarding separate schools for colored people." A week later on July 13, 1903, all white members of the board of education met to consider the advisability of building a new school of two rooms suitably located to accommodate the colored pupils of the city. At this meeting, the board of education decided to "employ two persons to circulate petitions among the colored people with a view to ascertain their desires regarding the new building."[39] Presumably the board members wanted to find out about the attitude of the blacks regarding a segregated school.

A second special meeting was held on July 16 to further consider the feasibility of a separate school, and a delegation of the African-Americans was present at that meeting. The "matter was discussed pro and con by them, after which the Board went into a secret session."[40] The board decided to postpone any decision at that time. Finally, at the school board meeting on August 3, 1903, a motion was made to build a two-room building. Following a deliberation, the motion was approved by a vote of six to one. The president of the school board and the building and grounds committee of the city were authorized to take preliminary steps toward the erection of the building. Requests for sealed bids for the construction of a ward school were published in the local newspaper and the building was completed at a cost of $3,828.[41]

The black community was not generally supportive of the idea of segregated education for their children. At the regular board meeting on September 7, 1903, "a committee of colored people was present and presented a remonstrance against the building of a separate building for the colored pupils."[42] The board of education nevertheless went ahead with its plan to construct a building for the black students. The minutes of the special meeting of the board on September 16, 1903, stated, "It was moved and seconded that the board proceed with the building of a new school house according to specification and that Smith and Correll be awarded the contract for the same."[43]

Upon the request of the African-American community, the board approved the name of the new Fifth Ward building as the Douglas School, after Frederick Douglass, the noted abolitionist and black advocate, and ordered that the name be cut on the stone.[44] The *Mercury* of January 13, 1904, reported that the new Douglas School opened with sixty children on January 4, 1904.

Some of the African-American senior citizens interviewed had a different perspective on the establishment of the Douglas School. They believed that the school was created to provide a job for Eli Freeman, a black teacher. Deola Bennett stated that "a man got a piece of money and lied, said that there is going to be a night school, and turned it into a nigger school."

Few parents of the interviewees ever attended primary school in Manhattan, unlike many of the interviewees, who attended the Douglas School. George Giles recalled that he was a student of Mr. Freeman, who taught first through third grades. The black students attended through the sixth grade in the Douglas School, after which they went to an integrated junior and senior high school. Some of the senior citizens we interviewed told us that their memories of the integrated school system at the junior and senior levels are filled with unpleasant experiences of stark racism. Remembering her high school days, Clara Settler stated:

> In high school when we went to the auditorium for the assembly, they would always sit us in the back. Even though the school was integrated. I remember that the day I graduated from junior high and also when we went from assembly, you were supposed to be seated alphabetically, but they would sit all the blacks together or at the back of the room.

Emma Parks recalled that most black boys did not go beyond seventh or eighth grade. Incentive for education did not exist for the blacks. Built-in social barriers to a decent and respectable livelihood for the blacks were the major impediment to seeking education. Clara Settler stated:

> Well, I really don't think it made much difference that whether if you [were] taught in the school. Course, wages were low at that time, so I really couldn't

say.... Most of the ladies cooked in the fraternities and sororities and the men were janitors. I don't think it made any difference about your education.

The fulfillment of ambition for the black people rested on opportunities to execute their skills, to acquire new crafts, and to develop talents that the society was ready to accept. Thus, the pattern and scope of employment that became available to the African-Americans provide an index to the narrative of their struggle to establish themselves in the society.

In 1865, the black population consisted of three men of working age, all of them were employed. Edom Thomas was a laborer, Oliver Simms a teamster, and J.S. Thomas a servant. None of the working age women were employed for wages. The employment patterns, opportunities, and preferences for members of the black community became more varied in the years following the development of the nucleus of this African-American community.

During the 1870s, the majority worked as laborers on surrounding farms or in the town. Several were self-employed as barbers and farmers. Stephen Steward and two of his family members worked as barbers. After working as a teamster in the 1860s, Oliver Simms became an owner of a farm on which he worked for the next couple of decades. Eighteen-year-old William Fields from Missouri worked for the G.F. Brown family—a white pioneer family in Manhattan. Richard Thomas and John Foreman worked as stone masons. Foreman himself employed James Alexander from Texas as a laborer. Noah Morgan from Indiana worked as a hotel cook. William Cox from Virginia was employed as hotel porter. Edom Thomas also worked as a hotel porter.

Only five of twenty-one black women were gainfully employed between 1865 and 1875. Working as domestics were Sally Breakbill, Sarah Craig from Missouri, Deborah Alexander from Indiana, and Eliza Mathews from Kentucky. Martha Mathews worked as a hotel cook.

In 1875 state census data showed that black men generally worked as laborers. Some, like Alfred Griggsby from Tennessee and Thomas Hill from Maryland, worked as craftsmen, carpenters, or harnessmakers. Jerry Mitchell, who once hauled material by wagon from Leavenworth to Fort Riley, settled in Manhattan after he met Rose Taylor. Jerry and Rose Mitchell raised their family of twelve children at 731 Pottawatomie, the site of present Bell Air Apartments. Later in his life, in 1912, Jerry Mitchell started the first garbage collection for the city of Manhattan. The Mitchells helped with the construction of the Shepard Methodist Chapel around 1916.[45]

In the 1870s, most of the African-American women did not work for wages. The few women who found employment opportunities worked largely as laundresses operating their businesses from home. In the 1870s, Kate Noris, Eliza Hill and Sally Breakbill, who previously worked as domestics, began to wash clothes for others at home. Hanna Noris, daughter of Kate Noris, began to work as a domestic at age seventeen.

The census data of 1880 revealed that nearly 84 percent of the employed black men worked as day laborers. In 1880, 20 percent of the women were employed and of those slightly more than half worked as laundresses, and the remaining either worked as domestics, midwives, or cooks. The census data of 1885 indicated that 77 percent of the working force among the African-American men served as day laborers. In 1985, men were still working primarily as day laborers, and some worked for the railroad. Although at this time very few women worked outside the home for wages, Selina Wilson of Arkansas was the first black teacher in Manhattan. About a year later, a second teacher, Eli Freeman, was employed, and in 1900, Hattie Jones joined Wilson and Freeman in teaching the African-American children.

Job opportunities for physically able black men were limited between the period of 1885 and 1895. In 1885, 64 percent of the working black men were employed. In 1895, less than 50 percent of them were employed. In the period between 1885 and 1895, less than 5 percent of black women worked outside the home for wages. The poor harvests and the national depression of the previous years were responsible for much of the unemployment in the African-American community. In 1910, over 45 percent of women worked outside their home to supplement their family income.

In the years following the 1890s, black men and women held varied occupations. Joseph Williams worked in 1900 as a traveling showman, and Andrew Lewis was a U.S. mail carrier. In 1915, Giles Cooper became the first black policeman in Manhattan. The 1910 census data revealed that a large segment of black working women were earning wages as laundresses either operating from their own homes or working at private homes. Mrs. Settler's maternal grandmother took in washing and ironing to put her daughter [Mrs. Settler's mother] through school. Mrs. Fulghem's and Mrs. Starnes's mothers also did ironing at home for college students. In the 1920s, George Giles's grandmother and mother worked as cooks for mess halls at Fort Riley, and during the same time period they owned a restaurant at 615 South Ninth Street. In the 1920s and 1930s, most of our female interviewees worked as domestics or as cooks. Deola Bennett reported that she did housework for an army couple for twenty-five cents per hour. In the 1930s, Iva Benjamin worked as a domestic for a family of four and received $5.00 per week, and her mother did housework for $4.50 per week. In the 1930s and 1940s, Mr. Lorraine Alexander ran the movie projector at Wareham Theater, and during the same time period George Giles played professional baseball with the Kansas City Monarchs of the Negro League. Another black family owned a restaurant at 721 Riley in the 1930s.

The history of the African-American community in Manhattan from 1865 to 1940 clearly indicates that racism dictated the terms of interracial relationship and the access of blacks to institutions in the society at large. Their churches and their own close communal bonds were major forces enabling the few hundred black men, women, and children to provide a strong foundation for the African-American ethnic community in Manhattan. About her life and experience Dorothy Fulghem stated, "I think we came a long ways, and I think back there in those times I lived there, I was satisfied because I didn't know any better." Regarding the present and future relationship between the blacks and the whites in Manhattan, Deola Bennett commented:

> I believe right now, a black man and the rest of the world can get along, cause the Bible is coming true. The dark race shall stretch forth their wings and rise. They doing it, ain't they? Slowly, slowly, goin' rise in the east and go to the west, yes sir. If the white man had kept his hand off the black man all of this, none of this would happen.

NOTES

This research was funded by a grant from the Kansas Committee for the Humanities. For their assistance, the author wishes to thank Lawrence P. Nicholson, director of the Douglass Community Center, Manhattan; Afro-American Senior Citizens, Manhattan; Jean Dallas and Cheryl Collins of the Riley County Historical Society Library and Archives; Geraldine Walton of Manhattan Public Library; and David Hacker and Bill Ferber of the *Manhattan Mercury*. Thanks also go to professors Homer E. Socolofsky and Marion W. Gray of Kansas State University for their advice and comments in preparing this article.

1. Some major studies on the settlement and activities of blacks in Kansas are Robert G. Athearn, *In Search of Canaan: Black Migration to Kansas, 1879-1880* (Lawrence: The regents Press of Kansas, 1978); Lee Ella Black, "The Great Exodus of 1879 and 1880 to Kansas," Master's thesis, Kansas State College, Manhattan, Kansas, 1928; James C. Carper, "The Popular Ideology of Segregated Schooling: Attitudes Towards the Education of Blacks in Kansas, 1854-1900," *Kansas History: A Journal of the Central Plains* 1 (Winter 1978): 254-65; Dudley Taylor Cornish, "Kansas Negro Regiments in the Civil War," *Kansas Historical Quarterly*, 20 (May 1953): 417-29; Willard B. Gatewood, Jr., "Kansas Negroes and the Spanish-American War," *Kansas Historical Quarterly*, 37 (Autumn 1971): 300-13; and Nell Irvin Painter, *Exodusters: Black Migration to Kansas After Reconstruction* (New York: Alfred A. Knopf, 1977).
2. Thomas Cooper Cox, *Blacks in Topeka, Kansas, 1865-1915: A Social History* (Baton Rouge: Louisiana State University, 1982); *The Afro-American Community in Kansas City Kansas: A History* (N.p.: City of Kansas City, Kansas, 1982).
3. David A. Gerber, "Local and Community History: Some Cautionary Remarks on an Idea Whose Time Has Returned," *The History Teacher*, 13 (November 1979): 25.
4. *Ibid.*, 26.
5. These interviews were conducted between September 1983 and September 1984, and the interviewees were over the age of sixty and had lived in Manhattan for more than fifty years. The tapes of these interviews are at the Riley County Historical Society Archives in Manhattan, Kansas (hereafter cited as RCHS Archives). Ten tapes are transcribed and one copy of each transcript is at the RCHS Archives. In this article no distinction has been made between blacks and mulattoes.
6. All the census data consulted are in the Kansas State Historical Society.
7. Records of marriage certificates are located in the RCHS Archives.
8. 1865 census does not spell out the names of the members of the Thomas family.
9. "Early Resident Relates History of Negro Pioneers in City," *Manhattan Tribune-News*, March 19, 1950.

10. For more information, see Athearn, *In Search of Canaan*; Black, "The Great Exodus of 1879 and 1880 to Kansas"; and Painter, *Exodusters*.

11. Athearn, *In Search of Canaan*, 42.

12. *Manhattan Enterprise*, May 2, 1879.

13. *Ibid.; Nationalist*, Manhattan, May 2, 1879.

14. For biographical information on the committee members, see *Pioneers of the Bluestem Prairie: Kansas Counties: Clay, Geary, Marshall, Pottawatomie, Riley, Wabaunsee, and Washington* (Manhattan: Riley County Genealogical Society, 1976).

15. *Nationalist*, September 12, 1879.

16. *Ibid.*, January 9, 1880.

17. Although the interviewees were describing conditions up to the 1940s, discrimination in housing lasted until mid-1960s.

18. *Manhattan Tribune-News*, March 19, 1950.

19. *Ibid.*

20. *Nationalist*, September 5, 1879.

21. *Benevolent Banner*, Topeka, October, 8, 1887. A shortlived (May 21-October 22, 1887) black newspaper established by Rev. P.W. Barker and S.O. Garrett.

22. *Nationalist*, August 5, 1880.

23. Harry Wareham's Scrapbook, RCHS Archives.

24. *Manhattan Republic and Manhattan Nationalist*, August 20, 1936.

25. For more information on Shepard Church see Homer E. Socolofsky, *From the Beginning: A History of the First United Methodist Church, Manhattan, Kansas 1855-1985* (Manhattan: First United Methodist Church, 1985).

26. Kansas Church Charts, v. 6, [1893], 20, Library, Kansas State Historical Society.

27. For more information on Pilgrim Baptist Church see Ruth Bayard, "History of Pilgrim Baptist Church," RCHS Archives.

28. Carper, "The Popular Ideology of Segregated Schooling," 255.

29. Quoted in *ibid*, 259.

30. Richard Klugler, *Simple Justice: The History of* Brown v. Board of Education *and Black America's Struggle for Equality* (New York: Alfred A. Knopf, 1976), 371.

31. *Nationalist*, February 12, 1875.

32. *Ibid.*, February 26, 1875. Similar views of segregation were expressed again in the *Nationalist* on March 5, 1875.

33. *Manhattan Tribune-News*, March 19, 1950.

34. *Manhattan Enterprise*, August 22, 1879.

35. *Mercury*, Manhattan, June 16, September 15, 1886.

36. *Ibid.*, January 23, 1896. Occupations of Edwin and Emma Thomas are listed in 1880 federal census.

37. *Manhattan Nationalist*, August 13, 1903.

38. Dedicatory Exercise for the New Douglas School Building, Manhattan: October, 1937.

39. *Ibid.*

40. *Ibid.*

41. *Manhattan Nationalist*, August 13, 1903.

42. *Ibid.*, September 10, 1903.

43. *Ibid.*, September 17, 24, 1903.

44. Although named for Frederick Douglass, the school's name is Douglas.

45. *Pioneers of the Bluestem Prairie*, 406.

32

Black Women Activists
and the Student Nonviolent
Coordinating Committee:
The Case of Ruby Doris Smith Robinson

Cynthia Griggs Fleming

Since their earliest days in American society, many people of African descent have worked to combat the racism and oppression confronting them. Some of these activists were women, and a select few of them even became famous. Names like Sojourner Truth and Harriet Tubman are familiar to most Americans. Yet, those few African-American female freedom fighters who have been elevated to legendary status have often been forced to confront a very personal issue in the midst of their efforts to free their people: the issue of redefining their womanhood. Against the backdrop of the peculiar status of African-American women in U.S. society, black female activist efforts have routinely been tied to a negative assessment of black womanhood.

This is a consequence of negative notions of African-American women that are firmly anchored in the nineteenth century and slavery. In fact, slaveholders defined African-American womanhood in their own best interests, shifting their treatment of female slaves to meet their needs:

> Where work was concerned, strength and productivity under the threat of the whip outweighed considerations of sex. In this sense, the oppression of women was identical to the oppression of men.
>
> But women suffered in different ways as well, for they were victims of sexual abuse and other barbarous mistreatment that could only be inflicted on women.[1]

In short, "when it was profitable to exploit them [slave women] as if they were men, they were regarded, in effect, as genderless, but when they could be exploited, punished and repressed in ways suited only for women, they were locked into their exclusive female roles."[2]

At the same time, critical nineteenth-century political and economic changes began to have a profound impact on definitions of white womanhood. It was at this time that sharply differentiated gender roles emerged. Many middle-class nineteenth-century white Americans became convinced that men and women were so different that their duties, obligations, and responsibilities

561

actually constituted "separate spheres."[3] In this context expectations of proper female behavior came to be defined by women's domestic duties. "Women's activities were increasingly limited to care of children, the nurturing of [the] husband, and the physical maintenance of the home."[4]

Negative views of African-American womanhood combined with restrictive notions of white womanhood persisted until well into the twentieth century. Both black and white women were affected by them—but in very different ways. Many white women were intent on questioning and testing the old established limits. At the same time, this white female restlessness contrasted sharply with black female aspirations. As black economic expectations rose during the post-World War II period, many African-American women would have been only too happy to stay home and cultivate a separate female sphere for a change.[5] Yet, at this time financial realities continued to push large numbers of African-American women out of the home and into the job market. In such an atmosphere questions about black womanhood and white womanhood persisted. It was a confusing and unsettling time.

In this volatile and fluid atmosphere one modern African-American female activist who sought to define her womanhood as she gained power within the Student Nonviolent Coordinating Committee (SNCC) was Ruby Doris Smith Robinson. Robinson began her activist career in the Atlanta Student Movement. She was a freshman at Spelman College in Atlanta when the sit-ins first started. Early on, though, Robinson began to look beyond Atlanta and concentrate her efforts on the national arena and SNCC. Over two decades after Robinson's most active period, many of her movement colleagues still have vivid memories of her. Friends and associates were able to recall with remarkable clarity a wealth of detail about Robinson's activist career and her personal life. Consequently, I conducted interviews with a number of those who were close to her, including family members, childhood friends, Atlanta University Center associates, and SNCC comrades.

Regardless of the circumstances of their relationship with Robinson, most associates identified her as a powerful woman. In many instances this identification resulted in curious perceptions of the importance of Robinson's gender in relation to her power. For example, co-worker Courtland Cox insisted that people in SNCC "didn't view her as a man or a woman, they viewed her as a strength."[6] SNCC organizer Mukasa (Willie Ricks) insisted that gender was not an issue since "her personality was so strong . . . didn't nothing else matter."[7] One of her earlier acquaintances, Reverend Albert Brinson, had a chance to observe Ruby when she was a Spelman College student just beginning her movement work. Brinson remembered that a typical Spelman student was "always taught to be a lady. A lady stood back and waited to be waited upon by a man." Robinson did not fit in this atmosphere, though, since "she was not the lady-like kind. . . . She was rather aggressive."[8]

The existence of such perceptions of Robinson raises crucial questions. How did she see this issue of gender in view of her growing power within the Student Nonviolent Coordinating Committee? Also, what influences in

Robinson's early life shaped the balance that she would eventually strike between her activism and her gender identity? Indeed, an examination of her upbringing reveals intriguing glimpses of the influences that provoked her activism and shaped her views of proper gender roles.

Ruby Doris Smith was born in Atlanta, Georgia, on April 25, 1942, the second oldest of seven children. She was raised in the city's black Summerhill neighborhood. The family home at 794 Fraser Street was a large frame structure that had both a store and a beauty shop attached to it. Ruby Smith's mother, Alice Smith, supplemented the family income by operating the beauty shop, while her father, J. T. Smith, operated the store and engaged in a variety of other occupations. Smith drove a cab, owned a used furniture store, tried his hand at the moving business, and operated a restaurant. Later, when Ruby Smith was in high school, her father became a Baptist minister. He eventually founded his own church.[9] Even though the family did not have a lot of money, J. T. and Alice Smith were able to provide a comfortable living for their children. Just as important as the income they provided was the example they set: the source of their income was dependent on black patronage rather than white support.

As Robinson grew to maturity she became involved in a variety of social activities. In 1958, with the enthusiastic blessing of her family, she became a debutante, just as her older sister, Mary Ann, had done a year earlier. The Smith sisters' formal introduction to African-American social life clearly indicates the family's and their daughters' acceptance of African-American middle-class standards for proper female behavior. Other actions and attitudes that characterized Robinson's formative years also suggest that she accepted the 1950s notions of proper African-American middle-class female behavior. For example, she was head majorette with the Prince High School marching band. She was very concerned about her appearance and particularly liked expensive clothes that would flatter her figure.

Ruby Smith and her sisters and brothers enjoyed a secure existence in their separate black world as they grew to maturity. They had strong adult support, and they had their own churches, schools, and social activities. Also, within the confines of the middle-class value system that governed their lives, the Smith children comfortably embraced the gender roles that were a part of that value system. No matter how insulated and comfortable they were, though, the reality of racism and segregation in the United States managed to intrude from time to time. Moreover, the injurious effects of segregation were equally traumatic for males and females. In the segregated South of the 1950s gender counted for much less than race.

African-American youngsters of this generation reacted in a variety of ways to the ugly reality of segregation. Ruby Smith's older sister Mary Ann (Wilson) remembered that she was aware of segregation, but "everything was so separated you just didn't think about it."[10] Despite this perception, confrontation was inevitable. Wilson sharply recalled the pain resulting from one of those confrontations. One day she boarded a bus on her way home from school. Since the bus on this route was usually filled with African-American passengers, most of them generally sat wherever they chose. Consequently, without even thinking, Wilson sat down right behind the driver. But there was a white woman sitting behind her, and when Wilson realized this, she jumped up and moved behind this woman. At that moment Wilson knew something was terribly wrong.[11]

When young Ruby Doris Smith encountered segregation she reacted to it quite strongly. Her younger sister Catherine witnessed one encounter that occurred in a drugstore located at the corner of Capitol and Georgia Avenue. The Smith children often bought ice cream from this drugstore. Catherine Robinson recalled the store clerks generally seemed reluctant to serve black customers. That reluctance was particularly apparent one day when the Smith sisters ordered an ice cream cone. "So, they pulled the cone down. . . . [Ruby] waited till they fixed it and got ready for her to pay. . . . She said, 'Oh, you can keep that one, I won't be eating that one.'" The baffled and annoyed clerk could not understand Ruby's behavior. She angrily insisted, "'You ordered this.'" An equally angry Ruby explained, "'But you're not going to put your hands on my cone.' She knew that when whites came in, they used a tissue to pull the cone down; and when blacks came in, they would just use their hands."[12] This was not the only time she confronted the reality of racism during her early years. Robinson recalled, "I was conscious of my blackness. Every young Negro growing up in the South has thoughts about the racial situation."[13] She also remembered her reaction to the white people with whom she came in contact when she was a youngster. "I didn't recognize their existence and they didn't recognize mine. . . . My only involvement was in throwing rocks at them."[14]

As Ruby Doris Smith Robinson passed through adolescence during the 1950s, she was keenly aware of the broader issues of racial injustice. She saw others suffer the same indignities that confronted her. Yet, she also saw the signs of change: the Montgomery Bus Boycott, the Brown Decision, and the integration of Little Rock's Central High School were powerful symbols for this generation. At the same time, the African-American teachers at Price High School where Robinson was a student routinely discussed issues of race with their students. They encouraged these youngsters to think critically and to consider possibilities for change.

This heightened consciousness regarding segregation that characterized the 1950s occurred amidst the growing interest in reassessing gender roles in the modern U.S. This juxtaposition of race and gender issues served to focus particular attention on African-American women. Consequently, the efforts of white journalists, scholars, and physicians to examine the female role generally were complemented by a special interest in black women's roles by various members of the African-American community. Studies produced by scholars along with articles in the African-American press during this era contained mixed signals about black female prospects and accomplishments.

An article in the popular black press entitled "What's Wrong with Negro Women?" provides a graphic example of the negative assessment accepted by some. The author of that article, Roi Ottley, criticized African-American women in practically every area of life. He declared that African-American women were not interested in furthering their education, and that they were culturally backward as well. He went on to insist that they were shallow dilettantes who were primarily interested in embracing the vulgar trappings of middle-class life. Above all, these women were not fulfilling one of their most important responsibilities, Ottley charged: *"Too few Negro women contribute to the race fight* [emphasis added]. Beyond one or two national organizations and sororities, they do not even organize for their own rights as women. . . ."[15]

While the Ottley article is extremely critical, it is also quite revealing. It clearly suggests that the proper role for the modern African-American woman should include civil rights activism and an emphasis on educational achievement. A more thoughtful and sympathetic view is provided by author Lerone Bennett in a 1960 edition of *Ebony* magazine. In an article entitled "The Negro Woman," Bennett asserted that most people accepted the notion that the African-American woman's role was one of domination. This history of domination resulted in a healthy sense of independence. Yet, it was that very independence that created a dilemma for African-American women. "Independence, as many white women have recently discovered, is not an unmixed blessing. . . . One result of the traditional independence of the Negro woman is that she is more in conflict with her innate biological role than the white woman."[16]

Thus, by the 1950s some members of the African-American community began to express concern about the issue of black women's roles. In many instances African-American sentiment tended to favor a far more inclusive role than the restrictive and traditional view that tied women's roles more firmly to the home. But, there was still a lot of uncertainty. It was during this volatile period that Ruby Doris Smith began her college career; she entered Spelman College as a freshman in the fall of 1959.

Even though there was a strain of conservatism at many black colleges and universities—including the Atlanta University Center schools[17]—this conservatism existed in the midst of an atmosphere that encouraged students to question the South's racial etiquette. Some faculty and administrators in Atlanta University Center schools regularly reminded students that they must play a role in their own liberation. Others, however, were not nearly as supportive as Howard Zinn, a Spelman history professor who noted that:

> The new Spelman girl is having an effect on faculty and administrators. Many who were distressed and critical when they first learned their sweet young things were sitting behind bars, later joined in the applause of the Negro community and the nation at large.[18]

While Spelman worked hard to provide a nurturing and supportive atmosphere that encouraged students to think critically and act assertively, it also provided training in etiquette that rivaled any charm school. Throughout the 1950s many of the college's faculty members and administrators clearly remained committed to training proper "ladies" for the black middle class. Thus, the Spelman College that shaped the young Ruby Doris Smith Robinson accepted expanded limits for African-American women's roles, but also expected traditional behavior. In short, young African-American women of this generation were told that they could and should do it all.

In this hospitable atmosphere Robinson, like many other young black people of her generation, became convinced that change was possible.[19] Furthermore, many saw themselves as the agents of that change. Then Greensboro happened. The start of sit-ins there galvanized black college students all over the South. Robinson immediately considered the prospect of sit-ins in Atlanta, but was not prepared to take the initiative. When the Atlanta University Center students formed the Atlanta Committee on Appeal for Human Rights, though, she enthusiastically joined. The group quickly staged its first demonstration at the state capitol, and Robinson was with them. She described the events:

> I went through the food line in the restaurant at the State Capitol with six other students, but when we got to the cashier, she wouldn't take our money. She ran upstairs to get the Governor. The Lieutenant-Governor came down and told us to leave. We didn't, and we went to the county jail.[20]

This was only the beginning of Robinson's activist career. She became heavily involved in the Atlanta student movement. While she did not assume a leadership role, she did gain a reputation for bravery and assertiveness. Atlanta Student Movement colleague Julian Bond witnessed one of the incidents that added to her reputation. Bond recalled that on one occasion a group of Atlanta students decided to desegregate Grady Hospital—a large, public hospital. Although Grady admitted African-American patients, it had segregated entrances. When black Atlanta students went in the hospital's white entrance the receptionist just inside the door immediately told them they could not enter on that side; "and besides," she insisted, "you're not sick anyway."[21] As the students stood in the entrance trying to decide how to proceed, Robinson boldly walked up to the receptionist's desk, looked her in the eye, bent over and vomited all over the desk, straightened up and demanded to know, "Is that sick enough for you?"[22]

While Robinson continued to work with the Atlanta Student Movement, she became involved on the national scene as early as February of 1961. At that time the new Student Nonviolent Coordinating Committee decided to initiate a "jail no bail" policy. The arrest of a group of Friendship College students, who were jailed for protesting in Rock Hill, South Carolina, provided the occasion for the initiation of this new policy. Throughout the fall of 1960 members of SNCC had debated the wisdom of pursuing this strategy. Most recognized that the increasing number of students jailed for protesting activities was beginning to strain the financial resources of the black community to the limit. In many instances member of these communities—even those in difficult financial circumstances—were generous contributors to bail funds. It was not uncommon for property owners to pledge their houses in an effort to raise bail money. By late 1960 some in SNCC expressed alarm that the depletion of community resources might begin to strangle the life out of the movement.

On the other hand, if protestors insisted on serving their full sentences, this could put pressure on the white community that might hasten movement victories. As white southerners were faced with the logistical and financial nightmare of housing and feeding increasing numbers of demonstrators serving jail time, many reasoned, white tax payers would become much more willing to accede to movement demands. Once SNCC voted to pursue the jail no bail strategy, the organization immediately dispatched a delegation to Rock Hill. They were directed to demonstrate and refuse bail once they were arrested. When the delegation was chosen, Robinson was not among them, but her older sister Mary Ann was. Mary Ann Wilson vividly recalled that when she went home to pack, she began to have second thoughts. At the same time, Robinson began to express an interest in going. "So what happened eventually is Ruby Doris talked it up, and I just bowed out and let her go."[23] After Robinson and the other students were arrested in Rock Hill, they spent thirty days in the York County, South Carolina, jail. Upon completion of her sentence, Robinson returned to Atlanta on March 18, 1961. At that time the *Atlanta Inquirer* reported that she was "ready, if necessary, to do it again."[24]

Ruby Doris Robinson soon got her chance to do it again. By May of 1961 she decided to join the Freedom Rides. After being menaced by white mobs, she and the other riders were arrested and jailed. She eventually served a sixty-day jail sentence in Mississippi. Shortly after her scheduled release on August 11, 1961, Robinson decided to work with some of her SNCC colleagues involved in voter registration in McComb, Mississippi.[25] She was always willing to volunteer for the most hazardous movement duty. Furthermore, in such circumstances colleagues could depend on Robinson to be bold and daring.

Because of her attitude and her actions, Ruby Doris Smith Robinson soon became a legend—even among the bold and brave young people of SNCC. Most people in the early days of SNCC could recount at least one Ruby Doris Robinson story. For example, Julian Bond remembered that when a delegation of SNCC staff was preparing to board a plane for Africa in the fall of 1964, an airline representative told them that the plane was full even though they had tickets. He wanted to know if they would wait and take a later flight. This angered Robinson so much that, without consulting the rest of the group, she went and sat down in the jetway and refused to move. They were given seats on that flight.[26]

James Bond, who worked in the SNCC print shop, witnessed another incident. The incident occurred when a group of SNCC staff, including Robinson, went to the airport to meet some of the organization's celebrity supporters. The first plane the group met had Marlon Brando and Tony

Franciosa on it. The group then went to a different gate to meet a second plane:

> And as we stood out at the gate waiting—and the first person to come off the plane was Governor [George] Wallace. And Ruby Doris went up to him and said "How are you Governor," and introduced herself and said, "I've spent some time in your jails." And he said, "Well, I hope they treated you well, and if you're ever back, look me up."[27]

She never did.

While Robinson's assertiveness, brashness, and courage were important, they were not unique. Rather, her actions and her attitude fit comfortably in a context of boldness displayed by many African-American women over time. A number of cases illustrating this attitude exist within the civil rights movement. Consider the example of Annie Pearl Avery. During the course of a demonstration in Montgomery, Alabama, Avery came face-to-face with a white policeman who had a billy club aimed straight at her head. He had already beaten several others. Avery "reached up, grabbed the club and said, 'Now what you going to do, motherfucker?'" The policeman was awed. Avery slipped back into the crowd of demonstrators.[28] Cynthia Washington, on the other hand, became a SNCC project director in a rural Alabama County where there had previously not been any civil rights workers. Because she was convinced that a car would make her too conspicuous a target for racist authorities, Washington ditched the car and organized the county from the back of a mule.[29]

Even though the behavior of African-American women activists like these did not always fit contemporary notions of proper female behavior, they still fit comfortably into that established tradition of African-American female assertiveness that came straight out of slavery. Yet, what was considered acceptable and normal in the black community was not necessarily acceptable to white American society. Consequently, African-American women whose actions were applauded by other African Americans received the message from the larger American society that those actions were somehow unladylike. Furthermore, regardless of how they acted, their race had always consigned black women to a category other than female. For over three centuries they had been treated differently from white women in a society that eagerly embraced a white female standard of beauty and propriety.

In view of such differential treatment, gender roles and black and white female perspectives on issues of oppression were necessarily quite different. As young white women of the sixties generation explored the gender limitations imposed by their society, they collided with African-American women who came out of a black tradition that had a less restricted vision. Cynthia Washington clearly recalled how different their perspectives were. In the fall of 1964 Washington's white co-worker Casey Hayden complained that women were being limited to office work. An exasperated Washington simply could not understand Hayden's complaint:

What she said didn't make any particular sense to me because, at the time, I had my own project in Bolivar County, Mississippi. A number of other black women also directed their own projects. What Casey and other white women seemed to want was an opportunity to prove they could do something other than office work. I assumed that if they could do something else, they'd probably be doing that.[30]

Washington recognized how hard the work of a project director was, and besides, "it wasn't much fun." Because of her insider's view, she was at a loss to understand why white women were complaining about their assignments. In fact, their discontent over such issues only convinced Washington "how crazy they [white women] were."[31]

While white women's perspectives were very difficult for African-American women to understand, white society's disrespect for their womanhood was almost too painful to bear. One African-American female civil rights worker frankly expressed that pain:

We've been getting beaten up for years trying to integrate lunch counters, movies, and so on, and nobody has ever paid us no attention or wrote about us. But these white girls come down here for a few months and get all the publicity. Everybody talks about how brave and courageous *they* are. What about us?[32]

Another black female civil rights worker was both angered and amazed by the treatment she received. When she was with a group demonstrating at a bus station "a cop grabbed me by the arm and slapped my face. I don't know why I was surprised, but I really was." She decided to remind him of a basic tenet of southern etiquette. "I looked at him and I say, 'Listen Man, take another look at me. I'm a woman! You don't hit a woman! Didn't they teach you that?' He looked kinda sorry, but he say, 'You're a niggah and that's all you are!' "[33]

Such a pervasive and negative view was bound to wound black women's views of their own womanhood. As a blunt, outspoken, black, female activist, Ruby Doris Smith Robinson was clearly the victim of such negative views. There is an additional factor in Robinson's case, however, that further reinforced negative views of her womanhood. That additional factor was her appearance. Robinson grew to maturity in a society that, from its earliest days, had judged African women by a European standard of beauty. Many women of African descent had only to look in the mirror to see that they could never measure up physically. But many tried, and it was often quite painful.

Zohara Simmons, one of Robinson's SNCC colleagues and a fellow Spelman student, was keenly aware of the European standard of beauty that was idealized by so many. That awareness was born of Simmons's painful experience on the Spelman campus. Spelman was famous for the beauty of its student body, which, translated, meant that a fairly high proportion of the students had light skin, keen features, and straight or nearly straight hair. Because Simmons was dark skinned, she experienced a great deal of pain. But, it was often caused less by white reaction than by black rejection. She insisted,

"Some of the Morehouse guys were so nasty to a person who looked like myself. OVERT. I mean, straight up. . . ."[34] Appearance was important, but African-American women were powerless to change their appearance, at least permanently. Feelings of insecurity about their looks could and did lead to the application of desperate measures: "Cosmetic preparations for lightening skin and straightening hair represent a multi-million dollar market among Negroes not favored with Caucasoid features." In fact, according to some, the African-American female concern about appearance led many women to pursue an "unending search for some approximation of the white ideal."[35] It was a terrible burden to carry around.

Ruby Doris Robinson had to carry her share of this black woman's burden. She was not particularly light skinned, she had broad features, and her hair was not naturally straight. Like so many African-American women of her generation she wrestled with negative views of who and what she was that were popularized by white society, but then embraced, at least in part, by African-American society. Evidence of black acceptance of such negative assessments was abundant and pervasive. In fact, the African-American author of one popular magazine article noted that such black acceptance had a profound impact:

> Negro women, according to the consensus of male opinion, have some sort of inferiority complex where white women are concerned. . . . Unwittingly, much of this feeling, if it exists is inspired by men themselves—at least, as far as I can see. Too many Negro men have loudly sang [sic] the praises of white women they have known.[36]

Such pervasive negative notions of black female character, combined with Robinson's assertive activist demeanor in the field, helped shape perceptions of her by movement colleagues in the early years. By late 1962, however, Robinson became much less active in the field. At that point she became a permanent fixture in SNCC's central office in Atlanta. In this setting colleagues continued to recognize her assertiveness; and she soon gained a reputation as an uncompromising administrator. She eventually became the only female Executive Secretary the organization ever had. Co-workers agreed that Robinson was an exceptionally talented administrator. "She had great facility with words. She had such quick ability to think and conceptualize."[37] Through it all, Robinson was tough. She demanded hard work and dedication from all of those around her. She would not allow anyone to shirk his or her responsibilities. Jack Minnis, a member of SNCC's research staff, insisted that people were never able to fool Ruby because she had a "100 percent effective shit detector."[38]

As SNCC's membership enlarged and its character changed over time, it became increasingly difficult to administer. But Robinson tried. She made hard decisions, and she eventually had a great deal of influence in SNCC. She used whatever tactics were necessary to keep people on the job so that the organization could continue to function. Robinson would threaten, cajole, insist, and demand. Such administrative tactics provoked a wide range of reactions from movement colleagues. Mukasa described some of those reactions. "She's nice, she was kind, she was in charge, she was hateful. She was mean, and at different points you would hate her. You dislike her, you disagreed with her, and you agreed with her, and you liked her, and you loved her."[39]

Robinson's reputation as a tough female administrator constituted an important challenge to general notions of woman's place in the 1960s in the U.S. At the same time, even in the context of more broadly defined women's roles in the African-American community, Robinson's position as a leader in a male-dominated organization still made her an anomaly. Of course, SNCC was more egalitarian in many respects than the other civil rights groups: the organization had a number of black female field secretaries, project directors, and local leaders. Yet, even in SNCC, there was a great deal of "male posturing" in the early 1960s, and "overt sexism" by the end of the decade when Black Power became popular.[40] Regardless of her gender, though, SNCC colleagues insist that Robinson was respected by her co-workers—both male and female. In an effort to keep that respect, some suspected that she carefully and consciously emphasized the assertive, blunt, and independent part of her nature.

On the other hand, some in SNCC looked beyond her leadership and observed another side of Ruby Doris Smith Robinson. Kwame Ture (Stokely Carmichael), for example, remembered, "I found Ruby Doris to be a real pretty sister with a pleasant smile. . . . If she wasn't my sister, you know, I'd say she had a fine body."[41] SNCC co-worker Mildred Forman recalled the tender and domestic side of Ruby that was especially evident after the birth of her son.

> That was, I think, one of the best moments of her life. She was ecstatic over the baby and the husband; and she was a good mother. And she was always mothering that baby. . . she just beamed and glowed with the baby.[42]

Ruby only knew Clifford Robinson a few months before she married him in 1963. In fact their courtship was so brief and so private that the two were married before many of Robinson's SNCC colleagues even realized they were seriously involved. SNCC co-worker Stanley Wise clearly recalled his surprise. "I mean I never saw them stand together, I never saw them hold hands, I mean I didn't even know they were married until I went to their house and saw that's who Cliff was."[43] SNCC staffer Bobbi Yancey recalled that secretive romances were not that uncommon among the organization's members. Furthermore, Yancey reasoned, Robinson may have been concerned about how marriage might affect her colleagues' perceptions of her. After all, the tough, blunt, and uncompromising image Ruby projected as a leader was incompatible with the qualities many Americans in the 1960s thought a good wife should possess. Yancey concluded, "She [Ruby] may have felt that it was going against her image to have this person on the side."[44]

Many were particularly surprised that Robinson's new husband was an outsider. Clifford Robinson did not remain an outsider very long, however. He soon joined the SNCC staff as a mechanic and worked on the cars in the Sojourner Motor Fleet. Even though he joined the organization, he was less committed to the movement than he was to his new wife. Many SNCC colleagues agree that he joined SNCC because he loved Ruby Smith and she was committed to the movement. Essentially, when Clifford Robinson married twenty-one-year-old Ruby Doris Smith, he also married the Student Nonviolent Coordinating Committee. By this time she had been working in SNCC for over three years and a large part of her identity was inextricably bound up in the organization. Movement co-worker Reginald Robinson remembered the way in which many of Robinson's colleagues viewed her husband. In Reginald Robinson's estimation, "he was not involved—he was Ruby's husband."[45] In fact, Clifford Robinson freely admitted that if he and Ruby Smith had not been married he never would have joined SNCC. Mukasa succinctly described the newlyweds' relationship to SNCC. "Cliff was the husband, but Ruby Doris was the boss [in the organization]."[46] Regardless of the extent of his involvement, Clifford Robinson had to cope with an uncommon situation. He was married to one of the most powerful women in a major civil rights organization, and that meant that he and his new wife faced a number of difficult issues. Strains were inevitable.

One of the most important issues the Robinsons had to resolve was the question of establishing a balance of power in their relationship. Obviously, Ruby Robinson exercised a fair amount of power in SNCC. But what about her power within the marriage? Some insist that she dominated the relationship. SNCC colleague Dorie Ladner agreed. She remarked, "He seemed to have been in awe of her, and under her spell."[47] Ladner continued:

> I was a little surprised that she got married as early as she did. I always [pictured] her staying single much longer and uh, being more or less the woman who was in charge and . . . see the other side of it was that she wanted a family . . . but her husband was also very supportive of her. And I saw him as being weaker than she. . . . And he looked up to her. . . . When I met Cliff and saw his bearing, I knew that she was in control.[48]

Others in the organization viewed the marriage very differently. Ruby Robinson's friend and colleague Freddie Biddle insisted that Ruby "had this husband who wanted to really dominate her."[49] According to Biddle, "she [Ruby] was definitely sensitive to what he liked and what he didn't like. But yet she tried as much as possible not to, not to be dominated by that whole process."[50] In all likelihood both descriptions of the Robinsons' relationship are accurate. As newlyweds they were undoubtedly testing limits and trying to establish a balance of power in their relationship. The fact of their unique position as a husband/powerful wife team in SNCC made the establishment of that balance a difficult proposition, indeed.

Regardless of how hard the Robinsons worked to keep their relationship in balance, evidence of strain soon became apparent. Movement colleague Emma Bell Moses clearly recalled witnessing incidents that indicated strains. Zohara Simmons also remembered seeing evidence of strains. She described a particularly illustrative incident:

> I can remember . . . , you run in the office and he's [Clifford] standing there waiting on her to go. And . . . everybody's saying, "Ruby Doris, so and so and so." And he's saying "Look, we got to go." And she's saying, "Cliff, wait a minute . . . I got to take care of this." And him stalking off mad. And she saying, "Oh God . . . later for him, then." I imagine she caught hell when she got home.[51]

Thus, even though her marriage was important, there were times when Ruby Robinson refused to let anything—including marriage—interfere with her SNCC duties.

Clifford Robinson freely acknowledged how consumed Ruby Robinson was by her work in SNCC. It seemed that she never had any free time. Rather, according to Clifford, "it [SNCC work] was going on all the time around the house."[52] In the midst of her responsibilities, however, there were instances when she made extraordinary efforts to plan activities with her SNCC friends that her husband enjoyed. Freddie Biddle clearly recalled that Ruby Robinson would often invite some of the people from the office to their house to play cards. She knew that Clifford enjoyed this and he would participate.

It is clear that there was more than one side to Ruby Doris Smith Robinson. Yet, those characteristics Robinson possessed that were most compatible with popular notions of proper female behavior were often submerged in the intensity of her work. Often, but not always. It would be misleading to try and fit Robinson's life into rigid categories. On the contrary, even in the office there were times when she displayed behavior that some might have considered contradictory to her tough leader image. Co-worker Dion Diamond had vivid recollections of such behavior:

> Ruby used her femininity. . . . Ruby was aware that aside from all of these macho men that they were in many respects chauvinist . . . and I think she was aware that her being female that there was something that she could utilize in terms of that chauvinism—she could manipulate the chauvinism.[53]

It seemed, then, that Robinson did not mind engaging in a little lighthearted bantering and mild flirtation of her own. Nevertheless, all agreed that she drew a line: she did not simper, she was not coquettish or coy.

Hence, given her personal characteristics, Robinson was quite comfortable in an assertive and commanding role, and she was equally comfortable with the other side of her personality. Even if people around her saw a contradiction between the various parts of Ruby Doris Smith Robinson, she did not. At the same time, it seemed that she was annoyed by people who attempted to categorize her based on their own limited notions of proper female behavior. Matthew Jones, one of the SNCC Freedom Singers, talked about his perceptions and Robinson's reactions: "Ruby Doris wasn't the kind of woman that you'd say . . . can I talk to her. You never thought that way." She found such perceptions exasperating, Jones remembered, since she really wanted to be treated like a "regular human being."[54]

Robinson's unconventional actions and demeanor were accompanied by attitudes that were a bit surprising and definitely unpredictable. For, despite her strength, her vision, and the reality of her life, Ruby Doris Robinson still embraced some very traditional attitudes about gender roles; and she was not alone. A chorus of strong black female voices echoed similar sentiments. For example, SNCC staffer Jennifer Lawson observed, "Often women might prefer *not* to lead, but there's a responsibility to black people at this time that must be met, and it overshadows this business of being a man or a woman."[55] Carolyn Rivers, a New Yorker working in the Alabama Black Belt, had no doubt that "if Negro men were able to assert themselves fully, they'd be willing to send all the women back home."[56] Rivers did not say whether she thought the women would be willing to go. Finally, Fannie Lou Hamer explained, "But as women, we feel we have done many things that have enabled us to open doors for our men and to show them that when they get their chance, we will be there to back them up all the way."[57]

Like her activist sisters, Robinson also expressed views that were sympathetic to the peculiar trials suffered by African-American men in U.S. society. She believed that the crusade for racial justice was really men's work, after all. Since African-American men had been so victimized by U.S. society, however, they were not yet ready to shoulder the whole burden. Robinson insisted that "fortunately, more men are becoming involved with the movement, and the day might come when women aren't needed for this type of work."[58] Because she was practical and realistic, though, Robinson realized that women would be in the movement for a long time: "But, I don't believe the Negro man will be able to assume his full role until the struggle has progressed to a point that can't even be foreseen—maybe in the next century or so."[59]

Clearly these women, including Ruby Doris Robinson, were suggesting that in the future men, not women, would be *the* leaders of the movement. Women were leading, they insisted, because in the United States of the 1960s this was the most practical approach. On one hand, Robinson and the others could have been reacting to the exhaustion and frustration that came with trying to juggle their traditional female family responsibilities with their leadership commitments. On the other hand, however, this assessment could have been influenced by the increasingly popular notion that black men had somehow been more victimized than black women. Above all, race loyalty undoubtedly overshadowed gender issues in the minds of most African-American female civil rights activists of this era. They wanted to lead but they did not wish to assert themselves at the expense of their men. Such a position was fraught with contradictions.

As Robinson and her colleagues reflected on the issue of gender roles in the movement, their views were filtered through the growing male chauvinism that accompanied the rise of Black Power. One of the distinctive rallying cries of Black Power advocates was black male dominance. For so long, these advocates insisted, African-American men had been virtually emasculated by white society in the U.S. Thus, they must assume leadership roles and reclaim their masculinity as a prerequisite to the empowerment of African-American people. According to some men, they could only assume their rightful place if women would step aside and stop interfering. Such a negative notion of black female leadership was inextricably bound to a twisted assessment that blamed African-American women rather that white society for black male subordination.

Thus, increasingly, strong African-American women were subjected to negative assessments of their character and accomplishments from the black community as well as from the larger white society. Yet, Ruby Doris Smith Robinson refused to surrender to society's negative and limited expectations. She was an extremely complex woman who fought against the stereotypes. But, she had to have been affected by them. Any effort to assess Robinson's contribution to the movement, and the movement's effect on her, must necessarily recognize that part of her struggle was a continuing effort to hang on to her own sense of self in the face of pervasive and pernicious stereotypical images. Despite what anyone else thought or expected, however, Ruby Doris Robinson acted in ways *she* defined as appropriate and did things *she* thought were important. If she had moments of hesitation or indecision, she did not let them stop her. Rather, she fulfilled the roles that were most important to her. She was a leader in the Student Nonviolent Coordinating Committee, and that was important to her. She was also a woman, a wife, and a mother, and that was also important to her. There were some who insisted that Ruby Doris Smith Robinson's refusal to limit her vision of her capabilities led to her premature death from cancer in 1967 at the age of 25:

> ... she died of exhaustion. ... I don't think it was necessary to assassinate her. What killed Ruby Doris was the constant outpouring of work, work, work, work with being married, having a child, the constant conflicts, the constant struggles that she was subjected to because she was a woman. ... She was destroyed by the movement.[60]

NOTES

1. Angela Davis, *Women, Race and Class* (New York: Vintage Books, 1983), 6.
2. *Ibid.*
3. Carl Degler, *At Odds: Women and the Family in America From the Revolution to the Present* (New York: Oxford University Press, 1980), 26.
4. *Ibid.*
5. William Chafe, *The Paradox of Change: American Women in the Twentieth Century* (New York: Oxford University Press, 1991), 176.
6. Courtland Cox, interview with author, Washington, D.C., December 16, 1988.
7. Mukasa (Willie Ricks), interview with author, Atlanta, Ga., April 8, 1990.
8. Albert Brinson, interview with author, Atlanta, Ga., November 10, 1990.
9. Mary Ann Wilson, interview with author, Atlanta, Ga., November 19, 1989.
10. *Ibid.*
11. *Ibid.*

12. Catherine Robinson and Ruby O'Neal, interview with author, Atlanta, Ga., March 3,1990.

13. Phyl Garland, "Builders of a New South," *Ebony* 21 (August 1966): 36.

14. *Ibid.*

15. Roi Ottley, "What's Wrong with Negro Women?" *Negro Digest* 9 (December 1950): 73.

16. Lerone Bennett, "The Negro Woman," *Ebony* 16/17 (August 1960): 40.

17. The Atlanta University schools at that time included all-female Spelman College, all-male Morehouse College, Morris Brown College, Atlanta University, Clark College, and Gammon Theological Seminary.

18. Howard Zinn, "Finishing School for Pickets," *The Nation* (August 6, 1960), 73.

19. Robinson, like many African-American women, did not see the two sides of herself, debutante and activist, as contradictory. She was comfortable with both roles.

20. Quoted in Howard Zinn, *SNCC, The New Abolitionists* (Boston: Beacon Press, 1964), 17-18.

21. Julian Bond, interview with author, Washington, D.C., December 16, 1988.

22. *Ibid.*

23. Benjamin Brown and Mary Ann Wilson, interview with author, Atlanta, Ga., November 11, 1990.

24. The *Atlanta Inquirer*, March 18, 1961.

25. Taylor Branch, *Parting the Waters* (New York: Simon and Schuster, 1988), 496.

26. Julian Bond interview.

27. James Bond, interview with author, Atlanta, Ga., February 8, 1991.

28. Paula Giddings, *When and Where I Enter* (New York: Bantam Books, 1984), 292.

29. *Ibid.*

30. Cynthia Washington, "We Started From Different Ends of the Spectrum," *Southern Exposure* 5 (Winter 1977): 14.

31. *Ibid.*

32. Alvin Poussaint, "The Stresses of the White Female Worker in the Civil Rights Movement in the South," *Journal of American Psychiatry* 123 (October 1966): 403.

33. Josephine Carson, *Silent Voices* (New York: Delacorte Press, 1969), 60.

34. Zohara Simmons, interview with author, Philadelphia, Pa., December 17, 1988.

35. Carson, *Silent Voices*, 160.

36. Roi Ottley, "What's Wrong with Negro Women?" 75.

37. Joyce Ladner, interview with author, Washington D.C., December 18, 1988.

38. Jack Minnis, interview with author, New Orleans, La., November 4, 1990.

39. Mukasa interview.

40. Jacqueline Jones, *Labor of Love, Labor of Sorrow: Black Women, Work and the Family, From Slavery to the Present* (New York: Vintage Books, 1985), 282.

41. Kwame Ture (Stokely Carmichael), interview with author, Knoxville, Tenn., March 14, 1990.

42. Mildred Forman, interview with author, Chicago, Ill., November 6, 1989.

43. Stanley Wise, interview with author, Atlanta, Ga., November 11, 1988.

44. Bobbi Yancey, interview with author, New York, N.Y., May 16, 1991.

45. Reginald Robinson and Charles Jones, interview with author, McComb, Miss., June 28, 1991.

46. Mukasa interview.

47. Dorie Ladner, interview with author, Washington, D.C., May 18, 1991.

48. *Ibid.*

49. Freddie Green Biddle, interview with author, McComb, Miss., June 29, 1991.
50. *Ibid.*
51. Simmons interview.
52. Clifford Robinson, interview with author, Atlanta, Ga., March 17, 1989.
53. Dion Diamond, interview with author, McComb, Miss., June 18, 1991.
54. Matthew Jones, interview with author, Knoxville, Tenn., April 24, 1989.
55. Garland, "Builders of a New South," 37.
56. *Ibid.*
57. *Ibid.*
58. *Ibid.*, 36.
59. *Ibid.*
60. Giddings, *When and Where I Enter*, 315.

Notes on Editors and Contributors

Editors

Darlene Clark Hine is John A. Hannah Professor of American History at Michigan State University. Her books include *The Rise and Fall of the White Primary in Texas* and *Black Women in White: Racial Conflict and Cooperation in the Nursing Profession, 1890-1950*. She is the Editor of the award-winning *Black Women in America: An Historical Encyclopedia* (Carlson Publishing, 1993). Her most recent book is *Hine Sight: Black Women and the Re-Construction of American History* (Carlson Publishing, 1994).

Wilma King is Associate Professor of History at Michigan State University. Her book *A Northern Woman in the Plantation South: Letters of Tryphena Blanche Holder Fox, 1856-1876* was published in 1993. She has two forthcoming books: *Africa's Progeny—America's Slaves: Children and Youth in Bondage in the Nineteenth-Century South* and *From Uncle Tom's Cabin to the Onset of the Civil War (1851-1861)*.

Linda Reed is an Associate Professor of History at the University of Houston, where she is also director of the African-American Studies Program. She is the author of *Simple Decency and Common Sense: The Southern Conference Movement, 1938-1963* and is working on a biography of Mississippi civil rights activist Fannie Lou Hamer.

Contributors

Andrea Starr Alonzo is a Lecturer at the Borough of Manhattan Community College in the English Department. She has published articles in *Hudson River*, *Women's Studies Quarterly*, and *Community Review*. She is currently working on a novel.

Gail Bederman is Assistant Professor of History at the University of Notre Dame. she is the author of *Manliness and Civilization: A Cultural History of Gender and Race in the United States, 1880-1917*.

Elsa Barkley Brown teaches in the Department of History and the Center for Afroamerican and African Studies, University of Michigan, Ann Arbor. Her articles have appeared in *Signs, SAGE, History Workshop Journal, Feminist Studies,* and *Public Culture.* She is associate editor of *Black Women in America: An Historical Encyclopedia* (Carlson Publishing, Inc., 1993).

Barbara Bush is Senior Lecturer in Social and Political Science at Parson Cross College in Sheffield, England.

Anne M. Butler is Professor of History at Utah State University. She is co-editor of the *Western Historical Quarterly.* Her publications include *Daughters of Joy, Sisters of Misery: Prostitutes in The American West, 1865-1890.*

Nupur Chaudhuri teaches at Kansas State University and is co-editor of *Western Women and Imperialism: Complicity and Resistance.* She has published articles in *Journal of Women's History, Victorian Studies,* and *National Women's Studies Association Journal.* She is the U.S. representative for the International Federation for Research in Women's History.

Beth Maclay Doriani is Assistant Professor of English and chair of the department at Northwestern College. Her publications include *Emily Dickinson, Daughter of Prophecy* and articles in *Studies in Puritan American Spirituality, The Emily Dickinson Journal,* and *Early American Literature.*

Cynthia Griggs Fleming is Director of African and African-American Studies and Associate Professor of History at the University of Tennessee, Knoxville. She has published articles in *Journal of Women's History; Southern Women: Hidden Histories,* edited by Virginia Bernhardt and Elizabeth Fox Genovese; and *Acculturation and Ethnicity in the United States,* edited by John Buenker and Larry Ratner.

Noralee Frankel is Assistant Director on Women and Minorities of the American Historical Association. She has completed a manuscript entitled *Brake Those Chains At Last: African Americans, 1860-1880.* She is the editor of *AHA Directory of Women Historians* and co-editor, with Nancy S. Dye, of *Gender, Class, Race, and Reform in the Progressive Era* (1991).

Linda Gordon is Florence Kelley Professor of History at the University of Wisconsin, Madison. Her publications include *Woman's Body, Woman's Right: The History of Birth Control in America; Heroes of their Own Lives: History and Politics of Family Violence;* and *Pitied But Not Entitled: Single Mothers and the History of Welfare.*

Joan Rezner Gundersen is Professor of History and Director of the Women's Studies Program at California State University, San Marcos.

Sharon Harley is acting director of the Afro-American Studies Program and Associate Professor of Afro-American Studies and History at the University of Maryland, College Park. She is coeditor of *The Afro-American Woman: Struggles* *and Images* (1978) and of *Women in Africa and the African Diaspora* (1987). Her articles have been published in *Signs* and *Nineteenth Century Black Leaders*.

Evelyn Brooks Higginbotham is Professor of Afro-American Studies and African American Religious History at Harvard University. She is the author of *Righteous Discontent: The Women's Movement in the Black Baptist Church, 1880-1920* (1993). Her articles on race and gender issues in America have been published in *Signs*, *Gender & History*, and *Journal of Religious Thought*.

Patricia K. Hunt is Assistant Professor of Textiles, Merchandising, and Interiors in the College of Family and Consumer Sciences at the University of Georgia. She specializes in the study of costume and textile history, particularly as it relates to the dress of African American women in the South. She has published articles in *Clothing and Textiles Research Journal*, *Cutter's Research Journal*, and *The Georgia Historical Quarterly*.

Tera W. Hunter is Assistant Professor of History at the University of North Carolina, Chapel Hill. She is finishing a book entitled *Contesting the New South: The Politics and Culture of Wage Household Labor in America, 1861-1920* which will be published by Harvard University Press.

Sylvia M. Jacobs is Professor of History and Chair of the Department at North Carolina Central University. She is the author of *The African Nexus: Black American Perspectives on the European Partitioning of Africa, 1880-1920* and the editor of *Black Americans and the Missionary Movement in Africa*. She has written nearly two dozen articles on the relationship of African-Americans with Africa and Africans.

Whittington B. Johnson is Associate Professor of History at the University of Miami. He is the author of *The Promising Years: The Emergence of Black Business and Labor, 1750-1830* and has published articles in *The Georgia Historical Quarterly*.

Herbert S. Klein is Professor of History at Columbia University. His publications include *African Slavery in Latin America and the Caribbean*; *Rural Society in The Bolivian Andes, Eighteenth and Nineteenth Centuries*; and *Haciendas and Ayllus*.

Mamie E. Locke is Assistant Dean and Associate Professor of Political Science in the School of Liberal Arts and Education at Hampton University. Her publications include "Outsiders in Insider Politics: Black Women and the American Political System," in *An American Government Reader* (Kendall Hunt Publishers, 1987) and "Is This America? Fannie Lou Hamer and the Mississippi Freedom Democratic Party," published in *Women in the Civil Rights Movement: Trailblazers and Torchbearers, 1941-1965* (Carlson Publishing, 1990).

Paul E. Lovejoy is Professor of History at York University in Canada. His publications include *Transformations in Slavery: A History of Slavery in Africa*;

Salt of the Desert Sun: History of Salt Production and Trade in the Central Sudan; and *Slow Death For Slavery: The Course of Abolition in Northern Nigeria, 1897-1936*.

Susan A. Mann is Professor and Chair of Sociology at the University of New Orleans and was formerly Director of Women's Studies. She is the author of *Agrarian Capitalism in Theory and Practice* and is currently co-authoring a textbook entitled *Lullabies and Lies: A Sociology of Families and Interpersonal Relationships*.

Debra L. Newman, specialist in Afro-American history and culture at the Library of Congress, is the author of *Black History: A Guide to Civilian Records in the National Archives* (1984). Her articles have appeared in *Sage*, *Minerva*, and the *Journal of Negro History*.

Nell Irvin Painter is the Edwards Professor of American History at Princeton University. Her books include *Exodusters: Black Migration to Kansas After Reconstruction*, *The Narrative of Hosea Hudson: His Life as a Negro Communist in the South*, and *Standing at Armageddon: The United States 1877-1919*.

Rhoda E. Reddock is Professor of Women's Studies at University of West Indies, Trinidad.

John B. Reid is completing his Ph.D. in history at Michigan State University. His dissertation is entitled "The Black Women Schoolteachers of the Midwest, 1860-1950."

Loren Schweninger is Professor of History at the University of North Carolina, Greensboro. His publications include *Black Property Owners in the South, 1790-1915*. He is currently editing a project entitled *Race Slavery and Free Blacks: Petitions to Southern Legislature County Courts, 1776-1867*.

Stephanie J. Shaw is Assistant Professor in the Department of History and the Center for Women's Studies at Ohio State University. Her research and teaching focuses on the experiences of Black women in the United States.

Rosalyn Terborg-Penn is Professor of History and Head of the Ph.D. Program in History at Morgan State University. Her books include *The Afro-American Woman: Struggles and Images*, (edited with Sharon Harley) and *Women in Africa and the African Diaspora*, (edited with Sharon Harley and Andrea Benton Rushing). She is a founder and first National Director of the Association of Black Women Historians. She is associate editor of *Black Women in America: An Historical Encyclopedia* (Carlson Publishing, Inc., 1993).

John Thornton is Associate Professor of History at Millersville University of Pennsylvania. He is the author of *The Kingdom of Kongo: Civil War and Transition, 1641-1718* and *Africa and Africans in the Making of the Atlantic World, 1450-1680*.

Lillian S. Williams is Assistant Professor of History, Department of Women's Studies at the University of Albany. Her publications have appeared in *Journal of Negro Education*, and *Afro-Americans in New York Life and History*. She is an Associate Editor of *Afro-Americans in New York Life and History* and Carlson Publishing's sixteen-volume series, *Black Women in United States History*.

Copyrights and Permissions

Alonzo, Andrea Starr. "A Study of Two Women's Slave Narratives: *Incidents in the Life of a Slave Girl* and *The History of Mary Prince*," *Women's Studies Quarterly* 17 (Fall/Winter 1989): 118-22. Reprinted by permission of the author.

Bederman, Gail. " 'Civilization,' The Decline of Middle Class Manliness, and Ida B. Wells's Antilynching Campaign (1892-94)," *Radical History Review* Vol. 52 (Winter 1992): 4-30. Reprinted by permission of Cambridge University Press.

Brown, Elsa Barkley. " 'What Has Happened Here': The Politics of Difference in Women's History and Feminist Politics," *Feminist Studies* Vol. 18 (Summer 1992): 295-312. Reprinted with the permission of the author.

Bush, Barbara. "Defiance or Submission? The Role of the Slave Woman in Slave Resistance in the British Caribbean," *Immigrants and Minorities*, Vol. 1, No. 12 (March 1992): 16-39.

Butler, Anne M. "Still in Chains: Black Women in Western Prisons, 1865-1910," *The Western Historical Quarterly* Vol 20 (February 1989): 18-35. Reprinted by permission of the author.

Chaudhuri, Nupur. " 'We All Seem Like Brothers and Sisters': The African-American Community in Manhattan, Kansas, 1865-1940," *Kansas History* Vol. 14, No. 4 (1991-92): 270-288. Reprinted by the permission of the Kansas State Historical Society.

Cooper, Afua. "The Search for Mary Bibb, Black Woman Teacher in Nineteenth-Century Canada West," *Ontario History* 83 (March 1991): 39-54. Reprinted by the permission of the Ontario Historical Society.

Doriani, Beth Maclay. "Black Womanhood in Nineteenth-Century America: Subversion and Self-Construction in Two Women's Autobiographies," *American Quarterly* Vol. 43, No. 2 (1991): 199-222. Reprinted by the permission of the author and The Johns Hopkins University Press, Baltimore/London.

Klein, Herbert S. "African Women in the Atlantic Slave Trade" in *Women and Slavery in Africa*, edited by Claire Robinson and Martin C. Klein (1983), pp. 29-38. Reprinted by permission of the University of Wisconsin Press.

Locke, Mamie E. "From Three-Fifths to Zero: Implications of the Constitution for African-American Women, 1787-1870," *Women, Politics and the Constitution* (Haworth Press, Inc., 1990), pp. 33-46. Reprinted by permission of Haworth Press.

Lovejoy, Paul E. "Concubinage and the Status of Women Slaves in Early Colonial Northern Nigeria," *Journal of African History* 29 (1988): 245-266. Reprinted by permission of the author and Cambridge University Press. [This article has been corrected for publication here.]

Mann, Susan A. "Slavery, Sharecropping and Sexual Inequality" *Signs*, Vol. 14 (Summer 1989): 774-98. Copyright © 1989, University of Chicago Press. Reprinted by permission.

Newman, Debra L. "Black Women in the Era of the American Revolution in Pennsylvania," *The Journal of Negro History* Vol. LXI, No. 3 (July 1976): 276-289. Copyright © Association for the Study of Afro-American Life and History. Reprinted by permission.

Painter, Nell Irvin. "Sojourner Truth in Life and Memory: Writing the Biography of an American Exotic," *Gender and History* Vol. 2 (Spring 1990): 3-16. Reprinted by permission of Blackwell Publishers, Oxford, England.

Reddock, Rhoda E. "Women and Slavery in the Caribbean: A Feminist Perspective," *Latin American Perspectives* Vol. 12 (Winter 1985): 63-80. Copyright © 1985 by Sage Publications, Inc. Reprinted by permission of Sage Publications, Inc.

Reid, John B. " 'A Career to Build, a People to Serve, a Purpose to Accomplish': Race, Class, Gender and Detroit's First Black Women Teachers, 1865-1916," *Michigan Historical Review* Vol. 18, No. 1 (Spring 1992): 1-27. Permission granted by *Michigan Historical Review*.

Rodrique, Jessie M. "The Black Community and the Birth Control Movement," in Kathy Peiss and Christina Simmons, *Passion and Power: Sexuality in History* (Temple University Press, 1989), pp. 138-154. Reprinted by permission from MARHO: The Radical Historians Organization. Copyright © MARHO.

Schweninger, Loren. "Property Owning Free African-American Women in the South, 1800-1870," *Journal of Women's History* Vol. 1, No. 3 (1990): 13-44. Reprinted by permission of the journal and the author.

Shaw, Stephanie J. "Black Club Women and the Creation of the National Association of Colored Women," *Journal of Women's History* Vol. 3 ,No. 2 (Fall 1991): 10-25. Reprinted by permission of the journal and the author.

Terborg-Penn, Rosalyn. "Discontented Black Feminists: Prelude and Postscript to the Passage of the Nineteenth Amendment," in *Decades of Discontent: The Women's Movement, 1920-1940*, ed. Lois Scharf and Joan Jensen (1983), pp. 261-278. Reprinted by permission of Greenwood Publishing Group, Inc.

Index